T0140192

Lecture Notes in Computer Science 3308

Commenced Publication in 1973
Founding and Former Series Editors:
Gerhard Goos, Juris Hartmanis, and Jan van Leeuwen

Jim Davies   Wolfram Schulte
Mike Barnett (Eds.)

Formal Methods and Software Engineering

6th International Conference
on Formal Engineering Methods, ICFEM 2004
Seattle, WA, USA, November 8-12, 2004
Proceedings

 Springer

Volume Editors

Jim Davies
University of Oxford, Software Engineering Programme
Wolfson Building, Parks Road, Oxford OX1 3QD, UK
E-mail: jim.davies@comlab.ox.ac.uk

Wolfram Schulte
Mike Barnett
Microsoft Research
One Microsoft Way, Cedar Court 113/4048, Redmond, WA 98052-6399, USA
E-mail: {schulte, mbarnett}@microsoft.com

Library of Congress Control Number: 2004114617

CR Subject Classification (1998): D.2.4, D.2, D.3, F.3

ISSN 0302-9743
ISBN 3-540-23841-7 Springer Berlin Heidelberg New York

Springer is a part of Springer Science+Business Media

springeronline.com

© Springer-Verlag Berlin Heidelberg 2004
Printed in Germany

Typesetting: Camera-ready by author, data conversion by Scientific Publishing Services, Chennai, India
Printed on acid-free paper   SPIN: 11348801   06/3142   5 4 3 2 1 0

Preface

Formal engineering methods are changing the way that software systems are developed. With language and tool support, they are being used for automatic code generation, and for the automatic abstraction and checking of implementations. In the future, they will be used at every stage of development: requirements, specification, design, implementation, testing, and documentation.

The ICFEM series of conferences aims to bring together those interested in the application of formal engineering methods to computer systems. Researchers and practitioners, from industry, academia, and government, are encouraged to attend, and to help advance the state of the art. Authors are strongly encouraged to make their ideas as accessible as possible, and there is a clear emphasis upon work that promises to bring practical, tangible benefit: reports of case studies should have a conceptual message, theory papers should have a clear link to application, and papers describing tools should have an account of results.

ICFEM 2004 was the sixth conference in the series, and the first to be held in North America. Previous conferences were held in Singapore, China, UK, Australia, and Japan. The Programme Committee received 110 papers and selected 30 for presentation. The final versions of those papers are included here, together with 2-page abstracts for the 5 accepted tutorials, and shorter abstracts for the 4 invited talks.

We would like to thank: Dines Bjørner, for his work in organizing speakers and sponsors; Jin Song Dong and Jim Woodcock, for an excellent handover from ICFEM 2003; Joxan Jaffar, J Strother Moore, Peter Neumann, and Amitabh Srivastava, for agreeing to address the conference; the authors, for submitting their work; the Programme Committee, and their colleagues, for their reviews; and Springer, for their help with publication.

ICFEM 2004 was organized by Microsoft Research in Seattle, with additional support and sponsorship from the University of Oxford, the United Nations University, Formal Methods Europe, NASA, and ORA Canada.

November 2004

Jim Davies
Wolfram Schulte
Mike Barnett

Organizing Committee

Conference Committee

Mike Barnett (Microsoft Research, USA)
  Local Organization
Dines Bjørner (National University of Singapore, Singapore)
  Conference Chair
Jim Davies (University of Oxford, UK)
  Programme Co-chair
Wolfram Schulte (Microsoft Research, USA)
  Programme Co-chair
Hongjun Zheng (Semantics Design, USA)
  Workshops and Tutorials Chair

Sponsors

Microsoft Research
  www.research.microsoft.com
Oxford University Software Engineering Programme
  www.softeng.ox.ac.uk
United Nations University–International Institute for Software Technology
  www.iist.unu.edu
Formal Methods Europe (FME)
  www.fmeurope.org
NASA–JPL Laboratory for Reliable Software
  eis.jpl.nasa.gov/lars/
ORA Canada
  www.ora.on.ca

Steering Committee

Keijiro Araki (Kyushu University, Japan)
Jin Song Dong (National University of Singapore, Singapore)
Chris George (United Nations University, Macau)
Jifeng He *(Chair)* (IIST, United Nations University, Macau)
Mike Hinchey (NASA, USA)
Shaoying Liu (Hosei University, Japan)
John McDermid (University of York, UK)
Tetsuo Tamai (University of Tokyo, Japan)
Jim Woodcock (University of York, UK)

Programme Committee

Adnan Aziz (University of Texas, USA)
Richard Banach (University of Manchester, UK)
Egon Börger (University of Pisa, Italy)
Jonathan Bowen (London South Bank University, UK)
Manfred Broy (University of Munich, Germany)
Michael Butler (University of Southampton, UK)
Ana Cavalcanti (University of Kent, UK)
Dan Craigen (ORA, Canada)
Jin Song Dong (National University of Singapore, Singapore)
Matthew Dwyer (Kansas State University, USA)
John Fitzgerald (University of Newcastle upon Tyne, UK)
David Garlan (Carnegie Mellon University, Pittsburgh, USA)
Thomas Jensen (IRISA/CNRS Campus de Beaulieu, Rennes, France)
Jim Larus (Microsoft Research, USA)
Mark Lawford (McMaster University, Canada)
Huimin Lin (Chinese Academy of Sciences, Beijing, China)
Peter Lindsay (University of Queensland, Australia)
Shaoying Liu (Hosei University, Japan)
Zhiming Liu (United Nations University, Macau SAR, China)
Brendan Mahony (Department of Defence, Australia)
Marc Frappier (Université de Sherbrooke, Québec, Canada)
William Bradley Martin (National Security Agency, USA)
David Notkin (University of Washington, USA)
Jeff Offutt (George Mason University, USA)
Harald Ruess (Computer Science Laboratory, SRI, USA)
Augusto Sampaio (Universidade Federal de Pernambuco, Brazil)
Thomas Santen (Technical University of Berlin, Germany)
Doug Smith (Kestrel Institute, USA)
Graeme Smith (University of Queensland, Australia)
Paul A. Swatman (University of South Australia, Australia)
Sofiene Tahar (Concordia University, Canada)
T.H. Tse (Hong Kong University, Hong Kong)
Yi Wang (Uppsala University, Sweden)
Farn Wang (National Taiwan University, Taiwan)
Jeannette Wing (Carnegie Mellon University, USA)
Jim Woodcock (University of York, UK)

Reviewers

Amr Abdel-Hamid; Isaam Al-azzoni; Adnan Aziz; Richard Banach;
Andreas Bauer; Jounaidi Ben Hassen; Egon Börger; Jonathan Bowen;
Peter Braun; Manfred Broy; Michael Butler; Colin Campbell; Ana Cavalcanti;
Alessandra Cavarra; Antonio Cerone; Yifeng Chen; Corina Cirstea;
David Clark; Dan Craigen; Charles Crichton; Jim Davies; Roger Duke;
Bruno Dutertre; Matthew Dwyer; Pao-Ann Eric Hsiung; Yuan Fang Li;
Bill Farmer; William M. Farmer; Carla Ferreira; Colin Fidge; John Fitzgerald;
Marc Frappier; Jorn Freiheit; David Garlan; Amjad Gawanmeh;
Frederic Gervais; Jeremy Gibbons; Uwe Glaesser; Andy Gravell;
Wolfgang Grieskamp; Ali Habibi; John Hakansson; Steve Harris; Jifeng He;
Maritta Heisel; Steffen Helke; Matthew Hennessy; Xiayong Hu;
Geng-Dian Huang; Chung-Yang Ric Huang; Van Hung Dang; Jiale Huo;
Cornelia P. Inggs; Jan Jürjens; Bart Jacobs; Thomas Jensen; Thierry Jeron;
Zhi Jin; Wolfram Kahl; Soon-Kyeong Kim; Soon Kyeong Kim; Leonid Kof;
Pushmeet Kohli; Pavel Krcal; Sy-Yen Kuo; Rom Langerak; James Larus;
Mark Lawford; Ryan Leduc; Karl Lermer; Guangyuan Li; Xiaoshan Li;
Huimin Lin; Peter Lindsay; Shaoying Liu; Zhiming Liu; Quan Long;
Marcio Lopes Cornelio; Dorel Lucanu; Anthony MacDonald; Brendan Mahony;
William Bradley Martin; Jim McCarthy; M. Meisinger; Yassine Mokhtari;
Leonid Mokrushin; Alexandre Mota; Muan Yong Ng; Sidney Nogueira;
David Notkin; Jeff Offutt; Chun Ouyang; Hong Pan; Jun Pang;
Paul Pettersson; Mike Poppleton; Steven Postma; Stephane Lo Presti;
Wolfgang Reisig; Abdolbaghi Rezazadeh; River; Harald Ruess; Heinrich Rust;
Vlad Rusu; Augusto Sampaio; Thomas Santen; Renate Schmidt;
Wolfram Schulte; Thorsten Schutt; Dirk Seifert; Laura Semini; Adnan Sherif;
Benjamin Sigonneau; Carlo Simon; Andrew Simpson; Doug Smith;
Graeme Smith; Doug Smith; Colin Snook; Jin Song Dong; Maria Sorea;
Mark Staples; Jun Sun; Paul A. Swatman; Sofiene Tahar; J.P. Talpin;
Rodrigo Teixeira Ramos; Nikolai Tillmann; T.H. Tse; Phillip J. Turner;
Margus Veanes; S. Vogel; Philip Wadler; Farn Wang; Bow-Yaw Wang;
Alan Wassyng; Jun Wei; Guido Wimmel; Jeannette Wing; Kirsten Winter;
Jim Woodcock; Wang Yi; Fang Yu; Mohamed Zaki; Wenhui Zhang;
Guangquan Zhang; Ning Zhang; Riley Zheng; Xiaocong Zhou; Jeff Zucker

Table of Contents

Tutorials

Invited Talks

Full Papers

Model-Based Development: Combining Engineering Approaches and Formal Techniques

Bernhard Schätz

Institut für Informatik, Technische Universität München,
80290 München, Germany

1   Model-Based Development

In a nutshell, a model-based approach offers several benefits:

Improved Product: By moving away from an implementation biased view of a system, the developer can focus on the important issues of the product under development. This results in
  - thinking in terms of the domain-specific conceptual model (state, interaction, etc.) instead of the coding level (objects, method calls, etc.)
  - narrowing the gap between informal specification and formal specification (since, e.g., notions like mode, event, or communication, appear in the informal specifications as well as in the model)
  - limiting the possibility of making mistakes while building models and refining them by ensuring consistency conditions (e.g. interface correctness, absence of undefined behavior)

Improved Process: Using a better structured product model helps to identify more defects earlier. Additionally, higher efficiency can be obtained by more CASE-supported process steps
  - mechanizing conceptual consistency conditions, either guaranteed by construction (e.g., interface correctness) or checked automatically on demand (e.g., completeness of defined behavior)
  - supporting semantical consistency conditions, either automatically (e.g., checking whether an EET can be performed by system), or interactively (e.g., by ensuring a safety condition of a system)
  - enabling transformations of specification (e.g. inserting standard behavior for undefined situations), interactively carried out by the CASE tool.

The limit of model-based support is defined by the sophistication of the underlying model: by adding more domain-specific aspects, more advanced techniques can be offered (e.g., reliability analysis, schedule generation).

2   Structured Development

Model-based development is all about adding the structuring and preciseness of formal approaches to the development process while being driven by the models of the application domain instead of mathematical formalisms.

J. Davies et al. (Eds.): ICFEM 2004, LNCS 3308, pp. 1–2, 2004.

Thus it helps reducing the complexity of the development process by clearly focusing on specific issues and offering suitable, generally CASE-supported techniques tailored for each step of the development (see also [1]):

Step 1: By linking informal requirements and the models of system and environment, we can check whether all informal requirements are covered or trace back from design to requirements; but most importantly, it helps to structure the requirements, get a better understanding, and identify open issues in the requirements.

Step 2: By modeling the environment and its interface to the system, we get a precise understanding of how the system influences the environment and how the environment reacts. Especially important, we precisely state what properties of the environment we take for granted and which possibly faulty behavior we must tolerate to establish the required safety behavior.

Step 3: By defining the abstract, possibly incomplete and non-deterministic behavior of the system, we describe a high-level initial design without already incorporating implementation details complicating the design or limiting further decision. Furthermore, we establish the basis for further analysis and development steps.

Step 4: By analyzing the models of system and environment for their validity, we ensure their usefulness for the following steps; using simulation or conceptual consistency checks, we identify open issues like unrealistic behavior of the environment, as well as undefined behavior of the system.

Step 5: By using even stronger techniques we establish whether the defined behavior of the system ensures the expected behavior of the environment. Using formal verification, we show that the system guarantees the safety requirements of the environment assuming optimal circumstances; furthermore, using failure analysis, we show that also mean time requirements are met using quantitative assumptions about the environment.

Step 6: By applying structural refinement, we add further design decisions concerning the architecture of a system by breaking it up into interacting sub-components. By adding behavior to each sub-component, we can make sure that the refined system implements the abstract one.

Step 7: By restricting non-deterministic or undefined behavior, we add further design decisions concerning underspecified behavior of the introduced components, resulting in a more optimized reaction of the system while maintaining the overall functionality.

Step 8: By checking the components of the system for possible undefined behavior we identify remaining open behavior to be resolved in the final implementation. By adding standard reactions for open behavior, we improve the robustness of the system against unexpected behavior.

References

1. B. Schätz. Mastering the Complexity of Embedded Systems - The AutoFocus Approach. In F. Kordon and M. Lemoine, editors, *Formal Techniques for Embedded Distributed Systems: From Requirements to Detailed Design*. Kluwer, 2004.

Tutorial on the RAISE Language, Method and Tools

Chris George

United Nations University, International Institute for Software Technology
(UNU-IIST), Macao
cwg@iist.unu.edu
http://www.iist.unu/~cwg

Abstract. RAISE — Rigorous Approach to Industrial Software Engineering — was first developed in European collaborative projects during 1985-94. Since then a new set of free, open-source, portable tools has been developed, and a range of developments have been carried out. This tutorial introduces the language and method, and demonstrates the range of software life-cycle activities supported by the tools. These include generation of specifications from UML class diagrams, validation and verification of specifications, refinement, prototyping, execution of test cases, mutation testing, generation of documents, proof by means of translation to PVS, and generation of program code in C++ by translation. A comprehensive user guide is also available.

It is a common perception that "formal methods" are difficult to use, involve a lot of proof, are expensive, and are only applicable to small, critical problems. The aim of this tutorial is to introduce a formal technology that is easy to learn, need involve no proof at all, is cheap to apply, and is intended in particular to deal with large, not necessarily critical problems.

The RAISE method [1] is extreme in its basic simplicity: you write a specification and then you produce the implementation (if possible, automatically from the specification). You may for a particular project want to do more than this: you may decide you want to produce a more abstract specification first, and then a more concrete one, and then perhaps assert (and even prove) some relation, such as refinement, between them. But for many projects one specification is enough [2]. If you find graphical approaches useful, you can start by drawing a UML class diagram and generate the first specification from it.

What this simple picture of the method hides is the urgent need to validate the specification. Many discussions on formal methods assume the specification is correct, is what you want, and concentrate on verification, on showing that it is properly implemented. But all this is wasted if the specification is wrong. Mistakes made at the beginning of a project (and not quickly noticed) cause many problems, at best time and cost overruns, and at worst complete failure. So a major aim of the RAISE method, and of the tools that support it, is exploring and finding problems with the specification.

J. Davies et al. (Eds.): ICFEM 2004, LNCS 3308, pp. 3–4, 2004.

Concretely we can, with the tools:

- write large specifications in modules that we can analyse separately;
- generate and inspect "confidence conditions" that subtype conditions are not violated, pre-conditions are satisfied by function calls, cases are complete, etc.;
- translate and execute test cases that are recorded with the specification;
- assess the adequacy of test cases by means of specification mutation testing;
- generate high quality documents that include the specifications; and even, for more critical applications,
- prove confidence conditions, refinement, or other properties that we choose to assert

The RAISE Specification Language (RSL) [3] is a "wide-spectrum" language. It supports "algebraic" as well as "model-oriented" styles, and also includes applicative, imperative and concurrent features. It is modular, and therefore supports the writing of a very wide range of specifications.

Introductory information on the language and method is available in a variety of papers [4–6]. There is also an extension to RSL to deal with time [7].

The RAISE tool is open source, comes ready built for Windows, Linux and Sparc-Solaris, and can be built in any environment where you can compile C. There is also a comprehensive user guide [8].

The tutorial covers RSL, the method, the tools, and gives an example of a large system specified using RAISE.

References

1. The RAISE Language Group. *The RAISE Development Method*. BCS Practitioner Series. Prentice Hall, 1995. Available from `ftp://ftp.iist.unu.edu/pub/RAISE/method_book`.
2. Hung Dang Van, Chris George, Tomasz Janowski, and Richard Moore. *Specification Case Studies in RAISE*. FACIT. Springer-Verlag, 2002.
3. The RAISE Language Group. *The RAISE Specification Language*. BCS Practitioner Series. Prentice Hall, 1992. Available from Terma A/S. Contact `jnp@terma.com`.
4. Chris George. A RAISE Tutorial. Technical Report 153, UNU-IIST, P.O.Box 3058, Macau, December 1998. Presented at the BRNS workshop *Verification of Digital and Hybrid Systems* at TIFR, Mumbai, India, 7–11 January 1999.
5. Chris George. Introduction to RAISE. Technical Report 249, UNU-IIST, P.O. Box 3058, Macau, April 2002.
6. Chris George and Anne E. Haxthausen. The Logic of the RAISE Specification Language. *Computing and Informatics*, 22(3–4), 2003.
7. Chris George and Xia Yong. An Operational Semantics for Timed RAISE. Technical Report 149, UNU-IIST, P.O.Box 3058, Macau, November 1998. Presented at and published in the proceedings of FM'99, Toulouse, France, 20–24 September 1999, LNCS 1709, Springer-Verlag, 1999, pp. 1008–1027.
8. Chris George. RAISE Tools User Guide. Technical Report 227, UNU-IIST, P.O. Box 3058, Macau, February 2001. The tools are available from `http://www.iist.unu.edu`.

Model-Based Testing with Spec#

Jonathan Jacky

University of Washington, Seattle, USA

1   Introduction

This half-day tutorial introduces model-based testing, using the Spec# modeling language and the Spec Explorer test tool.

We write a model program (an executable specification) in Spec# that models the implementation we wish to test. Then we use Spec Explorer to validate the model program, generate test suites from the model program, and execute conformance tests, using the model program again as the oracle.

2   The Spec# Language

The Spec# language is a superset of C# with additional constructs for contracts. A contract is (part of) a specification expressed in the programming language itself. Spec# provides two kinds of contracts: declarative contracts and model programs.

2.1   Declarative Contracts

A declarative contract is an assertion: a Boolean expression that describes a condition that should be true at certain times during program execution. Spec# provides several kinds of declarative contracts, including preconditions and post-conditions.

Each precondition and postcondition is associated with a method. A precondition is supposed to be true when execution enters its method. Preconditions often express requirements on method arguments. A postcondition should be true when its method exits. It expresses the intended result or effect of the method.

Spec# provides more Boolean operators (such as implication) and more kinds of Boolean expressions (such as quantified expressions) to make it easier to write expressive declarative contracts.

2.2   Model Programs

It can be quite difficult to write postconditions that express exactly what is intended. It is often easier and clearer to write a program that demonstrates the intended effect. A program written for this purpose is a kind of contract. It is called an executable specification or a model program.

J. Davies et al. (Eds.): ICFEM 2004, LNCS 3308, pp. 5–6, 2004.

In order to be useful, a model program must be shorter and clearer than the program it models. Spec# provides constructs that make this possible. In effect, Spec# is a very high level programming language. For example, it provides more collection types (sets, sequences, and maps) and expressions (comprehensions) that enable collections to be created and manipulated without coding loops, indices, or references.

3   The Spec Explorer Tool

The Spec Explorer tool can investigate the properties of model programs written in Spec#, using a process called exploration which is similar to model checking. It can also generate test suites and perform conformance tests.

3.1   Exploration

Exploration performs all possible executions of the model program (including all possible interleavings of operations), within a finite scope that is configured by the user. Exploration generates the graph of a finite (perhaps quite large) state machine which is a portion (an under-approximation) of the finite (but astronomically large) state machine that would be generated if the program could be explored completely (without any limitations on its scope). Each edge in the graph is a method invocation (including particular argument values).

Spec Explorer provides several ways for the user to limit exploration by configuring finite domains for each method argument, limitations on the sizes of data structures, equivalence classes on states (where only one representative state from each class will be explored), and various other stopping conditions.

Exploration can check safety properties by searching for unsafe states, and investigate liveness by searching for paths to goal states.

3.2   Test Suite Generation

Spec Explorer can generate test suites by traversing the graph of the finite state machine. Different traversal algorithms achieve different coverage. For example, a postman tour achieves full link coverage.

3.3   Conformance Testing

Spec Explorer can perform conformance tests. It includes a test harness that can execute generated test suites on the implementation and the model program in lockstep, using the model program as the oracle to check the implementation.

4   References

For more information about the Spec# language and Spec Explorer tool consult the Foundations of Software Engineering web site at Microsoft Research:
    http://research.microsoft.com/fse/

Formal Engineering for Industrial Software Development – An Introduction to the SOFL Specification Language and Method

Shaoying Liu

Department of Computer Science,
Faculty of Computer and Information Sciences,
Hosei University, Tokyo, Japan
`sliu@k.hosei.ac.jp`
`http://cis.k.hosei.ac.jp/~sliu/`

Formal methods have been developed as a rigorous approach to computer systems development over last three decades, but have been facing challenges in fighting for industrial acceptance in general. Most commonly used formal methods do not offer comprehensible structuring mechanism for building complex systems; formal refinement is not sufficient to deal with real development situations; and formal verification requires high skills and is time-intensive, and is therefore expensive to be adopted by industry.

Having mentioned these challenges, we do not mean to suggest the denial of the advantages of formal methods in achieving preciseness and conciseness of software systems. In fact, our position is in favour of adopting formal methods, but emphasize that it must be employed in an appropriate manner that can significantly improve the rigor, comprehensibility, and the controllability of the commonly used software engineering methods and processes. To this end, we believe that it is important to improve the languages and techniques for constructing formal specifications, refining specifications, and verifying and validating specifications and programs.

One effective way to realize this goal is to provide a formal but practical specification language and method by properly integrating existing formal methods and informal or semi-formal methods commonly used in industry. Such a method should allow developers to systematically carry out software development using a comprehensible notation in a rigorous and controllable process. It should also offer a means for effective cooperation among different people within the same software project, such as managers, analysts, designers, programmers, and testers. Furthermore, perhaps the most important feature of such a method would be the tool supportability; that is, the method should be easily supported in depth.

On the basis of our intensive research and application experience over the last fifteen years, we have developed the SOFL specification language and method for software development [1, 2, 3], aiming to address these problems. As a specification language, SOFL integrates VDM-SL, Data Flow Diagrams, and Petri Nets to provide an intuitive, rigorous, and comprehensible formal notation for specifications at different levels. Compared to UML (Unified Modeling Language), SOFL provides a simpler but systematic mechanism for *precisely* defining the

J. Davies et al. (Eds.): ICFEM 2004, LNCS 3308, pp. 7–8, 2004.

functions of system units and their integration, and therefore avoids the difficulty in managing different kinds of diagrams and their consistency in UML. As a method, it combines structured methods and object-oriented methods, and advocates an transformational and evolutionary approach to constructing formal specifications from informal and then semi-formal specifications; it integrates the idea of formal proof and commonly used verification and validation techniques, such as testing and reviews, to offer rigorous but practical verification techniques.

After a brief description of the general principle of Formal Engineering Methods, this tutorial offers a systematic introduction to the SOFL specification language, method, process, and supporting tools. Specifically, the tutorial is divided into three parts. The first part includes the brief introduction to Formal Engineering Methods and the SOFL specification language. In particular, we will focus on the explanation of the idea of using the graphical notation, known as Condition Data Flow Diagram (or CDFD for short), to model the architecture of a system, while using the pre-post notation to define the functionality of processes occurring in CDFDs. The second part explains the SOFL method and process: how SOFL can be used to construct a formal specification by taking a three-step: informal, semi-formal, and formal specifications. It also explains how structured abstract design can be smoothly transformed into object-oriented detailed design and programs. Furthermore, the role of each form of these specifications in the entire software development process is also elaborated. Finally, the third part of the tutorial presents Rigorous Review and Specification Testing as two practical techniques for verification and validation of specifications, and demonstrates several tools we have built to support SOFL.

References

[1] Shaoying Liu. *Formal Engineering for Industrial Software Development Using the SOFL Method*. Springer-Verlag, 2004.
[2] Shaoying Liu, Jeff Offutt, Chris Ho-Stuart, Yong Sun, and Mitsuru Ohba. SOFL: A Formal Engineering Methodology for Industrial Applications. *IEEE Transactions on Software Engineering*, 24(1):337–344, January 1998. Special Issue on Formal Methods.
[3] Shaoying Liu. Utilizing Specification Testing in Review Task Trees for Rigorous Review of Formal Specifications. In *Proceedings of 10th Asia-Pacific Software Engineering Conference (APSEC03), Chiangmai, Thailand, December 10–12 2003*. IEEE Computer Society Press.

Tutorial: Software Model Checking

Edmund Clarke[1] and Daniel Kroening[2,*]

[1] Department of Computer Science, Carnegie Mellon University,
Pittsburgh, PA, 15213
[2] Computer Systems Institute, ETH Zürich, Switzerland

Abstract. Model Checking is an automated technique for the systematic exploration ofu the state space of a state transition system. The first part of the tutorial
provides an introduction to the basic concepts of model checking, including BDD-
and SAT-based symbolic model checking, partial order reduction, abstraction, and
compositional verification. Model Checking has been applied sucessfully to hardware in the past. However, software has become the most complex part of safety
ciritcal systems. The second part of the tutorial covers tools that use Model Checking to formally verify computer software.

1 Introduction

Software has become the most complex part of today's safety critical embedded systems.
Testing methods can only provide very limited coverage due to the enormous state space
that needs to be searched. Formal verification tools, on the other hand, promise full
coverage of the state space. Introduced in 1981, *Model Checking* [1, 2] is one of the most
commonly used formal verification techniques in a commercial setting. The first part
of the tutorial reviews classical explicit state and symbolic model checking algorithms
with a focus on software.

The capacity of Model Checking algorithms is constrained by the state-space explosion problem. In case of BDD-based symbolic model checking algorithms, this problem
manifests itself in the form of unmanagbly large BDDs. Thus, techniques to reduce the
size of the state space, such as the partial order reduction, are discussed.

Abstraction and compositional verification techniques will also be covered briefly.

The second part of the tutorial discusses tools and algorithms for the model checking
computer software. We first cover explicit state methods and implementations such as
Spin, JPF [3], Bogor [4], and CMC [5]. We describe the area of application of each of

---

* This research was sponsored by the Gigascale Systems Research Center (GSRC), the National
Science Foundation (NSF) under grant no. CCR-9803774, the Office of Naval Research (ONR),
the Naval Research Laboratory (NRL) under contract no. N00014-01-1-0796, and by the Defense Advanced Research Projects Agency, and the Army Research Office (ARO) under contract
no. DAAD19-01-1-0485, and the General Motors Collaborative Research Lab at CMU. The
views and conclusions contained in this document are those of the author and should not be
interpreted as representing the official policies, either expressed or implied, of GSRC, NSF,
ONR, NRL, DOD, ARO, or the U.S. government.

J. Davies et al. (Eds.): ICFEM 2004, LNCS 3308, pp. 9–10, 2004.

these tools using a concrete example. However, the size of the software system is usually severely constrained when using explicit state model checker.

Software model checking has, in recent years, been applied successfully to large, real software programs, but within certain restricted domains. Many of the tools that have been instrumental in this success have been based on the Counterexample Guided Abstraction Refinement (CEGAR) paradigm [6, 7], first used to model check software programs by Ball and Rajamani [8]. Their SLAM tool [9] has demonstrated the effectiveness of software verification for device drivers. BLAST [10] and MAGIC [11] have been applied to security protocols and real-time operating system kernels.

A common feature of the success of these tools is that the programs and properties examined did not depend on complex data structures. The properties that have been successfully checked or refuted have relied on control flow and relatively simple integer variable relationships. SLAM, BLAST, and MAGIC rely on theorem provers to perform the critical refinement step. The tutorial covers some of the details of these implementations.

References

1. E. Clarke, O. Grumberg, and D. Peled. *Model Checking*. MIT Press, 2000.
2. E. M. Clarke and E. A. Emerson. Synthesis of synchronization skeletons for branching time temporal logic. In *Logic of Programs: Workshop*, volume 131 of *LNCS*. Springer-Verlag, 1981.
3. W. Visser, K. Havelund, G. Brat, S. Park, and F. Lerda. Model checking programs. *Automated Software Engineering*, 10(2):203–232, 2003.
4. Robby, E. Rodriguez, M. Dwyer, and J. Hatcliff. Checking strong specifications using an extensible software model checking framework. In *Tools and Algorithms for the Construction and Analysis of Systems*, pages 404–420, 2004.
5. M. Musuvathi, D. Park, A. Chou, D. Engler, and D. Dill. CMC: a pragmatic approach to model checking real code. In *Symposium on Operating System Design and Implementation*, 2002.
6. R. P. Kurshan. *Computer-Aided Verification of Coordinating Processes: The Automata-Theoretic Approach*. Princeton University Press, 1995.
7. E. Clarke, O. Grumberg, S. Jha, Y. Lu, and H. Veith. Counterexample-guided abstraction refinement. In *Computer Aided Verification*, pages 154–169, 2000.
8. T. Ball and S.K. Rajamani. Boolean programs: A model and process for software analysis. Technical Report 2000-14, Microsoft Research, February 2000.
9. T. Ball and S. Rajamani. Automatically validating temporal safety properties of interfaces. In *SPIN Workshop on Model Checking of Software*, pages 103–122, 2001.
10. T. A. Henzinger, R. Jhala, R. Majumdar, and G. Sutre. Lazy abstraction. In *Principles of Programming Languages*, pages 58–70, 2002.
11. S. Chaki, E. Clarke, A. Groce, S. Jha, and H. Veith. Modular verification of software components in C. *IEEE Transactions on Software Engineering*, 30(6):388–402, June 2004.

Engineering Quality Software

Amitabh Srivastava

Microsoft Corporation

Producing high performing, reliable and secure software is a challenging problem in the software industry. An important element in achieving this goal lies in the automation of the software development process, which currently is primarily manual. However, progress in program specification, verification, and testing is more rapid today than ever before. At Microsoft, we have developed innovative techniques to address some of these challenges. Our techniques scale to meet the requirements of real production environments and span the whole development process from software architecture to sustained engineering. These methodologies are making huge impact in the development of Windows and other products at Microsoft. This talk focuses on the challenges in software development, describes our progress and experience, and outlines remaining problems.

J. Davies et al. (Eds.): ICFEM 2004, LNCS 3308, p. 11, 2004.

When Can Formal Methods Make a Real Difference?

Peter G. Neumann

SRI International Computer Science Lab,
Menlo Park, CA 94025
Neumann@CSL.sri.com
http://www.csl.sri.com/neumann

This talk will consider a few cases from the ACM Risks Forum archives

http://www.risks.org

for which the sensible use of formal methods could have made a decisive difference in avoiding serious consequences – with respect to requirements, specifications, human interfaces, implementation, and even operation, typically in systems that were supposedly safe, reliable, or secure. This will provide a view to the future in terms of things we can learn about the past.

J. Davies et al. (Eds.): ICFEM 2004, LNCS 3308, p. 12, 2004.

On the Adoption of Formal Methods by Industry: The ACL2 Experience

J Strother Moore

Department of Computer Sciences,
University of Texas at Austin

Formal methods are gradually being adopted by industry. The complexity of industrial designs – often seen as an impediment to the use of formal methods – is actually one of the main arguments in favor of mechanized formal methods. No other tool is as good as mechanized mathematical modeling at capturing the complexity and giving the human designers the facilities for explaining the reasons their designs are correct and controlling the revelation of the relevant complexity.

In this talk I will describe the ongoing Boyer-Moore project, which for three decades has been concerned with the use of mechanized theorem proving to verify properties of hardware and software. The current theorem prover, ACL2, is the product of Matt Kaufmann and the speaker, and has been used to verify

- the correspondence of a bit- and cycle-accurate micro-architectural model of a Motorola digital signal processor and the microcode engine it implemented,
- the verification of some microcode for that Motorola dsp,
- the correctness, with respect to the IEEE 754 floating point standard, of the AMD K5's FDIV and FSQRT instructions,
- the correctness of the RTL implementing the elementary floating point operations on the AMD Athlon and other AMD fpu designs,
- process isolation properties of the microcode implementing a separation kernel on the Rockwell AAMP7 processor, and
- properties of JVM bytecode and of the JVM itself, including ongoing work on the bytecode verifier and class loader.

I will sketch how we got to this state of affairs and some of the key reasons ACL2 has been adopted for these and other projects.

J. Davies et al. (Eds.): ICFEM 2004, LNCS 3308, p. 13, 2004.

A CLP Approach to Modelling Systems

Joxan Jaffar*

School of Computing, National University of Singapore,
Republic of Singapore 117543

We present a formal method for modelling the operational behavior of various kinds of systems of concurrent processes. A first objective is that the method be broadly applicable. A system can be described in terms of its processes written in a traditional syntax-based manner, or in some non-traditional form such as a timed automaton. The number of processes may be fixed, or parameterized, or, because of dynamic process creation, unbounded. The communication and synchronization between processes may be synchronous or not, and via shared variables or some form of channels. We may have a traditional interleaving of processes, or use a specific scheduling strategy. The observables modelled should not be restricted to just the values of the program variables, but possibly other attributes of the system such as its registers and cache, its clock and battery values, etc. An example application area which touches upon these characteristics is that of determining worst-case execution time.

We choose to model a generic system S in the form of a CLP program P. The model-theoretic semantics of P shall characterize the "collecting" semantics of S, that is, those states that are observable. The proof-theoretic semantics of P, on the other hand, further characterize the "trace" semantics of S. An advantage of this CLP approach is that intricate details of the system can be captured in a familiar logical framework.

We then present a specification language for an extensive class of system behaviors. In addition to the traditional safety and liveness properties which specify the universality or eventuality of certain predicates on states, we introduce the notions of *relative safety* and *relative progress*. The former extends traditional safety assertions to accommodate non-behavioral properties such as symmetry, serializability and commutativity between processes. The latter provides for specifying progress properties. Our specification method is not just for stating the property of interest, but also for the *assertion* of properties held at various program points.

Finally, we present an inference method, based upon a notion of *inductive tabling*, for proving an assertion A. This method can use assertions that have already been proven, use the assertion A itself, in a manner prescribed by induction principles, and dynamically generate new assertions. All these properties are shown to be useful in preventing redundant computations, which then can lead to efficient proofs. Our proof method thus combines the search characteristic of model-checking and abstract interpretation, and methods of inductive assertions. We demonstrate a prototype implementation on some benchmark examples.

---

* Joint work with Andrew Santosa and Răzvan Voicu

J. Davies et al. (Eds.): ICFEM 2004, LNCS 3308, p. 14, 2004.
© Springer-Verlag Berlin Heidelberg 2004

Multi-prover Verification of C Programs

Jean-Christophe Filliâtre and Claude Marché

*PCRI — LRI (CNRS UMR 8623) — INRIA Futurs — Université Paris 11,
Bât 490, Université Paris-sud, 91405 Orsay cedex, France

Abstract. Our goal is the verification of C programs at the source code level using formal proof tools. Programs are specified using annotations such as pre- and post-conditions and global invariants. An original approach is presented which allows to formally prove that a function implementation satisfies its specification and is free of null pointer dereferencing and out-of-bounds array access. The method is not bound to a particular back-end theorem prover. A significant part of the ANSI C language is supported, including pointer arithmetic and possible pointer aliasing. We describe a prototype tool and give some experimental results.

Keywords: C programming language, Hoare logic, pointer programs, formal verification and proof.

1   Introduction

Using formal methods for verifying properties of programs at their source code level has gained more interest with the increased use of embedded programs, which are short programs where a high-level of confidence is required. Such embedded programs are no more written in assembly language but in C (plane command control, cars, etc.) or in JavaCard [21] (mobile phones, smart cards, etc.). This paper introduces a verification method for ANSI C source code, following the same approach as the one we used for Java [15, 16]. A prototype tool has been implemented, called Caduceus, freely available for experimentation [11]. This tool is currently under experimentation at Axalto (smart cards) and Dassault Aviation (aeronautics).

In the following, we assume the reader fairly familiar with ANSI C [13]. In our setting, the properties that may be checked are of two kinds: first, the program may be checked to be free of *threats* (null pointer dereferencing or out-of-bounds array access) and second, it may be proved satisfying functional properties given as functions's *postconditions*. These kinds of properties are not independent since they both usually need insertion of appropriate annotations (functions's *preconditions*, *global invariants*, *loop invariants*, etc.) as usual in a Hoare logic framework. In practice, these annotations are inserted in the source code as comments of a specific shape / * @ . . . * / . The specification language we use in those comments is largely inspired by the Java Modeling Language (JML) [14]. It has however significant differences, mainly due to the fact that unlike JML we do not seek runtime assertion checking.

* This research was partly supported by the "projet GECCOO de l'ACI Sécurité Informatique", CNRS & INRIA, http://gecco.lri.fr.

J. Davies et al. (Eds.): ICFEM 2004, LNCS 3308, pp. 15–29, 2004.

Once a C program is annotated, verification is done by running **Caduceus** on the sources in a way similar to a classical compiler but resulting in the generation of the so-called *verification conditions*: these are first-order predicate logic formulas whose validity implies the soundness of the program with respect to the absence of threat and to the functional properties given as annotations. At this point, a general purpose theorem prover must be used to establish those verification conditions. An original **Caduceus** feature is its independence with respect to the prover. It currently supports the Coq interactive proof assistant [7] and the Simplify automatic prover [1]. New provers may easily be added provided a suitable pretty-printer; support for PVS [18] and haRVey [19] are planned in a near future.

A significant part of ANSI C is supported. All control structures are supported except goto. Pointer programs are supported, including pointer arithmetics and possible pointer aliasing, using old ideas from Burstall [4] recently emphasized by Bornat [3] and used for a case study by Mehta and Nipkow [17]. The main unsupported feature is the cast of pointer (e.g. when pointers to void are used to write "polymorphic" functions).

In this paper we present both an overview of **Caduceus** from a user's point of view and the method used internally to generate the verification conditions. This method is very similar to the one we used for Java programs and a significant amount of work is shared: the generation of the conditions is indeed realized by a common intermediate tool called **Why** [9, 10] whose input language—also annotated with Hoare-like pre- and postconditions—is specifically designed for the purpose of verification conditions generation. In other words, **Caduceus** is a compiler from annotated C programs to the **Why** input language.

We seek for a method which guarantees soundness with the highest level of confidence, even if it is not fully automatic. In other words, our approach differs from static checking methods, which are always fully automated but may sometimes miss bugs.

This paper is organized as follows. Section 2 gives an overview of the use of **Caduceus** with a presentation of the specification language, examples and experimental results. In Section 3, we describe the internal approach used to perform verification, including the modeling of heap memory, the translation to **Why** and discussion about soundness. We conclude in Section 4 with a comparison to related works.

2   Overview of Caduceus and Its Specification Language

This section gives an overview of **Caduceus** from a user's point of view based on small examples. A comprehensive description of the annotation syntax can be found in the **Caduceus** reference manual [11].

2.1   A Simple Character Queue

We start with a very simple C program implementing a character queue within a circular array. The queue is a global structure q declared on Figure 1. The array q.contents contains the queue elements stored from index q.first included to index q.last excluded. q.length is the length of q.contents, that is the maximal capacity of the queue. The boolean fields q.empty and q.full indicate whether the queue is empty or full respectively.

```
struct queue {
  char *contents;
  int length;
  int first, last;
  unsigned int empty, full :1;
} q;
```

Fig. 1. A character queue within a circular array

It is natural to associate an invariant to such a global declaration. It avoids repeating the same properties in all functions's specifications. For instance, we may declare that q.contents points to a valid (i.e. allocated) array of at least q.length elements and that q.first and q.last are valid indexes within this array. This is done using the global declaration invariant as follows:

```
/*@ invariant q_invariant :
  @   \valid_range(q.contents, 0, q.length-1) &&
  @   0 <= q.first < q.length &&
  @   0 <= q.last < q.length
  @*/
```

Informally, such an invariant is added to the precondition of each function involving q and to the postcondition of each function possibly modifying q. The precise meaning of "involving" and "possibly modifying" is given below.

Annotations such as the above invariant are first-order logic predicates built from atoms and connectives such as &&, ||, !, etc. Atoms are built from side-effects free C expressions and predicate symbols. Here, \valid_range is a predefined predicate expressing that a given array range can be safely dereferenced.

A function specification is given right before the function definition and is composed of three (optional) clauses: a precondition introduced by the keyword requires, a side-effects clause introduced by the keyword assigns and a postcondition introduced by the keyword ensures. For instance, here is a possible specification/definition of a function push adding an element in q:

```
/*@ requires !q.full
  @ assigns   q.empty, q.full, q.last, q.contents[q.last]
  @ ensures   !q.empty && q.contents[\old(q.last)] == c
  @*/
void push(char c) {
  q.contents[q.last++] = c;
  if (q.last == q.length) q.last = 0;
  q.empty = 0;
  q.full = (q.first == q.last);
}
```

The requires clause is a predicate that must hold whenever the function is called; here it states that q must not be full.

The assigns clause indicates the set of locations possibly modified by the function call. More precisely, it says that any memory location already allocated before the function call and not mentioned in this set is left untouched by the function call.

The ensures clause is a predicate that must hold whenever the function returns. Values of expressions or predicates in the prestate—the program point corresponding to the function call—can be obtained using the \old() modifier. For instance we write here \old(q.last) to denote the value of q.last when push was called.

When run on the above code, Caduceus produces several verification conditions expressing that (1) the postcondition and the assigns clause of push are established, (2) the invariant q_invariant is preserved by push, and (3) the code of push contains no null pointer dereference (which means here that the assignment of q.contents[q.last++] is valid).

To establish the validity of these conditions, a theory (i.e. a set of axioms) is provided (see Section 3.4). Using the Simplify decision procedure with this theory, the three conditions for push are automatically discharged. With the Coq proof assistant, proofs are easily handled (6 lines of tactics to write).

A function specification can also be attached to a function declaration, this function being defined later or not. For instance we can declare a pop function together with its specification:

```
/*@ requires !q.empty
 @ assigns q.empty, q.full, q.first
 @ ensures !q.full && \result == q.contents[\old(q.first)]
 @*/
char pop();
```

Notice, in the postcondition, the use of \result to denote the returned value.

It is important to notice that our verification process is modular, in the sense that when another function calls push or pop, only their specifications are seen. In other words the implementation of push may be changed or the one of pop added without affecting the remaining of the verification process. Notice also that the assigns clauses are essential for modularity of the verification, not only because they specify what is modified, but mainly because they specify that everything else is unmodified (see Section 3.4).

2.2   In-place List Reversal

We continue with a now classical example: in-place list reversal [3, 4, 17]. The code is given Figure 2. It introduces a type list for linked list of integers and a function reverse that reverses a list in-place.

To write a specification for reverse we first need to express that the list p0 is finite. This cannot be expressed using a first-order predicate (assuming no primitive). A solution could have been to allow the use of side-effect free functions from the code itself, like in JML for instance. This would clearly make sense for runtime assertion checking, but for formal verification we think it is better to clearly separate the code side and the logic side. So instead, in our setting predicates and logical functions required to write specifications must be defined on the logic side, that is in the language of the backend theorem prover, and imported into the source code.

```
typedef struct struct_list {          list reverse(list p0) {
  int hd;                               list r = p0, p = NULL;
  struct struct_list *tl;               while (r != NULL) {
} *list;                                  list q = r;
                                          r = r->tl; q->tl = p; p = q;
                                        }
                                        return p;
                                      }
```

Fig. 2. In-place list reversal

For this example, we import a predicate is_list, supposed to characterize finite lists, with the following declaration:

```
/*@ predicate is_list(list l) reads l->tl */
```

The clause reads indicates the memory locations involved in the predicate definition. This is indeed mandatory for the predicate to be applied to the corresponding variables on the logic side. On this example, the definition of is_list obviously requires the knowledge of the tl fields of lists cells.

We need additional predicates to give reverse a postcondition. Indeed we must relate the returned list to the input list. Following [17] we introduce a predicate llist relating a C list p (a pointer) to the list of all its elements:

```
/*@ predicate llist(list p, plist l) reads l->tl */
```

Here plist is an abstract type of pointer lists defined on the logic side. With the additional declaration of a reverse function on type plist

```
/*@ logic plist rev(plist pl) */
```

it is then possible to write a specification for reverse:

```
/*@ requires is_list(p0)
  @ ensures \forall plist l0;
  @     \old(llist(p0, l0)) => llist(\result, rev(l0))   @*/
list reverse(list p0) { ...
```

It is important to note that the function symbol rev involved in the specification is not at all related to the C function reverse being defined.

As usual with Hoare-like annotations, we need to annotate the loop to be able to prove function reverse correct. We insert a loop invariant and a variant to ensure the termination, respectively introduced by the keywords invariant and variant:

```
...
/*@ invariant
      \exists plist lp; \exists plist lr;
        llist(p, lp) && llist(r, lr) && disjoint(lp, lr) &&
      \forall plist l;
        \old(llist(p0, l)) => app(rev(lr), lp) == rev(l)
```

```
  @ variant length(r) for length_order */
while (r != NULL) { ...
```

The invariant involves new importations:

```
/* app(l1,l2) is the concatenation of l1 and l2 */
/*@ logic plist app(plist l1, plist l2) */
/* disjoint(l1,l2) is true whenever l1 and l2 have no
   element in common */
/*@ predicate disjoint(plist l1, plist l2) */
```

and the variant also requires importations of length and length_order (see [11] for details).

With these annotations, Caduceus generates 7 verification conditions for the C function reverse. The Simplify prover only established 4 of them automatically, which is not surprising because indeed we did not provide a full theory for the new predicates such as llist. On the other hand, we defined in Coq a model for these predicates using the predefined Coq lists and all conditions have been proved correct. The proofs amount to 70 lines of tactics. The model for linked lists (definition of llist, etc.) is around 180 lines long and is reusable for other programs involving linked lists.

We are currently experimenting Caduceus on the Schorr-Waite algorithm which is considered as a benchmark for pointer programs verification [3, 17]. Compared to the proof in Isabelle/HOL [17], we also check the absence of threats. Since annotations from [17] fit in our specification language, we strongly believe that Isabelle/HOL proofs will be adapted to Coq without difficulty.

3   The Verification Technique

Our approach is to translate annotated C programs into Why's input language. The latter does not provide any data structure, but only applicative types (primitive types such as integers, booleans, etc. and *abstract* datatypes) and mutable variables containing applicative values. This means that Why has absolutely no knowledge of arrays, structures, pointers and memory heap in general, hence our translation mechanism needs to introduce definitions of abstract datatypes to model the memory state of a given C program. Then the semantics of C statements must be translated into Why statements operating on these abstract datatypes. In this section we proceed as follows: first we present Why's input language, then we describe our modeling of memory heaps, then we give the translation rules from C statements to Why's statements, then the background theory and finally we discuss about the soundness of the approach.

3.1   The Why Tool

Unlike usual approaches in Hoare logic, Why's core language is not Pascal-like but ML-like: there is no difference between expressions and statements (the latter are simply expressions of type unit, which is similar to void in C) and immutable variables are introduced by let..in.. constructs. On top of this side-effect free core language, modifiable variables are introduced using an explicit reference type ref as in SML or

OCaml. A feature of great importance for us is that Why rejects any variable aliasing (rejecting aliasing is required by Why to guarantee the soundness of verification condition generation), hence dealing with pointer programs requires an appropriate modeling of memory. Finally, beside usual imperative control statements (sequence, conditional and while loops) Why features exceptions with a try-catch mechanism. Exceptions will be used to encode return, break and continue C statements.

Why programs can be annotated using pre- and postconditions, loop invariants and intermediate assertions. Logical formulas are written in a (possibly polymorphic) typed first-order logic with built-in equality, booleans, infinite precision integers and real numbers with usual operations. Why performs an *effect analysis* (see below) on modifiable variables of programs, a classical weakest precondition computation [8] and generates proof obligations for various provers.

Why has a modular approach. New logic functions or predicate symbols can be introduced and freely used in the specification part. Sub-programs can also be introduced abstractly, by the mean of a full specification: type of input variables and result, pre- and postconditions, as well as its *effects*, that is the sets of global references possibly read and/or written by the subprogram.

In order to translate an annotated C program into Why, one needs to proceed the following way:

1. Find an appropriate modeling of C memory states using global Why variables which will never be aliased;
2. Translate C constructs into Why statements, with assignments over the global variables introduced above;
3. Translate annotations into Why predicates over those variables.

Because C functions can be mutually recursive, we first give a specification for all the functions as abstract Why subprograms with specifications. This abstract view is used to interpret function calls and suffices to ensure partial correctness of programs.

Figure 3 shows the Why abstract declaration of the subprogram corresponding to the push function of Section 2.1. It has one argument (the integer c) which is supposed to satisfy the precondition (first formula between curly braces). There is no result (output type is unit), it accesses nine global variables (listed after **reads**) and writes four (listed after **writes**). The postcondition (second pair of curly braces) uses the notation $x@$ to denote the value of variable x before the function application. The predicates valid, valid_range and assigns, and function symbols acc, shift and pointer_loc are easily understood as translation of specifications; they are formally introduced in the next sections.

3.2   Modeling C Memory Heap

The C memory is represented by a finite set of Why variables, each containing an applicative map. We adopt Burstall's approach [4], recently emphasized by Bornat [3] then Mehta and Nipkow [17]. The key idea is to have one Why variable for each structure field. Indeed, two structure fields cannot be aliased (as soon as one conforms to ANSI C). The very useful consequence is that whenever one structure field is updated, only the corresponding Why variable is modified and we have for free that any other field is left untouched. We extend this model to arrays and more generally to pointer arithmetic.

parameter push.parameter : c : int →
  { acc($full, q$) = 0 ∧ valid($alloc, q$)∧
    valid_range($alloc$, acc($contents, q$), 0, acc($length, q$) − 1)∧
    0 ≤ acc($first, q$) < acc($length, q$) ∧ 0 ≤ acc($last, q$) < acc($length, q$) }
  unit **reads** $alloc, contents, empty, first, full, intP, last, length, q$
  writes $empty, full, intP, last$
  { acc($empty, q$) = 0 ∧ acc($intP$, shift(acc($contents, q$), acc($last@, q@$))) = c∧
    assigns($alloc@, last@, last$, pointer_loc($q@$))∧
    assigns($alloc@, intP@, intP$,
          pointer_loc(shift(acc($contents@, q@$), acc($last@, q@$))))∧
    assigns($alloc@, full@, full$, pointer_loc($q@$))∧
    assigns($alloc@, empty@, empty$, pointer_loc($q@$))∧
    valid_range($alloc$, acc($contents, q$), 0, acc($length, q$) − 1)∧
    0 ≤ acc($first, q$) < acc($length, q$) ∧ 0 ≤ acc($last, q$) < acc($length, q$) }

Fig. 3. Why interpretation of push

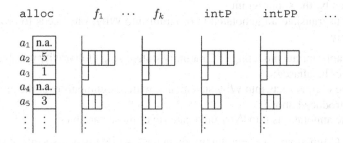

Fig. 4. Modeling of C memory heap

The set of variables representing the C memory is displayed on Figure 4. All these variables contain applicative maps indexed by addresses a_1, a_2, ... belonging to some abstract data type addr. The variable alloc on the left of the figure is the *allocation store* which tells for each address whether it is allocated and, when so, the size of the block it points to. All other variables map addresses to 1-dimensional arrays indexed by integers. A type pointer is introduced to represent C pointers. A value of type pointer is either the null pointer or a pair of an address and an integer index. For instance, address a_2 points to a block of length 5 according to alloc and thus the pointer $(a_2, 3)$ refers to the fourth element of each array $f_1(a_2)$, $f_2(a_2)$, ... The variable intP is used for arrays of integers i.e. pointers to int, intPP for pointers to pointers to int, etc. Similarly the variable pointerP is used for pointers to structures, pointerPP for pointers to pointers to structures, etc.

On the Why side, each of those applicative maps is of type α memory, an abstract polymorphic datatype equipped with the following side-effect free functions, to access a cell and to update it, respectively.

```
acc:  α memory, pointer → α
upd:  α memory, pointer, α → α memory
```

Depending on the memory used, α is either `int`, `float` or `pointer`. We also introduce one Why variable for each C global variable or static local variable. Finally, C local variables are represented using Why local variables since they cannot be aliased.

Effects Inference. Once we have determined the set of variables representing the memory state, a non-trivial step to be able to deal modularly with function calls is to statically compute the *effects* of each statement and each function. An effect is a pair of sets of Why variables respectively (possibly) accessed and modified. Such an effect appears on Figure 3 (the **reads** and **writes** clauses).

Computing statements effects is straightforward: it is only a matter of traversing statements and expressions recursively, collecting accessed and modified variables along and assuming known effects for all functions. Computing functions effects is then obtained by iterating effects inference on each function body until a fixpoint is reached, which is guaranteed to happen since the set of variables is finite and effects can only grow during this process.

3.3   Translating C Source Code

This section describes the translation from C source code to Why source code. The translation is realized through four mutually recursive interpretations:

- $[\![e]\!]$: the interpretation of a C expression e;
- $[\![e]\!]_b$: the interpretation of a C expression e as a Why boolean expression—though C does not have booleans, the translation is more natural when a C expression e used as a boolean is directly translated into a Why boolean;
- $[\![e]\!]_l$: the interpretation of a C *left value* e, i.e. an expression allowed on the left of an assignment;
- $[\![s]\!]$: the interpretation of a C statement s.

Left Values. The interpretation of a left value e is either a Why reference x or a pair (m, p) of a memory m and a pointer expression p. This interpretation is defined as follows:

- $[\![x]\!]_l = x$
- $[\![*e]\!]_l = (m, [\![e]\!])$, where m depends on the type of e, e.g. `intP` for `int*`, `intPP` for `int**`, etc.
- $[\![e\text{->}f]\!]_l = (f, [\![e]\!])$

Expressions. We only give the most significant constructs. Translation of memory access and assignment is done via two abstract Why programs

parameter access : $m : \alpha$ memory ref $\rightarrow p :$ pointer $\rightarrow$
   $\{\text{valid}(alloc, p)\}$ α **reads** $alloc, m$ $\{result = \text{acc}(m, p)\}$

parameter update : $m : \alpha$ memory ref $\rightarrow p :$ pointer $\rightarrow v : \alpha \rightarrow$
   $\{\text{valid}(alloc, p)\}$ unit **reads** $alloc, m$ **writes** m $\{m = \text{upd}(m@, p, v)\}$

where $\mathtt{valid}(alloc, p)$ expresses that p can be safely dereferenced according to $alloc$. The precise meaning of $\mathtt{valid}$ is given Section 3.4.

- $[\![x]\!] = \,!x$
- $[\![*e]\!] = \mathtt{access}\ m\ p$, when $[\![*e]\!]_l = (m, p)$
- $[\![e\text{->}f]\!] = \mathtt{access}\ f\ [\![e]\!]$
- $[\![x = e_2]\!] = x := [\![e_2]\!];\ !x$
- $[\![e_1 = e_2]\!] = \mathtt{let}\ v_1 = p_1\ \mathtt{in}\ \mathtt{let}\ v_2 = [\![e_2]\!]\ \mathtt{in}\ \mathtt{update}\ m\ v_1\ v_2;\ v_2,$
  when $[\![e_1]\!]_l = (m, p_1)$
- $[\![e_1 + e_2]\!] = \mathtt{shift}\ [\![e_1]\!]\ [\![e_2]\!]$, when e_1 is a pointer
- $[\![e_1\ op\ e_2]\!] = [\![e_1]\!]\ op\ [\![e_2]\!]$, with $op \in \{+, -, *, /, \%, \&, \hat{}, |\}$
- $[\![e_1\ op\ e_2]\!] = \mathtt{if}\ [\![e_1\ op\ e_2]\!]_b\ \mathtt{then}\ 1\ \mathtt{else}\ 0,$
  with $op \in \{==, !=, >, >=, <, <=, \&\&, ||\}$
- $[\![\mathtt{f}(e_1, \ldots, e_n)]\!] = \mathtt{f.parameter}([\![e_1]\!], \ldots, [\![e_n]\!])$

Boolean Expressions. The interpretation of a "boolean" expression is defined as follows:

- $[\![e_1\ op\ e_2]\!]_b = \mathtt{let}\ v_1 = [\![e_1]\!]\ \mathtt{in}\ \mathtt{let}\ v_2 = [\![e_2]\!]\ \mathtt{in}\ v_1\ op\ v_2,$
  with $op \in \{==, !=, >, >=, <, <=\}$
- $[\![e_1\ \&\&\ e_2]\!]_b = \mathtt{if}\ [\![e_1]\!]_b\ \mathtt{then}\ [\![e_2]\!]_b\ \mathtt{else}\ \mathtt{false}$
- $[\![e_1\ ||\ e_2]\!]_b = \mathtt{if}\ [\![e_1]\!]_b\ \mathtt{then}\ \mathtt{true}\ \mathtt{else}\ [\![e_2]\!]_b$
- $[\![!e]\!]_b = \mathtt{not}\ [\![e]\!]_b$
- $[\![e]\!]_b = [\![e]\!]\ \mathtt{<>}\ 0,$ otherwise

Statements. The translation of a C statement is defined as follows:

- $[\![e]\!] = \mathtt{let}\ \_ = [\![e]\!]\ \mathtt{in}\ \mathtt{void}$
- $[\![e_1;\ e_2]\!] = [\![e_1]\!];\ [\![e_2]\!]$
- $[\![\{\ \beta_1\ x_1 = e_1;\ \ldots\ \beta_n\ x_n = e_n;\ s\ \}]\!]$
  $= \mathtt{let}\ x_1 = \mathtt{ref}\ [\![e_1]\!]\ \mathtt{in}\ \ldots\ \mathtt{let}\ x_n = \mathtt{ref}\ [\![e_n]\!]\ \mathtt{in}\ [\![s]\!]$

  The translation above assumes that each variable x_i has an initializer e_i. If a local variable has no initializer, it is indeed initialized using a call to an unspecified function, thus simulating a random initialization.

- $[\![\mathtt{for}(e_1;\ e_2;\ s_3)\ s]\!] =$
  $\quad [\![e_1]\!];$
  $\quad \mathtt{try}$
  $\quad\quad \mathtt{while}\ [\![e_2]\!]\ \mathtt{do}\ \mathtt{try}\ [\![s;\ s_3]\!]\ \mathtt{with}\ \mathtt{Continue}\ \text{->}\ \mathtt{void}\ \mathtt{end}\ \mathtt{done}$
  $\quad \mathtt{with}\ \mathtt{Break}\ \text{->}\ \mathtt{void}\ \mathtt{end}$

  A similar translation is used for $\mathtt{while}$ and $\mathtt{do}$ loops.
- $[\![\mathtt{return}\ e]\!]_s = \mathtt{raise}\ (\mathtt{Return}\ [\![e]\!])$

Finally, a C function definition is interpreted as a **Why** function definition where the exception $\mathtt{Return}$ is caught appropriately:

$[\![\mathtt{f}(\tau_1\ x_1, \ldots, \tau_n\ x_n)\ \{\ s\ \}]\!] =$
$\quad \mathtt{let}\ \mathtt{f}\ (x_1\!:\![\![\tau_1]\!])\ \ldots\ (x_n\!:\![\![\tau_n]\!]) = \mathtt{try}\ [\![s]\!]\ \mathtt{with}\ \mathtt{Return}\ v\ \text{->}\ v\ \mathtt{end}$

Addresses. In order to interpret the C prefix operator & which returns the address of a left value, we first manage to have structures always referred to via pointers, artificially inserting pointers if needed. Therefore the expression $e.f$ is everywhere interpreted as $e\text{->}f$. Then we introduce a new interpretation $[\![e]\!]_a$ which stands for the memory location denoted by e. It is defined as follows:

- $[\![x]\!]_a = \ !\,x$, when x is a pointer
- $[\![*e]\!]_a = [\![e]\!]$
- $[\![e.f]\!]_a = [\![e\text{->}f]\!]_a = [\![e]\!]$, when field f is of numerical type
- $[\![e.f]\!]_a = [\![e\text{->}f]\!]_a = \text{access } f\ [\![e]\!]$, when field f is a pointer

This interpretation is the precise meaning of &, that is $[\![\&e]\!] = [\![e]\!]_a$.

3.4   Background Theory

To be able to prove the obligations generated from a given program, it remains to provide a suitable theory, i.e. a set of axioms giving a meaning to all logical predicates and function symbols introduced so far. We give here only the significant part of the theory.

Validity of Pointer Dereferencing. First, a theory is introduced in order to establish obligations required by pointer dereferencing, i.e. the valid(*alloc*, *p*) precondition to the Why functions access and update (Section 3.3). A pointer p is a pair of a base address, base_addr(p), and an offset inside the block, offset(p). Pointer arithmetic is only a matter of changing offsets inside a given block. If i is an integer then the pointer p+i has the same base address as p and offset offset(p)+i. This situation is illustrated below:

A memory block is constituted of zero, one or several elements; the length of the block p points at is block_length(alloc,p), where alloc is the allocation store. Consequently, valid is defined as

$$\text{valid}(a, p) \equiv p \neq \text{null} \ \wedge \ 0 \leq \text{offset}(p) < \text{block\_length}(a, p)$$

Additional predicates are introduced for convenience, to express that access to p+i and to the whole range p[i...j] are valid:

$$\text{valid\_index}(a, p, i) \equiv p \neq \text{null} \ \wedge \ 0 \leq \text{offset}(p) + i < \text{block\_length}(a, p)$$

$$\text{valid\_range}(a, p, i, j) \equiv p \neq \text{null} \ \wedge \ 0 \leq \text{offset}(p) + i \ \wedge \ i \leq j \ \wedge$$
$$\text{offset}(p) + j < \text{block\_length}(a, p)$$

Note that two different blocks are truly *separated* i.e. there is no way to access and/or modify any element of a block using a pointer related to another block. There is no way to express that two blocks allocated with two different calls to `malloc` are contiguous in memory. As specified in the ANSI C standard, pointer subtraction and pointer comparison are restricted to pointers with a same base address. When it is so, pointer subtraction (resp. comparison) corresponds to the subtraction (resp. comparison) of offsets.

Access and Update of Memories. The next set of axioms is related to the combination of accesses and updates within memories. As expected, we have the following two axioms defining the theory of arrays [12]:

axiom acc_upd : $\forall m : \alpha$ memory, $\forall p :$ pointer, $\forall a : \alpha,$
    $\mathrm{acc}(\mathrm{upd}(m, p, a), p) = a$
axiom acc_upd_neq : $\forall m : \alpha$ memory, $\forall p_1, p_2 :$ pointer, $\forall a : \alpha,$
    $p_1 \neq p_2 \rightarrow \mathrm{acc}(\mathrm{upd}(m, p_1, a), p_2) = \mathrm{acc}(m, p_2)$

These two axioms allow to handle pointer aliasing in a natural way: pointers are aliased iff they are equal. In other words, the second axiom simply says that the memory location $\mathrm{acc}(m, p_2)$ is unchanged by a memory update at location p_1 whenever $p_1 \neq p_2$.

Dealing with `Assigns` Clauses. `assigns` clauses are essential for reasoning modularly when several functions are involved. They are modeled using a Why predicate `assigns`. The postcondition of the translated function `f_parameter` of some C function `f` has one `assigns` predicate for each of the Why variables it modifies, as computed by the analysis of effects described in Section 3.2. The `assigns` clause is automatically split into various `assigns` predicates for each modified variable. See Figure 3 for example.

Formally, an `assigns` clause with location *loc* specifies that in the post-state of the considered function, every memory location which is already allocated in the pre-state and is not included in *loc* is unchanged. Thus `assigns` is defined as

assigns($a :$ alloc_table, $m_1, m_2 : \alpha$ memory, $loc :$ assign_loc) :=
  $\forall\, p :$ pointer,
    $\neg\mathrm{fresh}(a, p) \wedge \mathrm{unchanged}(p, loc) \rightarrow \mathrm{acc}(m_1, p) = \mathrm{acc}(m_2, p)$

where `assign_loc` is a type representing a set of modifiable locations. It remains to give axioms for the `unchanged` function, depending on the form of the locations set *loc*:

- The clause `assigns \nothing` specifies that nothing is modified. It is interpreted with a new constant `nothing_loc` of type `assign_loc` with the axiom:

    $\forall p :$ pointer, $\mathrm{unchanged}(p, \mathrm{nothing\_loc})$

- The clause `assigns p->f` specifies that the field `f` of `p` is modified. It is interpreted with a new function `pointer_loc` of type `pointer` $\rightarrow$ `assign_loc` with the axiom:

    $\forall p', p :$ pointer, $\mathrm{unchanged}(p', \mathrm{pointer\_loc}(p)) \leftrightarrow p' \neq p$

- The clauses assigns t[i..j] and assigns t[*] are interpreted using functions range_loc and all_loc with axioms

$$\forall p : \text{pointer}, \, n : \text{int}, \, t : \text{pointer}, \, i : \text{int}, \, j : \text{int},$$
$$\text{unchanged}(p, n, \text{range\_loc}(t, i, j)) \leftrightarrow p \neq t \lor n < i \lor n > j$$
$$\forall p : \text{pointer} \, n : \text{int} \, t : \text{pointer},$$
$$\text{unchanged}(p, n, \text{all\_loc}(t)) \leftrightarrow p \neq t$$

When a clause assigns l_1, l_2 specifies several (say two) locations l_1 and l_2, then two cases may occur: either l_1 and l_2 refer to locations represented by different variables and then a conjunction of two assigns assertions is built, or they refer to the same variable and then the clause is interpreted using the function union_loc satisfying

$$\forall p : \text{pointer}, \, l_1, l_2 : \text{assign\_loc},$$
$$\text{unchanged}(p, \text{union\_loc}(l_1, l_2)) \leftrightarrow \text{unchanged}(p, l_1) \land \text{unchanged}(p, l_2)$$

Finally if a variable is detected as written by the effects analysis but there is no assigns location referring to it, we add an assertion assigns(..., nothing_loc) for it.

As a toy example, let us imagine a test function on our queue data structure, given Figure 5. Proof of the postcondition needs the fact that q1 is not modified by the call to pop(). This is ensured by the precondition q1 != &q that forbids aliasing of q1 and q, and the assigns clause for pop. This is automatically proved by Simplify.

```
/*@ requires \valid(q1) && q1 != &q && !q.empty
  @ ensures \result == \old(q1->empty) */
int test(struct queue *q1) {
    pop();
    return q1->empty;
}
```

Fig. 5. A toy example requiring the use of assigns clauses

3.5   Soundness of the Approach

A main goal of our work is to guarantee the soundness with the highest level of confidence: contrary to some static checking methods, we ensure that if all proof obligations for a given function are proved valid, then the function is a correct implementation of its specification. However, this is only true for a restricted fragment of C. Indeed, possible source of bugs that are not yet covered by our tool include:

- Non-terminating recursive functions;
- Initialization of global variables not satisfying invariants;
- Arithmetic overflow;
- Use of & operator on stack-allocated variables.

The soundness of our method relies on both Why's own soundness and correctness of the translation from C to Why. Why's verification condition generator has been proved [9]. Moreover, each run of the Why tool produces a *validation*, which is an automatically checkable certificate. On the other hand, soundness of the translation from C is not formally proved, but we believe that it is clearly and simply enough stated in this paper to be trusted.

Notice that there exist another possible source of error: the axioms added by the user and the background theory may be inconsistent. To ensure consistency, it is always possible to realize these axioms (in Coq for example).

4   Conclusion

We proposed a method for verifying C programs with pointers and a prototype implementation. Our approach is based on Burstall's model for structures, which we extended to arrays and pointers. We could successfully apply our tool to non-trivial case studies [17], moreover checking the absence of null pointer dereferencing. We took advantage of the modular architecture of Why allowing verification condition generation for various provers.

Similar verification tools for C program exist, such as Astrée [2], CAVEAT [5] and SDV [6]. However, these tools are bounded to a specific prover, hence mostly do not allow to conduct a formal proof within an interactive proof assistant. Furthermore, our specification language has original features, such as assigns clauses, which allow modular reasoning with pointer aliasing. Compared to separation logic [20] which seeks the same goal, a clear advantage of our approach is that we still use a standard first-logic, so we are able to use existing provers. On the other hand, our specification language is probably not as powerful as separation logic.

In a near future, we plan to add support for bounded integer arithmetic and floating-point arithmetic, to disallow possible overflow. This is not hard at all because it is only a matter of interpreting arithmetic operators into new abstract Why functions with appropriate preconditions. Other plans include support for initialization code as mentioned in previous section, C union construct, library functions such as malloc and strcpy, which all require appropriate extensions to our specification language.

Other interesting issues include assistance to the construction of specifications. Suitable preconditions could be generated or at least suggested automatically, either by analysis of counter-examples provided by automatic provers, or by exploitation of Why weakest precondition calculus. There is also an interesting issue about the cooperation of output provers: it would be nice if automatic provers could generate traces of their proofs, which could be double-checked by a proof assistant: in this way, only proof obligations that cannot be solved automatically would need to be proved manually. To obtain such a trace, the use of the haRVey [19] tool is currently under investigation.

Current experiments with Caduceus on embedded programs for smart cards and avionics show some scaling up issues in our approach. We are now investigating techniques for integrating static analysis into the tool, both for solving those issues, and more generally to assist the user in adding annotations in its code.

Acknowledgments. We thank June Andronick from Axalto, Dillon Pariente and Emmanuel Ledinot from Dassault Aviation for their very useful feedback about the specification language and the Caduceus prototype.

References

1. The Simplify decision procedure (part of ESC/Java). `http://research.compaq.com/SRC/esc/simplify/`.

2. B. Blanchet, P. Cousot, R. Cousot, J. Feret, L. Mauborgne, A. Miné, D. Monniaux, and X. Rival. The ASTRÉE static analyzer. `http://www.astree.ens.fr/`.

3. R. Bornat. Proving pointer programs in Hoare logic. In *Mathematics of Program Construction*, pages 102–126, 2000.

4. R. Burstall. Some techniques for proving correctness of programs which alter data structures. *Machine Intelligence*, 7:23–50, 72.

5. CAVEAT project. `http://www-drt.cea.fr/Pages/List/lse/LSL/Caveat/index.html`.

6. B. Cook. Static driver verifier. `http://www.microsoft.com/whdc/devtools/tools/sdv.mspx`.

7. The Coq Proof Assistant. `http://coq.inria.fr/`.

8. P. Cousot. Methods and logics for proving programs. In J. van Leeuwen, editor, *Handbook of Theoretical Computer Science*, volume B, pages 841–993. North-Holland, 1990.

9. J.-C. Filliâtre. Verification of Non-Functional Programs using Interpretations in Type Theory. *Journal of Functional Programming*, 13(4):709–745, July 2003.

10. J.-C. Filliâtre. The why verification tool, 2002.

11. Jean-Christophe Filliâtre and Claude Marché. The Caduceus tool for the verification of C programs. `http://why.lri.fr/caduceus/`.

12. D. Kaplan. Some Completeness Results in the Mathematical Theory of Computation. *J. ACM*, 15(1):124–34, Jan 1968.

13. B. Kernighan and D. Ritchie. *The C Programming Language (2nd Ed.)*. Prentice-Hall, 1988.

14. G. T. Leavens, K. R. M. Leino, E. Poll, C. Ruby, and B. Jacobs. JML: notations and tools supporting detailed design in Java. In *OOPSLA 2000 Companion, Minneapolis, Minnesota*, pages 105–106, 2000.

15. C. Marché, C. Paulin, and X. Urbain. The KRAKATOA proof tool, 2002. `http://krakatoa.lri.fr/`.

16. C. Marché, C. Paulin-Mohring, and X. Urbain. The KRAKATOA tool for certification of JAVA/JAVACARD programs annotated in JML. *Journal of Logic and Algebraic Programming*, 58(1–2):89–106, 2004. `http://krakatoa.lri.fr`.

17. F. Mehta and T. Nipkow. Proving pointer programs in higher-order logic. In F. Baader, editor, *19th Conference on Automated Deduction*, Lecture Notes in Computer Science. Springer-Verlag, 2003.

18. The PVS system. `http://pvs.csl.sri.com/`.

19. S. Ranise and D. Deharbe. Light-weight theorem proving for debugging and verifying units of code. In *Proc. SEFM'03*, Canberra, Australia, Sept. 2003. IEEE Computer Society Press. `http://www.loria.fr/equipes/cassis/softwares/haRVey/`.

20. J. C. Reynolds. Separation logic: a logic for shared mutable data structures. In *17h Annual IEEE Symposium on Logic in Computer Science*. IEEE Comp. Soc. Press, 2002.

21. Sun Microsystems. The JavaCard^{TM} application programming interface (API). `http://java.sun.com/products/javacard/`.

Memory-Model-Sensitive Data Race Analysis[*]

Yue Yang[1], Ganesh Gopalakrishnan[2], and Gary Lindstrom[2]

[1] Microsoft Research, One Microsoft Way, Redmond WA 98052
jasony@microsoft.com
[2] School of Computing, University of Utah, Salt Lake City, UT 84112
{ganesh, gary}@cs.utah.edu

Abstract. We present a "memory-model-sensitive" approach to validating correctness properties for multithreaded programs. Our key insight is that by specifying both the *inter-thread* memory consistency model and the *intra-thread* program semantics as constraints, a program verification task can be reduced to an equivalent constraint solving problem, thus allowing an exhaustive examination of all thread interleavings precisely allowed by a given memory model. To demonstrate, this paper formalizes race conditions according to the new Java memory model, for a simplified but non-trivial source language. We then describe the implementation of a memory-model-sensitive race detector using constraint logic programming (CLP). In comparison with conventional program analysis, our approach does not offer the same kind of performance and scalability due to the complexity involved in exact formal reasoning. However, we show that a formal semantics can serve more than documentation purposes — it can be applied as a sound basis for *rigorous* property checking, upon which more scalable methods can be derived.

1 Introduction

Unlike a sequential program, which simply requires that each read observes the latest write on the same variable according to program order, a multithreaded program has to rely on a *memory model* (also known as *thread semantics*) to define its legal outcomes in a shared memory environment.

The most commonly known memory model is *sequential consistency* (SC) [1]. As a natural extension of the sequential model, sequential consistency requires that (i) operations of all threads can exhibit a total order, (ii) operations of each individual thread appear in this total order following program order, and (iii) a read observes the latest write on the same variable according to this total order. Motivated by various optimization needs, many weaker shared memory systems have also been developed (see [2] for a survey).

Java is the first widely deployed programming language that provides built-in threading support at the language level. Unfortunately, developing a rigorous

* This work was supported by a grant from the Semiconductor Research Corporation for Task 1031.001, and Research Grants CCR-0081406 and CCR-0219805 of NSF.

J. Davies et al. (Eds.): ICFEM 2004, LNCS 3308, pp. 30–45, 2004.

Thread 1	Thread 2
$r1 = x;$	$r2 = y;$
if($r1 > 0$)	if($r2 > 0$)
$y = 1;$	$x = 1;$

Thread 1	Thread 2
$r1 = x;$	$r2 = y;$
if($r1 > 0$)	if($r2 >= 0$)
$y = 1;$	$x = 1;$

(a) Program 1   (b) Program 2

Fig. 1. Initially, x = y = 0. Are these programs race-free?

and intuitive Java memory model (JMM) has turned out to be very difficult. The existing JMM is flawed [3] due to the lack of rigor. It is currently under an official revision process and a new JMM draft [4] is proposed for community review.

Although multithreading provides a powerful programming paradigm for developing well structured and high performance software, it is also notoriously hard to get right. For example, programmers are torn on the horns of a dilemma regarding the use of synchronization: too much may impact performance and risk deadlock, too little may lead to race conditions and application inconsistency. Therefore, a *formal analysis* about thread behavior is often needed to make a program more reliable. However, this can become a daunting task with a traditional pencil-and-paper approach.

One common analysis is *race detection*. Consider program 1 in Figure 1, where each thread issues a read and a conditional write. Does this program contain data races? At the first glance, it may appear that the answer is "yes" since it seems to fit the conventional intuition about a race condition — two operations from different threads (e.g., $r1 = x$ in thread 1 and $x = 1$ in thread 2) attempt to access the same variable without explicit synchronization, and at least one of them is a write. However, a more careful analysis reveals that the control flow of the program, which must be consistent with the read values allowed by the memory model, needs to be considered to determine whether certain operations will ever happen. Therefore, before answering the question, one must clarify what memory model is assumed. With sequentially consistent executions, for instance, the branch conditions in program 1 will never be satisfied. Consequently, the writes can never be executed and the code is race-free. Now consider program 2 in Figure 1, where the only difference is that the branch condition in Thread 2 is changed to $r2 >= 0$. Albeit subtle, this change would result in data races.

For multithreaded programs, data/control flow is interwoven with shared memory consistency requirements. This makes it extremely hard and error-prone to hand-prove thread behavior, even for small programs. From the above example, several conclusions can be drawn.

1. The precise thread semantics, in addition to the intra-thread program semantics, must be taken into account to enable a rigorous analysis of multithreaded software, because a property that is satisfied under one memory model can be easily broken under another.

2. Correctness properties such as race-freedom need to be formalized because informal intuitions often lead to inaccurate results.
3. An automatic verification tool with exhaustive coverage is extremely valuable for designers to test their detailed understanding.

Based on these observations, we develop a formal framework for reasoning about multithreaded software. By capturing thread semantics and correctness properties as constraints, we can pose a verification problem as a constraint satisfaction problem or an equivalent boolean satisfiability problem, thus allowing us to employ an existing constraint/SAT solver to automate the analysis. Using a verification tool embodying these techniques, we can configure the underlying memory model, select a program property of interest, take a test program as input, and verify the result automatically under all executions. Previous program analysis tools all rely on *simplifying assumptions* about the underlying execution platform and thereby introduce unsoundness. They tend to only concentrate on efficiency or scalability. While these are highly worthy goals, there is also a clear need for supporting exhaustive analysis. Our approach fills in this gap by providing the thread semantics explicitly.

This paper offers the following contributions. (i) We describe how to specify memory model rules while taking program value/control flow into account. As a concrete example, we formalize sequential consistency for a source language that supports the use of local variables, computations, control branches, and a monitor-like mechanism for mutual exclusion. To the best of our knowledge, no one has previously provided such a formal executable specification that combines memory model semantics and program semantics in the same setting. (ii) We show how to formulate program properties (or "programmer expectations") as constraints and automatically verify them using constraint solving. In particular, we provide the executable definition of race conditions according to the new Java memory model. (iii) We build a race detector using constraint logic programming (CLP) and report the experiences gained during the implementation. Previous tools aim at finding data races with minimal false alarms. A rigorous race detector, on the other hand, serves a different (but also important) purpose. That is, it allows a user to analyze a programming pattern under an exact memory model to gain deep insight into the implications of the underlying model.

The rest of the paper proceeds as follows. In Section 2, we provide an overview of our approach. Section 3 describes the source language used as the basis of our presentation. Data race is formalized in Section 4. We discuss the implementation of our prototype tool in Section 5. Related work is reviewed in Section 6. We conclude and explore future work in Section 7. The detailed formal specification is presented in the Appendix.

2   Framework Overview

Our approach is based on Nemos (Non-operational yet Executable Memory Ordering Specifications) [5] [6], our previously developed memory model specifica-

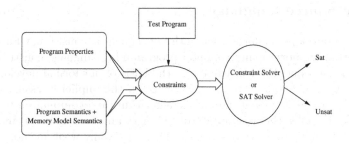

Fig. 2. The processing flow of our approach

tion framework. Nemos defines a memory model in a declarative style using a collection of ordering rules. The processing flow of our verification methodology is shown in Figure 2, which comprises the following steps: (i) capturing the semantics of the source language, including the thread semantics, as constraints, (ii) formalizing program properties as additional constraints, (iii) applying these constraints to a given test program and reducing the verification problem to a constraint satisfaction problem, and (iv) employing a suitable tool to solve the constraint problem automatically.

2.1   Specifying the Constraints

We use predicate logic to specify the ordering constraints imposed on a relation *order*. To make our specifications compositional and executable, our notation differs from previous formalisms in two ways. First, we employ a modest extension of predicate logic to higher order logic, i.e., *order* can be used as a parameter in a constraint definition so that new refinements to the ordering requirement can be conveniently added. This allows us to construct a complex model using simpler components. Second, our specifications are fully explicit about all ordering properties, including previously implicit requirements such as totality, transitivity, and circuit-freedom. Without explicating such "hidden" requirements, a specification is not complete for execution.

2.2   Solving the Constraints

The Algorithm: Given a test program $\mathcal{P}$, we first derive its execution *ops* (defined in Section 3.1) from the program text in a preprocessing phase. The initial execution is *symbolic*, that is, *ops* may contain free variables, e.g., for data values and ordering relations. Suppose *ops* has n operations, there are n^2 ordering pairs among these operations. We construct a $n \times n$ adjacency matrix $\mathcal{M}$, where the element $\mathcal{M}_{ij}$ indicates whether operations i and j should be ordered. We then go through each requirement in the specification and impose the corresponding propositional constraints with respect to the elements of $\mathcal{M}$. The goal is to find a binding of the free variables in *ops* such that it satisfies the conjunction of all specification requirements or to conclude that no such binding exists. This is automated using a constraint solver.

3 The Source Language

This section develops the formal semantics of sequential consistency for a source language that supports many common programming language constructs. The choice of using sequential consistency as the basis of our formal development is motivated by two major factors: (i) SC is often the implicitly assumed model during software development, i.e., many algorithms and compilation techniques are developed under the assumption of SC. Yet, an executable specification of SC for non-trivial languages has been lacking. (ii) Many weak memory models, including the new JMM draft, define pivotal properties such as race-freedom using SC executions. In Section 4, we will need the formal definition of SC to capture the notion of data races in the new JMM.

It should be emphasized that although this paper only formalizes SC, our framework is generic and allows many other memory models to be plugged-in. In our previous work, we have already applied Nemos to build a large collection of memory model specifications, including the Intel Itanium memory model [6] and a variety of classical memory models [5].

Our previous specification of sequential consistency in [5] only deals with normal read and write operations. While it is sufficient for most processor level memory systems, it is not enough for handling more realistic programs (e.g., those involving control branches), this paper extends the previous model by supporting a language that allows the use of local variables, computation operations, control branches, and synchronization operations.

3.1 Terminology

Variables: Variables are categorized as *global variables*, *local variables*, *control variables*, and *synchronization variables*. Control variables do not exist in the original source program — they are introduced by our system as auxiliary variables for control operations. Synchronization variables correspond to the locks employed for mutual exclusion.

Instruction: An *instruction* corresponds to a program statement from the program text. The source language has a syntax similar to Java, with *Lock* and *Unlock* inserted corresponding to the Java keyword *synchronized*. It supports the following instruction types[1]:

Read:	e.g., $r1 = x$	Control:	e.g., $if(r1 > 0)$
Write:	e.g., $x = 1$ or $x = r1$	Lock:	e.g., *Lock l1*
Computation:	e.g., $r1 = r2 + 1$	Unlock:	e.g., *Unlock l1*

Execution: An *execution* consists of a set of symbolic *operation* instances generated by program instructions. We assume that the expression involved in a computation or control operation only uses local variables.

---

[1] Currently, we do not handle loops in a general manner — see Section 3.3.

Operation Tuple: An operation i is represented by a tuple as follows:
$\langle t, pc, op, var, data, local, localData, cmpExpr, ctrExpr, lock, matchID, id \rangle$, where

t $i = t$:	thread ID
pc $i = pc$:	program counter
op $i = op$:	operation type
var $i = var$:	global variable
data $i = data$:	data value
local $i = local$:	local variable
localData $i = localData$:	data value for local variable
cmpExpr $i = cmpExpr$:	computation expression
ctrExpr $i = ctrExpr$:	path predicate
lock $i = lock$:	lock
matchID $i = matchID$:	ID of the matching lock
id $i = id$:	global ID of the operation

For every global variable x, there is a default write operation for x, with the default value of x and a special thread ID t_{init}.

3.2   Control Flow

In order to support memory-model-sensitive analysis, one key challenge is to specify control flow in the context of nondeterministic thread interleavings. Our insight is that path feasibility can be specified as another set of constraints (encoded in symbolic path predicates) and must be enforced so that it is mutually consistent with memory model constraints. We achieve this by (i) transforming control related operations to auxiliary reads and writes using control variables and (ii) imposing a set of consistency requirements on the "reads" and "writes" of control variables similar to that of normal reads and writes. The detailed steps are as follows:

- For each branch instruction i, say $if(p)$, add a unique auxiliary control variable c, and transform instruction i to an operation i' with the format of $c = p$. Operation i' is said to be a control operation (**op** $i' = Control$), and can be regarded as an *assignment* to the control variable c.
- Every operation i has a $ctrExpr$ field that stores its path predicate, which is a boolean expression on a set of control variables dictating the condition for i to be executed. An operation i can be regarded as a *usage* of the involved control variables in the path predicate.
- An operation i is *feasible* if its $ctrExpr$ field evaluates to $True$. We define a predicate **fb** to check the feasibility of an operation.
- In the memory ordering rules, feasibility of the involved operations is checked to make sure the consistency of control flow is satisfied.

By converting control blocks to assignments and usages of control variables, we can specify consistency rules for control flow in a fashion similar to data flow.

3.3   Loops

For the purpose of defining a memory model alone, our mechanism for handling control operations is sufficient for handling loops. This is because the task of a memory model specification can be regarded as answering the question of whether a given execution is allowed by the memory model. For any concrete execution, loops have already been resolved to a finite number of iterations.

To enable a fully automatic and exhaustive program analysis involving loops, however, one needs to develop another level of constraints in which the path predicate of an operation can conditionally grow until all constraints are satisfied (this is not currently supported by our specification). In practice, our experience shows that unwrapping a loop into fixed iterations is still effective (although this loses soundness) for property checking.

3.4   Formal Semantics

The detailed semantics of the source language is presented in Appendix A as a collection of constraints. For example, predicate legalSC is the overall constraint that defines the requirement of sequential consistency on an execution *ops* in which the operations follow an ordering relation *order*.

legalSC *ops order* ≡
   requireProgramOrder *ops order* ∧ **requireReadValue** *ops order* ∧
   requireComputation *ops order* ∧ **requireMutualExclusion** *ops order* ∧
   requireWeakTotalOrder *ops order* ∧ **requireTransitiveOrder** *ops order* ∧
   requireAsymmetricOrder *ops order*

Program Order Rule (Appendix A.1): Constraint requireProgramOrder formalizes program order via predicate orderedByProgram. In addition, the default writes are ordered before other operations.

Read Value Rules (Appendix A.2): Constraint requireReadValue enforces the consistency of data flow across reads and writes. The assignments and usages of local variables (data dependence) and control variables (control dependence) follow the similar guideline to ensure consistent data transfer. Therefore, requireReadValue is decomposed into three subrules for global reads, local reads, and control reads, respectively.

Computation Rule (Appendix A.3): Constraint requireComputation enforces that for every operation involving computations (i.e., when the operation type is *Computation* or *Control*), the resultant data must be obtained by properly evaluating the expression in the operation. For brevity, the Appendix omits some details of the standard program semantics that are commonly well understood. For example, we use a predicate eval to indicate that standard process should be followed to evaluation an expression. Similarly, getLocals and getCtrs are used to parse the *cmpExpr* and *ctrExpr* fields to obtain a set of ⟨variable, data⟩ entries involved in the expressions (these entries represent the local/control variables that the operation depends on and their associated data values), which can be subsequently processed by `getVar` and `getData`.

Mutual Exclusion Rule (Appendix A.4): Rule `requireMutualExclusion` enforces mutual exclusion for operations enclosed by matched Lock and Unlock operations.

General Ordering Rules (Appendix A.5): These constraints require *order* to be transitive, total, and asymmetric (circuit-free).

4   Executable Specification of Race Conditions

Our definition of a data race is according to [7], which has also been adopted by the new JMM draft [4]. In these proposals, a *happens-before* order (based on Lamport's *happened-before* order [8] for message passing systems) is used for formalizing concurrent memory accesses. Further, data-race-free programs (also referred to as *correctly synchronized programs*) are defined as being free of conflicting and concurrent accesses under all *sequentially consistent* executions. The reason for using SC executions to define data races is to make it easier for a programmer to determine whether a program is correctly synchronized.

We define constraint `detectDataRace` to catch any potential data races. This constraint attempts to find a total order *scOrder* and a happens-before order *hbOrder* such that there exists a pair of conflicting operations which are not ordered by *hbOrder*.

detectDataRace *ops* $\equiv \exists$ *scOrder, hbOrder.*
  legalSC *ops scOrder* $\wedge$ **requireHbOrder** *ops hbOrder scOrder* $\wedge$
  mapConstraints *ops hbOrder scOrder* $\wedge$ **existDataRace** *ops hbOrder*

Happens-before order is defined in `requireHbOrder`. Intuitively, it states that two operations are ordered by happens-before order if (i) they are program ordered, (ii) they are ordered by synchronization operations, or (iii) they are transitively ordered by a third operation.

requireHbOrder *ops hbOrder scOrder* $\equiv$
  requireProgramOrder *ops hbOrder* $\wedge$
  requireSyncOrder *ops hbOrder scOrder* $\wedge$
  requireTransitiveOrder *ops hbOrder*

Since sequential consistency requires a total order among all operations, the happens-before edges induced by synchronization operations must follow this total order. This is captured by `requireSyncOrder`. Similarly, `mapConstraints` is used to make sure *scOrder* is consistent with *hbOrder*.

requireSyncOrder *ops hbOrder scOrder* $\equiv \forall\ i\ j \in ops.$
     (**fb** $i\ \wedge$ **fb** $j\ \wedge$ **isSync** $i\ \wedge$ **isSync** $j\ \wedge$ **scOrder** $i\ j) \Rightarrow$ **hbOrder** $i\ j$

mapConstraints *ops hbOrder scOrder* $\equiv \forall\ i\ j \in ops.$
     (**fb** $i\ \wedge$ **fb** $j\ \wedge$ **hbOrder** $i\ j) \Rightarrow$ **scOrder** $i\ j$

With a precise definition of happens-before order, we can formalize a race condition in constraint `existDataRace`. A race is caused by two feasible operation that are (i) *conflicting*, i.e., they access the same variable from different threads (**t** $i \neq$ **t** j) and at least one of them is a write, and (ii) *concurrent*, i.e., they are not ordered by happens-before order.

existDataRace *ops hbOrder* $\equiv \exists\ i, j \in\ ops.$
     fb $i \wedge$ **fb** $j\ \wedge$ **t** $i \neq$ **t** $j\ \wedge$ **var** $i =$ **var** $j\ \wedge$
     (**op** $i = Write\ \wedge$ **op** $j = Write\ \vee$ **op** $i = Write\ \wedge$ **op** $j = Read\ \vee$
     op $i = Read\ \wedge$ **op** $j = Write) \wedge \neg($**hbOrder** $i\ j) \wedge \neg($**hbOrder** $j\ i)$

To support a full-featured Java race detector, this race definition needs to be extended, e.g., by adding semantics for volatile variable operations. This should be a relatively straightforward process.

5   Implementation of the Rigorous Race Detector

Constraint-based analyses can be quickly prototyped using a constraint logic programming language such as FD-Prolog[2]. We have built a tool named *DefectFinder*, written in SICStus Prolog [9], to test the proposed techniques.

Two mechanisms from FD-Prolog can be applied for solving the constraints in our specification. One applies backtracking search for all constraints expressed by logical variables, and the other uses non-backtracking constraint solving techniques such as *arc consistency* [10] for finite domain variables, which is potentially more efficient and certainly more complete (especially under the presence of negation) than with logical variables. In a sense, the built-in constraint solver from Prolog provides an effective means for bounded software model checking by explicitly exploring all program executions, but symbolically reasoning about the constraints imposed on free variables.

Translating the constraints specified in the Appendix to Prolog rules is straightforward. One caveat, however, is that most Prolog systems do not directly support quantifiers. While existential quantification can be realized via Prolog's backtracking mechanism, we need to implement universal quantification by enumerating the related finite domain. For instance, `requireWeakTotalOrder` is originally specified as follows:

---

[2] FD-Prolog refers to Prolog with a finite domain (FD) constraint solver. For example, SICStus Prolog and GNU Prolog have this feature.

Tinit	Thread 1	Thread 2
(1)wr(x,0);	(3)rd(x,r1);	(6)rd(y,r2);
(2)wr(y,0);	(4)ctr(c1,[r1>0]);	(7)ctr(c2,[r2>=0]);
	(5)wr(y,1,[c1]);	(8)wr(x,1,[c2]);

Fig. 3. The execution derived from program 2 in Figure 1

requireWeakTotalOrder *ops order* $\equiv \forall\ i, j \in ops.$
$\qquad$ (**fb** i $\wedge$ **fb** j $\wedge$ **id** $i \neq$ **id** j) $\Rightarrow$ (**order** $i\ j$ $\vee$ **order** $j\ i$)

In the Prolog code, predicate `forEachElem` is recursively defined to call the corresponding `elemProg` for every element in the adjacency matrix *Order* (variable names start with a capital letter in Prolog).

```
requireWeakTotalOrder(Ops,Order,FbList):-
    forEachElem(Ops,Order,FbList,doWeakTotalOrder).

elemProg(doWeakTotalOrder,Ops,Order,FbList,I,J):-
    const(feasible,Feasible), length(Ops,N),
    matrix_elem(Order,N,I,J,Oij), matrix_elem(Order,N,J,I,Oji),
    nth(I,FbList,Fi), nth(J,FbList,Fj),
    (Fi #= Feasible #/\ Fj #= Feasible #/\ I #\= J) #=> (Oij #\/ Oji).
```

One technique shown by the above example is particularly worth noting: the adjacency matrix *Order* and the feasibility list *FbList* are passed in as finite domain variables. The domain of the elements in these lists (which is *boolean* in this case) is previously set up in the top level predicate. Providing such domain information significantly reduces the solving time, hence is critical for the performance of the tool.

The search order among the constraints may also impact performance. In general, it is advantageous to let the solver satisfy the most restrictive goal first. For example, read value rules should precede the general ordering rules.

Example. DefectFinder enables *interactive* and *incremental* analyses, meaning it allows users to selectively enable or disable certain constraints to help them understand the underlying model piece by piece.

To illustrate how the tool works, recall program 2 in Figure 1. Figure 3 displays the corresponding execution (*ops*) derived from the program text (it only shows the operation fields relevant to this example). When checked for race conditions, our tool would report that program 2 contains data races. The conflicting operations (3 and 8 in this case) and an interleaving that leads to the race conditions are also displayed. The corresponding adjacency matrix is shown in Figure 4. On the other hand, if program 1 in Figure 1 is checked, DefectFinder would report that it is race-free.

Performance Analysis: Rigorous semantic analysis such as race detection is NP-hard in general [11]. Nonetheless, constraint-based methods have become

	1	2	3	4	5	6	7	8
1	0	1	1	1	1	1	1	1
2	0	0	1	1	1	1	1	1
3	0	0	0	1	1	0	0	0
4	0	0	0	0	1	0	0	0
5	0	0	0	0	0	0	0	0
6	0	0	1	1	1	0	1	1
7	0	0	1	1	1	0	0	1
8	0	0	1	1	1	0	0	0

Fig. 4. The adjacency matrix for the execution shown in Figure 3 under sequential consistency. A matrix element $\mathcal{M}_{ij}$ can have a value of 0 or 1, where 0 indicates i is not ordered before j and 1 indicates i must precede j. A possible interleaving *1 2 6 7 8 3 4 5* is also automatically derived from this matrix

very successful in practice, thanks to the efficient solving techniques developed in recent years. Using a Pentium 366 MHz PC with 128 MB of RAM running Windows 2000, with SICStus Prolog run under compiled mode, the above two analyses take 0.811 second and 6.810 seconds, respectively. As an orthogonal effort, our recent work in [12] has dramatically improved the scalability of our framework using an incremental SAT solver. Our prototype utility is available for download at http://www.cs.utah.edu/~yyang/DefectFinder.zip.

6   Related Work

Constraint solving was historically applied to AI planning problems. In recent years, it has started to show a lot of potential for program analysis as well, e.g., [13] [14] [15] [16]. To the best of our knowledge, our work is the first to apply the constraint-based approach for capturing language-level memory models and reasoning about correctness properties in multithreaded programs.

Extensive research has been done in model checking Java programs, e.g., [17] [18] [19] [20]. These tools, however, do not specifically address memory model issues. Therefore, they cannot precisely analyze fine-grained thread interleavings. We can imagine our method being incorporated into these tools to make their analyses more accurate.

There is a large body of work on race detection, which can be classified as static or dynamic analysis. The latter can be further categorized as on-the-fly or post-mortem, depending on how the execution information is collected. Netzer and Miller [21] proposed a detection algorithm using the post-mortem method. Adve and Hill proposed the *data-race-free* model [22] and developed a formal definition of data races under weak memory models [7]. Lamport's happened-before relation has been applied in dynamic analysis tools, e.g., [23] [11] [24]. Several on-the-fly methods, e.g., [25] [26] [27], exploited information based on the underlying cache coherence protocol. The drawback of these dynamic techniques is that they can easily miss a data race, depending on how threads are scheduled.

Unlike the dynamic approaches, we use a static method that examines a symbolic execution to achieve an exhaustive coverage.

Some race detectors, e.g., [28] [29] [30], were designed specifically for the lock-based synchronization model. Our approach is based on the definition given in [7], which employs the happened-before relation, hence it is more generic and is able to handle many different synchronization styles. Tools such as ESC/Java [31] and Warlock [32] rely on user-supplied annotations to statically detect data races. Type-based approaches, e.g., [33] [34] [35], have also been proposed for object-oriented programs. While effective in practice, these tools do not address the issue that we focus on in this paper, which is how to rigorously reason about multithreaded programs running in a complex shared memory environment.

7   Conclusions

We have presented a novel approach that handles both program semantics and memory model semantics in a declarative constraint-based framework. Our framework is particularly useful in helping people understand the underlying concurrency model and conduct verification for common programming patterns that, albeit small, can be extremely difficult to analyze by hand. To summarize, our system offers the following benefits:

- It is rigorous. Specifications developed in such a formal style can also be sent to a theorem proving utility, such as the HOL theorem prover [36], for proving generic properties.
- It is automatic. Our approach allows one to take advantage of the tremendous advances in constraint/SAT solving techniques. The executable thread semantics can also be treated as a "black box" whereby the users are not necessarily required to understand all the details of the model to benefit from the tool.
- It is generic. Since our method is not limited to a specific synchronization mechanism, it can be applied to reason about various correctness properties for different threading model, all using the same framework.

Future Work: Divide-and-conquer style verification methods may be helpful to make our system more scalable. Techniques developed in other tools, such as predicate abstraction, branch refinement, and assume-guarantee, can be integrated into our system. Furthermore, the structural information of the domain-specific constraints may be exploited for improving the solving algorithms.

References

1. Leslie Lamport. How to make a multiprocessor computer that correctly executes multiprocess programs. *IEEE Transactions on Computers*, 28(9):690–691, 1979.
2. S. V. Adve and K. Gharachorloo. Shared memory consistency models: A tutorial. *IEEE Computer*, 29(12):66–76, 1996.

3. W. Pugh. The Java memory model is fatally flawed. *Concurrency: Practice and Experience*, 12(1):1–11, 2000.
4. JSR133: Java memory model and thread specification. http://www.cs.umd.edu/~pugh/java/memoryModel.
5. Yue Yang, Ganesh Gopalakrishnan, Gary Lindstrom, and Konrad Slind. Nemos: A framework for axiomatic and executable specifications of memory consistency models. *In Proceedings of the 18th International Parallel and Distributed Processing Symposium (IPDPS)*, April 2004.
6. Yue Yang, Ganesh Gopalakrishnan, Gary Lindstrom, and Konrad Slind. Analyzing the Intel Itanium memory ordering rules using logic programming and SAT. In *Proceedings of the 12th Advanced Research Working Conference on Correct Hardware Design and Verification Methods (CHARME'03), LNCS 2860*, October 2003.
7. S. V. Adve, M. D. Hill, B. P. Miller, and R. H. B. Netzer. Detecting data races on weak memory systems. In *Proceedings of the 18th International Symposium on Computer Architecture (ISCA)*, pages 234–243, 1991.
8. L. Lamport. Time, clocks and ordering of events in distributed systems. In *Communications of the ACM*, volume 21, pages 558–565, July 1978.
9. SICStus Prolog. http://www.sics.se/sicstus.
10. J. Jaffar and J-L. Lassez. Constraint logic programming. In *Principles Of Programming Languages*, Munich, Germany, January 1987.
11. Robert H. B. Netzer. Race condition detection for debugging shared-memory parallel programs. Technical Report CS-TR-1991-1039, 1991.
12. Ganesh Gopalakrishnan, Yue Yang, and Hemanthkumar Sivaraj. QB or not QB: An efficient execution verification tool for memory orderings. In *Proceedings of Computer Aided Verification (CAV'04)*, July 2004.
13. Alexander Aiken, Manuel Fähndrich, and Zhendong Su. Detecting races in relay ladder logic programs. *LNCS*, 1384:184–200, 1998.
14. Etienne Gagnon, Laurie J. Hendren, and Guillaume Marceau. Efficient inference of static types for java bytecode. In *Static Analysis Symposium*, pages 199–219, 2000.
15. Atanas Rountev, Ana Milanova, and Barbara G. Ryder. Points-to analysis for Java using annotated constraints. In *Proceedings of Object-Oriented Programming Systems, Lanuages, and Applications*, pages 43–55, 2001.
16. Cormac Flanagan. Automatic software model checking using CLP. In *Proceedings of ESOP*, 2003.
17. Klaus Havelund and Thomas Pressburger. Model checking JAVA programs using JAVA PathFinder. *International Journal on Software Tools for Technology Transfer*, 2(4):366–381, 2000.
18. W. Visser, K. Havelund, G. Brat, and S. Park. Java PathFinder - second generation of a Java Model Checker. In *Post-CAV Workshop on Advances in Verification, Chicago*, 2000.
19. James C. Corbett, Matthew B. Dwyer, John Hatcliff, Shawn Laubach, Corina S. Pasareanu, Robby, and Hongjun Zheng. Bandera: extracting finite-state models from Java source code. In *International Conference on Software Engineering*, 2000.
20. D. Park, U. Stern, and D. Dill. Java model checking. In *Proceedings of the First International Workshop on Automated Program Analysis, Testing and Verification, Limerick, Ireland*, 2000.
21. R. H. Netzer and B. P. Miller. What are race conditions? Some issues and formalizations. *ACM Letters on Programming Languages and Systems*, 1(1):74–88, 1992.

22. S. V. Adve and M. D. Hill. A unified formalization of four shared-memory models. *IEEE Trans. on Parallel and Distributed Systems*, 4(6):613–624, 1993.
23. A. Dinning and E. Schonberg. Detecting access anomalies in programs with critical sections. In *Proceedings of the ACM/ONR Workshop on Parallel and Distributed Debugging*, pages 85–96, 1991.
24. D. Perkovic and P. Keleher. Online data-race detection via coherency guarantees. In *Proceedings of the 2nd Symposium on Operating Systems Design and Implementation (OSDI'96)*, pages 47–57, 1996.
25. S. L. Min and J.-D. Choi. An efficient cache-based access anomaly detection scheme. In *Proceedings of the 4th International Conference on Architectural Support for Programming Languages and Operating System (ASPLOS)*, pages 235–244, 1991.
26. B. Richards and J. R. Larus. Protocol-based data-race detection. In *Proceedings of the SIGMETRICS symposium on Parallel and distributed tools*, 1998.
27. Edmond Schonberg. On-the-fly detection of access anomalies. In *Proceedings of PLDI*, pages 285–297, 1989.
28. Stefan Savage, Michael Burrows, Greg Nelson, Patrick Sobalvarro, and Thomas Anderson. Eraser: A dynamic data race detector for multithreaded programs. *ACM Transactions on Computer Systems*, 15(4):391–411, 1997.
29. C. von Praun and T. Gross. Object-race detection. In *Proceedings of Object-Oriented Programming Systems, Lanuages, and Applications*, pages 70–82, 2001.
30. J. Choi, K. Lee, A. Loginov, R. O'Callahan, V. Sarkar, and M. Sridharan. Efficient and precise datarace detection for multithreaded object-oriented programs. In *Proceedings of PLDI*, 2002.
31. C. Flanagan, K. Leino, M. Lillibridge, C. Nelson, J. Saxe, and R. Stata. Extended static checking for Java, 2002.
32. N. Sterling. Warlock - a static data race analysis tool. *USENIX Winter Technical Conference*, pages 97–106, 1993.
33. Cormac Flanagan and Stephen N. Freund. Type-based race detection for Java. *Proceedings of PLDI*, pages 219–232, 2000.
34. David F. Bacon, Robert E. Strom, and Ashis Tarafdar. Guava: a dialect of Java without data races. In *Proceedings of Object-Oriented Programming Systems, Lanuages, and Applications*, 2000.
35. Chandrasekhar Boyapati and Martin Rinard. A parameterized type system for race-free Java programs. In *Proceedings of Object-Oriented Programming, Systems, Languages, and Applications*, 2001.
36. T. F. Melham M. J. C. Gordon. *Introduction to HOL: A theorem proving environment for higher order logic*. Cambridge University Press, 1993.

A   Sequential Consistency

legalSC *ops order* $\equiv$

> **requireProgramOrder** *ops order* $\wedge$ **requireReadValue** *ops order* $\wedge$
> **requireComputation** *ops order* $\wedge$ **requireMutualExclusion** *ops order* $\wedge$
> **requireWeakTotalOrder** *ops order* $\wedge$ **requireTransitiveOrder** *ops order* $\wedge$
> **requireAsymmetricOrder** *ops order*

A.1   Program Order Rule

requireProgramOrder *ops order* $\equiv \forall\, i, j \in ops.$

> (**fb** $i \wedge$ **fb** $j \wedge$ (**orderedByProgram** $i\, j \vee \mathbf{t}\, i = t_{init} \wedge \mathbf{t}\, j \neq t_{init})) \Rightarrow$ **order** $i\, j$

A.2   Read Value Rules

requireReadValue *ops order* ≡
    globalReadValue *ops order* ∧ **localReadValue** *ops order* ∧
    controlReadValue *ops order*

globalReadValue *ops order* ≡ ∀ k ∈ *ops*.
    (**fb** k ∧ **isRead** k) ⇒
    (∃ i ∈ *ops*. **fb** i ∧ **op** $i = Write$ ∧ **var** $i =$ **var** k ∧
    data $i =$ **data** k ∧ ¬(**order** k i) ∧
    (¬∃ j ∈ *ops*. **fb** j ∧ **op** $j = Write$ ∧ **var** $j =$ **var** k ∧ **order** i j ∧ **order** j k))

localReadValue *ops order* ≡ ∀ k ∈ *ops*. **fb** k ⇒
    (∀ e ∈ (**getLocals** k).
    (∃ i ∈ *ops*. (**fb** i ∧ **isAssign** i ∧ **local** $i =$ **getVar** e ∧
    data $i =$ **getData** e ∧ **orderedByProgram** i k) ∧
    (¬∃ j ∈ *ops*. (**fb** j ∧ **isAssign** j ∧ **local** $j =$ **getVar** e ∧
    orderedByProgram i j ∧ **orderedByProgram** j k))))

controlReadValue *ops order* ≡ ∀ k ∈ *ops*.
    (∀ e ∈ (**getCtrs** k).
    (∃ i ∈ *ops*. **op** $i = Control$ ∧ **var** $i =$ **getVar** e ∧
    data $i =$ **getData** e ∧ **orderedByProgram** i k))

A.3   Computation Rule

requireComputation *ops order* ≡ ∀ k ∈ *ops*.
    ((**fb** k ∧ **op** $k = Computation$) ⇒ (**data** $k =$ **eval** (**cmpExpr** k))) ∧
    ((**fb** k ∧ **op** $k = Control$) ⇒ (**data** $k =$ **eval** (**ctrExpr** k)))

A.4   Mutual Exclusion Rule

requireMutualExclusion *ops order* ≡ ∀ i, j ∈ *ops*.
    (**fb** i ∧ **fb** j ∧ **matchLock** i j) ⇒
    (¬∃ k ∈ *ops*. **fb** k ∧ **isSync** k ∧
    lock $k =$ **lock** i ∧ **t** $k ≠$ **t** i ∧ **order** i k ∧ **order** k j)

A.5   General Ordering Rules

requireWeakTotalOrder *ops order* ≡ ∀ i, j ∈ *ops*.
    (**fb** i ∧ **fb** j ∧ **id** $i ≠$ **id** j) ⇒ (**order** i j ∨ **order** j i)

requireTransitiveOrder *ops order* ≡ ∀ i, j, k ∈ *ops*.
    (**fb** i ∧ **fb** j ∧ **fb** k ∧ **order** i j ∧ **order** j k) ⇒ **order** i k

requireAsymmetricOrder *ops order* ≡ ∀ i, j ∈ *ops*.
    (**fb** i ∧ **fb** j ∧ **order** i j) ⇒ ¬(**order** j i)

A.6 Auxiliary Definitions

fb $i \equiv (\textbf{eval } (\textbf{ctrExpr } i) = True)$

orderedByProgram $i\ j \equiv (\textbf{t } i = \textbf{t } j\ \wedge\ \textbf{pc } i < \textbf{pc } j)$

isAssign $i \equiv (\textbf{op } i = Computation\ \vee\ \textbf{op } i = Read)$

isSync $i \equiv (\textbf{op } i = Lock\ \vee\ \textbf{op } i = Unlock)$

matchLock $i\ j\ \equiv \textbf{op } i = Lock\ \wedge\ \textbf{op } j = Unlock\ \wedge\ \textbf{matchID } j = \textbf{id } i$

Note: for brevity, the following predicates are not explicitly defined here since they are commonly well understood.

eval *exp*:	evaluate *exp* with standard program semantics;
getLocals *k*:	parse *k* and get the set of local variables that k depends on, with their associated data values;
getCtrs *k*:	parse the path predicate of *k* and get the set of control variables that k depends on, with their associated data values;
getVar *e*:	get variable from a ⟨variable, data⟩ entry;
getData *e*:	get data from a ⟨variable, data⟩ entry.

Formal Models for Web Navigations with Session Control and Browser Cache

Jessica Chen and Xiaoshan Zhao

School of Computer Science, University of Windsor,
Windsor, Ont. Canada N9B 3P4
{xjchen,zhaon}@cs.uwindsor.ca

Abstract. While providing better performance, transparency and expressiveness, the main features of the web technologies such as web caching, session and cookies, dynamically generated web pages etc. may also affect the correct understanding of the web applications running on top of them. From the viewpoint of formal verification and specification-based testing, this suggests that the formal models of the web applications we use for static analysis or test case generation should subsume the abstract behavior of their supporting environment. Here we provide the definition of such a model in terms of labelled transition systems from a given abstract description of the navigations of a web application by incorporating the abstract behavioral model of the web browsers in the presence of session control and browser cache. The significance of the work is twofold: on one hand, it provides a formal basis for better understanding of the web systems; on the other hand, it lays the ground work for both model checking and specification-based testing on the web applications where we take into account the affect of the internal mechanism to the correct web navigations, which can be quite sensitive to the security of the information they carry.

Keywords: Labelling Transition Systems, Operational Semantics, Model Checking, Specification-based Testing, Web Navigation, Web Caching.

1 Introduction

With the advance of networking and web technology, more and more information is being posted into and retrieved from the World Wide Web that the web systems are becoming the primary device for information sharing and retrieval. A web system can be as simple as a set of static web pages for information presentation. It can also be as complicate as a world wide banking system that handles all transaction requests from different machines in different countries in multiple languages. The diversity and the intensive use of the web systems are enabled by the advance of its emerging technologies such as web caching and dynamic web pages.

In web caching, cacheable web pages are stored between a web client and a web server, and they are sent directly to the clients on behalf of the web server

J. Davies et al. (Eds.): ICFEM 2004, LNCS 3308, pp. 46–60, 2004.
© Springer-Verlag Berlin Heidelberg 2004

whenever the same pages are requested again. The use of web caching mechanism can reduce the workload of web servers, and when the proxies are placed close to or right on the web browsers, it can also reduce network traffic. From the user's viewpoint, the effect is the shortening of the response time.

Dynamic web pages are generated on-the-fly by web servers according to the requested URLs. With the introduction of dynamic web pages, the use of web technology has moved from simple sets of hyperlinked web pages to complex web applications. Dynamic web pages are often used together with session/cookie techniques. A cookie is a small piece of data that is sent from a web server and stored in the local storage of a web browser. When a web browser sends out a web page request, a cookie may be included in the request message and arrives at the web server's hand. A web server can identify each browser by issuing different cookies on the browsers who have visited it. The use of cookies gives a web server the abilities to trace the status of its client browsers and maintain the communication sessions with them.

While providing better performance, transparency and expressiveness, the above features of the web technology have also raised some important issues and posed additional difficulties on the validation of the correctness of the web applications built upon it. In the presence of web browser cache, for example, the users can interact not only with the web pages but also with the web browser itself via the use of the special buttons such as *back, forward, refresh* or via URL rewriting. Such actions of the users may affect the overall navigations of the web pages, which can be quite sensitive to the security of the information they carry. Thus, the behavior of the web browsers may have impact on the correctness of the web applications: a web application providing all correct functionality by itself may however malfunction when it is put into its supporting environment. This leads us to the following two points:

1. Note that the behavior of the web browsers depends on how the web browser is implemented and configured, whether the cookie is enabled, etc., and the web developers have access to the configuration of the web browsers and cookies. From the viewpoint of software design, the above concern suggests that a web application should be carefully designed with correct configuration of the web browsers and of some important properties of the web pages such as secure page, cacheable page, etc.
2. From the viewpoint of validation/verification and specification-based testing, the formal model for static analysis or test case generation should contain enough details of the interactions between the users and the web system as a whole. For example, the user's possible interactions with the web browser should also be modeled and reflected in the design specification.

There exists a gap between a design specification in item 1 and the one in item 2: While it is reasonable to ask the web developers to provide the design specifications that contain the correct configuration and page properties, it is too demanding to ask them for the specification of the abstract behavior of the web application that subsumes the behavior of the supporting web system. Here we define the latter from the former: we provide the formal definition in terms of labelled transition system on the integrated model of the web application incorporating the abstract behavior of the internal session control and caching mechanism of web browser into the description of the web applications.

We assume the availability of the design specification of the web application in terms of what we call *page navigation diagrams*. Such a diagram shows all the desired or all the possible navigations among the web pages. We assume that among the pages in the application, some are *entry* ones, in the sense that their URLs do not contain any *search parameters* and users can access them from any page by typing in the host name and the path name. The home page of a web site is a typical entry page. For non-entry pages, their URLs in the page request consist of some search parameters from the previous pages and we assume that users are not able to type in the whole URL. In this setting, the users have to follow the navigations given in the page navigation diagram to access each non-entry page. We also assume that each page is associated with some properties to define whether it is a secure page and whether it is cacheable. A secure page should always be accessed with the *authentication session* open, in the sense that the user has successfully signed-in and has not yet signed-out for the secured pages in this application. A cacheable page can be stored in either browser cache or proxy cache. Here we model the browser cache and our model is abstracted from the implementations of existing commercial web browsers such as Microsoft's Internet Explorer, Netscape's Navigator.

Based on the information on the page navigation diagram, we define the labelled transition system, which on one hand, provides a formal basis for better understanding of the web system itself, and on the other hand, lays the ground work for both model checking and specification-based testing on the web applications where we take into account the affect of the internal session control and caching mechanism to the correct web page navigations.

In the following, we first give two motivating examples in Section 2 to illustrate the problem domain. Then we give a brief overview of the web systems in Section 3 with the focus on the aspects we are interested in. In Section 4, we explain the page navigation diagrams, and present the formal models of the web applications. How such a model can be used for specification-based testing and model checking is briefly discussed in Section 5. The related work is given in Section 6 followed by some final remarks.

2   Motivating Examples

Now we give two motivating examples. The first example demonstrates the so-called *unauthorized access* phenomenon (Figure 1(a)). Suppose the user is required to login to view certain secured pages. In page p_1, the user enters the user name and password, and clicks on the sign-in button. Upon this click, the user name and password are sent to the web server for authentication. When the authentication has passed, a secure page p_2 is loaded into the browser. Suppose in page p_2, the user clicks on the sign-out button and insecure page p_3 is shown.

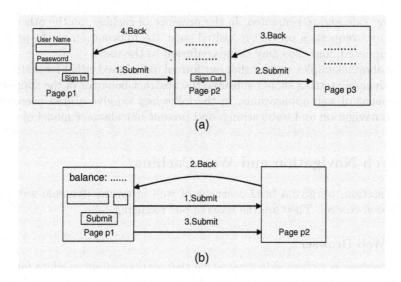

Fig. 1. The unauthorized-access and re-submit phenomena

With the caching mechanism, the *back* button may be enabled, and thus the user can actually click on it to view page p_2 again, without re-entering the user name and password. If this happens in an area where the machines can be publicly accessed, e.g. public library, airport internet zone, it will raise the issue that important information (such as visa card number) contained in a secure page p_2 may be viewed by wrong users.

This phenomenon can be avoided, for example, if page p_2 is defined as un-cacheable. In fact, the phenomenon does not appear in all applications: while it appears in the current University of Windsor Web Mail System, it does not show in the Microsoft's Hotmail.

The second example demonstrates the so-called *re-submit* phenomenon (Figure 1(b)). Suppose in an on-line banking system, the user clicked the submit button on page p_1 to confirm a transaction and waiting for page p_2 which somehow cannot be shown. As the *back* button is available, the user clicks on it to get back to page p_1. If page p_1 is a cached one, it will be identical to the previous one and thus the user cannot notice any change of the information on it. In particular, suppose the account balance is there and remains unchanged, the user will be confused whether the transaction is successful. Then the user may click on the submit button again. While the user needs only one transaction, the banking system will treat the two submit actions as different ones and processes both of them.

This phenomenon will not exhibit itself if there is no caching system involved: if the pages are not cached, the user will have to go through a sequence of given links to reach page p_1 again, just like the first time. Along the navigated pages, the user will normally be able to observe the updated information, e.g. the updated account balance, because the requests for the pages are always sent to the server side and re-generated. In the presence of caching, on the other hand, when a user requests a previously visited page, the information on the page will not be updated, and thus may cause confusion to the users.

The above examples suggest that our formal model used either for static analysis or dynamic testing should subsume the abstract behavior of the supporting environment of web applications. In the following, we give a brief overview of the web navigation and web caching, and present our abstract model of it.

3   Web Navigation and Web Caching

In this section, we give a brief overview of web browsers, dynamic web pages and session control. They are the basis of our modeling.

3.1   Web Browser

A web browser is a client side application that works as user interface for a web application. It provides a graphical interface to allow users to navigate web pages by clicking hyperlinks, toolbar buttons, or typing URLs in its *address textbox*. Here we give an abstract model of web browsers based on the interfaces of and some existing documents [7, 12] on two major web browsers, Netscape Navigator and Internet Explorer. Conceptually, a web browser consists of *a browser module*, *a network interface module*, *an HTML parser*, *a history stack* and *a local cache* (See Figure 2). The browser module is mainly responsible for presenting a web page, and processing user navigation events. The network interface module maintains communications between the browser and all web servers. It generates HTTP request messages and sends them to the designated web servers.

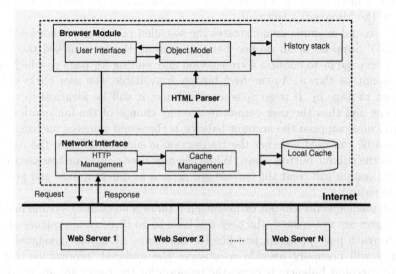

Fig. 2. Conceptual Architecture of Web Browser

When response messages are received, the network interface module retrieves the web pages embedded in response messages and performs operations on its local cache according to the parameters associated with HTTP response messages. The HTML parser parses HTML web pages, and constructs an object model for each web page. The presentation of a web page and the user's operations on it all rely on this object model. The history stack and local cache are maintained for reloading previously visited URLs and web pages: the former contains the previously visited URLs and the latter contains the previously visited cacheable pages. We give some more details on these two parts as our model is mainly based on their behavior.

History Stack. The history stack, as called in [7], is a kind of stack with similar operations as normal stacks. It maintains a stack pointer, a top pointer and a bottom pointer. The stack pointer of the browser's history stack always points to the current page, and it can be moved up and down between the top pointer and bottom pointer. The values of these variables determine whether a back or forward button can be enabled: If the stack has more than one item and the stack pointer does not point to the bottom item stored in the history stack, the back button is enabled. Similarly, the forward button is enabled when the stack has more than one item and the stack pointer does not point to the top item in the history stack.

Local Cache. Web cache is a manageable storage place that stores previously visited pages (For a detailed description on web caching, see [12]). If one of these visited pages is requested again, the page can be retrieved from the web cache instead of the web server. This can significantly reduce the serverload and response time to users, and smooth the network traffic when the cache is physically close to the users. There are two kinds of web caches, *proxy cache* and *browser's local cache*. Proxy cache is located between a web server and web browsers in a network and it provides services for all browsers within a local network. Browser cache provides the same functionality as a proxy cache does but it resides in a computer that a browser executes, and it only provides cacheable web pages for the specific browser running on the same computer.

The use of the browser's local cache depends on both the *cache settings* inside the browser and the *HTTP cache controls* associated with the received web page.

Cache Setting. A user can select a policy for the browser's cache setting. In each web browser of Microsoft's Internet Explorer 6.0, there are four options to define cacheable pages: *every visit to the page*, *every time you start Internet Explorer*, *automatically*, and *never*. For example, *automatically* means all cacheable web pages are valid: if a previously visited page is stored in the local cache and it is fresh, there is no need to check if there is any change.

HTTP Cache Control. A cacheable web page is considered fresh if the original page does not change in a certain time period and this time period is used to control the freshness of a web page. When a browser receives a web page from a web server, it must determine if it is cacheable and what its valid period is before saving the page into the local cache. The freshness of a web page is determined by the *expire time* of the page. Expire time of a web page can be set in the header part of the HTTP response message or in the web page itself with META tag. A page can be set *uncacheable* by defining its expire time as the same time it is created. Except for expire time, HTTP 1.1 introduced new cache control elements to provide more options in the control of cacheable web pages [8]: *max-age, s-maxage, public, no-cache, must-revalidate, proxy-revalidate*. Here *public* indicates the response page is cacheable, while *no-cache* means the web page received by a browser is not cacheable.

3.2   Web Server and Dynamic Web Page

When a request reaches a web server, the web server retrieves the URL from the request message. This URL is used to identify a unique web page in a web server: It contains the address of the web server and possibly with a *searchpart* that consists of search parameters a client passes to the web server. These parameters can be information needed to generate a new page, or can be information such as transaction data that needs to be processed by an application server.

If the requested web page is a static HTML page stored in a directory of the web server, the server reads the HTML file, encapsulates it in a response message and sends the message back to the requesting web browser. If the web server cannot locate a static web page in its local directory with the URL, it passes the request URL to a dynamic web page generating module. Typically, a dynamic web page generating module consists of a dispatcher and a set of page generating procedures. The dispatcher receives the request URL and calls the corresponding procedure to generate a web page. Each procedure contains a *page template* that predefines the layout, format, and static content in the page. While a procedure is called, a web page is assembled by adding dynamic content into the template. The dynamic content used for dynamic web page generation may depend on database servers or distributed objects that encapsulate the business logics.

3.3   Sessions and Cookies

Most web applications need to maintain communication sessions with their client browsers, and monitor each client's individual status and activities. An online banking system should maintain a communication session with a specific user during the time the user has logged in (and not yet logged out). The account information and transactions are restricted to this specific user, not others. Unfortunately, the communication protocol between web browser and web server (HTTP) is stateless and it does not provide the functionality on session control. The connection is only established during the time a browser sends out a request and receives a response message.

In order to maintain a logical session between a web browser and a web server, the identification as well as other kinds of information of a web client should be included in each request/response communication cycle. The cookie technique has emerged as such a solution to the user's session control: After receiving a page request from the browser, the web server generates a cookie and sends this cookie with the response message. The browser receives the response message and stores the cookie in its local storage place. When the same browser sends a page request to the server again, the cookie is sent within the request message. If the cookie contains unique identification information, the web server will be able to recognize the identity of the browser and trace the communication with the client.

4   Operational Semantics

Based on the actual systems explained above, we now present our modeling of the web applications. First, we explain the page navigation diagram that is given as its design specification. Then we define the integrated model in terms of labelled transition systems.

4.1   Page Navigation Diagram

As we explained before, a web application contains some procedures to generate the web pages, each of which consists of a static page template and some code to generate the dynamic content. The dynamic content can be dynamic links or dynamic texts. For the moment, we do not model the dynamic links, and we consider the dynamic texts as symbolic and finite output to be checked. Thus, each page template can be used to generate a finite set of predefined pages. In this way, we model the dynamic web pages in a web application as a finite set of *pages*. We assume that each page has a unique page id in the design specification.

The navigation among the pages is determined by the requested URL which consists of a hyperlink that the user has chosen, together with some possible input. We also assume that such navigations are predefined in the design specification:

– We consider a closed system, in the sense that the hyperlinks all point to the pages within the same web application. Thus, there is a given number of hyperlinks. An open system can be similarly modeled by augmenting an additional page to represent all the internet web pages beyond those in the application under consideration.
– The same hyperlink with different inputs (such as correct password and incorrect password) as *search parameters* may lead to different pages. We consider the user's input as abstract symbols that each of them, together with a hyperlink, can uniquely determine the page to be generated. We use a unique action to denote the pair of user's hyperlink choice and input for the navigation from one page to another.

There are pages that can be uniquely determined by their host name and path name, without any search parameters. We call them *entry pages* and we assume that the users can access entry pages directly by typing in the host and path names, without going through the hyperlinks. Pages that require search parameters on the other hand can be accessed only via the given navigations. The entry pages are identified in the design specifications.

For session control, we only model the sessions for the *authentications*, as we are interested in the correct access of the web pages in terms of the verification of the user's identifications. We do not consider the relationship between the cookie information and the dynamic content/link. We single out two special actions *SignIn* and *SignOut* to model a popular way of authentication: The former denotes the action that the user has entered the correct authentication information and requested to enter a secure page. After this action, the session will remain open for the consecutive accesses to secure pages until action *SignOut* is performed. Corresponding to this, we assume that it is also given in the design specification whether a page is secure or not. In addition, we assume that entry pages are by nature not secure.

For the *cache settings*, we have assumed that the given setting is *automatically* (see Section 3.1), which is widely used and which is the most complicated setting to model. According to this setting, a web page is considered as cacheable if the cacheable setting is included in the header part of the HTTP message containing the web page. For *HTTP cache control*, we do not model the expire time for cacheable pages: if a page is cacheable, the page is always fresh. Under these assumptions, we can consider that each page is associated with an attribute for cacheability.

With the above discussion, we assume that we are given a design specification $(P, EP, SP, CP, A, \Rightarrow)$ for a web application, where P, EP, SP, CP are the finite sets of ids of the pages, entry pages, secure pages and cacheable pages respectively. Obviously, EP, SP, $CP \subseteq P$, $EP \cap SP = \emptyset$. A is the finite set of symbols for the user's actions including special ones $SignIn$ and $SignOut$. $\Rightarrow \in P \times A \times P$ denotes the navigation relation between the pages.

4.2   The Integrated Model

Now, given a page navigation diagram $(P, EP, SP, CP, A, \Rightarrow)$, we define the operational semantics of the abstract behavior of the integrated web application in terms of labelled transition systems. We model the user's interactions with web browsers, the history stack and its impact on the navigation, the local cache and its influence on the freshness of the web pages, and the authentication sessions.

Basically, a labelled transition system is a quadruple *(State,Label,→,s_0)* where (i) *State* is the set of possible states of the program computation; (ii) *Label* is a set of labels showing the information about the state changes; (iii) $\rightarrow \subseteq State \times Label \times State$ is a transition relation that describes the system evolution. $(s, l, s') \in \rightarrow$ (also written as $s \xrightarrow{l} s'$) expresses that the system may evolve from state s to state s' with the information of the state change described in l. (iv) $s_0 \in State$ is the initial state.

A state contains all the information we are interested in for the computation of the navigations. In our current work, it consists of

- a page id to denote the current page we are in. Apart from the pages in P, we use an additional error page err. We will reach page err, for example, when attempting to access a secure page without an open session.
- a history stack variable for the current status of the URLs contained in the history stack. As in our case there is a one-to-one relationship between a URL and a page id, the history stack is a stack of page ids. Let p be a page id, hs be a stack variable, we will use $push(hs,p)$ to denote the history stack obtained from hs by pushing p onto the top of the stack, and move the related stack pointer and top pointer correspondingly. We will use $moveBack(hs)$ and $moveForward(hs)$ to denote the history stack obtained from hs by moving the stack pointer backward or forward one step respectively. We use $previous(hs)$ to denote the previous page id of the one pointed by the stack pointer.
- a variable of a set of page ids to denote the current status of the locally cached pages. Let lc be a local cache variable. We will use $add(lc,p)$ to denote the local cache obtained from lc by adding page id p to the set. We will use $inCache(lc,p)$ to denote the truth whether page p is contained in the local cache lc.
- a boolean variable to denote whether the authentication session is currently open.

The set of labels in the labelled transition system contains and only contains the information that we need to verify the correct navigations. Here we consider the set of labels as

$$L = \{(l, f) \mid l \in A \cup \{back, forward, entry, err\}, f = fresh \ or \ cache\}$$

For the interface offered by the web browsers, we model the user's operations as pressing the $back$ button, pressing the $forward$ button and typing the URLs (without the search parameters). $entry$ denotes that the user types in the URL. These actions are in addition to the user's interaction with the web application itself as given in A. We also have a special action err to denote that the navigation is directed to a special error page err.

As the erroneous navigations are very often due to the incorrect use of the cached versions of the pages, we use $fresh$ or $cache$ on the labels to denote whether the accessed page is from the origin server or from the local cache.

Now given a page navigation diagram $(P, EP, SP, CP, A, \Rightarrow)$, let $HS(P)$ denote the set of history stacks of P. Then the labelled transition system is a quadruple $\langle S, L, \rightarrow, s_0 \rangle$, where

- $S \subseteq (P \cup \{err\}) \times HS(P \cup \{err\}) \times 2^P \times Boolean$;
- $s_0 \in S$ is the initial state;
- $L \subseteq (A \cup \{back, forward, entry, err\}) \times \{fresh, cache\}$

The transition relation $\rightarrow$ is defined as the least relation satisfying 20 *structural rules*. All the structural rules have schema: $\dfrac{\text{ANTECEDENT}}{\text{CONSEQUENT}}$ which is interpreted logically as: $\forall(\text{ANTECEDENT} \longrightarrow \text{CONSEQUENT})$, where $\forall(\dots)$ stands for the universal closure of all free variables occurring in (...). Observe that, typically, ANTECEDENT and CONSEQUENT share free variables. When ANTECEDENT is missing, it is interpreted as *true*.

Due to the lack of the space, we only show some examples of the structural rules. In the following, $p, q \in P$ are page ids, $hs \in HS(P)$ denotes the history stack, $lc \in 2^P$ denotes the local cache, and *guard* denotes the session status. Suppose we are currently in page p with the history stack hs, local cache lc, and guard *guard*.

Rule 2.1

$$\frac{(p, SignIn, q) \in \Rightarrow \wedge inCache(lc, q) = true}{\langle p, hs, lc, guard\rangle \xrightarrow{(SignIn, cache)} \langle q, push(hs, q), lc, true\rangle}$$

Rule 2.1 shows an example of the structural rules for the transition relation corresponding to the user's sign-in action. If the user can sign-in from page p into page q, then we can derive the transition from the current state to the one with page q where q is put into the history stack. In the ending state, the guard *guard* is set *true* to indicate that the session for authentication is now open. The label on the transition shows that this is a sign-in action.

Rule 4.2

$$\frac{\begin{array}{l}previous(hs) = q \wedge q \notin CP \wedge \\ ((q \notin SP) \vee (q \in SP \wedge guard = true))\end{array}}{\langle p, hs, lc, guard\rangle \xrightarrow{(back, fresh)} \langle q, moveBack(hs), lc, guard\rangle}$$

Rule 4.2 shows an example corresponding to the user's action of pressing *back* button in the web browser. Suppose page q is on the top of the history stack (*previous(hs)=q*). If q is uncacheable, we use the URL contained in the history stack to retrieve the page from the origin server. Thus, page q is *fresh*. We can derive the corresponding transition from the state of p to the state of q under the condition that q is not a secure page ($q \notin SP$) or it is a secure page but the session is currently open (*guard=true*).

Given an initial state, the structural rules allow us to associate to it a labelled transition system whose states are those reachable from the initial state, via the transitions inferred by using these rules. Such a labelled transition system is finite as the page navigation diagram is finite and the history stack and browser cache are all of limited capacity.

The obtained labelled transition system is deterministic. This is based on the following two facts:

- the given page navigation diagram is deterministic in the sense that from each page, the input link uniquely determines the next page.
- for each state and each given action, there is exactly one rule to apply to derive the next state.

Since there is no nondeterminism involved, we can apply trace equivalence on the derived model for reduction.

5   Testing and Verification

Labelled transition systems are well defined models to describe the system's behavior at various levels of abstraction. It can be used for both specification-based testing and model checking.

In terms of testing, adopting labelled transition systems to conduct specification-based testing has been extensively studied in the past decade. For example, a test derivation algorithm is given [18] for conformance testing on labelled transition systems. How to use labelled transition system to express the possible internal choices of a program for reproducible testing is discussed in [3]. For an annotated bibliography on transition systems testing, see [2].

In terms of model checking and equivalence checking, many tools are based on the theory of labelled transition systems. Of course, to actually apply a particular verification tool will require that the model be specified according to a particular specification language such as CSP, Promela that can be recognized by the tool, and this is beyond the scope of the present work.

Now we revisit the previous two examples to illustrate how to express the desired properties in terms of temporal logics. Again, we do not follow the syntax of a particular temporal logic language as it depends on the tool selected.

For the unauthorized access problem, a requirement can be expressed as: *Any secure page (either cached or fresh) should be accessed when the session is open.* Of course, if a secure page is freshly retrieved, the session must be open, so this property essentially says that *Any cached secure page should be accessed when the session is open.* Since the status of the session guard depends only on the *SignIn* and *SignOut* actions, this is equivalent to saying that *access to any cached secure page (with label (a,cache)) should always be preceded by a SignIn action (with label (SignIn,*)) without a SignOut action (with label (SignOut,*)) in between,* where a links to a secure page and * denotes either *cache* or *fresh*.

For the *re-submit* phenomenon, let a_1 be the action for the form submission. We may require that after each submission, the user should visit a certain fresh page q before revisiting the page for the form submission, where q contains some information to convince the user of the submission status. Let a_2 be the action to link to page q. This property can be expressed as *after each $(a_1, *)$, there must be a $(a_2, *)$ before the next $(a_1, *)$.*

6   Related Work

In general, the design of web applications can follow the style of UML diagrams. Typically, the behavior of a web application can be described in finite state machines or statechart diagrams [5]. The use of finite state machines in describing the user's graphical interface is illustrated in [4] with a tool support to ease the editing of the specification.

In terms of testing, various issues in testing web sites or web applications have been addressed in the literature (See e.g. [9, 14, 15, 1, 19, 10, 11]). For example, Ricca and Tonella [14, 15] proposed a white-box testing strategy on web site analysis through web browser. A tool called *ReWeb* is developed to gather all web pages and their relations within a web site from source code, and a UML-based model for the web site is constructed. Using the derived UML models, a testing tool called *TestWeb* is developed to test the web application. Most of the previous work on testing web sites or web applications only considered the navigation behavior when a user clicks the links on the web pages, without considering the interface that the browser provides to the users.

As the web browser provides the interface to the web applications, the operations on a browser itself can change the navigation behavior while a user browses a web application. Correspondingly, the testing of a web application should consider the browser's influence on the navigation behavior of the web application. In this regard, the effect of user's actions of pressing back/forward buttons has been taken into account in generating test cases for bypass testing [13] by systematically altering the given transitions. In [19], Offutt et al. introduced a modeling and testing methodology where the user's capability of pressing the back/forward/refresh buttons or directly modifying the URLs are modeled as *operational transitions*. Lucca and Penta [11] proposed a *baseline testing* strategy which creates a testing model by adding browser's behavior to a series of pages with inter-related hyperlinks: For each navigation path called *baseline*, the testing model is a navigation tree generated by adding the user's actions on clicking *back* and *forward*. In their work, dynamic pages and session control are not modeled, and the proposed test case generation only applies to baselines: the browser's behavior is added to each *path* instead of the complete navigation model.

In terms of model checking, how to use existing model checker SMV in web applications is discussed in [16]. In [17], it has been proposed to use existing model checking technique where Petri Nets are used to describe the structure of the links in a hypertext and a variant of CTL^* is defined to describe the sequence of transitions between states. A model checker specially designed for web sites has been proposed in [6]. A common view we share is to use the state transformation to denote the page navigations: the states are pages and transitions between states are hyperlinks between the pages. While these approaches considered the verification of the correctness in the web applications themselves, our focus has been put in the modeling of some important aspects of the web systems.

7   Final Remarks

To adopt formal methods into a specific application domain, one needs to have not only a deep understanding of the domain itself, but also a careful analysis on the specific problems and a proper selection of the aspects to be modeled. Due to the state space problem in model checking, this is important in rendering the models reasonable enough for analysis: the model has to be suitable by abstracting away as much un-related details as possible. Much of our effort has been put to reach this. A web application is executed in an environment with integrated technologies in all different aspects: web browser, web server, distributed objects, middleware and databases, etc. We have considered here only its navigation behavior influenced by the session control and the browser caching mechanism. This is based on the problems on the correct navigations that we are interested in.

Of course, our model can be modified upon needs or extended to cover more features. For example,

- Our web caching model is based on a certain setting of the browser cache, and it only serves as an example of the formal models of the web caching. As we mentioned, the modeling of this setting is both the most difficult and the most significant one. It does not take much effort to tailor it into other settings.
- The information carried on the labels in the labelled transition system can be defined in different ways, according to the properties to be checked. For example, we may use a single action to represent all actions we are not interested in.
- We did not consider the dynamic links in the assumed page navigation diagram, and for the functionality provided by session/cookie techniques, we have chosen only the session control.

The extension of the present work to cover other features of dynamically generated pages are in progress. For the purpose of empirical studies, we are also interested in applying a particular model checking tool with the input model automatically generated.

Acknowledgements

The author would like to thank the anonymous reviewers for helpful comments on the preliminary version of this paper submitted to ICFEM 2004. This work is supported by the Natural Sciences and Engineering Research Council of Canada under grant number RGPIN 209774.

References

1. M. Benedikt, J. Freire, and P. Godefroid. VeriWeb: A platform for automating web site testing. In *Proc. of the World Wide Web Conference (Web Engineering Track)*, 2002.
2. E. Brinskma and J. Tretmans. Testing transition systems: An annotated bibliography. In *Lecture Notes in Computer Science Vol. 1067*, pages 187–195. Springer-Verlag, 2001.
3. J. Chen. Using formal methods to serialize synchronization events. In *Proc. of the International Conference on Formal Engineering Methods, LNCS 2885*, pages 34–47, 2003.

4. J. Chen and S. Subramaniam. Specification-based testing for GUI-based applications. *Software Quality Journal*, 10(3):205–224, 2002.
5. J. Conallen. Modelling web applications architectures with UML. *Communications of the ACM*, 42(10):63–70, 1999.
6. L. de Alfaro. Model checking the world wide web. In *Proc. of the 13th International Conference on Computer Aided Verification, Lecture Notes in Computer Science 2102*, pages 337–349, 2001.
7. S. Greenberg and A. Cockburn. Getting back to back: Alternate behaviors for a web browsers back button. In *Proc. of the 5th Annual Human Factors and the Web Conference*, Gaithersburg, Maryland, USA, June 1999.
8. IETF.   Hypertext   transfer   protocol – HTTP 1.1 (RFC2616).   http:// www.ietf.org/rfc/rfc2616.txt?number=2616, 1999.
9. D. C. Kung, C. Liu, and P. Hsia. An object-oriented web test model for testing web applications. In *The 1st Asia-Pacific Conference on Quality Software (APAQS 2000)*, pages 111–120, 2000.
10. S. C. Lee and J. Offutt. Generating test cases for XML-based web component interactions using mutation analysis. In *Proc. of the 12th IEEE International Symposium on Software Reliability Engineering (ISSRE'01)*, pages 200–209, Hong Kong, PRC, November 2001.
11. G. D. Lucca and M. D. Penta. Considering browser interaction in web application testing. In *Proc. of the 5th IEEE International Workshop on Web Site Evolution (WSE03)*, pages 74–83, 2003.
12. M. Nottingham.   Caching   tutorial   for   web   authors   and   webmasters. http://www.web-caching.com/mnot_tutorial, last access: July 2004.
13. J. Offutt, Y. Wu, X. Du, and H. Huang. Bypass testing of web applications. In *Proc. of the 15th IEEE International Symposium on Software Reliability Engineering (ISSRE'04)*, 2004. To appear.
14. F. Ricca and P. Tonella. Analysis and testing of web applications. In *Proc. of the 23rd IEEE International Conference on Software Engineering (ICSE'01)*, pages 25–34, Toronto, Canada, 2001.
15. F. Ricca and P. Tonella. Testing processes of web applications. *Annals of Software Engineering*, 14:93–114, 2002.
16. E. D. Sciascio, F. M. Donini, M. Mongiello, and G. Piscitelli. Web applications design and maintenance using symbolic model checking. In *Proc. of IEEE the 7th European Conference on Software Maintenance and Reengineering (CSMR'03)*, pages 63–72, 2003.
17. P. Stotts and J. Furuta. Hyperdocuments as automata: Verification of trace-based browsing properties by model checking. *ACM Transactions on Information Systems*, 16(1):1–30, 1998.
18. J. Tretmans. Testing transition systems: A formal approach. In *Proc. of the 10th International Conference on Concurrency Theory. Lecture Notes in Computer Science Vol. 1664*, pages 46–65. Springer-Verlag, 1999.
19. Y. Wu, J. Offutt, and X. Du. Modeling and testing of dynamic aspects of web applications. Submitted for publication. Technical report ISE-TR-04-01, www.ise.gmu.edu/techreps/, 2004.

Managing Verification Activities Using SVM

Bill Aldrich[1], Ansgar Fehnker[2], Peter H. Feiler[3], Zhi Han[2], Bruce H. Krogh[2], Eric Lim[1], and Shiva Sivashankar[4]

[1] The Mathworks, Inc., 3 Apple Hill Dr Natick, MA 01760-2098
[2] Dept. Elec. and Comp. Eng., Carnegie Mellon University Pittsburgh, PA 15213
[3] Software Engineering Institute, Carnegie Mellon University Pittsburgh, PA 15213
[4] Emmeskay, Inc., 44191 Plymouth Oaks Blvd Suite 300, Plymouth, MI 48170

Abstract. SVM (System Verification Manager) manages the application of verification methods for model-based development of embedded systems by providing integrated representations of requirements, system architecture, models and verification methods. Developed in Java within MATLAB®, SVM supports all types of tools for modelling and verification through an extensible framework of data and coding structures. This paper presents the main features of SVM and illustrates its application to embedded control and signal processing systems.

1 Introduction

SVM (System Verification Manager) supports model-based design of embedded system software by providing an integrated environment for specifying and managing the relationships between system requirements, system architectures, system models, verification methods, and results of verification activities. Implemented in Java within the MATLAB® environment, SVM is an extensible environment designed to support the use of multiple modelling, simulation, and verification tools. SVM objects encapsulate the information required for managing the development process with pointers to the actual models and tools used to carry out the design. Thus, SVM facilitates model-based development without imposing constraints on the models or methods used for design and implementation.

SVM provides multiple views that allow the system design process to evolve along several dimensions without advocating or enforcing a particular design process or methodology. Requirements, for example, can be entered, imported, updated, and elaborated as the system develops. New models and verification methods can be introduced whenever they are needed. Different representations (called variants) of components in the system architecture can be defined and invoked as the design moves from algorithm development to executable code for the target processor. SVM provides several features for model-based development that have not been integrated previously into a single tool, including: *requirements traceability, system architecture, model management, verification activities*, and *results management*.

J. Davies et al. (Eds.): ICFEM 2004, LNCS 3308, pp. 61–75, 2004.

Section 2 describes the main features of SVM. These features are then illustrated for an embedded controller in an automotive engine application (Sect. 3) and a signal processing application (Sect. 4). Section 5 summarizes the contributions of this work and plans for future development.

2   Overview of SVM

SVM does not prescribe a particular development approach. Instead, it supports a range of development processes. On one hand it supports the development of a system from requirements into a system architecture that gets realized through a series of models, and the specification of verification conditions that must be met in order to consider given requirements to be satisfied. On the other hand SVM supports the management of an existing set of models for a system by organizing them into a common system architecture, by keeping a record of the verification activities that are routinely performed on models through model analysis, simulation runs, and model execution, and by automating the bookkeeping of the verification results.

This section describes SVM features for defining verification activities and for managing their execution and results. Section 2.1 describes the representation of SVM requirements and how requirements are entered and associated with models and verification activities. Section 2.2 describes how models are represented in SVM and the relationships between SVM model objects and the actual models in the "native" tool environments. It also describes the representation of the system architecture and the concept of model variants whereby multiple models can be associated with components of the system architecture to reflect the evolution of the system development process, and how consistency between models and the architecture is checked and maintained. Section 2.3 presents the concepts of verification methods and verification activities, and describes how they are defined in SVM to be associated with particular models and requirements. Section 2.4 describes how SVM provides access to verification results and propagates the status of results through the requirements hierarchy.

2.1   Requirements Traceability

SVM supports requirements-driven verification. All verification activities are associated with and initiated from a specific requirement in a requirement tree that is displayed and managed through an interactive window. The requirements view, shown in Fig. 1, includes the name and description of the requirement, along with the status of its verification.

Requirements are entered, viewed and managed in a hierarchical tree structure. This allows the cascading of requirements into multiple sub-requirements, which in turn can be further partitioned into manageable sub-sub-requirement entities. A typical safety critical design process involves successive cycles of refining requirements from one level of abstraction into more detailed requirements at a lower level of abstraction. These processes are naturally represented with a requirements hierarchy. [6]. Such a requirement tree can be entered manually

	Name	Status	Description
System Requirements			
Performance requirement		FAILED	The perfomance requirements as descri...
Rise time requirement		PASSED	Rise time for step changes from closed ...
Settle time requirement		PASSED	Settle time is less than 40ms after eachi...
Percent overshoot		FAILED	ETC throttle plate shall never hit the stops
Steady state error		FAILED	State Tracking Error is within the +2% ra...
Throttle plate resolution		FAILED	Control the throttle plate angle with a res...
RRT Verification		PASSED	Use RRT to compute the set reachable ...
Reduced order		PASSED	
4th order		FAILED	Use a 4th order model
5th order		PASSED	Use a 5th order model

Fig. 1. SVM requirements view for an embedded control application (see Sect. 3)

or imported from an existing requirements document. Currently, the set of requirements (and all associated sub-requirements) beneath a given node in the
requirement tree in a project can be imported from (and exported to) a spread-
sheet in Excel format. A requirement is verified either by executing any directly
associated verification activities and/or by verifying any sub-requirements. The
verification activity for a requirement is chosen from the list of registered verification methods and is instantiated with specific values for its inputs. This
operation creates an association between the requirement and its verification activities. Typically, to verify a requirement, a test is executed on the work product
and the results of the test are analyzed to infer if the verification criteria have
been satisfied. SVM allows the user to import the work product as a system
model (or as an element within the system model) and then allows the user to
pick this system model during verification activity definition. SVM stores and
keeps track of such relationships to advise the user to re-verify requirements
when work products are changed.

As is frequently practiced, the partitioning (or cascading) of requirements
into sub-requirements generally follows the partitioning of the system into subsystems and components. SVM allows users to associate requirements and sub-
requirements with nodes in the system architecture. This relationship can be
used to guide the user in the system development and verification process. After
the verification activities are defined, the user can invoke verification at any requirement node from the context menu in the requirements view. When the user
requests verification on a particular requirement in SVM, the tool tries to verify
all the sub-requirements (including all nested levels) and then infers that the requirement has passed verification only if all of its sub-requirements have passed.
The verification status is tracked and displayed in the requirements view and
this status can be one of the following - passed, failed, in progress, TBD (To Be
Decided) or inspect. The inspect status flags verification activities whose results
must be manually inspected to determine if they passed. This status can also
be used when the verification activity aborts due to an error in the verification
script.

SVM maintains associations between different objects, such as requirements, verification activities, system models and system architecture. These associations are visually indicated with window synchronization and propagate changes to requirements that need re-verification. When the SVM windows (views) are synchronized and a node (or object) is selected in one of the views, the associated entities in other windows get highlighted. Change propagation enables SVM to advise the user to re-verify a requirement whenever it or one of its verification activities is updated or added or sub-requirement is added. In such instances, the status on the affected requirement and all of its ancestors are reset to TBD. Similarly, if the models in their native tool domains are changed, SVM associates these changes to affected system models and ultimately to the requirements which use these models for verification. Since models are usually assembled using reusable library components, this provides a powerful mechanism to trace the impact of changes at a component level (model) to verification of requirements at the system level.

2.2   Model Management

Embedded systems are typically designed to reflect a system architecture that identifies the functional components in the system. The architecture becomes the reference for identifying the roles of various models developed during the design process. Similarly, system requirements, both functional and para-functional, such as response time, latency, and tolerance of incomplete and inaccurate data streams, are typically expressed in terms of the system and its subsystems.

During the development additional claims and observations of functional and para-functional system properties may be made. This makes the architecture also a reference point for the requirements and claims hierarchy as discussed in Sect. 2.1. Finally, requirements and claims are validated through verification activities that are associated with requirements and claims (see section 4). Those verification activities are applied to models that represent the system or subsystem, whose requirement is to be validated. Thus, the system architecture provides a bridge between the verification of requirements and the models used in the verification - as shown in Fig. 2.

SVM provides two views of the system architecture, a tree view, and a block diagram view, both shown in Fig. 3. The tree view reflects the compositional hierarchy of the system. The graphical view reflects the interactions between system components, typically represented by ports and connections.

We have enhanced the basic system architecture description with semantic information about the application domain in order to support consistency analysis of system properties that otherwise are undocumented and result in hidden side effects. Examples of common problems are mistaking wheel speed for car speed, using meters instead of feet, or using an absolute coordinate system instead of a relative one. Figure 4 illustrates how SVM identifies these mismatches in the system architecture. Semantic information can also include bounds on values and rates of changes such as a constraint on a stream of setpoints, whose change in successive data values is expected to stay within bounds acceptable

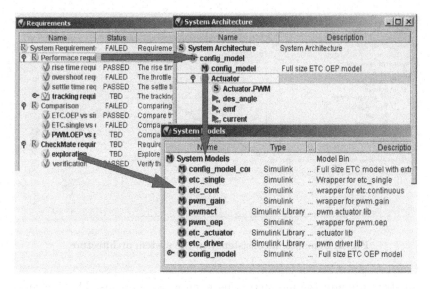

Fig. 2. SVM system architecture as reference point

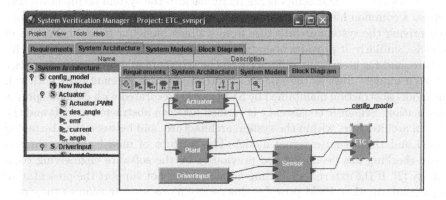

Fig. 3. Tree and block diagram view of the system architecture

to the receiving controller. System architectures decorated with such additional information can be checked for semantic consistency early in the development life cycle.

Such a model-based approach to architecture modelling and analysis is promoted by the Model-Driven Architecture initiative of the Object Management Group (OMG) [1] and is incorporated in the Society of Automotive Engineers (SAE) Architecture Analysis & Design Language (AADL) standard for embedded real-time systems currently in ballot [3]. This standard is targeted for the avionics, aerospace, and automotive industries. SVM maintains an abstraction of such models with information that is relevant to the verification of system requirements. The abstraction of these external models represents the modelled

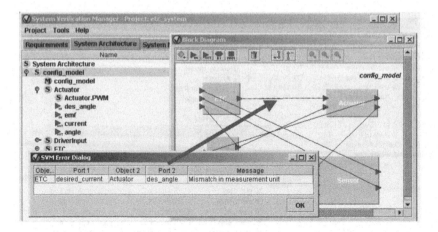

Fig. 4. Semantic inconsistency in the system architecture

system structure and the interaction between its subsystems. This information is automatically extracted from the external models.

All models and their components relate back to the system architecture that defines a common hierarchy and interaction topology. SVM provides operations for deriving the system architecture from a single model or from a collection of models. Similarly, it provides operations for comparing a model against its architecture, and for identifying differences in the structure and interaction topology between models. Just as the system architecture can be semantically enriched, the model abstraction maintained by SVM can be decorated with domain-specific information. Semantic consistency is verified between abstracted models and the system architecture, within the system architecture, and between the abstracted model and the actual external model. The concept of model abstraction and static checking has been explored previously by the software engineering community [2]. If the external modelling notation does not support the presentation of such information, SVM provides this capability as an extension to the external tool. For example, the current release of MathWorks Simulink has a limited data dictionary capability focusing on the consistent use of implementation types such as short and long integers, etc. SVM extends these models with information related to the application domain.

2.3   Verification Activities

The verification activities associated with SVM requirements are defined in two steps. First, verification methods (VMs), defined by MATLAB® m-code, are registered with unbound variables. Registered VMs are then invoked and instantiated as verification activities (VAs) by binding the VM variables to the models and signals associated with a particular requirement.

Figure 5 shows the VM registration user interface, which has three panes to define the variables in the VM (shown in Fig. 5), the VM code to be exe-

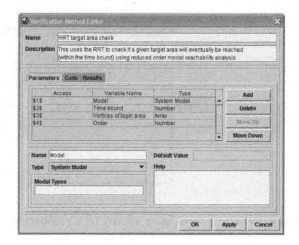

Fig. 5. Verification method registration interface

cuted, and the functions for reviewing results from the VM (also m-code). VM code can invoke any models and tools through the standard MATLAB® programming constructs. Verification parameters (unbound variables) are assigned names, types, and descriptions to assist the user when the VM is instantiated as a method. Several pre-registered VMs are available with SVM, including: step response analysis; comparative model simulation; discrete model checking (SMV); hybrid model checking (Checkmate); Dymola simulation; batch simulation on datasets; and mex compile. Users can add additional VMs. VMs are instantiated as VAs from the requirements window, as shown in Fig. 6. The user selects one of the registered VMs to be applied for the requirement and binds the variables that identify the models, signals and data to be used for the VA.

2.4 Results Management

SVM automatically manages the record keeping of the execution of verification activities and their results. It does so in three ways: it maintains the result status, it archives the results for later examination, and it manages the impact of changes in models and verification methods by invalidating previous verification results that are potentially affected by the changes.

A verification activity is in one of several states. It may need to be executed, its execution may be in progress, it may have completed by passing or failing, or it may require examination to determine whether it is satisfied. SVM allows verification activities of individual requirements to be organized into verification folders. Those folders can represent different life cycle phases, and contains different logic expressions to indicate the conditions under which the contained set of verification activities and folders is considered satisfied. This verification result status is not only propagated up the verification folder hierarchy, but also up the requirements hierarchy. Such accumulation of verification result status

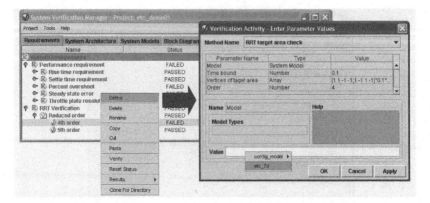

Fig. 6. Defining a verification activity for a requirement

provides a simple visual cue as to the degree to which requirements of a system are being satisfied as well as a quantification of such pass/fail coverage.

A verification activity that takes the form of model checking may produce counter examples when the model checking condition is not satisfied. A simulation run may produce logs of produced output, traces of state changes etc. Similarly, probes in the executing code of a system may produce a trail of its execution. This information may be evaluated during the execution of the verification activity to determine the results status. SVM keeps track of such information that is produced by external tools. It uses the file system to identify and archive results related to a particular verification method. Before executing a verification method the tool creates a new results directory and makes it the working MATLAB® directory. This allows verification methods to produce common output files without conflicting with the results of other verification methods. SVM users can later examine these results through manual inspection to review the automated evaluation of the verification condition and to draw additional conclusions.

SVM not only automates the recording of verification results, but it also can automate the identification and automatic execution of verification activities that have yet to be executed. Furthermore, SVM can manage the impact of changes made to models, library components of models, to configurations of models, to verification methods, to parameters and data sets that are input to the verification activity.

SVM tracks changes to external models and data files in two ways. First, it tracks such changes if they are initiated through SVM by the user opening a model or data file through SVM and making modifications. Second, changes made through an external tool without the involvement of SVM are identified by tracking mechanisms such as recording modification dates of files or checksums of file contents and comparing them to the actual files at startup of SVM or at user request. SVM also supports change impact management by incorporating ideas explored in previous research on this topic [9, 7, 4]. Since SVM has a record of relevant dependencies it can invalidate the result status of any previously completed verification activity whose result is potentially impacted by the change. SVM under user control automatically re-executes these verification activities to determine whether the requirements are still satisfied. The same dependency information can be used by SVM to provide what-if impact analysis, i.e., to predict the amount of reverification necessary as a result of a change before the change is made.

3   An Embedded Control Application

This section deals with an application from the DARPA project Model Based Integration of Embedded Software (MoBIES). This project proposed two automotive case studies, one of them is an Electronic Throttle Control (ETC) system. The ETC system is a component that replaces the mechanical link between the pedal and the throttle plate in an automobile.

Problem Statement. The ETC system was part of an Open Experimental Platform (OEP). The OEP was used to illustrate the model based approach to produce embedded code. In this section we will focus on the modelling phase, and illustrate the use of multiple models and verification folders.

Application of (SVM) System Verification Manager. Figure 1 depicts the requirements tree for the ETC system. The first set of requirements was part of the informal description of the ETC system. This description was provided by the OEP along with a Simulink and Stateflow model. Among the requirements were rise time, settle time and overshoot requirements. These requirements were defined for a single execution of the system with step input. Satisfaction of the requirement can typically be tested by single (or finitely many) runs of the simulation model. For this example we find that the rise time requirement is satisfied, whereas the steady state error requirement is violated.

The second set of requirements deal with a simplified version of the OEP model. Although the ETC system is essentially just a DC motor and a spring, controlled by a sliding mode controller, and a linear filter for the input, the OEP model contain more details. This mainly, because it served at the same time as blueprint for an implementation. For the verification we model the plant, the sliding model controller and the filter, but we omit for example details from actuator and sensors. This model is a piecewise linear time-invariant 7th-order system.

To formally verify requirements of the ETC system for a set of initial states, reachability analysis is performed on the 7th-order model using procedures from RRT (Reachability analysis in Reduced state space Toolbox) [5]. Complexity of reachability computations for continuous and hybrid dynamic systems typically grows dramatically with the dimension of the continuous state space. To avoid performing reachability analysis in the full-order state space, the tool RRT computes an over-approximation of the set reachable states using reduced-order models. The procedures in RRT first construct a reduced-order model using the balance and truncation (B&T) [8] method. It then estimates the upper-bound

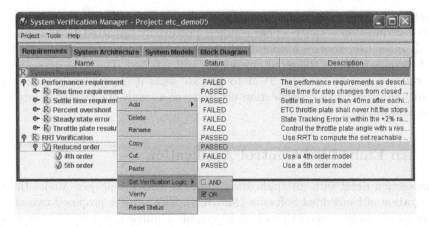

Fig. 7. The verification folders can be used to group verification activities

on the approximation error introduced by model reduction. Finally, conservative over-approximations of the reachable states are computed, which incorporate the error bounds.

The reduced order reachability analysis provides efficient analysis at the expense of bigger over-approximation errors. A drastic reduction of the order might may lead to a large approximation error, and thus to inconclusive results. On the other hand, if the procedure finds that the reduced order model satisfies the requirement, we know that the full order model satisfies the requirement. We define multiple verification activities with different choices of reduced orders. If any of these verification activities finds that the property is satisfied, we know that the overall requirement is satisfied. The verification folder Reduced order contains all verification activities. To reflect that only one of these activities has to return PASS, we select the option OR from the context menu Set Verification Logic (Fig. 7).

Future Work. The current implementation SVM evaluates all verification activities. If a verification folder contains multiple activities, of which only one has to pass, the SVM could stop as soon as one activity passes. The status of the folder will be PASSED regardless of the outcome of the remaining activities. Similarly, if all activities have to pass, the evaluation might stop as soon as one activity fails. A future release of the SVM should give the user the option to either evaluate all activities regardless of the result, or to stop evaluation as soon as the status of the folder can be determined.

4   A Signal Processing Application

In this section we consider the application of SVM to a signal classification development project. The goal of this project is to produce efficient embeddable code starting from a prototype design implemented in MATLAB® using the built-in language and signal processing functions. We need to ensure that the

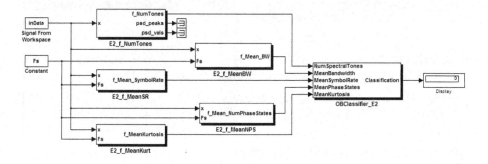

Fig. 8. Signal Classifier: Application Level

final implementation is able to generate embeddable code and is functionally equivalent to the prototype MATLAB® M code within an acceptable tolerance. SVM is used to precisely identify discrepancies between the implementations and to trace these to specific components in the design.

Problem Statement. This application classifies incoming signal as Phase Shift Keyed (PSK), Frequency Shift Keyed (FSK), or none of the above (NOTA) based on signal features such as bandwidth, symbol rate, kurtosis, number of spectral tones, and number of phase states. The model-based implementation is done in Simulink and Stateflow so that embeddable C-code can be automatically generated using Real-Time Workshop.

Design. The Simulink model is arranged in an application, component, and primitive block hierarchy. This arrangement is well suited to a model based implementation because it clearly illustrates the control and data flow. Figure 8 shows the top level Simulink diagram. The application is composed of five feature extractor components that processes input signals to produce signal characteristics that are used to determine signal modulation. These components are built with *primitive blocks*, each of which performs a specific signal operation.

The underlying implementation of the primitive blocks leverages the signal processing capabilities of Simulink and the Signal Processing Blockset extension product. In some cases the primitive block function requires some custom capability beyond the built-in library of signal processing components. Stateflow is used in many of these cases to incorporate arbitrary structured control flow such as while loops and nested if-then else constructs. Figure 9 shows two block implementations: OBFFT that simply encapsulates the built-in FFT, and OBBWest, the bandwidth estimator, that is a Stateflow chart.

Application of (SVM) System Verification Manager. Verifying the Simulink model implementation against the reference MATLAB® implementation can be tedious, considering the number of components that must be individually verified. SVM helps the user organizes requirements, verification activities and results all in one central point.

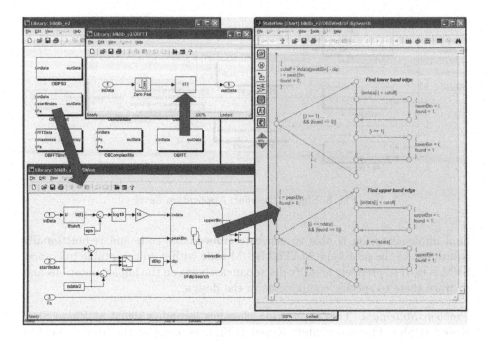

Fig. 9. Signal Classifier: Component Level

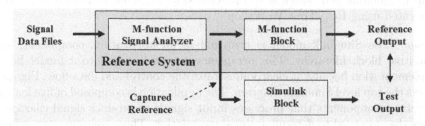

Fig. 10. Verification Method use to compare Simulink implementation against reference M-code implementation

To verify the Simulink component implementations, we need test inputs and output. We devised a system shown in Fig. 10 to capture these outputs as a side effect of executing the overall prototype signal classification application. The reference inputs drive the Simulink blocks to give test outputs that are compared against the reference M-functions blocks to determine if the results meet a specified tolerance.

This verification method is implemented as an M function registered within SVM. Registering a generic operation such as this enables us to instantiate and parameterize the function from within the SVM user interface. As shown in Fig. 11 each primitive and component block has an instantiation of the method with its own set if parameter values.

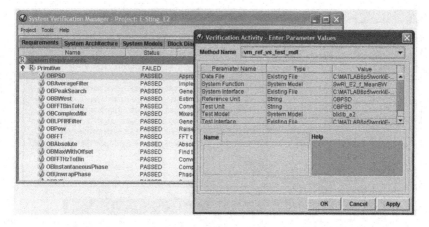

Fig. 11. Associating verification method for each block

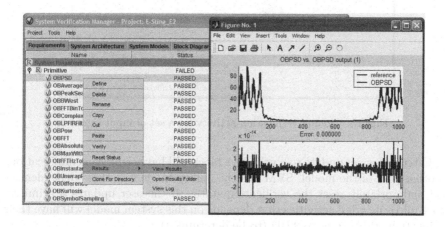

Fig. 12. Verification Results

After each verification activity, the results are automatically organized in a separate folder by SVM and can be easily accessed within the SVM environment. For example, the OBPSD primitive block, which computes the power spectrum density, follows the reference MATLAB® implementation very closely. The error is on the order of 10-14 which is close to floating point precision (Fig 12).

Verifying a block against one signal does not guarantee that the requirements will be met for an entire range of signals. SVM provides an easy method to repeat the verification for a set of signals by cloning the verification activity, as shown in Fig. 13. By breaking down the verifications to manageable model primitive components, the user can now easily locate and troubleshoot areas within a model that causes it to deviate from requirements. The verification activities are automatically organized within a verification folder to allow the user to easily browse the results.

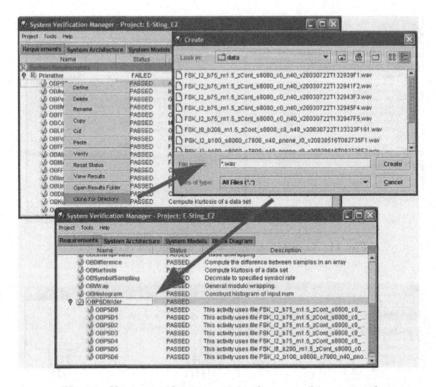

Fig. 13. Cloning verification activity for a set of input signals

Often times, an update to a primitive block will have significant ramifications to other part of the model. SVM has the ability to identify these dependencies and appropriately reset the verification status. If the user updates a primitive block all verification activities that depends on this system model will have their verification status reset to TBD (to be determined).

Future Work. The concept of cloning a verification activity for a set of input signals does not ensure every part of a model is tested. As part of the Simulink Performance Tools package there is a tool called Model Coverage, which records all simulation paths and generates a report indicating untested portions of a model for a given set of input signals. The SVM verification method will be enhanced to leverage this capability to give the user additional verification information to ensure the model will meet their specified requirements.

5   Discussion

This paper describes the features of the current beta version of SVM (available at http://www.ece.cmu.edu/~webk/svm). SVM has been applied to several examples in the DARPA MoBIES program, including the electronic throttle control (ETC) and a software radio digital signal processing system, described in this paper. Current development is focusing on enhancing the development environment for defining verification methods and verification activities.

We are also investigating methods for increasing the capability of SVM to support heterogeneous verification activities, by which we mean the application of multiple formalisms and tools to acquire information about the design and system performance. The current mechanisms for combining verification status information in the requirements tree are a first step in this direction. Requirements can be satisfied using a wide range of verification methods, including simulation, model checking, theorem proving, and designer evaluation of empirical results. We aim to increase the power of SVM by introducing richer representations of the relationships among models and verification activities so that further inferences could be obtained automatically. Towards that end, we are developing an ontology for hybrid system verification that will support combining and reasoning about information from heterogeneous verification activities.

References

1. OMG model driven architecture. http://www.omg.org/mda.
2. E.M. Clarke, O. Grumberg, and D.E. Long. Model checking and abstraction. In *Nineteenth Annual ACM Symposium on Principles of Programming Languages*, 1992.
3. P. Feiler, B. Lewis, and S. Vestal. The SAE Architecture Analysis & Design Language (AADL) Standard: A basis for model-based architecture-driven embedded systems engineering. In *IFIP World Computer Congress - Workshop on Architecture Description Languages (WADL04)*, 2004.
4. P.H. Feiler and Jun Li. Managing inconsistency in reconfigurable systems. In *IEE Proceedings Software*, pages 172–179, 1998.
5. Z. Han and B. H. Krogh. Using reduced-order models in reachability analysis of hybrid systems. In *IEEE Proc of American Control Conference*, 2004, to appear.
6. L.A. Johnson. Software considerations in airborne systems and equipment certification. Technical report, RTCA Inc., 1992. Document RTCA/DO-178B.
7. Jun Li and P.H. Feiler. Impact analysis in real-time control systems. In *Proceedings of International Conference on Software Maintenance (ICSM)*, pages 443–452. IEEE CS Press, 1999.
8. B. C. Moore. Principal component analysis in linear systems: Controllability, observability and model reduction. *IEEE Transaction on Automatic Control*, 26(1), Feb 1981.
9. D.E. Perry. The logic of propagation in the Inscape Environment. In *ACM SIGSOFT '89 Third Symposium on Software Testing, Analysis and Verification*, pages 114–21, 1989.

A General Model for Reachability Testing
of Concurrent Programs

Richard H. Carver[1] and Yu Lei[2]

[1] Dept. of Computer Science, MS 4A5,
George Mason University, Fairfax
VA 22030-4444
rcarver@cs.gmu.edu
[2] Dept. of Computer Science and Engineering,
The University of Texas at Arlington, Arlington, Texas, 76019
ylei@cse.uta.edu

Abstract. Reachability testing is a technique for testing concurrent programs. Reachability testing derives test sequences on-the-fly as the testing process progresses, and can be used to systematically exercise all the behaviors of a program. The main contribution of this paper is a general model for reachability testing. This model allows reachability testing to be applied to many different types of concurrent programs, including asynchronous and synchronous message passing programs, and shared-memory programs that use semaphores, locks, and monitors. We define a common format for execution traces and present timestamp assignment schemes for identifying races and computing race variants, which are a crucial part of reachability testing. Finally, we discuss a prototype reachability testing tool, called RichTest, and present some empirical results.

1 Introduction

Concurrent programming is an important technique in modern software development. Concurrency can improve computational efficiency and resource utilization. However, concurrent programs behave differently than sequential programs. Multiple executions of a concurrent program with the *same* input may exercise *different* sequences of synchronization events (or SYN-sequences) and produce *different* results. This non-deterministic behavior makes concurrent programs notoriously difficult to test.

A simple approach to dealing with non-deterministic behavior when testing a concurrent program CP is to execute CP with a fixed input many times and hope that faults will be exposed by one of these executions [18]. This type of testing, called *non-deterministic testing*, is easy to carry out, but it can be very inefficient. It is possible that some behaviors of CP are exercised many times while others are never exercised. An alternative approach is called *deterministic testing*, which forces a specified SYN-sequence to be exercised. This approach allows CP to be tested with carefully selected SYN-sequences. The test sequences are usually selected from a

J. Davies et al. (Eds.): ICFEM 2004, LNCS 3308, pp. 76–98, 2004.

static model of CP or of CP's design. However, accurate static models are often difficult to build for dynamic behaviors.

Reachability testing is an approach that combines non-deterministic and deterministic testing [9] [12] [19]. It is based on a technique called prefix-based testing, which controls a test run up to a certain point, and then lets the run continue non-deterministically. The controlled portion of the execution is used to force the execution of a "prefix SYN-sequence", which is the beginning part of one or more feasible SYN-sequences of the program. The non-deterministic portion of the execution exercises one of these feasible sequences.

A novel aspect of reachability testing is that it adopts a dynamic framework in which test sequences are derived automatically and on-the-fly, as the testing process progresses. In this framework, synchronization events (or SYN-events) are recorded in an execution trace during each test run. At the end of a test run, the trace is analyzed to derive prefix SYN-sequences that are "race variants" of the trace. A race variant represents the beginning part of a SYN-sequence that definitely could have happened but didn't, due to the way race conditions were arbitrarily resolved during execution. The race variants are used to conduct more test runs, which are traced and then analyzed to derive more race variants, and so on. If every execution of a program with a given input terminates, and the total number of SYN-sequences is finite, then reachability testing will terminate and every partially-ordered SYN-sequence of the program with the input will be exercised.

Reachability testing requires program executions to be modeled so that races can be identified and race variants can be generated. The execution model must also contain sufficient information to support execution tracing and replay. Models for tracing and replay have been developed for many synchronization constructs, including semaphores, locks, monitors, and message passing [4] [20]. However, these models do not support race analysis. Models for race analysis have been developed for message passing, but not for other synchronization constructs. The contributions of this paper are: (1) a general execution model for reachability testing that supports race analysis and replay for all of the synchronization constructs mentioned above. This model defines a common format for execution traces and provides a timestamp assignment scheme that assists in identifying races and computing race variants. (2) A race analysis method that can be used to identify races in executions captured by our execution model. This method can be used by an existing algorithm for generating race variants. (3) A Java reachability testing tool, called RichTest, that implements reachability testing without any modifications to the Java JVM or to the operating system.

The rest of this paper is organized as follows. The next section illustrates the reachability testing process. Section 3 presents an execution model for several commonly used synchronization constructs. Section 4 defines the notions of a race and a race variant, and discusses how to identify races and compute race variants. Section 5 describes the RichTest tool and reports some empirical results. Section 6 briefly surveys related work. Section 7 provides concluding remarks and describes our plans for future work.

2   The Reachability Testing Process

We use a simple example to illustrate the reachability testing process. Fig. 1 shows a program CP that consists of four threads. The threads synchronize and communicate by sending messages to, and receiving messages from, ports. Ports are communication objects that can be accessed by many senders but only one receiver. Each send operation specifies a port as its destination, and each receive operation specifies a port as its source.

Fig. 1 also shows one possible scenario for applying reachability testing to the example program. Each sequence and race variant generated during reachability testing is represented by a space-time diagram in which a vertical line represents a thread, and a single-headed arrow represents asynchronous message passing between a send and receive event. The labels on the arrows match the labels on the send and receive statements in program CP. The reachability testing process in Fig. 1 proceeds as follows:

- First, sequence Q0 is recorded during a non-deterministic execution of CP. Sequence V1 is a race variant of Q0 derived by changing the outcome of a race condition in Q0. That is, in variant V1, thread T3 receives its first message from T4 instead of T2. The message sent by T2 is left un-received in V1.
- During the next execution of CP, variant V1 is used for prefix-based testing. This means that variant V1 is replayed and afterwards the execution proceeds non-deterministically. Sequence Q1 is recorded during this execution. Sequence Q1 is guaranteed to be different from Q0 since V1 and Q0 differ on the outcome of a race condition and V1 is a prefix of Q1. Variant V2 is a race variant of Q1 in which T2 receives its first message from T3 instead of T1.
- When variant V2 is used for prefix-based testing, sequence Q2 is recorded. Reachability testing stops since Q0, Q1 and Q2 are all the possible SYN-sequences that can be exercised by this program.

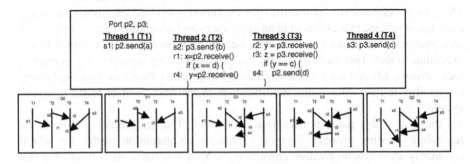

Fig. 1. The reachability testing process

For a formal description of the above process, the reader is referred to a reachability testing algorithm that we reported in [13]. The challenge for reachability testing is to identify races and derive race variants. This is discussed in the remainder of this paper.

3   Models of Program Executions

In this section, we present a general execution model for several commonly used synchronization constructs. This model provides sufficient information for replaying an execution and for identifying the race variants of an execution. Replay techniques have already been developed for these constructs [4] [20]. An algorithm for computing race variants is described in the next section.

3.1   Asynchronous Message Passing

Asynchronous message passing refers to non-blocking send operations and blocking receive operations. A thread that executes a non-blocking send operation proceeds without waiting for the message to arrive at its destination. A thread that executes a blocking receive operation blocks until a message is received. We assume that asynchronous ports (see Section 2) have unlimited capacity (which means that a send operation is never blocked) and use a FIFO (First-In-First-Out) message ordering scheme, which guarantees that messages passed between any two threads are received in the order that they are sent.

```
Port p;
Thread 1    Thread 2
p.send(msg)    msg = p.receive();
```

An execution of a program that uses asynchronous ports exercises a sequence of send and receive events. A send or receive event refers to the execution of a send or receive statement, respectively. A send event s and the receive event r it synchronizes with forms a synchronization pair $<s, r>$, where s is said to be the send partner of r, and r is said to be the receive partner of s. We use an event descriptor to encode certain information about each event. Each send event s is assigned an event descriptor (T, O, i), where T is the sending thread, O is the port, and i is the event index indicating that s is the i-th event in T. Each receive event r is assigned an event descriptor (T, O, i), where T is the receiving thread, O is the port name, and i is the event index indicating that r is the i-th event of T. A send event s is said to be open at a receive event r if $s.O = r.O$.

Fig. 2 shows a space-time diagram representing an execution with three threads. Thread $T2$ receives messages from ports $p1$ and $p2$. Thread $T1$ sends two messages to port $p1$. Thread $T3$ sends its first message to port $p1$ and its second message to port $p2$.

We note that in many applications a thread only has one port for receiving messages. In this special case, a thread identifier is usually specified as the destination of a send event, and the source of a receive event can be left unspecified. Also, a link-based communication scheme can be simulated by using ports that are restricted to having only one sender. We also point out that in practical implementations, ports are often implemented using bounded buffers that can only hold a fixed number of messages. In this case, a send operation can be blocked if the capacity of a buffer is reached. Our model can be applied to buffer-blocking ports without any modification.

3.2 Synchronous Message Passing

Synchronous message passing is the term used when the send and receive operations are both blocking. The receiving thread blocks until a message is received. The sending thread blocks until it receives an acknowledgement that the message it sent was received by the receiving thread.

A selective wait construct is commonly used in synchronous message passing to allow a combination of waiting for, and selecting from, one or more receive() alternatives [1]. The selection can depend on guard conditions associated with each alternative of the selective wait:

```
Port port1, port2;
select
   when (guard condition 1) => port1.receive();
or
   when (guard condition 2) => port2.receive();
end select;
```

A receive alternative is said to be *open* if it does not start with when(guard condition), or if the value of the guard condition is *true*. It is said to be *closed* otherwise. A select statement works as follows:

- an open receive-alternative (i.e., one with a *true* guard) is selected only if that alternative has a waiting message.
- if several receive-alternatives are open and have waiting messages, the alternative whose message arrived first is selected.
- if one or more receive-alternatives are open but none have a waiting message, select blocks until a message arrives for one of the open receive-alternatives.
- If none of the receive-alternatives are open, select throws an exception.

We make the restriction that there can be only one receive-alternative for a given port.

A send event s and the receive event r it synchronizes with form a rendezvous pair $<s, r>$, where s is the send partner of r and r is the receive partner of s. Each send event s is assigned an event descriptor (T, O, i), where T is the sending thread, O is the port, and i is the event index indicating that s is the i-th event of T. Each receive event r is assigned an event descriptor (T, L, i), where T is the receiving thread, L is the open-list of r, and i is the index indicating that r is the i-th event of T. The open-list of a receive event r is a list containing the ports that had open receive-alternatives at r. Note that this list includes the source port of r. For a simple receive statement that is not in a selective wait, the list of open alternatives consists of the source port of the receive statement only. Event s is said to be open at r if the port $s.O$ of s is in the open-list $r.L$ of r.

Fig. 3 shows a space-time diagram representing an execution with three threads. Thread T1 sends two messages to port $p1$, and thread T3 sends two messages to port *p2*. Thread T2 executes a selective wait with receive-alternatives for *p1* and *p2*. Assume that whenever *p2* is selected, the alternative for *p1* is open, and whenever *p1* is selected, the alternative for *p2* is closed. This is reflected in the open-lists for the receive events. Note that each solid arrow is followed by a dashed arrow in the opposite direction. The dashed arrows represent the updating of timestamps when the synchronous communication completes, and will be discussed in Section 4.

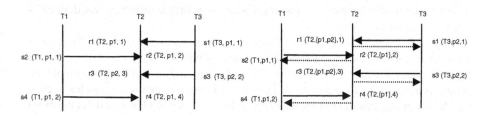

Fig. 2. A sequence of asynchronous send/ receive events

Fig. 3. A sequence of synchronous send/ receive events

3.3 Semaphores

A semaphore is a synchronization object that is initialized with an integer value and then accessed through two operations named *P* and *V*. Semaphores are provided in many commercial operating systems and thread libraries. There are two types of semaphores – counting semaphores and binary semaphores.

A $V()$ operation on a counting semaphore *s* increments the value of *s*. A $P()$ operation decrements the value of *s*, but if *s* is less than or equal to zero when the $P()$ operation starts, the $P()$ operation waits until *s* is positive. For a *counting semaphore* *s*, at any time, the following relation, called the semaphore invariant, holds:

(initial value of *s*) + (number of completed $s.V()$ operations) $\geq$ (number of completed $s.P()$ operations)

A thread that starts a $P()$ operation may be blocked inside $P()$, so the operation may not be completed right away. The invariant refers to the number of completed operations, which may be less than the number of started operations. For a counting semaphore, $V()$ operations never block their caller and are always completed immediately.

A *binary semaphore* must be initialized with the value 1 or the value 0 and the completion of $P()$ and $V()$ operations must alternate. ($P()$ and $V()$ operations can be started in any order, but their completions must alternate.) If the initial value of the semaphore is 1 the first completed operation must be $P()$. If a $V()$ operation is attempted first, the $V()$ operation will block its caller. Likewise, if the initial value of the semaphore is 0, the first completed operation must be $V()$. Thus, the $P()$ and $V()$ operations of a binary semaphore may block the calling threads. (Note that $V()$ operations are sometimes defined to be non-blocking – executing a non-blocking $V()$ operation on a binary semaphore has no effect if the value of the semaphore is 1. In this paper, we are using a blocking $V()$ operation. Our model can be easily adjusted if a non-blocking $V()$ operation is used.) We assume that the queues of blocked threads are FIFO queues.

We model the invocation of a *P()* or *V()* operation as a pair of call and completion events. When a thread *T* calls a *P()* or *V()* operation on a semaphore *S*, a "semaphore-call" event, or simply a "call" event, *c* is performed by *T*. When a *P()* or *V()* operation of a semaphore *S* is completed, a "semaphore-completion" event, or simply a "completion" event, *e* occurs on *S*. If the operation of a call event *c* is completed by a completion event *e*, we say that *c* and *e* form a completion pair <*c, e*>, where *c* is the call partner of *e* and *e* is the completion partner of *c*. This model is intentionally similar to the model for message passing where a synchronization pair was defined as a pair of send and receive events.

Each call event *c* is assigned a descriptor *(T, S, op, i)*, where *T* is the calling thread, *S* is the destination semaphore, *op* is the called operation (*P()* or *V()*), and *i* is the event index indicating that *c* is the *i*-th (call) event performed by *T*. A completion event *e* is assigned a descriptor *(S, L, i)*, where *S* is the semaphore on which *e* occurs, *L* is the list of operations (*P()* and/or *V()*) that can be completed at *e*, and *i* is the event index indicating that *e* is the *i*-th (completion) event that occurs on *S*. *L* is also called the open-list of *e*. A call event *c* is open at a completion event *e* if *c.S* = *e.S*, and the operation *c.op* of *c* is in the open-list *e.L* of *e*.

Fig. 4 shows a space-time diagram representing an execution with two threads *T1* and *T2*, and a binary semaphore *S* initialized to 1. Each of *T1* and *T2* performs a *P()* and *V()* operation on *S*. In this diagram, semaphore *S* is also represented as a vertical line, which contains the entry events that occurred on *S*. A solid arrow represents the completion of a *P()* or *V()* operation. The open-lists for the completion events model the fact that P and V operations on a binary semaphore must alternate. Note that each solid arrow is followed by a dashed arrow in the opposite direction. The dashed arrows represent the updating of timestamps when operations complete, and will be discussed in Section 4.

3.4 Locks

A mutex (for "*mut*ual *ex*clusion") lock is a synchronization object that is used to create critical sections. The operations on a mutex lock are named *lock()* and *unlock()*. Unlike semaphores, a mutex lock has an owner, and ownership plays an important role in the behavior of a mutex lock:

- A thread requests ownership of mutex lock *K* by calling *K.lock()*.
- A thread that calls *K.lock()* becomes the owner if no other thread owns the lock; otherwise, the thread is blocked.
- A thread releases its ownership of *K* by calling *K.unlock()*. If the thread does not own *K*, the call to *K.unlock()* generates an error.
- A thread that already owns lock *K* and calls *K.lock()* again is not blocked. In fact, it is common for a thread to request and receive ownership of a lock that it already owns. But the thread must call *K.unlock()* the same number of times that it called *K.lock()*, before another thread can become *K*'s owner.

Our model for *lock()* and *unlock()* operations on mutex locks is similar to our model for *P()* and *V()* operations on semaphores. When a thread *T* calls a *lock()* or *unlock()* operation on mutex lock *K*, a "mutex-call" event, or simply a "call" event, *c* occurs on *T*. When *T* eventually finishes a *lock()* or *unlock()* operation, a "mutex-completion" event, or simply a "completion" event, *e* occurs on *K*. If the operation of a call event *c* is completed by a completion event *e*, we say that *c* and *e* form a completion pair <*c,e*>, where *c* is the call partner of *e* and *e* is the completion partner of *c*.

Each call event *c* is assigned a descriptor *(T, K, op, i)*, where *T* is the calling thread, *K* is the destination lock, *op* is the called operation *(lock()* or *unlock())*, and *i* is the event index indicating that *c* is the *i*-th (call) event performed by *T*. A completion event *e* is assigned a descriptor *(K, L, i)*, where *K* is the lock on which *e* occurs, *L* is the list of operations *(lock()* and/or *unlock())* that can be completed at *e*, and *i* is the event index indicating that *e* is the *i*-th (completion) event that occurs on *K*. *L* is also called the open-list of *e*. If the lock is owned by some thread *T* when *e* occurs, then each operation in *L* is prefixed with *T* to indicate that only *T* can perform the operation. This is because if a thread *T* owns lock *L*, then only *T* can complete a *lock()* or *unlock()* operation on *L*. For example, if the open-list *L* of an entry event *e* on a lock *K* contains two operations *lock()* and *unlock()*, and if *K* is owned by a thread *T* when *e* occurs, then *L = {T:lock(), T:unlock()}*. A call event *c* executed by thread *T* is open at a completion event *e* if *c.K = e.K*, and the operation *c.op* of *c* is in the open-list *e.L* of *e*, and if *K* is owned when *e* occurs then *T* is the owner.

Fig. 5 shows a space-time diagram representing an execution with two threads and a mutex lock *K* initialized to 1. Thread *T1* performs two *lock()* operations followed by two *unlock()* operations on *K*, and thread *T2* performs one *lock()* operation followed by one *unlock()* operation on *K*.

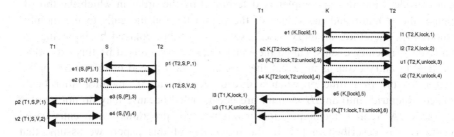

Fig. 4. A sequence of P and V events   **Fig. 5.** A sequence of lock and unlock events

3.5 Monitors

A monitor is a high-level synchronization construct that supports data encapsulation and information hiding and is easily adapted to an object oriented environment. We use an object oriented definition of a monitor in which a monitor is a synchronization object that is an instance of a special "monitor class". The data members of a monitor represent shared data. Threads communicate by calling monitor methods that access the shared data.

At most one thread is allowed to execute inside a monitor at any time. Mutual exclusion is enforced by the monitor's implementation, which ensures that each monitor method is a critical section. If a thread calls a monitor method, but another thread is already executing inside the monitor, the calling thread must wait outside the monitor. A monitor has an *entry* queue to hold the calling threads that are waiting to enter the monitor.

Condition synchronization is achieved using condition variables and operations *wait()* and *signal()*. A condition variable denotes a queue of threads that are waiting to be signaled that a specific condition is true. (The condition is not explicitly specified as part of the condition variable.) There are several different types of signaling disciplines. When the *Signal-and-Continue* (*SC*) discipline is used, the signaling thread continues to execute in the monitor, and the signaled thread does not reenter the monitor immediately. We assume that the signaled thread joins the entry queue and thus competes with calling threads to enter the monitor. When the *Signal-and-Urgent-Wait* (*SU*) discipline is used, the signaling thread is blocked in a queue called the *reentry* queue and the signaled thread reenters the monitor immediately. The difference between the *entry* and *reentry* queues is that the former holds calling threads that are waiting to enter the monitor for the first time while the latter holds threads that have entered the monitor, executed a *signal* operation, and are waiting to reenter the monitor. The *SU* discipline assigns a higher priority to the reentry queue, in the sense that a thread in the entry queue can enter the monitor only if the reentry queue is empty.

We assume that a monitor's entry queue and the queues associated with condition variables are FIFO queues. Thus, the only non-determinism that is present in a monitor is the order in which threads (re)enter the monitor. Such monitors enjoy a beneficial property called entry-based execution, i.e., the execution behavior of threads inside a monitor is completely determined by the order in which the threads (re)enter the monitor and the values of the parameters on the calls to the monitor methods [4]. Therefore, an entry-based execution can be replayed by replaying the sequence of (re)entry events, called the Entry-sequence, exercised by this execution. Note that an entry event is an event that occurs when a thread enters an *SU* or *SC* monitor for the *first* time or when a thread reenters an *SC* monitor after being signaled. Reentries into an *SU* monitor are not modeled because they do not involve any races. A replay technique for monitor-based programs with entry-based executions was described in [4]. In the remainder of this paper, we assume that monitor-based programs have entry-based executions and the order of the entries is the sole source of non-determinism in the programs.

Characterizing a monitor-based execution as an Entry-sequence is sufficient for replaying executions, but not for identifying races. When two or more threads call a monitor at the same time, they race to see which one will enter first. Thus, we model the invocation of a monitor method as a pair of monitor-call and monitor-entry events:

- *SU Monitors*: When a thread T calls a method of monitor M, a monitor-call event, or simply a call event, c occurs on T. When T eventually enters M, a monitor-entry event, or simply an entry event, e occurs on M, and then T starts to execute inside M.
- *SC Monitors*: When a thread T calls a method of monitor M, a monitor-call event, or simply a call event, c occurs on T. A call event also occurs when T tries to reenter a monitor M after being signaled. When T eventually (re)enters M, a

monitor-entry event, or simply an entry event, e occurs on M, and T starts to execute inside M.

In these scenarios, we say that T is the calling thread of c and e, and M is the destination monitor of c as well as the owning monitor of e. We also say that c and e form an entry pair $<c, e>$, where c is the call partner of e and e is the entry partner of c.

Each call event c is assigned an event descriptor (T, M, i), where T is the calling thread, M is the destination monitor, and i is the event index indicating that c is the i-th (call) event of T. Each entry event e is assigned an event descriptor (M, i), where M is the owning monitor, and i is the event index indicating that e is the i-th event of M. A call event c is open at an entry event e if the destination monitor of c is the owning monitor of e, i.e., $c.M = e.M$.

Fig. 6 shows a space-time diagram, which represents an execution involving three threads $T1$, $T2$, and $T3$, and two SC monitors $M1$ and $M2$. Thread $T1$ enters $M1$ first and executes a $wait()$ operation. The second call event performed by $T1$ occurs when $T1$ reenters $M1$ after being signaled by $T2$. Note that if $M1$ were an SU monitor, there would be no $c3$ event representing reentry. After $T1$ exits from $M1$, $T1$ enters and exits $M2$. This is followed by thread $T3$ entering and exiting $M2$ and then entering and exiting $M1$.

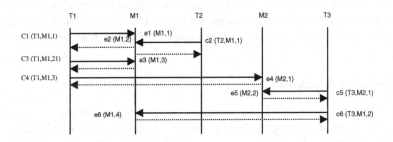

Fig. 6. A sequence of monitor call and entry events

3.6 A General Model

In the models presented above, a program execution is characterized as a sequence of event pairs. For asynchronous and synchronous message-passing programs, an execution is characterized as a sequence of send and receive events. For semaphore-, lock-, and monitor-based programs, an execution is characterized as a sequence of call and completion events. In the remainder of this paper, we will refer to a send/call event as a sending event, and a receive/completion event as a receiving event. We also refer to a pair of sending and receiving events as a synchronization pair.

The event descriptors for the sending and receiving events defined above all fit into a single general format:

- A descriptor for a sending event s is denoted by (T, O, op, i), where T is the thread executing the sending event, O is the destination object, op is the operation performed, and i is the event index indicating that s is the i-th event of T. Note that for message passing, *op* is always a send operation, and for monitors, *op* is the called method.

- A descriptor for a receiving event *r* is denoted by *(D, L, i)*, where *D* is the destination thread or object, *L* is the open-list, and *i* is the event index indicating that *r* is the *i*-th event of *D*. Note that for asynchronous message-passing, *L* contains the source port of *r* only, and is thus represented as a single port. For a monitor, *L* contains all of the methods defined on the monitor since entry into a monitor is never guarded. (A thread may be blocked after it enters a monitor, but a thread that calls a monitor method is guaranteed to eventually enter the method.)

In programs that use shared variables, we assume that accesses to shared variables are always protected by semaphores, locks, or monitors. To enforce this, reachability testing can be used in conjunction with the techniques used in data race detection tools for multithreaded programs [16].

4   Race Analysis of SYN-Sequences

In this section, we show how to perform race analysis on SYN-sequences. Section 4.1 presents two schemes for assigning logical timestamps to determine the happened-before relation between events. Section 4.2 defines the notion of a race and shows how to identify races based on the happened-before relation. Section 4.3 defines the notion of a race variant and uses an example to illustrate how to compute race variants.

4.1   Timestamp Assignment

As we will see in Section 4.2, the definition of a race between events in a SYN-sequence is based on the happened-before relation, which is a partial order defined in the traditional sense [11]. Simply put, an event *a* happens before another event *b* in a *SYN*-sequence *Q* if *a* could potentially affect *b*. We denote this as $a \rightarrow_Q b$, or simply $a \rightarrow b$ if *Q* is implied. In a space-time diagram, if we take into account the direction of the (solid and dashed) arrows, *a* happens before *b* if there exists a path from *a* to *b*.

Vector timestamps are frequently used to capture the happened-before relation between events. In this section, we present thread-centric and object-centric timestamp assignment schemes. A *thread-centric* timestamp has a dimension equal to the number of threads involved in an execution. An *object-centric* timestamp has a dimension equal to the number of synchronization objects involved. Therefore, a thread-centric scheme is preferred when the number of threads is smaller than the number of synchronization objects, and an object-centric scheme is preferred otherwise. In the remainder of this section, we will use *v[i]* to denote the *i*-th component of a vector *v*, and $max(v_1, v_2)$ to denote the component-wise maximum of vectors v_1 and v_2.

4.1.1   A Thread-Centric Scheme
A vector timestamp scheme for asynchronous message passing programs has already been developed [6][14]. This scheme is thread-centric by our definition and can be

used for race analysis. In this scheme, each thread maintains a vector clock. A vector clock is a vector of integers used to keep track of the integer clock of each thread. The integer clock of a thread is initially zero, and is incremented each time the thread executes a send or receive event. Each send and receive event is also assigned a copy of the vector clock as its timestamp.

Let $T.v$ be the vector clock maintained by a thread T. Let $f.ts$ be the vector timestamp of an event f. The vector clock of a thread is initially a vector of zeros. The following rules are used to update vector clocks and assign timestamps to the send and receive events in asynchronous message passing programs:

1. When a thread T_i executes a non-blocking send event s, it performs the following operations: (a) $T_i.v[i] = T_i.v[i] + 1$; (b) $s.ts = T_i.v$. Thread T_i also sends $s.ts$ along with the message sent by s.
2. When a thread T_j executes a receive event r, it performs the following operations: (a) $T_j.v[j] = T_j.v[j] + 1$; (b) $T_j.v = max(T_j.v, s.ts)$; (c) $r.ts = T_j.v$, where s is the synchronization partner of r.

Fig. 7(a) shows the timestamps for the asynchronous message passing program in Fig. 2.

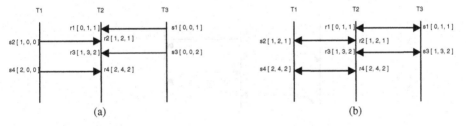

Fig. 7. Traditional timestamp schemes for asynchronous and synchronous message passing

A timestamp scheme for synchronous message passing has also been developed [6], but this scheme must be extended for race analysis. The traditional timestamp scheme for synchronous message passing is to assign the same timestamp to send and receive events that are synchronization partners:

1. When a thread T_i executes a blocking send event s, it performs the operation $T_i.v[i] = T_i.v[i] + 1$. Thread T_i also sends $T_i.v$ along with the message sent by s.
2. When a thread T_j executes a receiving event r that receives the message sent by s, it performs the following operations: (a) $T_j.v[j] = T_j.v[j] + 1$; (b) $T_j.v = max(T_j.v, T_i.v)$; (c) $r.ts = T_j.v$. Thread T_j also sends $T_j.v$ back to thread T_i.
3. Thread T_i receives $T_j.v$ and performs the following operations (a) $T_i.v = max(T_i.v, T_j.v)$; (b) $s.ts = T_i.v$.

The exchange of vector clock values between threads T_i and T_j represents the synchronization that occurs between them, which causes their send and receive events to be completed at the same time. Fig. 7b shows the timestamps for the synchronous message passing program in Fig. 3.

In our execution model for synchronous message passing, we model the start of a send event, not its completion. For send and receive events that are synchronization partners, the start of the send is considered to happen before the receive event with which the send eventually synchronizes. This means that the timestamps for send and receive partners should not be the same. Thus, we use the timestamp of the receive event to update the vector clock of the sending thread, but not the timestamp of the send event, when the synchronization completes:

1. When a thread T_i executes a blocking send event s, it performs the following operations: (a) $T_i.v[i] = T_i.v[i] + 1$. (b) $s.ts = T_i.v$. Thread T_i also sends $T_i.v$ along with the message sent by s.
2. When a thread T_j executes a receiving event r that receives the message sent by s, it performs the following operations: (a) $T_j.v[j] = T_j.v[j] + 1$; (b) $T_j.v = max(T_j.v, T_i.v)$; (b) $r.ts = T_j.v$. Thread T_j also sends $T_j.v$ back to thread T_i.
3. Thread T_i receives $T_j.v$ and performs the operation (a) $T_i.v = max(T_i.v, T_j.v)$.

Fig. 8 shows the timestamps that are assigned so that race analysis can be performed on the synchronous message passing program in Fig. 3. Note that the dashed arrows represent the execution of rule 3.

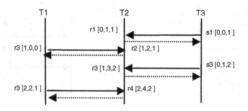

Fig. 8. Timestamp scheme for race analysis of synchronous message passing programs

Below we describe a new thread-centric timestamp scheme for semaphores, locks, and monitors. We refer to semaphores, locks, and monitors generally as "synchronization objects". In this scheme, each thread and synchronization object maintains a vector clock. (As before, position i in a vector clock refers to the integer clock of thread T_i; synchronization objects do not have integer clocks and thus there are no positions in a vector clock for the synchronization objects.) Let $T.v$ (or $O.v$) be the vector clock maintained by a thread T (or a synchronization object O). The vector clock of a thread or synchronization object is initially a vector of zeros. The following rules are used to update vector clocks and assign timestamps to events:

1. When a thread T_i executes a sending event s, it performs the following operations: (a) $T_i.v[i] = T_i.v[i] + 1$; (b) $s.ts = T_i.v$;
2. When a receiving event r occurs on a synchronization object O, the following operations are performed: (a) $O.v = max(O.v, s.ts)$; (b) $r.ts = O.v$, where s is the sending partner of r;

3. Semaphore/Lock: When a thread T_i finishes executing an operation on a semaphore or lock O, it updates its vector clock using the component-wise maximum of $T_i.v$ and $O.v$, i.e., $T_i.v = max(T_i.v, O.v)$.

SU Monitor: When a thread T_i finishes executing a method on a monitor O, it updates its vector clock using the component-wise maximum of $T.v$ and $O.v$, i.e., $T.v = max(T.v, O.v)$.

SC Monitor: When a thread T_i finishes executing a method on a monitor O, or when a thread T_i is signaled from a condition queue of O, it updates its vector clock using the component-wise maximum of $T_i.v$ and $O.v$, i.e., $T_i.v = max(T_i.v, O.v)$.

Figs. 9a and 9b shows the thread-centric timestamps assigned for the executions in Figs. 4 and 6, respectively. Again, dashed arrows are also shown to indicate applications of the third rule.

Thread-centric timestamps can be used to determine the happened-before relation between two arbitrary events, as shown below.

Proposition 1. Let X be an execution involving threads $T_1, T_2, ..., T_n$ and semaphores, locks, or monitors. Let Q be the SYN-sequence exercised by X. Assume that every event in Q is assigned a thread-centric timestamp. Let $f.tid$ be the (integer) thread ID of thread $f.T$ for an event f. Let f_1 and f_2 be two events in Q. Then, $f_1 \rightarrow f_2$ if and only if

(1) $<f_1, f_2>$ is a synchronization pair; or
(2) $f_1.ts[f_1.tid] \leq f_2.ts[f_1.tid]$ and $f_1.ts[f_2.tid] < f_2.ts[f_2.tid]$.

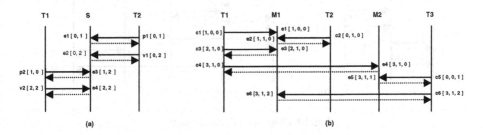

(a)   (b)

Fig. 9. Timestamp scheme for race analysis of semaphore-based and monitor-based programs

4.1.2 Object-Centric Scheme

In this scheme, each thread and synchronization object (port, semaphore, lock, or monitor) maintains a version vector. A version vector is a vector of integers used to keep track of the version number of each synchronization object. The version number of a synchronization object is initially zero, and is incremented each time a thread performs a sending or receiving event. Each sending and receiving event is also assigned a version vector as its timestamp.

Let $T.v$ (or $O.v$) be the version vector maintained by a thread T (or a synchronization object O). Initially, the version vector of each thread or synchronization object is a vector of zeros. The following rules are used to update version vectors and assign timestamps to events:

1. When a thread T executes a sending event s, T assigns its version vector as the timestamp of s, i.e., $s.ts = T.v;$.
2. When a receiving event r occurs on a synchronization object O_i, letting s be the sending partner of r, the following operations are performed: (a) $O_i.v = max(O_i.v, s.ts)$; (b) $r.ts = O_i.v$.
3. Semaphore/Lock: When a thread T finishes a called operation on a semaphore or lock O, T updates its version vector using the component-wise maximum of $T.v$ and $O.v$, i.e., $T.v = max(T.v, O.v)$.

   SU Monitor: When a thread T finishes executing a method on a monitor O, T updates its version vector using the component-wise maximum of $T.v$ and $O.v$, i.e., $T.v = max(T.v, O.v)$.

   SC Monitor: When a thread T finishes executing a method on a monitor O, or when a thread T is signaled from a condition queue of O, T updates its version vector using the component-wise maximum of $T.v$ and $O.v$, i.e., $T.v = max(T.v, O.v)$.

   Timestamps assigned using the above rules are called object-centric timestamps. Note that this scheme is preferred only if the number of synchronization objects is smaller than the number of threads. Considering that in a message-passing program, each thread usually has at least one port, we do not expect that this scheme will be frequently used for message passing programs. Fig. 10 shows object-centric timestamps assigned for the executions in Fig 9.

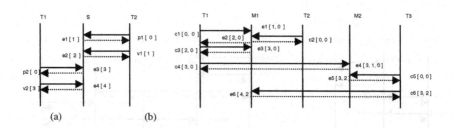

Fig. 10. Object-centric timestamps

Object-centric timestamps cannot be used to determine the happened-before relation between two arbitrary events. However, they can be used to determine the happened-before relation between two events if at least one of the events is a receiving event, which is sufficient for our purposes.

Proposition 2. Let X be an execution involving synchronization objects O_1, O_2, ..., O_m. Let Q be the SYN-sequence exercised by X. Assume that every event in Q is assigned an object-centric timestamp. Let r be a receiving event on O_i, and f a receiving event on O_j, where $1 \le i, j \le m$. Then, $e \rightarrow f$ if and only if $e.ts[i] \le f.ts[i]$ and $e.ts[j] < f.ts[j]$.

Proposition 3. Let X be an execution involving synchronization objects O_1, O_2, ..., O_m. Let Q be the *SYN*-sequence exercised by X. Assume that every event in Q is assigned an object-centric timestamp. Let r be a receiving event on O_i, and s a sending event on O_j, where $1 \leq i, j \leq m$. Then, $r \rightarrow s$ if and only if $r.ts[i] \leq s.ts[i]$.

In Fig. 10b, entry e_3 happens before entry e_4 since $e_3.ts[1] = e_4.ts[1]$ and $e_3.ts[2] < e_4.ts[2]$. Entry e_3 happens before call c_6 since $e_3.ts[1] = e_6.ts[1]$.

4.2 Race Detection

As we described in Section 3.6, we can characterize a program execution as a sequence of sending and receiving events. Intuitively, there exists a race between two sending events if they can synchronize with the same receiving event in different executions. In order to accurately determine all the races in an execution, the program's semantics must be analyzed. Fortunately, for the purpose of reachability testing, we only need to consider a special type of race, called a lead race. Lead races can be identified solely based on the SYN-sequence of an execution, i.e., without analyzing the program's semantics.

Definition 1. Let Q be a *SYN*-sequence exercised by an execution of a concurrent program CP. Let s be a sending event and r a receiving event in Q such that $<s, r>$ is a synchronization pair. Let s' be another sending event in Q. There exists a lead race between s' and $<s, r>$ in Q if s' and r can form a synchronization pair during some other execution of CP provided that all the events that happen before s' or r in Q are replayed in that execution.

Note that Definition 1 requires all events that can potentially affect s' or r in Q to be replayed and thus ensures the existence of c' or e, regardless of the program's implementation. As a result lead races can be identified solely based on information encoded in Q. In the remainder of this paper, a race is assumed to be a lead race unless otherwise specified.

Next, we define the notion of a race set of a receiving event. Let Q be a *SYN*-sequence. Let r be a receiving event and s a sending event in Q such that $<s, r>$ is a synchronization pair. The race set of r in Q, denoted as *race(r, Q)* or *race(r)* if Q is implied, is the set of sending events in Q that have a race with $<s, r>$. Formally, *race(r, Q) = {s'* $\in Q$ *| there exists a lead race between s' and <s, r>}.*

The following proposition describes how to compute the race set of a receiving event.

Proposition 4. Let Q be a *SYN-sequence* exercised by a program execution. A sending event s is in the race set of a receiving event r if (1) s is open at r; (2) r does not happen before s; (3) if $<s, r'>$ is a synchronization pair, then r happens before r'; and (4) s and r are consistent with FIFO semantics (i.e., all the messages that were sent to the same destination as s, but were sent before s, have already been received before r).

Race Set Examples:

- *Asynchronous Message Passing.* The race set of each receive event in Fig. 2 is as follows: *race(r1) = {s2}, race(r2) = race(r3) = race(r4) = {}*. Note that *s3* is not in the race set of *r1* because *s3* is sent to a different port and thus *s3* is not open at *r1*. For the same reason, *s4* is not in the race set of *r3*. Also note that *s4* is not in the race set of *r1*, because FIFO semantics ensures that *s1* is received before *s4*.

- *Synchronous message passing.* The race set of each receive event in Fig. 3 is as follows: *race(r1)* = *{s2}*, *race(r2)* = *{ }*, *race(r3)* = *{s4}*, and *race(r4)* = *{ }*. Since the alternative for *p2* is open whenever *T2* selects the receive-alternative for *p1*, the race set for *r1* contains *s2* and the race set for *r3* contains *s4*. On the other hand, since the alternative for *p1* was closed when *T2* selected the receive-alternative for *p2* at *r2*, the race set for *r2* does not contain *s3*.

- *Semaphores.* The race set of each completion event in Fig. 4 is as follows: *race(e1)* = *{p2}*, *race(e2)* = *race(e3)* = *race(e4)* = *{ }*. Note that since *P()* was not in the open-list of *e2*, the race set for *e2* does not contain *p2*. This captures the fact that the *P()* operation by *T1* could start but not complete before the *V()* operation by *T2* and hence that these operations do not race.

- *Locks.* The race set of each completion event in Fig. 5 is as follows: *race(e1)* = *{l3}*, *race(e2)* = *race(e3)* = *race(e4)* = *race(e5)* = *race(e6)* = *{}*. Note that since *T2* owned lock *K* when the operations for events *e2*, *e3*, and *e4* were started, the race sets for *e2*, *e3*, and *e4* are empty. This represents the fact that no other thread can complete a *lock()* operation on *K* while it is owned by *T2*.

- *Monitors.* The race set of each entry event in Fig. 6 is as follows: *race(e1)* = *{c2}*, race(e2) = race(e3) = { }, race(e4) = {c5}, and race(e5) = race(e6) = { }. Sending event *c3* is not in the race set of *e2* since *c3* happened after *e2*. (Thread T2 entered monitor *m* at *e2* and executed a signal operation that caused *T1* to issue call *c3*.)

4.3 Computing Race Variants

Let *CP* be a concurrent program. Let *Q* be the *SYN*-sequence exercised by an execution of *CP*. Informally, a race variant of *Q* is the beginning part of one or more *SYN*-sequences of *CP* that could well have occurred but didn't, due to the way races were arbitrarily resolved during execution.

Definition 2. Let *Q* be a *SYN*-sequence and *V* be a race variant of *Q*. Let *partner(r, Q)* (or *partner(r, V)*) be the sending partner of a receiving event *r* in *Q* (or in *V*). Variant *V* is another *SYN*-sequence that satisfies the following conditions:

1. Let *r* be a receiving event in *Q*. If *r* is also in *V*, and if *call(r, Q) != call(r, V)*, then *call(r, V)* must be in *race(r, Q)*.
2. Let *f* be a sending or receiving event in *Q*. Then, *f* is not in *V* if and only if there exists a receiving event *r* in *Q* such that $r \rightarrow_Q f$ in *Q* and *partner(r, Q) != partner(r, V)*.
3. There exists at least one receiving event *r* in both *Q* and *V* such that *partner(r, Q) != partner(r, V)*.

The first condition says that if we change the sending partner of a receiving event *r*, the new sending partner must be a sending event in the race set of *r*. The second condition says that if and only if we change the sending partner of a receiving event *r*, we remove all the events that happen after *r*. The third condition says that there must be at least one difference between *Q* and *V*.

Note that the second condition is a conservative approach to ensuring that a race variant is always feasible (i.e., it can be exercised by at least one program execution), regardless of the program's control and data flow. This condition is necessary since after the sending partner of a receiving event r is changed, all the events that happen after r could potentially be affected. That is, what happens after r might depend on the program's control and data flow. Note that this is a conservative approach since it removes events that happen after r even if they are not affected and are still feasible.

An algorithm for computing race variants of semaphore-based programs was described in [13]. This algorithm is easily adapted to the general execution model presented in this paper so we briefly describe it here. The race variants of a SYN-sequence are generated by building a so-called "race table", where each row of a race table corresponds to a race variant. The composition of a race table is described as follows. There is a column for each receiving event whose race set is non-empty. Let r be the receiving event corresponding to column j, V the race variant to be derived from row i, and v the value at row i, column j. Value v indicates how receiving event r is changed in variant V:

1. $v = -1$ indicates that r is removed from V
2. $v = 0$ indicates that the sending partner of r is left unchanged in V
3. $v > 0$ indicates that, in V, the sending partner of r is changed to the v-th event in $race(r)$, where the sending events in $race(r)$ are arranged in an arbitrary order and the index of the first event in $race(r)$ is 1.

Note that when we change the sending partner of event r, we need to remove all the events that happened after r in the original execution. This is to be consistent with the second condition in Definition 2. The algorithm in [13] generates a race table whose rows contain all possible combinations of values for the receiving events.

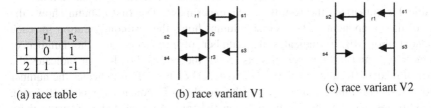

	r_1	r_3
1	0	1
2	1	-1

(a) race table   (b) race variant V1   (c) race variant V2

Fig. 11. Race variant examples

Fig. 11(a) shows the race table for the sample execution in Fig. 3. Recall that r_1 and r_3 are the only receiving events whose race sets are non-empty: $race(r_1) = \{s_2\}$ and $race(r_3) = \{s_4\}$. Fig. 11(b) shows the variant derived from the first row, where the sending partner of r_3 is changed from s_3 to s_4. Fig. 11(c) shows the variant derived from the second row, where the sending partner of r_1 is changed from s_1 to s_2, and event r_3 is removed since r_3 happened after r_1. See [13] for details about this algorithm.

5 Empirical Results

We implemented our reachability testing algorithms in a prototype tool called RichTest. RichTest is developed in Java, and consists of three main components: a synchronization library, a race variant generator, and a test driver. The synchronization library provides classes for simulating semaphores, locks, monitors, and message passing with selective waits. The synchronization classes contain the necessary control for replaying variants and tracing SYN-sequences. The race variant generator inputs a SYN-sequence and generates race variants of the sequence as discussed in Sections 4. The test driver is responsible for coordinating the exchange of variants and SYN-sequences between the synchronization classes and the variant generator. These three components and the application form a single Java program that performs the reachability testing process presented in Section 2.

   We wish to stress that RichTest does not require any modifications to the JVM or the operating system. Instead, the synchronization classes contain the additional control necessary for reachability testing. In trace mode, the synchronization classes record synchronization events at appropriate points and assign timestamps to these events. In replay mode, the synchronization classes implement the replay techniques that have been developed for the various constructs. We are applying this same approach to build portable reachability testing tools for multithreaded C++ programs that use thread libraries in Windows, Solaris, and Unix.

   As a proof-of-concept, we conducted an experiment in which RichTest was used to apply reachability testing to several components. The components chosen to carry out the experiment include: (1) BB – a solution to the bounded-buffer problem where the buffer is protected using either semaphores, an SC monitor, an SU monitor, or a selective wait; (2) RW – a solution to the readers/writers problem using either semaphores, an SU monitor, or a selective wait; (3) DP – a solution that uses an SU monitor to solve the dining philosophers problem without deadlock or starvation.

   Table 1 summarizes the results of our experiment. The first column shows the names of the components. The second column shows the test configuration for each component. For BB, it indicates the number of producers (P), the number of consumers (C), and the number of slots (S) in the buffer. For RW, it indicates the number of readers (R) and the number of writers (W). For DP, it indicates the number of processes. The third column shows the number of sequences generated during reachability testing. To shed some light on the total time needed to execute these sequences, we observe that, for instance, the total execution time for the DP program with 5 philosophers is 7 minutes on a 1.6GHz PC with 512 MB of RAM.

   Note that RichTest implements the reachability testing algorithm presented in [13]. The algorithm has a very low memory requirements, but it could generate duplicate SYN-sequences (i.e., exercise a given SYN-sequence more than once) for certain communication patterns. The reader is referred to [13] for more discussion on duplicates. In our experiment, the only case where duplicates were generated was for program BB-Semaphore. Since the number of duplicates may vary during different applications of reachability testing, we performed reachability testing on BB-Semaphore ten times and reported the average number of sequences exercised. We note that the program has 324 unique sequences, and thus, on average, 64 sequences (or 18% of the total sequences) exercised during reachability testing were duplicates.

Table 1. Experimental Results

Program	Config.	# Seqs.	Program	Config.	# Seqs.	Program	Config.	# Seqs.
BB-Select	3P + 3C + 2S	144	RW-Semaphore	2R + 2W	608	DP-MonitorSU	3	30
BB-Semaphore	3P + 3C + 2S	384 (avg.)	RW-Semaphore	2R + 3W	12816	DP-MonitorSU	4	624
BB-MonitorSU	3P + 3C + 2S	720	RW-Semaphore	3R + 2W	21744	DP-MonitorSU	5	19330
BB-MonitorSC	3P + 3C + 2S	12096	RW-MonitorSC	3R + 2W	70020			
			RW-MonitorSU	3R + 2W	13320			
			RW-Select	3R + 2W	768			

The results in Table 1 show that the choice of synchronization construct has a big effect on the number of sequences generated during reachability testing. SC monitors generate more sequences than SU monitors since SC monitors have races between signaled threads trying to reenter the monitor and calling threads trying to enter for the first time. SU monitors avoid these races by giving signaled threads priority over calling threads. Selective waits generated fewer sequences than the other constructs. This is because the guards in the selective waits are used to generate open-lists that reduce the sizes of the race sets.

6   Related Work

The simplest approach to testing concurrent programs is *non-deterministic testing*. The main problem with non-deterministic testing is that repeated executions of a concurrent program may exercise the same synchronization behavior. Most research in this area has focused on how to increase the chances of exercising different synchronization behaviors, and thus the chances of finding faults, when a program is repeatedly executed. This is typically accomplished by inserting random delays [23] or calls to a randomized scheduling function [17] into carefully selected program locations.

An alternative approach is *deterministic testing*, which is used to determine whether a specified sequence can or cannot be exercised. The main challenge for deterministic testing is dealing with the test sequence selection problem. A common method for selecting test sequences for deterministic testing is to derive a global state graph of a program (or of a model of the program) and then select paths from this graph [21]. This method, however, suffers from the state explosion problem. Moreover, it is possible to select two or more paths that correspond to the same partial order, which is inefficient. Most research [10] [22] in this area has focused on how to address these two problems.

Reachability testing combines non-deterministic and deterministic testing. In [9], a reachability testing technique was described for multithreaded programs that use read and write operations. A reachability testing approach for asynchronous message-passing programs was reported in [19] and was later improved in [12]. These two approaches use different models to characterize program executions as well as different algorithms for computing race variants. Our work in this paper presents a general model for reachability testing. In addition, these approaches compute race variants by considering all possible interleavings of the events in a SYN-sequence. This is less efficient than our table-based algorithm where we deal with partial orders directly.

Recently, there is a growing interest in techniques that can systematically explore the state space of a program or a model of the program. The main challenge is dealing with the state explosion problem. The tools Java PathFinder I [8] and Bandera [5] first derive an abstract model of a Java program and then use model checkers such as SPIN to explore a state graph of the model. Techniques such as slicing and abstraction are used to reduce the size of the state graph. One problem these tools encounter is the semantic gap between programming languages and modeling languages, which makes some programming language features difficult to model. To overcome this problem, tools such as Java PathFinder II, VeriSoft [7] and ExitBlock [3] directly explore the state space of actual programs, i.e., without constructing any models. These tools use partial order reduction methods to reduce the chances of executing sequences that only differ in the order of concurrent events.

Reachability testing also directly explores the state space of actual programs. However, unlike VeriSoft, ExitBlock, and Java PathFinder II, our reachability testing algorithm deals with partial orders directly. In contrast, partial order reduction still generates total orders but tries to reduce the chances of generating total orders that correspond to the same partial order. In addition, the SYN-sequence framework used by reachability testing is highly portable. This is because the definition of a SYN-sequence is based on the language-level definition of a concurrency construct, rather than the implementation details of the construct. Our Java reachability testing tools do not require any modifications to the Java Virtual Machine (JVM) or the thread scheduler, and are completely portable. Our C/C++ tools for Windows, Unix, and Solaris, do not require any modifications to the thread scheduler either. In contrast, VeriSoft, ExitBlock and Java PathFinder II all rely on access to the underlying thread scheduler to control program execution, and the latter two tools also rely on a custom JVM to capture program states. As a result, these tools have limited portability.

7 Conclusion and Future Work

In this paper, we described a general model for reachability testing of concurrent programs. The main advantages of reachability testing can be summarized as follows:

- Reachability testing uses a dynamic framework to derive test sequences. This avoids the construction of static program models, which are often inaccurate and may be too large to build.

- If desired, reachability testing can systematically exercise all the behaviors of a program. This maximizes test coverage and has important applications in program-based verification.
- Reachability testing tools can be implemented in a portable manner, without modifying the underlying virtual machine, runtime-system or operating system.

We note that since reachability testing is implementation-based, it cannot by itself detect "missing sequences", i.e., those that are valid according to the specification but are not allowed by the implementation. In this respect, reachability testing is complimentary to specification-based approaches that select valid sequences from a specification and determine whether they are allowed by the implementation [10].

We are continuing our work on reachability testing in the following directions. First, we are considering additional synchronization constructs, such as else/delay alternatives in selective wait statements. Second, exhaustive testing is not always practical due to resource constraints. Towards a more scalable solution, we are developing algorithms that can *selectively* exercise a set of SYN-sequences according to some coverage criteria. Third, there is a growing interest in combining formal methods and testing. Formal methods are frequently model based, which means that a model must be extracted from a program. Static analysis methods for model extraction have difficulty handling dynamic activities like creating threads and heap management. These things are easier to handle in a dynamic framework. Since reachability testing is dynamic and can be exhaustive, we are investigating the use of reachability testing to construct complete models of the communication and synchronization behavior of a concurrent program.

References

1. Ada Language Reference Manual, January 1983.
2. A. Bechini and K. C. Tai, Timestamps for Programs using Messages and Shared Variables, 18th Int'l Conf. on Distributed Computing Systems, 1998.
3. D. L. Bruening. Systematic testing of multithreaded Java programs. Master's thesis, MIT, 1999.
4. R. Carver and K. C. Tai, "Replay and Testing for Concurrent Programs," IEEE Software, Vol. 8 No. 2, Mar. 1991, 66-74.
5. J. Corbett, Matthew Dwyer, John Hatcliff, Corina Pasareanu, Robby, Shawn Laubach, and Hongjun Zheng. Bandera: Extracting Finite-state Models from Java Source Code, In Proceedings of the 22nd International Conference on Software Engineering, June, 2000.
6. C. J. Fidge, Logical Time in Distributed Computing Systems, IEEE Computer, Aug. 1991, pp. 28-33.
7. P. Godefroid. Model Checking for Programming Languages using VeriSoft. Proceedings of the 24th ACM Symposium on Principles of Programming Languages, pages 174-186, Paris, January 1997.
8. K. Havelund and Tom Pressburger. Model Checking Java Programs Using Java PathFinder. International Journal on Software Tools for Technology Transfer (STTT) 2(4): 366-381, April 2000.

9. G. H. Hwang, K. C. Tai, and T. L. Huang. Reachability testing: An approach to testing concurrent software. International Journal of Software Engineering and Knowledge Engineering, 5(4):493-510, 1995.

10. Koppol, P.V., Carver, R. H., and Tai, K. C., Incremental Integration Testing of Concurrent Programs, IEEE Trans. on Software. Engineering, Vol. 28, No. 6, June 2002, 607-623.

11. L. Lamport. Time, Clocks, and the Ordering of Events in a Dist. System, Comm. ACM, July 1978, pp. 558-565.

12. Yu Lei and Kuo-Chung Tai, Efficient reachability testing of asynchronous message-passing programs, Proc. 8th IEEE Int'l Conf. on Engineering for Complex Computer Systems, pp. 35-44, Dec. 2002.

13. Yu Lei and Richard H. Carver, "Reachability testing of semaphore-based programs", to be published in Proc. of the 28th Computer Software and Applications Conference (COMPSAC), September, 2004.

14. F. Mattern, Virtual Time and Global States of Distributed Systems, Parallel and Distributed Algorithms (M. Cosnard et al.), Elsevier Science, North Holland, 1989, pp. 215-226.

15. R. H. B. Netzer. Optimal tracing and replay for debugging shared-memory parallel programs. Proc. of 3rd ACM/ONR Workshop on Parallel and Dist. Debugging, pp. 1-11, 1993.

16. S. Savage, M. Burrows, G. Nelson, P. Sobalvarro, and T. Anderson, "Eraser: A dynamic race detector for multithreaded programs," Transactions on Computer Systems 15, 4 (November 1998), 391-411

17. S. D. Stoller. Testing concurrent Java programs using randomized scheduling. In Proc. of the Second Workshop on Runtime Verification (RV), Vol. 70(4) of Electronic Notes in Theoretical Computer Science. Elsevier, 2002.

18. K. C. Tai. Testing of concurrent software. Proc. of the 13th Annual International Computer Software and Applications Conference, pp. 62-64, 1989.

19. K. C. Tai. Reachability testing of asynchronous message-passing programs. Proc. of the 2nd International Workshop on Software Engineering for Parallel and Distributed Systems, pp. 50-61, 1997.

20. K. C. Tai, R. H. Carver, and E. Obaid, "Debugging concurrent Ada programs by deterministic execution," IEEE Trans. Software Engineering, 17(1):45-63, 1991.

21. R. N. Taylor, D. L. Levine, and Cheryl D. Kelly, Structural testing of concurrent programs, IEEE Transaction on Software Engineering, 18(3):206-214, 1992.

22. A. Ulrich and H. Konig, Specification-based Testing of Concurrent Systems, Proceedings of the IFIP Joint International Conference on Formal Description Techniques and Protocol Specification, Testing, and Verification (FORTE/PSTV '97), 1997.

23. C. Yang and L. L. Pollock. Identifying redundant test cases for testing parallel language constructs. ARL-ATIRP First Annual Technical Conference, 1997.

A Knowledge Based Analysis of Cache Coherence[*]

Kai Baukus[1] and Ron van der Meyden[2]

[1,2] School of Computer Science and Engineering,
University of New South Wales
[2] National ICT Australia
{kbaukus,meyden}@cse.unsw.edu.au

Abstract. This paper presents a case study of the application of the knowledge-based approach to concurrent systems specification, design and verification. A highly abstract solution to the cache coherence problem is first presented, in the form of a knowledge-based program, that formalises the intuitions underlying the MOESI [Sweazey & Smith, 1986] characterisation of cache coherency protocols. It is shown that any concrete implementation of this knowledge-based program, which relates a cache's actions to its knowledge about the status of other caches, is a correct solution of the cache coherence problem. Three existing protocols in the MOESI class are shown to be such implementations. The knowledge-based characterisation furthermore raises the question of whether these protocols are optimal in their use of information available to the caches. This question is investigated using by the model checker MCK, which is able to verify specifications in the logic of knowledge and time.

1 Introduction

Reasoning about knowledge [FHMV95] provides an approach to concurrent system specification, development, and verification that focuses on information flow in the system and how information relates to action. The approach promises a number of advantages: a high level of abstraction in specification, ease of verification and a methodology for the development of protocols that make optimal use of information. This paper presents a case study of the approach in a recently developed formulation, and uses for part of the effort a new tool that enables model checking specifications in the logic of knowledge and time [GM04].

The focus of the case study is cache coherence protocols for multi-processor systems. Numerous cache coherency solutions have been proposed [AB86], and the area has been a popular target for the application of model checking systems [CGH+95]. Often, the literature on verification of such protocols has concentrated on verifying specific concrete protocols rather than a more abstract

---

[*] Work supported by an Australian Research Council Discovery Grant. National ICT Australia is funded through the Australian Government's *Backing Australia's Ability* initiative, in part through the ARC.

J. Davies et al. (Eds.): ICFEM 2004, LNCS 3308, pp. 99–114, 2004.

design level. One exception is the work of Sweazey and Smith [SS86], who have given an abstract characterisation of a class of cache coherency protocols in order to show that these protocols can be implemented on the FutureBus. They show that several of the protocols in the literature can be implemented as concrete instances of their general scheme. However, their presentation is informal and does not provide a rigorous relationship between their intuitions and the concrete transition tables by which they present the concrete protocols.

We show in this paper that the knowledge-based approach provides the means to formalise the abstract intuitions of Sweazey & Smith, enabling their relationship to the concrete protocols to be precisely defined and justified. We describe how this implementation relationship can be verified. Our characterisation clarifies some aspects of Sweazey and Smith's intuitions. Moreover, our formulation raises the interesting question of whether these concrete protocols make optimal use of the information generated in running them. We investigate this question using a newly developed tool, MCK, a model checker for the logic of knowledge and time [GM04]. In some cases, we find that the protocols do make optimal use of information, but we also identify ways in which they do not. In some cases, this is because our analysis takes into account aspects not considered by the protocol designers. In one case, however, the Synapse protocol, this is much less clear, and our analysis points to a way to optimize the protocol.

2   Framework: Syntax and Semantics

In this section we recall some definitions from the literature on reasoning about knowledge, and sketch the process notation we use in the paper. For more detailed exposition and motivation on reasoning about knowledge, we refer the reader to [FHMV95].

2.1   Reasoning About Knowledge

Consider a concurrent system comprised of a set of processes. Each process is associated with a set of variables that we call its *local variables*. A *global state* is an assignment of values to each of the local variables of each process. Executing the processes from some initial state produces a *run*, a mapping from natural numbers to global states. If r is a run and $n \in \mathbf{N}$ a time, then $r(n)$ denotes the global state at time n. A *point* is a pair (r, n) consisting of a run r and a time $n \in \mathbf{N}$.

A *system* is a set of runs. If *Prop* is a set of atomic propositions, an *interpretation* of *Prop* in a system $\mathcal{R}$ is a mapping π associating each point in $\mathcal{R}$ with the set of $p \in Prop$ it satisfies. An *interpreted system* is a pair $(\mathcal{R}, \pi)$ where $\mathcal{R}$ is a system and π is an interpretation for $\mathcal{R}$.

The logic of knowledge contains a modal operator K_i, intuitively representing the expression "process i knows that", as well as the usual boolean operators. If ϕ is a formula then so is $K_i\phi$, where i is a process. The semantics of the logic of knowledge is usually defined in interpreted systems as follows. First, each process i is associated with a *local state* at each point (r, n) — this local state is denoted by $r_i(n)$, and intuitively captures all the information available to the process for determining what it knows at that time. Two points (r, n) and (r', n') are said to be *indistinguishable* to process i, written $(r, n) \sim_i (r', n')$, if $r_i(n) = r_i(n')$. Formulas are given semantics by means of a relation of satisfaction of a formula ϕ at a point (r, n) in an interpreted system $\mathcal{I}$, written $\mathcal{I}, (r, n) \models \phi$. If $\mathcal{I} = (\mathcal{R}, \pi)$, this relation is defined inductively by

1. $\mathcal{I}, (r, n) \models p$, for $p \in Prop$, if $p \in \pi(r, n)$,
2. $\mathcal{I}, (r, n) \models K_i\phi$, if $\mathcal{I}, (r', n') \models \phi$ for all points $(r', n') \sim_i (r, n)$ in $\mathcal{R}$,

and the obvious clauses for the boolean operators. Intuitively, this definition says that process i knows ϕ if ϕ holds at all points it is unable to distinguish from the current point. We write $\mathcal{I} \models \phi$ if ϕ is valid in the structure $\mathcal{I}$, i.e, $\mathcal{I}, (r, n) \models \phi$ for all points (r, n) in $\mathcal{I}$.

The local state can be defined in a number of ways. One, which we call the *observational* interpretation of knowledge, defines $r_i(n)$ to be the restriction $r(n) \upharpoonright Vars_i$ of the global state $r(n)$ to the set $Vars_i$ of local variables of process i. (We could furthermore restrict to a smaller set of variables if the question of what information is carried by that smaller set of variables is of interest). Another, the *asynchronous perfect recall* semantics inductively defines the local state as a sequence of assignments as follows: $r_i(0) = r(0) \upharpoonright Vars_i$ and $r_i(n + 1) = r_i(n)$ if $r(n) \upharpoonright Vars_i = r(n + 1) \upharpoonright Vars_i$ and $r_i(n + 1) = r_i(n) \cdot (r(n + 1) \upharpoonright Vars_i)$ otherwise. Intuitively, in this interpretation, process i remembers its complete history of observations except that due to asynchrony it is unable to distinguish stuttering equivalent sequences of observations.

The semantics above has formed the basis of much of the literature on the knowledge-based approach, but has been generalised [EMM98] in order to provide a framework that provides greater flexibility. The generalisation uses the notion of *sound local propositions*. We formulate this here as follows. Introduce a set of atomic propositions of the form $\mathbf{k}_i\phi$, where ϕ is a formula, with the semantics of these atomic propositions given by the *first* of the two clauses above. To retain some of the key aspects of the usual semantics of the knowledge operator, we impose the following constraints:

Locality: If $r_i(n) = r'_i(n')$, then $\mathbf{k}_i\phi \in \pi(r, n)$ iff $\mathbf{k}_i\phi \in \pi(r', n')$.
Soundness: $\mathcal{I} \models \mathbf{k}_i\phi \Rightarrow \phi$

Intuitively, locality says that the proposition $\mathbf{k}_i\phi$ is a function of process i's local state. Sound local propositions generalise the logic of knowledge: it can be seen that soundness and locality implies that $\mathcal{I} \models \mathbf{k}_i\phi \Rightarrow K_i\phi$, so if an interpretation of the extended set of atomic propositions also satisfies

Completeness: $\mathcal{I} \models K_i\phi \Rightarrow \mathbf{k}_i\phi$

then we have $\mathcal{I} \models \mathbf{k}_i\phi \Leftrightarrow K_i\phi$.

It has been noted [EMM98] that much of the work of knowledge formulas in the knowledge-based approach can be done with sound local propositions, and a formal refinement calculus embodying this generalisation of the approach is under development [EMM01, Eng02]. We use some ideas from this calculus in the present paper.

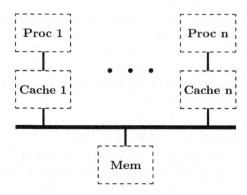

Fig. 1. Caches connected via a bus

2.2   Process Notation

We will describe systems at a number of levels of abstraction. Most concretely, we use a process algebraic notation to describe the implementation level. Variables may be updated by assignments. We use standard nondeterministic programming constructs, and a parallelism operator ||, the semantic details of which we omit for space reasons. The overall semantics is non-deterministic and asynchronous in the sense that at any time, up to one of the possible events is nondeterministically selected for execution. The choice is fair, in the sense that a continuously enabled event is eventually selected.

The communication mechanism in the notation is by a synchronous handshake between some set of processes. This may be a two-way handshake passing a value v from process A to B, which we represent by having A perform the event $B!v$ and having B perform $A?x$, writing the value v into $B's$ variable x. This handshake event is treated as causing a single transition in the global state of the system. In order to model communication on the bus, we also need a handshake involving more than two processes. Such handshake events also cause a single transition in the system state, and may change any of the local variables of the participating processes. We define the semantics of such handshakes by providing sequential code used by each of the participating processes to update its local variables: this code is interpreted to run atomically.

3   The Cache Coherence Problem

We study cache coherence protocols in the standard setting of several processors that access their data indirectly through caches, connected via a bus to each other and the main memory. The situation is depicted in Figure 1. The processors access memory locations via **read** and **write** requests. In a system without caches, the requests would be queued to access the main bus sequentially. Caches are fast memories introduced to speed up access to frequently used locations.

The direct communication between processor and cache is much faster than the main bus serving all parties connected to it. When the requested data value exists as a *valid* copy in the cache, the cache answers the request immediately. Otherwise, the cache has to request the corresponding location via the main bus. A *cache coherence protocol* is a protocol run by the caches on the main bus in order to guarantee consistency between the copies of data values that they maintain.

A variety of different cache coherence protocols have been designed, that have been placed into a general framework by Sweazey and Smith [SS86], who identify the following attributes as being of relevance in the family of cache-coherence protocols they consider:

1. **Ownership/Modification:** The owner of a memory line is responsible for the value of that line. When the owner is a cache, it is the owner just when it holds a modified value of the memory line.
2. **Exclusiveness:** Copies of the memory line may be held simultaneously by a number of caches. If it is held by just one, that cache holds it exclusively. A non-exclusive line is said to be *shared.*
3. **Validity:** The copy held by a cache may be valid (equal to the copy of the owner) or invalid.

These three attributes give 8 possible states, but ownership and exclusivity are not of interest for invalid memory lines, so [SS86] aggregate the four invalid cases into one, leaving five states, which they call M (exclusive modified), O (shared modified), S (shared unmodified), E (exclusive unmodified) and I (invalid). These states are updated as a result of bus communications, where in addition to the memory value, six different boolean signals are communicated across the bus: each is associated with an intuitive meaning, and the possible patterns of communication of these signals in each of the MOESI states and the resulting state updates are described in a set of tables. The tables allow for some choice of action in a number of states, and [SS86] show that a number of existing cache-coherency protocols can be modelled by appropriate choice of a subset of the MOESI states and a choice of the associated actions.

The MOESI states are not given a formal specification in [SS86], and the associated tables are justified only by some text that provides some informal motivation. We propose here a higher level view of the MOESI states and the associated protocols, by describing a knowledge-based program that captures the underlying reasons for correctness of the MOESI protocols. This will have the benefit not just of providing a clearer exposition of the protocol, but also of opening the way for an investigation of whether the existing protocols make optimal use of the information being communicated across the bus (something we investigate by model checking some particular cases) and permitting the exploration of alternative implementations that make greater use of the pattern of communication across the bus.

4   Knowledge-Based Specification

We now give an abstract, knowledge-based specification of cache coherence. We consider a single memory line, which we model using a single bit. The abstract behaviour of the processors is to non-deterministically choose between modifying the value arbitrarily and reading/writing of the value back to memory, represented by the following term:

$P_i \equiv$ **do** $value := 0$
    [] $value := 1$
    [] $C_i!$ **write**($value$); C_i? **ack**
    [] $C_i!$ **read**; C_i? $value$
  od

We denote the set of caches by Cache. Each cache $i \in$ Cache has associated with it the following variables:

1. a variable c_i denoting the value i has for the memory line. This might be $\perp$ if the cache does not have any value registered. It is convenient to denote the main memory by m and the value of the main memory by c_m, but this variable will never take the value $\perp$.
2. a variable $pending_i$ which has as value either the action that process i has requested to be performed (**read** or **write**(v), for $v \in \{0, 1\}$), or the value $\perp$, indicating that all requests have been processed.

At each moment of time, either one of the caches or the main memory is designated as the owner of the memory line; we represent the current owner by the variable o, with domain Cache $\cup \{m\}$. Exactly how the owner is determined at each moment of time is a matter of implementation detail - we provide some examples of particular implementations later.

A cache's actions in response to its processors read and write requests depend on what the cache knows about the state of the system, in particular, what it knows about the three attributes identified above. We represent this knowledge by means of three atomic propositions: $\mathbf{k}_i(\mathbf{excl}_i)$, $\mathbf{k}_i(o = i)$ and $\mathbf{k}_i(c_i = c_o)$, which we will require to be given a sound interpretation local to cache i (see Section 2). The meaning of the formulas in these proposition names is as follows:

1. We write $\mathbf{excl}_i$ for $c_i \neq \perp \wedge \bigwedge_{j \in \text{Cache} \setminus \{i\}} c_j = \perp$, i.e., cache i is the only cache with a copy of the line; thus $\mathbf{k}_i(\mathbf{excl}_i)$ intuitively says that cache i knows that it has an exclusive copy;
2. $o = i$ says that cache i is the owner, hence $\mathbf{k}_i(o = i)$ intuitively says that cache i knows that it is the owner;
3. $c_i = c_o$ says that cache i's copy of the data value is equal to the owner o's copy, hence $\mathbf{k}_i(c_i = c_o)$ intuitively says that cache i knows that its copy is valid.

We relate these local propositions to the cache's actions by the following specification of the cache's behaviour, in the form of a guarded do loop that runs forever. The clauses of this do loop have been labelled for reference, e.g. the first is labelled "{Get request}". Intuitively, the treatment of the variable $pending_i$ ensures that this variable acts as a flag indicating whether there exists a pending request from the processor. Requests to read are cleared by the cache by executing the {Read Hit} or {Read Miss} clauses and requests to write are cleared by executing the clause {Write Local} or {Write Bus}. The memory line is cleared from the cache by executing the {Copy back} or {Flush} clause. The reason we have two clauses to achieve each effect is that one involves a bus event and the other can be achieved locally.

$\mathcal{C}_i \equiv$ **do**

$\qquad$ {Get request}
$\qquad pending_i = \bot \rightarrow \mathcal{P}_i?pending_i$
$\quad$ [] $\quad$ {Read Hit}
$\qquad pending_i = \mathbf{read} \wedge \mathbf{k}_i(c_i = c_o) \qquad\qquad \rightarrow \mathcal{P}_i!\, c_i;\ pending_i := \bot$
$\quad$ [] $\quad$ {Read Miss}
$\qquad pending_i = \mathbf{read} \wedge \neg\mathbf{k}_i(c_i = c_o) \qquad \rightarrow [c_o = X,\ c_o = X \wedge K_i(c_i = c_o)]_B;$
$\qquad\qquad\qquad\qquad\qquad\qquad\qquad\qquad\qquad\qquad \mathcal{P}_i!\, c_i;\ pending_i := \bot$
$\quad$ [] $\quad$ {Write Local}
$\qquad pending_i = \mathbf{write}(v) \wedge \mathbf{k}_i(\mathbf{excl}_i) \quad \rightarrow [\text{TRUE}, c_i = v \wedge o = i]_L;$
$\qquad\qquad\qquad\qquad\qquad\qquad\qquad\qquad\qquad \mathcal{P}_i!\,\mathbf{ack};\ pending_i := \bot$
$\quad$ [] $\quad$ {Write Bus}
$\qquad pending_i = \mathbf{write}(v) \wedge \neg\mathbf{k}_i(\mathbf{excl}_i) \rightarrow [\text{TRUE}, c_o = v \wedge c_i = v]_B;$
$\qquad\qquad\qquad\qquad\qquad\qquad\qquad\qquad\qquad \mathcal{P}_i!\,\mathbf{ack};\ pending_i := \bot$
$\quad$ [] $\quad$ {Copy Back}
$\qquad pending = \bot \wedge \mathbf{k}_i(o = i) \qquad\qquad\quad \rightarrow [c_i = X,\ i \neq o \wedge c_o = X \wedge$
$\qquad\qquad\qquad\qquad\qquad\qquad\qquad\qquad\qquad\qquad\qquad pending_i = \bot]_B$
$\quad$ [] $\quad$ {Flush}
$\qquad pending = \bot \wedge \neg\mathbf{k}_i(o = i) \qquad\qquad \rightarrow [i \neq o,\ c_i = \bot \wedge pending_i = \bot]_L;$
$\quad$ [] $\quad$ {Bus Observation}
$\qquad [pending_i = X, pending_i = X]_B$
$\quad$ **od**

This specification is in the spirit of knowledge-based programs in the sense of [FHMV95, FHMV97], in that it relates the cache's actions to its knowledge. However, it also draws on elements of the knowledge based refinement calculus under development [EMM98, MM00, EMM00, EMM01, Eng02]. One of these elements is the use of sound local propositions $\mathbf{k}_i\phi$ as guards, where the [FHMV95, FHMV97] knowledge-based programs would require use of sound and complete guards $K_i\phi$. As we will show in the next section, soundness of the guards suffices for correctness of the specification. This makes our specification more general. (The astute reader may have noticed that we do use the classical notion of knowledge in the {Read Miss} clause. We comment on the reasons for this later.)

Another difference from the knowledge-based programs of [FHMV95, FHMV97] is that in addition to having concrete actions in the clauses, we also make use of *specification statements* $[\phi, \psi]$. These are pre- and post-condition specifications: they stand for some code, to be determined, that when executed from a state satisfying ϕ terminates in a state satisfying ψ. (The subscripts B and L are explained below.) We give a formal definition below. The variable X is used in the specification statements as an implicitly universally quantified frame variable, which is required to assume the same value in the pre-condition and the post-condition. That is, the specification in this case is required to be satisfied for all values of X.

We place some further constraints on the code implementing the specification statements in the program:

I1. We assume that this code does not involve any communication actions between the cache and its processor, so that the only such events in the implementation are those already visible in the program above.

I2. Statements of the form $[\phi, \psi]_L$ must be implemented by a program that takes only actions *local* to the cache.

I3. Statements of the form $[\phi, \psi]_B$ must be implemented by a single bus event.

I4. The variable c_i cannot change from having value $\bot$ to having a value not equal to $\bot$ without a bus event occurring.

I5. During the execution of $[i \neq o, \ c_i = \bot \wedge pending_i = \bot]_L$, $i \neq o$ remains true.

The intuition for I5 is that the clause containing this statement is intended to flush the data value from the cache, and it does not make sense for the cache to acquire ownership in order to do so. (This condition is also required for technical reasons below.)

The {Bus Observation} clause is included to deal with the cache's observations (*snooping*, in the terminology of the literature) of bus events generated by other caches. The cache may update its own state as a result of observing such events. It is assumed that all caches participate in each bus event, either by causing it, or by observing it. Observers may also exchange information during the bus event, e.g., by declaring that they retain a copy of the memory line. There is a further requirement that each event observed on the bus be caused by the action of one of the caches on the bus. Formally, we capture this by the following conditions:

BObs. Each bus event in a run of the system corresponds to the simultaneous execution by each cache of a bus event specification statement $[\alpha, \beta]_B$. At least one of these is not the {Bus_Observation} specification statement.

We also need some constraints on the definition of ownership:

O1. The owner's value for the memory line is never $\bot$, i.e., $\Box\, c_o \neq \bot$

O2. It is always the case that the owner, if a cache, knows that it is the owner, i.e., $\bigwedge_{i \in Cache} \Box\, (o = i \Rightarrow \mathbf{k}_i(o = i))$

O3. If a cache is the owner, it remains the owner until a bus event occurs.

We note that O3 permits that ownership can be transferred from the main memory to a cache without a bus event occurring. We later give an example where this occurs.

An *candidate implementation* of the above specification consists of the following:

1. A set of concrete processes C_i for each of the cache specifications C_i, obtained by substituting specific code for the specification statements in the process terms C_i, in accordance with constraints I1-I3. These concrete processes may make use of variables additional to those mentioned above, in order to maintain information about the state of other caches.
2. A concrete process $\mathcal{M}$ for the memory.
3. A definition of the semantics of any handshake actions used in these processes, defining which combinations may occur in a handshake, and what the effect is on the local states.
4. A definition of the local propositions $\mathbf{k}_i\phi$: these should depend only on the local variables of cache i in the implementation. These definitions should be substituted in the guards of C_i in constructing the implementation C_i.
5. A definition of the ownership as a function of global state.

Given a candidate implementation, let $S = M \parallel (P_1 \parallel C_1) \parallel \cdots \parallel (P_n \parallel C_n)$ be the parallel composition of all the components, and let $\mathcal{I}$ be the system consisting of the set of runs of S, with propositions interpreted in accordance with their interpretations in the candidate implementation. Then the candidate implementation is an *implementation* if the following hold in $\mathcal{I}$.

1. Constraints I4-I5, O1-O3 and BObs are satisfied.
2. The specification constraints are satisfied: for any run r of $\mathcal{I}$, for any interval (m, n) such that the code implementing the statement $[\phi, \psi]$ runs over interval (m, n) in r, if $\mathcal{I}, (r, m) \models \phi$ then $\mathcal{I}, (r, n) \models \psi$. (Note that because the underlying semantics is asynchronous, actions of other processes may occur during the interval $[m, n]$.)

For the purposes of the above definition, the knowledge operator in {Read Miss} should be interpreted according to the observational semantics of knowledge.

We now show that any implementation of the knowledge-based specification solves the cache coherence problem, by establishing that a strong type of sequentiality holds if one observes the system at the level of bus events. Say that a *write event (of cache i)* is an event involving cache i, such that the next event involving cache i is $P_i!\mathbf{ack}$. That is, a write event of a cache i is the final event of the implementation of one of the specification statements $[\text{TRUE}, c_i = v \wedge o = i]_L$ or $[\text{TRUE}, c_o = v \wedge c_i = v]_B$. We say that the value v is the *value written* in this write event. We call events of the form $P_j!w$ where w is a memory line value, *read events*, with value w. The following result states that values read are always equal to the last value written. When an event corresponds to the transition between times n and $n + 1$, we say it occurs at time n.

Lemma 1 (Sequentiality). *Let $\mathcal{I}$ be a system implementing the knowledge-based specification, and let r be a run of $\mathcal{I}$. If a write event with value v occurs at time m in r, a read event with value w occurs at time $n > m$, and no write event occurs at times p with $m < p \leq n$, then $v = w$.*

It is worth remarking that the specification statement for the {Read Miss} clause could have used the local proposition $\mathbf{k}_i(c_i = c_o)$ in place of $K_i(c_i = c_o)$, but this would be less general by validity of $\mathbf{k}_i(\phi) \Rightarrow K_i(\phi)$. In practice, however, $\mathbf{k}_i(c_i = c_o)$ could well be the postcondition established, and would have the benefit of matching the guard of the {Read Hit} statement. If one were to weaken $K_i(c_i = c_o)$ in the postcondition of the {Read Miss} clause to $c_i = c_o$, the sequentiality result would no longer hold, intuitively because there is then no guarantee that the owner does not perform a local write interleaved between execution of the bus event and the handshake $P_i!c_i$. However, a closely related result, stating that observations of reads and writes at the level of the processors are *linearisable* [HW90] could still be proved with this weakening.

5   Implementation of the Cache Protocols

One of the benefits of the knowledge-based approach is that it enables high level descriptions capturing the underlying reasons for correctness of a variety of protocols. We illustrate this by showing that three known cache coherence protocols are implementations of our knowledge-based program for cache coherence. We refer the reader to [AB86] for a detailed presentation of these protocols.

The first protocol is the so-called *Write-Once* protocol, which gets its name from the fact that the first write hit is performed as a write-through to the memory and gives the other caches the information to invalidate their copies. After this write-through, reads and writes can be performed locally, and the cache can also be flushed without a write-back if there has been no second write. See Figure 2(a) for a graphical representation. The cache line can be in four different states: Invalid (Inv), Valid (Vld), Reserved (Rsv), or Dirty (Drty). Writes and reads in state Inv lead to a *Write-Miss (wm)* resp. *Read-Miss (rm)*. In all other states the protocol reacts with a hit action, e.g., *Write-Hit (wh)* resp. *Read-Hit (rh)*. Other caches observe the miss actions, and take in response the transitions labelled *wmo* (write miss observed) *rmo* (read miss observed), and also observe the write-hit in state Vld, taking the transition *woo* (write once observed).

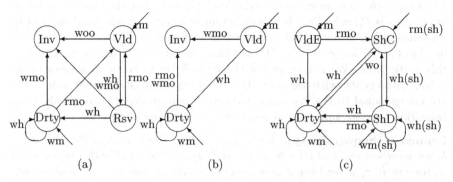

(a)   (b)   (c)

Fig. 2. State graphs of the (a) Write-Once, (b) Synapse, and (c) Dragon protocols

The *Synapse* protocol on the other hand gets by with only three states as shown in Figure 2(b). There is no Rsv state, hence all miss actions of other caches result in invalidation of the cache line.

The *Dragon* protocol uses both a write-through and a copy-back approach. It needs 5 local states, but Figure 2(c) shows only 4: the invalid state is omitted. Once loaded, the value is always kept up-to-date until the line is flushed. If the cache holds the line exclusively, then all reads and writes are local. When other caches may also have a copy of the line, all activities go over the bus to update all of them. After supplying the line, the main memory is involved only when the owning cache flushes the line. The four possible states of a loaded line are: Valid-Exclusive (VldE), Shared-Clean (ShC), Shared-Dirty (ShD), and Dirty (Drty). Both dirty states imply ownership and copy-back responsibility.

The added *(sh)* at some labels indicates that other caches indicated (via the so-called shared-line) that they share the line. For the owning cache this means further updates need to be communicated via the bus. The protocol is written for special hardware that features such shared-lines and offers an inter-cache communication that is much faster than write-cycles involving the main memory.

In order to show that these protocols are implementations of the knowledge-based program, we define additional local variables required for the processes, and instantiate the various components in the knowledge-based program. By way of the additional variables, it suffices to associate a variable s_i with each cache C_i. The variable s_i is used to indicate the state the protocol associates with the memory line in the cache. The following table shows how the propositions in the knowledge-based program are defined.

	$o = i$	$\mathbf{k}_i(o = i)$	$\mathbf{k}_i(c_i = c_o)$	$\mathbf{k}_i(\text{excl}_i)$
Write-Once	$s_i = \text{Drty}$	$s_i = \text{Drty}$	$s_i \neq \text{Inv}$	$s_i \in \{\text{Rsv}, \text{Drty}\}$
Synapse	$s_i = \text{Drty}$	$s_i = \text{Drty}$	$s_i \neq \text{Inv}$	$s_i = \text{Drty}$
Dragon	$s_i \in \{\text{Drty}, \text{ShD}\}$	$s_i \in \{\text{Drty}, \text{ShD}\}$	$s_i \neq \text{Inv}$	$s_i \in \{\text{VldE}, \text{Drty}\}$

The implementation of the locally executed specification statements turns out to be the same in all the protocols: the {Flush} statement $[o \neq i, c_i = \bot \wedge pending_i = \bot]$ is implemented by $c_i := \bot; s_i := \text{Inv}$, and the {Write Local} statement $[\text{TRUE}, c_i = v \wedge o = i]$ is implemented by $c_i := v; s_i := \text{Drty}$. Using the above table, it can be seen directly that, for each protocol, these implementations ensure that the postcondition is satisfied.[1]

The remaining statements requiring definition are the bus event specification statements. Recall that these execute as a handshake between all caches and the memory, with all but one of the caches executing the {Observe} statement. The following table describes, for each of the protocols, the atomic state transitions resulting from the {Write Bus} statement. One column describes the effects at

---

[1] For the variable $pending_i$ we need to use the context in which the statement occurs.

the cache initiating the bus event, the other describes the transition at each of the caches observing the bus event.

{Write Bus}	$[\text{TRUE}, c_o = v \wedge c_i = v]_B$	Observer j
Write-Once	$c_i := v$; if $s_i = \text{Inv}$ then $s_i := \text{Drty}$ else if $s_i = \text{Vld}$ then $\{c_m := v; s_i := \text{Rsv}\}$	$c_j := \bot; s_j = \text{Inv}$
Synapse	$c_i := v; s_i := \text{Drty}$	$c_j := \bot; s_j = \text{Inv}$
Dragon	$c_i := v;$ *if Sh then* $s_i := \text{ShD}$ *else* $s_i := \text{Drty}$	*if* $s_j \neq \text{Inv}$ *then* $\{c_j := v; s_j = \text{ShC}\}$

In this table, Sh abbreviates $\exists j \neq i(s_j \neq \text{Inv})$, and corresponds to the SharedLine used by the caches to indicate that they have a copy of the memory line. The table for the {Read Miss} statement is as follows.

{Read Miss}	$[c_o = X, c_o = X \wedge K_i(c_i = c_o)]_B$	Observer j
Write-Once	$c_i := c_o; s_i := \text{Vld}$	if $s_j = \text{Drty}$ then $c_m := c_j$; if $s_j \in \{\text{Rsv}, \text{Drty}\}$ then $s_j := \text{Vld}$
Synapse	$c_i := c_o; s_i := \text{Vld}$	if $s_j = \text{Drty}$ then $\{\, c_m := c_j; c_j := \bot; s_j = \text{Inv}\}$
Dragon	$c_i := c_o;$ if Sh then $s_i := \text{ShC}$ else $s_i := \text{VldE}$	if $s_j \in \{\text{VldE}, \text{ShC}\}$ then $s_j := \text{ShC}$; if $s_j = \text{Drty}$ then $s_j := \text{ShD}$

In the case of the Synapse protocol, our modelling of the {Read Miss} condenses two bus events into one: the actual protocol does not allow the memory line to be read from another cache: if some cache has a Drty copy, it must first write this back to memory, and the cache requesting a read must then reissue its request and obtain the line from the memory.

In case of the {Copyback} statement, the implementation in all the protocols is by $c_m := c_i; c_i := \bot; s_i := \text{Inv}$ at the cache performing the copyback, and no action at the observers. We remark that this implementation satisfies a stronger postcondition than is required by our knowledge-based specification, which does not require that $c_i = \bot$ after a copyback. This suggests the existence of protocols that separate copyback from flush operations. We return to this point later. Some other opportunities for alternate implementations are apparent: e.g., the specification permits the copyback to transfer ownership to another cache rather than the memory.

Another point needs to be noted concerning our modelling: by representing the memory line as a single variable, we do not distinguish between reads and writes of blocks versus single memory locations. Some changes would be required to capture this: for example, in the write-once protocol, a Drty cache observing a write must write the block back to memory, but the writing cache then need only write through the particular memory location being written.

6   Correctness of the Implementations

In order to verify that a concrete program is a correct implementation of the knowledge based-program, we need to check that each of the specification statements is satisfied by the code implementing that statement, that the test for knowledge are interpreted by sound conditions for knowledge, and that the other constraints noted are satisfied. This verification could be carried out by any standard means, e.g., theorem proving or model checking technology, and once carried out, implies, by the correctness theorem, that the implementation satisfies the correctness condition for cache coherence. (We can, of course, also verify this condition directly on the concrete code.)

We have conducted the verification by model checking using the model checker MCK [GM04]. In addition to providing standard temporal logic model checking capabilities, MCK enables model checking formulas of the logic of knowledge and time.[2] This makes it possible to check not just for correctness but also to determine if protocols are making optimal use of the information encoded in the local states. We illustrate our methodology in this section.

6.1   Global Consistency

As an example of the global consistency properties we check, consider the requirement that there be a unique owner at all times. In the Write-Once protocol, we wish to define cache i to be the owner if $status_i = Drty$ and the owner to be the main memory otherwise. To check that this definition makes sense, we first model check the following formula $\Box\,(status_0 \neq Drty \vee status_1 \neq Drty)$. This implies that the definition of ownership assigns a unique owner in all circumstances. Model checking other properties of this kind also provides a useful means to detect a variety of basic implementation errors.

6.2   Soundness

Although it may appear to involve model checking knowledge, verifying soundness of a concrete interpretation of the knowledge formulas can be carried out using only temporal logic model checking technology. For example, to obtain the Synapse protocol we interpret the local proposition $\mathbf{k}_i(\mathtt{excl}_i)$ by the test $s_i = \mathtt{Drty}$. Thus, soundness of this interpretation amounts to the claim $\Box\,(s_i = \mathtt{Drty} \Rightarrow (c_i \neq \bot \wedge \bigwedge_{j \neq i} c_j = \bot))$, which is a pure temporal logic formula.

6.3   Completeness

The most significant novelty of our methodology concerns cases where we model check knowledge formulas using the capabilities MCK provides for this purpose. In particular, for some simple configurations of the 3 protocols, we have checked the following:

---

[2] We extended MCK to handle the asynchronous perfect recall semantics for knowledge in order to do so - the details will be reported elsewhere.

K1 A {Read Miss} establishes the postcondition $K_i(c_i = c_o)$, with respect to the observational (and hence also the perfect recall) interpretation of knowledge.

K2 Does the formula $\Box \, (\mathbf{k}_i(\phi) \Leftrightarrow K_i \phi)$ hold for each of the local propositions $\mathbf{k}_i \phi$ in the specification, with respect to the asynchronous perfect recall semantics of knowledge?

The variables observable to the caches for these results included variables recording information potentially available to the caches in bus event, such as the transition being performed by the cache initiating the bus event. See the discussion above for the significance of property **K1**. A positive answer for Property **K2** shows that the protocols are *optimal* in their use of information, in the sense that the variables s_i store *all* the information available to the caches that they could use to determine whether the formulas ϕ hold. The answer to the question turns out to be yes in all three protocols when the formula ϕ is $o = i$. This is to be expected, since for each protocol, $\mathbf{k}(o = i)$ and $o = i$ are identical and i-local, from which soundness and completeness can easily be seen to follow.

However, when the formula ϕ is $\mathtt{excl}_i$, we find that the i-local interpretation for $\mathbf{k}_i(\phi)$ is sound but *not* complete in the Write-Once and Synapse protocols. A scenario showing incompleteness is where the first action in a run is for a cache to issue a {Read Miss}. Upon receipt of the value, the cache will be in state $\mathtt{Vld}$, but will know from a log of its observations that no other cache has a copy, since it would have observed a read or write attempt by any other cache. To some extent this negative result is to be expected, since the Write-Once and Synapse protocols make no attempt to maintain exclusiveness information. The Dragon protocol *does* maintain information about whether the value is shared, and our model checking results indicate that whenever the Dragon cache could know that it has an exclusive copy from a complete log of its observations of bus events, it already knows this fact from just its Dragon state.

When the formula ϕ is $c_o = c_i$, things are more subtle. In this case, the interpretations we gave for $\mathbf{k}_i(\phi)$ turn out to be sound and complete for all three protocols as we have described them. However, this conclusion hinges on the fact that we perform the assignment $c_i := \bot$ whenever we perform $s_i := Inv$. An alternate interpretation of the protocols would rely on the Flush operation to perform $c_i := \bot$, and execute just $s_i := Inv$ at other times.[3] This allows us to ask the question: are there situations where a cache could know that a value that it has kept is valid, even though the protocol has marked it as invalid?

Our model checking experiments discovered that there is indeed such a situation. In the Synapse protocol, note that a cache in state $\mathtt{Drty}$, on observing a {Read Miss}, writes the value back to memory and goes to state $\mathtt{Inv}$. In fact, it could know that the value it has remains valid, since any subsequent write would still have to involve a bus transaction. This suggests a change to the Synapse protocol, in which the *rmo* transition from $\mathtt{Drty}$ in Figure 2(b) goes to $\mathtt{Vld}$ instead of $\mathtt{Inv}$. This observation has been previously made in the

---

[3] As we noted above, the knowledge-based specification allows us to distinguish between a copyback and a flush.

literature ([Han93], p. 175), but the point we wish to make is that model checking knowledge provides an automated way to discover such lack of optimality in protocols.[4] If we make the proposed change to the Synapse protocol, we then find that the interpretation for $\mathbf{k}_i(c_o = c_i)$ is both sound and complete.

7   Conclusion

The literature on the knowledge-based approach to the design and analysis of distributed systems provides comparatively few examples from which to generalise in development of the approach. Our results in this paper provide a new case study, which illuminates a number of key points. In particular, we see here an example where correctness of an implementation of a knowledge-based program requires only soundness of the knowledge test, and can be separated from the issue of optimality in use of information, which corresponds to completeness.

We have also clarified Sweazey and Smiths analysis of cache coherence, by giving it a highly abstract, knowledge-theoretic presentation, that highlights a number of subtleties and reveals some design alternatives for the development of new cache coherence protocols. We remark that there has been a previous analysis of cache coherence using epistemic logic [MWS94]. The key differences to our work is that it considers a somewhat different class of protocols for network rather than hardware settings, and uses a logic of belief rather than a logic of knowledge. Neiger [Nei95] has also considered, from a knowledge theoretic perspective, distributed shared memory satisfying weaker properties than cache coherence.

Verification of cache coherence protocols has previously been approached by refinement, e.g. [BDG$^+$94]. What distinguishes our approach is that it allows us to automatically discover situations where protocols are not optimal in their use of information. It also opens up avenues for synthesis of implementations. For example, after providing implementations of the specification statements, we could try to determine sound and complete interpretations of the knowledge conditions by automated synthesis. We leave this as a question for future work.

References

[AB86]   James Archibald and Jean-Loup Baer. Cache coherence protocols: evaluation using a multiprocessor simulation model. *ACM Transactions on Computer Systems (TOCS)*, 4(4):273–298, 1986.

[BDG$^+$94] E. Brinksma, J. Davies, R. Gerth, S. Graf, W. Janssen, B. Jonsson, S.Katz, G. Lowe, M. Poel, A. Pnueli, C. Rump, and J. Zwiers. Verifying sequentially consistent memory. Computing Science Reports 94-44, Eindhoven University of Technology, 1994.

---

[4] How to modify a protocol in such a situation is an interesting but much more subtle question, that we leave for the future.

[CGH+ 95] E.M. Clarke, O. Grumberg, H. Hiraishi, S. Jha, D.E. Long, K.L McMillan, and L.A. Ness. Verification of the Futurebus+ cache coherence protocol. *Formal Methods in System Design*, 6:217–232, 1995.

[EMM98] Kai Engelhardt, Ron van der Meyden, and Yoram Moses. Knowledge and the logic of local propositions. In Itzhak Gilboa, editor, *Theoretical Aspects of Rationality and Knowledge, Proceedings of the Seventh Conference (TARK 1998)*, pages 29–41. Morgan Kaufmann, July 1998.

[EMM00] Kai Engelhardt, Ron van der Meyden, and Yoram Moses. A program refinement framework supporting reasoning about knowledge and time. In *Foundations of Software Science and Computation Structures*, pages 114–129, 2000.

[EMM01] Kai Engelhardt, Ron van der Meyden, and Yoram Moses. A refinement theory that supports reasoning about knowledge and time for synchronous agents. In *Proceedings LPAR 2001*, pages 125–141, 2001.

[Eng02] Kai Engelhardt. Towards a refinement theory that supports reasoning about knowledge and time for multiple agents. In John Derrick, Eerke Boiten, Jim Woodcock, and Joakim von Wright, editors, *Electronic Notes in Theoretical Computer Science*, volume 70. Elsevier, 2002.

[FHMV95] Ronald Fagin, Joseph Y. Halpern, Yoram Moses, and Moshe Y. Vardi. *Reasoning About Knowledge*. MIT Press, 1995.

[FHMV97] Ronald Fagin, Joseph Y. Halpern, Yoram Moses, and Moshe Y. Vardi. Knowledge-based programs. *Distributed Computing*, 10(4):199–225, 1997.

[GM04] Peter Gammie and Ron van der Meyden. MCK — Model-checking the logic of knowledge. In *Proc. Computer Aided Verification: 16th International Conference, CAV*, pages 479 – 483. Springer LNCS No. 3114, 2004.

[Han93] J. Handy. *The Cache Memory Book*. Academic Press, 1993.

[HW90] Maurice P. Herlihy and Jeannette M. Wing. Linearizability: a correctness condition for concurrent objects. *ACM Transactions on Programming Languages and Systems (TOPLAS)*, 12(3):463–492, 1990.

[MM00] Ron van der Meyden and Yoram Moses. On refinement and temporal annotations. In *Formal Techniques in Real-Time and Fault-Tolerant Systems, 6th International Symposium, FTRTFT 2000 Pune, India, September 20–22, Proceedings*, pages 185–201, 2000.

[MWS94] Lily B. Mummert, Jeannette M. Wing, and M. Satyanarayana. Using belief to reason about cache coherence. In *Proc. ACM Symposium on Principles of Distributed Computing*, pages 71–80, 1994.

[Nei95] Gil Neiger. Simplifying the design of knowledge-based algorithms using knowledge consistency. *Information and Computation*, 119(2):283–293, 1995.

[SS86] P. Sweazey and A. J. Smith. A class of compatible cache consistency protocols and their support by the IEEE futurebus. In *Proceedings of the 13th Annual International Symposium on Computer architecture*, pages 414–423. IEEE Computer Society Press, 1986.

A Propositional Logic-Based Method for Verification of Feature Models

Wei Zhang, Haiyan Zhao, and Hong Mei

Institute of Software,
School of Electronics Engineering and Computer Science,
Peking University, Beijing, 100871, China
{zhangw, zhhy}@sei.pku.edu.cn, meih@pku.edu.cn

Abstract. The feature model is a domain/product-line oriented requirements model based on hierarchical structure and explicit variability modeling, and has been adopted by several important software reuse methods. However, with respect to the problem of verification of constraints on features and verification of partially customized feature models, these methods tend to be semi-formal and offer little formal assistance. In this paper, we propose a propositional logic-based method for the verification of feature models at different binding times. The most important characteristic of this method is that it integrates the logical verification with binding times, which makes it can be used to verify any partially customized feature models at any binding time (except run-time). In this method, constraints on features are formalized by logical sentences. Thus, the verification of feature models is converted into satisfaction problems in the logic. With this formal method, verification problems such as the detection of inconsistent constraints or the detection of conflicting or unnecessary binding resolutions can be automatically revealed.

1 Introduction

One practical approach to software reuse is to produce general purpose (i.e., reusable) software artifacts, followed by customization to accommodate different situations. To facilitate the customization of reusable software artifacts, elements in these artifacts should be cohesive enough, and dependencies between elements should be specified clearly.

Feature-oriented methods [1,2,3,4] have been proposed to improve the customization of the problem space of software. These methods treat features as the basic elements in the problem space, and use features, relationships (i.e. refinements and constraints) between features (called feature model) to structure the problem space. In the development for reuse phase [5, 9], a domain feature model is first constructed by exploring commonality and variability in a software domain. Then, in the later development with reuse phase, the domain feature model is customized into application feature models according to different reuse contexts. Those still undecided features in application feature models will be gradually bound or removed through a series of binding times (e.g. compile-time, install-time, load-time, and run-time).

J. Davies et al. (Eds.): ICFEM 2004, LNCS 3308, pp. 115–130, 2004.

Constraints specified in the domain feature model then provide criteria to verify the completeness and consistency of those customized feature models. In such a way, customization of the domain feature model is operated.

However, as far as we know, all these feature-oriented methods lack effective measures to verify partially customized feature models. A real customization process often includes a series of binding times, in each of which, certain customizing resolutions are decided and a partially customized feature model is obtained. The inability to verify partially customized feature models increases the difficulty of customization. As feature models become larger and constraints on features become more complex, the cost of constraints modeling and maintenance will also increase considerably. In addition, constraints defined by these methods currently are too simple to describe complex constraints involving three or more features.

In this paper, we propose a propositional logic-based method for the verification of feature models at different binding times. In this method, the statement "a feature is in the bound state" is regard as a two-value proposition in the logic. These propositions can further be combined with basic logical connectives to represent complex constraints on features. By this way, constraints in a feature model are formalized by a set of logical sentences. Then, at each binding time, after an undecided feature is bound or removed, the truth value of this feature will become the logical constant True or False respectively. Thus, the verification of feature models is converted into satisfaction problems in the logic. Therefore, verification problems such as the detection of inconsistent constraints or the detection of conflicting or unnecessary binding resolutions can be automatically revealed.

The rest of this paper is organized as follows. Basic knowledge about feature models is given in Section 2. Section 3 presents a propositional logic based verification method in detail. Two case studies are illustrated in Section 4. Related work is discussed in Section 5. Finally, Section 6 concludes this paper with a short summary.

2   Context: A Metamodel of Feature Models

The focus of this paper is on the verification of feature models. Hence, we need to first give an introduction about feature models. In the remainder of this section, we introduce a metamodel of feature models. The content of this section is mainly based on our previous work on feature modeling [12] and other related literature [1, 2, 3, 4, 7].

Figure 1 shows a metamodel of feature models. This metamodel consists of three basic concepts: Feature, Refinement, and Constraint. All these concepts are subclasses of the two concepts: Classifier and Relationship in UML Core Package [22].

2.1   Feature

A feature describes a product characteristic from user or customer views [2, 16], which essentially consists of a cohesive set of individual requirements [17, 18, 19]. In feature models, a feature is characterized by a set of attributes: *name, description, optionality, binding-time* and *binding-state*.

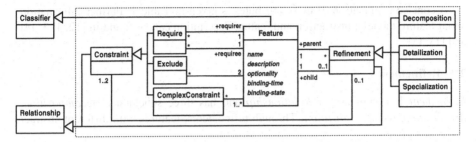

Fig. 1. A MetaModel of Feature Models

Name is a short character string. Its main purpose is to facilitate the communication between stakeholders. In this paper, we also use the name of a feature to denote the logic proposition of *"this feature is in the bound state"*. *Description* is a detailed representation of a feature.

Optionality describes whether a feature has the chance to be removed from the current feature model when its parent feature (if has) has been bound. This attribute has two values: *mandatory* and *optional*.

Binding-time is an attribute related to optional features. It describes a phase in the software life-cycle when an optional feature should either be bound or removed form the current feature model. Typical binding-times include *reuse-time, compile-time, deploy-time, load-time,* and *run-time.*

The attribute *binding-state* has three values: *bound, removed* and *undecided*. A *bound* feature means that if its trigger conditions and pre-conditions are satisfied, this feature will be executed. A *removed* feature means that it will never be bound again. An *undecided* feature means that it is currently not in the *bound* state, but still has the chance to be bound or removed in later binding-times. In this paper, we use *"tailoring"* to denote the action of changing a feature's *binding-state* from *undecided* to *removed,* use *"binding"* to denote the action of changing a feature's *binding-state* from *undecided* to *bound,* and also use *"binding resolution"* to denote the decision of whether to bind or tailor a feature from the current feature model in a specific binding-time.

Table 1. Explanation of Feature Attributes

Attribute	Description	Value Range
name	The denotation of a feature	possible meaningful character strings
description	The detailed representation of a feature	{informal, semi-formal, formal}
optionality	Whether a feature must also be bound when its parent feature is bound	{*mandatory, optional*}
binding-time	The phase when a feature must be bound or removed	{*construct-time, reuse-time, compile-time, install-time, load-time*}
binding-state	Whether a feature has been bound or removed, or is waiting for being decided	{*bound, removed, undecided*}

A concise explanation of these attributes is given in Table 1. Further information about feature model construction and feature description can be found in [12, 1, 3, 14] and [13, 15].

2.2 Refinement

Refinement is a subclass of *Relationship* and has three subclasses: *decomposition*, *detailization* and *specialization*. Through refinements, features with different abstract levels and granularities form a hierarchy structure.

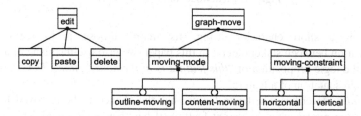

Fig. 2. Examples of decomposition, detailization and specialization

Refining a feature into its constituent features is called *decomposition* [1]. For example, the *edit* feature in many software systems is often decomposed into three sub-features: *copy*, *paste* and *delete* (see Fig. 2). Refining a feature by identifying its attribute features is called *detailization*. For example, in *graph editor* domain, the *graph-move* feature can be detailized by two attribute features: *moving-mode* and *moving-constraint*. The difference between *decomposition* and *detailization* is often omitted by most feature modeling methods, but the distinguishing between them does have necessity for binding resolutions verification, because of the different constraints implied by them: a fully decomposed feature must be removed if all its constituent features have been removed; while a feature may still be bound, even if all its attribute features have been removed. Refining a general feature into a feature incorporating further details is called *specialization* [1]. *Specialization* is often used to represent a set of variants of a general feature in feature models. A general feature is also called a *variation point feature* (*vp-feature*) in [3].

Features with different abstract levels and granularities form a hierarchy structure through refinement relationships between them. More strictly, most feature modeling methods limit this hierarchy structure to be one or more feature trees. This limitation contributes to the simplicity and understandability of feature models. [20] and [21] present guidelines on transforming general structures into tree structures and maintaining tree structures in feature modeling process.

2.3 Constraint

Constraint captures static dependencies between features. And these dependencies must be satisfied when customizing feature models. In other words, constraints provide criteria to verify the results of customization of feature models (i.e. *application feature models*). Only those results that don't violate constraints on features are the candidates of valid application feature models.

Require and *exclude* are two kinds of binary constraint on features [1]. For features A and B, "A *require* B" indicates the rule that B cannot be removed from the current feature model when A hasn't been removed. "A *exclude* B" means that the two features can not coexist in a same context.

Besides binary constraints *require* and *exclude*, this metamodel also define two kinds of *ComplexConstraint* on a set of features: *GroupConstraint* and *CompositeConstraint* (Figure 3).

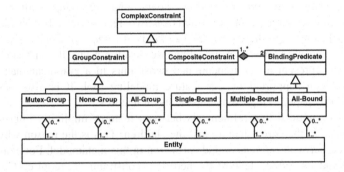

Fig. 3. Complex Constraints

GroupConstraint is a kind of constraint on a set of feature. It has three subclasses: *Mutex-Group*, *None-Group* and *All-Group*. *Mutex-Group* indicates that there is an *exclude* constraint on any two elements in a feature set. *None-Group* means there is no *require* and *exclude* constraints on any two elements in a feature set. Thus, features in a *None-Group* set can be bound or unbound freely without considering the *binding-state* of other features in this set. *All-Group* indicates a kind of strong constraint on a feature set: features in this set must be all in the bound state, or all in the unbound state.

CompositeConstraint is a kind of constraint on two feature sets, and the two feature sets themselves are constrained by some kinds of *GroupConstraint*. For example, binding one feature in a *Mutex-Group* set may require binding one or more features in another *None-Group* set. To represent such kind of constraint, we need to define three *binding predicates* corresponding to the three *GroupConstraints* respectively. For a *Mutex-Group* set, there are two possible binding results which satisfy the *Mutex-Group* constraint. One result is that no feature in the set is in the bound state, the other is that only one feature in the set is in the bound state. Hence, the predicate *single-bound* is derived to indicate whether no feature or exactly one feature in a feature set is in the bound state. Similarly, predicates *multiple-bound* and *all-bound* can be derived from *None-Group* and *All-Group*.

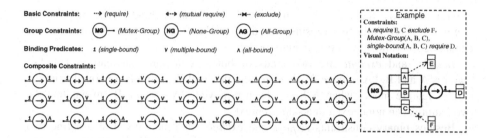

Fig. 4. Visual Constraint Notation

By composing *single-bound*, *multiple-bound* and *all-bound* with *require* or *exclude*, we thus can represent constraints on two feature sets. If considering *the mutual require* constraint, there are totally 27 kinds of *CompositeConstraint*.

For convenience of constraint modeling, we develop a visual constraint notation (Figure 4), to represent all aforementioned constraints in a graphical manner. This notation has been supported by our feature modeling tool. It is also used in the remainder of this paper to represent constraints on features.

It should be noticed that refinements between features implicitly impose one or two constraints on the parent feature and the children. This is the reason why there is an association between *refinement* and *constraint* in this metamodel. For example, for a feature *P* and its refined feature *C*, there is a constraint "*C* require *P*" on them, which means that if you want to bind *C*, you must firstly bind its parent *P*. Such constraints are called *refinement imposed constraints* in this paper, to distinguish them from those *constructor imposed constraints*. The issue of extracting refinement imposed constraints from refinements is addressed in section 3.

3   Formal Verification of Feature Models

3.1   An Overview of the Process

The process of feature model verification is depicted in Figure 5. There are five main steps in the process. The first step is feature model construction. In this step, features, refinement relations between features and constraints on features associated with a software domain/product-line are systematically identified as in [12, 1, 3, 14]. Most feature-oriented reuse approaches have provided tool supporting to this step. The second step is to formalize constraints on features into logic sentences, which will be presented in section 3.3. The third step is to compute atomic-sets contained in a feature model, and use these atomic-sets to simplify constraints by replacing features involved in constraints with their corresponding atomic-sets (see section 3.4). In our approach, the second and third steps can be automated by tool supporting. After the third step, operators can apply the *SUS* criteria to verify constraints on features (the fourth step, see section 3.5), and further take *binding resolutions* at each binding-time (the fifth step) and repeatedly apply the *SUS* criteria to verify these resolutions. The fourth step can be automated by using model checkers, such as SMV [11].

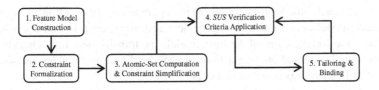

Fig. 5. The Process of Feature Model Verification

3.2 Partition Features in Feature Models

As discussed above, tailoring and binding features in different binding times can be viewed as changing the binding states of features. Usually, features in a feature model can be partitioned into three sets according to their *binding-states*: *BFSet*, *UFSet* and *RFSet*. The definition of the three set is:

$BFSet = \{ f \mid f.binding\text{-}state = bound \}$;
$UFSet = \{ f \mid f.binding\text{-}state = undecided \}$;
$RFSet = \{ f \mid f.binding\text{-}state = removed \}$;

The partition of features among the three sets may not be stable when current binding time changes. Features in *UFSet* may move to the other two sets after tailoring or binding actions. Once a feature moves to *BFSet* or *RFSet*, the **truth value** of this feature will become the logical constant of **True** or **False**. Figure 6 shows the transition of a feature's *binding-state* between different binding times.

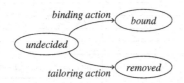

Fig. 6. Feature Binding-State Transition Diagram

The three feature sets combined with the feature binding-state transition provide a uniform view of these tailoring and binding actions which are taken both at the development for reuse phase (i.e. *construct-time*) and at the development with reuse phase (such as *reuse-time, compile-time*, and so on). At the beginning, all features in a feature model belong to *UFSet*, and each feature's *binding-time* is carefully decided. Then, at the *construct-time*, feature model constructors put those *construct-time* bound features into *BFSet* through *binding* actions. The set of *construct-time* bound features is also called the commonality of a feature model, because these features will exist in every application feature models. The *construct-time* is the only binding time at the development for reuse phase. After the *construct-time* is the *reuse-time*. At this time, requirement analyzers for individual applications will take some tailoring and binding actions according their current reuse contexts. The result is that some features in *UFSet* are partitioned into *BFSet* or *RFSet*. Similar tailoring and binding actions can be taken at each binding time, although the operators of these actions may change from feature model constructors to requirement analyzers, even to end users at *run-time*. Thus, the verification of feature models is transformed into checking the rationality of tailoring and binding actions at each binding time, besides checking the consistency of constraints in feature models.

3.3   Formalize Constraints on Features

To achieve the above-mentioned verification, we need to transform the constraints into a form that can be processed by model checkers. According to the cause of constraints, constraints in a feature model can be roughly divided into two categories. Constraints in the first category are imposed explicitly by feature model constructors. Constraints in the second category are imposed implicitly by feature refinements.

For the explicit constraints, we can formalize typical constraints on features [1, 2, 3] and binding predicates into the propositional logic. Table 2 shows the results of our formalization. For conciseness, only one kind of Composite Constraint's formalization is given in this table. Others can be deduced in a similar way.

Table 2. Formalization of Typical Constraints

Constraint/Predicate	Formalization
f_1 require f_2	$f_1 \rightarrow f_2$
f_1 mutex f_2	$\neg(f_1 \cap f_2)$
Mutex-Group$(f_1, f_2, \ldots f_n)$	$\forall f_j, f_k \in \{f_1, f_2, \ldots f_n\}, j \neq k, \neg(f_j \cap f_k)$
None-Group$(f1, f2, \ldots fn)$	True
All-Group$(f_1, f_2, \ldots f_n)$	$(\cap_{1 \leq i \leq n} f_i) \cup (\cap_{1 \leq i \leq n} \neg f_i)$
single-binding$(f_1, f_2, \ldots f_n)$	$\exists 1 \leq i \leq n (\cap_{1 \leq j \leq n, j \neq i} \neg f_j) \cap f_i$
multiple-binding$(f_1, f_2, \ldots f_n)$	$\cup_{i=1, \ldots, n} f_i$
all-binding$(f_1, f_2, \ldots f_n)$	$\cap_{i=1, \ldots, n} f_i$
single-bound$(f_1, \ldots f_n)$ require multiple-bound$(g_1, \ldots g_n)$	single-bound$(f_1, \ldots f_n) \rightarrow$ multiple-bound$(g_1, \ldots g_n)$

For the implicit constraints, we can represent them as the following rules. These rules essentially reflect constraints imposed by refinements.

- A pre-condition of binding a feature is that its parent must have been bound.
- A post-condition of binding a feature is that all its mandatory children must also be bound.
- A post-condition of binding a fully decomposed feature is that at least one of its constituent features must also be bound.

Similarly, there are also two kinds of rules when unbinding a feature:

- A pre-condition of unbinding a feature is that all its children must have been unbound.
- A post-condition of unbinding a mandatory feature is that its parent must also be unbound.

Table 3 shows constraints implied by typical refinement scenarios.

Table 3. Constraints Implied by Typical Refinement Scenarios

Refinement Scenario	Implied Constraints
fp: a feature; *{fm₁,fm₂...fmᵢ}*: the set of mandatory refinement features of *fp*; *{ fo₁,fo₂...foⱼ }*: the set of optional refinement features of *fp*; And there is no decomposition feature of *fp*;	$fp \rightarrow all\text{-}binding(fm_1,fm_2...fm_i)$, $multiple\text{-}binding(fm_1,fm_2...fm_i) \rightarrow fp$, $multiple\text{-}binding(fo_1,fo_2...fo_j) \rightarrow fp$
fp: a feature; *{fm₁,fm₂...fmᵢ}*: the set of mandatory refinement features of *fp*; *{ fo₁,fo₂...foⱼ }*: the set of optional refinement features of *fp*; *{ fd₁,fd₂...fdₖ }*: the set of decomposition features of *fp*;	$fp \leftrightarrow all\text{-}binding(fm_1,fm_2...fm_i)$, $multiple\text{-}binding(fm_1,fm_2...fm_i) \rightarrow fp$, $multiple\text{-}binding(fo_1,fo_2...fo_j) \rightarrow fp$, $fp \rightarrow multiple\text{-}binding(fd_1,fd_2...fd_k)$
fvp: a vp-feature; *{ fv₁,fv₂...fvₙ }*: the set of *Mutex-Group* specialized features of *fvp*;	$fvp \leftrightarrow single\text{-}binding(fv_1,fv_2...fv_n)$
fvp: a vp-feature; *{ fv₁,fv₂...fvₙ }*: the set of *None-Group* specialized features of *fvp*;	$fvp \leftrightarrow multiple\text{-}binding(fv_1,fv_2...fv_n)$

3.4 Atomic Feature Sets in *Tailoring* and *Binding* Actions

In above discussions, features are the basic units in tailoring and binding actions. However, considering those pre-/post-conditions of binding or unbinding features (see section 3.3), we can find that for any feature f, all its mandatory child features, its parent feature (if f is a mandatory feature) and f itself can be treated as a whole in tailoring and binding actions if the constraints implied by refinements are not broken. Thus, features that can be treated as a whole in tailoring and binding actions can be viewed as an atomic set, which is represented as atomic-set in this paper. More formally, the atomic-set containing feature f can be constructed by the following four rules:

1. Create an empty set *atomic-set*, put *f* into it.
2. If mandatory feature $g \in atomic\text{-}set$, and this feature' parent $g_p \notin atomic\text{-}set$, then put g_p into *atomic-set*.
3. If feature $g \in atomic\text{-}set$, feature g_c is a mandatory child of *g*, and $g_c \notin atomic\text{-}set$, then put g_c into *atomic-set*.
4. Repeat rules 2 and 3, until no feature in *atomic-set* satisfies the two rules.

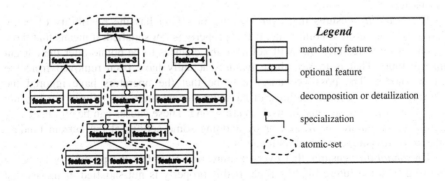

Fig. 7. Atomic-Sets in a Feature Tree

Based on the four rules, general algorithms to compute atomic-sets of feature models can be further developed. Figure 7 shows atomic-sets derived from a possible feature tree by following the atomic-set construction rules presented above.

Atomic-sets derived from a feature tree compose a partition of features in this feature tree. Any feature is only contained by one atomic-set.

The reason for using atomic-sets as the basic units in tailoring and binding is that the granularity of atomic-sets is often larger than that of features, and thus, tailoring or binding will become more efficient. The transition to using atomic sets as the basic units can be achieved by simply replacing features in a constraint with their corresponding atomic sets.

3.5 The *SUS* Verification Criteria

To evaluate whether the proper tailoring and/or binding actions have been taken in each binding time, we propose three properties (i.e. *Satisfiability*, *Usability* and *Suitability*) to verify feature models. We call them "the *SUS* verification criteria" in this paper.

Suppose $\{C_1, C_2, ..., C_n\}$ is the set of logic sentences capturing all constraints in a feature model and $UFSet^I$ denotes the set of all possible interpretations of the proposition symbols in *UFSet*. After tailoring and binding actions at each binding time, features in *UFSet* should satisfy the *SUS* verification criteria to ensure the rationality of those tailoring and binding actions.

>   **Satisfiability:**
> $\exists\, I \in UFSet^I, I \models \cap_{i=1,...,n} C_i$
>   **Usability:**
> $\forall\, f \in UFSet, \exists\, I \in UFSet^I, I \models (\cap_{i=1,...,n} C_i) \cap f$
>   **Suitability:**
> $\forall\, f \in UFSet, \exists\, I \in UFSet^I, I \models (\cap_{i=1,...,n} C_i) \cap (\neg f)$

The *Satisfiability* ensures that there is no inconsistency in tailoring and binding actions. If this property is not satisfied, constraints on features or those tailoring and binding actions of the current binding time should be reconsidered to eliminate inconsistencies.

The *Usability* ensures that every feature in *UFSet* has the possibility of being bound in some future binding time. If this property is not satisfied, it means that there are one or more features that will not have the chances to be bound after the current binding time. That is to say, these features actually have been removed from the feature model. The possible causes may be that the operators have ignored the tailoring actions on these features, or have done some improper tailoring or binding actions, or some constraints themselves are wrong. These causes can be eliminated by putting these features to *RFSet*, or by undoing some actions at the current binding time, or by revising constraint on features.

The *Suitability* ensures that every feature in *UFSet* has the possibility of being removed in some future binding time. If this property is not satisfied, it means that there are one or more features that will not have the chances to be removed after the current binding time. That is to say, these features actually have been bound. The possible causes may be that the operators have ignored the binding of these features, or have done some improper tailoring or binding actions, or some constraints themselves are wrong. These causes can be eliminated by putting these features to *BFSet*, or by undoing some actions of the current binding time, or by revising constraint on features.

4 Case Studies

We applied our method to two real feature models which we have found in the literature. The first one is the feature model of Lambda Feedback Control (LFC), which is presented in [10]. The second one is the feature model of Window Management Systems, which is presented in [1] as a case study of the FODA method. In these two case studies, we use the model checker SMV to automate the fifth step of feature model verification.

4.1 Verification of the Feature Model of Lambda Feedback Control (LFC)

Figure 8 depicts the feature model of LFC. Table 4 shows the 6 atomic sets in the feature model. In these atomic sets, only the atomic-set as_0 contains 4 features, while others contain only 1 feature.

After steps 2 and 3, we get the simplified constraints using atomic-sets as basic variables (see the SPEC section in Figure 9). In this case, the number of refinement imposed constraints decreases from 7 to 4 after step 3, and the number of constructor-imposed constraints is unchanged. Then, we put these constraints to SMV to check the three properties in the SUS verification criteria. Figure 9 shows the input files to SMV.

Table 4. Atomic-sets in the LFC Feature Model

Atomic-Set	Features Contained by Atomic-Set
as_0	*Lambda-Feedback-Control, First-Sensor-Feedback-Control, Main-Sensor-Feedback-Control, Continous-Feedback-Control-Main-Sensor*
as_1	*Two-State-Feedback-Control-First-Sensor*
as_2	*Continous-Feedback-Control-First-Sensor*
as_3	*Catalyst-Outcome-Feedback-Control*
as_4	*Middle-Sensor-Feedback-Control*
as_5	*Continous-Feedback-Control-Middle-Sensor*
as_6	*Natural-Frequency-Feedback-Control*

The result of this verification is that constraints in the feature model satisfy the *Satisfiability* and the *Suitability*, but as_3, as_5 violate the *Usability*. As we are not familiar with LFC domain, we do not know what the cause of these two violations is. However, as an experiment, we omit the two violations and further verify the feature model at the *construct-time*. At this *binding-time*, all *construct-time* binding (mandatory) features are partitioned to *BFSet*. Besides the two violations having been found, we further identify that as_4, as_6 violate the *Suitability* after these *construct-time* binding actions.

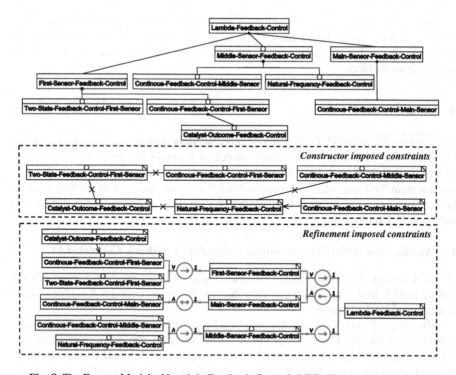

Fig. 8. The Feature Model of Lambda Feedback Control (LFC) (Recreated from [10])

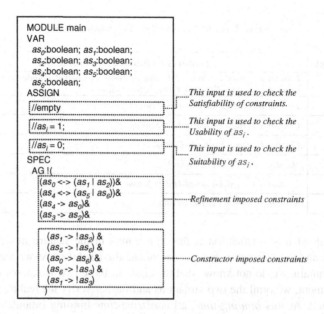

Fig. 9. Input Files to the Model Checker SMV

4.2 Verification of the Feature Model of Window Management Systems (WMS)

The feature model of WMS is relatively a large and complex one, which contains 117 features, and about 12 constructor-imposed constraints involving 33 features. The number of atomic-sets in this feature model is 93.

After the third step of feature model verification, constraints on features are transformed into constraints on atomic sets. Figure 10 shows constraints in the form of atomic sets. Although the number of possible variables in constraints has decreased form 117 (*features* as the variables) to 93 (*atomic-sets* as the variables), the number of constructor-imposed constraints does not decrease in this case. The reason for this is that each atomic set, which is involved in constructor-imposed constraints, contains only one feature. However, the number of refinement-imposed constraints does decrease, since there are 5 atomic-sets that contain more than one features, and refinement-imposed constraints on features in these atomic sets will be eliminated after using atomic sets as the variables.

Then we apply the *SUS* verification criteria to the feature model before and at the *construct-time* respectively, which is automated by using SMV. The result is that no constraint or feature in the feature model violates the *SUS* criteria at these two phases.

Refinement imposed constraints (part)   *Constructor imposed constraints*

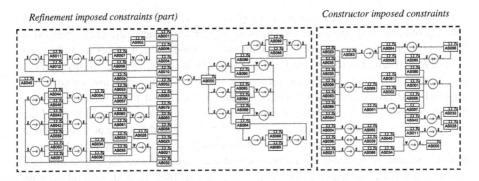

Fig. 10. Constraints in the Form of Atomic-Sets

5 Related Work

In [6], a first-order logic based variability validation method was proposed. In fact, this method only employs those propositional constructs of the first-order logic to capture constraints on features. The style of constraint representation adopted by this method is, to some extent, different from the conventional propositional logic. Thus, this style may not be directly parsed by those general-purpose model checkers. Moreover, this method does not consider the *binding-time* property of features, i.e. it does not distinguish between *bound* features and *undecided* features. Hence, this method may not apply well when some features in a feature model are in the undecided states.

[7] proposes the concept of "commonality of a feature", which is slightly different from the concept of atomic set in our approach. In most cases, the commonality of a feature can be constructed by following the construction rules of atomic-sets (not including the second rule, see section 3.4). Although the commonality of a feature also possesses the atomic property in tailoring or binding actions, its granularity is less than that of the *atomic-set* in most cases.

A discriminant-based tailoration method has been proposed by [8]. A discriminant corresponds to an optional feature in feature models. This method mainly focuses on refinement-imposed constraints and some simple constructor-imposed constraints. However, this method adapts a different way from our method to ensure that any application feature model will not violate these constraints. This method fully employs the tree structure of feature models and these pre-/post-conditions when binding or unbinding features, while our method transforms such knowledge into formal logic sentences. Our method further identifies the atomic feature sets in tailoring or binding actions, and translates constraints on features into constraints on atomic feature sets.

6 Conclusions

A propositional logic-based method is proposed for verification of feature models at different binding times in this paper. The most important characteristic of this method is that it integrates the logical verification with binding times, which makes it can be used to verify any partially customized feature models at any binding time. In this method, constraints on features, including refinement-imposed constraints and constructor-imposed constraints, are firstly formalized into propositional logic sentences. Then, three properties (i.e. *Satisfiability*, *Usability* and *Suitability*) are proposed to checking the consistency of constraints and rationality of tailoring and binding actions taken at each binding time. This method also employs atomic feature sets in tailoring or binding actions to decrease the complexity of constraints. Since all constraints in a feature model are formalized into logic sentences in this method, general-purpose model checkers can be easily used to automate the verification process.

We also applied our method to two real feature models, and some errors were detected in one of them. A phenomenon we have found in the two case studies is that, although using atomic sets can decrease the number of possible variables involved in constraints in the two case studies (one from 10 to 7, and the other from 117 to 93), the complexity of constructor-imposed constraints does not decrease. The reason is that each atomic set involved in constructor-imposed constraints in the two feature models accidentally contains only one feature. Hence, we still believe that replacing features with atomic sets in constraints can decrease the complexity of constraints in general.

Acknowledgements

This work is supported by the National Grand Fundamental Research 973 Program of China under Grant No. 2002CB31200003, the National Natural Science Foundation of China under Grant No. 60233010, 60125206, and the Research Fund for the Doctoral Program of Higher Education under Grant No. 20010001001.

The authors would like to thank Lu Zhang for his invaluable advice and help in polishing this paper.

References

1. Kyo C. Kang, Sholom G. Cohen, James A. Hess, William E. Novak, A. Spencer Peterson, "Feature-Oriented Domain Analysis Feasibility Study", SEI-90-TR-21, Software Engineering Institute, Carnegie Mellon University, Nov. 1990.
2. Kyo C. Kang, Sajoong Kim, Jaejoon Lee, Kijoo Kim, Euiseob Shin, Moonhang Huh, "FORM: A Feature-Oriented Reuse Method with Domain-Specific Architecture", Annals of Software Engineering, 5:143-168, September, 1998.
3. Martin L.Griss, John Favaro, Massimo d'Alessandro, "Integrating Feature Modeling with the RSEB", in Proceedings of Fifth International Conference on Software Reuse, pp.76-85, IEEE Computer Society, Canada, June 1998.
4. Gray Chastek, Patrick Donohoe, Kyo C. Kang, Steffen Thiel, "Product Line Analysis: A Practical Introduction", SEI-2001-TR-001, Software Engineering Institute, Carnegie Mellon University, 2001.
5. Even-André Karlsson (editor) "Software Reuse: A Holistic Approach", REBOOT Methodology Handbook, John Wiley & Sons, 1995.
6. Mike Mannion, "Using First-Order Logic for Product Line Model Validation", The Second Software Product Line Conference 2002, LNCS 2379, pp.176–187, August 2002.
7. Dániel Fey, Róbert Fajta, and András Boros, "Feature Modeling: A Meta-Model to Enhance Usability and Usefulness", The Second Software Product Line Conference 2002, LNCS 2379, pp.198–216, August 2002.
8. Mike Mannion, Barry Keepence, Hermann Kaindl, Joe Wheadon, "Reusing Single System Requirements from Application Family Requirements", in Proceedings of the International Conference on Software Engineering, pp.453-462, 1999.
9. Hafedh Mili, Fatma Mili, Ali Mili, "Reusing Software: Issues and Research Directions", IEEE TRANSACTIONS ON SOFTWARE ENGINEERING, VOL. 21, NO. 6, JUNE 1995.
10. Stefan Ferber, Jürgen Haag, Juha Savolainen, "Feature Interaction and Dependencies: Modeling Features for Reengineering a Legacy Product Line", The Second Software Product Line Conference 2002, LNCS 2379, pp.235–256, August 2002.
11. SMV, "Model Checking @CMU, The SMV System", http://www-2.cs.cmu.edu/~modelcheck/smv.html.
12. Hong Mei, Wei Zhang, Fang Gu, "A Feature Oriented Approach to Modeling and Reusing Requirements of Software Product Lines", The 27th Annual International Computer Software and Applications Conference, pp.250-255, November, 2003.
13. D. Amyot, L. Charfi, N. Gorse, T. Gray, L. Logrippo, J. Sincennes, B. Stepien, T. Ware, "Feature Description and Feature Interaction Analysis with Use Case Maps and LOTOS", FIW'00, Glasgow, May, 2000.
14. Kwanwoo Lee, Kay C. Kang, Jaejoon Lee, "Concepts and Guidelines of Feature Modeling for Product Line Software Engineering", ICSR-7, pp. 62-77, 2002.
15. P. Zave, "Feature interactions and formal specifications in telecommunications", IEEE Computer, 26(8):20-29, August, 1993.

16. Martin L. Griss, "Implementing Product-Line Features with Component Reuse", in Proceedings of Sixth International Conference on Software Reuse, pp. 137–152, LNCS 1844,Vienna, June, 2000.
17. C. Reid Turner, Alfonso Fuggetta, Luigi Lavazza, Alexander L.Wolf, "A Conceptual Basis for Feature Engineering", Journal of Systems and Software, VOL. 49, NO. 1, December 1999.
18. Karl E.Wiegers, "Software Requirements", Microsoft Press, 1999.
19. Alok Mehta, George T. Heineman, "Evolving Legacy System Features into Fine-Grained Components", Proceedings of the 24th international conference on Software engineering, Orlando, Florida, 2002.
20. Kyo C. Kang, Kwanwoo Lee, Jaejoon Lee, Sajoong Kim, "Feature Oriented Product Line Software Engineering: Principles and Guidelines". A chapter in "Domain Oriented Systems Development – Practices and Perspectives", UK, Gordon Breach Science Publishers, 2002.
21. Stefan Ferber, Jürgen Haag, Juha Savolainen, "Feature Interaction and Dependencies: Modeling Features for Reengineering a Legacy Product Line", The Second Software Product Line Conference 2002, LNCS 2379, pp.235–256, August 2002.
22. Unified Modeling Language (UML), Version 1.5, http://www.omg.org/technology/documents/formal/uml.htm.

Deriving Probabilistic Semantics
Via the 'Weakest Completion'

He Jifeng[1,*,**], Carroll Morgan[2], and Annabelle McIver[3]

[1] International Institute for Software Technology, United Nations University, Macau
[2] Department of Computer Science and Engineering,
The University of New South Wales, Sydney, Australia
[3] Department of Computing, Macquarie University, Sydney, Australia

1 Introduction

A theory of programming is intended to aid the construction of programs that meet their specifications; for such a theory to be useful it should capture (only) the essential aspects of the program's behaviour, that is only those aspects which one wishes to observe. And it should do so in a mathematically elegant – hence tractable – way.

For conventional imperative sequential programs there are these days two principal theories: the relational[1] and the predicate transformer. Because they have been reasonably successful, each has been used many times as a starting point for extensions: well-known examples include treating *timing* and allowing *concurrency*. In each case the extension somehow elaborates the model on which it is based.

In this paper we investigate two aspects of such semantic extensions, one general and one specific. The specific is that we concentrate on adding *probabilistic* behaviour to our programs. The more important general point however is to extend the theories in some sense "automatically" as far as possible. That is, we wish to make only a few explicit assumptions and then to "generate" the rest by following principles. We illustrate such principles with two case studies: the relational (Sec. 3) and predicate-transformer (Sec. 4) approaches to imperative programming.

There are two stages. In the first we extend the "base type" of the model – the states, for relational, and the predicates for transformers – by adding probabilistic information, and as part of that we give an explicit link between the original type and its probabilistic extension (*i.e.* either an injection from the former to the latter, or a retraction in the opposite direction). From that link between the base and the extended type we then attempt to induce automatically an embedding of *programs* over the base type: the technique is to consider the "weakest completion" of a sub-commuting diagram.

---

* On leave from the SEI of East China Normal University.
** Partly supported by Research Grant 02104 of MoE and 973 project 2002CB312001 of MoST of China.
[1] We take relational to include for example the "programs are predicates" [9, 10] view.

J. Davies et al. (Eds.): ICFEM 2004, LNCS 3308, pp. 131–145, 2004.

The second stage is to examine the image, in the extended space of programs, of the original (probability-free) model and to determine what algebraic characteristics define it. Such characteristics, often called "healthiness conditions", both reflect the behaviour of "real" programs and allow us to formulate and prove further algebraic laws that are of practical use in program derivation.

In Sec. 3 we use the weakest completion to derive a semantic definition of a probabilistic programming language from the relational semantics [12, 13] of the "standard", that is non-probabilistic, guarded command language; we relate computations of probabilistic programs to computations of imperative programs. In Sec. 4 we show how to use the weakest completion again, this time to generate probabilistic transformer semantics, our second example, for which our staring point is standard predicate-transformer semantics [3].

2   Probabilistic Program Syntax

The language examined in this paper extends the guarded command language [3] by including the probabilistic choice operator $P \,_r\oplus Q$ which chooses between programs P and Q with probabilities r and $1-r$ respectively. The abstract syntax of the programming language is given below.

$$
\begin{aligned}
P ::= \ &\bot & &\text{primitive aborting program} \\
&\mathit{II} & &\text{'skip' program} \\
&x := e & &\text{assignment} \\
&P \lhd b \rhd P & &\text{conditional} \\
&P \sqcap P & &\text{demonic choice} \\
&P \,_r\oplus P & &\text{probabilistic choice} \\
&P; P & &\text{sequential composition} \\
&(\mu X \bullet P(X)) & &\text{recursion}
\end{aligned}
$$

For ease of exposition we have included an explicit demonic choice operator $\sqcap$ and used a conventional 'if-then-else' conditional: that gives a convenient separation of the two concepts, combined in Dijkstra's general **if** $\cdots$ **fi**.

3   Relational Semantics

Our first example uses weakest completion to extend a relational semantics for the standard language (Sec. 2 without $_r\oplus$) to a semantics for the probabilistic language (Sec. 2 with its $_r\oplus$). We use Hoare's 'design' notation [12] to describe relations.

3.1   Standard Semantics

A standard sequential program starts its execution in an initial state, and terminates (if it ever does) in one of a set of final states. We give the relational meaning of a program by a pair of predicates p, R, *design*, with this syntax and interpretation:

$$p(s) \vdash R(s, s') \quad =_{\mathrm{df}} \quad (ok \wedge p) \Rightarrow (ok' \wedge R)$$

where

- ok records the observation that the program has been properly started,
- ok' records the observation that the program has terminated normally (without 'error messages'), and
- s and s' respectively denote the initial and final states of the program, mappings from the set of program variables to their values.

Thus if the program starts in an initial state satisfying the *precondition* p, it will terminate in a final state satisfying the *postcondition* R.

The effect of the 'design' notation $\cdots \vdash \cdots$ is thus to adjoin a Boolean ok to the state space, for the description of proper termination: if the previous command has terminated (ok in the antecedent) and the precondition p holds of the passed-on state, then this command will establish relation R between s and s', and will itself terminate too (ok' in the consequent).

The approach used in the refinement calculus and in VDM [12, 13, 21] for example gives semantics to programs by associating them with designs according to this scheme:

$$\bot =_{\mathrm{df}} \mathbf{false} \vdash \mathbf{true}$$

$$II =_{\mathrm{df}} \mathbf{true} \vdash (s' = s)$$

$$x := e =_{\mathrm{df}} \mathbf{true} \vdash (s' = s[e/x])$$

$$P \sqcap Q =_{\mathrm{df}} P \vee Q$$

$$P \lhd b \rhd Q =_{\mathrm{df}} (b \wedge P) \vee (\neg b \wedge Q)$$

$$P; Q =_{\mathrm{df}} P \circ Q$$

$$(\mu X \bullet P(X)) =_{\mathrm{df}} \bigvee \{Q \mid \forall ok, s, ok', s' \bullet (Q \Rightarrow P(Q))\}$$

where $\circ$ stands for the (relational) composition of designs defined

$$P \circ Q =_{\mathrm{df}} \exists \hat{ok}, \hat{s} \bullet P(\hat{ok}, \hat{s}/ok', s') \wedge Q(\hat{ok}, \hat{s}/ok, s) ,$$

and $s[e/x]$ denotes the new state obtained by updating s at x with e in the usual way.

We mention here some logical properties of designs that will be useful in later calculations; they are proved elsewhere [12].

Theorem 3.1

1. $(p0 \vdash R0) \vee (p1 \vdash R1) \quad = \quad (p0 \wedge p1) \vdash (R0 \vee R1)$
2. $(p0 \vdash R0) \wedge (p1 \vdash R1) \quad = \quad (p0 \vee p1) \vdash (p0 \Rightarrow R0) \wedge (p1 \Rightarrow R1)$
3. $(p0 \vdash R0) \circ (p1 \vdash R1) \quad = \quad (p0 \wedge \neg(R0 \circ \neg p1)) \vdash (R0 \circ R1)$
4. $(p0 \vdash R0) \lhd b \rhd (p1 \vdash R1) \quad = \quad (p0 \lhd b \rhd p1) \vdash (R0 \lhd b \rhd R1)$

$\square$

A program *refines* another if it terminates more often and behaves less non-deterministically than the other. We write $\sqsubseteq$ for "is refined by"; for predicates[2] P and Q it is defined by

$$P \sqsubseteq Q \quad =_{\text{df}} \quad \forall \, s, s', ok, ok' \bullet (Q \Rightarrow P) \,.$$

Theorem 3.2 (Top and Bottom Designs). For all designs D,

$$\bot \;=\; (\text{false} \vdash \text{true}) \;\sqsubseteq\; D \;\sqsubseteq\; (\text{true} \vdash \text{false}) \;=\; \top \,.$$

$\square$

3.2   Probabilistic Semantics

We extend our standard states to probabilistic states by replacing the final state s' with a final *distribution* which we call *prob'*. Maintaining the structure of designs in other respects, we say that a probabilistic program P can be identified as a design with *ok, s, ok'* and *prob'* as free variables.

Definition 3.3 (Probabilistic Distributions and Designs). Let S be a state space. The set of distributions over S is the set of total functions from S into the closed interval of reals $[0, 1]$,

$$PROB \quad =_{\text{df}} \quad S \to [0, 1]$$

We insist further that for any member *prob* of *PROB* the probabilities must sum to 1:

$$\Sigma_{s \in S} \; prob(s) \;=\; 1 \,.$$

For any subset X of S we define

$$prob(X) \quad =_{\text{df}} \quad \Sigma_{s \in X} \, prob(s) \,.$$

We use $\mathcal{P}$ to denote the set of *probabilistic designs* $p(s) \vdash R(s, prob')$.

We begin our extension by postulating a retraction from probabilistic to standard states; from that (below) we will induce an embedding of programs (designs).

The difference between the standard and the probabilistic semantics is that the former tells us which final states are or are not possible, whereas the latter tells us the probability with which they may occur. Thus to relate the latter to the former we take the view that a final state is possible iff it has positive probability of occurrence:

---

[2] Although strictly speaking we are concerned only with the predicates defined in our design notation, this definition applies for all predicates provided the right-hand universal quantification is understood to be over all free variables. We use that in Definition 3.5 below.

Definition 3.4 (Retraction of States). The design ρ relates a probabilistic state *prob* to a set of standard states s' according to the definition

$$\rho(ok, prob, ok', s') \quad =_{\mathrm{df}} \quad \mathbf{true} \vdash prob(s') > 0 .$$

Note that we have expressed the retraction — though not properly a computation — in the design notation as well, complete with its implicit *ok* variables; that allows us to use design composition in the construction of our sub-commuting diagram below, from which we extract the embedding of designs.

Now, based on our injection ρ, we seek an embedding of designs:

Definition 3.5 (Embedding of Programs). For any standard design D, we identify its embedding $\mathcal{K}(D)$, which will be a probabilistic design, as the *weakest solution* in X of the equation

$$X \circ \rho \;=\; D .$$

Thus define

$$\mathcal{K}(D) \;=_{\mathrm{df}}\; D/\rho ,$$

where the notation D/ρ represents the *weakest pre-specification*[11] of D through ρ:

$$(X \circ \rho) \sqsupseteq D \qquad \mathbf{iff} \qquad X \sqsupseteq D/\rho, \qquad \text{for all predicates } X .$$

The following theorem shows that $\mathcal{K}(D)$ is indeed a probabilistic design.

Theorem 3.6.

$$\mathcal{K}(p(s) \vdash R(s, s')) \;=\; p(s) \vdash (prob'(R) = 1) ,$$

where $prob'(R)$ abbreviates $prob'(\{t \mid R(s, t)\})$.

Proof:

$$\mathcal{K}(p \vdash R)$$
$$= \quad p(s) \vdash (R/(prob(s') > 0)) \qquad\qquad (p \vdash R)/(\mathbf{true} \vdash Q) = p \vdash (R/Q)$$

$$= \qquad\qquad\qquad\qquad X/(prob(s') > 0 = \neg(\neg X \circ (prob(s') > 0))$$
$$p(s) \vdash prob'(\{t \mid R(s, t)\}) = 1 .$$

$\square$

Corollary 3.7 (Inverse of $\mathcal{K}$). For all designs D we have

$$\mathcal{K}(D) \circ \rho \;=\; D .$$

Proof: From Theorems 3.1(3) and 3.6. $\square$

3.3   Preservation of Program Structure

We now examine the distribution of $\mathcal{K}$ through the program constructors of our language. First we note the effect of $\mathcal{K}$ on primitive designs.

Theorem 3.8 (Primitive Probabilistic Designs).

1. $\mathcal{K}(\bot) \;=\; \bot.$
2. $\mathcal{K}(x := e) \;=\; \textbf{true} \vdash prob'(s[e/x]) = 1.$

$\square$

Now we show that $\mathcal{K}$ distributes through conditional choice.

Theorem 3.9 (Conditional Choice).

$$\mathcal{K}(D0 \lhd b \rhd D1) \;=\; \mathcal{K}(D0) \lhd b \rhd \mathcal{K}(D1) \,.$$

Proof: From Theorems 3.1(4) and 3.6. $\square$

We now use $\mathcal{K}$ to discover the appropriate definition for demonic choice between probabilistic designs.

Theorem 3.10 (Demonic Choice).

$$\mathcal{K}(D0 \sqcap D1) \;=\; \mathcal{K}(D0) \vee \mathcal{K}(D1) \vee \bigvee_{0 < r < 1} (\mathcal{K}(D0) \|_{M_r} \mathcal{K}(D1)) \,,$$

where M_r is a 'coupling predicate' in the style of [12] used in this case as

$$(p0 \vdash R0) \|_{M_r} (p1 \vdash R1)$$
$$=_{\mathrm{df}} ((p0 \wedge p1) \vdash (R0(s, 0.prob') \wedge R1(s, 1.prob'))) \circ M_r$$

and $M_r \;=_{\mathrm{df}} \; \textbf{true} \vdash prob' = r \times 0.prob + (1 - r) \times 1.prob.$

Proof: Let $D0 = p0 \vdash R0$ and $D1 = p1 \vdash R1$, then proceed

RHS

$=$ Def. of $\|_{M_r}$ and Theorem 3.1(3)

$\quad p0 \vdash prob'(R0) = 1$
$\vee\ (p1 \vdash prob'(R1) = 1)$
$\vee\ \ \bigvee_{0 < r < 1}(p0 \wedge p1)$
$\qquad \vdash \exists 0.prob, 1.prob \bullet 0.prob(R0) = 1$
$\qquad\qquad\qquad \wedge\ 1.prob(R1) = 1$
$\qquad\qquad\qquad \wedge\ prob' = r \times 0.prob + (1 - r) \times 1.prob$

$\sqsupseteq$ $(r \times 0.prob + (1 - r) \times 1.prob)(R0 \vee R1) = 1$
$\quad (p0 \vdash prob'(R0 \vee R1) = 1$
$\vee\ (p1 \vdash prob'(R0 \vee R1) = 1)$
$\vee\ (p0 \wedge p1) \vdash prob'(R0 \vee R1) = 1$

$=$ $(p0 \wedge p1) \vdash prob'(R0 \vee R1) = 1$ Theorem 3.1(1)

$=$ $\mathcal{K}((p0 \wedge p1) \vdash (R0 \vee R1))$ Theorem 3.6

$=$ LHS Theorem 3.1(1)

$=$ Theorem 3.6 and case analysis

$$(p0 \wedge p1) \vdash \quad prob'(R0) = 1 \ \vee \ prob'(R1) = 1$$
$$\vee \ \exists \alpha, \beta > 0 \bullet prob'(R0 \vee R1) = 1$$
$$\wedge \ prob'(R0 \wedge \neg R1) = \alpha$$
$$\wedge \ prob'(R1 \wedge \neg R0) = \beta$$

$\sqsupseteq$
$$\begin{cases} r = \alpha/(\alpha + \beta) \\ 0.prob(R0 \wedge \neg R1) = \alpha + \beta \\ 0.prob(R0 \wedge R1) = 1 - (\alpha + \beta) \\ 1.prob(R1 \wedge \neg R0) = \alpha + \beta \\ 1.prob(R0 \wedge R1) = 1 - (\alpha + \beta) \end{cases}$$

$$(p0 \wedge p1) \vdash prob'(R0) = 1$$
$$\vee \ prob'(R1) = 1$$
$$\vee \ \exists r \in (0, 1), 0.prob, 1.prob \bullet$$
$$0.prob(R0) = 1 \wedge$$
$$1.prob(R1) = 1 \wedge$$
$$prob' = r \times 0.prob + (1 - r) \times 1.prob$$

$=$ RHS Theorem 3.1(1) and Def. $\|_{M_r}$

For sequential composition we follow the Kleisli-triple approach to semantics of programming languages [20], introducing a function $\uparrow$ to deal with sequential composition, which maps a probabilistic design taking (ok, s) to $(ok', prob')$ to a 'lifted' design taking $(ok, prob)$ to $(ok', prob')$.

Definition 3.11 (Kleisli Lifting).

$$\uparrow (p \vdash R)$$
$$=_{df} \quad (prob(p) = 1)$$
$$\vdash \ \exists Q \in (S \to PROB) \bullet$$
$$\forall s \bullet prob(s) > 0 \Rightarrow R(s, Q(s)) \wedge prob' = \Sigma_{t \in S}(prob(t) \times Q(t))$$

From the facts that $prob \in PROB$ and that for all $t \in S$ we have $Q(t) \in PROB$ we conclude that

$$\Sigma_{t \in S} prob(t) \times G(t) \ \in PROB .$$

Theorem 3.12 (Sequential Composition).

$$\mathcal{K}(D0; D1) \ = \ \mathcal{K}(D0) \circ \uparrow \mathcal{K}(D1)$$

Proof:

RHS

$=$ Theorem 3.6

$$p0(s) \vdash prob'(\{t \mid R0(s,t)\}) = 1$$
$$\circ \; prob(p1) = 1 \vdash$$
$$\exists Q \bullet \forall t \bullet prob(t) > 0 \Rightarrow \quad Q(t)(\{s' \mid R1(t,s')\}) = 1$$
$$\wedge \; prob' = \Sigma_t(prob(t) \times Q(t)))$$

$=$ Theorem 3.1(3)

$$p0(s) \wedge \neg(prob'(\{t \mid R0(s,t)\}) = 1 \circ prob(p1) < 1)$$
$$\vdash \exists \rho \bullet \quad \rho(\{t \mid R0(s,t)\}) = 1$$
$$\wedge \; prob' = \Sigma_s\{\rho(t) \times Q(t) \mid \rho(t) > 0$$
$$\wedge \; Q(t)(\{s' \mid R1(t,s')\}) = 1\}$$

$\Rightarrow$ $prob'(R0 \circ R1) = \Sigma_t\{\rho(t) * Q(t)(\{s' \mid R1(t,s')\}) \mid R0(s,t) \wedge \rho(t) > 0$

$$p0(s) \wedge \neg(R0 \circ p1) \; \vdash \; prob'(R0 \circ R1) = 1$$

$=$ LHS Theorems 3.1(3) and 3.6

$\Rightarrow$ $\begin{cases} f(u,v) =_{df} prob'(v)/(\#\{t \mid R0(s,t) \wedge R1(t,v)\}) \; R0(s,u) \wedge R1(u,v) \; 0 \\ \rho(u) =_{df} \Sigma_v f(u,v) \\ Q(u)(v) =_{df} f(u,v)/\rho(u) \text{ if } \rho(u) > 0 \end{cases}$

$$p0(s) \wedge \neg(R0 \circ \neg p1)$$
$$\vdash \exists \rho \bullet \rho(\{t \mid R0(s,t)\}) = 1 \wedge$$
$$prob' = \Sigma_s\{\rho(t) * \times Q(t) \mid \rho(t) > 0 \wedge Q(t)(\{s' \mid R1(t,s')\}) = 1\}$$

$=$ RHS .

□

Theorem 3.13 (New Unit).

1. $\uparrow \mathcal{K}(II) \;\;=\;\; \mathbf{true} \vdash (prob' = prob)$
2. $\mathcal{K}(II) \circ \uparrow P \;\;=\;\; P$

□

Following Theorems 3.6 to 3.12 we conclude by adopting the following definition for the probabilistic programming language semantics.

Definition 3.14 (Probabilistic Programs).

$$\perp =_{df} \mathcal{K}(\mathbf{true})$$
$$II =_{df} \mathcal{K}(\mathbf{true} \vdash (s' = s))$$
$$x := e =_{df} \mathcal{K}(\mathbf{true} \vdash (s' = s[e/x]))$$

$$P \lhd b \rhd Q =_{df} (b \wedge P) \vee (\neg b \wedge Q)$$
$$P \sqcap Q =_{df} P \vee Q \vee \bigvee_{0<r<1} (P\|_{M_r}Q)$$
$$P_r \oplus Q =_{df} P\|_{M_r}Q, \qquad \text{when } 0 < r < 1$$
$$P_1 \oplus Q =_{df} P$$
$$P_0 \oplus Q =_{df} Q$$
$$P; Q =_{df} P \circ \uparrow Q$$
$$(\mu X \bullet P(X)) =_{df} \bigvee \{Q \mid Q \sqsupseteq P(Q)\}$$

4 Predicate-Transformer Semantics

4.1 Introduction: Embedding Predicates

In Sec. 3 it was shown that a postulated retraction into the standard state space from the probabilistic state space could, with a small number of reasonable assumptions, be used to induce an embedding of standard programs into a space of probabilistic programs. The principal tool was the 'weakest completion' of a sub-commuting diagram, for which we used the weakest pre- and post-specifications.

In this section we apply the weakest completion to probabilistic transformer (as opposed to relational) semantics, for which our starting point is standard predicate-transformer semantics [3].

As before, we have a standard state space S; and for standard predicate transformer semantics we are interested in predicates over S, which we will take to be members of the powerset $\mathbb{P}S$. Given a predicate $P \subseteq S$ and a state s we can say with certainty whether P holds ($s \in P$) or does not hold ($s \notin P$) at s.

In contrast, a 'probabilistic predicate' A holds at s only with some probability: thus the type of A should be $S \to [0,1]$, which we write $\mathbb{E}S$. (Note that members of $\mathbb{E}S$ are not distributions over S.)

For example, let S be the three-element state space $\{-1, 0, 1\}$ and consider this probabilistic predicate in $\mathbb{E}S$ over the initial state of a given program:

executing the program

$$s := -s \quad _{1/3}\oplus \quad s := +s$$

will establish the postcondition $s \geq 0$.

In (initial) states $-1, 0, 1$ that probabilistic predicate has value $1/3, 1, 2/3$ respectively. (Note that those values do not sum to 1.)

Standard predicates in $\mathbb{P}S$ are injected into $\mathbb{E}S$ simply by converting them to characteristic functions: writing P^* for that injection of P, we note that P holds at s if the probability that P^* holds at s is 1, and that P does not hold at s if the probability that P^* holds at s is 0.

4.2   Embedding Programs

Based on our injection $()^*$ of predicates, we now seek an embedding of programs: for standard transformer t in $\mathbb{P}S \to \mathbb{P}S$ we want a definition of its embedding t^*, which will be a probabilistic predicate transformer in $\mathbb{E}S \to \mathbb{E}S$. For that we use the techniques of Sec. 3.

First we note that the injection of programs should be related to the injection of predicates by

$$t^*(P^*) \quad = \quad t(P)^* \, , \tag{1}$$

since it should not matter whether we analyse standard programs in their 'native' standard space or in the extended probabilistic space. That tells us immediately the action t^* has on *standard elements* of $\mathbb{E}S$, those that are purely $\{0,1\}$-valued (equivalently are P^* for some P).

More challenging is to deduce reasonable behaviour for t^* on *proper* elements of $\mathbb{E}S$, those that are not standard. Take for example the program t to be $s := -s$, acting (as before) over the space $S = \{-1, 0, 1\}$. From (1) we know

$$t^* \begin{pmatrix} -1 \rightsquigarrow 0 \\ 0 \rightsquigarrow 0 \\ 1 \rightsquigarrow 1 \end{pmatrix} \quad = \quad \begin{pmatrix} -1 \rightsquigarrow 1 \\ 0 \rightsquigarrow 0 \\ 1 \rightsquigarrow 0 \end{pmatrix} ;$$

But we do not know the value of say

$$t^* \begin{pmatrix} -1 \rightsquigarrow 1/2 \\ 0 \rightsquigarrow 0 \\ 1 \rightsquigarrow 1 \end{pmatrix} .$$

Applying the technique of Sec. 3 directly we would choose t^* to be the least transformer satisfying (1), suggesting the result of applying it to the above should be

$$\begin{pmatrix} -1 \rightsquigarrow 0 \\ 0 \rightsquigarrow 0 \\ 1 \rightsquigarrow 0 \end{pmatrix} ,$$

But that 'brute force' technique of taking all proper arguments of t^* to the everywhere-0 expectation is unlikely to be useful: for example we would not even have that t^* was monotonic in general.

We turn therefore to 'healthiness conditions' on $\mathbb{E}S \to \mathbb{E}S$, making explicit which conditions — like monotonicity — we will impose.

4.3   Healthiness Conditions

In the minimalist spirit we impose only one principal condition on the probabilistic transformers: continuity. For any u in $\mathbb{E}S \to \mathbb{E}S$ and any directed subset $\mathcal{A}$ of $\mathbb{E}S$ we require

$$t(\sqcup \mathcal{A}) \quad = \quad \sqcup \{t(A) \mid A \in \mathcal{A}\} \, , \tag{2}$$

where the order $\leq$ over which $\sqcup$ is taken is just the normal $\leq$ relation over $[0, 1]$ extended pointwise to $\mathbb{E}S$. (Note that it acts as the injection of implication.)

From (2) we extract two more-specialised conditions: monotonicity, and 'scaling'. Monotonicity follows in the usual way from continuity: and as it is $\leq$-monotonicity, it agrees with the usual $\Rightarrow$-monotonicity of standard transformers when restricted to their embeddings.

To 'discover' scaling we apply continuity to a c-indexed subset $\mathcal{A}$ of $\mathbb{E}S$, with c varying over reals in $[0, 1]$: for arbitrary fixed A in $\mathbb{E}\mathcal{A}$ and state s we must have that

$$t(c \times A)(s)$$

varies smoothly, passing through each value between $0 = t(0)(s) = t(0 \times A)(s)$ and $t(A)(s)$, as c itself is varied from 0 to 1. The simplest hypothesis is to suppose that the multiplication by c distributes directly, which is the property we call *scaling*:

for all c in $[0, 1]$, probabilistic predicate A in $\mathbb{E}S$ and transformer u in $\mathbb{E}S \to \mathbb{E}S$ we have

$$u(c \times A) \quad = \quad c \times u(A) \,. \tag{3}$$

4.4   Completing the Embedding

We now define t^*, for t in $\mathbb{P}S \to \mathbb{P}S$, to be the least monotonic and scaling transformer in $\mathbb{E}S \to \mathbb{E}S$ that satisfies (1). (It will turn out as a consequence that t^* is continuous as well, so satisfying (2).) This section is devoted to exhibiting a constructive definition of t^*.

Lemma 4.1. Let t be a predicate transformer in $\mathbb{P}S \to \mathbb{P}S$. Then for any expectation A we have

$$t^*(A) \quad = \quad \sqcup_{P \in \mathbb{P}S} (\sqcap_P A) \times t(P)^* \,,$$

where $\sqcap_P A$ denotes the infimum of A over the subset P of S.

Proof: Clearly the right-hand side defines a transformer that is monotonic and scaling (in A); to see that it satisfies (1) we take A to be P^* (renaming the bound P to P'), and reason

$$
\begin{aligned}
& \sqcup_{P' \in \mathbb{P}S} (\sqcap_{P'} P^*) \times t(P')^* \\
= \quad & \sqcup_{P' \in \mathbb{P}P} (\sqcap_{P'} P^*) \times t(P')^* && \text{if } P' \not\subseteq P \text{ then } \sqcap_{P'} P^* = 0 \\
= \quad & \sqcup_{P' \in \mathbb{P}P} t(P')^* && \text{if } P' \subseteq P \text{ then } \sqcap_{P'} P^* = 1 \\
= \quad & t(P)^* \,. && \text{monotonicity of } t
\end{aligned}
$$

Now consider any (other) u in $\mathbb{E}S \to \mathbb{E}S$ satisfying the three conditions; we have

$$
\begin{aligned}
& u(A) \\
\geq && u \text{ monotonic and scaling}
\end{aligned}
$$

$$\sqcup\{c \times u(P^*) \mid c \in [0,1]; P \in \mathbb{P}S; c \times P^* \le A\}$$

$$
\begin{aligned}
=\quad & \sqcup\{c \times t(P)^* \mid c \times P^* \le A\} && \text{Property (1)} \\
=\quad & \sqcup\{c \times t(P)^* \mid c \le \sqcap_P A\} && \text{rewrite condition} \\
=\quad & \sqcup\{(\sqcap_P A) \times t(P)^* \mid P \in \mathbb{P}S\} && c \times t(P)^* \text{ is monotonic in } c \\
=\quad & \sqcup_{P \in \mathbb{P}S} (\sqcap_P A) \times t(P)^* \;,
\end{aligned}
$$

which shows the right-hand side indeed satisfies the definition of t^*.

As remarked above, we should have t^* continuous if t itself is. Take directed set $\mathcal{A}$ of expectations, let $\mathbb{F}S$ denote the finite subsets of S, and reason

$$
\begin{aligned}
& t^*(\sqcup\mathcal{A}) \\
=\quad & \sqcup_{P \in \mathbb{P}S} (\sqcap_P(\sqcup\mathcal{A})) \times t(P)^* && \text{Lem. 4.1} \\
\le\quad & \sqcup_{P \in \mathbb{F}S} (\sqcap_P(\sqcup\mathcal{A})) \times t(P)^* && t \text{ continuous} \\
=\quad & \sqcup_{P \in \mathbb{F}S; A \in \mathcal{A}} (\sqcap_P A) \times t(P)^* && P \text{ finite, } \mathcal{A} \text{ directed} \\
\le\quad & \sqcup_{A \in \mathcal{A}} \sqcup_{P \in \mathbb{P}S} (\sqcap_P A) \times t(P)^* && \mathbb{F}S \subseteq \mathbb{P}S \\
=\quad & \sqcup_{A \in \mathcal{A}} t^*(A) \;, && \text{Lem. 4.1}
\end{aligned}
$$

with the opposite inequality immediate from monotonicity of t^*.

4.5   Program Structure Is Preserved

The previous section obtained the main result, that an embedded t^* can be induced from the embedding of predicates. Here we verify the technical details of the embedding, in particular (as in Sec. 3.3 earlier) investigating the effect on the elementary program structures (Lem. 4.4 below); for convenience we give a technical lemma that characterises ()*-images.

Definition 4.2. A transformer u in $\mathbb{E}S \to \mathbb{E}S$ is said to be *semi-linear* if for all c, c' in $[0,1]$ and A in $\mathbb{E}S$ we have

$$u(c \times A \ominus \underline{c'}) \quad=\quad c \times u(A) \ominus \underline{c'}\;,$$

where *truncated subtraction* $a \ominus b$ is defined $(a - b) \sqcup 0$ with lowest syntactic precedence, and $\underline{c'}$ is the constant function in $\mathbb{E}S$ taking the value c' everywhere.   □

Lemma 4.3. A continuous transformer u in $\mathbb{E}S \to \mathbb{E}S$ is semi-linear iff it is the image t^* of some standard transformer in $\mathbb{P}S \to \mathbb{P}S$.

Proof: For *if* note that Lem. 4.1 allows $t^*(A)(s)$ to be written

$$(\sqcup P \mid s \in t(P) \bullet \sqcap_P A)\;,$$

and both $(c \times)$ and $(\ominus \underline{c'})$ distribute through $\sqcap_P$ and $\sqcup$. For *only if* the proof is given elsewhere [23].

We now deal with the elementary program structures.

Lemma 4.4. The following structure-preservation laws hold for program embedding.

1. $\perp$ is the least program: $\perp^*(A) = \underline{0}$.
2. Assignment acts as composition, in the usual way: $(x := e)^*(A) = A \circ (\lambda s \bullet s[e/x])$.
3. For state-to-Boolean conditional B we have the usual $(t_1 \lhd B \rhd t_2)^* = t_1^* \lhd B \rhd t_2^*$.
4. Demonic choice, acting as conjunction for standard transformers, becomes *minimum* for probabilistic transformers:

$$(t_1 \square t_2)^*(A) = t_1^*(A) \sqcap t_2^*(A) \; ;$$

5. Sequential composition remains composition of transformers:

$$(t_1 ; t_2)^* = t_1^* ; t_2^* \; .$$

Proof: Properties 1 and 3 come directly from Lem. 4.1. For Property 2 we argue

$$
\begin{array}{lll}
& (x := e)^*(A)(s) & \\
= & \sqcup_{P \in \mathbb{PS}} (\sqcap_P A) \times ((x := e)(P))^*(s) & \text{Lem. 4.1} \\
= & \sqcup_{P \in \mathbb{PS}} (\sqcap_P A) \times P^*(s[x/e]) & s \in (x := e)(P) \text{ iff } s[e/x] \in P \\
= & \sqcup_{P \ni s[x/e]} \sqcap_P A & P^*(s[x/e]) \text{ is 0 otherwise} \\
= & A(s[x/e]) \; . &
\end{array}
$$

Properties 4 and 5 require Lem. 4.3. For the first, we have that t_1^* and t_2^* are semi-linear (Lem. 4.3 *if*); and then it is easy to check that semi-linearity is preserved by $\sqcap$. Thus $t_1^*(A) \sqcap t_2^*(A)$ is semi-linear in A, and so for all A equals $t^*(A)$ for some standard t (Lem. 4.3 *only if*). But since the two sides of Property 4 agree on standard arguments, the two standard transformers of which they are images, that is $t_1 \square t_2$ (*lhs*) and t (*rhs*), must themselves agree on all (standard) arguments. Hence they are equal.

For Property 5 the argument is similar, relying this time on preservation of semi-linearity by composition.

5   Conclusion

Choosing the 'right' semantic extension can be a tricky business, to some extent a lucky guess.[3] Here we have isolated a principle that can reduce the guesswork.

In our two examples (Sections 3, 4) we postulated an extension of the 'base' type to include the desired new information — in this case probability. Although the base types differ — states on the one hand, and predicates (sets of states)

---

[3] Consider for example the great variety of bisimulations in demonic process algebras, each one (via the quotient) inducing a slightly different semantic model.

on the other — the subsequent procedure was broadly the same[4] in each case: to induce a corresponding embedding of programs, take the weakest completion of a certain sub-commuting diagram.

We have shown in this paper that the embedding is actually a homomorphism, *i.e.* it distributes over appropriately-defined programming operators. As a result, most of the algebraic laws, which were established in the original semantical framework and were used to capture the properties of the programming operators, remain valid in the enriched model.

The resulting probabilistic models have each been shown independently to be useful in their own right [7, 23]; and in further work [8] it is hoped that the value of the technique will be further demonstrated.

The weakest completion approach has been used for in support of data refinement in VDM and other state-based development methods, where the link is designed to connect abstract data type with its concrete representation. It is also used for data abstraction in model checking by dramatically reducing the size of state space. This paper illustrates another way of using simulation to derive enriched semantics.

References

1. J.C.M. Baeten, J.A. Bergstra and S.A. Smolka. *Axiomatizing Probabilistic Processes ACP with Generative Probabilities.* LNCS 630, (1993).
2. R.-J.R. Back. *A calculus for program derivations,* Acta Informatica 25, 593-624, (1988).
3. E.W. Dijkstra. *A Discipline of Programming,* Prentice-Hall, (1976).
4. R. Fagin, J.Y. Halpern and N. Meggido. *A logic for reasoning about probabilities,* Information and Computation, 78-128, (1990).
5. Michele Giry. *A categorical approach to probability theory,* LCM 915, 68–85, (1975).
6. H. Hansson and B. Jonsson. *A calculus for communicating systems with time and probabilities.* In Proceedings of the 11th IEEE Symposium on Real-time systems (1990).
7. He Jifeng, K. Seidel and A. McIver. *Probabilistic models for the Guarded Command Language* Science of Computer Programming, 28:171–192, (1997).
8. He Jifeng. *Derive Enriched Semantics by Simulation.* To appear in the Proceedings of the Workshop of Refinement and Abstraction, ETL, Osaka, (1999).
9. E.C.R. Hehner. *Predicative Programming: Part 1 and 2.* Communications of the ACM, Vol 27(2): 134–151, (1984).
10. E.C.R. Hehner. *A Practical Theory of Programming.* Springer-Verlag, (1993)
11. C.A.R. Hoare and He Jifeng *Weakest prespecifications.* Fundamenta Informaticae IX, 51–84, 217–252, (1986).
12. C.A.R. Hoare and He Jifeng *Unifying theories of programming,* Prentice-Hall, (1998).
13. C.B. Jones. *Systematic Software Development Using VDM.* Prentice-Hall, (1986).
14. C. Jones and G. Plotkin. *A probabilistic power domain of evaluations,* In Proceedings of 4th IEEE Symposium on Logic in Computer Science, 186-195, Cambridge, Mass., (1989)

---

[4] For the predicates we imposed 'scaling' additionally.

15. C. Jones. *Probabilistic Nondeterminism*, Doctoral Thesis, Edinburgh University.
16. D. Kozen. *Semantics of probabilistic programming.* Journal of Computer Systems Science 22, 328–350, (1981).
17. D. Kozen. *a probabilistic PDL.* Proceedings of the 15th ACM Symposium on Theory of Computing. (1983)
18. K.G. Larsen and A. Skou. *Bisimulation through probabilistic testing.* Information and Computation 94(1), (1991).
19. F.W. Lawvere. *The category of probabilistic mappings*, Preprint, (1962).
20. E. Moggi. *Notations of computation and monads.* Information and Computation 93, 55–92, (1986).
21. C.C. Morgan. *Programming from Specifications*, Prentice-Hall, Second edition, (1994).
22. C.C. Morgan, A. McIver, K. Seidel and J.W. Sanders. *Refinement-oriented Probability for CSP*, Technical Report PRG-TR-12-94, Oxford University Computing Laboratory, (1994).
23. C.C. Morgan, A. McIver, K. Seidel and J.W. Sanders. *Probabilistic predicate transformers* Technical Report PRG-TR-5-95, Oxford University Computing Laboratory, (1995).
24. J.M. Morris. *A theoretical basis for stepwise refinement and the programming calculus*, Science of Computer Programming, 9(3): 287-306, (1987).
25. J.R. Rao. *Reasoning about probabilistic parallel programs.* ACM Transactions on Programming Language and Systems, 16(3), (1994)
26. M. Sharir, A. Pnueli and S. Hart. *Verification of probabilistic programs.* SIAM Journal on Computing 13(2), 292–314, (1984).

CSP Representation of Game Semantics for Second-Order Idealized Algol[*]

Aleksandar Dimovski and Ranko Lazić

Department of Computer Science,
University of Warwick,
Coventry CV4 7AL, UK
{aleks,lazic}@dcs.warwick.ac.uk

Abstract. We show how game semantics of an interesting fragment of Idealised Algol can be represented compositionally by CSP processes. This enables observational equivalence and a range of properties of terms-in-context (i.e. open program fragments) to be checked using the FDR tool. We have built a prototype compiler which implements the representation, and initial experimental results are positive.

1 Introduction

Context. One of the main breakthroughs in theoretical computer science in the past decade has been the development of game semantics (e.g. [11,1]). Types are modelled by games between Player (i.e. term) and Opponent (i.e. context or environment), and terms are modelled by strategies. This has produced the first accurate (i.e. fully abstract and fully complete) models for a variety of programming languages and logical systems.

It has recently been shown that, for several interesting programming language fragments, game semantics yields algorithms for software model checking. The focus has been on Idealised Algol (IA) [14] with active expressions. IA is similar to Core ML. It is a compact programming language which combines the fundamental features of imperative languages with a full higher-order procedure mechanism. For example, simple forms of classes and objects may be encoded in IA.

For second-order recursion-free IA with iteration and finite data types, [9] shows that game semantics can be represented by regular expressions, so that observational equivalence between any two terms can be decided by equality of regular languages. For third order and without iteration, it was established in [13] that game semantics can be represented by deterministic pushdown automata, which makes observational equivalence decidable by equality of deterministic context-free languages. Classes of properties other than observational

---

[*] We acknowledge support by the EPSRC (GR/S52759/01). The first author was also supported by the Intel Corporation.

equivalence can also be checked algorithmically, such as language containment or Hoare triples (e.g. [2]).

In recent years, software model checking has become an active research area, and powerful tools have been built (e.g. [4]). Compared with other approaches to software model checking, the approach based on game semantics has a number of advantages [3]:

- there is a model for any term-in-context, which enables verification of program fragments which contain free variable and procedure names;
- game semantics is compositional, which facilitates verifying a term to be broken down into verifying its subterms;
- terms are modelled by how they interact with their environments, and details of their internal state during computations are not recorded, which results in small models.

Our Contribution. In this paper, we show how game semantics of second-order recursion-free IA with iteration and finite data types can be represented in the CSP process algebra. For any term-in-context, we compositionally define a CSP process whose terminated traces are exactly all the complete plays of the strategy for the term. Observational equivalence between two terms can then be decided by checking two traces refinements between CSP processes.

Compared with the representation by regular expressions (or automata) [9], the CSP representation brings several benefits:

- CSP operators preserve traces refinement (e.g. [17]), which means that a CSP process representing a term can be optimised and abstracted compositionally at the syntactic level (e.g. using process algebraic laws), and its set of terminated traces will be preserved or enlarged;
- the ProBE and FDR tools [7] can be used to explore CSP processes visually, to check traces refinements automatically, and to debug interactively when traces refinements do not hold;
- compositional state-space reduction algorithms in FDR [16] enable smaller models to be generated before or during refinement checking;
- composition of strategies, which is used in game semantics to obtain the strategy for a term from strategies for its subterms, is represented in CSP by renaming, parallel composition and hiding operators, and FDR is highly optimised for verification of such networks of processes;
- parameterised terms (as a simple example, a program which reverses an array of values of an arbitrary data type α) can be interpreted by single parameterised processes, which can then be verified e.g. using techniques from the infinite-state model checking literature.

We have implemented a prototype compiler which, given any IA term-in-context, outputs a CSP process representing its game semantics. We report some initial experimental results, which show that for model generation, FDR outperforms the tool based on the representation by regular expressions [8].

Organisation. In the next section, we present the fragment of IA we are addressing. Section 3 contains brief introductions to game semantics, CSP and FDR.

In section 4, we define the CSP representation of game semantics for the IA fragment. Correctness of the CSP model, and decidability of observational equivalence by traces refinement, are shown in section 5. We present the experimental results in section 6. Finally, in section 7, we conclude and discuss future work.

Further proof details and examples can be found in the full paper [5].

2   The Programming Language

Idealized Algol [14] is a functional-imperative language with usual imperative features as iteration, branching, assignment, sequential composition, combined with a function mechanism based on a typed call-by-name lambda calculus. We consider only the recursion-free second-order fragment of this language. We will only work with finite data sets.

The language has basic data types τ, which are a finite subset of the integers and the booleans. The phrase types of the language are expressions, commands and variables, plus first-order function types.

$$\tau ::= int \mid bool$$
$$\sigma ::= exp[\tau] \mid comm \mid var[\tau]$$
$$\theta ::= \sigma \mid \sigma \times \sigma \times \cdots \sigma \to \sigma$$

Terms are introduced using type judgements of the form:

$$\Gamma \vdash M : \theta, \text{ where } \Gamma = \{\iota_1 : \theta_1, \cdots, \iota_k : \theta_k\}$$

For the sake of simplicity, we assume that terms are β-normal, so there is no λ abstractions, and also function application is restricted to free identifiers. The terms of the language and their typing rules are given in Table 1.

For type $exp[int]$, the finitary fragment contains constants n belonging to a finite subset of the set of integers, and for type $exp[bool]$ there are constants *true* and *false*. For type *comm*, there are basic commands *skip*, to do nothing, and *diverge* which causes a program to enter an unresponsive state similar to that caused by an infinite loop. The other commands are assignment to variables, $V := E$, conditional operation, *if B then C else C'*, and while loop, *while B do C*. Also, we have sequential composition of commands $C \, \fatsemi \, C'$ as well as sequential composition of a command with an expression or a variable. There are also term formers for dereferencing variables, !V, application of first-order free identifiers to arguments $\iota M_1 \cdots M_k$, and local variable declaration $new[\tau] \, \iota \, in \, C$. Finally, we have a function definition *let* constructor.

3   Background

3.1   Game Semantics

We give an informal overview of game semantics and we illustrate it with some examples. A more complete introduction can be found in [2].

As the name suggests, game semantics models computation as a certain kind of game, with two participants, called Player(P) and Opponent(O). P represents

Table 1. Terms and typing rules

$$\overline{\Gamma \vdash true : exp[bool]} \qquad \overline{\Gamma \vdash n : exp[int]}$$

$$\overline{\Gamma \vdash skip : comm} \qquad \overline{\Gamma \vdash diverge : comm}$$

$$\overline{\Gamma, \iota : \theta \vdash \iota : \theta} \qquad \frac{\Gamma \vdash V : var[\tau]}{\Gamma \vdash !V : exp[\tau]}$$

$$\frac{\Gamma \vdash E_1 : exp[int] \quad \Gamma \vdash E_2 : exp[int]}{\Gamma \vdash E_1 + E_2 : exp[int]} \qquad \frac{\Gamma \vdash E_1 : exp[int] \quad \Gamma \vdash E_2 : exp[int]}{\Gamma \vdash E_1 = E_2 : exp[bool]}$$

$$\frac{\Gamma \vdash B_1 : exp[bool] \quad \Gamma \vdash B_2 : exp[bool]}{\Gamma \vdash B_1 \ and \ B_2 : exp[bool]} \qquad \frac{\Gamma \vdash B : exp[bool]}{\Gamma \vdash not \ B : exp[bool]}$$

$$\frac{\Gamma \vdash V : var[\tau] \quad \Gamma \vdash E : exp[\tau]}{\Gamma \vdash V := E : comm} \qquad \frac{\Gamma \vdash C : comm \quad \Gamma \vdash M : \sigma}{\Gamma \vdash C \, \S \, M : \sigma}$$

$$\frac{\Gamma \vdash B : exp[bool] \quad \Gamma \vdash M_1 : \sigma \quad \Gamma \vdash M_2 : \sigma}{\Gamma \vdash if \ B \ then \ M_1 \ else \ M_2 : \sigma} \qquad \frac{\Gamma \vdash B : exp[bool] \quad \Gamma \vdash C : comm}{\Gamma \vdash while \ B \ do \ C : comm}$$

$$\frac{\Gamma \vdash \iota : \sigma_1 \times \cdots \times \sigma_k \to \sigma \quad \Gamma \vdash M_i : \sigma_i}{\Gamma \vdash \iota(M_1, M_2, \ldots, M_k) : \sigma} \qquad \frac{\Gamma, \iota : var[\tau] \vdash C : comm}{\Gamma \vdash new[\tau] \ \iota \ in \ C : comm}$$

$$\frac{\Gamma, \iota : \sigma_1 \times \cdots \times \sigma_k \to \sigma' \vdash M : \sigma \quad \Gamma, \iota_1 : \sigma_1, \ldots, \iota_k : \sigma_k \vdash N : \sigma'}{\Gamma \vdash let \ \iota \ (\iota_1 : \sigma_1, \ldots, \iota_k : \sigma_k) \ = \ N \ in \ M : \sigma}$$

the term (program), while O represents the environment, i.e. the context in which the term is used. A play between O and P consists of a sequence of moves, governed by rules. For example, O and P need to take turn and every move needs to be justified by a preceding move. The moves are of two kinds, questions and answers.

To every type in the language corresponds a game — the set of all possible plays (sequences of moves). A term is represented as a set of all complete plays in the appropriate game, more precisely as a strategy for that game — a predetermined way for P to respond to O's moves.

For example, in the game for the type $exp[\tau]$, there is an initial move q and corresponding to it a single response to return its value. So a complete play for a constant $\vdash c : exp[\tau]$ is:

O: q (opponent asks for value)
P: c (player answers to the question)

Consider a more complex example $\iota : exp[int] \to exp[int] \vdash \iota(2) : exp[int]$, where the identifier ι is some non-locally defined function. A play for this term begins with O asking for the value of the result expression by playing the question move q, and P replies asking for the returned value of the non-local function ι, move q^ι. In this situation, the function ι may need to evaluate its argument, represented by O's move $q^{\iota 1}$ — what is the value of the first argument to ι. P will respond with answer $2^{\iota 1}$. Here, O could repeat the question $q^{\iota 1}$ to represent the function which evaluates its argument more than once. In the end, when O plays the move n^ι — the value returned from ι, P will copy this value and answer to the first question with n. A sample complete play for this term, when the function ι evaluates only once its argument, is:

O: q (asks for result value)
P: q^{ι} (P asks for value returned from function ι)
O: $q^{\iota 1}$ (O questions what is the first argument to ι)
P: $2^{\iota 1}$ (P answers: 2)
O: n^{ι} (O supplies the value returned from ι)
P: n (P gives the answer to the first question)

In the game for commands, there is an initial move run to initiate a command, and a single response $done$ to signal termination of the command. Thus the only complete play for the command $\vdash skip : comm$ is:

O: run (start executing)
P: $done$ (terminate command)

Variables are represented as objects with 2 methods: the "read method" for dereferencing, represented by an initial move $read$, with response an element of τ, and the "write method", for assignment, represented by an initial move $write(x)$ for any element x of τ, to which there is only one possible response ok. For example, a complete play for the command $v : var[\tau] \vdash v :=!v + 1 : comm$ is:

O: run
P: $read_v$ (what is the value of v)
O: 2 (O supplies the value 2)
P: $write(3)_v$ (write 3 into v)
O: ok_v (the assignment is complete)
P: $done$

When P asks to read from v, O can return an arbitrary value, i.e. not necessarily the last value P wrote into v. This is because, in general, the value of v can also be modified by the context into which the term will be placed. However, when a variable is declared, "good variable" behaviour is enforced within the scope of the declaration.

3.2   CSP

CSP (Communicating Sequential Processes) is a language for modelling interacting components. Each component is specified through its behaviour which is given as a process. This section only introduces the CSP notation and the ideas used in this paper. For a fuller introduction to the language the reader is referred to [17].

CSP processes are defined in terms of the events that they can perform. The set of all possible events is denoted Σ. Events may be atomic in structure or may consist of a number of distinct components. For example, an event $write.1$ consists of two parts: a channel name $write$, and a data value 1. If N is a set of values that can be communicated down the channel $write$, then $write.N$ will be the set of events $\{write.n \mid n \in N\}$. Given a channel c, we can define the set of all events that can arise on the channel c, by $\{\mid c \mid\} = \{c.w \in \Sigma\}$.

We use the following collection of process operators:

$$P ::= p \mid STOP \mid SKIP \mid RUN_A \mid ?x : A \rightarrow P \mid \mu\,p.P \mid P_1 \square P_2$$
$$\mid P_1 \triangleleft b \triangleright P_2 \mid P_1 \underset{A}{\parallel} P_2 \mid P \setminus A \mid P\,[a/b] \mid P_1\,{}^\circ_\circ P_2$$

where A represents a set of events, P a process expression and p is a process name (or identifier).

The process $STOP$ performs no actions and never communicates. It is useful for providing a simple model of a deadlocked system. $SKIP$ is a process that successfully terminates causing the special event $\checkmark$ ($\checkmark$ is not in Σ). RUN_A can always communicate any event of set A desired by the environment. A choice process, $?x : A \rightarrow P$, can perform any event from set A and then behaves as P. For example, $RUN_A = ?x : A \rightarrow RUN_A$. Process $\mu\,p.P$, where P is any process involving p, represents recursion. It can return to its initial state and in that way communicate forever. The process $P_1 \square P_2$ can behave either as P_1 or as P_2, its possible communications are those of P_1 and those of P_2. Conditional choice process $P_1 \triangleleft b \triangleright P_2$ means the same as *if b then P else Q*, and has the obvious meaning as in all programming languages. Process $P_1 \underset{A}{\parallel} P_2$ runs P_1 and P_2 in parallel, making them synchronise on events in A and allowing all others events freely. The parallel combination terminates successfully when both component processes do it. This is known as distributed termination. Process $P \setminus A$, behaves as P except that events from A become invisible events τ (τ is not in Σ). The renaming operator $[\,]$ is used to rename some events of a given process. We will only use injective renaming and notation $P[a/b]$ to mean that the event or channel b in P is replaced by a, and all others remain the same. Sequential composition $P_1\,{}^\circ_\circ P_2$ runs P_1 until it terminates successfully producing the special event $\checkmark$, and then runs P_2.

CSP processes can be given semantics by sets of their traces. A trace is a finite sequence of events. A sequence tr is a trace of a process P if there is some execution of P in which exactly that sequence of events is performed. Examples of traces include $\langle\rangle$ (the empty trace, which is possible for any process) and $\langle a_1, a_2 \rangle$ which is a possible trace of RUN_A, if $a_1, a_2 \in A$. The set $traces(P)$ is the set of all possible traces of process P.

Using traces sets, we can define traces refinement. A process P_2 is a traces refinement of another, P_1, if all the possible sequences of communications which P_2 can do are also possible for P_1. Or more formally:

$$P_1 \sqsubseteq_T P_2 \;\Leftrightarrow\; traces(P_2) \subseteq traces(P_1) \tag{1}$$

CSP processes can also be described by transition systems or state machines. The transition system of a process is a directed graph showing the states which the process can go through and the events from $\Sigma \cup \{\checkmark, \tau\}$ that it can perform to get from one to another state. The successful termination $\checkmark$ is always the last event and leads to an end state Ω.

The FDR tool [7] is a refinement checker for CSP processes. It contains several procedures for compositional state-space reduction. Namely, before generating a transition system for a composite process, transition systems of its component processes can be reduced, while preserving semantics of the composite process [16]. FDR is also optimised for checking refinements by processes which consist of a number of component processes composed by operators such as renaming, parallel composition and hiding.

4   CSP Representation of Game Semantics

With each type θ, we associate a set of possible events: an alphabet $\mathcal{A}_\theta$. The alphabet of a type contains events $\mathbf{q} \in \mathbb{Q}_\theta$ called questions, which are appended to channel with name Q, and for each question $\mathbf{q}$, there is a set of events $\mathbf{a} \in \mathbb{A}_\theta^{\mathbf{q}}$ called answers, which are appended to channel with name A.

$$\mathcal{A}_{int} = \{0, \cdots, N_{max} - 1\}, \quad \mathcal{A}_{bool} = \{true, false\}$$
$$\mathbb{Q}_{exp[\tau]} = \{q\}, \quad \mathbb{A}_{exp[\tau]}^{q} = \mathcal{A}_\tau$$
$$\mathbb{Q}_{comm} = \{run\}, \quad \mathbb{A}_{comm}^{run} = \{done\}$$
$$\mathbb{Q}_{var[\tau]} = \{read, write.x \mid x \in \mathcal{A}_\tau\}, \quad \mathbb{A}_{var[\tau]}^{read} = \mathcal{A}_\tau, \quad \mathbb{A}_{var[\tau]}^{write.x} = \{ok\}$$
$$\mathbb{Q}_{\sigma_1 \times \cdots \times \sigma_k \to \sigma_0} = \{j.\mathbf{q} \mid \mathbf{q} \in \mathbb{Q}_{\sigma_j}, 0 \le j \le k\},$$
$$\mathbb{A}_{\sigma_1 \times \cdots \times \sigma_k \to \sigma_0}^{j.\mathbf{q}} = \{j.\mathbf{a} \mid \mathbf{a} \in \mathbb{A}_{\sigma_j}^{\mathbf{q}}\}, \text{for } 0 \le j \le k$$
$$\mathcal{A}_\theta = Q.\mathbb{Q}_\theta \cup A.\bigcup_{\mathbf{q} \in \mathbb{Q}_\theta} \mathbb{A}_\theta^{\mathbf{q}}$$

We now define, for any typed term-in-context $\Gamma \vdash M : \sigma$, a CSP process which represents its game semantics. This process is denoted $[\![\Gamma \vdash M : \sigma]\!]^{CSP}$, and it is over the following alphabet $\mathcal{A}_{\Gamma \vdash \sigma}$:

$$\mathcal{A}_{\iota:\theta} = \iota.\mathcal{A}_\theta = \{\iota.\alpha \mid \alpha \in \mathcal{A}_\theta\}$$
$$\mathcal{A}_\Gamma = \bigcup_{\iota:\theta \in \Gamma} \mathcal{A}_{\iota:\theta}$$
$$\mathcal{A}_{\Gamma \vdash \sigma} = \mathcal{A}_\Gamma \cup \mathcal{A}_\sigma$$

4.1   Expression Constructs

$[\![\Gamma \vdash v : exp[\tau]]\!]^{CSP} = Q.q \to A.v \to SKIP$, $v \in \mathcal{A}_\tau$ is a constant

$[\![\Gamma \vdash not\ B : exp[bool]]\!]^{CSP} =$
$\quad [\![\Gamma \vdash B : exp[bool]]\!]^{CSP}[Q_1/Q, A_1/A] \quad \underset{\{|Q_1, A_1|\}}{\|}$
$\quad (Q.q \to Q_1.q \to A_1?v : \mathcal{A}_{bool} \to A.(not\ v) \to SKIP) \setminus \{|\ Q_1, A_1\ |\}$

$[\![\Gamma \vdash E_1 \bullet E_2 : exp[\tau]]\!]^{CSP} =$
$\quad [\![\Gamma \vdash E_1 : exp[\tau]]\!]^{CSP}[Q_1/Q, A_1/A] \quad \underset{\{|Q_1, A_1|\}}{\|}$
$\quad ([\![\Gamma \vdash E_2 : exp[\tau]]\!]^{CSP}[Q_2/Q, A_2/A] \quad \underset{\{|Q_2, A_2|\}}{\|}$
$\quad (Q.q \to Q_1.q \to A_1?v1 : \mathcal{A}_\tau \to Q_2.q \to A_2?v2 : \mathcal{A}_\tau \to$
$\quad\quad A.(v1 \bullet v2) \to SKIP) \setminus \{|\ Q_2, A_2\ |\}) \setminus \{|\ Q_1, A_1\ |\}$

$[\![\Gamma \vdash \iota : exp[\tau]]\!]^{CSP} = Q.q \to \iota.Q.q \to \iota.A?v : \mathcal{A}_\tau \to A.v \to SKIP$

Any constant $v : exp[\tau]$ is represented by a process which communicates the events: a question q (what is the value of this expression), an answer v — the value of that constant, and then terminates successfully. The process that represents any arithmetic-logic operator $\bullet$ is defined in a compositional way, by parallel combination of the processes that represents both operands and a process that gets the operands values by synchronisation on the corresponding channels and returns the expected answer ($v1 \bullet v2$). All events that participate in synchronisation are hidden. Arithmetic operators over a finite set of integers are interpreted as modulo some maximum value. The last process interprets a free identifier ι of type $exp[\tau]$ by a copycat strategy.

4.2   Command Constructs

$[\![\Gamma \vdash skip : comm]\!]^{CSP} = Q.run \rightarrow A.done \rightarrow SKIP$

$[\![\Gamma \vdash diverge : comm]\!]^{CSP} = STOP$

$[\![\Gamma \vdash C \,\S\, M : \sigma]\!]^{CSP} =$

$\quad [\![\Gamma \vdash C : comm]\!]^{CSP}[Q_1/Q, A_1/A] \quad \underset{\{|Q_1,A_1|\}}{\|}$

$\quad ([\![\Gamma \vdash M : \sigma]\!]^{CSP}[Q_2/Q, A_2/A] \quad \underset{\{|Q_2,A_2|\}}{\|}$

$\quad (Q?\mathbf{q} : \mathbb{Q}_\sigma \rightarrow Q_1.run \rightarrow A_1.done \rightarrow Q_2.\mathbf{q} \rightarrow A_2?\mathbf{a} : \mathbb{A}_\sigma^{\mathbf{q}} \rightarrow A.\mathbf{a} \rightarrow SKIP)$
$\quad\quad \setminus \{|\, Q_2, A_2 \,|\}) \setminus \{|\, Q_1, A_1 \,|\}$

$[\![\Gamma \vdash if\ B\ then\ M_1\ else\ M_2 : \sigma]\!]^{CSP} =$

$\quad [\![\Gamma \vdash B : exp[bool]]\!]^{CSP}[Q_0/Q, A_0/A] \quad \underset{\{|Q_0,A_0|\}}{\|}$

$\quad (([\![\Gamma \vdash M_1 : \sigma]\!]^{CSP}[Q_1/Q, A_1/A] \,\square\, (A?\mathbf{a} : \bigcup_{\mathbf{q}\in\mathbb{Q}_\sigma} \mathbb{A}_\sigma^{\mathbf{q}} \rightarrow SKIP)) \quad \underset{\{|Q_1,A_1,A|\}}{\|}$

$\quad (([\![\Gamma \vdash M_2 : \sigma]\!]^{CSP}[Q_2/Q, A_2/A] \,\square\, (A?\mathbf{a} : \bigcup_{\mathbf{q}\in\mathbb{Q}_\sigma} \mathbb{A}_\sigma^{\mathbf{q}} \rightarrow SKIP)) \quad \underset{\{|Q_2,A_2,A|\}}{\|}$

$\quad (Q?\mathbf{q} : \mathbb{Q}_\sigma \rightarrow Q_0.q \rightarrow A_0?v : A_{bool} \rightarrow (Q_1.\mathbf{q} \rightarrow A_1?\mathbf{a} : \mathbb{A}_\sigma^{\mathbf{q}} \rightarrow A.\mathbf{a} \rightarrow SKIP$
$\quad\quad \lessdot v \gtrdot Q_2.\mathbf{q} \rightarrow A_2?\mathbf{a} : \mathbb{A}_\sigma^{\mathbf{q}} \rightarrow A.\mathbf{a} \rightarrow SKIP))$
$\quad\quad\quad\quad \setminus\{|\, Q_2, A_2 \,|\})\setminus\{|\, Q_1, A_1 \,|\})\setminus\{|\, Q_0, A_0 \,|\}$

$[\![\Gamma \vdash while\ B\ do\ C : comm]\!]^{CSP} =$

$\quad (\mu\, p'.([\![B : comm]\!]^{CSP}[Q_1/Q, A_1/A] \,\S\, p') \,\square\, (A.done \rightarrow SKIP)) \quad \underset{\{|Q_1,A_1,A|\}}{\|}$

$\quad ((\mu\, p''.([\![C : comm]\!]^{CSP}[Q_2/Q, A_2/A] \,\S\, p'') \,\square\, (A.done \rightarrow SKIP)) \quad \underset{\{|Q_2,A_2,A|\}}{\|}$

$\quad (Q.run \rightarrow \mu\, p.Q_1.q \rightarrow A_1?v : A_{bool} \rightarrow (Q_2.run \rightarrow A_2.done \rightarrow p \lessdot v \gtrdot$
$\quad\quad A.done \rightarrow SKIP)) \setminus \{|\, Q_2, A_2 \,|\}) \setminus \{|\, Q_1, A_1 \,|\}$

$[\![\Gamma \vdash \iota : comm]\!]^{CSP} = Q.run \rightarrow \iota.Q.run \rightarrow \iota.A.done \rightarrow A.done \rightarrow SKIP$

The command *skip* is represented by the question and answer events for commands followed by the ✓ event. The command *diverge* is represented by the deadlocked process $STOP$, which matches with its game semantics, namely there is not any complete play for *diverge*. The process for a sequential composition $\Gamma \vdash C \,\S\, M : \sigma$ is a parallel composition of the processes for the command

C and term M, and a "control" process which accepts a question for type σ, runs C, then passes the original question to M, and finally copies any answer from M as the overall answer. The synchronisations between the latter process and the processes for C and M are hidden. The interpretations of branching and iteration are similar. In the case of branching, choice is used to enable the parallel composition to terminate without executing one of the processes for M_1 and M_2. For iteration, the processes for B and C are in general executed zero or more times. A free identifier is interpreted by a copycat strategy.

4.3   Variable Constructs

For a free identifier of type $var[\tau]$, the copycat strategy is a choice between two processes: the first for reading from the variable, and the second for writing.

$$\llbracket \Gamma \vdash \iota : var[\tau] \rrbracket^{CSP} =$$
$$(Q.read \to \iota.Q.read \to \iota.A?v : \mathcal{A}_\tau \to A.v \to SKIP) \;\square$$
$$(Q.write?v : \mathcal{A}_\tau \to \iota.Q.write.v \to \iota.A.ok \to A.ok \to SKIP)$$

The process for an assignment $V := M$ is a parallel composition of the processes for V and M, and a process which starts with a *run* (as the assignment is a command), evaluates M, then writes the obtained value to V, and finishes with *done*. The synchronisations with the former two processes are hidden. Note that V can be an arbitrary term of type $var[\tau]$, perhaps containing side-effects.

$$\llbracket \Gamma \vdash V := M : comm \rrbracket^{CSP} =$$
$$\llbracket \Gamma \vdash M : exp[\tau] \rrbracket^{CSP}[Q_1/Q, A_1/A] \underset{\{|Q_1,A_1|\}}{\|}$$
$$(\llbracket \Gamma \vdash V : var[\tau] \rrbracket^{CSP}[Q_2/Q, A_2/A] \underset{\{|Q_2,A_2|\}}{\|}$$
$$(Q.run \to Q_1.q \to A_1?v : \mathcal{A}_\tau \to Q_2.write.v \to A_2.ok$$
$$\to A.done \to SKIP) \setminus \{| Q_2, A_2 |\}) \setminus \{| Q_1, A_1 |\}$$

A dereference expression $!V$ is interpreted by reading from V:

$$\llbracket \Gamma \vdash !V : exp[\tau] \rrbracket^{CSP} =$$
$$\llbracket \Gamma \vdash V : var[\tau] \rrbracket^{CSP}[Q_1/Q, A_1/A] \underset{\{|Q_1,A_1|\}}{\|}$$
$$(Q.q \to Q_1.read \to A_1?v : \mathcal{A}_\tau \to A.v \to SKIP) \setminus \{| Q_1, A_1 |\}$$

The semantics of a local variable block consists of two operations: imposing the "good variable" behaviour on the local variable, and removing all references to the variable to make it invisible outside its binding scope. The first condition is accomplished by synchronising the process for the scope with a "cell" process $U_{\iota:var[\tau],a_\tau}$ which keeps the current value of ι. The initial value a_τ is defined by $a_{int} = 0$ and $a_{bool} = false$.

$$U_{\iota:var[\tau],v} = (\iota.Q.read \to \iota.A!v \to U_{\iota:var[\tau],v}) \;\square$$
$$(\iota.Q.write?v' : \mathcal{A}_\tau \to \iota.A.ok \to U_{\iota:var[\tau],v'}) \;\square$$
$$(A.done \to SKIP)$$

The second condition is realised by hiding all interactions between the process for the scope and the cell process:

$$[\![\Gamma \vdash new[\tau] \ \iota \ in \ M : comm]\!]^{CSP} =$$
$$\left([\![\Gamma \vdash M : comm]\!]^{CSP} \underset{\{|\iota,A|\}}{\|} U_{\iota:var[\tau],a_\tau}\right) \setminus \{|\iota|\}$$

4.4   Application and Functions

Application $\iota(M_1 \ldots M_k)$, where ι is a free identifier, is represented by a process that communicates the usual question and answer events for the return type of the function on the channel $\iota.0$, and runs zero or more times any processes of the function arguments. Arguments events are appended on the channels comprised of the function name followed by the index of that argument.

$$[\![\Gamma \vdash \iota(M_1 \ldots M_k) : \sigma]\!]^{CSP} = Q?\mathbf{q} : \mathbb{Q}_\sigma \to \iota.0.Q.\mathbf{q} \to$$
$$\mu L. \left(\left(\square_{j=1}^{k} \left([\![\Gamma \vdash M_j : \sigma_j]\!]^{CSP} \underset{\{|Q,A|\}}{\|} (\iota.j.Q?\mathbf{q}:\mathbb{Q}_{\sigma_j} \to Q.\mathbf{q} \to A?\mathbf{a}:\mathbb{A}^{\mathbf{q}}_{\sigma_j}\right.\right.$$
$$\left.\left.\to \iota.j.A.\mathbf{a} \to L)) \setminus \{| Q, A |\}\right) \square SKIP\right) \ {}^{\circ}_{9} \ \iota.0.A?\mathbf{a} : \mathbb{A}^{\mathbf{q}}_\sigma \to A.\mathbf{a} \to SKIP$$

Finally, we give a CSP representation for the *let* construct. The process for the scope M is put in parallel with the process for the definition term N, where the latter is enabled to execute zero or more times. Synchronisation is on interactions of M with the defined identifier ι, which are then hidden.

$$[\![\Gamma \vdash let \ \iota(\iota_1 : \sigma_1, \ldots, \iota_k : \sigma_k) = N \ in \ M : \sigma]\!]^{CSP} =$$
$$\left([\![\Gamma \vdash M : \sigma]\!]^{CSP} \underset{\{|\iota|\}}{\|}\right.$$
$$\left(\mu p.([\![\Gamma \vdash N : \sigma']\!]^{CSP}[\iota.0.Q/Q, \iota.1/\iota_1, \ldots, \iota.k/\iota_k, \iota.0.A/A] {}^{\circ}_{9} p) \square SKIP)\right)$$
$$\setminus \{|\iota|\}$$

5   Correctness and Decidability

Our first result is that, for any term, the set of all terminated traces of its CSP interpretation is isomorphic to the language of its regular language interpretation, as defined in [9].

Theorem 1. *For any term* $\Gamma \vdash M : \sigma$, *we have:*

$$\mathcal{L}_R(\Gamma \vdash M : \sigma) \overset{\phi}{\cong} \mathcal{L}_{CSP}(\Gamma \vdash M : \sigma) \tag{2}$$

where

$$\mathcal{L}_R(\Gamma \vdash M : \sigma) = \mathcal{L}([\![\Gamma \vdash M : \sigma]\!]^R) \quad (defined \ in \ [9]) \tag{3}$$
$$\mathcal{L}_{CSP}(\Gamma \vdash M : \sigma) = \{tr \mid tr^\frown\langle\checkmark\rangle \in traces([\![\Gamma \vdash M : \sigma]\!]^{CSP})\} \tag{4}$$

and ϕ is defined by:

$$\phi(\langle a_1, \ldots, a_k \rangle) = \phi(a_1) \cdot \ldots \cdot \phi(a_k)$$
$$\phi(Q.m) = m \qquad \phi(A.n) = n$$
$$\phi(\iota.Q.m) = m^\iota \quad \phi(\iota.A.n) = n^\iota$$

Proof. The proof of this Theorem is by induction on the typing rules defined in Table 1. □

Two terms M and N in type context Γ and of type σ are observationally equivalent, written $\Gamma \vdash M \equiv_\sigma N$, iff for any term-with-hole $C[-]$ such that both $C[M]$ and $C[N]$ are closed terms of type *comm*, $C[M]$ converges iff $C[N]$ converges. It was proved in [1] that this coincides to equality of sets of complete plays of the strategies for M and N, i.e. that the games model is fully abstract. (Operational semantics of IA, and a definition of convergence for terms of type *comm* in particular, can be found in the same paper.)

For the IA fragment treated in this paper, it was shown in [9] that observational equivalence coincides with equality of regular language interpretations. By Theorem 1, we have that observational equivalence corresponds to two traces refinements:

Corollary 1 (Observational Equivalence).

$$
\begin{aligned}
\Gamma \vdash M \equiv_\sigma N \ \Leftrightarrow\ & [\![\Gamma \vdash M : \sigma]\!]^{CSP} \ \square \ RUN_\Sigma \ \sqsubseteq_T \ [\![\Gamma \vdash N : \sigma]\!]^{CSP} \ \wedge \\
& [\![\Gamma \vdash N : \sigma]\!]^{CSP} \ \square \ RUN_\Sigma \ \sqsubseteq_T \ [\![\Gamma \vdash M : \sigma]\!]^{CSP}
\end{aligned}
\tag{5}
$$

Proof.

$$
\begin{aligned}
\Gamma \vdash M \equiv_\sigma N \ &\overset{(i)}{\Leftrightarrow}\ \mathcal{L}([\![\Gamma \vdash M : \sigma]\!]^R) \ = \ \mathcal{L}([\![\Gamma \vdash N : \sigma]\!]^R) \\
&\overset{(ii)}{\Leftrightarrow}\ \mathcal{L}_{CSP}(\Gamma \vdash M : \sigma) \ = \ \mathcal{L}_{CSP}(\Gamma \vdash N : \sigma) \\
&\overset{(iii)}{\Leftrightarrow}\ [\![\Gamma \vdash M : \sigma]\!]^{CSP} \ \square \ RUN_\Sigma \ \sqsubseteq_T \ [\![\Gamma \vdash N : \sigma]\!]^{CSP} \ \wedge \\
&\qquad\ \ [\![\Gamma \vdash N : \sigma]\!]^{CSP} \ \square \ RUN_\Sigma \ \sqsubseteq_T \ [\![\Gamma \vdash M : \sigma]\!]^{CSP}
\end{aligned}
$$

where (i) is shown in [9], (ii) holds by Theorem 1, and (iii) is straightforward. □

Refinement checking in FDR terminates for finite-state processes, i.e. those whose transition systems are finite. Our next result confirms that this is the case for the processes interpreting the IA terms. As a corollary, we have that observational equivalence is decidable using FDR.

Theorem 2. *For any term $\Gamma \vdash M : \sigma$, the CSP process $[\![\Gamma \vdash M : \sigma]\!]^{CSP}$ is finite state.*

Proof. This follows by induction on typing rules, using the fact that a process can have infinitely many states only if it uses either a choice operator $?x : A \to P$, where A is an infinite set and P varying with x, or certain kinds of recursion. □

Corollary 2 (Decidability). *Observational equivalence between terms of second-order recursion-free IA with iteration and finite data types is decidable by two traces refinements between finite-state CSP processes.* □

We now consider an example equivalence and prove it using the CSP model.

Example 1. $\Gamma \vdash while\ true\ do\ C \equiv_{comm} diverge.$

We prove the first traces refinement of the equivalence (5), i.e.
$$[\![\Gamma \vdash while\ true\ do\ C : comm]\!]^{CSP} \sqcap RUN_{\Sigma} \sqsubseteq_T [\![\Gamma \vdash diverge : comm]\!]^{CSP} \quad (*)$$
Since $[\![\Gamma \vdash diverge : comm]\!]^{CSP} = STOP$, and the process $STOP$ traces refines any other process, it implies that $(*)$ holds.

The second traces refinement is:

$$[\![\Gamma \vdash diverge : comm]\!]^{CSP} \sqcap RUN_{\Sigma} \sqsubseteq_T [\![\Gamma \vdash while\ true\ do\ C : comm]\!]^{CSP} \quad (**)$$

We have:

$$traces([\![\Gamma \vdash while\ true\ do\ C : comm]\!]^{CSP}) =$$
$$= \{\langle\rangle, \langle Q.run\rangle, \langle Q.run\rangle^\frown tr', \langle Q.run\rangle^\frown tr, \langle Q.run\rangle^\frown tr^\frown tr', \ldots \mid$$
$$\langle Q.run\rangle^\frown tr^\frown \langle A.done\rangle^\frown \langle\checkmark\rangle \in traces([\![\Gamma \vdash C]\!]^{CSP}), tr' \leqslant tr\}$$

Since there is not any sequence with successful termination in the traces set of $[\![\Gamma \vdash while\ true\ do\ C : comm]\!]^{CSP}$, all sequences from this traces set will be also in the traces set of RUN_{Σ} process, so $(**)$ holds too. □

5.1   Property Verification

Suppose ϕ is any property of terms with type context Γ and type σ such that the set of all behaviours which satisfy ϕ is a regular language $\mathcal{L}(\phi)$ over $\mathcal{A}_{\Gamma \vdash \sigma}$. A finite-state CSP process whose set of terminated traces equals $\mathcal{L}(\phi)$ can then be constructed. Thus, we can verify whether a term $\Gamma \vdash M : \sigma$ satisfies ϕ by checking the traces refinement:

$$P_\phi \sqcap RUN_{\Sigma} \sqsubseteq_T [\![\Gamma \vdash M : \sigma]\!]^{CSP} \qquad (6)$$

Example 2. Consider a term $x : var[\tau], c : comm \vdash M : comm$. We want to check the property "a value is written into x before c is called". A CSP process which interprets this property is:

$$P_\phi = \mu\,p.\Big((?e : \mathcal{A}_{comm} \cup \mathcal{A}_{x:var[\tau]\setminus\{|x.Q.write|\}} \to p) \sqcap \big(x.Q.write?v : \mathcal{A}_\tau \to$$
$$\mu\,p'.(?e : \mathcal{A}_{comm} \cup \mathcal{A}_{x:var[\tau]} \to p') \sqcap (c.Q.run \to$$
$$\mu\,p''.(?e : \mathcal{A}_{\Gamma \vdash comm} \to p'') \sqcap SKIP)\big)\Big) \sqcap$$

6   Experimental Results

We have implemented a compiler from IA terms-in-context into CSP processes which represent their game semantics. The input to the compiler is code, with some simple type annotations to indicate what finite sets of integers will be used to model integer variables.

Here, we discuss the modelling of a sorting program, report the results from our tool and compare them with the tool based on regular expressions [8]. We will analyse the bubble-sort algorithm, whose implementation is given in Figure 1. The code includes a meta variable n, representing array size, which will be replaced by several different values. The integers stored in the array are of type $int\%3$, i.e. 3 distinct values 0, 1 and 2, and the type of index i is $int\%n+1$, i.e. one more than the size of the array. The program first copies the input array $x[\,]$ into a local array $a[\,]$, which is then sorted and copied back into $x[\,]$. The array being effectively sorted, $a[\,]$, is not visible from the outside of the program because it is locally defined, and only reads and writes of the non-local array $x[\,]$ are seen in the model. The transition system of final (compressed) model process for $n = 2$ is shown in Figure 2. It illustrates the dynamic behaviour of the program, where the left-side half of the model reads all possible combinations of values from $x[\,]$, while the right-side half writes out the same values, but in sorted order.

```
var int% 3 x[n]; ⊢
new int% 3 a[n] in
new int% n+ 1 i in
while (i < n)  {a[i] := x[i];   i := i + 1; }
new boolean flag := true in
while(flag){
        i := 0;
        flag := false;
        while (i < n − 1)  {
            if (a[i] > a[i + 1])  {
                flag := true;
                new int% 3 temp in
                temp := a[i];
                a[i] := a[i + 1];
                a[i + 1] := temp;  }
            i := i + 1;  } }
i := 0;
while (i < n)  {x[i] := a[i];   i := i + 1; }
: comm
```

Fig. 1. Implementation of bubble-sort algorithm

Table 2 contains the experimental results for model generation. We ran FDR on a Research Machines Xeon with 2GB RAM. The results from the tool based on regular expressions were obtained on a SunBlade 100 with 2GB RAM [8]. We list the execution time, the size of the largest generated state machine during model generation, and the size of the final compressed model. In the CSP

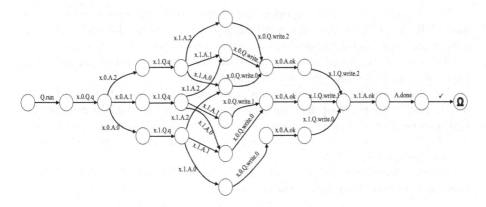

Fig. 2. A transition system of the model for $n = 2$

Table 2. Experimental results for minimal model generation

n	CSP			Regular expressions		
	Time (min)	Max. states	Model states	Time (min)	Max. states	Model states
5	6	1 775	164	5	3 376	163
10	20	18 752	949	10	64 776	948
15	50	115 125	2 859	120	352 448	2 858
20	110	378 099	6 394	240	1 153 240	6 393
30	750	5 204 232	20 339	failed		

approach, the process output by our compiler was input into FDR, which was instructed to generate a transition system for it by applying a number of compositional state-space reduction algorithms. The results confirm that both approaches give isomorphic models, where the CSP models have an extra state due to representing termination by a ✓ event.

We expect FDR to perform even better in property verification. For checking refinement by a composite process, FDR does not need to generate an explicit model of it, but only models of its component processes. A model of the composite process is then generated on-the-fly, and its size is not limited by available RAM, but by disk size.

7   Conclusion

We presented a compositional representation of game semantics of an interesting fragment of Idealised Algol by CSP processes. This enables observational equivalence and a range of properties of terms-in-context (i.e. open program fragments) to be checked using the FDR tool.

We also reported initial experimental results using our prototype compiler and FDR. They show that, for minimal model generation, the CSP approach outperforms the approach based on regular expressions.

As future work, we plan to compare how the two approaches perform on a range of equivalence and property checking problems.

We also intend to extend the compiler so that parameterised IA terms (such as parametrically polymorphic programs) are translated to single parameterised CSP processes. Such processes could then be analysed by techniques which combine CSP and data specification formalisms (e.g. [6, 15]) or by algorithms based on data independence [12].

Another important direction is dealing with concurrency (e.g. [10]) and further programming language features.

References

1. S.Abramsky and G.McCusker. Linearity, sharing and state: a fully abstract game semantics for Idealized Algol with active expressions. In P.W.O'Hearn and R.D.Tennent, editors, *Algol-like languages*. Birkhaüser, 1997.
2. S.Abramsky. Algorithmic game semantics: A tutorial introduction. Lecture notes, Marktoberdorf International Summer School 2001, 2001.
3. S.Abramsky, D.Ghica, A.Murawski and C.-H.L.Ong. Applying Game Semantics to Compositional Software Modeling and Verifications. In Proceedings of TACAS, LNCS 2988, March 2004.
4. T.Ball and S.K.Rajamani. The SLAM Project: Debugging System Software via Static Analysis. In Proceedings of POPL, ACM SIGPLAN Notices 37(1), January 2002.
5. A.Dimovski and R.Lazić. CSP Representation of Game Semantics for Second-order Idealized Algol. Research Report, Department of Computer Science, University of Warwick, May 2004.
6. A.Farias, A.Mota and A.Sampaio. Efficient CSP-Z Data Abstraction. In Proceedings of IFM, LNCS 2999, April 2004.
7. Formal Systems (Europe) Ltd. Failures-Divergence Refinement: FDR2 Manual. 2000.
8. D.Ghica. Game-based Software Model Checking: Case Studies and Methodological Considerations. Oxford University Computing Lab, Technical Report PRG-RR-03-11, May 2003.
9. D.Ghica and G.McCusker. The Regular-Language Semantics of Second-order Idealized Algol. Theoretical Computer Science 309(1–3): 469–502, 2003.
10. D.Ghica, A.Murawski and C.-H.L.Ong. Syntactic Control of Concurrency. In Proceedings of ICALP, LNCS 3142, July 2004.
11. J.M.E.Hyland and C.-H.L.Ong. On full abstraction for PCF: I, II and III. Information and Computation 163: 285–408, 2000.
12. R.Lazić. A Semantic Study of Data Independence with Applications to Model Checking. DPhil thesis, Computing Laboratory, Oxford University, 1999.
13. C.-H.L.Ong. Observational equivalence of 3rd-order Idealised Algol is Decidable. In Proceedings of LICS, IEEE, July 2002.
14. J.C.Reynolds. The essence of Algol. In Proceedings of ISAL, 345–372, Amsterdam, Holland, 1981.

15. M.Roggenbach. CSP-CASL — A new Integration of Process Algebra and Algebraic Specification. In Proceedings of AMiLP, TWLT 21, Universiteit Twente, 2003.
16. A.W.Roscoe, P.H.B. Gardiner, M.H.Goldsmith, J.R.Hulance, D.M.Jackson and J.B.Scattergod. Hierarchical compression for model-checking CSP or how to check 10^{20} dining philosophers for deadlock. In Proceedings of TACAS, LNCS 1019, May 1995.
17. A.W.Roscoe. The Theory and Practice of Concurrency. Prentice Hall, 1998.

An Equational Calculus for Alloy

Marcelo F. Frias[*,1], Carlos G. López Pombo[2], and Nazareno M. Aguirre[3]

[1]Department of Computer Science, School of Exact and Natural Sciences,
University of Buenos Aires, Argentina, and CONICET
{mfrias,clpombo}@dc.uba.ar
[2]Department of Computer Science, School of Exact and Natural Sciences,
University of Buenos Aires, Argentina
[3]Department of Computer Science, FCEFQyN,
Universidad Nacional de Río Cuarto, Argentina
aguirre@dc.exa.unrc.edu.ar

Abstract. In this paper we show that, by translating Alloy formulas to formulas in the language of fork algebras, we obtain a complete, equational, and purely relational calculus for Alloy.

1   Introduction

Alloy [10] is a formal modeling language that is gaining acceptance within the formal methods community. Its main feature is its tool support. The Alloy Analyzer [8] performs a kind of bounded model checking that allows one to find counterexamples of supplied assertions within a model description written in Alloy. Another important feature of Alloy is its amenable language, which incorporates constructs ubiquitous in object modeling notations. Also, its easy to understand semantics, based on relations, makes the language appealing.

Contributions of This Paper: At the same time a vast research has been carried on about the analysis of Alloy specifications using SAT solving [9, 10], not much research has been done so far on the analysis of Alloy specifications using theorem proving. In order to prove Alloy assertions from Alloy specifications, in this paper we propose the following procedure:

1. Translate both the assertions and the specification to equations in the language of fork algebras [4].
2. Verify equationally whether the translated assertions can be derived from the translation of the specification.

The language of fork algebras is quite similar to Alloy in that it predicates exclusively about relations (binary in this case). The advantage of moving to fork algebras comes from the fact there is a complete (equational) calculus for reasoning about this class of algebras. Therefore, proving an Alloy formula reduces to proving its translation in this complete equational calculus.

---

[*] Research partially funded by Antorchas foundation and project UBACYT X094.

J. Davies et al. (Eds.): ICFEM 2004, LNCS 3308, pp. 162–175, 2004.

Relevance to Formal Engineering Methods: The Alloy modeling language and the Alloy Analyzer are being applied in domains such as air traffic control [3] or verification of medical software [12]. While the kind of analysis provided by Alloy is extremely useful, it does not substitute analysis techniques such as theorem proving. There has been a growing interest in combining the SAT-solving approach of Alloy with theorem proving (we will elaborate on this in the next paragraph), and our hope is that new tools developed in this direction take into account the limitations pointed out here, as well as the possible solutions we offer.

Comparison with Previous Work: Since a broad comparison with other formal methods that combine model checking and theorem proving might make us loose focus, we will compare with the specific work that has already been done on theorem proving from Alloy specifications. Prioni [2] is a tool that combines the model checking capabilities offered by Alloy with the theorem proving capabilities provided by the (semi-automatic) theorem prover Athena [1]. Athena's characterisation of Alloy allows one to reason about specifications, using (semi automatic) theorem proving. However, the proposed characterisation does not capture well some features of Alloy and its relational logic, such as, for instance, the uniform treatment for scalars, singletons and relations. Quoting the authors,

> "Recall that all values in Alloy are relations. In particular, Alloy blurs the type distinction between scalars and singletons. In our Athena formalization, however, this distinction is explicitly present and can be onerous for the Alloy user." (cf. [2, p. 6])

Prioni has also a number of further shortcomings, such as the, in our opinion, awkward representations of *Alloy*'s composition operation '.' and of ordered pairs [2, p. 4]. This tool, however, manages to integrate the use of theorem proving with the SAT solving based analysis of the Alloy Analyzer, cleverly assisting theorem proving with SAT solving and vice versa. The mechanisms used to combine SAT solving and theorem proving are independent of the theorem prover used and the axiomatic characterisation of Alloy. Thus, they could also be employed to combine the Alloy Analyzer with other approaches to reasoning about Alloy specifications, such as, for instance, the one presented in this paper.

In a previous paper [6] we presented a semantics for Alloy based on fork algebras. In that paper, the way in which we assigned semantics to quantification followed Alloy's definition, which is not equational. In this paper we present a complete and equational calculus for reasoning about Alloy assertions, in the context of Alloy specifications. Moreover, the language of fork algebras is closer to Alloy than the language used in Prioni because fork algebras talk about relations at the same level of abstraction that Alloy does.

Structure of the Paper: In Section 2 we present the syntax and semantics of Alloy, as well as a sample of Alloy specification that will be used in Section 3.4. In Section 3 we present the main results of the paper. It contains a description of fork algebras, including ways to deal with relations that are not binary.

It presents the translation of Alloy formulas to fork algebra equations, and a theorem that shows that the translation indeed captures the meaning of Alloy formulas. The section finishes with an example. Finally, in Section 4, we state our conclusions about the presented work.

2   Syntax and Semantics of Alloy

In this section we present the syntax and semantics of Alloy's relational logic as extracted from [10]. The relational logic is the kernel of Alloy. The language is then defined by means of extensions of the kernel that can be reduced to relational logic formulas. Constructs such as 'Functions' allow one to define abbreviations for formulas. 'Facts' are axioms constraining the model, and 'Assertions' are properties intended to hold that are subject to analysis within the model. For a careful description of these concepts, the reader is directed to [10]. A good source of information on Alloy is the paper [9], but the semantics is given in terms of binary relations unlike the latest version of Alloy [10], where relations have arbitrary finite ranks. In Fig. 1, we present the grammar and semantics of *Alloy*'s relational logic. Composition of binary relations is well understood; but for relations of higher rank, the following definition for the composition of relations has to be considered:

$$R; S = \{\langle a_1, \ldots, a_{i-1}, b_2, \ldots, b_j \rangle :$$
$$\exists b \left(\langle a_1, \ldots, a_{i-1}, b \rangle \in R \ \wedge \ \langle b, b_2, \ldots, b_j \rangle \in S \right) \} \ .$$

Example 1. Let us consider the following fragment of Alloy specification for memories, extracted from [10].

sig Addr { }   sig Data { }

These are basic signatures. We do not assume any special properties regarding the structures of data and addresses.

A possible way of defining memories is by saying that a memory consists of set of addresses, and a (total) mapping from these addresses to data values:

sig Memory {
addrs: set Addr
map: addrs ->! Data
}

The symbol "!" in the above definition indicates that "map" is functional and total (for each element a of addrs, there exists exactly one element d in *Data* such that $\mathrm{map}(a) = d$).

Alloy allows for the definition of signatures as subsets of the set denoted by other "parent" signature. This is done via what is called *signature extension*. For the example, one could define other (perhaps more complex) kinds of memories as extensions of the *Memory* signature:

$problem ::= \text{decl}^* form$
$decl ::= var : typexpr$
$typexpr ::=$
$type$
$| \ type \rightarrow type$
$| \ type \Rightarrow typexpr$

$M : \text{form} \rightarrow env \rightarrow Boolean$
$X : \text{expr} \rightarrow env \rightarrow value$
$env = (var + type) \rightarrow value$
$value = (atom \times \cdots \times atom) +$
$\quad (atom \rightarrow value)$

form ::=
expr *in* expr (subset)
|!form (neg)
| form && form (conj)
| form || form (disj)
| all $v : type$/form (univ)
| some $v : type$/form (exist)

$M[a \ in \ b]e = X[a]e \subseteq X[b]e$
$M[!F]e = \neg M[F]e$
$M[F\&\&G]e = M[F]e \wedge M[G]e$
$M[F \ || \ G]e = M[F]e \vee M[G]e$
$M[all \ v : t/F] =$
$\quad \bigwedge\{M[F](e \oplus v \mapsto \{ x \})/x \in e(t)\}$
$M[some \ v : t/F] =$
$\quad \bigvee\{M[F](e \oplus v \mapsto \{ x \})/x \in e(t)\}$

expr ::=
expr + expr (union)
| expr & expr (intersection)
| expr − expr (difference)
|∼ expr (transpose)
| expr.expr (navigation)
| +expr (closure)
| $\{v : t/form\}$ (set former)
| Var

$X[a + b]e = X[a]e \cup X[b]e$
$X[a\&b]e = X[a]e \cap X[b]e$
$X[a - b]e = X[a]e \setminus X[b]e$
$X[\sim a]e = (X[a]e)^{\smile}$
$X[a.b]e = X[a]e ; X[b]e$
$X[+a]e = $ the smallest r such that
$\quad r ; r \subseteq r$ and $X[a]e \subseteq r$
$X[\{v : t/F\}]e =$
$\quad \{x \in e(t)/M[F](e \oplus v \mapsto \{ x \})\}$
$X[v]e = e(v)$
$X[a[v]]e = \{\langle y_1, \ldots, y_n\rangle /$
$\quad \exists x. \langle x, y_1, \ldots, y_n\rangle \in e(a) \wedge \langle x \rangle \in e(v)\}$

$Var ::=$
var (variable)
| $Var[var]$ (application)

Fig. 1. Grammar and semantics of Alloy

sig *MainMemory* extends *Memory* {}

sig *Cache* extends *Memory* {
    dirty: set addrs
}

With these definitions, *MainMemory* and *Cache* are special kinds of memories. In caches, a subset of addrs is recognised as *dirty*.

A system might now be defined to be composed of a main memory and a cache:

sig *System* {
    cache: *Cache*
    main: *MainMemory*
}

3   A Complete Equational Calculus for Alloy, Based on Fork Algebras

We begin this section by introducing in Section 3.1 the class of fork algebras. Fork algebras are closely related to Alloy's semantics because they provide a formalism for dealing with (binary) relations. Actually, fork algebras are even closer to NP [7], a specification language also developed by Jackson and that later evolved to Alloy. Since fork algebras allow us to deal with binary relations and Alloy handles relations of arbitrary arity, in Sections 3.2 and 3.3 we show how to emulate these kinds of relation in fork algebras. Finally, in Section 3.4 we present the mapping and present a theorem connecting Alloy terms with their translation. Finally, we present an example illustrating the way the translation works.

3.1   Fork Algebras

Fork algebras [4] are described through few equational axioms. The intended models of these axioms are structures called *proper fork algebras*, in which the domain is a set of binary relations (on some base set, let us say B), closed under the following operations for sets:

- *union* of two binary relations, denoted by $\cup$,
- *intersection* of two binary relations, denoted by $\cap$,
- *complement* of a binary relation, denoted, for a binary relation r, by $\bar{r}$,
- the *empty* binary relation, which does not relate any pair of objects, and is denoted by $\emptyset$,
- the *universal* binary relation, usually $B \times B$, that will be denoted by 1.

Besides the previous operations for sets, the domain has to be closed under the following operations for binary relations:

- *transposition* of a binary relation. This operation swaps elements in the pairs of a binary relation. Given a binary relation r, its transposition is denoted by $\breve{r}$,
- *composition* of two binary relations, which, for binary relations r and s is denoted by $r\,;s$,
- *reflexive–transitive closure*, which, for a binary relation r, is denoted by r^*,
- the *identity* relation (on B), denoted by Id.

Finally, a binary operation called *fork* is included, which requires the base set B to be closed under an injective function $\star$. This means that there are elements x in B that are the result of applying the function $\star$ to elements y and z. Since $\star$ is injective, x can be seen as an encoding of the pair $\langle y, z \rangle$. The application of fork to binary relations R and S is denoted by $R \nabla S$, and its definition is given by:

$$R \nabla S = \{ \langle a, b \star c \rangle : \langle a, b \rangle \in R \text{ and } \langle a, c \rangle \in S \} \ .$$

The operation *cross* (denoted by $\otimes$) performs a kind of parallel product. Its set-theoretical definition is given by:

$$R \otimes S = \{ \langle a \star c, b \star d \rangle : \langle a, b \rangle \in R \wedge \langle c, d \rangle \in S \} \ .$$

Once the class of proper fork algebras has been presented, the class of fork algebras is axiomatized with the following formulas:

1. Your favorite set of equations axiomatizing Boolean algebras. These axioms define the meaning of union, intersection, complement, the empty set and the universal relation.

2. Formulas defining composition of binary relations, transposition, reflexive–transitive closure and the identity relation:

$$x; (y;z) = (x;y) ;z,$$
$$x;Id = Id;x = x,$$
$$(x;y) \cap z = \emptyset \text{ iff } (z;\breve{y}) \cap x = \emptyset \text{ iff } (\breve{x};z) \cap y = \emptyset,$$
$$x^* = Id \cup (x;x^*),$$
$$x^*;y;1 \leq (y;1) \cup \left(x^*;(\overline{y;1} \cap (x;y;1))\right).$$

3. Formulas defining the operator ∇:

$$x \nabla y = (x; (Id\nabla 1)) \cap (y; (1\nabla Id)),$$
$$(x \nabla y) ;(w \nabla z)^\vee = (x;\breve{w}) \cap (y;\breve{z}),$$
$$(Id\nabla 1)^\vee \nabla (1\nabla Id)^\vee \leq Id.$$

The axioms given above define a class of models. Proper fork algebras satisfy the axioms [5], and therefore belong to this class. It could be the case that there are models for the axioms that are not proper fork algebras. Fortunately, as was proved in [5], [4, Thm. 4.2], if a model is not a proper fork algebra then it is isomorphic to one.

In Section 3.4 we will need to handle fork terms involving variables denoting relations. Following the definition of the semantics of Alloy, we define a mapping Y that, given an environment in which these variables get values, homomorphically allows to calculate the values of terms. The definition is given in Fig. 2. The set U is the domain of a fork algebra, and therefore a set of binary relations.

$$Y : \text{expr} \rightarrow \text{env} \rightarrow U$$
$$\text{env} = (\text{var} + \text{type}) \rightarrow U.$$

$$Y[\emptyset]e = \text{smallest element in } U$$
$$Y[1]e = \text{largest element in } U$$
$$Y[\overline{a}]e = \overline{Y[a]e}$$
$$Y[a \cup b]e = Y[a]e \cup Y[b]e$$
$$Y[a \cap b]e = Y[a]e \cap Y[b]e$$
$$Y[\breve{a}]e = (Y[a]e)^\vee$$
$$Y[Id]e = Id$$
$$Y[a;b]e = Y[a]e;Y[b]e$$
$$Y[a \nabla b]e = Y[a]e \nabla Y[b]e$$
$$Y[a^*]e = (Y[a]e)^*$$
$$Y[v]e = e(v)$$

Fig. 2. Semantics of fork terms involving variables

3.2   Representing Objects and Sets

We will represent sets by binary relations contained in the identity relation. Thus, for an arbitrary type t and an environment env, $env(t) \subseteq Id$ must hold. That is, for a given type t, its meaning in an environment env is a binary relation contained in the identity binary relation. Similarly, for an arbitrary variable v of type t, $env(v)$ must be a relation of the form $\{\langle x, x \rangle\}$, with $\langle x, x \rangle \in env(t)$. This is obtained by imposing the following conditions on $env(v)$[1]:

$$env(v) \subseteq env(t),$$
$$env(v); 1; env(v) = env(v),$$
$$env(v) \neq \emptyset \,.$$

Actually, given binary relations x and y satisfying the properties:

$$y \subseteq Id, \quad x \subseteq y, \quad x; 1; x = x, \quad x \neq \emptyset, \tag{1}$$

it is easy to show that x must be of the form $\{\langle a, a \rangle\}$ for some object a. Thus, given an object a, by a we will also denote the binary relation $\{\langle a, a \rangle\}$. Since y represents a set, by $x : y$ we assert the fact that x is an object of type y, which implies that x and y satisfy the formulas in (1).

3.3   Representing and Navigating Relations of Higher Rank in Fork Algebras

In a proper fork algebra the relations π and ρ defined by

$$\pi = (1' \nabla 1)^{\smile}, \quad \rho = (1 \nabla 1')^{\smile}$$

behave as projections with respect to the encoding of pairs induced by the injective function $\star$. Their semantics in a proper fork algebra $\mathfrak{A}$ whose binary relations range over a set B, is given by

$$\pi = \{\langle a \star b, a \rangle : a, b \in B\},$$

$$\rho = \{\langle a \star b, b \rangle : a, b \in B\}\,.$$

From the definitions of fork, π and ρ, operation $\otimes$ is definable as follows:

$$R \otimes S = (\pi; R) \nabla (\rho; S)\,.$$

Given a n-ary relation $R \subseteq A_1 \times \cdots \times A_n$, we will represent it by the binary relation

$$\{\langle a_1, a_2 \star \cdots \star a_n \rangle : \langle a_1, \ldots, a_n \rangle \in R\}\,.$$

---

[1] The proof requires relation 1 to be of the form $B \times B$ for some nonempty set B.

This will be an invariant in the representation of n-ary relations by binary ones.

For instance, given an Alloy ternary relation

$$\text{map} \subseteq \textit{Memory} \times \text{addrs} \times \text{Data},$$

in our framework it is encoded as a binary relation map whose elements are pairs of the form $\langle m, a \star d \rangle$ for $m : \textit{Memory}$, $a : \text{Addr}$ and $d : \text{Data}$. We will in general denote the encoding of a relation C as a binary relation, by C. Given an object (in the relational sense — cf. 3.2) $m : \text{Memory}$, the navigation of the relation map through m should result in a binary relation contained in Addr $\times$ Data. Given a relational object $a : t$ and a binary relation R encoding a relation of rank higher than 2, we define the navigation operation $\bullet$ by

$$a \bullet R = \breve{\pi} \,; Ran\,(a\,;R) \,; \rho \,. \tag{2}$$

Operation Ran in (2) returns the range of a relation as a partial identity. It is defined by

$$Ran\,(x) = (x\,;1) \cdot 1' \,.$$

Its semantics in terms of binary relations is given by

$$Ran\,(R) = \{\, \langle a, a \rangle : \exists b \text{ s.t. } \langle b, a \rangle \in R \,\} \,.$$

If we denote by $x \xrightarrow{R} y$ the fact that x and y are related via the relation R, then Fig. 3 gives a graphical explanation of operation $\bullet$.

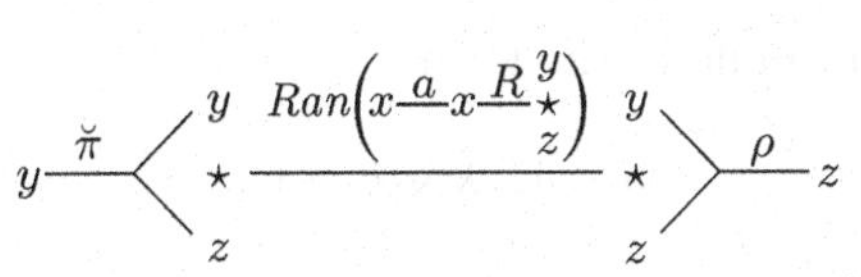

Fig. 3. Semantics of $\bullet$

For a binary relation R representing a relation of rank 2, navigation is easier. Given a relational object $a : t$, we define

$$a \bullet R = Ran\,(a\,;R) \,.$$

Going back to our example about memories, it is easy to check that for a relational object $m' : \textit{Memory}$ such that $m' = \{\, \langle m, m \rangle \,\}$,

$$m' \bullet \text{map} = \{\, \langle a, d \rangle : a \in Addr, d \in Data \text{ and } \langle m, a \star d \rangle \in \text{map} \} \,.$$

3.4   Translating Alloy Formulas to Fork Algebra Equations

It is well known [13, p. 26] that Boolean combinations of relation algebraic equations can be translated into a single equation of the form $R = 1$. Since

Alloy terms are typed, the translation must be modified slightly. We denote by 1 the untyped universal relation. By 1_k we will denote the universal k-ary relation, and by Id_k we denote the k-ary identity relation. The transformation, for n-ary Alloy terms a and b, is:

$$a \text{ in } b \rightsquigarrow 1_n - (a - b) = 1_n$$

For a formula of the form $!(a = 1_n)$, we reason as follows:

$$!(a = 1_n) \iff !(1_n - a = 0) .$$

Now, from a nonempty n-ary relation, we must generate a universal n-ary relation. Notice that if $1_n - a$ is nonempty, then $1_1 . (1_n - a)$ is nonempty, and has arity $n - 1$. Thus, the term

$$\underbrace{1_1 . (\cdots . (1_1 . (1_n - a)) \cdots)}_{n-1}$$

yields a nonempty 1-ary relation. If we post compose it with 1_2, we obtain the universal 1-ary relation. If the resulting relation is then composed with the $(n+1)$-ary universal relation, we obtain the desired n-ary universal relation. We then have

$$!(a = 1_n) \rightsquigarrow \underbrace{(1_1 . (\cdots . (1_1 . (1_n - a)) \cdots).1_2).1_{n+1}}_{n-1} = 1_n .$$

If we are given a formula of the form

$$a = 1_n \text{ \&\& } b = 1_m,$$

with $n = m$, then the translation is trivial:

$$a = 1_n \text{ \&\& } b = 1_m \rightsquigarrow a\&b = 1_n .$$

If $m > n$, we will convert a into a m-ary relation a' such that $a' = 1_m$ if and only if $a = 1_n$. Let a' be defined as

$$a.Id_3.1_{m-n+1} .$$

Then,

$$a = 1_n \text{ \&\& } b = 1_m \rightsquigarrow a'\&b = 1_m .$$

Therefore, we will assume that whenever a quantifier occurs in a formula, it appears being applied to an equation of the form $R = 1_n$, for some n. Since variables in RL stand for single objects, we will first convert term R into a term of the form

$$(Id_{S_1} \otimes \cdots \otimes Id_{S_k}) \otimes R .$$

Intuitively, the term $Id_{S_1} \otimes \cdots \otimes Id_{S_k}$ allows us to pass on the value of the free variables occurring in R so that the values can be retrieved at any time. If we define relations $X_i (1 \leq i \leq k)$ by

$$X_i = \begin{cases} \rho^{;(i-1)};\pi & \text{if } 1 \leq i < k, \\ \rho^{;(i-1)} & \text{if } i = k, \end{cases}$$

an input $a_1 \star \cdots \star a_k$ is related through term X_i to a_i. Notice then that the term $Dom\,(\pi;X_i \cap \rho)$ filters those inputs $(a_1 \star \cdots \star a_k) \star b$ in which $a_i \neq b$ (i.e., the value b is bound to be a_i). The translation is defined as follows:

$$\begin{aligned}
T(C) &= (Id_{S_1} \otimes \cdots \otimes Id_{S_k}) \otimes C, \\
T(x_i) &= Dom\,(\pi;X_i \cap \rho), \\
T(r+s) &= T(r) \cup T(s), \\
T(r\&s) &= T(r) \cap T(s), \\
T(r-s) &= T(r) \cap \overline{T(s)} \cap ((Id_{S_1} \otimes \cdots \otimes Id_{S_k}) \otimes 1), \\
T(\sim r) &= T(r)^{\smile}, \\
T(+r) &= T(r);T(r)^{*}.
\end{aligned}$$

In order to define the translation for navigation $r.s$ and application $s[v]$, we need to distinguish whether s is a binary relation, or if it has greater arity. The definition is as follows:

$$T(r.s) = \begin{cases} T(r) \bullet T(s) & \text{if } s \text{ is binary,} \\ T(r) \bullet (T(s); ((Id \otimes \pi) \nabla (Id \otimes \rho))) & \text{otherwise.} \end{cases}$$

$$T(s[v]) = \begin{cases} T(v) \bullet T(s) & \text{if } s \text{ is binary,} \\ T(v) \bullet (T(s); ((Id \otimes \pi) \nabla (Id \otimes \rho))) & \text{otherwise.} \end{cases}$$

In case there are no quantified variables, there is no need to carry the values on, and the translation becomes:

$$\begin{aligned}
T(C) &= C, \\
T(r+s) &= T(r) \cup T(s), \\
T(r\&s) &= T(r) \cap T(s), \\
T(r-s) &= T(r) \cap \overline{T(s)}, \\
T(\sim r) &= T(r)^{\smile}, \\
T(+r) &= T(r);T(r)^{*}, \\
T(r.s) &= T(r) \bullet T(s), \\
T(s[r]) &= T(r) \bullet T(s).
\end{aligned}$$

It is now easy to prove a theorem establishing the relationship between Alloy terms and the corresponding translation. Notice that:

- Given a type T, $e(T)$ is a nonempty set.
- Given a variable v, $e(v)$ is a n-ary relation for some $n \in \mathbb{N}$.

We define the environment e' by:

- Given a type T, $e'(T) = \{\langle a, a \rangle : a \in e(T)\}$.
- Given a variable v such that $e(v)$ is a n-ary relation,

$$e'(v) = \begin{cases} \{\langle a, a \rangle : a \in e(v)\} & \text{if } n = 1, \\ \{\langle a_1, a_2 \star \cdots \star a_n \rangle : \langle a_1, a_2, \ldots, a_n \rangle \in e(v)\} & \text{otherwise.} \end{cases}$$

Theorem 1 establishes the relationship between the semantics of Alloy terms and their translation, and allows us to assess that the translation is sound in the sense that it captures the semantics of Alloy terms. For the theorem we assume that whenever the transpose operation or the transitive closure occur in a term, they affect a binary relation. Notice that this is the assumption in [10]. We also assume that whenever the navigation operation is applied, the argument on the left-hand side is a unary relation (set). This is because our representation of relations of arity greater than two makes defining the generalized composition more complicated than desirable. At the same time, use of navigation in object-oriented settings usually falls in the situation modeled by us. In order to simplify notation, we will denote by $b^\star$ the element $b_1 \star \cdots \star b_m$.

Theorem 1. *For every Alloy term t such that:*

1. *$X[t]e$ defines a n-ary relation,*
2. *there are m free variables $x_1, \ldots, x_m$ in t,*

$$Y[T(t)]e' = \begin{cases} \{\langle b^\star \star a, b^\star \star a \rangle : \\ \quad a \in X[t]e(\overline{b} \mapsto \overline{x})\} & \text{if } n = 1 \\ \{\langle b^\star \star a_1, b^\star \star (a_2 \star \cdots \star a_n) \rangle : \\ \quad \langle a_1, \ldots, a_n \rangle \in X[t]e(\overline{b} \mapsto \overline{x})\} & \text{if } n > 1 \end{cases}$$

Proof. (Sketch of the proof) With the aim of using a shorter notation, the value (according to the standard semantics) of an Alloy term t in an environment e will be denoted by $e(t)$ rather than by $X[t]e$. Similarly, the value of a fork algebra term t in an environment e' will be denoted by $e'(t)$ rather than by $Y[t]e'$. The proof follows by induction on the structure of term t. As a sample we prove it for the variables, the remaining cases end up being simple applications of the semantics of the fork algebra operators.

If v is a quantified variable (namely, x_i), then $e(t)$ is a unary relation.

$$\begin{aligned} & e'\left(T(x_i)\right) \\ & = e'\left(Dom\left(\pi; X_i \cap \rho\right)\right) && \text{(by def. } T) \\ & = \{\langle b^\star \star a, b^\star \star a \rangle : a = b_i\} && \text{(by semantics)} \\ & = \{\langle b^\star \star a, b^\star \star a \rangle : a \in \{b_i\}\} && \text{(by set theory)} \\ & = \{\langle b^\star \star a, b^\star \star a \rangle : a \in \left(e(\overline{b} \mapsto \overline{x})\right)(x_i)\} \; . && \text{(by def. } e(\overline{b} \mapsto \overline{x})) \end{aligned}$$

If v is a variable distinct of $x_1, \ldots, x_m$, there are two possibilities.

1. $e(v)$ denotes a unary relation.
2. $e(v)$ denotes a n-ary relation with $n > 1$.

If $e(v)$ denotes a unary relation,

$$
\begin{aligned}
e'\left(T(v)\right) &= e'\left(\left(Id_{S_1} \otimes \cdots \otimes Id_{S_m}\right) \otimes v\right) && \text{(by def. } T) \\
&= \left(Id_{S_1} \otimes \cdots \otimes Id_{S_m}\right) \otimes e'(v) && \text{(by semantics)} \\
&= \left(Id_{S_1} \otimes \cdots \otimes Id_{S_m}\right) \otimes \left\{\, \langle a, a \rangle : a \in e(v) \,\right\} && \text{(by def. } e') \\
&= \left\{\, \langle b^\star \star a, b^\star \star a \rangle : a \in e(v) \,\right\} && \text{(by semantics)} \\
&= \left\{\, \langle b^\star \star a, b^\star \star a \rangle : a \in (e(\overline{b} \mapsto \overline{x})))(v) \,\right\} \ . && \text{(by def. } e(\overline{b} \mapsto \overline{x}))
\end{aligned}
$$

If $e(v)$ denotes a n-ary relation $(n > 1)$,

$$
\begin{aligned}
e'\left(T(v)\right) &= e'\left(\left(Id_{S_1} \otimes \cdots \otimes Id_{S_m}\right) \otimes v\right) && \text{(by def. } T) \\
&= \left(Id_{S_1} \otimes \cdots \otimes Id_{S_m}\right) \otimes e'(v) && \text{(by semantics)} \\
&= \left(Id_{S_1} \otimes \cdots \otimes Id_{S_m}\right) \otimes \left\{\, \langle a_1, a_2 \star \cdots \star a_n \rangle : \langle a_1, \ldots, a_n \rangle \in e(v) \,\right\} && \\
&&& \text{(by def. } e') \\
&= \left\{\, \langle b^\star \star a_1, b^\star \star (a_2 \star \cdots \star a_n) \rangle : \langle a_1, \ldots, a_n \rangle \in e(v) \,\right\} && \text{(by semantics)} \\
&= \left\{\, \langle b^\star \star a_1, b^\star \star (a_2 \star \cdots \star a_n) \rangle : \langle a_1, \ldots, a_n \rangle \in (e(\overline{b} \mapsto \overline{x})))(v) \,\right\} \ . && \\
&&& \text{(by def. } e(\overline{b} \mapsto \overline{x}))
\end{aligned}
$$

∎

From the set-theoretical definition of fork and the remaining relational operators, it follows that[2]

$$
(x_1 \star \cdots \star x_n) \star x \ T(t) \ (x_1 \star \cdots \star x_n) \star y \iff
$$
$$
(x_1 \star \cdots \star x_n) \star x \star y \in \mathsf{ran}\left(Id \ \nabla \ T(t); \rho\right) \ . \quad (3)
$$

Now, it only remains to adequately quantify, using relational expressions, variables $x_1, \ldots, x_n, x, y$. We define the relational term $\exists_{x_i}$ as follows:

$$
\exists_{x_i} = X_1 \nabla \cdots \nabla X_{i-1} \nabla 1_S \nabla X_{i+1} \nabla \cdots \nabla X_k \ .
$$

For instance, if $k = 3$, we have $\exists_{x_2} = X_1 \nabla 1_S \nabla X_3$. This term defines the binary relation

$$
\left\{\, \langle a_1 \star a_3, a_1 \star a_2 \star a_3 \rangle : a_2 \in S \,\right\} \ .
$$

Notice that the term generates all possible values for variable x_2. The term

$$
\exists_{x_2} ; Ran\left(Id \ \nabla \ T(t(x_1, x_2, x_3)); \rho\right) ; 1
$$

describes the binary relation

---

[2] Given a binary relation R, $\mathsf{ran}\,(R)$ denotes the set $\{\, b : \exists a \text{ such that } \langle a, b \rangle \in R \,\}$.

$$\{ \ \langle (a_1 \star a_3) \star a \star b, c \rangle : (\exists a_2 : S)\, (\langle a_1 \star a_2 \star a_3 \rangle \star a, b) \in T(t(x_1, x_2, x_3)) \ \} \ .$$

This term allows us to quantify over the right domain. Profiting from the interdefinability of $\exists$ and $\forall$, the term

$$\overline{\exists_{x_2}; \overline{T(t)}}$$

allows us to quantify variable x_2 universally. We will denote such a term as $\forall_{x_2} T(t)$.

Since variables x and y abstract the input and output values for term $T(t)$ (cf. (3)) and the original equation is of the form $T(t) = 1$, variables x and y must be quantified universally.

Example 2. Let us consider the following Alloy assertion, to be understood in the context of the specification for memories provided in Section 2.

$$\text{some } s : System \mid s.cache.map \text{ in } s.main.map \ . \tag{4}$$

Once converted to an equation of the form $R = 1$, assertion (4) becomes

$$\text{some } s : System \mid 1_2 - (s.cache.map - s.main.map) = 1_2 \ . \tag{5}$$

If we apply translation T to the term on the left-hand side of the equality in (5), it becomes

$$\overline{Dom\,(\pi; X_s \cap \rho) \bullet \begin{matrix} Id_S \\ \otimes \\ cache \end{matrix} \bullet \begin{pmatrix} Id_S & Id \otimes \pi \\ \otimes & ; & \nabla \\ map & Id \otimes \rho \end{pmatrix}} \cap \begin{pmatrix} Id_S \\ \otimes \\ 1 \end{pmatrix}$$

$$\cup \ Dom\,(\pi; X_s \cap \rho) \bullet \begin{matrix} Id_S \\ \otimes \\ main \end{matrix} \bullet \begin{pmatrix} Id_S & Id \otimes \pi \\ \otimes & ; & \nabla \\ map & Id \otimes \rho \end{pmatrix} \ . \tag{6}$$

Since s is the only variable, $X_s = \rho^0 = Id$, and therefore (6) becomes

$$\overline{Dom\,(\pi \cap \rho) \bullet \begin{matrix} Id_S \\ \otimes \\ cache \end{matrix} \bullet \begin{pmatrix} Id_S & Id \otimes \pi \\ \otimes & ; & \nabla \\ map & Id \otimes \rho \end{pmatrix}} \cap \begin{pmatrix} Id_S \\ \otimes \\ 1 \end{pmatrix}$$

$$\cup \ Dom\,(\pi \cap \rho) \bullet \begin{matrix} Id_S \\ \otimes \\ main \end{matrix} \bullet \begin{pmatrix} Id_S & Id \otimes \pi \\ \otimes & ; & \nabla \\ map & Id \otimes \rho \end{pmatrix} \ . \tag{7}$$

Certainly (7) is harder to read than the equation in (4). This can probably be improved by adding adequate syntactic sugar to the language. Let us denote by E the term in (7). Following our recipe, we arrive to the following equation

$$\exists_s; \forall_x \forall_y \,(Ran\,(Id \ \nabla \ E; \rho)\,; 1) = 1 \ . \tag{8}$$

4   Conclusions

Even although theorem proving was not considered a critical issue during the development of Alloy, it has been lately recognized as a significant problem that deserves to be addressed. The tool Prioni allows one to prove properties from Alloy specification but at the expense of requiring the user to learn another language conceptually different of Alloy in order to understand proof steps. Although the language of fork algebras is not the same as Alloy, from a conceptual viewpoint the language of fork algebras shares common principles with Alloy, as for instance the fact that objects are relations. This is one of the cornerstones of Alloy, and is shared by fork algebras but not by the language used in Athena.

References

1. Arkoudas K., *Type-ω DPLs*, MIT AI Memo 2001-27, 2001.
2. Arkoudas K., Khurshid S., Marinov D. and Rinard M., *Integrating Model Checking and Theorem Proving for Relational Reasoning*, to appear in Proceedings of RelMiCS'03.
3. Gregory Dennis, *TSAFE: Building a Trusted Computing Base for Air Traffic Control Software*. MIT Masters Thesis, January 2003.
4. Frias M., *Fork Algebras in Algebra, Logic and Computer Science*, World Scientific Publishing Co., Series Advances on Logic, 2002.
5. Frias, M. F., Haeberer, A. M. and Veloso, P. A. S., *A Finite Axiomatization for Fork Algebras*, Logic Journal of the IGPL, Vol. 5, No. 3, 311–319, 1997.
6. Frias M., López Pombo C., Baum G., Aguirre N. and Maibaum T., *Taking Alloy to the Movies*, in Proceedings of FME'03, Pisa, Italy, 2003, LNCS 2805, pp. 678–697.
7. Jackson D., *Nitpick: A checkable specificacion language*, in proceedings of Formal Methods in Software Practice, January 1996.
8. Jackson D., *Micromodels of Software: Lightweight Modelling and Analysis with Alloy*, 2002.
9. Jackson D., *Alloy: A Lightweight Object Modelling Notation*, ACM Transactions on Software Engineering and Methodology (TOSEM), Volume 11, Issue 2 (April 2002), pp. 256-290.
10. Jackson, D., Shlyakhter, I., and Sridharan, M., *A Micromodularity Mechanism*. Proc. ACM SIGSOFT Conf. Foundations of Software Engineering/European Software Engineering Conference (FSE/ESEC '01), Vienna, September 2001.
11. Maddux R., *Pair-Dense Relation Algebras*, Transactions of the American Mathematical Society, Vol. 328, N. 1, 1991.
12. Andrew Rae, Prasad Ramanan, Daniel Jackson, and Jay Flanz. *Critical feature analysis of a radiotherapy machine*. International Conference of Computer Safety, Reliability and Security (SAFECOMP 2003), Edinburgh, September 2003.
13. Tarski, A. and Givant, S., *A Formalization of Set Theory without Variables*, A.M.S. Coll. Pub., vol. 41, 1987.

Guiding Spin Simulation*

Nicolae Goga and Judi Romijn

Department of Mathematics and Computer Science,
Eindhoven University of Technology,
P.O. Box 513, NL–5600 MB Eindhoven,
the Netherlands
{goga, jromijn}@win.tue.nl

Abstract. In this paper we present a technique for the Spin tool, inspired by practical experiences with Spin and a FireWire protocol. We show how to guide simulations with Spin, by constructing a special *guide* process that limits the behaviour of the original system. We set up a theoretical framework in which we prove under some sufficient conditions that the adjusted system (with the added *guide* process) exhibits a subset of the behaviour of the original system, and has no new deadlocks. We have applied this technique to a Promela specification of the IEEE 1394.1 FireWire net update algorithm. The experiment shows that this technique increases the error detecting power of Spin in the sense that we found errors in the guided specification, which could not be discovered with Spin simulation and validation in the original specification.

1 Introduction

When validating designs using exhaustive verification methods, one can nowadays employ a wealth of model checking tools and methods, such as Spin [8], CADP [5], μCRL [1], Murphi [4], SMV [3], HyTech [7], Kronos [16], TVS [2], and Uppaal [12]. However, for real-life designs of complex systems, one quickly encounters the limits of what these tools and methods can handle, and exhaustive verification of the full required functionality often turns out to be infeasible.

An alternative method in such cases is to perform experiments rather than to do a verification, which may help to find errors. Many verification tools provide this possibility in the form of simulation. Often, simulation helps in finding errors in two ways: (1) by experimenting with the model interactively, the user obtains a better understanding of the behaviour of his/her system and can check specific scenarios, and (2) by random simulations, unpredicted situations can be found. Based upon these findings, the model of the system can be improved.

The major drawback of such an experimenting approach is of course that coverage of the full behaviour is not achieved: when no (more) errors are found

---

* This research is supported by NWO under project 016.023.015 "Improving the Quality of Protocol Standards", URL: http://www.win.tue.nl/oas/iqps/index.html.

using simulation, there is no guarantee whatsoever that a system is correct. But if verification is infeasible, experimenting may be the only way to gain confidence.

This paper presents a technique for lifting a practical drawback of simulation with the tool Spin, which allows a mixture of interactive and automated simulation by adjusting the Promela code to be simulated. This approach is useful when ordinary interactive simulation requires a disproportionate number of simulation steps and automated (random) simulation does not cover enough of the interesting parts of the state space. Our technique, called guiding, consists of adjusting the Promela specification somewhat, and most importantly, constructing a special extra process called Guide. The Guide restricts the behaviour of the system that it is added to, such that by some sufficient conditions no new behaviour and no new deadlocks are introduced. The Guide can be employed to drive the simulations into interesting parts of the state space, and enables a user to experiment with certain (types of) scenarios.

In order to guide sensibly, the direct intervention and judgement of the user are needed: it is not possible to decide automatically how arbitrary Promela code should be guided. However, it is likely that such interesting scenarios can often easily be determined by the user who has a good understanding of at least part of his/her specification. We do not provide an automation of the adjustment itself, since this would introduce more overhead and limit the freedom for the user to use Promela language constructs freely.

Besides simulation, it is also possible to perform verification on the guided Promela code. The guiding construction is such that whenever a safety property is violated in the guided Promela, this holds for the original Promela as well.

Related Work. In [6], a high-level approach to guiding is taken, called *temporal debugging*. Here, a property in the temporal logic LTL is used to restrict the system behaviour and an exploration algorithm is developed that allows for interactive simulation with backtracking facilities. This approach has the advantage of a high abstraction level that is independent of the actual specification language and supporting tools used. However, since there is no implementation available, it is hard to assess its practical value. For instance, we wonder if one can guide inter-process communication and scheduling as naturally as in our lower-level approach. It may be very cumbersome to express guiding properties in LTL, especially if all basic properties must be expressed in state formulas. Also, it seems that any implementation of the exploration algorithm in [6] would add quite a lot of overhead due to its model checking-like features. This would be very undesirable for the specifications we are interested in, which are too large and complicated for the current model checkers.

Our work can be seen as a dedicated instantiation of the superimposition approach as described in [14], in sequential order with specific constraints and properties for the Promela syntax and semantics.

Further, our approach to guiding may seem similar to techniques based on *monitoring*. In Spin, the Promela `trace` proctype can be used for this purpose. However, when monitoring, the behaviour of a specification is not limited or steered (as we intend to do), but rather observed. Another Promela construct,

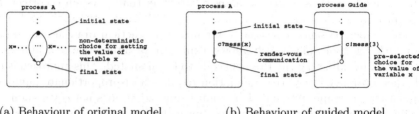

(a) Behaviour of original model   (b) Behaviour of guided model

Fig. 1. Guiding non-determinism in internal computation

the STDIN channel, does resemble our guiding approach, because it allows to mix user (or application) interaction with automated simulation. However, here only one parameter per communication is allowed on the one special channel. In our approach, as many parameters as desired are allowed. Moreover, we allow to pre-select in a set of possible rendez-vous communications, to schedule internal activity among different processes, and even to attempt verification, all of which cannot be done with the STDIN channel. The *breakpoints* present in Spin which can be used during random simulation can help in monitoring, but not in guiding since it is not possible to switch to interactive simulation.

Finally, tools exist in which during simulation, a special *environment* process is always present, and user interaction at certain points is possible. One of these tools is Telelogic/Tau [15]. In such a tool, the specification is an open system, where the environment must guide everything (with or without user interaction). We are interested in guiding only part of the behaviour of Promela specifications, which are closed, and in opening up such a closed system only partly.

Our approach has been applied in Spin simulation of a Promela specification of the net update protocol from the IEEE P1394.1 FireWire Bridges draft standard [11]. This has resulted in the detection of errors that were not found with ordinary Spin simulation and verification.

Organization. Section 2 presents the idea and techniques of guiding on the Promela level, which is rather informal. Section 3 presents the theoretic framework and the proofs. Finally, Section 4 describes our experiments with the net update algorithm from the IEEE P1394.1 draft standard.

Acknowledgements. We thank Arjan Mooij and the anonymous referees for useful comments on this paper, and Gia Tagviashvili for his input in an early stage of this research.

2   Guiding Promela

In this section, we explain what we mean with guiding Promela specifications, and what we intend to achieve. We present our examples, definitions, sufficient conditions, and desired properties informally, on the level of Promela code. This

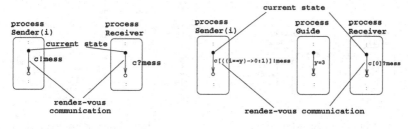

(a) Behaviour of original model   (b) Behaviour of guided model

Fig. 2. Guiding rendez-vous communication possibilities

yields a compact, understandable view, which can also serve as instruction for a user who would like to guide Spin simulations with the techniques presented. It is, however, too informal for actual proof. Section 3 presents the same definitions, sufficient conditions and desired properties, now on the level of the automata that provide semantics to Promela specifications. That section is harder to read, but does show the theoretic soundness and feasibility.

Familiarity is assumed with Promela language constructs such as assignments (with =), conditions ((c)), conditional expressions ((c->e1:e2)), selection statements (if ... fi), loops (do ... od) and grouping (atomic{...}). We refer to the Spin book and web site [8].

What we want in Spin simulation is control over what happens, without having to perform all simulation steps interactively, by fixing some choices which are left open in the Promela specification. We signal three important kinds of choices that we intend to guide: (1) non-determinism inside a process, (2) multiple rendez-vous communication possibilities between sending and receiving processes, and (3) scheduling possibilities between different processes. We guide these choices by adding an extra Guide process that interferes and provides pre-selected fixed values. The definitions of processes to be guided are altered a little. The guided Promela specification is simulated without user interaction, exhibiting only the restricted behaviour, and can even be model checked for safety properties, where each erroneous behaviour found in the guided Promela is also present in the original Promela (but not the other way around).

The Guide process can interfere with the original processes only through communication and the values of global variables. In order to only restrict behaviour and not introduce new behaviour, the Guide can only use communication channels and affect global variables that are not present in the original Promela specification. We choose to guide non-determinism inside a process by having it communicate with the Guide process, and to guide multiple rendez-vous communication possibilities and scheduling possibilities by having the communication and process enabling depend on fresh global variables which are controlled by the Guide process. All of these are depicted in Figures 1, 2, and 3.

In the first example, the behaviour of process A (Figure 1(a)) can be restricted by adding a Guide process that fixes a value (3, in this case) and communicates

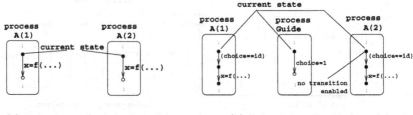

(a) Behaviour of original model   (b) Behaviour of guided model

Fig. 3. Guiding scheduling possibilities

with process A. In process A, the internal computation fragment is replaced with this new communication (Figure 1(b)).

In the second example, there are many instances of a Sender proctype that can communicate with one Receiver process (Figure 2(a)). The multiple communication possibilities can be restricted by adding a fresh global variable (y in this case) which is controlled by the Guide process, changing the type of the channel in question to an array with an extra index, and adding an expression index for each Sender that depends on the new global variable. The Receiver is modified such that it expects the communication on index 0. Now the Guide process can control for which Sender process the index expression evaluates to *true*, and thus enable the communication with the Receiver for only that Sender process. All other Sender process try to send on a channel which has no receiver.

In the third example, there are many instances of a proctype A. In Figure 3(a) two of these are represented. Each instance can execute a transition labelled with an assignment to variable x. In the guided model (Figure 3(b)) only instance A(1) will be scheduled to execute this transition. This is realized by adding a transition before the assignment, labelled with a condition that uses the new global variable **choice**, whose preset value is fixed by the Guide process.

Isolated Fragment. In order to guide internal non-determinism, it is necessary to identify the fragment of Promela code in which the non-determinism is present. An *isolated fragment* is a valid sequence of Promela statements that does not contain: (1) communication; (2) assertions; (3) goto statements that jump outside the sequence (the end state of the sequence is allowed). Also, the fragment may not be a part of a larger atomic sequence, when one or more statements precede it in this atomic sequence.

Guiding Promela. Here we describe the three types of guiding. Consider Promela specifications S, S', a proctype definition G, and sets of global variables V and channels C that are not used in S. We call S' a *guided version* of S if S' can be obtained by adjusting S a number of times with any of the following constructions, and adding the extra proctype G, which is instantiated exactly once.

```
proctype A(...) {
...
x=0; /* start of fragment F */
do
:: (x<N) -> x++;
:: (true) -> break;
od; /* end of fragment F */
...
}
```

```
proctype A(...) {
...
chan?mess(x); /* F replaced by rendez-vous receive */
...
}
proctype Guide() {
...
chan!mess(3); /* pre-selected value for x */
...
}
```

(a) Original Promela   (b) Guided Promela

Fig. 4. Type I Guiding in Promela

```
proctype Sender(i:ID) {
...
chan!mess; /* unconditional send */
...
}
proctype Receiver() {
...
chan?mess;
...
}
```

```
ID y; /* fresh global variable */
proctype Sender(i:ID) {
...
c[((i==y)->0:1)]!mess; /* send on c[0] or c[1] */
...
}
proctype Receiver() {
...
c[0]?mess; /* nobody receives on c[1] */
...
}
proctype Guide() {
...
y=3; /* selecting sender A(3) */
...
}
```

(a) Original Promela

(b) Guided Promela

Fig. 5. Type II Guiding in Promela

1. *Type I: Guiding internal non-determinism.* In the Promela code of a proctype, an isolated fragment of Promela may be replaced with a rendez-vous receive statement on a fresh channel $c \in C$.
2. *Type II: Guiding rendez-vous communication possibilities.* If the Promela code of proctype P contains a send (resp. receive) statement on rendez-vous channel (array) c, the specification may be adjusted as follows, where e' is an expression involving local variables of P and global variables from V:
   - If c is an array with range $0..R-1$, and is indexed in P as $c[e]$, then c must become an array with range $0..R$, and be indexed in P as $c[(e'->e:R)]$.
   - If c is not an array, then c must become an array with range $0..1$, and c be indexed in P as $c[(e'->0:1)]$. Any other occurrence of c in any proctype must be indexed as $c[0]$.
3. *Type III: Guiding scheduling possibilities.* In the Promela code of proctype P, an isolated fragment F may be guided by adding a condition e':
   - If the first statement of F is a condition (e) then it is changed to $(e \wedge e')$.
   - If the first statement of F is an assignment then it is preceded by a new condition statement (e') such that the new statement plus the original isolated fragment are contained in one atomic block.

The guide process G may modify global variables in V, perform rendez-vous send actions on channels in C, and perform any internal activity.

```
proctype A(id) {
    ...
    atomic{(id==choice); /* guided assignment */
        x=f(...)} ;
    ...
}
proctype Guide() {
    ...
    choice=1; /* selection of A(1) */
    ...
}
```

```
proctype A(id) {
    ...
    x=f(...); /* assignment */
    ...
}
```

(a) Original Promela

(b) Guided Promela

Fig. 6. Type III Guiding in Promela

The Promela code corresponding to the examples in Figures 1, 2 and 3 is depicted in Figures 4, 5 and 6.

Desired Properties. The following two properties express that the guided Promela specification does not exhibit new behaviour or new deadlocks. Let S, S' be Promela specifications such that S' is a guided version of S. (1) When only observing communication and global variables from S, all behaviour exhibited by S' is also exhibited by S, and (2) whenever S' encounters a deadlock state, in the corresponding original state S also deadlocks. If these properties hold, we can conclude that each safety property that holds for S, must also hold for S'. Hence, if a simulation or verification finds an error in S' (a deadlock or assertion violation S), the same error must be present in S as well.

Sensible Guiding. In order to conclude that the desired properties hold, some sufficient conditions must be met. Let S, S' be Promela specifications such that S' is a guided version of S. S' is *guided sensibly* if the following holds for the behaviour exhibited by S and S'.

- *(Type I Guiding does not introduce new behaviour).* Whenever process instance p can communicate with the Guide in S', it must be possible for p to execute the corresponding isolated fragment in S, such that the effect of the communication on the global variables and the local variables of p in S' is contained in the possible end states of the fragment in S.
- *(The guided processes do not introduce new deadlocks).* Whenever process instance p can execute some statement in S that was adjusted or replaced in S', either some non-guided statement must be executable in S as well, or it must be possible in S' to execute an adjusted or newly added statement.
- *(The Guide process does not introduce new deadlocks).* Whenever S' reaches a state for which the counterpart in S is a valid end state, then in S', the Guide must be in a valid end state as well.

These sufficient conditions require a good understanding of the dynamic behaviour of both the original and the guided system. This may be a problem since the original specification is being debugged. However, in some cases one can decide purely on the syntax of the Promela code that it is guided sensibly. The following conditions imply that the sufficient conditions are satisfied.

- *(Type I Guiding does not introduce new behaviour)*. If process instance p has been adjusted with Type I Guiding, and no variables occur in any expression in the isolated fragment, nor in the rendez-vous send communication of the Guide, then it can be decided statically whether the values communicated by the Guide in the guided specification are contained in the possible outcomes of the isolated fragment in the original specification.
- *(No new deadlocks)*. In each state of the Guide proctype definition, both of the following hold. (1) There is a statement possible that is not a condition or a rendez-vous send communication, and (2) the state is a valid end-state.

Note that if these very restrictive conditions are not met, it is still possible that the Promela is guided sensibly. For example, even if Type I Guiding involves expressions with variables, the user might know with certainty some of the values that these variables can obtain and use these values for guiding. In such a case the Promela is still guided sensibly.

3   Theory Section

In this section, we will provide the theoretic framework for guiding a Promela specification. All the elements of the previous section reappear, and particularly the two desired properties are proved to hold.

We rely on the Promela semantics defined in terms of automata, as presented in the Spin book [8] in Chapters 7, 8 and 16 and Appendix A, with as little detail as possible from the semantics engine. This is the most straightforward way to define precisely what we mean by guiding, and to construct the proofs.

3.1   Preliminaries

We assume the notions of (finite state) automaton, run, asynchronous product, and the semantics for Promela basic statements as defined in the Spin book [8] in Chapters 7, 8 and 16 and Appendix A.

Since we are only considering safety properties, we may assume for sake of simplicity that there is no never claim or trace process present. We also abstract from the details of dynamic process instantiation and termination.

For our purposes, it is convenient to characterize a system with the global variables V, global channels C, and automata $A_1, \ldots, A_n$ that are used to build it (skipping details such as the global handshake, timeout, else variables), and keep the array structures on the channels. So a *system* $\Sigma = (V, C, A_1, \ldots, A_n)$ is assumed to generate the asynchronous product of the automata $A_1, \ldots, A_n$ with semantics provided by the semantics engine.

We will characterize an automaton (generated from a Promela proctype) as a tuple (W, L, l_0, F, R), where W is the set of local variables, L is the set of locations[1], $l_0 \in L$ is the initial location, $F \subseteq L$ is the set of final locations, and R is the set of transitions. Transitions are denoted $l_1 \xrightarrow{a} l_2$, where the action

---

[1] To avoid confusion, we call the abstract states in automata *locations*.

label a can be an assignment, a condition, an assertion or a communication send/receive part. For automaton A, we denote its components with $A.W$, $A.L$, etc. Moreover, for system $\Sigma = (V, C, A_1, \ldots, A_n)$ we often use the abbreviations $\Sigma.R$ for $A_1.R \cup \ldots \cup A_n.R$ and $\Sigma.F$ for $A_1.F \cup \ldots \cup A_n.F$.

A *global system state* s of Σ is a tuple containing (1) for each variable $v \in V \cup A_i.W \cup \ldots \cup A_n.W$, a value: $s.v$, (2) for each buffered channel $c \in C$, the buffer status: $s.c$, and (3) for each automaton A_i, a location of $A_i.L$: $s.A_i$. For the *initial* global system state s_0 we assume that each variable $v \in (V \cup A_i.W \cup \ldots \cup A_n.W)$ has a preset initial value v_0, and we assume that $s_0.A_i$ is $A_i.l_0$. Given global system states s, t, a step of a system is denoted $s \to t$ *with transition* $l_1 \overset{a}{\to} l_2$ to indicate both the effect on the global system state, and the (uninterpreted) automaton transition that governs it. A *run* σ of the system from global system state s to t is denoted $s \overset{\sigma}{\Rightarrow} t$. A global system state s is *reachable* if there is a run from the initial global system state to s. A global system state s is said to *deadlock* if there is no step possible from s and at least one automaton A_i is not in a final location, that is, $s.A_i \notin A_i.F$.

In order to relate the behaviour of the original and the guided Promela system, we need some notion of observable behaviour. We will require the two systems to exhibit the same communication behaviour (channel names and message values per communication, and ordering in a run), and the assertions. The latter is implied if related states have the same values for state variables. We denote an observable step of a system with $s \overset{a}{\rightsquigarrow} t$, where a is the label for the combined send and receive part in case of a rendez-vous communication, or the label of either the send or the receive part in case of buffered communication. In all other cases, a is ϵ (the empty label). The reflexive transitive closure is denoted with $s \overset{ab\cdots}{\rightsquigarrow}{}^* t$.

Promela Language Constructs. Here we list the most important Promela language constructs and indicate their counterparts in the generated automaton in our framework. Constructions such as selections (if ... fi), loops (do ... od), interrupts (...unless...), and jumps (goto ... and break) are encoded in the structure of the automaton. Grouping with dstep{...} is encoded in one transition, whereas each basic statement in an atomic{...} group gives rise to a separate transition in the automaton, with a special mark to be recognised as atomic. Basic statements such as assignments (with =), conditions ((c)), communication on channels (c!m(...) and c?m(...)) and assertions (assert(...)) each give rise to a separate transition in the automaton that is labelled with the statement itself. Note the use of array variables var[index] and conditional expressions (c->a:b).

3.2   Guiding

We start with the definition of an isolated fragment, needed for the first type of guiding. For this definition, we assume that given an automaton, it can be decided syntactically for each location whether it is contained in an atomic sequence (i.e. not the start or the end location of the atomic sequence). We call a location atomic if it is, and non-atomic otherwise.

Definition 1 (Isolated Fragment). *Let A be an automaton, $l_1, l_2 \in A.L$, and $T \subseteq A.R$, such that each transition in T starts in l_1. If each run in A that begins with a transition from T, either contains l_2 or can be extended in A such that it ends in l_2, then we say that the combination of l_1, l_2, T isolates fragment T' of A, where $T' \subseteq A.R$ is the set of all transitions occurring in any run in A that begins with a transition from T, ends in l_2, and does not visit l_2 in between. We demand that fragment T' contains only conditions and assignments, and that location l_1 is non-atomic.*

If the conditions for isolating a fragment are met, it is easy to compute the fragment by finding the fixpoint of k-step reachable transitions in A for arbitrary k, starting with T and $k = 1$.

Now the three types of guiding follow.

Definition 2 (Guiding). *Let $\Sigma = (V, C, A_1, \ldots, A_n)$ be a system, G an automaton, and V' a fresh set of global variables.*

Σ can be guided yielding system $\Sigma' = (V \cup V', C' \cup C_G, A'_1, \ldots, A'_n, G)$ iteratively in m steps, as follows. We call Σ' a guided version of Σ.

To start: $C^0 = C$ and $C_G^0 = \emptyset$, and each $A_i^0 = A_i$. To end: $C' = C^m$, $C_G = C_G^m$, and each $A'_i = A_i^m$. In each step $j + 1$, C^{j+1}, C_G^{j+1}, and each A_i^{j+1} can be constructed from C^j, C_G^j, and A_i^j in any of the following ways[2] (only describing the components that change, any component not mentioned is assumed to stay the same in step $j + 1$).

1. *(Type I: Guiding internal non-determinism). Let l_1, l_2, T isolate fragment T' of A_i^j, and c be a fresh rendez-vous channel. Then A_i^{j+1} is A_i^j where the set T' is deleted from the transitions, and a transition from l_1 to l_2 is added, with a rendez-vous receive action on channel c, with as message parameters only variables in $V \cup A_i^j.W$, and $C_G^{j+1} = C_G^j \cup \{c\}$.*

    The freshly introduced channel may also be an array, with appropriate index expressions on the sending and receiving parts.

2. *(Type II: Guiding rendez-vous communication possibilities). Let $l_1 \xrightarrow{a} l_2$ be a transition of A_i^j with rendez-vous communication on channel (array) c from C^j. Let e' be an expression over variables in $V \cup V' \cup A_i^j$.*

    (a) *If c is an array with range $0..R - 1$ and is indexed on the transition as $c[e]$, then A_i^{j+1} is A_i^j where on the adjusted transition c is indexed as $c[(e' -> e : R)]$. Further, in C^{j+1}, c has range $0..R$.*

    (b) *If c is not an array then A_i^{j+1} is A_i^j where on the adjusted transition c is indexed as $c[(e' -> 0 : 1)]$. Further, in C^{j+1}, c is an array with range $0..1$, and for each occurrence of channel c in another transition of any A_k^j is replaced in A_k^{j+1} by $c[0]$.*

3. *(Type III: Guiding scheduling possibilities). Let $l_1, l_2, \{l_1 \xrightarrow{a} l_3\}$ isolate fragment T' of A_i^j, such that l_1 and l_2 are non-atomic and either all other loca-*

---

[2] Each step may be performed simultaneously on a set of automata $A_{i_1}^j, \ldots, A_{i_h}^j$ provided these automata are equal (i.e. generated from one Promela proctype).

tions in T' are atomic or $l_2 = l_3$ (i.e. T' consists of one transition). Let e' be an expression over variables in $V \cup V' \cup A_i^j.W$.

(a) If the transition $l_1 \xrightarrow{a} l_3$ is a condition with label $a = (e)$, then A_i^{j+1} is A_i where transition $l_1 \xrightarrow{(e)} l_3$ is replaced by $l_1 \xrightarrow{(e \wedge e')} l_3$.

(b) If the transition $l_1 \xrightarrow{a} l_3$ is an assignment, then A_i^{j+1} is A_i where transition $l_1 \xrightarrow{a} l_3$ is replaced by two transitions: $l_1 \xrightarrow{(e)} l_4$ and $l_4 \xrightarrow{a} l_3$, such that l_4 is a fresh location which is atomic in A_i^{j+1}.

The guide automaton G may contain conditions over and assignments to variables in $V' \cup G.W$, as well as rendez-vous send actions on channels from C_G. We assume a function map that maps each channel from C' and each transition from A_i' (except rendez-vous communication with Guide G) to their original counterpart in C and A_i, respectively. Moreover, we extend map to global system states such that for global system state s' of Σ', $s = map(s')$ is the global system state of Σ with the values of s' for each global variable, each channel, and the local variables and current state for each automaton. Note that we may have added locations in Type III Guiding for A_i' that are not present in A_i. Given newly added location l_4 for transitions $l_1 \xrightarrow{(e)} l_4$ and $l_4 \xrightarrow{a} l_3$, if $s'.A_i' = l_4$, then we let $map(s').A_i = l_1$ (i.e. we map back to the starting location[3]).

We need some sufficient conditions to prove the desired properties of guiding.

Definition 3 (Sensible Restriction). *Let system $\Sigma' = (V', C', A_1', \ldots, A_n', G)$ be a guided version of system $\Sigma = (V, C, A_1, \ldots, A_n)$ with mapping map.*

This guided version is sensible if the following holds for each reachable global system state s' of Σ' and global system state s of Σ where $s = map(s')$.

1. *(Type I Guiding, no new behaviour). If $s' \to t'$ with some transition in $G.R$ labelled with a rendez-vous send action and $t' \to u'$ with transition $l_1 \xrightarrow{b} l_2$ in A_i', which is the result of Type I Guiding of isolated fragment T in A_i, then there is a run σ of transitions in T such that $s \xRightarrow{\sigma} u$, $u.A_i = l_2$, and for each variable $v \in V \cup A_i.W$, $u.v = u'.v$.*

2. *(No new deadlocks in guided automata) If $s \to t$ with transition $l_1 \xrightarrow{a} l_2$ in $A_i.R - A_i'.R$ then either (1) $s \to u$ with some transition(s) in $A_i.R \cap A_i'.R$, or (2) $s' \to t'$ with some transition(s) in $\Sigma'.R - \Sigma.R$.*

3. *(No new deadlocks in Guide) If for each A_i, $s.A_i$ is a final location of A_i ($s.A_i \in A_i.F$), then $s'.G$ is a final location as well ($s'.G \in G.F$).*

The next two propositions ensure that the guided system does not exhibit new behaviour (Proposition 1) or new deadlocks (Proposition 2). The proofs are in Appendix A.

---

[3] This will not cause problems when Type III Guiding is applied more than once, since new locations are only added for assignment transitions with a non-atomic starting location which rules out assignment transitions that have already been guided.

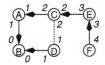

Fig. 7. An example spanning tree in a bus-based view

Proposition 1. *Let system* $\Sigma' = (V', C', A'_1, \ldots, A'_n, G)$ *be a sensibly guided version of system* $\Sigma = (V, C, A_1, \ldots, A_n)$, *with mapping map.*

Then for each reachable global system state s' *of* Σ' *and global system state* $map(s')$ *of* Σ, *the following holds. (1) If* s' *is the initial global system state of* Σ', *then* $map(s')$ *is the initial global system state of* Σ. *(2) If* $s' \overset{a}{\leadsto} t'$ *in* Σ' *then* $map(s') \overset{\hat{a}}{\leadsto}{}^* t$ *in* Σ, *and* $t = map(t')$. *Here,* $\hat{a} = map(a)$ *if* $map(a)$ *is an assertion or a communication on a channel from* C, *and* $a = \epsilon$ *(empty) otherwise.*

Proposition 2. *Let system* $\Sigma' = (V', C', A'_1, \ldots, A'_n, G)$ *be a sensibly guided version of system* $\Sigma = (V, C, A_1, \ldots, A_n)$, *with mapping map. Then whenever* Σ' *deadlocks in reachable global system state* s', Σ *deadlocks in global system state* $map(s')$.

In the following section we describe an experiment where we successfully applied the theory from this section.

4 The IEEE 1394.1 Case Study

This section reports on our experience in guiding a Promela specification of the IEEE 1394.1 FireWire net update algorithm. Section 4.1 summarizes relevant details of the net update algorithm. Section 4.2 shortly describes the Promela specification of the net update algorithm (for better descriptions see [11, 13, 10]), and our Spin experiences. Section 4.3 describes the error Spin could not find, and Section 4.4 reports the guiding process.

4.1 Introduction to the Net Update Algorithm

A 1394 *bus* consists of a number of connected *nodes* that communicate as described by the IEEE 1394 standard. An IEEE 1394.1 *net* [10] consists of IEEE 1394 buses [9] connected with *bridges*. The bridges themselves consist of two nodes, called *portals*, connected with some fabric. Each portal acts as an ordinary 1394 node on the bus that it is connected to.

A 1394.1 net is supposed to be "plug-and-play", which means that devices (including bridges!) can be connected and disconnected at all times, and the resulting net is expected to continue to function without too much disruption. Whenever the connection state of any of the nodes on a bus changes, then immediately a 1394.1 algorithm called net update starts to process the new net topology. This algorithm maintains a spanning tree which is used to give the net

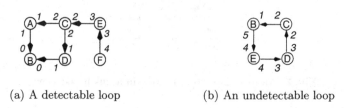

(a) A detectable loop   (b) An undetectable loop

Fig. 8. Examples of loops

an identity and to deal with cycles in the net topology. The root of the tree is called the *prime* portal. See Figure 7 for an example. Here, each node represents a bus, and each arrow represents a bridge with a direction. The bridge connecting bus C and bus D is not part of the spanning tree: it has no direction as indicated with the dotted line. The numbers indicate the distance to the root bus.

4.2   Using Spin

The Promela Specification. The Promela specification models the spanning tree functionality of net update. In the code, there are ten bridge portals, constituting five bridges, expressed in a total of twenty processes which are all active all along. Another process models the changes in the network topology, by nondeterministically connecting and disconnecting bridge portals to buses. A bus is not modelled separately by a process, it can be identified through the connection state of the portals. Safety properties are added in assertions to check the successful termination of net update, and the spanning tree.

Verification Experience. All verification experiments were done on an Intel i686 dual CPU, running Linux RedHat 7, with 2 Gbyte main memory and 3 Gbyte swap memory. We tried both exhaustive and approximative verification. The former did not complete. None of the experiments detected an error.

Simulation Experience. Apart from our verification attempts, we tried many simulations in order to find errors. This led to many modelling errors being detected and fixed. All simulation experiments were done on an i686 647 MHz CPU, with 256 Mbyte main memory and 870 Mbyte swap memory.

After many adjustments, we had a version of the specification in which we did not find errors with random simulation anymore, (seemingly) however many random seed numbers we supplied. At first, we were inclined to trust our specification, but as explained in the following section, this confidence was misplaced.

4.3   An Error Spin Could not Find

An Error Found by Spin. Not all loops are detected by the original net update protocol, and the algorithm may not terminate at all. The basic criterion for detecting a loop in the network is that on a bus, there either are two bridges

```
                                         proctype AllBuses(...) {
                                           int i,j;
                                           do
                                           :: ...
  proctype AllBuses(...) {                 :: fromGuide?Choose(i,j);
    int i,j;                                  ...
    do                                     :: ...
    :: ...                                 od;
    :: atomic {                           }
        (!TopologyMayChange);            proctype Guide() {
        choose(i,j); } /* inline macro */    ...
        ...                                  fromGuide!Choose(0,1);
    :: ...                                   ...
    od;                                   }
  }
```

     (a) Original Promela   (b) Guided Promela

Fig. 9. Type I Guiding in FireWire Promela specification

pointing away from that bus into the direction of the same prime portal or the bus has a prime portal and a bridge pointing away to that same prime portal, see Figure 8(a). However, after some network topology changes, a loop can exist in the network where this criterion is not met: all buses on the loop have exactly one portal pointing towards the prime portal, but the prime portal itself is not there. This can be seen by observing the information of the distance of each portal to the prime portal. There must be at least one bus that has an outgoing bridge with a distance larger than a corresponding incoming bridge, see Figure 8(b). Here, all bridge portals belong with the same prime portal, and on bus B, the loop could be detected with an adjusted loop detection criterion.

In this situation, the net update algorithm as presented in the current draft does not terminate, but keeps being executed on consecutive buses in the loop, and the distances keep increasing. This is a major error. It was discovered by extensive simulation with Spin.

An Error not Found by Spin. Upon discovering this erroneous behaviour, we tried a small adjustment of the algorithm, by undirecting the incoming bridge with the erroneous distance. We simulated with Spin and verified the new specification. No error was found. The new specification seemed to eliminate the possibility of having non-present prime portal identities in the net. Consequently, the loop detection problem seemed to be solved. But later it turned out that the new specification still has the same problem as the old one.

We were rather surprised that in our verification and extensive simulation experiments with Spin, no error was reported. Suspecting that the error is there, and knowing what behaviour should produce it, we tried to guide our Promela specification by constructing an extra process Guide and pre-selecting the topology changes in the net. How we proceeded is explained in the next section.

4.4   Guiding Net Update

In the new specification a new process called Guide was added. It suffhced to only restrict the internal non-determinism with Type I Guiding, for steering the

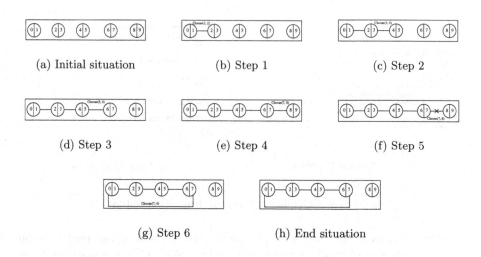

(a) Initial situation   (b) Step 1   (c) Step 2

(d) Step 3   (e) Step 4   (f) Step 5

(g) Step 6   (h) End situation

Fig. 10. Guiding net update to find an error

simulation in the desired direction. The Promela construction is demonstrated in Figure 9. The guided scenario is depicted in Figure 10.

The Guide process sends inputs to the topology process via a new channel, deciding which pair of portals connects or disconnects at a given time. In the original model the portals connect and disconnect completely at random. The message used is $Choose(x, y)$ where x and y are portal identities. In the network there are five bridges formed from the following pairs of portals: 0/1, 2/3, 4/5, 6/7, and 8/9. In the beginning, the Guide connects the bridges in the following order: $Choose(1, 2)$; $Choose(3, 4)$; $Choose(5, 6)$; $Choose(7, 8)$. Then the Guide waits for some time to let the network form the spanning tree. After stabilization the portal with the greatest identity, 9, is the prime portal. The rest of the portals have the following distances to the prime: 8 and 7 (being on the same bus) both have distance 1; 6 and 5 have distance 2; 4 and 3 have distance 3; 2 and 1 have distance 4; 0 has distance 5. Now the Guide sends two inputs: first $Choose(7, 8)$ which acts as a disconnection of portals 7 and 8, and then $Choose(0, 7)$ which creates a loop. The portal identity 9, of the bridge which is now disconnected, is still present as a prime portal identity in all bridge portals on the loop. The bridges in the loop are: 0/1; 2/3; 4/5; 6/7.

As a result of the new situation created, two waves of net update are active, and they are chasing each other's tail: one wave with messages transporting the new prime portal identity 7, and one wave transporting the absent prime portal identity 9. Each bridge portal on the loop keeps changing its prime portal identity between 7 and 9. The configuration does not stabilize and the distance of each portal to the prime portal increases to values which are not allowed, causing an assertion violation. This behaviour reveals that the guided Promela specification does not adequately handle the scenario created by the Guide.

The violated assertions show the errors in the model which are errors of the net update protocol. In the current 1394.1 draft standard, which is being finalized, an extra protocol has been added to deal with the mistakes we found.

We finally discuss shortly why our Promela specification is guided sensibly and hence assertion violations found in the guided Promela exist in the behaviour of the original Promela as well. The first major point is that the Guide limits the number and timing of the topology changes which in the original Promela are unlimited. This may be a source of deadlocks for the guided process that communicates with the Guide about topology changes. However, this process can also at any point decide not to accept topology changes anymore. Hence our Guide satisfies the condition 2.(1) of Definition 3. Deadlocks in the Guide itself are prevented by labelling each Promela statement that may block with an **end** label to accomodate condition 3 of Definition 3. Finally, since we know that each topology change in the original Promela is possible for all portal identities (which is easy to prove), we can be sure that replacing the isolated fragment does not introduce new behaviour, and condition 1 of Definition 3 is satisfied. Hence, our Promela is guided sensibly.

References

1. S.C.C. Blom, W.J. Fokkink, J.F. Groote, I.A. van Langevelde, B. Lisser, and J. van de Pol. mCRL: A toolset for analysing algebraic specifications. In *Proceedings of CAV'01*, volume 2102 of *LNCS*, pages 250–254. Springer, 2001.
2. A. Burns, R.L. Spelberg, H. Toetenel, and T. Vink. Modeling and verification using XTG and PMC. *Proc. of the 5th annual conf. of ASCI*, 1999.
3. E. Clarke, O. Grumberg, and D. Long. Verification Tools for Finite State Concurrent Systems. In *A Decade of Concurrency-Reflections and Perspectives*, volume 803, pages 124–175. Springer, 1993.
4. L.D. David, J.D. Andreas, J.H. Alan, and C.H. Yang. Protocol verification as a hardware design aid. *IEEE International Conference on Computer Design: VLSI in Computers and Processors*, pages 522–525, 1992.
5. H. Garavel, F. Lang, and R. Mateescu. An overview of CADP 2001. *EASST Newsletter*, 4:13–24, 2002. Also available as INRIA Technical Report RT-254.
6. E. Gunter and D. Peled. Temporal debugging for concurrent systems. In *Proceedings of TACAS'02*, LNCS, pages 431–444. Springer, 2002.
7. T.A. Henzinger, P.H. Ho, and H. Wong-Toi. Hytech: The next generation. *Proc. of RTSS'95*, pages 56–65, 1995.
8. G.J. Holzmann. *The Spin Model Checker–Primer and Reference Manual*. Addison-Wesley, 2003. See also URL http://www.spinroot.com/.
9. The Institute of Electrical And Electronics Engineers, Inc. *IEEE Standard for a High Performance Serial Bus*, August 1996. IEEE Std 1394-1995.
10. The Institute of Electrical And Electronics Engineers, Inc. *IEEE P1394.1 Draft Standard for High Performance Serial Bus Bridges*, November 2003. Version 1.05.
11. I.A. van Langevelde, J.M.T Romijn, and N. Goga. Founding firewire bridges through promela prototyping. In *Proc. of FMPPTA'03*. IEEE CS Press, 2003.
12. K.G. Larsen, P. Pettersson, and W. Yi. UPPAAL in a Nutshell. *Int. Journal on Software Tools for Technology Transfer*, 1(1–2):134–152, October 1997.

13. J.M.T. Romijn. Improving the quality of protocol standards: Correcting IEEE 1394.1 firewire net update. *Newsletter of the NVTI*, 8:23–30, 2004.
14. M. Sihman and S. Katz. A calculus of superimpositions for distributed systems. In *Proceedings of AOSD'02*, pages 28–40. ACM Press, 2002.
15. Sweden Telelogic AB. *Telelogic Tau Guide*. 1998.
16. S. Yovine. A verification tool for real-time systems. *International Journal of Software Tools for Technology Transfer*, 1:123–133, 1997.

A   Proofs

Proof of Proposition 1. Let s' be a global system state of Σ', and s a global system state of Σ such that $s = map(s')$.

- Suppose s' is the initial global system state of Σ'. By the properties of map, the values of s and s' are the same for all global variables, channels, and the local variables and current location of each process of Σ. So trivially, s must be the initial global system state of Σ.
- Suppose $s' \overset{a}{\rightsquigarrow} t'$ in Σ'.
    - *(Unchanged transitions).* If this step is caused by one transition $l_1 \overset{a}{\rightarrow} l_2$ that is not new in Σ' (i.e. $l_1 \overset{a}{\rightarrow} l_2 \in \Sigma.R \cap \Sigma'.R$), then by the properties of map, trivially $s \overset{\hat{a}}{\rightsquigarrow}^* t$ in Σ and $t = map(t')$.

      If this step is a rendez-vous communication, caused by two transitions $l_1 \overset{a}{\rightarrow} l_2$ and $l_3 \overset{b}{\rightarrow} l_4$ which are not new in Σ' (i.e. $\{l_1 \overset{a}{\rightarrow} l_2, l_3 \overset{b}{\rightarrow} l_4\} \subseteq \Sigma.R \cap \Sigma'.R$), then again by the properties of map, trivially $s \overset{\hat{a}}{\rightsquigarrow}^* t$ in Σ and $t = map(t')$.
    - *(Type I guided transitions).* Suppose a is a rendez-vous communication label that was introduced by Type I Guiding. Then this step is caused by a rendez-vous send transition $l_1 \overset{a}{\rightarrow} l_2$ of Guide G, and a rendez-vous receive transition $l_3 \overset{b}{\rightarrow} l_4$ of A_i', and both these transitions are new (i.e. $\{l_1 \overset{a}{\rightarrow} l_2, l_3 \overset{b}{\rightarrow} l_4\} \subseteq \Sigma'.R - \Sigma.R$), and $\hat{a} = \epsilon$. Let transition $l_3 \overset{b}{\rightarrow} l_4$ be the result of applying Type I Guiding to A_i for isolated fragment T. By Definition 3, and since s' and u' agree on all variables in $V \cup A_i.W$ and on the current location of A_i', there is a run σ of transitions in T such that $s \overset{\sigma}{\Rightarrow} t$ and for each variable $v \in V \cup A_i.W$, $t.v = t'.v$. Since the communication of G and A_i' can only affect variables in $V \cup A_i'.W$ and the current location of A_i' and G, and σ can only affect variables in $V \cup A_i.W$ and the current location of A_i, no other part of s and s' is altered to reach t and t'. By all the above, $t = map(t')$. Trivially, σ contains no communication, $\hat{\epsilon}$ is ϵ, and $s \overset{\hat{a}}{\rightsquigarrow}^* t$.
    - *(Type II guided transitions).* Suppose a is a rendez-vous communication label that was adjusted by Type II Guiding. Whatever has been altered is the addition of conditions to the channel array index expression. Hence, if in s' this expression evaluates to an index for which another process is actually ready to receive rendez-vous communication, the same can be

executed in s for the original channel (array). So $s \stackrel{\hat{a}}{\rightsquigarrow}^* t$. Since the effect has not been altered, certainly $t = map(t')$.

- *(Type III guided transitions)*. Suppose a is a condition that was adjusted by Type III Guiding. Whatever has been altered is the addition of a conjunct to the condition expression. Hence, if in s' this expression evaluates to true, the condition expression without the conjunct (which is weaker) evaluates to true in s since s and s' agree on all variables occurring in the original condition. So $s \stackrel{\hat{a}}{\rightsquigarrow}^* t$. Since the effect has not been altered, certainly $t = map(t')$.

  Suppose a is a condition that was added by Type III Guiding to A_i. Clearly, the original system should not perform a step. Since $\hat{a} = \epsilon = \hat{\epsilon}$ and $s \stackrel{\hat{\epsilon}}{\rightsquigarrow}^* s$ by not performing a transition, it is enough to show that $s = map(t')$. The only effect of the transition on the global system state is that the current location of A_i' is changed to the location that was freshly added. The function map has been defined such that it maps that current location, $t'.A_i'$ onto the same location as $s'.A_i'$ which is exactly what is needed. Since t' and s' agree on all other parts, clearly $s = map(t')$.

  Suppose a is an assignment that was adjusted by Type III Guiding for A_i. The assignment transition is present in A_i and A_i', and differs only in its starting location. Since an assignment is always enabled, $s \stackrel{\hat{a}}{\rightsquigarrow}^* t$. Since the effect of this assignment is equal on s and s', $t = map(t')$.

- *(Remaining transitions of the Guide)*. Suppose a is a condition or assignment in the Guide G. Clearly, the original system should not perform a step. Since $\hat{a} = \epsilon = \hat{\epsilon}$ and $s \stackrel{\hat{\epsilon}}{\rightsquigarrow}^* s$ by not performing a transition, it is enough to show that $s = map(t')$. The effect of any such transition of the Guide on the global system state is that the new global variables and the local variables and current location of the Guide are changed. These have nothing to do with the parts of s', t' which are mapped to global system states of the original system. Hence $s = map(t')$. $\boxtimes$

Proof of Proposition 2. Suppose Σ' deadlocks in reachable global system state s'. By Definition 3, at least one A_i' is not in a final location (otherwise G would be in a final location and there would not be a deadlock). By definition of map, no transition in $\Sigma.R \cap \Sigma'.R$ is enabled in $map(s')$ (otherwise it would be enabled in s' as well).

Suppose $map(s')$ enables a transition in $\Sigma.R - \Sigma'.R$. Then by Definition 3, either $map(s')$ also enables a transition in $\Sigma.R - \Sigma'.R$ or s' enables a transition in $\Sigma'.R - \Sigma.R$. Both cases lead to a contradiction, so $map(s')$ does not enable a transition in $\Sigma.R - \Sigma'.R$. $\boxtimes$

Linear Inequality LTL (*iLTL*):
A Model Checker for
Discrete Time Markov Chains*

YoungMin Kwon and Gul Agha

Open Systems Laboratory,
Department of Computer Science,
University of Illinois at Urbana Champaign
{ykwon4,agha}@cs.uiuc.edu

Abstract. We develop a way of analyzing the behavior of systems modeled using Discrete Time Markov Chains (DTMC). Specifically, we define *iLTL*, an LTL with linear inequalities on the pmf vectors as atomic propositions. *iLTL* allows us to express not only properties such as the expected number of jobs or the expected energy consumption of a protocol during a time interval, but also inequalities over such values. We present an algorithm for model checking properties of DTMCs expressed in *iLTL*. Our model checker differs from existing probabilistic ones in that the latter do not check properties of the transitions on the probability mass function (pmf) itself. Thus, *iLTLChecker* can check, given an interval estimate of current pmf, whether future pmfs will always satisfy a specification. We believe such properties often arise in distributed systems and networks and may, in particular, be useful in specifying requirements for routing or load balancing protocols. Our algorithm has been implemented in a tool called *iLTLChecker* and we illustrate the use of the tool by means of some examples.

1   Introduction

Many aspects of the behavior of distributed and embedded systems are stochastic and memoryless in nature; *Markov chains* provide a good model to analyze such behavior. In particular, queueing systems and network protocols are often analyzed using Markov chains [14, 4]. We develop a simple and efficient algorithm for model checking the behavior of such systems. An advantage of using Markov chains is that one can directly obtain the model from a system by estimating the *probability mass functions (pmf)* over time. For example, in a sensor network, we can obtain a sequence of pmfs of sensor states by taking successive snapshots.

We are interested in the temporal behavior of a system that can be expressed by *linear inequalities* over the pmfs. For example, such inequalities may be used to compose

* This research has been supported by the DARPA IXO NEST Award F33615-01-C-1907 and the DARPA/AFOSR MURI Award F49620-02-1-0325.

J. Davies et al. (Eds.): ICFEM 2004, LNCS 3308, pp. 194–208, 2004.

the expected queue length of a queueing system or the expected energy consumption of a network protocol. We define a *Linear Temporal Logic*, *iLTL*, which expresses properties of a Markov chain; the atomic propositions of *iLTL* include linear inequalities over pmfs. We develop a method for model checking formulae in this logic given the Markov chain representation of a system and implement the method in a tool called *iLTLChecker*.

iLTLChecker may also be used as a run-time safety checker. For example, by analyzing a snapshot, we can get an interval estimate of the probability distribution of current states. Since such an interval estimate may be expressed as a set of linear inequalities about the pmf, we can check with certain confidence level whether some (possibly future) safety property may be violated.

A number of useful probabilistic logics and associated model checkers have been developed based on logics. In particular, model checking logics pCTL and pCTL* are probabilistic extensions of the Computation Tree Logic (CTL). They express quantitative bounds on the probabilities of correct behavior [1]. Continuous-time Stochastic Logic (CSL) is a logic for Continuous Time Markov Chains (CTMC) which has an operator to reason about the steady-state probabilities of a system [13].

PRISM is a tool that can model check DTMC, CTMC and Markov Decision Processes for specifications written in pCTL or CSL [16]. Alfaro introduces nondeterminism, or *strategy*, in pCTL and pCTL* [2]. A strategy is expressed as a conditional probability and his model checker checks the worst case and the best case probabilities. Recently, Andova *et al.* [19] extended pCTL to model check a Markov reward model. With their logic, we can specify such characteristics as the expected value. An LTL model checker for Markov chains has been developed by Vardi which checks whether the probability measure of the paths that do not satisfy a specification is zero [17]. However, all the above model checkers use logics that cannot express dynamic behaviors of Markov processes: using these logics, one cannot compare one probability directly with another probability. For example, in pCTL we can express the property "The probability that a process p will eventually terminate is larger than 0.9." Similarly, in CSL we can express "The probability that in the long run the queue will be full is 0.5" [16]. But in neither logic can we express the property "Eventually the probability of p in a busy state will be at least 10% larger than the probability of p in a terminating state." Although extended logic in Andova *et al.* [19] can express these properties through a Markov reward model, it cannot express the reward in terms of a current pmf. In particular, it cannot model check a property such as "Given an interval estimate of the current pmf, the energy consumption of the network will be within [30 mW, 50 mW]." Such properties are often of interest in practical systems.

The essential idea behind our approach is quite simple. Inequalities combined by logical connectives are expressive enough to specify a finite union or complement of polytopes in the pmf space. Using temporal operators, we can also specify the time in which the sequence pmf's of a Markov chain should remain in a given polytope. Since the pmf sequence of a Markov chain is a function of the initial pmf, model checking is about determining whether there is an initial pmf that may violate the specification. In our model checking algorithm, we find the monotonic bounding functions that bound the left-hand side of inequalities. Together with the boundedness of the initial pmf, these bounding functions make the model checking a finite procedure. The model checking is done by feasibility checking for the sets of inequalities.

2   The Discrete Time Markov Chain Model

A Markov process is a stochastic process whose past has no influence on the future if its present is specified and a Markov chain is a Markov process having a countable number of states [5]. In this paper we represent a Discrete Time Markov Chain (DTMC) X as a tuple $(S, \mathbf{M})$ where S is a finite set of states $S = \{s_1, s_2, \ldots s_n\}$ that X can take and $\mathbf{M}$ is a Markov transition matrix that governs the transitions of X's probability mass function (pmf). We also use a column vector $\mathbf{x}(t) = [x_1(t), x_2(t), \ldots, x_n(t)]^T$ to represent the pmf of X at time t such that $x_i(t) = P\{X(t) = s_i\}$. Thus,

$$\mathbf{x}(t + 1) = \mathbf{M} \cdot \mathbf{x}(t).$$

Since $\mathbf{M}$ is a Markov matrix, the sum of each column is one. This guarantees that $\mathbf{M}$ has an eigenvalue $\lambda_1 = 1$ [11]. We consider only the Markov matrices which are diagonalizable, and their eigenvalues λ_i have absolute values strictly less than 1 except $\lambda_1 = 1$ ($|\lambda_i| < 1$ for $i \in [2, n]$). Since all the eigenvalues other than λ_1 have absolute values less than 1, regardless of the initial pmf $\mathbf{x}(0)$, there is a unique final pmf $\mathbf{x}(\infty)$ which is a multiple of the eigenvector $\zeta^1 = [\zeta_1^1, \zeta_2^1, \ldots, \zeta_n^1]^T$ corresponding to the eigenvalue λ_1. That is, $\mathbf{M} \cdot \zeta^1 = 1 \cdot \zeta^1$ and $\mathbf{x}(\infty) = \zeta^1 / \sum_{i=1}^n \zeta_i^1$ [11]. The constraint about the eigenvalues is a necessary and sufficient condition for the existence of a unique steady state pmf of X. Note that an ergodic Markov chain satisfies this eigenvalue constraint and the irreducibility and aperiodicity are the necessary and sufficient conditions for the ergodicity of X since $|S|$ is finite [15]. This condition is generally true in practical systems [14]. The diagonalizability constraint can be easily enforced even if the original Markov matrix is not diagonalizable by adding and subtracting small random numbers from its elements [11]. Observe that such very small perturbation to the probability values do not change the behavior significantly.

A Markov process is a deterministic system in the sense that once the initial pmf $\mathbf{x}(0)$ is given, the rest of the transitions $\mathbf{x}(t)$, $t \geq 1$ are uniquely determined by the Markov matrix $\mathbf{M}$: $\mathbf{x}(t) = \mathbf{M}^t \cdot \mathbf{x}(0)$.

3   Specification Logic

Because we are interested in the temporal behavior of the pmf, the specification logic should be able to express properties of the transitions of the pmf. The sort of properties we are interested in compare a probability that a DTMC will be a particular state with a constant or with another such probability possibly at a different time. We use linear inequalities about the pmf vectors as atomic propositions of our specification logic.

3.1   Syntax

We use LTL as the specification logic where the atomic propositions of the LTL are linear inequalities about the pmf $\mathbf{x}(t)$. The syntax of the specification logic is:

$$\psi ::= T \mid F \mid ineq \mid$$
$$\neg\psi \mid \psi \vee \phi \mid \psi \wedge \phi \mid$$
$$\mathbf{X}\,\psi \mid \psi\,\mathbf{U}\,\phi \mid \psi\,\mathbf{R}\,\phi$$
$$ineq ::= \sum_{i=1}^{n} a_i \cdot P\{X = s_i\} < b,$$

where $X = (\{s_1, \ldots, s_n\}, \mathbf{M})$, $a_i \in \mathbb{R}$ and $b \in \mathbb{R}$. As usual, $\rightarrow$, $\square$ and $\diamond$ are defined as follows:

$$\psi \rightarrow \phi \equiv \neg\psi \vee \phi,$$
$$\square\psi \equiv F\,\mathbf{R}\,\psi,$$
$$\diamond\psi \equiv T\,\mathbf{U}\,\psi.$$

Observe that the comparison between two probabilities at different times can be expressed by the linear inequalities of the form *ineq*. For example, given the DTMC $X = (\{s_1, \ldots, s_n\}, \mathbf{M})$, the probability that X is in state s_i at time $t + k$ is given by

$$P\{X(t + k) = s_i\} = x_i(t + k) = \mathbf{M}_i^k \cdot \mathbf{x}(t),$$

where $\mathbf{M}_i^k$ is the ith row of $\mathbf{M}^k$ and $\mathbf{x}(t)$ is the pmf at time t.

Predicates about a Markov reward process [10] can also be expressed by linear inequalities. We consider only a constant reward function $\rho : S \rightarrow \mathbb{R}$ for each state. A performance metric is an accumulated reward over time. A predicate about an expected accumulated reward can be expressed as follows:

$$\sum_{k=0}^{T} \sum_{s_i \in S} \rho(s_i) \cdot P\{X(t + k) = s_i\} = \mathbf{r} \cdot \left(\sum_{k=0}^{T} \mathbf{M}^k\right) \cdot \mathbf{x}(t)$$
$$= \mathbf{r} \cdot \mathbf{S} \cdot \left(\sum_{k=0}^{T} \mathbf{\Lambda}^k\right) \cdot \mathbf{S}^{-1} \cdot \mathbf{x}(t)$$

where $\rho(s_i)$ is a reward function associated with a state s_i, $\mathbf{r}$ is a row vector $[\rho(s_1), \ldots, \rho(s_n)]$, $\mathbf{M} = \mathbf{S} \cdot \mathbf{\Lambda} \cdot \mathbf{S}^{-1}$ with $\mathbf{\Lambda}$ a diagonal matrix of eigenvalues of $\mathbf{M}$ and the T on the summation is an upper bound of the accumulation interval. It can be ∞ if the reward vector $\mathbf{r}$ is orthogonal to the steady state pmf vector.

3.2   Semantics

A ternary satisfaction relation $\models$ over tuples consisting of a Markov matrix, an initial pmf vector and an LTL formula is recursively defined as:

$$\mathbf{M}, \mathbf{x} \models T$$
$$\mathbf{M}, \mathbf{x} \not\models F$$
$$\mathbf{M}, \mathbf{x} \models \Sigma a_i \cdot P\{X = s_i\} < b \text{ iff } \Sigma a_i \cdot x_i < b$$
$$\mathbf{M}, \mathbf{x} \models \neg \phi \quad \text{iff } \mathbf{M}, \mathbf{x} \not\models \phi$$
$$\mathbf{M}, \mathbf{x} \models \phi \vee \psi \text{ iff } \mathbf{M}, \mathbf{x} \models \phi \text{ or } \mathbf{M}, \mathbf{x} \models \psi$$
$$\mathbf{M}, \mathbf{x} \models \phi \wedge \psi \text{ iff } \mathbf{M}, \mathbf{x} \models \phi \text{ and } \mathbf{M}, \mathbf{x} \models \psi$$
$$\mathbf{M}, \mathbf{x} \models X \phi \quad \text{iff } \mathbf{M}, \mathbf{M} \cdot \mathbf{x} \models \phi$$
$$\mathbf{M}, \mathbf{x} \models \phi U \psi \text{ iff there exists an } i \geq 0 \text{ such that } \mathbf{M}, \mathbf{M}^i \cdot \mathbf{x} \models \psi \text{ and}$$
$$\text{for all } 0 \leq j < i, \mathbf{M}, \mathbf{M}^j \cdot \mathbf{x} \models \phi$$
$$\mathbf{M}, \mathbf{x} \models \phi R \psi \text{ iff for all } j \geq 0, \text{ if for every } i < j \, \mathbf{M}, \mathbf{M}^i \cdot \mathbf{x} \not\models \phi \text{ then.}$$
$$\mathbf{M}, \mathbf{M}^j \cdot \mathbf{x} \models \psi$$

A binary satisfaction relation $\models$, over tuples of a Markov chain and an LTL formula is define as follows:

$$X \models \psi \text{ iff for all initial pmf } \mathbf{x}(0), \ \mathbf{M}, \mathbf{x}(0) \models \psi,$$

where $\mathbf{M}$ is the Markov matrix of X. The model checking problem to find out whether a given tuple (X, ψ) is in the binary relation $\models$ above.

3.3   Example

We give a simple example of a send/ack protocol to illustrate the notation. The protocol is represented by a state transition diagram where the transition labels are probabilities and the labels of the state include the reward (energy consumption in this example) in that state.

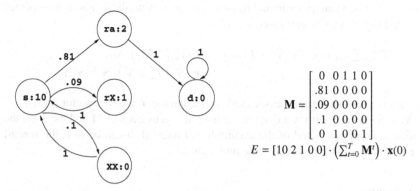

Fig. 1. A simple send/ack protocol (left) and its Markov matrix (**M**) and expected energy consumption (E) during the interval 0 and T (right)

The LHS of Figure 1 shows a simple send/ack network protocol. In this protocol, a sender sends a packet and a receiver, on receiving the packet, replies an ack. If the sender does not receive the ack during a certain period of time it sends the packet again. The states s, ra, rX, XX and d represent 'sent', 'received and acknowledged', 'received but not acknowledged', 'not received' and 'done'. The Markov matrix of this process and the expected energy consumption during the interval 0 and T with initial pmf $\mathbf{x}(0)$ are on the RHS of Figure 1. Because the reward vector [10 2 1 0 0] is orthogonal to the steady state pmf vector [0 0 0 0 1], the expected energy consumption is bounded even if T is infinite.

4   Model Checking

Let $s_X(\mathbf{x}(0))$ be a string whose alphabet is $\Sigma = 2^{AP}$ and its ith alphabet is $\{ineq \in AP : ineq(\mathbf{M}^i \cdot \mathbf{x}(0))\}$ where X is a DTMC, $\mathbf{x}(0)$ is an initial pmf and AP is a set of inequalities. Let $L_X \subseteq \Sigma^*$ be a set of strings $s_X(\mathbf{x}(0))$ for all $\mathbf{x}(0)$. Then our model checker checks whether $L_X \subseteq L_\psi$ where L_ψ is a language accepted by the Büchi automata built from an LTL formula ψ. More specifically, for a given specification ψ, it checks whether any $s_X \in L_X$ is in $L_{\neg\psi}$.

Our model checking algorithm has two steps. First, we build a Büchi automaton for the negated normal form of a given LTL specification ψ using the *expand* algorithm [18]. Second, we check the feasibility of the initial pmf $\mathbf{x}(0)$ against the set of inequalities collected along finite paths obtained from the automaton. From the set of inequalities, if there is a feasible solution, then a counterexample that does not satisfy the specification ψ is found. Otherwise, the DTMC X satisfies the given specification. Note that given the linear inequalities of an LTL formula ψ and a Markov matrix $\mathbf{M}$, we can compute an upper bound N on the number of time steps after which the atomic propositions of ψ become constant. The following section derives the upper bound.

4.1   Computation of Search Depth

Since we consider only Markov matrices $\mathbf{M}$ that are diagonalizable and whose eigenvalues have absolute values strictly less than 1 (except for $\lambda_1 = 1$), there is a stationary final pmf $\mathbf{x}(\infty)$. That is, $\mathbf{x}(\infty) = \mathbf{S} \cdot \mathbf{\Lambda}^\infty \cdot \mathbf{S}^{-1} \cdot \mathbf{x}(0) = \zeta^1 / \sum_{i=1}^n \zeta_i^1$, where $\mathbf{S} = [\zeta^1, \dots, \zeta^n]$, ζ^i is the eigenvector corresponding to λ_i, $\mathbf{\Lambda}$ is a diagonal matrix whose diagonal is $[\lambda_1, \dots \lambda_n]$ [11]. Furthermore, since $\mathbf{x}(t)$ is a pmf, $0 \le x_i(t) \le 1$ for all t. This constraint on the initial pmf and the existence of the final stationary pmf leads to bounding functions within which left-hand side of the inequalities, $\mathbf{a} \cdot \mathbf{x}(t) < b$, will remain for $t \ge 0$. So, for the set of inequalities of a given LTL specification, there is a number N after which the truth values of the inequalities become constant for every initial pmf $\mathbf{x}(0)$. This guarantees the termination of the model checking procedure.

Theorem 1. *Let* $\mathbf{M} \in [0, 1]^{n \times n}$ *be a Markov matrix which is diagonalizable with eigenvalues* $|\lambda_i| < 1$ *for* $i = 2 \dots n$ *and* $\lambda_1 = 1$, *and let* $\mathbf{x}(t) \in [0, 1]^{n \times 1}$ *be the pmf at* t *transited by* $\mathbf{M}$. *Then for all inequalities* $\sum_{j=1}^n a_{ij} \cdot x_j(t) < b_i$ *of a given LTL formula* ψ, *if* $\sum_{j=1}^n a_{ij} \cdot x_j(\infty) \ne b_i$ *then there is an integer* N *such that for any integer* $N' \ge N$,

$$\sum_{j=1}^n a_{ij} \cdot x_j(N') < b_i \text{ iff } \sum_{j=1}^n a_{ij} \cdot x_j(N) < b_i.$$

Proof. For an inequality $\sum_{i=1}^{n} a_i \cdot x_i(t) < b$, let $\mathbf{a}$ be the row vector $[a_1, \ldots, a_n]$ and let b^{∞} be the inner product of $\mathbf{a}$ and the final pmf of $\mathbf{M}$ such that $b^{\infty} = \mathbf{a} \cdot \mathbf{M}^{\infty} \cdot \mathbf{x}(0)$ where $\mathbf{x}(0)$ is any initial pmf. From both sides of the inequality at step t, $\mathbf{a} \cdot \mathbf{x}(t) < b$ we subtract the equality $\mathbf{a} \cdot \mathbf{x}(\infty) = b^{\infty}$. Thus

$$\mathbf{a} \cdot (\mathbf{M}^t \cdot \mathbf{x}(0) - \mathbf{x}(\infty)) < b - b^{\infty}.$$

Since the left hand side of the inequality tends to 0 as $t \to \infty$ and $b \neq b^{\infty}$, for a given $\mathbf{x}(0)$ there is a bound n' after which the truth value of the inequality becomes a constant (true if $b^{\infty} < b$, false otherwise).

Now, we show that for all initial pmf $\mathbf{x}(0)$ there is a bound N after which the inequality become a constant. The bound N can be a value of t such that $|\mathbf{a} \cdot (\mathbf{M}^t \cdot \mathbf{x}(0) - \mathbf{x}(\infty))| < |b - b^{\infty}|$ even though this bound may not be minimal. The fact that $\mathbf{x}(0)$ is a pmf ($0 \leq x_i(0) \leq 1$) leads to a monotonically decreasing function which is larger than the left side of the previous inequality regardless the choice of $\mathbf{x}(0)$.

$$
\begin{aligned}
\left| \mathbf{a} \cdot (\mathbf{M}^t \cdot \mathbf{x}(0) - \mathbf{x}(\infty)) \right| &= \left| \mathbf{a} \cdot \left(\mathbf{S} \cdot \mathbf{\Lambda}^t \cdot \mathbf{S}^{-1} \cdot \mathbf{x}(0) - \mathbf{x}(\infty) \right) \right| \\
&= \left| \sum_{i=2}^{n} c_i \cdot \lambda_i^t \cdot \sum_{j=1}^{n} S_{ij}^{-1} \cdot x_j(0) \right| \\
&\leq \sum_{i=2}^{n} |c_i| \cdot |\lambda_i|^t \cdot \sum_{j=1}^{n} |S_{ij}^{-1}| \cdot x_j(0) \\
&\leq \sum_{i=2}^{n} |c_i| \cdot |\lambda_i|^t \cdot \sum_{j=1}^{n} |S_{ij}^{-1}| \cdot 1,
\end{aligned}
$$

where $\mathbf{M} = \mathbf{S} \cdot \mathbf{\Lambda} \cdot \mathbf{S}^{-1}$, $\mathbf{\Lambda}$ is the diagonal matrix of eigenvalues λ_i and $\mathbf{S}$ is the eigenvector matrix $[\zeta^1, \zeta^2, \ldots, \zeta^n]$ and $\mathbf{c} = [c_1, c_2, \ldots, c_n] = \mathbf{a} \cdot \mathbf{S}$. Since $\sum_{i=2}^{n} |c_i| \cdot |\lambda_i|^t \cdot \sum_{j=1}^{n} |S_{ij}^{-1}|$ is a monotonically decreasing function of t which is larger than $|\mathbf{a} \cdot (\mathbf{M}^t \cdot \mathbf{x}(0) - \mathbf{x}(\infty))|$, the integer N is the maximum N_i of all inequalities in ψ such that N_i is the minimum t that satisfies $\sum_{i=2}^{n} |c_i| \cdot |\lambda_i|^t \cdot \sum_{j=1}^{n} |S_{ij}^{-1}| < |b - b^{\infty}|$. ∎

Given a DTMC $X = (S, \mathbf{M})$, an initial pmf $\mathbf{x}(0)$ and an LTL formula, because we can compute the bound after which the truth value of the inequalities in the LTL formula become constants, after a finite expansion of the LTL formula, we can evaluate it. Recall that the 'until' and 'release' operators may be rewritten as

$$\phi \, \mathsf{U} \, \psi \equiv \psi \wedge (\phi \vee \mathbf{X}(\phi \, \mathsf{U} \, \psi))$$
$$\phi \, \mathsf{R} \, \psi \equiv (\phi \wedge \psi) \vee (\phi \wedge \mathbf{X}(\phi \, \mathsf{R} \, \psi)).$$

However, because *iLTL* uses a Büchi automaton for a given LTL formula, we do not explicitly expand the formula as above.

4.2   Model Checking as Feasibility Checking

In order to check the model X against a specification ψ, we first build a Labeled Generalized Büchi Automata (LGBA) by the expansion algorithm in [18]. The LGBA is a 6-tuple $\mathcal{A} = (S, R, S_0, F, D, L)$ where S is a set of states, $R \subseteq S \times S$ is a transition relation, $S_0 \subset S$ is a set of initial states, $F \in 2^{2^S}$ is a set of sets of final states, D is a set of inequalities and $L : S \to 2^D$ is a labeling function that returns a set of inequalities that a state should satisfy. Note that $\neg(\mathbf{a} \cdot \mathbf{x} < b)$ is converted to the inequality $-\mathbf{a} \cdot \mathbf{x} < -b$ while finding the negation normal form of ψ.

We call a (possibly infinite) sequence of states $q = q_0 q_1 \cdots q_\omega$ a *sequence of $\mathcal{A}$* if $(q_i, q_{i+1}) \in R$ for $i \geq 0$. For each final set $F_i \in F$, if some elements of the set appear infinitely often in q then we call q an *accepting sequence of $\mathcal{A}$*. A sequence q of $\mathcal{A}$ is an *execution of $\mathcal{A}$* if $q_0 \in S_0$. We say that a *sequence q of $\mathcal{A}$ accepts a pmf $\mathbf{x}(t)$* if $\mathbf{x}(t + \tau)$ satisfies all inequalities of $L(q_\tau)$ for $\tau \geq 0$. An LGBA $\mathcal{A}$ *accepts a pmf $\mathbf{x}(0)$* if there is an accepting execution of $\mathcal{A}$ that accepts $x(0)$.

Let $F' = \{q_i :$ an accepting sequence of $\mathcal{A}$ $(q_1, \ldots, q_i, \ldots, q_k)^*$ accepts the pmf $\mathbf{x}(\infty)\}$ where q^* means an infinite concatenation of q. And, let $F^+ = \{q_i :$ a sequence of $\mathcal{A}$ $q_1, \ldots, q_i, \ldots, q_k$ accepts the pmf $\mathbf{x}(\infty)$, and $q_k \in F'\}$. Note that any state in F^+ is reachable to an accepting sequence of $\mathcal{A}$. So, we check only those search paths of length N that ends with a state in F^+.

Theorem 2. *Let $\mathcal{A}$ be an LGBA (S, R, S_0, F, D, L) for a specification ψ, let M be the Markov matrix of X and let a set of inequalities $I(q)$ for an execution q be $I(q) = \{\mathbf{a} \cdot M^i \cdot \mathbf{x} < b : \mathbf{a} \cdot \mathbf{x} < b \in L(q_i), i \in [0, N]\}$ where the N is the bound computed in theorem 1.*

A pmf $\mathbf{x}(0)$ is accepted by $\mathcal{A}$ iff there is an execution $q = q_0 q_1 \cdots q_\omega$ of $\mathcal{A}$ with $q_N \in F^+$ and $\mathbf{x}(0)$ is a feasible point of $I(q)$.

Proof. $\rightarrow$: Since $\mathcal{A}$ accepts $\mathbf{x}(0)$ there is an accepting execution q of $\mathcal{A}$ that accepts $\mathbf{x}(0)$. That is, $\mathbf{x}(t)$ satisfies all inequalities in $L(q_t)$ for $t \geq 0$. Since $\mathbf{a} \cdot \mathbf{x}(t) < b \equiv \mathbf{a} \cdot M^t \cdot \mathbf{x}(0) < b$, $\mathbf{x}(0)$ is a feasible point of $I(q)$

Let q^N be the suffix of q after first N elements. Since q^N is an accepting sequence of $\mathcal{A}$ with infinite length over a finite set of states, there is a loop in the sequence that includes at least one elements of F_i for all $F_i \in F$. Since some states of the loop are in F', and since q_N is reachable to that states $q_N \in F^+$.

$\leftarrow$: Since $\mathbf{x}(0)$ satisfies all inequalities of $I(q)$, q accepts $\mathbf{x}(0)$ and since $q_N \in F^+$, q is an accepting execution of $\mathcal{A}$. Hence, $\mathcal{A}$ accepts $\mathbf{x}(0)$.   ∎

Since $\mathcal{A}$ accepts exactly those executions that satisfy ψ [18] if there is a feasible solution for $I(q)$ of an execution q of $\mathcal{A}$ with $q_n \in F^+$ then $\mathbf{M}, \mathbf{x}(0) \models \psi$. Hence, $\mathbf{x}(0)$ is a counterexample of the specification $\neg\psi$ the original specification. The feasibility can be checked by solving a linear programming problem with artificial variables [7]. Since we check the feasibility by linear programming we have a problem dealing with inequality. For example $\neg(a > b)$ will be translated as $-a < -b$ instead of $-a \leq -b$. However, because we are dealing with continuous values, precise equality is not meaningful. Instead, we can check properties such as, $|a - b| < \epsilon$ or $|a - b| > \epsilon$.

Figure 2 shows a Büchi automaton for the negation of []a. Let us assume that $\neg a$ is true for the final pmf. Then all three states are in $F^+ = \{\{T\}, \{\neg a\}, \{\}\}$ and after N transitions the model checker will decide []a false. If $\neg a$ is false for the final pmf then the only state in F^+ is the final state with an empty set of atomic propositions

($F^+ = \{\{\}\}$). So, if F^+ is reachable by N transitions then []a is false, otherwise it is true.

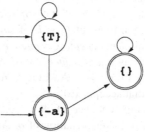

Fig. 2. A Büchi automaton for an LTL formula ¬[]a

One difficulty in the DTMC model checking is the size of the initial pmf space. Since $\mathbf{x}(0) \in [0, 1]^n$ with $\sum_{i=1}^n x_i(0) = 1$, we cannot build an automaton for the intersection of X and an LTL formula ψ as is done in [8]. Instead, we check the feasibility of the initial distribution against the transformed inequalities (i.e., consider the inequalities as linear constraints).

Let $\mathcal{A}$ be the Büchi automaton for an LTL formula $\neg\psi$ and let N be the bound for a DTMC X and the inequalities in ψ. Then the LTL DTMC model checking can be done by a depth-first-search for a sequence $q = q_0 q_1 \cdots q_N$ of $\mathcal{A}$ with $q_0 \in S_0$ and $q_N \in F^+$ and has a feasible solution $\mathbf{x}(0)$ for the set of inequalities $I(q)$. Thus, $X \models \psi$ iff there is a such sequence q. If $X \not\models \psi$ then $\mathbf{x}(0)$ is a counterexample.

Since we depth-first search the sequences, if infeasibility is found early in the search tree by the set $\cup_{i=0}^k \{\mathbf{a} \cdot \mathbf{M}^{k-1} \cdot \mathbf{x} < b : \mathbf{a} \cdot \mathbf{x} < b \in L(q_i)\}$ with a small k then we can skip checking large sub-branches. One small but very efficient optimization is checking the newly added inequalities with the feasible vector from the previous state before doing the linear programming. In many cases we can skip the linear programming.

As an example of the model checking let us consider the the Büchi automaton of Figure 2. Assume that N is 3 and ¬a is false by the final pmf $\mathbf{x}(\infty)$. Then F^+ is the states labeled by $\{\{\neg a\}, \{\}\}$. All paths of length 3 that end with the closure are:

$$(\neg a, \phi, \phi), (T, \neg a, \phi), (T, T, \neg a).$$

So the set of inequalities to check are (let ¬a is $\mathbf{c} \cdot \mathbf{x} < b$):

$$\{\mathbf{c} \cdot \mathbf{x} < b\}, \{\mathbf{c} \cdot \mathbf{M} \cdot \mathbf{x} < b\}, \{\mathbf{c} \cdot \mathbf{M}^2 \cdot \mathbf{x} < b\}$$

If there is a feasible solution vector $\mathbf{x}(0)$ that satisfies any of the three sets of inequalities, then $\mathbf{x}(0)$ is a counterexample that satisfies the negated specification ¬[]a. That is, the initial pmf $\mathbf{x}(0)$ violates the specification []a.

5   *iLTLChecker*: A Markov Chain Model Checker

The syntax of *iLTLChecker* is straight forward; it has two main blocks: corresponding to the model and to the specification. We input the states of a DTMC and its Markov transition matrix in the model block. In the specification block, we write optional inequality definitions followed by an *iLTL* formula. Figure 3 shows a snapshot of the execution of

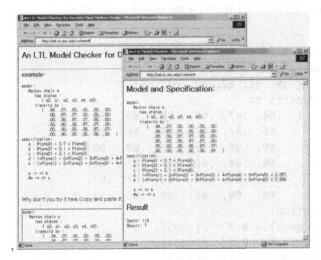

Fig. 3. *iLTLChecker*: a snapshot of an execution of *iLTLChecker*

iLTLChecker. It is available from the web site *http://osl.cs.uiuc.edu/~ykwon4*.

5.1   Example: An M/M/1 Queueing System

Consider a queuing system of Figure 4. It is an M/M/1 queueing system [12] with capacity 5, arrival rate $\lambda = 60/sec$ and service rate $\mu = 70/sec$. To simplify the discretization process, we over-sample the system (1000 sample/sec) and assume that on each sample a single new job arrives or a single job is finished with the probability of 0.06 (λ) and 0.07 (μ) each. If a new job arrives when the queue is full, it will be dropped.

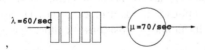

Fig. 4. A queueing system example: M/M/1 queue with capacity 5, $\lambda = 60/sec$ and $\mu = 70/sec$

Let $q = (\{q_0, q_1, q_2, q_3, q_4, q_5\}, \mathbf{M})$ be the DTMC for the queueing system. Each state of q represents the number of jobs in the queue. The Markov transition matrix $\mathbf{M}$ can be obtained from the following probability equations:

$$P\{q(t+1) = q_i\} = \lambda \cdot P\{q(t) = q_{i-1}\} + \mu \cdot P\{q(t) = q_{i+1}\}$$
$$+(1 - \lambda - \mu) \cdot P\{q(t) = q_i\} \text{ where } i \in \{1, \ldots, 4\}$$
$$P\{q(t+1) = q_0\} = \mu \cdot P\{q(t) = q_1\} + (1 - \mu) \cdot P\{q(t) = q_0\}$$
$$P\{q(t+1) = q_5\} = \lambda \cdot P\{q(t) = q_4\} + (1 - \lambda) \cdot P\{q(t) = q_5\}.$$

The steady state pmf vector of q is [0.24 0.20 0.17 0.15 0.13 0.11] and the expected number of jobs in the queue at the steady state is 2.0569.

Our model checker description for the system is as follows:

```
model:
    Markov chain q
        has states :
            { q0, q1, q2, q3, q4, q5},
        transits by :
            [  .94, .07, .00, .00, .00, .00;
               .06, .87, .07, .00, .00, .00;
               .00, .06, .87, .07, .00, .00;
               .00, .00, .06, .87, .07, .00;
               .00, .00, .00, .06, .87, .07;
               .00, .00, .00, .00, .06, .93  ]
    specification:
    a : P{q=q4} + 0.7 < P{q=q5},
    b : P{q=q3} + 0.1 < P{q=q4},
    c : P{q=q2} + 0.1 < P{q=q3},
    d : 1*P{q=q1} + 2*P{q=q2} + 3*P{q=q3}
                  + 4*P{q=q4} + 5*P{q=q5} < 2.057,
    e : 1*P{q=q1} + 2*P{q=q2} + 3*P{q=q3}
                  + 4*P{q=q4} + 5*P{q=q5} < 2.056
    a -> <> b
```

The `model` block of the checker defines the DTMC for the diagram: the states and the Markov transition matrix. The 'has states' block specifies an ordered set of the states of the Markov process q. The 'transits by' block defines the Markov matrix that governs the transitions of the pmf of q. The rows and columns are ordered according to the order of the state set defined previously. That is, the $(i, j)^{th}$ element of the matrix m_{ij} is the probability $P[q(t + 1) = s_i | q(t) = s_j]$.

The first part of the `specification` block contains optional inequality definitions. The time index of the random variable is omitted from the inequalities for convenience. The second part of the `specification` block is an LTL formula against which the model will be checked. Its atomic propositions are either T, F or the inequalities defined previously.

The LTL formula a-><>b checks whether once $P\{q = q5\}$ is at least 0.7 larger than $P\{q = q4\}$ then eventually $P\{q = q4\}$ will be at least 0.1 larger than $P\{q = q3\}$. The following is the result of the model checking.

```
Depth:  138
Result: T
```

The depth value 138 is the search depth. Since the depth appears before the actual model checking algorithm begins, a user can abort the model checking and adjust the specification if the bound is too large. The result of the model checking is *true* meaning the DTMC q satisfies the formula a-><>b.

Again we checked the formula a->c. The formula checks a similar condition with the previous example except $q4$ is replaced by $q3$ and $q3$ is replaced by $q2$. The model checking result is:

```
Depth:   95
Result: F
counterexample: [ 0.30 0.00 0.00 0.00 0.00 0.70 ]
```

The checker disproves the property by providing a counterexample above. Figure 6 shows the probability transitions. It shows that once the inequality a is satisfied, $P\{q = q3\}$ is never larger than $P\{q = q2\}$ by 0.1.

Finally, the specification <>[](d /\ ~e) checks whether the expected number of entities in the queue at the steady state is in between 2.057 and 2.056. Since the computed value of it is 2.0569, the checker should return *true*. However, the required depth to check the specification is 630 and it cannot be checked easily because the number of paths to be searched is exponential in N. In this example, the early checking strategy does not prune many branches. As a result the checking did not finish in 10 minutes with a 1.2GHz Pentium III machine. However, since the eigenvalues of the Markov matrix are { 1.0,0.98,0.93,0.87,0.80,0.76 } the Markov process has a unique steady state pmf. So, for the purpose of steady state expected queue length, we can check <>[]~(d /\ ~e) instead of <>[](d /\ ~e). The result is as follows:

```
Depth:   630
Result: F
counterexample: [ 0.13 0.21 0.12 0.53 0.00 0.00 ]
```

Since there is a steady state expected value and the expected value is not outside of the interval (2.057,2.056), it must be in the interval. Figure 5 shows how the expected value changes from the initial pmf of the counterexample. The value always eventually

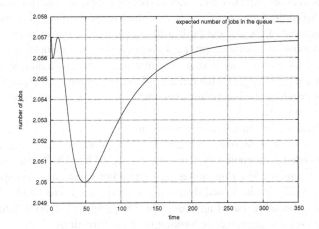

Fig. 5. The transition of the expected number of jobs in the queue beginning with the counter example discovered by the model checker

remains in the interval. So the model does not satisfy the specification, and we can infer that the steady state expected value will remain in the interval.

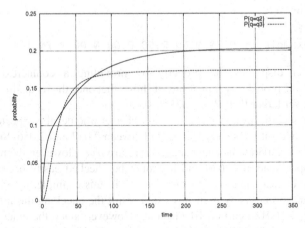

Fig. 6. The transition of the probabilities $P\{q = q2\}$ and $P\{q = q3\}$ beginning with the counter example discovered by the model checker

6   Conclusions

We have developed an LTL model checking algorithm for discrete time Markov chain models. To specify the temporal behavior of Markov chains, we add linear inequalities about pmf vectors to the atomic propositions of LTL. Such inequalities combined with logical connectives are expressive enough to specify temporal behavior of a Markov re-ward model. Since the future rewards are expressed in terms of initial pmfs, we can use an interval estimate of the current pmf in the specification. For example, an expected energy consumption of a network protocol given current pmf about states can be speci-fied and checked. Given a Markov transition matrix, we can find a monotonic bounding function within which the pmf must remain. With the bounding function, we can find a time bound after which the inequalities become constant. Hence the model checking is guaranteed to terminate.

In a practical system like wireless sensor network (WSN), modeling states of the network as they are will encounter a state-explosion problem. For example, a WSN of 100 nodes modeled as queueing systems of capacity 10 has 10^{100} states which cannot be represented directly. For this matter, state lumping techniques and space efficient structures like MDD (multi-valued decision diagram) are introduced [3]. There also is a probabilistic simulation based approach for this problem [6]. As a future work for verifying large scale system, we are looking for these directions.

Although model checking is expensive, some preliminary experiments with a tool based on our model checker suggests that it may be useful for a number of practical examples. Recall that the model checker does a depth-search for a counterexample over the executions of the Buchi automata of the specification. A bound for the length of executions is found; this bound is a function of the Markov matrix M and the inequalities used in the specification. The time complexity of our algorithm is $O((\text{maximum out degree of the nodes in Büchi automaton})^N)$. However, in practice the model checker skips many branches of the search tree by checking the feasibility early in the path. We are planning to introduce the partial order reduction technique used in the SPIN model checker which can reduce the search space substantially [9].

We describe a queueing system and model check several properties for this system as a way to illustrate the usefulness of our model checking tool. We are currently carrying out further work on the tool and applying it to other applications.

References

1. Adnan Aziz, Vigyan Singhal and Felice Balarin. It usually works: The temporal logic of stochastic systems. In *Proc. CAV'95, LNCS 939*, pages 155–165, 1995.
2. Andrea Bianco, Luca de Alfaro. Model checking of probabilistic and nondeterministic systems. In *Proceedings of Conferenco on Foundations of Software Technology and Theoretical Computer Science, Lecturenotes in Computer Science*, volume 1026, pages 499–513, 1995.
3. Andrew S. Miner and Gianfranco Ciardo. Efficient reachability set generation and storage using decision diagrams. In *Int. Conf. on Applications and Theory of Petri Nets*, pages 6–25. LNCS 1639, Springer-Verlag, 1999.
4. Andrew S. Tanenbaum. *Computer Networks*. Prentice Hall PTR, 4th edition, 2003.
5. Athanasios Papoulis. *Probability, Random Variables, and Stochastic Processes*. McGraw-Hill, 3rd edition, 1991.
6. Christel Baier, Joost-Pieter Katoen, Holger Hermanns and Boudewijn Haverkort. Simulation for continuous-time markov chains. In *Proc. CONCUR*, pages 338–354. Springer LNCS 2421, 2002.
7. David G. Luenberger. *Linear and Nonlinear Programming*. Addison Wesley, 2nd edition, 1989.
8. Edmund Clarke, Orna Grumberg, Doron Peled. *Model Checking*. MIT-Press, 2000.
9. Gerard J. Holzmann. The model checker spin. In *IEEE Transactions on Software Engineering*, volume 23, pages 279–295, May 1997.
10. Gianfranco Ciardo, Raymond A. Marie, Bruno Sericola and Kishor S. Trivedi. Performability analysis using semi-markov reward process. In *IEEE Transactions on Computers*, volume 39, pages 1251–1264, October 1990.
11. Gilbert Strang. *Linear Algebra and Its Applications*. Harcourt Brace Jovanovich, 3rd edition, 1988.
12. Henry Start, John W. Woods. *Probability and Random Processes with Applications to Signal Processing*. Prentice-Hall, 3rd edition, 2002.
13. Holger Hermanns, Joost-Pieter Katoen, Joachim Meyer-Kayser and Markus Siegle. A markov chain model checker. In *S. Graf and M. Schwartzbach, editors, TACAS'2000*, pages 347–362, 2000.
14. J.R. Norris. *Markov Chains*. Cambridge University Press, 1997.
15. Julian Keilson. *Markov Chain Models-Rarity and Exponentiality*. Springer-Verlag, 1979.
16. Marta Kwiatkowska, Gethin Norman and David Parker. Prism: Probabilistic symbolic model checker. In *Proc. TOOLS*, volume 2324, pages 200–204. LNCS, Springer-Verlag, April 2002.

17. Moshe Y. Vardi. Probabilistic linear-time model checking: an overview of the automata-theoretic approach. In *Proc. 5th Int. AMAST Workshop Formal Methods for Real-Time and Probabilistic Systems*, volume 1601, May 1999.
18. R. Gerth, D. Peled, M.Y. Vardi and P. Wolper. Simple on-the-fly automatic verification of linear temporal logic. In *IFIP/WG*, volume 6.1, pages 3–18, 1995.
19. Suzana Andova, Holger Hermanns and Joost-Pieter Katoen. Discrete-time rewards model-checked. In *Formal Modeling and Analysis of Timed Systems 2003*, pages 88–104. LNCS, Springer-Verlag, 2003.

Software Model Checking Using Linear Constraints[*]

Alessandro Armando, Claudio Castellini, and Jacopo Mantovani

Artificial Intelligence Laboratory,
DIST, Università degli Studi di Genova,
Viale F. Causa 13, 16145 Genova, Italy
{armando,drwho,jacopo}@dist.unige.it

Abstract. Iterative abstraction refinement has emerged in the last few years as the leading approach to software model checking. In this context Boolean programs are commonly employed as simple, yet useful abstractions from conventional programming languages. In this paper we propose Linear Programs as a finer grained abstraction for sequential programs and propose a model checking procedure for this family of programs. We also present the eureka toolkit, which consists of a prototype implementation of our model checking procedure for Linear Programs as well as of a library of Linear Programs to be used for benchmarking. Experimental results obtained by running our model checker against the library provide evidence of the effectiveness of the approach.

1 Introduction

As software artifacts get increasingly complex, there is growing evidence that traditional testing techniques do not provide, alone, the level of assurance required by many applications. To overcome this difficulty, a number of model checking techniques for software have been developed in the last few years with the ultimate goal to attain the high level of automation achieved in hardware verification. However, model checking of software is a considerably more difficult problem as software systems are in most cases inherently infinite-state, and more sophisticated solutions are therefore needed. In this context, iterative (predicate) abstraction refinement has emerged as the leading approach to software model checking. Exemplary is the technique proposed in [2]: given an imperative program P as input,

Step 1 (Abstraction). The procedure computes a boolean program B having the same control-flow graph as P and whose program variables are restricted to range over the boolean values T and F. By construction, the execution traces of B are a superset of the execution traces of P.

---

[*] We are indebted to Pasquale De Lucia for his contribution to the development of a preliminary version of the model checker described in this paper.

J. Davies et al. (Eds.): ICFEM 2004, LNCS 3308, pp. 209–223, 2004.

Step 2 (Model Checking). The abstract program B is then model-checked and if the analysis of B does not reveal any undesired behaviour, then the procedure can successfully conclude that also P enjoys the same property. Otherwise an undesired behaviour of B is detected and scrutinised in order to determine whether an undesirable behaviour of P can be derived from it. If this is the case, then the procedure halts and reports this fact; otherwise,

Step 3 (Counterexample-Driven Refinement). B is refined into a new boolean program with the help of a theorem prover. The new program does not exhibit the spurious execution trace detected in the previous step; then go to Step 2.

While the approach has proven very effective on specific application areas such as device drivers programming [2, 20], its effectiveness on other, more mundane classes of programs has to be ascertained. Notice that since the detection of a spurious execution trace leads to a new iteration of the check-and-refine loop, the efficiency of the approach depends in a critical way on the number of spurious execution traces allowed by the abstract program. Of course, the closer is the abstraction to the original program the smaller is the number of spurious execution traces that it may be necessary to analyse.

In this paper we propose Linear Programs as an abstraction for sequential programs and propose a model checking procedure for this family of programs. Similarly to boolean programs, Linear Programs have the usual control-flow constructs and procedural abstraction with call-by-value parameter passing and recursion. Linear Programs differ from boolean programs in that program variables range over a numeric domain (e.g. the integers or the reals); moreover, all conditions and assignments to variables involve linear expressions, i.e. expressions of the form $c_0 + c_1 x_1 + \cdots + c_n x_n$, where $c_0, \ldots, c_n$ are numeric constants and $x_1, \ldots, x_n$ are program variables ranging over a numeric domain. Linear Programs are considerably more expressive than boolean programs and can encode explicitly complex correlations between data and control that must necessarily be abstracted away when using boolean programs.

The model checking procedure for Linear Programs presented in this paper is built on top of the ideas presented in [1] for the simpler case of boolean programs and amounts to an extension of the inter-procedural data-flow analysis algorithm of [25]. We present the eureka toolkit, which consists of a prototype implementation of our model checking procedure for Linear Programs as well as of a library of Linear Programs. We also show the promising experimental results obtained by running eureka against the library.

2   Linear Programs

Most of the notation and concepts introduced in this Section are inspired by, or are extensions of, those presented in [1]. A Linear Program basically consists of global variables declarations and procedure definitions; a procedure definition is a sequence of statements; and a statement is either an assignment, a conditional (if/then/else), an iteration (goto/while), an assertion or a skip (;), much like in ordinary C programs. Variables are of type int, and expressions can be built employing $+$, $-$ and the usual arithmetic comparison predicates $=, \neq, <, >, \leq, \geq$.

Given a Linear Program P consisting of n statements and p procedures, we assign to each statement a unique index from 1 to n, and to each procedure a unique index from $n+1$ to $n+p$. With s_i we denote the statement at index i. For the sake of simplicity, we assume that variable and label names are globally unique in P. We also assume the existence of a procedure called main: it is the first procedure to be executed.

We define $Globals(P)$ as the set of global variables of P; $Formals_P(i)$ is the set of formal parameters of the procedure that contains the statement s_i; $Locals_P(i)$ is the set of local variables and formal parameters of the procedure that contains the statement s_i, while $sLocals_P(i)$ is the set of strictly local variables (i.e. without the formal parameters) of the procedure that contains statement s_i; $InScope_P(i)$ is the set of variables that are in scope at statement s_i. Finally, $First_P(pr)$ is the index of the first statement of procedure pr and $ProcOf_P(i)$ the index of the procedure belonging to the statement s_i.

The Control Flow Graph. The *Control flow Graph* of a Linear Program P is a directed graph $G_P = (V_P, Succ_P)$, where $V_P = \{0, 1, \ldots, n, n+1, \ldots, n+p\}$ is the set of vertices, one for each statement (from 1 to n) and one $Exit_{pr}$ vertex for each procedure pr (from $n+1$ to $n+p$). Vertex 0 is used to model the failure of an assert statement. Vertex 1 is the first statement of procedure main: $First_P(\text{main}) = 1$. To get a concrete feeling of how a linear program and its control flow graph look like, the reader may refer to the program parity.c, given in Figure 1.

As one can see, parity(n) looks reasonably close to a small, real C procedure recursively calling upon itself 10 times (the actual parameter x is set to 10) whose task is to determine the parity of its argument by "flipping" the global variable even, which ends up being 1 if and only if x is even. Again Figure 1 gives an intuition of how the function $Next_P(i)$ and $sSucc_P(i)$ behave. Roughly speaking, given a vertex i, $sSucc_P(i)$ follows the execution trace of the program,[1] while $Next_P(i)$ is the *lexical* successor of i.

Valuations and Transitions. We now informally define valuations and transitions for a Linear Program. The reader may find more formal and precise definitions in a longer version of this article [22]. Let $\mathcal{D}$ be a numerical domain, called the domain of computation. Given a vertex $i \in V_P$, a *valuation* is a function $\omega : InScope_P(i) \to \mathcal{D}$ (it can be extended to expressions inductively, in the usual way), and a *state* of a program P is a pair $\langle i, \omega \rangle$. A state $\langle i, \omega \rangle$ is *initial* if and only if $i = 1$. State transitions in a linear program P are denoted by $\langle i_k, \omega_1 \rangle \to_P^\alpha \langle i_{k+1}, \omega_2 \rangle$ where i_{k+1} is one of the successors of i and α is a label ranging over the set of terminals:

---

[1] Conditional statements represent the only exception: there, $Tsucc_P(i)$ and $Fsucc_P(i)$ denote the successors in the *true* and *false* branch, respectively.

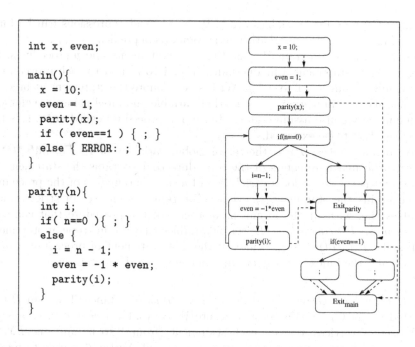

Fig. 1. parity.c and its control flow graph. The dashed lines show the $Next_P$ function, while the continuous lines show the successor relations between the vertices

$$\Sigma(P) = \{\sigma\} \cup \{\langle \text{call}, i, \delta \rangle, \langle \text{ret}, i, \delta \rangle : \exists j \in V_P \text{ s.t.}$$
$$s_j = \text{call}, i = Next_P(j), \delta : Locals_P(j) \to \mathcal{D}\}.$$

Terminals of the form $\langle \text{call}, i, \delta \rangle$ and $\langle \text{ret}, i, \delta \rangle$ represent, respectively, entry and exit points of the procedure invoked by s_j. A *path* is a sequence $\langle i_0, \omega_0 \rangle \to_P^{\alpha_1}$ $\langle i_1, \omega_1 \rangle \to_P^{\alpha_2} \cdots \to_P^{\alpha_n} \langle i_n, \omega_n \rangle$ such that $\langle i_k, \omega_k \rangle \to_P^{\alpha_{k+1}} \langle i_{k+1}, \omega_{k+1} \rangle$ for $k = 0, \ldots, n-1$. Notice that not all paths represent potential execution paths: in a transition like $\langle Exit_{pr}, \omega_1 \rangle \to_P^{\langle \text{ret}, i_2, \delta \rangle} \langle i_2, \omega_2 \rangle$, the valuation δ can be chosen arbitrarily and therefore ω_2 is not guaranteed to coincide with ω_1 on the locals of the caller, as required by the semantics of procedure calls. To rectify this, the notion of same-level valid path is introduced. A valid path from $\langle i_0, \omega_0 \rangle$ to $\langle i_n, \omega_n \rangle$ describes the transmission of effects from $\langle i_0, \omega_0 \rangle$ to $\langle i_n, \omega_n \rangle$ via a sequence of execution steps which may end with some number of activation records on the call stack; these correspond to "unmatched" terminals of the form $\langle \text{ret}, i, \delta \rangle$ in the string associated with the path. A same-level valid path from $\langle i_0, \omega_0 \rangle$ to $\langle i_n, \omega_n \rangle$ describes the transmission of effects from $\langle i_0, \omega_0 \rangle$ to $\langle i_n, \omega_n \rangle$—where $\langle i_0, \omega_0 \rangle$ and $\langle i_n, \omega_n \rangle$ are in the same procedure—via a sequence of execution steps during which the call stack may temporarily grow deeper (because of procedure calls) but never shallower than its original depth, before eventually returning to its original depth. A state $\langle i, \omega \rangle$ is *reachable* iff there exists a valid path from some initial state to $\langle i, \omega \rangle$. A vertex $i \in V_P$ is *reachable* iff there exists a valuation ω such that $\langle i, \omega \rangle$ is reachable.

3   Symbolic Model Checking of Linear Programs

The reachability of a line in a program can be reduced to computing the set of valuations Ω_i such that $\langle i, \omega \rangle$ is reachable iff $\omega \in \Omega_i$, for each vertex i in the control flow graph of the program: the statement associated to vertex i is reachable iff Ω_i is not empty. Following [1], our model checking procedure computes *(i)* "path edges" to represent the reachability status of vertices and *(ii)* "summary edges" to record the input/output behaviour of procedures.

Let $i \in V_P$ and $e = First_P(ProcOf_P(i))$. A *path edge* $\pi_i = \langle \omega_e, \omega_i \rangle$ of i is a pair of valuations such that there is a valid path $\langle 1, \omega_0 \rangle \rightarrow_P^{\alpha_1} \cdots \rightarrow_P^{\alpha_k} \langle e, \omega_e \rangle$ and a same-level valid path $\langle e, \omega_e \rangle \rightarrow_P^{\alpha_{k+1}} \cdots \rightarrow_P^{\alpha_n} \langle i, \omega_i \rangle$ for some valuation ω_0. In other words, a path edge represents a suffix of a valid path from $\langle 1, \omega_0 \rangle$ to $\langle i, \omega_i \rangle$.

Let $i \in V_P$ be such that $s_i = pr(e_1, \ldots, e_n)$, let $y_1, \ldots, y_n$ be the formal parameters of pr associated to the actuals $e_1, \ldots, e_n$ respectively, and let $\pi = \langle \omega_i, \omega_o \rangle$ be a path edge of a vertex $Exit_{pr}$. A *summary edge* $\sigma = \langle \omega_1, \omega_2 \rangle$ of π is a pair of valuations such that

1. $\omega_1(g) = \omega_i(g)$ and $\omega_2(g) = \omega_o(g)$ for all $g \in Globals(P)$, and
2. $\omega_1(y_j) = \omega_i(e_j) = \omega_o(e_j)$ for $j = 1, \ldots, n$.

The computation of the summary edges is one of the most important parts of the algorithm. Summary edges record the output valuation ω_2 of a procedure for a given input valuation ω_1. Therefore, there is no need to re-enter a procedure for the same input, since the output is known already. In some cases of frequently called procedures and of recursion, this turns into a great improvement in performance. We represent path edges and summary edges symbolically, by means of Abstract Disjunctive Linear Constraints. In the rest of this section we give the formal definitions needed and define the operations over them.

3.1   Representing Path Edges and Summary Edges Symbolically

A *linear expression* over $\mathcal{D}$ is an expression of the form $c_0 + c_1 x_1 + \ldots + c_n x_n$, where $c_0, c_1, \ldots, c_n$ are constants and $x_1, x_2, \ldots, x_n$ are variables, both ranging over $\mathcal{D}$. A *linear constraint* is a relation of the form $e \leq 0$, $e = 0$, $e \neq 0$, where e is a linear expression over $\mathcal{D}$. A *linear formula* is a boolean combination of linear constraints. A *Disjunctive Linear Constraint D* (DLC for short) is a linear formula in disjunctive normal form (that is, a disjunction of conjunctions of linear constraints). Formally, $D = \bigvee_i \bigwedge_j c_{ij}$, where c_{ij} are linear constraints. The symbol $\top$ stands for a tautological linear formula, while $\bot$ stands for an unsatisfiable linear formula. An *Abstract Disjunctive Linear Constraint* (ADLC for short) is an expression of the form $\lambda \mathbf{x} \lambda \mathbf{x}'.D$, where D is a DLC, and $\mathbf{x}, \mathbf{x}'$ are all and the only variables in D.[2] The following operations over DLCs are defined:

---

[2] For sake of simplicity, in the rest of the paper we will write $\lambda \mathbf{x} \mathbf{x}'.D$ instead of $\lambda \mathbf{x} \lambda \mathbf{x}'.D$.

- *Application.* Let $\lambda\mathbf{xx}'.D$ be an ADLC and $\mathbf{s}$ and $\mathbf{t}$ be vectors of linear expressions with the same number of elements as $\mathbf{x}$. The *application of $\lambda\mathbf{xx}'.D$ to $(\mathbf{s}, \mathbf{t})$* is the DLC obtained by simultaneously replacing the i-th element of $\mathbf{x}$ ($\mathbf{x}'$) with the i-th element of $\mathbf{s}$ ($\mathbf{t}$ resp.).
- *Conjunction.* Let D_1 and D_2 be two DLCs, then $D_1 \sqcap D_2$ is any DLC for $D_1 \wedge D_2$. Conjunction is extended to ADLCs as follows. Let δ_1 and δ_2 be two ADLCs. Then, $\delta_1 \sqcap \delta_2 = \lambda\mathbf{xx}'.(\delta_1(\mathbf{x}, \mathbf{x}') \sqcap \delta_2(\mathbf{x}, \mathbf{x}'))$.
- *Disjunction.* Let D_1 and D_2 be two DLCs, then $D_1 \sqcup D_2$ is $D_1 \vee D_2$. Disjunction is extended to ADLCs in the following way. Let δ_1 and δ_2 be two ADLCs. Then, $\delta_1 \sqcup \delta_2 = \lambda\mathbf{xx}'.(\delta_1(\mathbf{x}, \mathbf{x}') \sqcup \delta_2(\mathbf{x}, \mathbf{x}')) = \lambda\mathbf{xx}'.(\delta_1(\mathbf{x}, \mathbf{x}') \vee \delta_2(\mathbf{x}, \mathbf{x}'))$.
- *Negation.* Let D be a DLC. Then $\sim D$ is obtained by putting the negation $\neg D$ of D in disjunctive normal form. Negation is extended to ADLCs in the following way: $\sim\delta = \lambda\mathbf{xx}'.(\sim\delta(\mathbf{x}, \mathbf{x}'))$.
- *Quantifier Elimination.* Let D be a DLC, then $\exists\mathbf{x}.D$ is any DLC equivalent to D obtained by eliminating from D the variables $\mathbf{x}$.
- *Entailment.* Let δ_1 and δ_2 be two ADLCs, $\delta_1 \sqsubseteq \delta_2$ iff all the pairs of valuations satisfying δ_1 satisfy also δ_2: $\delta_1 \sqsubseteq \delta_2$ iff $\delta_1(\mathbf{x}, \mathbf{x}') \models_{\mathcal{D}} \delta_2(\mathbf{x}, \mathbf{x}')$. With the subscript $\mathcal{D}$ in $\models_{\mathcal{D}}$ we denote that assignments over variables range over $\mathcal{D}$ and that the symbols $+, -, *, =, \neq, \leq$ have the intended interpretation.

Summary Edges. Let c be a vertex of V_P for a procedure call, say $s_c = pr(\mathbf{a})$, and let i be the exit vertex of pr. Let $\mathbf{y} = Formals_P(i)$, $\mathbf{x} = InScope_P(i)$, $\mathbf{z} = sLocals_P(i)$, $\mathbf{g} = Globals(P)$; then $Lift_c(\delta) = \lambda\mathbf{gg}'\mathbf{y}.\exists\mathbf{zz}'\mathbf{y}'.\delta(\mathbf{x}, \mathbf{x}')$. A summary edge of a procedure pr records the "behaviour" of pr in terms of the values of the global variables just before the call (i.e. $\mathbf{g}$) and after the execution of pr (i.e. $\mathbf{g}'$). These valuations depend on the valuations of the formal parameters (i.e. $\mathbf{y}$) of pr.

Transition Relations. From here on, we will use the expression $\mathbf{x}' = \mathbf{x}$ as a shorthand for $x'_1 = x_1 \wedge \ldots \wedge x'_n = x_n$. Let $Exit_P$ be the set of exit vertices in V_P, $Cond_P$ be the set of conditional statements in V_P, and $Call_P$ be the set of all procedure calls in V_P. We associate with each vertex i of $V_P \setminus Exit_P$ a transfer function, defined as follows: if s_i is a ; or a `goto` statement, then $\tau_i = \lambda\mathbf{xx}'.(\mathbf{x}' = \mathbf{x})$ where $\mathbf{x} = InScope_P(i)$; if s_i is an assignment of the form `y=e`, then $\tau_i = \lambda\mathbf{xx}'\lambda\mathbf{yy}'.(\mathbf{y}' = \mathbf{e} \wedge \mathbf{x} = \mathbf{x}')$ where $\mathbf{x} = InScope_P(i) \setminus \mathbf{y}$; if $i \in Call_P$, i.e. s_i is of the form $pr(\mathbf{a})$, then $\tau_i = \lambda\mathbf{y}'\mathbf{gg}'.\exists\mathbf{yzz}'.(\mathbf{y}' = \mathbf{a} \wedge \mathbf{x} = \mathbf{x}')$ where $\mathbf{y} = Formals_P(First_P(pr))$, $\mathbf{z} = Locals_P(i)$, $\mathbf{x} = InScope_P(i)$ and $\mathbf{g} = Globals(P)$; finally, if $i \in Cond_P$, that is, s_i is of the form `if(d(x))`, `while(d(x))` or `assert(d(x))`, then $\tau_{i,true} = \lambda\mathbf{xx}'.(d(\mathbf{x}') \sqcap \mathbf{x}' = \mathbf{x})$, and $\tau_{i,false} = \lambda\mathbf{xx}'.((\sim d(\mathbf{x}')) \sqcap \mathbf{x}' = \mathbf{x})$, where $\mathbf{x} = InScope_P(i)$.

The Join Functions. We now define the *Join* and the *SEJoin* functions. The first one applies to a path edge the given transition relation for a vertex, while the second one is used only during procedure calls, adopting the summary edge as a (partial) transition relation.

Let δ be an ADLC representing the path edges for a given vertex i and let τ be an ADLC representing the transition relation associated with i; then $Join(\delta, \tau)$ computes and returns the ADLC representing the path edges obtained by extending the path edges represented by δ with the transitions represented by τ. Formally, $Join(\delta, \tau) = \lambda\mathbf{xx'}.\exists\mathbf{x''}.(\delta(\mathbf{x}, \mathbf{x''}) \sqcap \tau(\mathbf{x''}, \mathbf{x'}))$.

Let δ be an ADLC representing the path edges for $s_i = pr(\mathbf{a})$ and let σ be an ADLC representing the summary edges for pr. The $Join$ operation between δ and σ is defined as follows. Let $\mathbf{g} = Globals(P)$, $\mathbf{y} = Formals_P(First_P(pr))$, $\mathbf{z} = Locals_P(i)$; then $SEJoin(\delta, \sigma) = \lambda\mathbf{gg'zz'}.\exists\mathbf{g''}.(\exists\mathbf{y'}.(\sigma(\mathbf{g'}, \mathbf{g''}, \mathbf{y'}) \sqcap \mathbf{a'} = \mathbf{y'})) \sqcap \delta(\mathbf{g}, \mathbf{g''}, \mathbf{z}, \mathbf{z'})$.

Self Loops. $SelfLoop(\delta)$ is used to model the semantics of procedure calls, by making self loops with the target of the path edges. Formally, given an ADLC δ, $SelfLoop(\delta) = \lambda\mathbf{xx'}.\exists\mathbf{x''}.(\delta(\mathbf{x}, \mathbf{x''}) \sqcap \mathbf{x''} = \mathbf{x'})$.

3.2   The Model Checking Procedure

The Model Checking procedure works by incrementally storing in a worklist the next statement to be analyzed, by computing path edges and summary edges accordingly, and by removing the processed statement from the worklist. Let W be the worklist, P be an array of $n + p + 1$ ADLCs, and let S be an array of p ADLCs[3]. P collects the path edges of each vertex of the control flow graph, and S collects the summary edges of each procedure.

We define the initial state of our procedure as a triple $(1.\epsilon, P^1, S^1)$, where $P_1^1 = \lambda\mathbf{xx'}.(\mathbf{x} = \mathbf{x'})$ with $\mathbf{x} = InScope_P(1)$ and $P_i^1 = \lambda\mathbf{yy'}.\bot$ for each $0 \leq i \leq (n + p)$ such that $i \neq 1$, and $S_j^1 = \lambda\mathbf{yy'}.\bot$ for each $1 \leq j \leq p$.

We also need to define a function that updates the array P of the path edges and the worklist W, when needed. Given a vertex j (the next to be verified), the current worklist $W = i.is$, an ADLC D (the one just computed for vertex i), and the array P of path edges, the function returns the pair containing the updated worklist W' and the updated array P' of path edges, according to the result of the entailment check $D \sqsubseteq P_j$. We refer to this function as the "propagation" function $prop$.[4]

$$prop(j, i.is, D, P) = \begin{cases} (Insert(j, is), P\,[(D \sqcup P_j)/j]) & \text{if } D \not\sqsubseteq P_j \\ (is, P) & \text{otherwise.} \end{cases}$$

A generic transition of the procedure is of the form $(W, P, S) \rightarrow (W', P', S')$, where the values of W', P', S' depend on the vertex being valuated, that is, on the vertex on top of the worklist. Let i be the vertex on top of W, that is, $W = i.is$. The procedure evolves according to the following cases.

---

[3] We recall that n is the number of statements, and p is the number of procedures. With P_i and S_i we denote the i-th element of the arrays.

[4] The function $Insert(El, List)$ returns a new list in which El is added to $List$ in a non-deterministic chosen position.

Procedure Calls. Let $s_i = pr(\mathbf{a})$, $p = Exit_{pr}$, $l_i = SelfLoop(Join(P_i, \tau_i))$, and $r_i = SEJoin(P_i, S_p)$. In this case the procedure is entered only if no summary edge has been built for the given input. This happens if and only if l_i does not entail $P_{sSucc_P(i)}$; otherwise the procedure is skipped, using r_i as a (partial) transition relation. The call stack is updated only if the procedure is entered. If $l_i \not\sqsubseteq P_{sSucc_P(i)}$, then

$$W' = Insert(sSucc_P(i), is),$$
$$P' = P[(P_{sSucc_P(i)} \sqcup l_i)/sSucc_P(i)],$$
$$S' = S.$$

Otherwise, $(W', P') = prop(Next_P(i), W, r_i, P)$ and $S' = S$.

Return from Procedure Calls. Let $i \in Exit_P$. When an exit node is reached, a new summary edge s is built for the procedure. If it entails the old summary edges S_i, then $S' = S$; otherwise s is added to S_i. For each $w \in Succ_P(i)$ let $c \in Call_P$ such that $w = Next_P(c)$, and let $s = Lift_{\mathbf{c}}(P_i)$. If $s \not\sqsubseteq S_i$ then for each w,

$$(W', P') = prop(w, W, SEJoin(P_i, S_i \sqcup s), P),$$
$$S' = S[(S_i \sqcup s)/i].$$

Otherwise, $W' = W$, $P' = P$, and $S' = S$.

Conditional Statements. Both of the branches of the conditional statements have to be analyzed. Therefore, the worklist and the array of path edges have to be updated twice, according to the propagation function. Let $i \in Cond_P$, then

$$(W'', P'') = prop(Fsucc_P(i), W, Join(P_i, \tau_{i,false}), P),$$
$$(W', P') = prop(Tsucc_P(i), W'', Join(P_i, \tau_{i,true}), P''),$$
$$S' = S.$$

Other Statements. In all other cases the statements do not need any special treatment, and the path edges are simply propagated the single successor. If $i \in V_P \setminus Cond_P \setminus Call_P \setminus Exit_P$, then

$$(W', P') = prop(sSucc_P(i), W, Join(P_i, \tau_i), P),$$
$$S' = S.$$

When no more rules are applicable, P contains the valuations of all the vertices of the control flow graph and S contains the valuations that show the behaviour of every procedure given the values of its formal parameters. As a result, if the ADLC representing a path edge for a vertex is $\bot$, then that vertex is not reachable.

4   The **eureka** Toolkit

We have implemented the procedure described in Section 3 in a fully automatic prototype system called **eureka** which, given a Linear Program as input, first generates the control flow graph and then model-checks the input program. The most important operations involved in the procedure, namely quantifier elimination and entailment check, are taken care of, respectively, by a module called QE, employing the Fourier-Motzkin method (see, e.g.,[24])[5], and ICS 2.0 [15], a system able to decide satisfiability of ground first-order formulae belonging to several theories, among which Linear Arithmetic.

In order to qualitatively test the effectiveness and scalability properties of our approach, we have devised a library of Linear Programs called *eureka Library*. As a general statement, the library consists of Linear Programs reasonably close to real C language, and easily synthesizable in different degrees of hardness; in this initial version, it is organised in six parametrized families; for each family, a non-negative number N is used to generate problems which stress one or more aspects of the computation of Linear Programs:

Data. The use of arithmetic reasoning, e.g., summing, subtracting, multiplying by a constant and comparing;
Control. The use of conditionals, e.g., if, assert and the condition test of while;
Iteration. The number of iterations done during the execution;
Recursion. The use of recursion.

This classification is suggested by general considerations about what kind of data- and control-intensiveness is usually found in C programs in verification. For example, the corpus analysed by SLAM, consisting of device drivers [2, 20], is highly control-intensive but not data-intensive; arithmetic reasoning is usually considered hard to reason about; and recursion is usually considered harder than iteration.

A problem is generated by instantiating the family template according to N, and a line of the resulting program, tagged with an error label, is then tested for reachability. For each family, increasing N increases the hardness of the problem by making one or more of the above aspects heavier and heavier. Table 1 gives an account of which aspects are stressed in each family. A full account of the structure of the Library is available in [22], as well as at the URL http://www.ai.dist.unige.it/eureka.

For example, swap_seq.c(N) consists of a simple procedure swap() which swaps the values of two global variables, and is called upon $2N$ times. In this case, increasing N stresses the capacity of the system to deal with arithmetic reasoning. On the other side, swap_iter.c(N) does basically the same, but using an iterative cycle; therefore increasing N also forces more and more iterations.

As another example, parity.c(N) is the template version of the program in figure 1; here N is the number whose parity we want to evaluate. Making N bigger involves more and more arithmetic reasoning, and it also forces the system to follow more recursive calls.

---

[5] the Fourier-Motzkin method works on the real numbers, whereas Linear Programs variables range over the integers; this may lead to false negatives, but the problem has not arisen in practice so far.

Table 1. The eureka Library of Linear Programs. Each family stresses on or more aspects of the computation of Linear Programs, as N grows

Family	data	control	iteration	recursion
swap_seq.c(N)	√			
swap_iter.c(N)	√		√	
delay_iter.c(N)	√	√	√	
delay_recur.c(N)	√	√	√	√
parity.c(N)	√			√
sum.c(N)	√		√	

5   Experimental Results

In our experimental analysis we have tried to identify how our system scales on each family of Linear Programs in the eureka Library, as N grows, and why. An initial set of tests has revealed that, unsurprisingly, the hardest operations the system performs are *(i)* the *Join* operation, involving quantifier elimination, and *(ii)* the entailment check. Moreover, some of the programs in the library have proved to be particularly hard because of the number of redundant constraints generated during the conjunction of two ADLCs into a new ADLC, required again by *Join*. This can potentially make path edges and summary edges unmanageable.

Figure 2 shows the experimental results. The x-axis shows N for each family of programs, while the y-axis shows the total CPU time required, on a linear scale. Additionally, we show the time spent by ICS and by the QE module. All tests have been performed on Pentium IV 1.8GHz machines equipped with Linux RedHat 7.2; the timeout was set to 3600 seconds and the memory limit was set to 128MB.

A quick analysis of the results follows. First of all, let us note that in all cases except one the hardness of the problems grows monotonically with N; this indicates that, at least for our procedure, stressing the above mentioned aspects of computation actually makes the problems harder and harder. The only remarkable exception, presenting a strong oscillating behaviour, is parity.c(N); as one can see by looking at the graph, ICS is entirely responsible for it. Moreover, a more detailed analysis reveals that the *number of calls* to ICS grows monotonically; this means that some instances of the problems given to ICS are actually easier than those for a smaller N. We argue that this is due to the way constraints are stored in the summary edge during the calls to parity(n): in some cases they ease ICS's search, whereas in others they do not.

Secondly, the only family whose hardness seems to grow linearly with N is swap_seq.c(N). This is reasonable, since once the summary edges for the swapping procedure have been calculated twice, they need not be re-calculated any longer. Quantifier elimination is irrelevant.

Thirdly, swap_iter.c(N), delay_iter.c(N) and delay_recur.c(N) grow more than linearly with N, with ICS time dominating quantifier elimination but

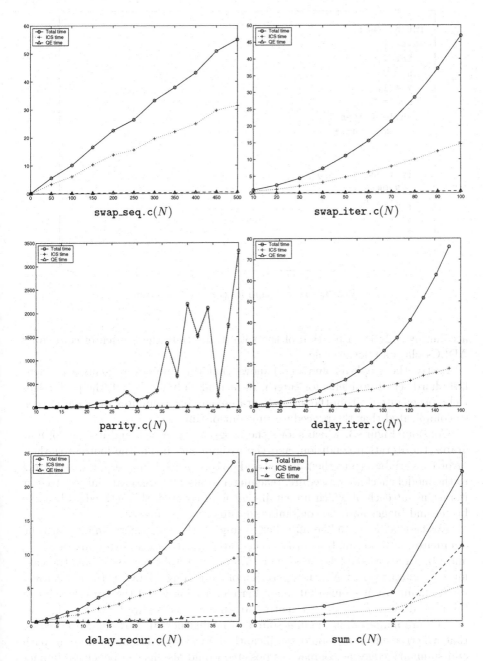

Fig. 2. Experimental results. Each graph shows the total CPU time, the time spent by ICS and the time required by the QE module, as N; each caption indicates the related program family

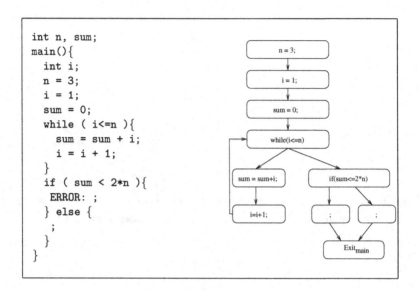

```
int n, sum;
main(){
  int i;
  n = 3;
  i = 1;
  sum = 0;
  while ( i<=n ){
    sum = sum + i;
    i = i + 1;
  }
  if ( sum < 2*n ){
  ERROR: ;
  } else {
    ;
  }
}
```

Fig. 3. sum.c(3) and its control flow graph

accounting only for a fraction of the total time. Here the burden of conjoining ADLCs plays a relevant role.

Lastly, the graph for sum.c(N) shows that this family represents a particularly hard set of problems for eureka. In fact, already for $N = 4$, the path edges to be propagated within the while() statement that computes the sum become so complicated that the procedure runs out of time.

Consider Figure 3, which shows the program for $N = 3$ and its control flow graph; the iteration condition, and the assignments inside the loop altogether, involve 3 variables (plus their primed and doubly primed counterparts, according to the model checking procedure, reaching a total of 9 variables). Subject to four iterations, at each of which no entailment is discovered, the path edges become bigger and bigger and the conjoining machinery goes timeout.

Notice that here, unlike all other examples, the quantifier elimination time dominates; still, an analysis of the failed attempt at sum.c(4) reveals that ICS and QE times account for less than 15% of the total time. As it was the case for, e.g., swap_iter.c(N), the operation of conjoining ADLCs is the bottleneck.

Summing up: it seems that quantifier elimination is *not* the hardest point of the procedure; rather, the way path and summary edges are built, that is, how ADLCs are managed, is the first source of inefficiency. In particular, we believe that a better encoding would significantly improve performance; keeping path and summary edges as compact as possible would also have a beneficial impact on ICS, since the problems it must solve could be significantly simpler.

Comparative Results. Only a few comparative tests have been possible, since one of the main systems able to tackle Linear Programs, namely SLAM [2], is not publicly available; we compared our results with the BLAST toolkit [20] instead. The input language of BLAST is a superset of that of Linear Programs, but the tool lacks support for recursion. We have run BLAST on the non-recursive programs of the eureka Library; but even for small instances (namely swap_seq.c(1), swap_iter.c(2) and sum.c(3)) the system stopped, reporting the infeasibility of discovering new predicates during its refinement process. Only on delay_iter.c(N) BLAST scales very well, exhibiting an almost constant behaviour.

6   Related Work

The Boolean *Abstraction/Refinement* paradigm is a common approach to Software Model Checking of C programs. It has been successfully applied to device drivers in the Slam toolkit [2] and in Blast [20]. The latter is a so-called "lazy" model checker, since if it finds an error in the model, it does not refine the whole abstraction that has been built, but only the fragment of code that generated the spurious error. Other model checkers for C that perform abstraction and refinement are MAGIC [7], Boop [9], and Moped [17]. Moreover, Flanagan [11] proposes both a technique and a tool that translate imperative programs to CLP. Each procedure is translated into two CLP relations, an *error* and a *transfer* relation. The program is then verified by performing a depth-first search trying to satisfy the error relation of the main procedure. Since the proposed tool is in a too preliminary stage for testing,[6] we plan to compare eureka with it as soon as the first release will be distributed.

FeaVer and Modex [12] provide support for the translation of C programs to input languages of verification tools like SPIN [4]. Basically they abstract a C program to a finite model that can then be verified. Two other tools do the same for Java software: Bandera [5] and Java PathFinder [6].

Various tools and approaches have been applied to programming languages other than C and to different systems. Bultan et al. [3] have developed a Model Checking procedure for concurrent systems that encodes constraints in Presburger Arithmetic and applies widening operators in order to enforce termination. The Kiss [19] toolkit is devoted to analyze concurrent software. It reduces the input program to a sequential program that simulates a large subset of behaviours of the original, concurrent one. Kiss uses the Slam toolkit as back-end.

7   Conclusions and Future Work

We have proposed Linear Programs as an alternative model for sequential programs to be used in the context of the abstraction/refinement paradigm. Linear Programs are a less abstract and more expressive model than boolean programs, and can explicitly encode complex correlations between data and control, allowing a great reduction of the inefficiencies due to the iterative refinement process.

---

[6] Personal communication by Cormac Flanagan.

We have also described and implemented a model checking procedure for Linear Programs. The eureka prototype has been tested against the eureka library, a set of benchmark programs built to stress different aspects of computation. As shown in section 5, the experimental results are promising, since they reveal good scalability properties of our approach.

Future Work. Since the eureka model checker is a prototype tool, it can be heavily optimized, for example by adopting Gaussian elimination for resolving equalities instead of the Fourier-Motzkin method or, more radically, by replacing it with the *Omega library* [21]. Also, since the reachability problem becomes undecidable if applied to Linear Programs, we plan to cope with the non termination of our model checking procedure by investigating the use of widening techniques [14, 3]. In doing so, one has to be aware that the procedure may terminate with some false positive results. Lastly, we are also working on abstraction. Since eureka only works on Linear Programs, we argue it may be possible to build a tool able to abstract from "usual" C programs (for instance including structures, pointers and array) to Linear Programs. The improvements described above, when done, will be tested against the eureka library, that will be growing with new programs of increasing difficulty and new categories.

References

1. Ball, T., Rajamani, S.K.: Bebop: A symbolic model checker for boolean programs. In: Proc. of SPIN 2000. (2000) 113–130
2. Ball, T., Rajamani, S.K.: Automatically validating temporal safety properties of interfaces. In: Proc. of SPIN 2001, Springer-Verlag New York, Inc. (2001) 103–122
3. Bultan, T., Gerber, R., Pugh, W.: Model-checking concurrent systems with unbounded integer variables: symbolic representations, approximations, and experimental results. ACM Transactions on Programming Languages and Systems **21** (1999) 747–789
4. Holzmann, G.J.: The model checker spin. IEEE Trans. Softw. Eng. **23** (1997) 279–295
5. Corbett, J.C., Dwyer, M.B., Hatcliff, J., Laubach, S., Pasareanu, C.S., Robby, Zheng, H.: Bandera: extracting finite-state models from java source code. In: Proc. of the 22nd int. conf. on Software engineering, ACM Press (2000) 439–448
6. Visser, W., Havelund, K., Brat, G., Park, S.: Java pathfinder - second generation of a java model checker (2000)
7. Chaki, S., Clarke, E., Groce, A., Jha, S., Veith, H.: Modular verification of software components in c. In: Proc. of the 25th int. conf. on Software engineering, IEEE Computer Society (2003) 385–395
8. Clarke, E.M., Grumberg, O., Jha, S., Lu, Y., Veith, H.: Counterexample-guided abstraction refinement. In: CAV. (2000) 154–169
9. Clarke, E., Kroening, D., Lerda, F.: A tool for checking ANSI-C programs. In Jensen, K., Podelski, A., eds.: TACAS 2004. Volume 2988 of Lecture Notes in Computer Science., Springer (2004) 168–176
10. Clarke, E., Kroening, D., Sharygina, N., Yorav, K.: Predicate abstraction of ANSI-C programs using SAT. FMSD (2004) To appear.

11. Flanagan, C.: Automatic software model checking using clp. In: Proc. of ESOP 03. Volume 2618 of LNCS., Springer (2003) 189–203
12. Holzmann, G.J., Smith, M.H.: Software model checking: extracting verification models from source code. Software Testing, Verification and Reliability **11** (2001) 65–79
13. Cousot, P., Halbwachs, N.: Automatic discovery of linear restraints among variables of a program. In: Conference Record of the Fifth Annual ACM SIGPLAN-SIGACT POPL Symposium, ACM Press, New York, NY (1978) 84–97
14. Cousot, P., Cousot, R.: Comparison of the Galois connection and widening/narrowing approaches to abstract interpretation. JTASPEFL '91, Bordeaux. BIGRE **74** (1991) 107–110
15. de Moura, L., Ruess, H., Shankar, N., Rushby, J.: The ICS decision procedure for embedded deduction. To appear at the IJCAR, Cork, Ireland (2004)
16. Chen, H., Wagner, D.: MOPS: an infrastructure for examining security properties of software. In: Proceedings of the 9th ACM Conference on Computer and Communications Security, Washington, DC (2002) 235–244
17. Schwoon, S.: Model-Checking Pushdown Systems. PhD thesis, Technische Universität München (2002)
18. Weissenbacher, G.: An Abstraction/Refinement Scheme for Model Checking C Programs. PhD thesis, Technische Universität Graz (2003)
19. Qadeer, S., Wu, D.: Kiss: keep it simple and sequential. In: Proceedings of the ACM SIGPLAN 2004 conference on Programming language design and implementation, ACM Press (2004) 14–24
20. Henzinger, T.A., Jhala, R., Majumdar, R., Sutre, G.: Lazy abstraction. In: POPL 2002. (2002) 58–70
21. Kelly, W., Maslov, V., Pugh, W., Rosser, E., Shpeisman, T., Wonnacott, D.: The omega library interface guide. Technical report, Univ. of Maryland at College Park (1995)
22. Armando, A., Castellini, C., Mantovani, J.: Introducing full linear arithmetic to symbolic software model checking. Technical report, available at URL: http://www.ai.dist.unige.it/eureka. University of Genova (2004)
23. Armando, A., de Lucia, P.: Symbolic model-checking of linear programs. Technical report, Datalogiske Skrifter, Technical Report No. 94, Roskilde University (2002)
24. Lassez, J.L., Maher, M.: On Fourier's Algorithm's for Linear Arithmetic Constraints. JAR **9** (1992) 373–379
25. Reps, T., Horwitz, S., Sagiv, M.: Precise interprocedural dataflow analysis via graph reachability. POPL **95** (1995) 49–61

Counterexample Guided Abstraction Refinement Via Program Execution

Daniel Kroening, Alex Groce, and Edmund Clarke*

Department of Computer Science,
Carnegie Mellon University,
Pittsburgh, PA, 15213

Abstract. Software model checking tools based on a Counterexample Guided Abstraction Refinement (CEGAR) framework have attained considerable success in limited domains. However, scaling these approaches to larger programs with more complex data structures and initialization behavior has proven difficult. Explicit-state model checkers making use of states and operational semantics closely related to actual program execution have dealt with complex data types and semantic issues successfully, but do not deal as well with very large state spaces. This paper presents an approach to software model checking that actually *executes* the program in order to drive abstraction-refinement. The inputs required for the execution are derived from the abstract model. Driving the abstraction-refinement loop with a combination of constant-sized (and thus scalable) Boolean satisfiability-based simulation and actual program execution extends abstraction-based software model checking to a much wider array of programs than current tools can handle, in the case of programs containing errors. Experimental results from applying the CRunner tool, which implements execution-based refinement, to faulty and correct C programs demonstrate the practical utility of the idea.

1   Introduction

Software model checking has, in recent years, been applied successfully to real software programs — within certain restricted domains. Many of the tools that have been most notable as contributing to this success have been based on the Counterexample Guided Abstraction Refinement (CEGAR) paradigm [20, 11], first used to model check software programs by Ball and Rajamani [4]. Their SLAM tool [5] has demonstrated the effectiveness of software verification for device drivers. BLAST [18] and MAGIC [8], making use of similar techniques, have been applied to security protocols and real-time operating system kernels.

* This research was sponsored by the Gigascale Systems Research Center (GSRC), the National Science Foundation (NSF) under grant no. CCR-9803774, the Office of Naval Research (ONR), the Naval Research Laboratory (NRL) under contract no. N00014-01-1-0796, and by the Defense Advanced Research Projects Agency, and the Army Research Office (ARO) under contract no. DAAD19-01-1-0485, and the General Motors Collaborative Research Lab at CMU. The views and conclusions contained in this document are those of the author and should not be interpreted as representing the official policies, either expressed or implied, of GSRC, NSF, ONR, NRL, DOD, ARO, or the U.S. government.

J. Davies et al. (Eds.): ICFEM 2004, LNCS 3308, pp. 224–238, 2004.

A common feature of the success of these tools is that the programs and properties examined did not depend on complex data structures. The properties that have been successfully checked or refuted have relied on control flow and relatively simple integer variable relationships. For device drivers, and at least certain properties of some protocols and embedded software systems, this may be sufficient. However, even the presence of a complex static data structure can often render these tools ineffective. SLAM, BLAST, and MAGIC rely on theorem provers to perform the critical refinement step: the logics used do not lend themselves to handling complex data structures, and may generally face difficulties scaling to very large programs.

Explicit-state model checkers that (in a sense) actually *execute* a program, such as JPF [24], Bogor [23], and CMC [21], on the other hand, can handle complex data structures and operational semantics effectively, but do not scale well to proving properties over large state spaces, unless abstractions are introduced.

This paper describes a variation on the traditional counterexample guided abstraction-refinement method and its implementation in the tool CRunner. Our approach combines the advantages of the abstraction-based and execution-based approaches: an abstract model is produced and refined based on information obtained from *actually running* the program being verified. The abstract model is used to provide inputs to drive execution and the results of execution are used to refine the abstract model. Although this does not reduce the difficulty of proving a program correct (the model must eventually be refined to remove all spurious errors), this method can be used to find errors in large programs that were not previously amenable to abstraction-refinement-based model checking. Section 1.3 describes more precisely where CRunner fits in the larger context of software model checkers.

1.1   Counterexample Guided Abstraction Refinement

The traditional Counterexample Guided Abstraction Refinement framework (Figure 1) consists of four basic steps:

1. **Abstract:** Construct a (finite-state) abstraction $A(P)$ which safely abstracts P by construction.

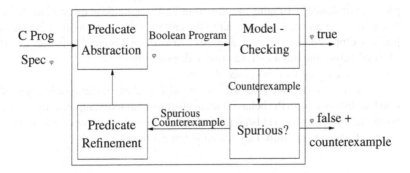

Fig. 1. The Counterexample Guided Abstraction Refinement Framework

2. **Verify:** Use a model checker to verify that $A(P) \models \varphi$: i.e., determine whether the abstracted program satisfies the specification of P. If so, P must also satisfy the specification.

3. **Check Counterexample:** If $A(P) \not\models \varphi$, a counterexample C is produced. C may be *spurious*: not a valid execution of the concrete program P. SLAM, BLAST, and MAGIC generally use theorem prover calls and propagation of weakest preconditions or strongest postconditions to determine if C is an actual behavior of P. If C is not spurious, P does not satisfy its specification.

4. **Refine:** If C is spurious, refine $A(P)$ in order to eliminate C, which represents behavior that does not agree with the actual program P. Return to step 1[1].

1.2   Counterexample Guided Abstraction Refinement Via Program Execution

The *Abstract*, *Verify*, *Check*, and *Refine* steps are also present in our execution-based adaptation of the framework. However, the *Check* stage relies on program execution to refine the model. The method presented in this paper can be seen as embedding these steps in a depth-first search algorithm more typical of explicit-state model checkers.

Figure 2 presents a high level view of the execution-based refinement loop.

Consider the simple example program shown in Figure 3. In order to model check this program, the first step in the execution based approach is to *compile* the program — a marked difference from most abstraction-based tools, which rely only on the source text. The `compile program` step in the diagram refers to a modified compilation, in that all calls to library routines (here, `getchar`) are replaced by calls to the model checker (this process is described in detail in Section 2). Where the original program would receive input from standard I/O, the recompiled program will receive input from the CRunner tool. The only restrictions on programs to be checked are that (1) all potential non-determinism in the program has been replaced with calls to CRunner, (2) no execution path enters an infinite loop without obtaining input, and (3) the program does not make use of recursion. If these conditions are violated, it is possible to miss errors. For the class of programs we have investigated, these restrictions are easily met; in particular, utilities written in C seldom make use of recursion. It is always, as with any abstraction-based scheme, possible that a correct program cannot be verified due to undecidability.

After compilation, the next step is `execute program`. The CRunner verification process is initiated by running the new compiled executable of the program to be checked. Execution will proceed normally until the call to `getchar` on line 4 is reached. At this point, we proceed to `program does input` in Figure 2. Had an assertion been violated before the input call was reached, execution would have terminated, reporting the sequence of inputs that caused the error.

Flow proceeds to `refine if necessary`. Refinement is only required if execution has diverged from the behavior of an abstract counterexample. In this case, however, no model checking has yet been performed, so refinment is unnecessary. The details of when refinement is required are presented in Section 3.

---

[1] This process may not terminate, as the problem is in general undecidable.

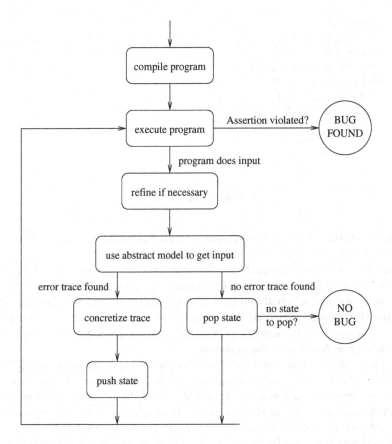

Fig. 2. Counterexample Guided Abstraction Refinement via Program Execution

The next step is use abstract model to get input. An initially coarse abstract model of the program is generated and model checked. The initial state for the abstract model is not the first line of the main, but the point at which the library call to obtain input appears. Note that in the case of programs with pointers or complex data structures, this can be a significant advantage for initial alias analysis.

Because the initial abstraction contains no information about the value of i, the model checker will report a counterexample in which the while condition is satisfied and the assertion on line 6 is violated.

Had no counterexample been produced, the algorithm would have proceeded to the pop state step. No states would have been on the stack, so verification would have terminated, proving the program error free. Changing line 5 to read:

```
5      while((ch != EOF) && (i < 100)) {
```
would produce this result.

Concretization of the abstract counterexample (concretize trace) shows that the assertion can be violated from the initial state of the abstract model if any input other than EOF is produced by the getchar call (and i is 100 or greater). Recall that the abstract state contains no information about the value of i.

```
1   int main() {
2     char buffer[100];
3     unsigned i = 0;
4     int ch = getchar();
5     while(ch != EOF) {
6       assert(i<100);
7       buffer[i]=ch;
8       i++;
9       ch = getchar();
10    }
11  }
```

Fig. 3. example.c

The current (initial) concrete program state is pushed on the stack, and control returns to example.c, with an arbitrary non-EOF value assigned to ch.

Execution of the program continues to line 9, with the assertion not violated. When execution reaches line 9, another input call is made. The program state does not match the initial state of the abstraction (the program counter is different), so a new abstraction (with a new initial state) is generated. Again, a counterexample is produced, and concretization indicates that any non-EOF input can violate the assertion. The algorithm passes through the same steps as before after the input call.

Execution reaches line 9 again, with another call for input. This time, when the use abstract model to get input step is reached, CRunner will make use of the fact that the program state matches the initial state of the current abstract model, and has not deviated from the model's behavior. The cached model checking results can be *reused without building a new abstraction or running the model checker again*. A non-EOF input is provided for the getchar call again, and the same loop is traversed. This will occur until i has reached a value of 100, and an error is detected. CRunner will then provide the sequence of inputs that produces the error, in lieu of a counterexample.

CRunner detects a buffer overflow in this program with only two calls to the expensive abstraction, model checking, and simulation algorithms, and *without adding any predicates to the abstract model*. Other abstraction based model checkers would require a series of predicates describing the value of i in order to produce a non-spurious counterexample. The speed of CRunner in this case is comparable to actual execution speed. Model checkers requiring the addition of new predicates on i would require many expensive refinement steps. It is likely that either memory or user patience would be exhausted before termination. Section 4 compares CRunner with an abstraction-refinement scheme without execution, supporting this claim, and presents experimental results for real-world examples.

1.3   Related Work

The verification approach presented in this paper is based on a Counterexample Guided Abstraction Refinement framework [11, 20] in which spurious counterexamples are detected and eliminated by a combination of Bounded Model Checking and program execution. Abstraction-refinement for software programs was introduced by Ball and

Rajamani [4], and is used by the well known SLAM, BLAST and MAGIC tools [5, 18, 8]. These tools all rely on theorem provers to determine if an abstract counterexample CE represents an actual behavior of a program P [6, 22, 9].

A second popular approach to software model checking is to rely on either actual execution of a program or a model with an execution-like operational semantics. Tools in this category include VeriSoft [16], JPF [24], Bogor [23], and CMC [21]. While some of these tools allow some kind of automated abstraction, it is not an essential part of their model checking process.

This paper presents a meeting of these two approaches: a program is *executed* in order to drive the refinement of an abstract model of that program, and the inputs provided to the executing program are derived from the abstract model.

Predicate-complete test coverage [1, 2] is conceptually related in that it combines predicate abstraction with a testing methodology. However, the final aims are fundamentally different: the coverage approach, as the name suggests, seeks to build a better test suite by using a measure of coverage. The BLAST model checker has also been extended to produce tests suites providing full coverage with respect to a given predicate [7]. The method presented in this paper executes a program, but uses the information obtained to guide an abstraction refinement framework towards exhaustive verification or refutation of properties rather than to produce test cases.

2   Preparing the Program

The first step is to recompile the program that is to be verified. As a pre-processing step, certain changes are made to the source before compilation:

1. For each function, a variable is added. This variable is set to a unique constant prior to each call of the function. The constant is derived from the position of the call in program order. The information maintained in these variables roughly corresponds to the call stack, and allows CRunner to distinguish the various instances of the functions at runtime without function inlining. As we do not permit recursion, one variable per function is sufficient.
2. Any calls to operating system input or output (I/O) functions are replaced by calls to CRunner. The CRunner code is linked with the program that is to be verified. Examples of I/O functions are printf, getc, and time.

Functions in the I/O library are replaced by prefixing the function name with CRUNNER_. For example, printf becomes CRUNNER_printf. For each I/O function within the I/O library, CRunner provides a replacement. If a function performs output, the output is discarded. If a function performs input, the model checker is called to obtain a value. To be precise, each nondeterministic choice to be made is replaced with a call to the model checker[2]:

```
unsigned char crunner_get_byte();
int crunner_get_int();
_Bool crunner_get_bool();
```

---

[2] _Bool is the C99 standard Boolean type.

We collectively refer to these functions as the `crunner_get_` functions.

Consider the implementation that replaces `fgetc` in figure 4. It may either return an error, indicated by return value −1, or return a byte corresponding to data from an input stream. The first choice is made by a call to `crunner_get_bool`, while the data value is obtained from `crunner_get_byte`. The CRunner version of `fgetc` can be extended in order to catch more program errors — e.g. to assert that `stream` is actually a valid pointer to a `FILE` object.

Figure 5 shows the replacement for `fprintf`. The data that is to be written is discarded. The function `crunner_get_int` is used to obtain a return value. Again, more errors could be detected by checking the arguments passed to the function using assertions.

```
int CRUNNER_fgetc(FILE *stream) {
  // EOF or not?
  if(crunner_get_bool()) return -1;
  return crunner_get_byte();
}
```

Fig. 4. Replacement for `fgetc`

```
int CRUNNER_fprintf(FILE *stream, const char *format, ...) {
  return crunner_get_int();
}
```

Fig. 5. Replacement for `fprintf`

3   Abstraction-Refinement with Program Execution

3.1   Overview

CRunner is structurally similar to an explicit state model checker performing depth-first-search (DFS): it maintains a stack of states and performs backtracking after exhaustively exploring branches of the search tree. CRunner does not store all visited states on the stack — it is only necessary to store states prior to input library calls.

3.2   Execution with Trapping of Input

As described in the previous section, all calls to system I/O library routines are replaced with versions that invoke CRunner.

The program is executed precisely as usual until I/O is performed or an assertion is violated (as shown in Figure 2). The restriction against infinite loops without input is necessary as CRunner cannot detect and abort such behavior.

Assertions include explicit assertions included within the program being verified, and automatically generated assertions introduced by the CRunner pre-processing step.

Automatically generated assertions are used to detect errors such as dereferencing of NULL pointers, out of bounds array indexing, and dereferencing of objects that have exceeded their lifetime.

When an assertion violation occurs, CRunner reports the error condition and terminates. In contrast to most other software model checkers, CRunner does not produce a complete counterexample trace. Rather, it outputs the sequence of inputs necessary to produce the error. If all nondeterminism has been trapped by CRunner, this will be sufficient to reproduce the error, but will lack the detail of a model checking counterexample. In this sense, CRunner is more akin to exhaustive testing than to more traditional model checking.

If the program produces output, the output data is simply discarded. There is no need to invoke the model checker in these cases, unless the output function also returns a value that is used. File system function calls such as remove are treated in a similar manner.

When the program requires an input, execution is suspended and the model checker is used to guide execution. CRunner uses the abstract model in order to provide an input value to the running program. The remainder of this section describes the generation and use of the abstract model.

3.3   Generating the Abstract Model

Existential Abstraction. CRunner performs a predicate abstraction [17] of the ANSI-C program: i.e., the variables of the program are replaced by Boolean variables that correspond to predicates over the original variables. The control flow of the program remains essentially unaltered — because CRunner does not use pushdown automata to represent control flow, an inlining step (at the abstract model level, rather than at the executing program level: see Section 2) is necessary.

Formally, we assume that the algorithm maintains a set of n predicates $\pi_1, \ldots, \pi_n$. Let S denote the set of concrete states. Each predicate is a function that maps concrete states $x \in S$ into Boolean values. When applying all predicates to a specific concrete state, one obtains a vector of n Boolean values, which represents an abstract state $\hat{x}$. We denote this function by $\alpha(x)$. It maps a concrete state into an abstract state and is therefore called the *abstraction function*.

We perform an existential abstraction [12], i.e., the abstract machine can make a transition from an abstract state $\hat{x}$ to $\hat{x}'$ iff there is a transition from x to x' in the concrete machine, x is abstracted to $\hat{x}$, and x' is abstracted to $\hat{x}'$. Let R denote the transition relation of the concrete program. We denote the transition relation of the abstract program by $\hat{R}$:

$$\hat{R} := \{(\hat{x}, \hat{x}') \mid \exists x, x' \in S : xRx' \wedge \\ \alpha(x) = \hat{x} \wedge \alpha(x') = \hat{x}'\} \tag{1}$$

Abstraction Using SAT. A Boolean satisfiability (SAT) solver can be used to compute $\hat{R}$ [13]. The computation relies on a SAT equation containing all the predicates, a basic block, and two symbolic variables for each predicate: one variable for the state before the execution of the basic block, and one variable for the state after its execution. The equation constrains the before and after values so that the second value is the result of applying the operations of the basic block to the original. When CRunnerproduces this equation, any calls to the `crunner_get_` functions are replaced by unique free variables $v_1, \ldots, v_q$. A SAT solver is used to obtain all satisfying assignments in terms of the the symbolic variables, which produces a precise abstract transition relation for the code in the basic block. This technique has also been applied to SpecC [19], which is a concurrent version of ANSI-C.

One advantage of this technique is that it models all ANSI-C bit-vector operators precisely. In contrast, tools using theorem provers such as Simplify [15] model the program variables as unbounded integers, and do not model the proper semantics for overflow on arithmetic operators. These tools typically treat bit-vector operators such as shifting and the bit-wise operators as uninterpreted functions.

However, the execution time of the SAT-based existential abstraction typically grows exponentially with the number of predicates. Most tools therefore do not compute a precise existential abstraction, but compute an over-approximation of the existential abstraction. One approach to over-approximation is to partition the set of predicates into subsets of limited size. Abstraction is then carried out for each of the subsets separately. The resulting transition relations are then conjoined. Note that this over-approximation results in additional spurious behavior. In particular, we use the set of variables mentioned in each predicate in order to group together related predicates. However, techniques for computing over-approximations of the existential abstraction are beyond the scope of this paper.

Verification of the Abstract Model. The result of the SAT-based abstraction is a symbolic transition relation for each basic block of the program. The program is transformed into a guarded `goto` program, in which all control constructs (e.g. `if`, `while`, and `for` statements) are replaced by guarded `goto` commands. The basic block transitions plus a program counter (PC) are combined with this control flow representation to produce a transition relation for the entire program.

Note that the initial program counter is not the location of the first instruction in the concrete program. Instead, we use the *location of the current input call as the initial PC*. This location can be determined at runtime using the values that are set for each function prior to function calls, as described above. By reading pointer values from memory, a very precise abstraction of this initial state can be efficiently computed.

We use the NuSMV [10] symbolic model checker to perform the actual verification. NuSMV will either verify that the abstract model does not contain any errors, or will produce an abstract counterexample (which may or may not be a possible behavior of the original program).

Because the abstraction used by CRunner is an existential over-approximation of all program behaviors, if the model checker determines that the a property violation cannot be reached from the input location, this result is reliable: from the current initial state, the original program cannot reach an error state.

If NuSMV determines that the property does hold from the current initial state, CRunner cannot conclude that the program is error free, but only that no error is reachable from the current initial state. Other states may remain to be explored. CRunner examines the stack, just as an explicit-state model checker would after finishing with a branch of the search tree:

- If the stack contains a state, let s denote the state on top of the stack, and s' denote the current state of the program (from which model checking has just completed). CRunner has exhaustively searched all paths originating from the state s'. The path from s to s' is removed from the abstract model in order to avoid re-opening this portion of the search tree. CRunner backtracks to state s, popping the search stack and restoring the program state from s. The process repeats from the input request in s.
- If the stack contains no more states, all possible paths have been explored, and CRunner reports that the program is error free.

On the other hand, if NuSMV does discover a counterexample, CRunner must attempt to concretize this abstract error trace in order to generate actual program inputs.

3.4   Concretizing the Abstract Trace

If the model checker finds an error trace in the abstract model, this does not imply that such a trace also exists in the concrete model. This is due to the fact that the abstract model is an over-approximation of the original program. An abstract trace without any corresponding trace in the concrete model is called a spurious trace.

Existing tools for predicate abstraction of C programs build a query for a theorem prover by following the control flow of the abstract error trace. If this query is satisfiable, a concrete error trace exists. The data values assigned along the trace and input values read along the trace can be extracted from the satisfying assignment. This is usually called simulation of the abstract trace on the concrete program, and is implemented as described above by SLAM, BLAST, and MAGIC. Incremental SAT has also been used to perform the simulation step [13], but the underlying principle is unchanged.

In large programs, in particular in the presence of dynamic data structures, error traces may easily have a thousand or more steps. The simulation of these long abstract traces quickly becomes infeasible as the program size and complexity increases. This fundamental issue of scalability motivates our efforts to avoid attempting to simulate the entire abstract counterexample using a theorem prover or SAT solver.

CRunner, in place of this large simulation step, attempt to continue executing the program at the current input location. The goal is to find an input value that guides the executing program along the abstract trace to the error location found in the abstract model.

CRunner produces this input value by building a simulation query, in a similar manner to existing tools. However, CRunner *limits the depth of the query* to a few steps. This should reduce the computational effort required in order to compute the simulation, but provide sufficient information to compute the next input value. This works in practice because programs often perform control flow decisions based on the input values immediately after obtaining the input.

Partial Simulation Using SAT. Let the counterexample trace have k steps, and let $k' \leq k$ be the depth (number of steps) used to obtain the input value. Simulation requires a total of k' SAT instances. Each instance adds constraints for one more step of the abstract counterexample trace. Let V denote the set of concrete program variables. We denote the value of the (concrete) variable $v \in V$ after step i by v_i. All the variables v inside an arbitrary expression e are renamed to v_i using the function $\rho_i(e)$.

The SAT instance number i is denoted by Σ_i and is built inductively as follows: Σ_0 (for the empty trace) is defined to be true. For $i \geq 1$, Σ_i depends on the type of statement in state i in the counterexample trace. Let p_i denote the statement executed in the step i. As described above, guarded goto statements are used to encode the control flow.

Thus, if step i is a guarded goto statement, then the (concrete) guard g of the goto statement is renamed and used as a conjunct in Σ_i. Furthermore, Σ_{i-1} is added as a conjunct in order to constrain the values of the variables to be equal to the previous values:

$$p_i = (\texttt{goto}, g, l) \longrightarrow \Sigma_i := \Sigma_{i-1} \wedge \rho_i(g) \wedge$$
$$\bigwedge_{u \in V} u_i = u_{i-1}$$

If step i is an assignment statement, the equality for the assignment statement is renamed and used as conjunct:

$$p_i = (\texttt{v:=exp}) \longrightarrow \Sigma_i := \Sigma_{i-1} \wedge$$
$$\rho_i(v) = \rho_{i-1}(exp) \wedge$$
$$\bigwedge_{u \in V \setminus \{v\}} u_i = u_{i-1}$$

As in the abstraction phase, any calls to the crunner_get_ functions on a right hand side are simply replaced by unique free variables $v_1, \ldots, v_u$.

Note that in case of assignment statements, Σ_i is satisfiable if the previous instance Σ_{i-1} is satisfiable. A SAT check is only necessary when the last step is a guarded goto statement. If the last instance $\Sigma_{k'}$ is satisfiable, the partial simulation is successful.

In this case, the SAT solver provides CRunner with a satisfying assignment containing values for all variables in $\Sigma_{k'}$. This includes, in particular, a value for the first input v_1. CRunner uses this value as the return value of the crunner_get_ function call, and returns control to the program being verified. Prior to returning control, CRunner saves the input value, the state, and the abstract trace on the DFS stack.

If the partial simulation fails, the abstract counterexample is spurious, and the abstract model must be refined, as described in the next section. After refinement, CRunner attempts to find another abstract error trace starting from the same concrete state.

3.5   Refining the Abstract Model

There are two ways to detect spurious behavior in the abstract model: first, as in the traditional refinement loop, the simulation step may fail.

The second way to detect spurious behavior is during execution: if the executed trace diverges from the expected abstract trace, CRunner checks to determine if the abstract trace is spurious.

Following a distinction introduced in the context of hardware verification [14], we distinguish two potential sources of spurious behavior in the abstract model:

1. The abstract counterexample may be spurious because we are not performing a precise existential abstraction. Partitioning the predicates may result in *spurious transitions* in the abstract model.

2. The abstract counterexample may be spurious because the abstraction is based on an insufficient set of predicates. This is referred to as a *spurious prefix* [14].

Microsoft's SLAM model checker uses the following approach to distinguish these two cases [3]: first, SLAM assumes that the spurious counterexample is caused by a lack of predicates and attempts to compute new predicates using weakest preconditions of the last guard in the query. If new predicates are added, the refinement loop continues as usual. However, if the refinement process fails to add new predicates, a separate refinement procedure, called *Constrain* is invoked in order to refine the approximation of the abstract transition relation.

CRunner, in contrast, following Wang, et al. [14] first checks whether any transition in the abstract trace is spurious. If so, CRunner refines the abstract model. The conflict graph from simulation is analyzed in order to eliminate multiple spurious transitions with one SAT solver call [14]. The details of this refinement process, as applied to software, are beyond the scope of this paper.

If no transitions are spurious, the spurious counterexample must be caused by a lack of predicates. In this case, CRunner computes new predicates by means of weakest preconditions in a similar fashion to the various existing predicate abstraction tools.

4   Experimental Results

We applied out prototype CRunner tool to a number of ANSI-C programs. All experiments were performed on a 1.5 GhZ AMD machine with 3 GB of RAM, running Linux.

We first investigated a scalable, artificial example in which a buffer overflow occurs after n bytes of input from a file. Existing tools usually require an abstract trace of at least n steps in order to find such an error. Furthermore, they rely on using a theorem prover or SAT solver to concretize a large abstract trace. The execution time of these tools is typically exponential in n.

Table 1 contains execution times for the artificial benchmark for various increasing values of n. Times are presented for CRunner and for a conventional implementation using the SMV model checker and a SAT-based abstraction-refinement. Note that for this example, most of the results used by CRunner can be cached, avoiding multiple expensive model checking or simulation runs. Even for very large n, the execution time is completely dominated by the compilation.

On the other hand, the performance of the conventional implementation degrades very quickly. It must refine the abstraction n times, adding a single new predicate for the array index in each step. The final result is a complete counterexample trace, rather than a set of inputs, but the cost for this precision is very high.

We also report the time to verify a correct version of the code in which a guard is added to prevent the buffer overflow. The conventional refinement loop is faster in this case, as no compilation is needed. However, after compilation, CRunner is comparable. For correct code, neither approach depends on the value of n.

Table 1. Comparison of CRunner prototype and conventional abstraction-refinement on an artificial example with a buffer overflow after *n* bytes of input from a file. The execution times include the compilation time for CRunner. A star * denotes a time-out

Method	*n*						no bug
	10	50	100	1000	10,000	100,000	
CRunner	1.5s	1.5s	1.5s	1.5s	1.5s	1.5s	1.5s
Conventional	41.4s	700s	*	*	*	*	0.01s

We also experimented with more realistic open source examples. Spamassassin is a tool for filtering email messages. Most of the system is written in Perl, but the front-end is coded in ANSI-C for efficiency reasons. Version 2.43 contains a (previously known) off-by-one error in the BSMTP interface. Figure 6 shows the relevant parts of the code.

The buffer overflow is triggered due to the special treatment of the dot in BSMTP. Due to the large size of the buffer (1024), a long input stream is required to trigger the bug. The conventional predicate refinement loop could not detect this overflow error in a reasonable amount of time. CRunner required 3 seconds (most of which are spent in compilation) to detect the error and to produce an input stream that triggers it.

We also experimented with `sendmail`, a commonly used mail gateway for Unix machines. We were able to reproduce previously known errors that are triggered by specially crafted email-messages. For example, due to a faulty type conversion, the ASCII character 255 was used to exploit older versions of `sendmail`. CRunner was able to generate the necessary input sequence to trigger this bug, while the conventional implementation was unable to find it due to the required length of the traces.

```
char buffer[1024];
[...]
switch(m->type){
  [...]
  case MESSAGE_BSMTP:
    total = full_write(fd, m->pre, m->pre_len);
    for(i = 0; i < m->out_len; ) {
      jlimit = (off_t) (sizeof(buffer) /
               sizeof(*buffer) - 4);
      for(j = 0; i < (off_t) m->out_len && j < jlimit; ) {
        if(i + 1 < m->out_len && m->out[i] == '\n' &&
          m->out[i+1] == '.') {
          if(j > jlimit - 4)
            break;  /* avoid overflow */
          buffer[j++] = m->out[i++];
          buffer[j++] = m->out[i++];
          buffer[j++] = '.';
        } else {
          buffer[j++] = m->out[i++];
    [...]
```

Fig. 6. Code from spamc

5   Conclusions and Future Work

This paper presents a variation of the counterexample guided predicate abstraction framework introduced for software by Ball and Rajamani [4]. Abstraction-refinement based model checkers have traditionally dealt poorly with complex data types and lengthy counterexamples. Explicit-state model checkers making use of states and operational semantics closely related to actual program execution have dealt with complex data types and semantic issues successfully, but do not deal well with very large state spaces. We therefore combine techniques from abstraction-refinement and explicit state model checking: exploration, meant to discover errors, is based on actual program execution, guided by abstraction that can prove the program correct, or prune the search space.

Experimental results indicate that no advantage over the existing methods in the case of correct programs, but demonstrate the power of our approach for finding errors.

Extending this work to a larger body of operating system libraries and allowing for some form of message-passing concurrency are topics for future research. We would also like to investigate whether predicate selection can be improved by using information from the program execution.

References

1. T. Ball. Abstraction-guided test generation: A case study. Technical Report 2003-86, Microsoft Research, November 2003.
2. T. Ball. A theory of predicate-complete test coverage and generation. Technical Report 2004-28, Microsoft Research, April 2004.
3. T. Ball, B. Cook, S. Das, and S. Rajamani. Refining approximations in software predicate abstraction. In *Tools and Algorithms for the Construction and Analysis of Systems (TACAS)*, pages 388–403. Springer-Verlag, 2004.
4. T. Ball and S. Rajamani. Boolean programs: A model and process for software analysis. Technical Report 2000-14, Microsoft Research, February 2000.
5. T. Ball and S. Rajamani. Automatically validating temporal safety properties of interfaces. In *SPIN Workshop on Model Checking of Software*, pages 103–122, 2001.
6. T. Ball and S. Rajamani. Generating abstract explanations of spurious counterexamples in C programs analysis. Technical Report 2002-09, Microsoft Research, January 2002.
7. D. Beyer, A. Chlipala, T. Henzinger, R. Jhala, and R. Majumdar. Generating tests from counterexamples. In *International Conference of Software Engineering*, 2004. To appear.
8. S. Chaki, E. Clarke, A. Groce, S. Jha, and H. Veith. Modular verification of software components in C. *IEEE Transactions on Software Engineering*, 30(6):388–402, June 2004.
9. S. Chaki, E. Clarke, A. Groce, J. Ouaknine, O. Strichman, and K. Yorav. Efficient verification of sequential and concurrent C programs. *Formal Methods in System Design*, 2004. To appear.
10. A. Cimatti, E. Clarke, E. Giunchiglia, F. Giunchiglia, M. Pistore, M. Roveri, R. Sebastiani, and A. Tacchella. NuSMV 2: An OpenSource tool for symbolic model checking. In *Computer Aided Verification*, pages 359–364, 2002.
11. E. Clarke, O. Grumberg, S. Jha, Y. Lu, and H. Veith. Counterexample-guided abstraction refinement. In *Computer Aided Verification*, pages 154–169, 2000.
12. E. Clarke, O. Grumberg, and D. Long. Model checking and abstraction. In *POPL*, January 1992.

13. E. Clarke, D. Kroening, N. Sharygina, and K. Yorav. Predicate abstraction of ANSI-C programs using SAT. *Formal Methods in System Design*, 2004. To appear.
14. E. Clarke, M. Talupur, and D. Wang. SAT based predicate abstraction for hardware verification. In *Proceedings of SAT'03*, May 2003.
15. D. Detlefs, G. Nelson, and J. B. Saxe. Simplify: A theorem prover for program checking. Technical Report HPL-2003-148, HP Labs, July 2003.
16. P. Godefroid. VeriSoft: a tool for the automatic analysis of concurrent reactive software. In *Computer Aided Verification*, pages 172–186, 1997.
17. S. Graf and H. Saidi. Construction of abstract state graphs with PVS. In O. Grumberg, editor, *Proc. 9th INternational Conference on Computer Aided Verification (CAV'97)*, volume 1254, pages 72–83. Springer Verlag, 1997.
18. T. A. Henzinger, R. Jhala, R. Majumdar, and G. Sutre. Lazy abstraction. In *Principles of Programming Languages*, pages 58–70, 2002.
19. H. Jain, D. Kroening, and E. Clarke. Verification of SpecC using predicate abstraction. In *MEMOCODE 2004*. IEEE, 2004.
20. R. P. Kurshan. *Computer-Aided Verification of Coordinating Processes: The Automata- Theoretic Approach*. Princeton University Press, 1995.
21. M. Musuvathi, D. Park, A. Chou, D. Engler, and D. Dill. CMC: a pragmatic approach to model checking real code. In *Symposium on Operating System Design and Implementation*, 2002.
22. T. B. A. Podelski and S. K. Rajamani. Relative completeness of abstraction refinement for software model checking. In *Tools and Algorithms for the Construction and Analysis of Systems*, pages 158–172, 2002.
23. Robby, E. Rodriguez, M. Dwyer, and J. Hatcliff. Checking strong specifications using an extensible software model checking framework. In *Tools and Algorithms for the Construction and Analysis of Systems*, pages 404–420, 2004.
24. W. Visser, K. Havelund, G. Brat, S. Park, and F. Lerda. Model checking programs. *Automated Software Engineering*, 10(2):203–232, 2003.

Faster Analysis of Formal Specifications*

Fabrice Bouquet[1], Bruno Legeard[1], Mark Utting[2], and Nicolas Vacelet[1]

[1] Laboratoire d'Informatique (LIFC),
Université de Franche-Comté - CNRS - INRIA,
16, route de Gray - 25030 Besançon, France
{bouquet,legeard,vacelet}@lifc.univ-fcomte.fr
[2] University of Waikato,
Hamilton, New Zealand
marku@cs.waikato.ac.nz

Abstract. When animating a formal model for validation or test generation purposes, scalability is a key issue. This paper describes a graph-based representation for the operations of state-based formal models. This representation makes it possible to handle large models efficiently and perform a variety of transformations, such as splitting an operation into separate behaviours, implementing various test coverage criteria for complex conditionals, removing inconsistent paths, factoring out common calculations, and executing the final operation using a customized constraint logic programming solver. The result is a fully automatic execution engine for state-based formal models such as B [Abr96], Z [Spi92] and UML with OCL preconditions and postconditions. It can be used for animation, test generation and other verification or validation purposes. Our experimental results on large industrial applications show that the transformations result in significant speedups.

1 Introduction

Formal modeling of systems is an important technique in software engineering. Complementary to proof techniques, animation of a model provides early feedback on requirements problems, and test generation provides a cost-effective way of cross-checking the model against an implementation.

Scalability is the key issue to be able to apply these techniques to real systems. The industrial case studies we are working on have many operations whose postconditions are more than two pages and whose disjunctive normal form (DNF) would contain millions of disjuncts.

This paper describes a graph-based representation for operations of state-based models. The various source languages (B, Z, UML/OCL) are transformed into precondition/postcondition format, where primed variables are used to represent the state after the operation and unprimed variables represent the state before the operation. However, to preserve the control structure of the operation,

---

* This work is partially supported by Schlumberger/Axalto Smart Card R&D and by PSA Peugeot Citroën.

J. Davies et al. (Eds.): ICFEM 2004, LNCS 3308, pp. 239–258, 2004.

the postcondition is represented as a graph, rather than a flat predicate. For example, this enables `if-then-else` structures to be represented as alternative paths in the graph. Similarly the translation from Z transforms schema operators into branches in the graph, and the `CASE`, `SELECT` and `CHOICE` operators of B are translated into multiway branches.

This graph-based representation is a superior representation for postconditions compared to the common approach of expanding the postcondition out into disjunctive normal form [DF93]. The graph-based representation enables various transformations that take advantage of the structure of the postcondition to avoid repeatedly analyzing or executing the same predicate multiple times.

Our goal has been to develop a powerful execution engine for such formal models. We use a customized Constraint Logic Programming (CLP) solver [BLP02] to evaluate predicates and detect inconsistencies. This execution engine is embedded in the BZ-Testing-Tools (BZ-TT) environment [ABC+02, LPU04], which supports animation and test generation from B [Abr96] abstract machines, Z [Spi92] specifications and UML class diagrams with OCL pre/post specifications of methods [RJB99, WK98]. The environment and solver could also be used to support other kinds of formal specification analysis such as invariant verification and counter-example generation.

The main contributions of this paper are to give clear descriptions of the various optimizations that we perform on the graph-based representation, and to give experimental results that illustrate their efficacy. The optimizations are general, many of them are applicable to other formal specification tools or to other CLP-based tools. Embedded in the BZ-Testing-Tools environment, the different levels of optimization have been evaluated on real-size industrial applications in three domains: smart cards, payment terminals and automobile embedded software.

This paper is structured as follows. Section 2 defines the graph-based representation and describes how the input notations are translated into graphs. Section 3 gives an overview of how the graph is finally translated into constraints and evaluated by the solver. Section 4 describes the optimizations and Section 5 gives the experimental results on several case studies. Section 6 discusses related work and Section 7 gives conclusions and further work.

2   The Graph Representation

This section defines the graph representation and its semantics, and gives an overview of how formal models are translated into the graph representation.

2.1   Graph Representation

The graphs can be drawn as diagrams, or written in textual form using two operators: $\dot{\vee}$ to represent branching and $\wedge$ to represent juxtaposition. This is possible because we consider only a restricted set of graphs that are properly nested and connected. Figure 1 shows the graph representing the following example:

$$(w \wedge (x \vee y)) \vee (z1 \wedge z2 \wedge z3)$$

The numbers within the nodes are not important – they just give us a way of naming particular arcs. However, we always follow the convention that the *start node* is numbered 1 and the *end node* is numbered 0.

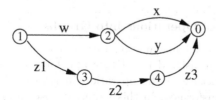

Fig. 1. An Example Graph

More precisely, graphs are formed from *arbitrary predicates* (which label the arcs of the graph) using the two operators, $\dot{\vee}$ and $\dot{\wedge}$. These operators are associative, symmetric and idempotent. The set of predicates that may appear as arguments includes all the usual relations $(=, \in, \subseteq, <, \le$, etc) that one finds in set-oriented formal specification languages, the usual predicate calculus quantifiers and propositional operators, and two special atoms called *fail* and *skip*, which are the identities of $\dot{\vee}$ and $\dot{\wedge}$, respectively. In addition, $\dot{\wedge}$ distributes over $\dot{\vee}$ and *fail* is a zero for $\dot{\wedge}$. Table 1 shows the laws that the graph operators satisfy. With these laws, graphs form a semiring algebraic structure known as a *dioid* [CL99].

Table 1. Laws of the Graph Operators

Idempotence	$x \dot{\vee} x = x$
	$x \dot{\wedge} x = x$
Associativity	$(x \dot{\vee} y) \dot{\vee} z = x \dot{\vee} (y \dot{\vee} z)$
	$(x \dot{\wedge} y) \dot{\wedge} z = x \dot{\wedge} (y \dot{\wedge} z)$
Symmetry	$x \dot{\vee} y = y \dot{\vee} x$
	$x \dot{\wedge} y = y \dot{\wedge} x$
Unit	$fail \dot{\vee} x = x \dot{\vee} fail = x$
	$skip \dot{\wedge} x = x \dot{\wedge} skip = x$
Zero	$fail \dot{\wedge} x = x \dot{\wedge} fail = fail$
Distributivity	$x \dot{\wedge} (y \dot{\vee} z) = (x \dot{\wedge} y) \dot{\vee} (x \dot{\wedge} z)$
	$(x \dot{\vee} y) \dot{\wedge} z = (x \dot{\wedge} z) \dot{\vee} (y \dot{\wedge} z)$

Intuitively, the operators $\dot{\vee}$ and $\dot{\wedge}$ correspond to disjunction and conjunction, and *fail* and *skip* correspond to false and true. However, there are some differences from the usual boolean algebra properties, since some properties, such as $x \dot{\vee} skip = skip$, are not always true. This is because our semantics for predicates uses an implicit frame, so that the appearance of x' within a predicate means that the state variable x may change value, whereas if no x' appears, it is implicit that x does not change. Thus the graph $(x' = x + 1)\ \dot{\vee}\ skip$ stands for two possible state updates, one in which just x is incremented, and the other in which no variables change value. These two state updates are not equivalent to *skip* (which means no-change), so the property $x\ \dot{\vee}\ skip = skip$ is not included in Table 1.

2.2   Translation of Operations into Graphs

The body of a B abstract machine operation, a Z schema or an OCL method specification can be translated into this graph format. The goal is to capture the control flow structure of the operation in a form that can be efficiently manipulated and transformed. In this paper, we use the B operation in Fig. 2 as an example.

As described in the introduction, the input formal models are transformed into before and after predicates, like $x' = x + 1$. In B, operations are written using a generalized substitution language which is similar to an abstract programming language, with IF and CASE statements, as well as non-deterministic SELECT, CHOICE and ANY statements. We use the standard rules from the B-Book [Abr96] to transform these generalized substitutions into before-after predicates. However, the conjunctions and disjunctions that come from the control structure of these generalized substitutions are translated into graph operators, $\dot{\vee}$ and $\dot{\wedge}$, rather than $\vee$ and $\wedge$. This preserves the control structure, and keeps it separate from other disjunctions that appear in the decisions of conditional statements. Figure 3 shows the graph that results from translating our example operation.

Similarly the translation from Z transforms schema operators into graph operators ($\dot{\vee}$ and $\dot{\wedge}$), and the translation from OCL transforms if-then-else constructs into graph operators.

$$r \leftarrow op(a, b, c)$$
$$\textbf{PRE}$$
$$a \subseteq 0\mathinner{\ldotp\ldotp}10 \wedge b \subseteq 0\mathinner{\ldotp\ldotp}10 \wedge c \subseteq 0\mathinner{\ldotp\ldotp}10$$
$$\textbf{THEN}$$
$$\textbf{IF}\ \ v \subseteq a \cup b \wedge v \subseteq a \cup c$$
$$\textbf{THEN}\ \ r := v$$
$$\textbf{ELSE}$$
$$\textbf{IF}\ \ v = a \cup b \cup c \vee v = a \cup b$$
$$\textbf{THEN}\ \ r := 0\mathinner{\ldotp\ldotp}10$$
$$\textbf{ELSE}\ \ r := \{\}$$
$$\textbf{END}$$
$$\textbf{END}$$
$$\textbf{END}$$

Fig. 2. An Example B operation: a, b and c are inputs, r is an output and v is a state variable. All are sets of integer

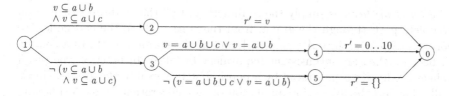

Fig. 3. Graph Representation of Example B Operation

Notice that the graph is similar to a control flow graph, but that all conditions and statements (represented by before-after predicates) appear on the arcs. Furthermore, there are no loops and no sequential composition ($\dot\wedge$ represents conjunction or parallelism)[1].

In practice, the postconditions of operations can contain more complex operators than just $\wedge$ and $\vee$. Table 2 shows how the conversion into graph format uses the De Morgan rules ($\neg\,(A \vee B) = \neg A \wedge \neg B$ etc.) to push negations inwards and rewrite $\Rightarrow$ and $\Leftrightarrow$ in terms of $\dot\wedge$ and $\dot\vee$. It also converts existential quantifiers into skolem constants. Universal quantifiers are left unchanged, as they are treated as a single constraint by the solver.

Table 2. Postcondition to Graph Translation Rules

$trans(p)$	p, if p is an atomic predicate
$trans(p \Rightarrow q)$	$not(\neg\, trans(p)) \dot\vee trans(q)$
$trans(p \Leftrightarrow q)$	$trans(p \wedge q) \dot\vee trans(\neg q \wedge \neg p)$
$trans(p \vee q)$	$trans(p) \dot\vee trans(q)$
$trans(p \wedge q)$	$trans(p) \dot\wedge trans(q)$
$trans(\neg\, p)$	$not(\neg\, trans(p))$
$not(\neg\,(p \dot\wedge q))$	$not(\neg\, p) \dot\vee not(\neg\, q)$
$not(\neg\,(p \dot\vee q))$	$not(\neg\, p) \dot\wedge not(\neg\, q)$
$not(\neg\, p)$	$\neg\, p$, if p is not an $\dot\vee$ / $\dot\wedge$ term.

2.3   Effect Predicates

Our primary goal is to be able to partition the postcondition of each operation in order to achieve test coverage of all the behaviours of the operation [LPU04]. Informally, the possible behaviours of an operation are all the possible paths through the control structure of the operation. The graph represents these paths in a compact way, but it is useful to be able to extract each behaviour as a separate predicate. We call these *effect predicates*. The BZ-TT test generation method generates one or more tests for each effect predicate, typically by using boundary analysis on the predicate [LPU02] and by computing a preamble (sequences of operation invocations) to reach each effect predicate [CLP03].

---

[1] Note that sequential composition does not appear in B abstract machines. It is introduced only in refined machines, which are not allowed as input to BZ-TT.

An *effect predicate* is simply the conjunction of all the predicates that lie on a complete path through the graph, from the start node to the end node. We ignore any *skip* arcs, since $A \wedge skip = A$, and we do not allow paths that contain *fail*, because they are inconsistent (equivalent to false). In practice, the set of all effect predicates is generated by a depth-first traversal of the graph. This is usually done on the fly, during animation or test generation. Table 3 shows all the effect predicates from the example.

Table 3. Effect Predicates from the Example

1 $v \subseteq a \cup b \wedge v \subseteq a \cup c \wedge r' = v$
2 $\neg (v \subseteq a \cup b \wedge v \subseteq a \cup c) \wedge (v = a \cup b \cup c \vee v = a \cup b) \wedge r' = 0 .. 10$
3 $\neg (v \subseteq a \cup b \wedge v \subseteq a \cup c) \wedge \neg (v = a \cup b \cup c \vee v = a \cup b) \wedge r' = \{\}$

Note that if all the predicates in a graph are *atomic* (contain no quantifiers or propositional operators), then the set of effect predicates is the same as the DNF form of the postcondition. But this is rare, since the decisions in the conditional constructs are usually complex predicates involving several conditions. One major advantage of this graph format is that it represents the set of effect predicates more efficiently than the common technique of expanding the postcondition into DNF form. This is because:

- distinguishing the $\dot{\vee}$ and $\dot{\wedge}$ graph operators from other disjunctions and conjunctions separates the control structure from the structure of complex conditions, which means that the set of effect predicates is usually much smaller than the number of disjuncts in the DNF partitioning.
- the graph structure allows common conjuncts to be shared between several effect predicates. This reduces the size of the graph (a minor benefit), but also reduces the amount of computation needed when evaluating all the effect predicates (a major benefit). Indeed, the goal of some of the transformations in the next section is to maximize this sharing, to further reduce the cost of evaluating all effects.

3   Evaluation by Constraints

This section describes how the graph representation can be executed by a constraint solver. This is done for many different purposes, including supporting interactive animation of specifications, supporting graph transformations and test generation, searching for preamble sequences and calculating oracle results.

3.1   Graph Traversal

The basic idea is to perform a depth-first traversal of the graph, passing each predicate to the constraint solver. The constraint solver maintains a set of possible solution states, but does this in symbolic form rather than enumerating them [MS98, AB98]. This is much more efficient than exploring one state at a time, since the constraint solver effectively executes many states in parallel. This increases scalability compared with a value-based enumeration of the states. It also enables us execute an operation with its input represented by a constraint variable – the precondition constrains the allowable values of that variable and the postcondition constrains how the outputs relate to it. This is a form of symbolic execution, which is ideal for supporting test generation.

As the depth-first traversal goes deeper into the graph, constraints are added to the solver. If these constraints become inconsistent, the solver fails, which leads to *backtracking* up the graph and trying an alternative path. This allows the different effect predicates to be explored one by one.

Too much backtracking is undesirable, because it forces a large number of case analyses, which makes execution very slow. For example, if each operation introduces several cases, a sequence of operations can quickly produce an exponential number of cases. Backtracking can also be introduced when complex predicates on the arcs of the graph are translated into constraints. The next subsection discusses this important issue further. Several of the optimizations in section 4 are intended to minimize backtracking or control its cost.

3.2   Translation of Predicates into Constraints

This section discusses how the predicates on the arcs of the graph are translated into constraints. The BZ-TT constraint solver, called CLPS [BLP02], supports constraints over integers, atoms, pairs, sets, relations and functions, including equality, inequality, membership, subset, range and domain constraints and many more. There are three aspects to the transformation of predicates into constraints:

- each boolean operator ($\land$, $\lor$, $\Rightarrow$, etc) must be translated into a conjunction or disjunction of constraints.
- each atomic predicate ($=$, $\in$, etc) must be translated into one or more constraints.
- the expressions that appear as the arguments of atomic predicates must be translated into forms that the constraint solver understands.

In BZ-TT, this translation is done by a recursive Prolog predicate called `reduce`, which takes a predicate or expression as input, adds constraints to the current constraint store, and either fails (which means that the constraints are inconsistent) or returns a constraint variable that represents the result of evaluating the expression. It also returns the type of the expression and maintains an *environment*, which maps each specification variable to its corresponding Prolog constraint variable.

The effect of the recursive *reduce* translation is to flatten an expression into a sequence of constraints. For example, if we call:

$$reduce(y \cup (y \cap z) \cup \{i + 2\}, Env, Env', Result, Type)$$

where *Env* is the environment $\{y \mapsto Y1, z \mapsto Z1, i \mapsto I1\}$ (we use uppercase names to indicate constraint variables), then reduce will succeed with *Type* = *set(integer)*, *Result* = *Tmp4* and *Env'* = *Env*, but will have added the following sequence of constraints to the constraint store (union and inter are internal operators of the CLPS solver) :

```
Tmp1  =  Y1 inter Z1
Tmp2  =  Y1 union Tmp1
Tmp3  =  I1+2
Tmp4  =  Tmp2 union {Tmp3}
```

Aside: *Env'* records the primed variables that appear in the predicate. This is used to determine the *frame* of each operation. If a given primed variable does *not* appear in the postcondition of an operation, it is assumed to not change. This is convenient for modelling assignment statements and B substitutions. The translation of Z schemas adds the state invariant to each postcondition, which means that every primed state variable appears, which is the correct semantics for Z. **End of Aside**

The reducer handles atomic predicates by translating their arguments, then converting the predicate into CLPS constraints. Some predicates, like equality, inequality, membership, subset etc, can be translated directly into CLPS constraints. Others are expanded into several simpler constraints. For example, $X \subset Y$ is expanded into $X \subseteq Y \wedge card(X) < card(Y)$.

Finally, the boolean operators are translated into Prolog conjunction and disjunction: $\wedge$ is implemented by Prolog conjunction, $\vee$ is implemented by Prolog disjunction (see Section 4.5). Other boolean operators are translated similarly to the transformations shown in Table 2.

The result of this translation is a series of Prolog choicepoints, with each choicepoint having its own constraint store. For example, the predicate

$$y \neq \{\} \Rightarrow y = z \cup \{i\} \wedge i < 100$$

(using the environment described earlier) will produce two choicepoints, with the following constraint stores:

```
1.  Y1   = {}
2.  TMP1 = Z1 union {I1}, Y1 = TMP1, I1 < 100
```

4   Graph Optimizations

This section describes the various transformation and optimization that can be applied to the postcondition graphs. First we give a decomposition theorem that is used by several transformations.

Theorem 1. *Given a graph G and a predicate P which may label some of the arcs within G, the following recursive decomposition function called "decomp"* *transforms G into an equivalent graph* $(P \wedge G_1) \dot{\vee} G_2$, *where* G_1 *and* G_2 *do not contain* P.

$$decomp(fail) = (P \dot{\wedge} fail) \dot{\vee} fail$$
$$decomp(skip) = (P \dot{\wedge} fail) \dot{\vee} skip$$
$$decomp(A) = \begin{cases} (P \dot{\wedge} skip) \dot{\vee} fail, & \text{if } P = A \\ (P \dot{\wedge} fail) \dot{\vee} A & \text{if } P \neq A \end{cases}$$
$$decomp(A \dot{\vee} B) = (P \dot{\wedge} (A_p \dot{\vee} B_p)) \dot{\vee} (A_{np} \dot{\vee} B_{np})$$
$$decomp(A \dot{\wedge} B) = (P \dot{\wedge} ((A_p \dot{\wedge} B_p)$$
$$\dot{\vee} (A_p \dot{\wedge} B_{np})$$
$$\dot{\vee} (A_{np} \dot{\wedge} B_p)))$$
$$\dot{\vee} (A_{np} \dot{\wedge} B_{np})$$
$$\text{where} \quad (P \dot{\wedge} A_p) \dot{\vee} A_{np} = decomp(A)$$
$$(P \dot{\wedge} B_p) \dot{\vee} B_{np} = decomp(B)$$

Proof: By induction over the structure of the graph. Using the rules from Table 1 it is easy to show that the input and output of each *decomp* rule is equivalent. □

Note that the $\dot{\wedge}$ case duplicates some subgraphs. This makes the graph bigger, but the resulting graph is still smaller than the complete set of effect predicates. In practice, we apply the Unit and Zero simplification rules from Table 1 to the result of the *decomp* function and this helps to keep the graph smaller.

4.1   Multi-condition Expansion

For test generation, the test engineer can select different coverage criteria for complex decisions that contain multiple conditions. These include *decision coverage* (DC), *Decision/Condition Coverage* (D/CC), *full predicate coverage* (FPC) and *multiple condition coverage* (MCC). Each of these is implemented by applying rewriting rules to complex decisions which contain disjunctions (or implications etc.). The theory and justification for these rules is described elsewhere [LPU04]. As an example, D/CC coverage rewrites a decision $C_1 \vee C_2$ to $C_1 \dot{\vee} C_2$, whereas FPC coverage rewrites it to $(C_1 \wedge \neg C_2) \dot{\vee} (C_2 \wedge \neg C_1)$. These rewriting rules can be applied *with* or *without* distribution. The former produces a small number of tests which is just sufficient to satisfy the coverage criteria, while the latter produces more tests to explore interactions between separate decisions.

The rewrite rules with distribution perform only a local transformation on the graph: one arc is replaced by several arcs. Unfortunately, for large postconditions this usually produces an exponential number of effects. For example, if we have $D_1 \dot{\wedge} D_2 \dot{\wedge} D_3$, where each of the D_i complex decisions is expanded into 5 branches, then the total number of effects increases from 1 to $5 * 5 * 5 = 125$.

To apply the rewrite rules without distribution, we use a more sophisticated rewriting algorithm which avoids the combinatorial case explosion. The algorithm recurses through the graph from the start node towards the end node, and rewrites at most *one* complex decision along each path. The following simplified extract of the algorithm illustrates the key idea: each complex decision D is rewritten into $D_1 \dots D_n$ and combined with the *unchanged* remainder of the graph (R). Also, the *unchanged* D is combined with a *rewritten* version of R.

$$nondist(D \mathbin{\dot\wedge} R) = (D \mathbin{\dot\wedge} nondist(R))$$
$$\mathbin{\dot\vee} (D_1 \mathbin{\dot\wedge} R) \mathbin{\dot\vee} \dots (D_n \mathbin{\dot\wedge} R)$$

The number of effects produced by this non-distribution algorithm is linear in the number of branches produced by the rewrite rules, rather than exponential. For example, applying this algorithm to the $D_1 \mathbin{\dot\wedge} D_2 \mathbin{\dot\wedge} D_3$ example above we get $5 + 5 + 5 = 15$ effects, rather than 125.

Fig. 4 shows the result of applying the D/CC rewrite rule with distribution to our running example.

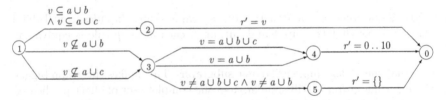

Fig. 4. After applying D/CC test coverage rule with distribution

4.2   Common Subexpression Elimination (CSE)

The goal of common subexpression elimination (CSE) is to factor out repeated calculations. This is similar to the common subexpression optimization used within compilers.

The form of a graph after this optimization is an equivalent graph in which repeated subexpressions have been factorized and moved slightly earlier in the graph (that is, closer to the start node). This can be done by applying theorem 1 to factor out any predicate or subexpression that appears many times in the graph. This avoids repeated recalculation and helps to decrease the number of internal variables created inside the constraint solver.

In practice, our implementation of the CSE algorithm takes a more conservative approach than applying theorem 1 blindly. It first works on chains of predicates, $P_1 \mathbin{\dot\wedge} \dots \mathbin{\dot\wedge} P_n$ where all the P_i are predicates, not subgraphs. It analyzes the subexpressions of $P_1 \dots P_n$ and counts the number of times each complex subexpression appears (a complex subexpression is any expression that is not just a simple constant or variable). For each complex subexpression E that appears more than once, a new predicate $\alpha = E$ is added to the front of the chain (where α is a fresh variable), and all the original occurrences of E in the P_i predicates are replaced by α. However, there are two conditions which can prevent subexpressions within complex predicates P_i from being extracted. Firstly, if P_i contains a quantifier, the algorithm must not move a subexpression out of the scope of the quantifier if that subexpression involves the bound variables. Secondly, it does not consider expressions inside operators that generate choicepoints, such as disjunctions and implications, since those expressions are not always executed. For example, if P_i is a complex predicate like $X \in A \cup B \wedge (X = f(E) \Rightarrow X \in T \cup U)$, it is safe to move $A \cup B$, but not $f(E)$ or $T \cup U$, because they are inside a choicepoint. Moving them outside the choicepoint would be semantically safe, but might result in decreased performance, so this is avoided.

A similar technique is applied to branches $G_1 \dot\vee \ldots \dot\vee G_n$. If a complex subexpression E appears on *every* path through *all* the G_i subgraphs, then this graph is rewritten to

$$\alpha = E \dot\wedge ((G_1 \dot\vee \ldots \dot\vee G_n)[E := \alpha])$$

where $[E := \alpha]$ means replace each occurrence of E by α.

The resulting of applying the CSE algorithm to our example is shown in Fig. 5.

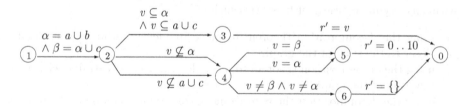

Fig. 5. After the elimination of the common subexpression

4.3   Removal of Inconsistent Paths

As mentioned in Sect. 2.3, paths through the graph that contain *fail* are discarded, because they are equivalent to false. However, other paths may also be inconsistent, if they contain contradictory predicates. This corresponds to dead-path [GBF97] removal in the control flow graphs of programs.

We transform the graph to delete such inconsistent paths. This is an expensive process (satisfiability checking is often expensive), so is done as a separate pass, rather than on-the-fly during animation or test generation.

To detect inconsistent paths, we perform a depth-first traversal of the graph, passing the predicates to the constraint solver, and pruning any subtree that the solver reports as being inconsistent. This expands the graph into a tree-like structure[2] of repeated predicates near the leaves, but decreases the number of effect predicates.

---

[2] In fact, the leaves of the tree are all linked to the end node (0), so it remains a graph.

For the running example, the predicates $v \not\subseteq \alpha$ and $v = \alpha$ are inconsistent, so the path that goes through these predicates is deleted, as giving Fig. 6.

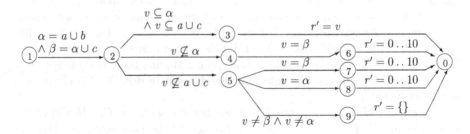

Fig. 6. After deleting inconsistent paths

4.4   Reordering the Graph

A common optimization in constraint programming is to reorder constraints so that deterministic constraints, or constraints with a small number of solutions, are placed before other constraints [MS98]. We have experimented extensively with this, trying a variety of heuristics such as:

1. using the decomposition theorem to move frequently occuring constraints closer to the start of the graph.
2. using the decomposition theorem to move deterministic constraints closer to the start of the graph.
3. using the decomposition theorem to move constraints with a small number of solutions closer to the start of the graph.

Surprisingly, all these heuristics resulted in worse performance. We believe that this is because the original order of the constraints in the graph is usually near optimal, due to the way the graph is constructed from the B substitution commands. For example, the decision parts of IF, SELECT or CASE statements always come earlier in the graph than the translated bodies of those statements. Most specifications seem to be written in a style that tests or constrains the inputs and local variables, before assigning results to output variables.

4.5   Avoiding Duplicates and Minimizing Choicepoints (NODUPS)

Section 3.2 described a simplistic technique for translating complex predicates (which appear on the arc of the graphs) into constraints and choicepoints. For example, $A \vee B$ is translated into the Prolog choicepoint A_c; B_c, where A_c and B_c are the constraints that result from the translation of A and B, respectively. A problem with this simplistic translation is that A_c and B_c constraints may return the same solution. This is an important issue in practice, because a few duplicate solutions from each operation in a sequence of operations can dramatically increase the search space.

Furthermore, it is difficult to remove duplicates after generating them, because the most efficient way to search for solutions is to use the depth-first search supported by Prolog (possibly with a depth bound, or using iterative deepening), and it is not possible to efficiently detect duplicate solutions with this approach. To do so would require storing all the solutions from the different choicepoints (which is quite impractical due to the space required) then searching for duplicates (which is $O(N^2)$ in the number of solutions).

Many industry case studies have thousands or millions of potential solutions. So, it is important to eliminate duplicates by avoiding creating them. One simple technique for ensuring that no duplicates are created is to force each disjunct to be mutually exclusive. There are three obvious alternative laws we could use to do this:

$$P \vee Q = P \vee (Q \wedge \neg P)$$
$$P \vee Q = (P \wedge \neg Q) \vee Q$$
$$P \vee Q = (P \wedge \neg Q) \vee (P \wedge Q) \vee (Q \wedge \neg P)$$

Initially, we used the third of these laws, because it is symmetric in P and Q.

The problem is that the use of these laws can sometimes result in a large number of choicepoints, because if P contains many conjuncts, then $\neg P$ turns into lots of disjuncts. To avoid this, we use the following cp function to calculate the number of choicepoints for each translation, then choose the translation that minimizes the number of choicepoints. Note: as well as the cases shown here, we use de Morgan rules to push negations inwards to the atomic predicates.

$$cp(A) = 1, \quad \text{if } A \text{ is an atomic predicate}$$
$$cp(\neg A) = 1, \quad \text{if } A \text{ is an atomic predicate}$$
$$cp(P \wedge Q) = cp(P) \times cp(Q)$$
$$cp(P \Rightarrow Q) = cp(\neg P \vee Q)$$
$$cp(P \Leftrightarrow Q) = cp(P \wedge Q \vee \neg P \wedge \neg Q)$$
$$cp(P \vee Q) = min \ \{ \ cp(P) + cp(Q \wedge \neg P),$$
$$cp(Q) + cp(P \wedge \neg Q),$$
$$cp(P \wedge \neg Q) + cp(P \wedge Q) + cp(\neg P \wedge Q) \}$$
$$cp(\exists x : T \bullet P) = cp(P)$$
$$cp(\forall x : T \bullet P) = 1$$

To illustrate the result of such an optimization we consider an effect predicate $(a_1 \wedge ... \wedge a_n) \vee (b_1 \wedge ... \wedge b_m)$, where a_i and b_j are atomic predicates.

- If we use the rule $P \vee (\neg P \wedge Q)$, the number of choicepoints is n.
- If we use the rule $Q \vee (\neg Q \wedge P)$, the number of choicepoints is m.
- If we use the rule $(P \wedge Q) \vee (\neg P \wedge Q) \vee (P \wedge \neg Q)$, the number of choicepoints is $2^n + 2^m - 2$.

Our algorithm takes the solution which gives the expression a minimal number of choicepoints. This NODUPS optimization is applied to every arc of the graph, and conceptually splits each arc into one or more arcs, corresponding to the number of choicepoints of the predicate on the arc. In practice, for efficiency reasons, we apply this optimization on the fly during the reduce process, rather than rewriting the graph. As reduce transforms each disjunctive predicate $P \vee Q$ into constraints, it uses the cp function to calculate how many choicepoints will result from each of the three $P \vee Q$ translation laws above, and uses one that produces the minimum number of choicepoints. This gives a translation that guarantees no duplicate solutions will be generated, while minimizing the number of choicepoints. The cost of a such computation is linear in term of number of atomic presdicates.

4.6   Delaying Choicepoints (DELAY)

It is well known in constraint logic programming that it is generally better to execute deterministic constraints before non-deterministic constraints.

Consider any path $P_1 \wedge \ldots \wedge P_n$ through the graph. Conceptually, we sort the predicates in this path so that they are ordered by increasing $cp(P_i)$ values.

In practice, this transformation is done on-the-fly during the reduce process. As reduce traverses the graph, any predicate P that requires choicepoints ($cp(P) > 1$) is delayed by putting it into a list, rather than converting it into Prolog choicepoints immediately. Once the end node of the graph is reached, the list of delayed predicates is sorted by the number of choicepoints, so that predicates with fewer choicepoints appear earlier, then the predicates are processed in that order.

Of course, this changes the order of predicates, which we have carefully optimized above. But a predicate P with n choicepoints can be considered as an equivalent predicate $P_1 \vee P_2 \ldots \vee P_{n+1}$. Then the previously computed order is not optimal. The idea is to delay the predicates that require choicepoints later in the graph.

For example, if w, x, y and z are any atomic predicates, then $cpt_1 = (w \wedge x) \vee (w \wedge y \wedge z)$ is an effect predicate in DNF form. After translating this into graph format and applying the CSE optimization, we get the equivalent graph $G1 = w \wedge (x \vee (y \wedge z))$. Note that w appears first because it is common to all the disjuncts.

Now consider the case where reduce expands y into three choicepoints ($y = y_1 \vee y_2 \vee y_3$), giving the graph G1a shown in Fig. 8. The graph is no longer optimal in terms of the number of executed predicates, because z may be executed three times. The DELAY optimization effectively transforms the G1a graph into the G2, by delaying y. Fig. 7 shows the number of atomic predicates executed during a depth-first traversal of these graphs. The optimal representation is G2, where each atomic predicate is executed only once.

At. Pred.	DNF	G1	At. Pred.	DNF	G1a	G2
w	2	1	w	4	1	1
x	1	1	x	1	1	1
y	1	1	y_1	1	1	1
			y_2	1	1	1
			y_3	1	1	1
z	1	1	z	3	3	1
Total	5	4		11	8	6

Fig. 7. Number of executed predicates using a depth-first search approach

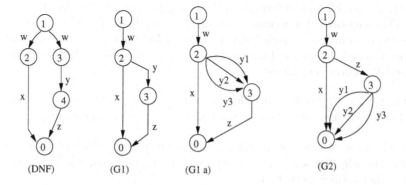

(DNF)   (G1)   (G1 a)   (G2)

Fig. 8. Different representations of a disjunctive effect predicate with choicepoints

5   Experimental Results

The graph-based representation and optimizations are used in the BZ-Testing-Tools environment [BZT03]. This environment has been used for formal model animation and test generation in several industry case studies, particularly for smart card software and automotive embedded software applications. In this section, we compare the efficiency of the different optimizations of four real-size B formal models. We first briefly describe the different formal specifications and then give performance results for the various optimizations.

- GSM 11-11 smart card software [BLLP04]: The GSM 11-11 standard defines an interface between a SIM[3] card and a ME[4]. This standard is used mainly in the mobile phone industry and describes the logical design of the SIM, its functionality and secure access to the data. Our B specification of a subset of the GSM 11.11 standard is composed of 11 operations and 10 state variables with an average domain size of 5 elements. The model contains 36 effect predicates.

---

[3] Subscriber Identification Module.
[4] Mobile Equipment.

- The CEPS (Common Electronic Purse Specifications) [cep01] specifications define a standard for electronic purse applications, and form the basis of a globally interoperable electronic purse standard which is widely accepted in the world. Our B formal model has 18 operations and 42 state variables with an average domain size of 10 elements and contains 63 effect predicates.
- CADSET is a formal model of an electronic payment transaction system compliant with the EMV[5] 2000 standard [cad00]. This standard defines the transaction during the payment protocol. More precisely, the goal of our formal model is to generate test cases to validate a Point of Sale terminal. The B formal model contains one big operation which leads to 2592 effect predicates.
- The SIM-KEY model formalizes the key management of a 2G/3G universal SIM smart card. The model defines all the commands that allow one to create security domains, to verify and to change PIN[6] code or to load applications on the card. This formal model, written in the B notation, has 16 operations and 173 effect predicates.

The tables (Fig. 9, Fig. 10) illustrate the time to execute all the behaviours of all the operations of each specification, using a variety of optimizations:

- DNF is the case where the effect predicate is in its disjunctive normal form. It is usually the worst way to represent postconditions, but has been used in other formal methods tools.
- G+CSE is our "Graph representation", with the CSE optimization, which means that the more frequently appearing atomic predicates are positioned earlier in the graph (so are executed fewer times).
- G+CSE+DELAY is the graph representation with the CSE optimization and the delaying choicepoint algorithm.
- G+CSE+NODUPS is the graph representation with CSE, plus the NODUPS optimization which minimizes the number of choicepoints and eliminates redundant solutions.
- The G+CSE+DELAY+NODUPS is the graph representation with CSE, plus both the DELAY and NODUPS optimizations.

The two tables give the results of applying the execution of all the effect predicates for all the operations of the B formal models described earlier. Figure 9 shows the total execution time in seconds and Figure 10 shows total number of atomic predicates executed. We saw earlier that the order of appearance of the atomic predicate is important.

We discuss first the results of Figure 9. These experiments show that, of course, the DNF representation is the worst we can use if the specification is big enough. For smaller specifications, the time spent applying the algorithm can outweigh the improvement from the optimizations. The DELAY and

---

[5] Europay Mastercard Visa.
[6] Personal Identifier Number.

NODUPS optimizations both usually give significant speedups, and applying both these optimizations is usually better than applying just one of them. Note that the columns with the NODUPS optimizations have the additional property that they guarantee that no duplicate solutions are produced, and this can lead to significant performed improvements when operations are composed sequentially. Compared with the DNF representation, the average speedup of the G+CSE+DELAY+NODUPS optimizations is $4522/487 = 9.3$ times faster. Even if we exclude the CADSET results, on the grounds that it gives unusually large improvements, the average speedup is $(48 + 330 + 528)/(6 + 64 + 376) = 2.0$, which is still very significant.

The results of the second table (Figure 10) are not surprising. The number of atomic predicates executed gradually decreases with the number of optimizations applied. Comparing the results for CADSET and SIM-KEY shows that the speedup in execution time is not always proportional to the reduction of the number of atomic predicates executed. CADSET has more atomic predicates than SIM-KEY, but is executed faster. This is due to the complexity of the specification–some operators take more time to be executed than others. The last result column (G+CSE+DELAY+NODUPS) of both these tables shows that complex formal models can be processed in reasonable execution times. (SIM-KEY is composed of 70 pages of B statements which is rather big).

Specification	DNF+CSE	G+CSE	G+CSE+DELAY	G+CSE+NODUPS	ALL = G+CSE+DELAY+NODUPS	Speedup (DNF/ALL)
GSM 11.11	48	46	5	6	6	8.0
CEPCARD	330	322	51	67	64	5.2
CADSET	3616	98	70	43	41	88.2
SIM-KEY	528	536	471	409	376	1.4
Total	4522	1002	597	525	487	9.3

Fig. 9. Execution time (in seconds) of all the effect predicates of the specification

Specification	DNF+CSE	G+CSE	G+CSE+DELAY	ALL = G+CSE+DELAY+NODUPS	Ratio (DNF/ALL)
GSM 11.11	3155	3103	1078	985	3.2
CEPCARD	5847	5782	5782	2411	2.4
CADSET	195585	96772	82725	32280	6.1
SIM-KEY	38858	30517	30499	24957	1.6

Fig. 10. Number of atomic predicates executed

6   Related Work

A graph-based representation of logical formulae, called Binary Decision Diagrams (BDD) was introduced by [Bry86]. A BDD has two different types of vertices. The terminal vertices represent the Boolean values, 0 and 1, while the non-terminal vertices represent variables of the boolean formula represented by the BDD. Each non-terminal vertex has exactly two outgoing edges, one of which is labeled by the Boolean constant 1 (or then) and the other by the Boolean constant 0 (or else). The graph begins at a single non- terminal node, known as the root, which has no incoming edges. Each path (sequence of nodes) ending with the termial node 1 is a solution of the boolean formula. All the others are counter-examples.

The graph structure described in this article does not represent a set of solutions of a program, but the set of potentially executable behaviors. With our dioid structure algebra, none of the BDD optimizations can be applied, because the structure of our graphs is different in two ways: first, each non terminal node can have one or more outgoing edges. Second, the graph has exactly one terminal node. So no direct comparison can be made with the BDD representation.

Control flow diagram (CFD) is a graph based approach to represent program statements. Usually, CFD is used to represent programs (implementations) for static analysis, especially for loops. Then some compilation optimizations can be applied to minimize the execution time of a program (for example, dead code elimination, constant folding, common sub expression elimination). Our graph representation is similar to a CFD applied to a formal model (which can be seen as an abstraction of an implementation). Part of the originality of our approach is the use of this CFD-like representation to animate formal models using constraint logic programming techniques.

During the 1990s, Constraint Logic Programming (CLP) was shown to be a powerful technique for analyzing complex scheduling and optimization problems [MS98]. More recently, CLP techniques are being applied to formal specifications and used in software validation and verification tools, including model checking e.g. [DP99], formal model animation e.g. [Gri00] and automated test generation that is either code-based e.g. [GBR00] or specification-based e.g. [MA00, ABlM97]. Our graph-based representation makes it possible to apply these CLP techniques to large specifications more efficiently.

7   Conclusions

In this paper, we have presented a symbolic execution approach based on Constraint Logic Programming for pre/post formal specification notations such as B, Z and UML/OCL. Executing the specification without computing all the reachability graph is a key issue in various formal verification and validation techniques, particularly for animation and test generation. This symbolic execution engine is embedded in the model-based animation and test generation environment BZ-Testing-Tools [BZT03] which has been used for a half a dozen of industrial applications between 1999 and 2003 in the area of smart cards software, automotive embedded systems and electronic bank payment. All these real size formal models involve large combinatorial state space. Mastering the execution time for test generation requires efficiently dealing with paths and alternatives in the control flow graphs of the post-conditions.

Our graph-based representation makes various optimizations possible. It allows us to factorize the various sub-predicates, to minimize choice-points, to efficiently discard inconsistent paths in the graph and therefore to optimize the constraint generation for the solver. These optimizations give huge improvements in efficiency both during model evaluation and test generation. In fact, real applications are often not practical with DNF, but are practical with this graph based representation and constraint solving.

The BZ-Testing-Tools technology is now mature enough to be used in industrial setting for animation and model-based testing. So, this technology is being transferred to a start-up company, LEIRIOS Technologies [LEI03], which is industrializing the tool, marketing it and using it for outsourced testing. This industrial tool, called Leirios Test Generator, also uses the same process for Statecharts Statemate [LBL04] formal models.

References

[AB98]   K. R. Apt and M. A. Bezem. Formulas as programs. In *194*, page 26. Centrum voor Wiskunde en Informatica (CWI), ISSN 1386-3711, 31 1998.

[ABC⁺02]   F. Ambert, F. Bouquet, S. Chemin, S. Guenaud, B. Legeard, F. Peureux, N. Vacelet, and M. Utting. BZ-TT: A tool-set for test generation from Z and B using constraint logic programming. In *Proceedings of the CONCUR'02 Workshop on Formal Approaches to Testing of Software (FATES'02)*, pages 105–120, Brnö, Czech Republic, August 2002. INRIA Technical Report.

[ABlM97]   L. Van Aertryck, M. Benveniste, and D. le Metayer. CASTING: a formally based software test generation method. *In 1ˢᵗ IEEE International Conference on Formal Engineering Methods (ICFEM'97)*, pages 99–112, 1997.

[Abr96]   J-R. Abrial. *The B-BOOK: Assigning Programs to Meanings*. Cambridge University Press, 1996. ISBN 0 521 49619 5.

[BLLP04]   E. Bernard, B. Legeard, X. Luck, and F. Peureux. Generation of test sequences from formal specifications: GSM 11.11 standard case-study. *The Journal of Software Practice and Experience*, 2004. Accepted for publication.

[BLP02]   F. Bouquet, B. Legeard, and F. Peureux. CLPS-B – A constraint solver for B. In *Proceedings of the ETAPS'02 International Conference on Tools and Algorithms for the Construction and Analysis of Systems (TACAS'02)*, volume 2280 of *LNCS*, pages 188–204, Grenoble, France, April 2002. Springer-Verlag.

[Bry86]   R.E. Bryant. Graph-based algorithms for boolean function manipulatio. *IEEE Transactions on Computers*, C-35(8):677–691, August 1986.

[BZT03]   The BZ-TT web site. http://lifc.univ-fcomte.fr/~bztt, September 2003.

[cad00]   Emv 2000 specifications version 4.0, December 2000. http://www.emvco.com.

[cep01]   Common electronic purse specifications version 2.3, March 2001. http://www.cepsco.com.

[CL99]   C.G. Cassandra and S. Lafortune. *Introduction to Discrete Event Systems.* KLUWER ACADEMIC PUBLISHER, September 1999.

[CLP03]   S. Colin, B. Legeard, and F. Peureux. Preamble computation in automated test generation using Constraint Logic Programming. In *Proceedings of UK-Test Workshop*, York, UK, September 2003.

[DF93]   J. Dick and A. Faivre. Automating the generation and sequencing of test cases from model-based specifications. In *Methods Europe (FME'93)*, volume 670 of *LNCS*, pages 268–284. Springer Verlag, April 1993.

[DP99]   G. Delzanno and A. Podelski. Model Checking in CLP. In *Proc. Tools and Algorithms for Construction and Analysis of Systems (TACAS'99)*, pages 223–239, 1999.

[GBF97]   R. Gupta, D. A. Berson, and J. Z. Fang. Path profile guided partial dead code elimation using predication. In *International Conference on Parallel Architectures and Compilation Techniques*, pages 102–113, November 10-14 1997.

[GBR00]   A. Gotlieb, B. Botella, and M. Rueher. A CLP framework for computing structural test data. In *Proceedings of the First International Conference on Computational Logic (CL'00)*, pages 399–413, London, UK, July 2000. Springer-Verlag.

[Gri00]   W. Grieskamp. A computation model for Z based on concurrent constraint resolution. In *Proceedings of the International Conference of Z and B Users (ZB'00)*, volume 1878 of *LNCS*, pages 414–432, September 2000.

[LBL04]   B. Legeard, F. Bouquet, and F. Lebeau. Automated Test Generation and Execution for Automtive Embeded Software. In International Council on Systems Engineering, editor, *INCOSE 2004, Annual International Symposium 4th European Systems Engineering Conference*, page To appear, 20-24 June 2004.

[LEI03]   The Leirios web site. http://www.leirios.com, September 2003.

[LPU02]   B. Legeard, F. Peureux, and M. Utting. Automated Boundary Testing from Z and B. In *Proceedings of the International Conference on Formal Methods Europe (FME'02)*, volume 2391 of *LNCS*, pages 21–40, Copenhagen, Denmark, July 2002. Springer-Verlag.

[LPU04]   Bruno Legeard, Fabien Peureux, and Mark Utting. Controlling test case explosion in test generation from b formal models. *The Journal of Software Testing, Verification and Reliability*, 14(2):1–23, 2004. To appear.

[MA00]   B. Marre and A. Arnould. Test Sequence generation from Lustre descriptions: GATEL. In *Proceedings of the 15th International Conference on Automated Software Engineering (ASE'00)*, pages 229–237, Grenoble, France, 2000. IEEE Computer Society Press.

[MS98]   K. Marriott and P. J. Stuckey. *Programming with Constraints: An Introduction.* MIT Press, Cambridge, Massachusetts, 1998.

[RJB99]   J. Rumbaugh, I. Jacobson, and G. Booch. *The Unified Modeling Language Reference Manual*, addison-wesley edition, 1999.

[Spi92]   J.M. Spivey. *The Z notation: A Reference Manual.* Prentice-Hall, 2nd edition, 1992. ISBN 0 13 978529 9.

[WK98]   J. Warmer and A. Kleppe. *The Object Constraint Language: Precise Modeling with UML.* Addison-Wesley, 1998.

Bridging Refinement of Interface Automata to Forward Simulation of I/O Automata*

Yanjun Wen, Ji Wang, and Zhichang Qi

National Laboratory for Parallel and Distributed Processing,
Hunan 410073, P.R. China
{y.j.wen,ji.wang}@263.net

Abstract. Interface automata is a formal model to be used for describing the temporal interface behaviors of software components. It adopts an *alternating* approach to design refinement, which is significantly different with the traditional use of automata. In this paper, it is proven that an interface automaton *refines* another if and only if there exists a special kind of *forward simulation* between their corresponding I/O automata, which shows the essential relation between interface automata and I/O automata on refinements.

1   Introduction

1.1   Background

Interface automata [1] has been introduced as a light-weight formalism that captures the *temporal* aspects of software component interfaces, in which environment assumptions can be modelled explicitly. Automatic compatibility checking and refinement checking can be made. It has been applied in several cases as a method for modelling the interface behavior of software [2–6].

Concretely, interface automata adopts an *optimistic* approach to composition, and an *alternating* approach to design refinement. The traditional I/O automata [7] are *input-enabled*, which means that an I/O automaton must be able to accept all input actions at all states and correspondingly, output actions will never be blocked when several I/O automata are composed. The property does not hold in CSP [8], in which a process can reject some input actions and output actions may be blocked until some parallel process enters a state that can accept those actions. As to interface automata, things change again. An optimistic approach is adopted for the composition. On the one hand, input actions may be blocked. But on the other hand, it is required that output actions must not be blocked. So roughly speaking, interface automata lie between CSP and I/O automata.

While a new semantics is adopted for the composition of interface automata, an alternating approach is used for the refinement. An interface automaton Q

---

* Supported by National Natural Science Foundation of China under the grants 60233020, 90104007, and 60303013, and by the National Hi-Tech Programme of China under the grant 2001AA113202.

J. Davies et al. (Eds.): ICFEM 2004, LNCS 3308, pp. 259–273, 2004.

refines another P if all input steps of P can be simulated by Q and all the output steps of Q can be simulated by P. In other words, an interface automaton refines another if it has weaker input assumptions and stronger output guarantees. This *contravariant* requirement on input actions and output actions is described by a new simulation relation: *alternating simulation* [6], which is greatly different with the traditional definitions of simulations [9]. The new refinement has some good properties: for example, we can always replace an interface automaton with a more refined version, provided that they are connected to the environment by the same inputs.

The new approaches to composition and refinement make interface automata significantly different with the traditional use of automata. In [6], interface automata is considered as a kind of interface model while I/O automata is considered as a kind of component model. And the refinement of interface automata, which is based on alternating simulation, is considered suitable for component-based design while the refinements of I/O automata, such as *forward simulation* [9], are considered suitable for component-based verification. So the two kinds of refinements seem quite distinct from each other. However, as shown in this paper, when we return back to the traditional perspective of view and think about interface automata again, it can be found that there is an intrinsic connection between the refinement of interface automata and the forward simulation of the traditional I/O automata.

We find that the refinement problem of interface automata can be transformed equivalently to the forward simulation problem of I/O automata. Concretely speaking, an interface automaton can be transformed equivalently to an I/O automaton by adding a special "exception" state. Whenever the automaton can not accept an input action, it enters the "exception" state. The primary theorem of this paper states that an interface automaton refines another if and only if there exists a special kind[1] of forward simulation between their corresponding I/O automata. For example, consider the interface automata *Comp* in Figure 1(a), which is introduced in [1] originally, and *QuickComp* in Figure 2(a). *Comp* describes the behavior of a software component that implements a message-transmission service, and *QuickComp* is one of its variants. Their corresponding I/O automata are presented in Figure 1(b) and Figure 2(b)[2] respectively. It can be seen that *QuickComp* refines *Comp* while $IO(Comp)$ forward simulates $IO(Hid(QuickComp, \{once\}))$[2](denoted as $QuickComp'$). There is a forward simulation from $QuickComp'$ to $IO(Comp)$ that relates i with i' for $i \in \{0 \ldots 6\}$ and relates Err with all states of $QuickComp'$. The key idea comes from the observation that after introducing the "exception" states, the contravariant requirement on input and output actions of interface automata can be converted to a *covariant* requirement on those of I/O automata if we require that the "exception" state of the implementation automaton can only be simulated by the "exception" state of the specification automaton.

---

[1] See Theorem 1.

[2] A "hiding" operation has been made to *QuickComp* (See Theorem 1).

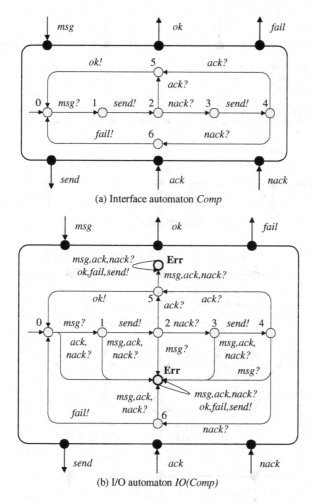

(a) Interface automaton *Comp*

(b) I/O automaton *IO(Comp)*

Fig. 1. Interface and I/O automata of *Comp*

Therefore, the essential relation between interface automata and I/O automata suggests that these two formalisms can work together nicely in a unified framework for component-based software development. In addition, by bridging refinement of interface automata to forward simulation of I/O automata, we may reuse the fruitful I/O automata tools for refinement checking between interface automata.

1.2   Related Works

The related works can be divided into three categories: I/O automata related, interface automata related, and the connections related between them.

There are a lot of works on I/O automata. We just mention those about forward simulation and tool supports. IOA Toolkit [10] is developed by the IOA

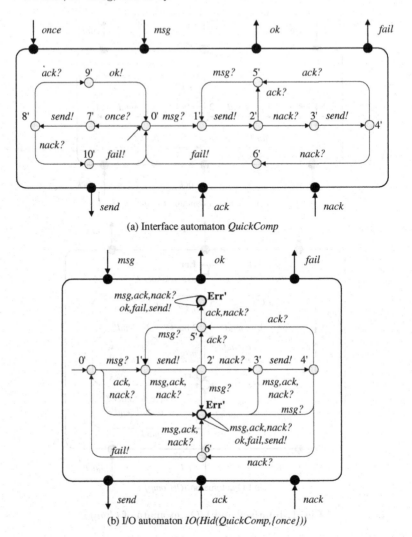

(a) Interface automaton *QuickComp*

(b) I/O automaton *IO(Hid(QuickComp,{once}))*

Fig. 2. Interface and I/O automata of *QuickComp*

project at MIT, and it includes analysis tools such as the simulator and interfaces to theorem-proving tools. Bogdanov [11] provides a way to verify simulations between I/O automata by transforming IOA specifications to LSL [12] and then using Larch Prover(LP). Müller [13] introduces a verification framework for I/O automata in Isabelle.

Interface automata is introduced by Alfaro and Henzinger in [1]. In [3,4], it is extended to describe more complicated behaviors of software module interfaces. In [5], it is used to extend the concept of type systems in programming languages to capture the dynamic interaction in component-based design. And in [6], Alfaro and Henzinger further extend the idea of interface automata to general cases and bring forward the classification of component models and interface models.

The closest work to ours is done by [2], which makes use of interface automata for the analysis of dataflow process networks. It introduced the notation of *input-universal RTS* of an interface automaton, which is similar to our definition of *the corresponding I/O automaton* of an interface automaton. However, their aim of introducing the new notation is to check the refinement relation between a special kind of interface automaton and a discrete-event component(DEC), not to bridge interface automata and I/O automata on refinements. Furthermore, in the domain of compositional reachability analysis(CRA), similar techniques are used. In [14], to check subsystem safety properties in CRA framework, the state machine model is augmented with a special state π to model the possible violation of safety properties. And in their definition of weak semantic equivalence between processes, state π can only be simulated by itself, which is similar to the relation between exception states that appears in Theorem 1. Similar techniques are also used in [15] and [16] to control the state explosion problem by interface specification.

1.3   Paper Outline

The rest of the paper is organized as follows. After Section 2 gives some concepts of interface automata and I/O automata, Section 3 introduces the transformation from interface automata to I/O automata. Then, Section 4 establishes the relation between the refinement of interface automata and the forward simulation of their corresponding I/O automata. The conclusion is summarized finally.

2   Preliminary

The actions of an automaton can be partitioned to describe the interface between the automaton and its environment. This interface is referred to as the action signature [7] of the automaton.

Definition 1 (Action Signature). *An* action signature *is a structure*

$$S = <in(S), out(S), int(S) >$$

where

- $in(S)$ *is an action set of* input actions,
- $out(S)$ *is an action set of* output actions,
- $int(S)$ *is an action set of* internal actions.

  It is required that $in(S)$, $out(S)$ *and* $int(S)$ *are disjoint with each other.*

The input actions and output actions are called *external actions* uniformly $(ext(S) = in(S) \cup out(S))$ while output actions and internal actions are called *locally-controlled actions* $(local(S) = out(S) \cup int(S))$. All actions, as a whole, is denoted by $act(S) = in(S) \cup out(S) \cup int(S)$.

I/O automata has been introduced as a formalism for modelling concurrent and distributed discrete event systems.

Definition 2 (I/O Automata). *An* input/output automaton (I/O automaton) *is a structure*

$$A =< sig(A), states(A), starts(A), steps(A), part(A) >$$

where

- *$sig(A)$ is the action signature of A.*
- *$states(A)$ is a set of* states.
- *$starts(A) \subseteq states(A)$. It is a nonempty set of* start states.
- *$steps(A) \subseteq states(A) \times act(sig(A)) \times states(A)$. It gives a transition relation with the property that for every state s and an input action π there is a transition (s, π, s') in $steps(A)$.*
- *$part(A)$ is an equivalence relation partitioning the set $local(sig(A))$ into at most a countable number of equivalence classes.*

The element $part(A)$ is used for modelling fairness conditions. In this paper, the fairness conditions are treated trivially and $part(A)$ will be omitted in the remainder of the paper.

Interface automata has been presented as a light-weight formalism for modelling the interface behavior of software components.

Definition 3 (Interface Automata). *An* interface automaton *is a structure*

$$A =< sig(A), states(A), starts(A), steps(A) >$$

where

- *$sig(A)$ is the action signature of A.*
- *$states(A)$ is a set of* states.
- *$starts(A) \subseteq states(A)$. It contains at most one state. If $starts(A) = \emptyset$, then A is called* empty.
- *$steps(A) \subseteq states(A) \times act(sig(A)) \times states(A)$. It gives a transition relation which is a set of* steps.

For an I/O automaton or interface automaton A, $act(sig(A))$, $in(sig(A))$, $out(sig(A))$, $int(sig(A))$, $local(sig(A))$ and $ext(sig(A))$ are denoted as $act(A)$, $in(A)$, $out(A)$, $int(A)$, $local(A)$ and $ext(A)$ respectively.

For an I/O automaton or interface automaton A, two states $s_1, s_2 \in states(A)$, two actions $a \in act(A)$, $a_x \in ext(A)$, and two finite action sequences $\alpha = a_1 a_2 \cdots a_n \in (act(A))^n$ and $\beta = b_1 b_2 \cdots b_n \in (ext(A))^n$, we define operator $\hat{a}$ and several relations as follows.

- $\hat{a} = \varepsilon$ if $a \in int(A)$ and $\hat{a} = a$ otherwise. $\hat{\alpha} = \hat{a_1}\hat{a_2} \cdots \hat{a_n}$.
- $s_1 \xrightarrow{a}_A s_2$ iff $(s_1, a, s_2) \in steps(A)$.
- $s_1 \xrightarrow{\tau}_A s_2$ iff $s_1 \xrightarrow{b}_A s_2$ for some $b \in int(A)$.
- $s_1 \xrightarrow{\alpha}_A s_2$ iff $s_1 \xrightarrow{a_1}_A \xrightarrow{a_2}_A \cdots \xrightarrow{a_n}_A s_2$. Especially, $s_1 \xrightarrow{\varepsilon}_A s_1$.
- $s_1 \xRightarrow{\varepsilon}_A s_2$ iff $s_1(\xrightarrow{\tau}_A)^* s_2$.
- $s_1 \xRightarrow{a_x}_A s_2$ iff $s_1 \xRightarrow{\varepsilon}_A \xrightarrow{a_x}_A \xRightarrow{\varepsilon}_A s_2$.
- $s_1 \xRightarrow{\beta}_A s_2$ iff $s_1 \xRightarrow{b_1}_A \xRightarrow{b_2}_A \cdots \xRightarrow{b_n}_A s_2$.

where $*$ is reflexive and transitive closure and juxtaposition is a composition of relations. We omit the subscript A when it is clear from the context.

3   From Interface Automata to I/O Automata

An interface automaton can be transformed equivalently and straightforwardly to an I/O automaton by adding a special "exception" state to the state set. Specifically, we require that the "exception" state has a self transition that can be triggered by all *external* actions.

Definition 4 (From Interface Automata to I/O Automata). *Given an interface automaton A, the* corresponding I/O automaton $IO(A)$ *is defined as follows.*

- $sig(IO(A)) = sig(A)$.
- $states(IO(A)) = states(A) \cup \{Err_A\}$, *where* Err_A *is a new state, called the* exception state *of* $IO(A)$.
- $starts(IO(A)) = starts(A)$.
- $steps(IO(A))$ *is composed of all the steps* (s, a, s') *such that*
  - $s = s' = Err_A$ *and* $a \in ext(A)$, *or*
  - $(s, a, s') \in steps(A)$, *or*
  - $s \in states(A)$, $a \in in(A)$, $s' = Err_A$ *and for any* $s'' \in states(A)$, $(s, a, s'') \notin steps(A)$.

We illustrate the notion by applying them to the examples introduced in [1], whose figure style is followed as well. In Figures 1 and 2, multiple occurrences of the exception state are allowed for the clarity of graphs. Moreover, the transitions with the same source and sink states are merged.

Example 1. Figure 1(a) gives the interface automaton *Comp*. Its corresponding I/O automaton *IO(Comp)* is given in Figure 1(b), where the exception state *Err* is circled in a thicker line. One may find that at every state of the interface automaton *Comp* only those transitions triggered by valid input actions are drawn, while at every state of the I/O automaton *IO(Comp)* all actions are allowed and every unexpected input action triggers a transition to the exception state *Err*, which means the occurrence of an exception. Obviously, both automata have described the same behavior.

4   Bridging Refinement of Interface Automata to Forward Simulation of I/O Automata

In this section, it will be shown that the refinement problem of interface automata can be transformed equivalently to the forward simulation problem of I/O automata.

Firstly we introduce the notion of hiding of interface automata on input actions. Some input actions of an interface automaton can be hidden by the "hiding" operation, which describes the composition with the environment that never outputs those actions.

Definition 5 (Hiding of Interface Automata on Input Actions). *Given an interface automaton P and an action set $X \subseteq in(P)$, the* hiding *of P on input actions X, denoted as $Hid(P, X)$, is the interface automaton $P \parallel Env(X)$, where $Env(X)$ is the interface automaton that never outputs any actions in X, and is defined as follows.*

- *$in(Env(X)) = int(Env(X)) = \emptyset$, $out(Env(X)) = X$.*
- *$states(Env(X)) = starts(Env(X)) = \{Idle\}$, where $Idle$ is a state.*
- *$steps(Env(X)) = \emptyset$.*

The lemma below shows that the "irrelevant" input actions can be hidden without affecting the refinement relation between interface automata. Its proof can be done straightforwardly according to the definitions.

Lemma 1. *Given two interface automata P and Q, let action set $X = in(Q) - in(P)$. Q refines P iff $Hid(Q, X)$ refines P.*

Now, we can express clearly the connection between interface automata and I/O automata on refinements. The key point of the following theorem lies in the requirement that the exception state $Err_{Q'}$ can only be simulated by the exception state Err_P.

Theorem 1. *Consider two nonempty interface automata P and Q such that $in(P) \subseteq in(Q)$ and $out(P) \supseteq out(Q)$. Let $X = in(Q) - in(P)$ and $Q' = Hid(Q, X)$. Then the following two propositions are equivalent:*

1. *Q refines P.*
2. *There exists a forward simulation $\succeq$ from $IO(Q')$ to $IO(P)$ such that $\{v|(v, Err_{Q'}) \in \succeq\} = \{Err_P\}$.*[3]

The proof is done by introducing a new refinement notion of I/O automata, similarly to that of interface automata. Then the new refinement can act as a medium between the refinement of interface automata and the forward simulation of I/O automata. Lemma 4 is the key point, where the relation between the alternating simulation of interface automata and the simulation (NOT alternating) of I/O automata is established.

First, we define the new notions of simulation and refinement of I/O automata in a similar way to those of interface automata.

Similar to the definitions in [1], the notions, ε-*closure* (ε-$closure_P$), *externally enabled output* ($ExtEn_P^O$), *externally enabled input* ($ExtEn_P^I$) and *external destination* ($ExtDest_P$), can be defined on an I/O automaton P, where the notable difference is that I/O automata are *input-enabled*: for every I/O automaton P and every state $v \in states(P)$, $ExtEn_P^I(v) = in(P)$.

---

[3] Here, for the consistency of styles, we make a trivial adjustment to the definition of forward simulation in [9]: we require $\succeq \subseteq states(P) \times states(Q)$ instead of $\succeq \subseteq states(Q) \times states(P)$ and have corresponding modification to the other parts of the definition without changing the semantics of forward simulation.

Definition 6 (Simulation Between I/O Automata). *Consider two I/O automata P and Q. A binary relation $\succeq \subseteq states(P) \times states(Q)$ is a simulation from Q to P if for all states $v \in states(P)$ and $u \in states(Q)$ such that $v \succeq u$, the following conditions hold:*

- $(in(Q) \cup ExtEn_Q^O(u)) \subseteq (in(P) \cup ExtEn_P^O(v))$.
- *For all actions $a \in in(Q) \cup ExtEn_Q^O(u)$ and all states $u' \in ExtDest_Q(u, a)$, there is a state $v' \in ExtDest_P(v, a)$ such that $v' \succeq u'$.*

Definition 7 (Refinement Between I/O Automata). *An I/O automaton Q refines an I/O automaton P, written $P \succeq Q$, if there is a simulation $\succeq$ from Q to P such that for every state $u \in starts(Q)$ there is a state $v \in starts(P)$ such that $v \succeq u$. Such a simulation is also called a* refinement *from Q to P.*

This definition of refinement of I/O automata is consistent with the definition of forward simulation in [9]. Both of the approaches describe the simulation relation between I/O automata on external behaviors. The difference lies in the way that they handle internal transition steps. In the "refinement" approach, a macro-step of the concrete automaton is simulated by a macro-step of the abstract automaton, while in the "forward simulation" approach, a micro-step of the concrete automaton is simulated by a macro-step of the abstract automaton. The lemma below makes precise the relationship between them.

Lemma 2. *Given two I/O automata P and Q, there exists a refinement from Q to P iff there exists a forward simulation from Q to P.*

Proof. First, we prove the forward direction. Suppose that $\succeq$ is a refinement from Q to P. A forward simulation $\succeq_F$ from Q to P can be constructed as follows. $\succeq_F$ is the minimal set satisfying the following two conditions.

- $\succeq \subseteq \succeq_F$.
- If $(v, u) \in \succeq_F$ and $u' \in \varepsilon\text{-}closure_Q(u)$, then $(v, u') \in \succeq_F$.

We will prove that $\succeq_F$ constructed above is indeed a forward simulation from Q to P. Before going into the details of the proof, let us recall the definition of forward simulation in [9]. A forward simulation from I/O automata B to A is a relation f from $states(A)^4$ to $states(B)$ that satisfies:

1. If $u \in starts(B)$ then there exists a state $v \in starts(A)$ such that $(v, u) \in f$.
2. If $u' \xrightarrow{a}_B u$ and $(v', u') \in f$, then there exists a state v such that $(v, u) \in f$ and $v' \xRightarrow{\hat{a}}_A v$.

Since $\succeq \subseteq \succeq_F$, the proof of the first condition of forward simulation is immediate from the definition of refinement of I/O automata. Now, we consider the second condition. Suppose $u' \xrightarrow{a}_Q u$ (i.e. $(u', a, u) \in steps(Q)$) and $(v', u') \in \succeq_F$. Thus $u' \xRightarrow{\hat{a}}_Q u$. By the construction procedure of $\succeq_F$, we know there are only two cases:

---

[4] See Footnote 3.

1. $(v', u') \in \succeq$. In this case, we distinguish two subcases further.
   - If $a \in int(Q)$, then $u \in \varepsilon - closure_Q(u')$. Since $(v', u') \in \succeq$, by the construction procedure of $\succeq_F$ we know $(v', u) \in \succeq_F$. Obviously, $v' \overset{\varepsilon}{\Longrightarrow}_P v'$. Let $v = v'$, and we know $(v, u) \in \succeq_F$. So the second condition of forward simulation is satisfied.
   - If $a \in ext(Q)$, then it can be known that $a \in in(Q) \cup ExtEn_Q^O(u')$ and $u \in ExtDest_Q(u', a)$ since $u' \overset{\hat{a}}{\Longrightarrow}_Q u$. Because $(v', u') \in \succeq$, by the definition of $\succeq$ there exists some state $v'' \in ExtDest_P(v', a)$ such that $(v'', u) \in \succeq$. Since $\succeq \subseteq \succeq_F$, $(v'', u) \in \succeq_F$ holds. So the second condition is also satisfied if letting $v = v''$.
2. There exists some u'' such that $u' \in \varepsilon\text{-}closure_Q(u'')$ and $(v', u'') \in \succeq$. Thus, we have $u'' \overset{\hat{a}}{\Longrightarrow}_Q u$. Similar to the first case, it can be proved that the second condition holds.

Therefore the second condition holds.

Next, we prove the opposite direction. If $\succeq_F$ is a forward simulation from Q to P, then it can be shown directly that $\succeq_F$ is also a refinement from Q to P. $\qquad \square$

Hence we have introduced an alternative way to define the forward simulation between I/O automata. Furthermore, by the proof procedure above, the following lemma can be proven easily.

Lemma 3. *Given two interface automata P and Q, the following two propositions are equivalent:*

1. *There exists a refinement $\succeq$ from $IO(Q)$ to $IO(P)$ such that*
   $\{v|(v, Err_Q) \in \succeq\} = \{Err_P\}$
2. *There exists a forward simulation $\succeq'$ from $IO(Q)$ to $IO(P)$ such that*
   $\{v|(v, Err_Q) \in \succeq'\} = \{Err_P\}$.

The next lemma shows the connection between interface automata and I/O automata on the refinement relations. Especially, it shows the relation between the alternating simulation of interface automata and the simulation of I/O automata. It is the key lemma for the proof of Theorem 1.

Lemma 4. *Given two nonempty interface automata P and Q such that $in(P) = in(Q)$ and $out(P) \supseteq out(Q)$, the following two propositions are equivalent:*

1. *Q refines P.*
2. *There exists a refinement $\succeq$ from $IO(Q)$ to $IO(P)$ such that*
   $\{v|(v, Err_Q) \in \succeq\} = \{Err_P\}$.

Proof. First, we deduce the proposition (2) from (1). Suppose Q refines P. Then there must exist an alternating simulation $\succeq_A$ from Q to P such that for every state $u \in starts(Q)$ there exists a state $v \in starts(P)$ that satisfies $v \succeq_A u$.[5] Let

---

[5] This condition is equivalent with the condition (2) of the definition of refinements [1] between interface automata on the premise that P and Q are nonempty.

$\succeq = \succeq_A \cup (\{Err_P\} \times states(IO(Q)))$. Obviously, $\{v|(v, Err_Q) \in \succeq\} = \{Err_P\}$. So it is sufficient to prove that $\succeq$ is a refinement from $IO(Q)$ to $IO(P)$. We prove it according to the definition of refinement of I/O automata in the following steps.

1. Because the start-state set of $IO(Q)$ (resp. $IO(P)$) is equal to the one of Q (resp. P), thus for every start state u of $IO(Q)$ there must exist a start state v of $IO(P)$ such that $(v, u) \in \succeq_A$ (so $\in \succeq$). So it remains to prove that $\succeq$ is a simulation from $IO(Q)$ (denoted as Q') to $IO(P)$ (denoted as P').

2. For all states $v \in states(P')$ and $u \in states(Q')$ such that $v \succeq u$, and for all actions $a \in in(Q') \cup ExtEn^O_{Q'}(u)$ and all states $u' \in ExtDest_{Q'}(u, a)$, we will show that $(in(Q') \cup ExtEn^O_{Q'}(u)) \subseteq (in(P') \cup ExtEn^O_{P'}(v))$ and there is a state $v' \in ExtDest_{P'}(v, a)$ such that $v' \succeq u'$. By the premise, $in(Q) = in(P)$. So $in(Q') = in(P')$. Since $\succeq_A$ is an alternating simulation from Q to P, we have $ExtEn^I_P(v) \subseteq ExtEn^I_Q(u)$ and $ExtEn^O_Q(u) \subseteq ExtEn^O_P(v)$. By the definition, it can be seen that $ExtEn^O_{Q'}(u) = ExtEn^O_Q(u)$ and $ExtEn^O_{P'}(v) = ExtEn^O_P(v)$. Thus $ExtEn^O_{Q'}(u) \subseteq ExtEn^O_{P'}(v)$. So $(in(Q') \cup ExtEn^O_{Q'}(u)) \subseteq (in(P') \cup ExtEn^O_{P'}(v))$ holds. It remains to show that there is a state $v' \in ExtDest_{P'}(v, a)$ such that $v' \succeq u'$. We distinguish four cases according to a and (v, u).

   - If $(v, u) \in \succeq_A \wedge a \in ExtEn^O_{Q'}(u)$, then u' must be unequal to Err_Q. And so $u' \in ExtDest_Q(u, a)$. and by the definition of alternating simulation there must exist a state $v' \in ExtDest_P(v, a)$ (so $\in ExtDest_{P'}(v, a)$) such that $v' \succeq_A u'$ (so $v' \succeq u'$).
   - If $(v, u) \in \succeq_A \wedge a \in in(Q') \wedge a \in ExtEn^I_P(v)$, then we know $a \in ExtEn^I_Q(u)$ and $u' \neq Err_Q$. Similar to the previous case, it can be proved that there exists a state $v' \in ExtDest_{P'}(v, a)$ such that $v' \succeq u'$.
   - If $(v, u) \in \succeq_A \wedge a \in in(Q') \wedge a \notin ExtEn^I_P(v)$, then there exists a state $v' \in \varepsilon{-}closure_P(v)$ such that $(v', a, Err_P) \in steps(P')$. Thus $Err_P \in ExtDest_{P'}(v, a)$. Since $\{Err_P\} \times states(Q') \subseteq \succeq$, we have $Err_P \succeq u'$. Thus Err_P is the appropriate state.
   - If $(v, u) \notin \succeq_A$, then $v = Err_P$. Since $(Err_P, a, Err_P) \in steps(P')$, we know $Err_P \in ExtDest_{P'}(v, a)$. Furthermore, we have $Err_P \succeq u'$. Thus Err_P is the appropriate state.

3. Thus, $\succeq$ is a simulation from Q' to P'. The forward direction is proved.

Next, we will prove the opposite direction. Suppose there exists a refinement $\succeq$ from Q' to P' such that $\{v|(v, Err_Q) \in \succeq\} = \{Err_P\}$. Then by the definition of refinement of I/O automata, the following two propositions hold.

1. $\succeq$ is a simulation from Q' to P'.
2. For every state $u \in starts(Q')$ there is a state $v \in starts(P')$ such that $v \succeq u$.

By the premise of the lemma, we have $in(P) \subseteq in(Q)$ and $out(P) \supseteq out(Q)$. So it remains to prove that there is an alternating simulation $\succeq_A$ from Q to P

such that for every start state u of Q there is a start state v of P satisfying $(v, u) \in \succeq_A$.[6]

Let $\succeq_A = \succeq \setminus \{(Err_P, u) \mid u \in states(Q')\}$. In the following, we will show that the relation $\succeq_A$ constructed above is the appropriate one.

Since $starts(P') = starts(P)$ and $starts(Q') = starts(Q)$, by the clause (2) above we know that for every start state u of Q there is a start state v of P such that $v \succeq u$. And since $Err_P \notin starts(P')$, $v \succeq_A u$ holds. So it is sufficient to prove that $\succeq_A$ is an alternating simulation from Q to P. We prove it according to the definition of alternating simulation.

For all states $v \in states(P)$ and $u \in states(Q)$ such that $(v, u) \in \succeq_A$, the following holds.

1. Since $\succeq$ is a simulation from Q' to P', we have $(in(Q') \cup ExtEn_{Q'}^O(u)) \subseteq (in(P') \cup ExtEn_{P'}^O(v))$. By the premise of the lemma, we know $in(P) = in(Q)$. Thus $in(P') = in(Q')$ and $ExtEn_{Q'}^O(u) \subseteq ExtEn_{P'}^O(v)$. Moreover, we know $ExtEn_{Q'}^O(v) = ExtEn_Q^O(v)$ and $ExtEn_{P'}^O(u) = ExtEn_P^O(u)$. So we have $ExtEn_Q^O(u) \subseteq ExtEn_P^O(v)$.

2. We will show that $ExtEn_P^I(v) \subseteq ExtEn_Q^I(u)$. Assume to the contrary that there is an action a' that satisfies $a' \in ExtEn_P^I(v) \wedge a' \notin ExtEn_Q^I(u)$. So for all states $v'' \in \varepsilon{-}closure_P(v)$, $(v'', a', Err_P) \notin steps(P')$ holds. And there must exist a state $u'' \in \varepsilon{-}closure_Q(u)$ such that $(u'', a', Err_Q) \in steps(Q')$. Thus $Err_P \notin ExtDest_{P'}(v, a')$ and $Err_Q \in ExtDest_{Q'}(u, a')$. So there does not exist a state $v' \in ExtDest_{P'}(v, a')$ such that $v' \succeq Err_Q$ because $v' \succeq Err_Q$ only if $v' = Err_P$. However, as we have showed, $Err_Q \in ExtDest_{Q'}(u, a')$ and $v \succeq u$ hold. It is contradictive with the assumption that $\succeq$ is a simulation from Q' to P'. So $ExtEn_P^I(v) \subseteq ExtEn_Q^I(u)$ holds.

3. For all actions $a \in ExtEn_P^I(v) \cup ExtEn_Q^O(u)$ and all states $u' \in ExtDest_Q(u, a)$, we will show that there is a state $v' \in ExtDest_P(v, a)$ such that $v' \succeq_A u'$. From the construction algorithm of $IO(Q)$, we know $ExtEn_{Q'}^O(v) = ExtEn_Q^O(v)$ and $ExtDest_Q(u, a) \subseteq ExtDest_{Q'}(u, a)$. Thus $a \in in(P) \cup ExtEn_Q^O(u)$, i.e. $a \in in(Q') \cup ExtEn_{Q'}^O(u)$, and $u' \in ExtDest_{Q'}(u, a)$. Moreover, because $v \succeq_A u$ and $\succeq_A \subseteq \succeq$, we have $v \succeq u$. Since $\succeq$ is a simulation from Q' to P' and $v \succeq u$, there must exist a state $v'' \in ExtDest_{P'}(v, a)$ such that $v'' \succeq u'$. So it is sufficient to prove that $v'' \in ExtDest_P(v, a)$ and $v'' \succeq_A u'$. We distinguish two cases.
   - If $a \in ExtEn_Q^O(u)$, then $a \in ExtEn_P^O(u)$ since $ExtEn_Q^O(u) \subseteq ExtEn_P^O(v)$. Thus $a \in ExtEn_{P'}^O(u)$. Moreover, as we know, $v'' \in ExtDest_{P'}(v, a)$, $v \in states(P)$ and so $v \neq Err_P$. Thus it is obvious that $v'' \neq Err_P$. Because all the transitions that are added to P when constructing $IO(P)$ have Err_P as their target states, we have $v'' \in ExtDest_P(v, a)$. Furthermore, since all the state-pairs removed from $\succeq$ when constructing $\succeq_A$ are of the form $(Err_P, \ldots)$, and v'' is unequal to Err_P, we know $(v'', u') \in \succeq_A$, i.e. $v'' \succeq_A u'$.

---

[6] See Footnote 5.

- If $a \in ExtEn_P^I(v)$, then for all states $w \in \varepsilon\text{-}closure_P(v, a)$ there is a state $w' \in states(P)$ such that $(w, a, w') \in steps(P)$. By the construction algorithm of $IO(P)$ we can see that $Err_P \notin ExtDest_{P'}(v, a)$. Thus $v'' \neq Err_P$. Similar to the deduction steps in the previous case, we can prove $v'' \in ExtDest_P(v, a)$ and $v'' \succeq_A u'$.

By the above, $\succeq_A$ is an alternating simulation from Q to P. The opposite direction is also proved.   □

Now, we can prove Theorem 1 by synthesizing Lemma 1, Lemma 3 and Lemma 4.

Proof. By Lemma 1 we have that Q refines P iff Q' refines P. By the premise, we know $in(P) \subseteq in(Q)$ and $out(P) \supseteq out(Q)$. Thus $in(P) = in(Q')$ and $out(P) \supseteq out(Q')$. By Lemma 4 we know that Q' refines P iff there exists a refinement $\succeq$ from $IO(Q')$ to $IO(P)$ such that $\{v|(v, Err_{Q'}) \in \succeq\} = \{Err_P\}$. Moreover, by Lemma 3 we know that the latter is further equivalent to that there exists a forward simulation $\succeq'$ from $IO(Q')$ to $IO(P)$ such that $\{v|(v, Err_{Q'}) \in \succeq'\} = \{Err_P\}$. Summing the results up, we know that Q refines P iff there exists a forward simulation $\succeq$ from $IO(Q')$ to $IO(P)$ such that $\{v|(v, Err_{Q'}) \in \succeq\} = \{Err_P\}$.   □

Example 2. Recall the example presented in Section 1. It can be seen that there exists an alternating simulation from $QuickComp$ to $Comp$ that relates i with i' for $i \in \{0 \ldots 6\}$. Moreover, as we have shown, there exists a forward simulation from $IO(Hid(QuickComp, \{once\}))$ to $IO(Comp)$.

From Theorem 1, it can be concluded that the refinement problem of interface automata can be equivalently transformed to the forward simulation problem of I/O automata, which has been studied extensively [9, 11, 17]. This enables us to reuse the theory and tool supports of I/O automata to solve the refinement problem of interface automata. For example, in [11], a proof method of forward simulation of I/O automata is provided based on a transformation from IOA [18] language to LSL. And then, Larch Prover(LP) is used to formally verify the forward simulation relation. Thus by Theorem 1, this method can also be used to verify refinements of interface automata.

5   Conclusion

The essential relation between interface automata and I/O automata has been investigated in the paper. We have shown that the refinement problem of interface automata can be equivalently transformed to the forward simulation problem of I/O automata. So the theory of interface automata and I/O automata can work together nicely in a unified framework for formal development of component-based systems, such as web services. In [6], Alfaro and Henzinger classify component-based models into component models and interface models, where I/O automaton is considered as a component model while interface automaton is considered as an interface model. So by the result of this paper, in a sense, not only a connection between I/O automata and interface automata on refinements is established, but also a connection between component models and interface models.

References

1. de Alfaro, L., Henzinger, T.A.: Interface automata. In: 9th Symposium on Foundations of Software Engineering, ACM Press (2001)
2. Jin, Y., Esser, R., Lakos, C., Janneck, J.W.: Modular analysis of dataflow process networks. In Pezzè, M., ed.: Proceedings of the 6th International Conference on Fundamental Approaches to Software Engineering (FASE'03), Held as Part of the Joint European Conferences on Theory and Practice of Software (ETAPS'03). Volume 2621 of LNCS., Warsaw, Poland, Springer-Verlag (2003) 184–199
3. Chakrabarti, A., de Alfaro, L., Henzinger, T.A., Jurdzinski, M., Mang, F.Y.C.: Interface compatibility checking for software modules. In: Proceedings of the 14th International Conference on Computer-Aided Verification. Volume 2404 of LNCS., Springer-Verlag (2002)
4. Chakrabarti, A., de Alfaro, L., Henzinger, T.A., Mang, F.Y.: Synchronous and bidirectional component interfaces. In: Proceedings of the 14th International Conference on Computer-Aided Verification. Volume 2404 of LNCS., Springer-Verlag (2002) 414–427
5. Lee, E.A., Xiong, Y.: Behavioral types for component-based design. In: Memorandum UCB/ERL M02/29. University of California, Berkeley, CA 94720, USA (2002)
6. de Alfaro, L., Henzinger, T.A.: Interface theories for component-based design. In: Proceedings of the First International Workshop on Embedded Software (EMSOFT). Volume 2211 of LNCS., Springer-Verlag (2001) 148–165
7. Lynch, N., Tuttle, M.: An introduction to input/output automata. CWI Quarterly **2** (1989) 219–246
8. Brookes, S.D., Hoare, C.A.R., Roscoe, A.W.: A theory of communicating sequential processes. Journal of the ACM (JACM) **31** (1984) 560–599
9. Lynch, N., Vaandrager, F.: Forward and backward simulations part 1: Untimed systems. Information and Computation **121** (1995) 214–233
10. Garland, S.J., Lynch, N.A.: The IOA language and toolset: Support for mathematics-based distributed programming. Technical Report MIT-LCS-TR-762, Laboratory of Computer Science, Massachusetts Institute of Technology, Cambridge, MA (1998)
11. Bogdanov, A.: Formal verification of simulations between I/O automata. Master's thesis, Massachusetts Institute of Technology (2001)
12. Guttag, J.V., Horning, J.J., Modet, A.: Report on the larch shared language: Version 2.3. Technical Report Technical Report 58, Digital Equipment Corporation, Systems Research Center, 130 Lytton Avenue, Palo Alto, CA 94301 (1990)
13. Mueller, O.: A Verification Environment for I/O Automata Based on Formalized Meta-Theory. PhD thesis, Technische Universitaet Muenchen (1998)
14. Cheung, S.C., Kramer, J.: Checking subsystem safety properties in compositional reachability analysis. In: Proceedings of the 18th international conference on Software engineering, Berlin, Germany (1996) 144–154

15. Cheung, S.C., Kramer, J.: Compositional reachability analysis of finite-state distributed systems with user-specified constraints. In: Proceedings of the 3rd ACM SIGSOFT symposium on Foundations of software engineering, Washington, D.C., United States (1995) 140–150
16. Graf, S., Steffen, B., Lüttgen, G.: Compositional minimization of finite state systems using interface specifications. Technical Report MIP-9505, Universität Passau, Passau, Germany (1995)
17. Schellhorn, G.: Verification of ASM refinements using generalized forward simulation. Journal of Universal Computer Science **7** (2001) 952–979
18. Garland, S.J., Lynch, N.A., Vaziri, M.: IOA: a language for specifying, programming, and validating distributed systems. MIT Laboratory for Computer Science (1997)

Learning to Verify Safety Properties

Abhay Vardhan, Koushik Sen, Mahesh Viswanathan, and Gul Agha*

Department of Computer Science,
University of Illinois at Urbana-Champaign, Urbana, IL, USA
{vardhan,ksen,vmahesh,agha}@cs.uiuc.edu

Abstract. We present a novel approach for verifying safety properties of finite state machines communicating over unbounded FIFO channels that is based on applying machine learning techniques. We assume that we are given a model of the system and learn the set of reachable states from a sample set of executions of the system, instead of attempting to iteratively compute the reachable states. The learnt set of reachable states is then used to either prove that the system is safe or to produce a valid execution of the system leading to an unsafe state (*i.e.* a counterexample). We have implemented this method for verifying FIFO automata in a tool called LEVER that uses a regular language learning algorithm called RPNI. We apply our tool to a few case studies and report our experience with this method. We also demonstrate how this method can be generalized and applied to the verification of other infinite state systems.

1 Introduction

Software systems are often abstracted as infinite state systems at the design and modeling stage. A popular model for a variety of such systems comprises of finite state machines communicating over unbounded FIFO (first in first out) channels (*FIFO automata*). Examples of such abstraction include: networking protocols where unbounded buffers are assumed, languages like Estelle and SDL (Specification and Description Language) in which processes have infinite queue size, distributed systems and various *actor* systems. A generic task in the automated verification of safety properties of any system is to compute a representation for the set of reachable states. For finite state systems, this is typically accomplished by doing an exhaustive exploration of the state-space. However, for FIFO automata (and most other infinite state systems) exhaustive exploration of the state space is impossible; and in fact the verification problem in general can shown to be undecidable.

We develop a novel *machine learning* based procedure for verifying safety properties of FIFO automata. We assume that the reachable states of the system is a regular set (or is contained in a regular set) which is a fixpoint with respect

* The third author was supported in part by DARPA/AFOSR MURI Award F49620-02-1-0325. The other three authors were supported in part by DARPA IPTO TASK Program (contract F30602-00-2-0586), ONR Grant N00014-02-1-0715, and Motorola Grant MOTOROLA RPS #23 ANT.

J. Davies et al. (Eds.): ICFEM 2004, LNCS 3308, pp. 274–289, 2004.

to the transition relation of the system. Instead of trying to compute the set of reachable states iteratively, we *learn* the set of reachable states from sample runs of the system being verified. If the set of reachable states turns out to be closed (fixpoint) under the transition relation of the system and does not contain any unsafe state, we deem the system to be correct. On the other hand, unsafe states in the learned reachable set are used to obtain executions that might lead to the unsafe state (*i.e.* a counterexample). The counterexample may or may not represent valid executions of the system because we may over-generalize while learning. If the counterexample turns out to be valid then we have discovered a bug in our system. On the other hand, if the counterexample is invalid, then we use it to refine the learnt set of reachable states. We repeat the process until we have either proved the system to be correct or discovered a buggy execution. Figure 1 shows the overall framework of the *learning to verify* procedure.

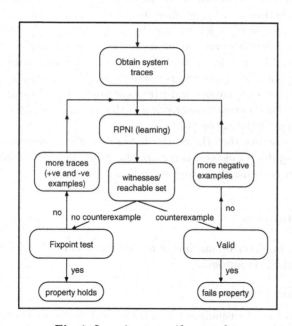

Fig. 1. Learning to verify procedure

Similar to regular model checking [1], we represent states of the system by strings and expect the set of reachable states of practical systems to be structured and representable as regular languages. We then use a modified version of the algorithm RPNI [2, 3], that learns regular languages, to identify the set of reachable states. We show that the algorithm that we present is a *complete verification* method for systems with regular reachable sets[1]; in other words, for

---

[1] Actually, we require the reachable states along with witness executions to form a regular language; for a precise condition see Section 4.

such systems we will eventually either find a buggy execution that violates the safety property, or will successfully prove that no unsafe state is reachable. We have implemented our algorithm in Java, and demonstrated the feasibility of this method by running the implementation on simple examples and network protocols such as the alternating-bit protocol and the sliding window protocol. Our approach is complementary to previous methods for algorithmic verification that have been proposed, and we present examples of FIFO automata that our method successfully verifies but on which other approaches fail (see Section 7 on related work). We also give the requirements under which classes of infinite state systems other than FIFO automata can be verified using the learning approach.

The rest of the paper is organized as follows. We first (Section 2) introduce the learning framework and recall the definition of FIFO automata. In Section 3, we describe the verification procedure for FIFO automata. Then, (in Section 4) we give the proof of soundness of the method and completeness under certain conditions. In Section 5, we generalize from FIFO automata to give a learning based paradigm for verification of infinite state systems. Finally, in Section 6, we give details of our Java implementation with experimental results, and conclude with overall lessons learnt and directions for future research (Section 8). Relationship of our work to previous research on the algorithmic verification of infinite state systems in general, and FIFO automata in particular, is deferred to Section 7. Proofs and detailed description of the examples analyzed are available in the full version of the paper [4].

This paper assumes that the reader is familiar with finite automata theory, in particular, *regular languages, deterministic finite automata* and *rational* sets. Some textbooks covering these topics are [5, 6].

2   Preliminaries

In this section, we describe machine learning framework that we use and recall the definition of FIFO automata.

2.1   Learning Framework

A learning algorithm is usually set in a framework which describes the types of input data and queries available to the learner. The framework sometimes includes a knowledgeable teacher (student-teacher framework [7]) which provides answers to membership queries (whether a given example belongs to a given concept) and equivalence queries (whether a given hypothesis matches the concept). However, in practice, such a teacher may not be available. Therefore, a more general framework for learning assumes that the learner is simply given examples included in the target concept (positive examples) and examples not included in the target concept (negative examples). One such framework called *language identification in the limit* was introduced by Gold [8] for inference of infinitary languages. In Gold's framework, the learner is given successively larger sequences of positive and negative examples. If the learner is able to converge on the target language after being given a sufficiently large sample of positive and negative examples, it is said to identify the language in the limit. The sample that is needed to guarantee this identification is said to be *characteristic*.

In our setting, we do not have access to a teacher which can answer equivalence queries. Therefore, we restrict ourselves to Gold's framework of identification in the limit. Moreover, in this paper we focus on learning of regular languages; based on the experience of *regular model checking* [1], regular languages are often sufficient to capture the behavior of an interesting class of infinite state systems. A well-known algorithm for the inference of regular languages in Gold's framework is RPNI (regular positive and negative inference) [2,3]. In this algorithm, the target concept to be learned is a *deterministic finite automata* (DFA) which accepts a regular language. The input consists of a set of positive samples S^+ accepted by the target DFA and a set of negative samples S^- rejected by the target DFA. We use a modified version of the RPNI algorithm which is described in more detail later.

2.2   FIFO Automata

A FIFO automaton [9] is a 6-tuple $(Q, q_0, C, M, \Theta, \delta)$ where Q is a finite set of *control states*, $q_0 \in Q$ is the initial control state, C is a finite set of *channel names*, M is a finite alphabet for contents of a channel, Θ is a finite set of transitions names, and $\delta : \Theta \to Q \times ((C \times \{?, !\} \times M) \cup \{\tau\}) \times Q$ is a function that assigns a *control transition* to each transition name. For a transition name θ, if the associated control transition $\delta(\theta)$ is of the form $(q, c?m, q')$ then it denotes a *receive* action, if it is of the form $(q, c!m, q')$ it denotes a *send* action, and if it is of the form (q, τ, q') then it denotes an *internal* action. The channels are considered to be perfect and messages sent by a sender are received in the order in which they were sent. The formal operational semantics, given by a labelled transition systems, is defined below.

A FIFO automaton $F = (Q, q_0, C, M, \Theta, \delta)$ defines a labelled transition system $\mathcal{L} = (S, \Theta, \to)$ where

- The set of states $S = Q \times (M^*)^C$; in other words, each state of the labelled transition system consists of a control state q and a C-indexed vector of words w denoting the channel contents.
- If $\delta(\theta) = (q, c?m, q')$ then $(p, w) \xrightarrow{\theta} (p', w')$ iff $p = q$, $p' = q'$ and $w = w'[c \mapsto m \cdot w'[c]]$
- If $\delta(\theta) = (q, c!m, q')$ then $(p, w) \xrightarrow{\theta} (p', w')$ iff $p = q$, $p' = q'$ and $w' = w[c \mapsto m \cdot w[c]]$
- If $\delta(\theta) = (q, \tau, q')$ then $(p, w) \xrightarrow{\theta} (p', w')$ iff $p = q$, $p' = q'$ and $w' = w$.

Here $w[i \mapsto s]$ stand for the C-indexed vector which is identical to w for all channels except i, where it is s; $w[i]$ denotes the contents of the channel i. We say $(p, w) \to (p', w')$ provided there is some θ such that $(p, w) \xrightarrow{\theta} (p', w')$. As usual, $\to^*$ will denote the reflexive transitive closure of $\to$. For $\sigma = \theta_1 \theta_2 \cdots \theta_n \in \Theta^*$, we say $(p, w) \xrightarrow{\sigma} (p', w')$ when there exist states $(p_1, w_1) \ldots (p_{n-1}, w_{n-1})$ such that $(p, w) \xrightarrow{\theta_1} (p_1, w_1) \xrightarrow{\theta_2} \cdots (p_{n-1}, w_{n-1}) \xrightarrow{\theta_n} (p', w')$. The trace language of the FIFO automaton is

$$L(F) = \{\sigma \in \Theta^* \mid \exists s = (p, w).\ s_0 \xrightarrow{\sigma} s\}$$

where $s_0 = (q_0, (\epsilon, \ldots, \epsilon))$, i.e., the initial control state with no messages in the channels.

3   Verification Procedure

We now describe the verification procedure in detail with reference to FIFO automata.

The central idea in our approach is to learn the set of reachable states instead of computing it by iteratively applying the transition relation. Once the set of reachable states is learnt, we can verify if the safety property is violated by checking if an unsafe state is among the set of reachable states. However, in order to ensure the soundness of our results, we need a mechanism to check if the output of the learning algorithm is indeed correct. Observe that if the set of states learnt is closed under the transition relation then it means that the learnt set of states contains all the reachable states, and if, in addition, none of the states in the learnt set are unsafe then we can conclude that the system satisfies the safety property. On the other hand, if one of the states in the learnt set is unsafe, then we need a mechanism to check whether the learning algorithm over-generalized, i.e., added states that are not reachable. One way to accomplish this is by producing a candidate execution to the unsafe state, and checking if that execution is indeed a valid execution of the system. Therefore, instead of learning the set of reachable states directly, we learn a language which allows us to identify both the reachable states and witnesses to these in terms of transitions executed by the system.

Let us now consider the language which can allow us to find both reachable states and their witnesses. The first choice that comes to mind is the language of the traces, $L(F)$. Since each trace uniquely determines the final state in the trace, $L(F)$ has the information about the states that can be reached. While it is easy to compute the state s such that $s_0 \xrightarrow{\sigma} s$ for a *single* trace σ, it is not clear how to obtain the set of states reached, given a *set of traces*. In fact, even if $L(F)$ is regular, there is no known algorithm to compute the corresponding set of reachable states of the labelled transition system.[2] The main difficulty is that determining if a receive action can be executed depends non-trivially on the sequence of actions executed before the receive. We overcome this difficulty by annotating the traces in a way that makes it possible to compute the set of reachable states.

---

[2] This can sometimes be computed for simple loops using meta-transitions.

Trace Annotation for FIFO: Consider a set $\overline{\Theta}$ of *co-names* defined as follows:

$$\overline{\Theta} = \{\overline{\theta} \mid \theta \in \Theta \text{ and } \delta(\theta) \neq \tau\}$$

In other words, for every send or receive action in our FIFO automaton, we introduce a new transition name with a "bar". We say $s \xrightarrow{\overline{\theta}} s'$ if $s \xrightarrow{\theta} s'$; executions over sequences in $(\Theta \cup \overline{\Theta})^*$ are defined naturally. The intuition of putting the annotation of a "bar" on some transitions of a trace is to indicate that the message sent or received as a result of this transition does not play a role in the channel contents of the final state. In other words, a "barred" transition $\overline{\theta}$ in an annotated trace of the system denotes either a message sent that will later be received, or the receipt of a message that was sent earlier in the trace. Thus, annotated traces of the automaton will be obtained by marking send-receive pairs in a trace exhibited by the machine. Let $\mathcal{A}$ be the function that correctly annotates an execution to produce a string over $\Sigma = \Theta \cup \overline{\Theta}$. Observe, that each execution is annotated uniquely, or to put it formally, $\mathcal{A}$ is an injective function. The *annotated trace language* of the automaton F is $AL(F) = \{\mathcal{A}(t) \mid t \in L(F)\}$ and consists of all strings in $(\Theta \cup \overline{\Theta})^*$ that denote correctly annotated traces of F. For example, consider the FIFO automaton shown in Figure 2(a). Some of the words in $AL(F)$ are: θ_1, $\theta_1\theta_1$, $\theta_1\theta_1\theta_1$, $\overline{\theta_1\theta_2}$, $\overline{\theta_1\theta_2}\theta_1$.

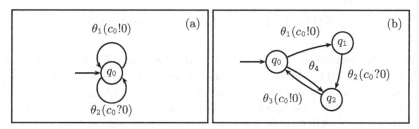

Fig. 2. Example FIFO automata. θ_4 does not change channel contents

Finding Reachable States from Annotated Traces: Since our objective is to identify the reachable region, we need a way to find the reachable states corresponding to a set of annotated traces. For a channel c, consider a function $h_c : (\Theta \cup \overline{\Theta}) \to M^*$ defined as follows:

$$h_c(t) = \begin{cases} m & \text{if } t \in \Theta \text{ and } \delta(t) = c!m \\ \epsilon & \text{otherwise} \end{cases}$$

Let h_c also denote the unique homomorphism from $(\Theta \cup \overline{\Theta})^*$ to M^* that extends the above function. Given an annotated trace ρ, the contents of channel c in the final state are clearly given by $h_c(\rho)$.

FIFO Automata with One Channel: Let $F = (Q, q_0, \{c_0\}, M, \Theta, \delta)$ be a single channel FIFO automaton, with c_0 being the only channel. As usual $s_0 = (q_0, \epsilon)$ will denote the starting state of F. Given a set of annotated traces L, let $L_q \subseteq L$

be the set of annotated traces in L whose last transition ends in control state q. Now the set of states reached (by traces in L) is given by

$$\mathcal{R}(L) = \{(q, m) \mid q \in Q \text{ and } m \in h_{c_0}(L_q)\}$$

For a regular set L, then it can be seen that L_q is regular, and $\mathcal{R}(L)$ can be computed by a simple homomorphism, and so $\mathcal{R}(L)$ is regular.

Multi-channel FIFO Automata: Consider a FIFO automaton $F = (Q, q_0, C, M, \Theta, \delta)$ communicating over channels $C = \{c_0, c_1, \ldots c_k\}$. Now the set of states reached (by traces in L) is given by

$$\mathcal{R}_m(L) = \{(q, (h_{c_0}(\sigma), h_{c_1}(\sigma), \ldots, h_{c_k}(\sigma))) \mid$$
$$q \in Q \text{ and } \sigma \in L_q\}$$

As we will see shortly, we need a test for inclusion for the reachable states corresponding to a set of annotated traces. In this respect, we cannot hope to work with $\mathcal{R}_m(L)$, since as soon as have even two channels, given a regular L, $\mathcal{R}_m(L)$ can be seen to be a rational relation for which inclusion is undecidable [6]. However, if we compute the contents of each channel independently of others, we can compute an upper approximation of $\mathcal{R}_m(L)$ as follows:

$$\mathcal{R}(L) = \bigcup_{q \in Q} \{q\} \times h_{c_0}(L_q) \times h_{c_1}(L_q) \cdots h_{c_k}(L_q)$$

It can be easily seen that $\mathcal{R}(L)$ is a regular language if L is regular. In general, $\mathcal{R}_m(L) \subseteq \mathcal{R}(L)$, however for many FIFO systems encountered in practice (most network protocols like Alternating Bit Protocol, Sliding Window Protocol), this gives the exact reachable region when applied to $AL(F)$, *i.e.* $\mathcal{R}_m(AL(F)) = \mathcal{R}(AL(F))$. We show later that this is sufficient for the applicability of our learning approach.

Recovering a Witness from an Unsafe State: If the reachable states corresponding to a learned set of annotated traces have a nonempty intersection with the set of "unsafe" states (which violate the safety property), we would like to extract a sequence of transitions of the system which witnesses the reachability of some unsafe state. The motivation is that such a sequence can then be used as a counterexample demonstrating the violation of the safety property or a negative example for the learning algorithm.

We assume that for each control state q, we are given the unsafe channel contents as a product of regular languages $U(q, c_0), U(q, c_1), \ldots, U(q, c_n)$ corresponding to channels $0 \ldots n$, *i.e.*, the unsafe states are given by $S_u = \bigcup_{q \in Q} \{(q, u_0, u_1, \ldots, u_n) \mid u_i \in U(q, c_i)\}$. Given a regular set of annotated traces, L, recall that $L_q \subseteq L$ represents the set of annotated traces in L whose last transition ends in control state q. For each control state q, for each channel i, we can find the intersection of $h_{c_i}(L_q)$ and $U(q, c_i)$ and calculate the traces $L_{q_i} \in L_q$ such that $h_{c_i}(L_{q_i}) = h_{c_i}(L_q) \cap U(q, c_i)$. Intuitively, this gives us annotated traces which lead to a potential unsafe configuration for channel c_i. Now, if the intersection $\bigcap_{i \in 0 \ldots n} L_{q_i}$ is non empty, an annotated trace t in this intersection leads to an unsafe configuration for each channel and hence an unsafe state in S_u. Let us call $\mathcal{W}$ the function which outputs t given L and S_u.

From Annotated Trace to System Execution: In order to convert $\mathcal{W}(L) \in \Sigma^*$ into a sequence of transitions, we need a way to extract the presumed system execution from a given annotated trace. Essentially, we want a substitution $RevA : \Sigma \mapsto \Theta^*$ which "reverses" the annotation $\mathcal{A}$. This can be done simply by removing the "bars" on the annotated trace. Formally, we can define $RevA(\overline{\theta}) = RevA(\theta) = \theta$ for all $\theta \in \Theta$. Extending $RevA$ to strings in the usual way, it can be seen that that $RevA(\mathcal{A}(t)) = t$.

---

algorithm *learnToVerify*
Input:
  F : model of system,
  S_u : regular set of "unsafe states"
Output: Property valid OR
  path to an unsafe state
begin
  $S_{2b}^- = \emptyset$
  $(S^+, S_1^-, S_{2a}^-) = GetTraces()$
  while(true)do
    $L = modifiedRPNI(S^+, S_1^-, S_{2a}^- \cup S_{2b}^-)$
    if $\mathcal{R}(L) \cap S_u \neq \emptyset$
      $l_c = \mathcal{W}(L, S_u)$
      if $RevA(l_c)$ valid execution of F
        Output $RevA(l_c)$; stop
      else
        $S_{2b}^- = S_{2b}^- \cup l_c$
    else
      if $\mathcal{R}(L)$ is a fixpoint
        Output "Property holds"; stop
      else
        $T_{new} = GetTraces()$
        add T_{new} to (S^+, S_1^-, S_{2a}^-)
end

algorithm *modifiedRPNI*
Input: $S^+ \in \Sigma^*$, $S_1^- \in \Theta^*$, $S_2^- \in \Sigma^*$
Output: a regular language L
begin
  $D \leftarrow PTA(S^+)$
  for $i = 2$ to $|D|$ do
    for $j = 1$ to $i - 1$ do
      if q_i, q_j not merged with smaller state then
        $D' \leftarrow merge(D, q_i, q_j)$
        $D' \leftarrow determinize(D', q_j)$
        $D'' \leftarrow RevA(D')$; all states in D'' made final
        if $compatible(D'', S_1^-)$ && $compatible(D', S_2^-)$
          D = D';exit j-loop
  return language defined by D
end

algorithm *determinize*
Input: A, x; **Output:** A
begin
  for any $x \xrightarrow{\theta} x_1, x \xrightarrow{\theta} x_2$ and $x_1 \neq x_2$
    $A \leftarrow merge(A, x_1, x_2)$
    $A \leftarrow determinize(A, $ smaller of $x_1, x_2)$
  return A
end

Fig. 3. Learning to verify algorithm

Verification Algorithm. We are now ready to formally describe the *learning to verify* procedure as shown in Figure 3. We first collect positive and negative examples of labels in Σ^* as follows. A set T of sequences of transitions that can be exhibited by the system is obtained by invoking a function *GetTraces*. Positive examples, S^+ are simply the correct "annotations" which put bars on the send-receive pairs in the strings in T, i.e. $S^+ = \{\mathcal{A}(t) \mid t \in T\}$. There are three sets of negative examples. The first set $S_1^- = \{t\theta_d \mid t \in T$ and θ_d is a disabled transition$\}$ consists of sequences of transitions extended by a disabled transition (a transition that cannot be taken at a certain state). The second set $S_{2a}^- = \{\sigma \in \Sigma^* \mid \exists t \in T$ such that $RevA(\sigma) = t$ and $\sigma \neq \mathcal{A}(t)\}$ corresponds to "incorrect" annotations. Notice that since $\mathcal{A}$ is injective, all annotations of a trace $t \in T$ other than $\mathcal{A}(t)$ cannot be exhibited by the system.

The third set, S_{2b}^-, is a collection of spurious counterexamples; initially this is empty.

The positive and negative examples are given to a learning algorithm based on RPNI. Similar to RPNI, this algorithm first constructs a *prefix tree automata* (PTA) from S^+. The PTA is simply a collection of the strings in S^+ as paths with common prefixes merged together. Each state in the PTA is associated with the string generated by following the path to that state from the initial state. The states are assigned numbers according to the standard ordering[3] imposed by the associated strings. The learning algorithm attempts to generalize from the positive examples by merging states in the PTA in a *specific order*: for i going from 1 to the largest state in the PTA, it attempts to merge q_i with all states less than q_i in ascending order. A merge may cause non-determinism which is removed by further merges using the operation *determinize* which results in a finite automaton D'. Another finite automaton D'' is obtained from D' by applying the substitution $RevA$ and making all states final. If D'' is compatible with the negative set S_1^- (all strings in S_1^- are rejected by D'') and D' is compatible with the negative set $S_2^- = S_{2a}^- \cup S_{2b}^-$, the merge is accepted. The learning algorithm is essentially the same as the traditional RPNI algorithm except for the the use of the additional kind of negative examples corresponding to S_1^-. For a detailed explanation of the RPNI algorithm itself, the reader is referred to [2, 3].

Let the output of the modified RPNI algorithm be the regular language L. If $\mathcal{R}(L)$ intersects with the unsafe states S_u, then a counterexample l_c ($= \mathcal{W}(AL(F), S_u)$) is obtained. By attempting to simulate the counterexample on the system, we can check if $RevA(l)$ is executable. If yes, then we have found a real counterexample and are done, otherwise l_c is added to S_{2b}^-. If $\mathcal{R}(L)$ does not intersect with the unsafe states S_u, then it is tested for being a fixpoint under the reachability relation by checking the following condition:

$$\{s_0\} \cup \{s \mid \exists s' \in \mathcal{R}(L). \ s' \to s\} = \mathcal{R}(L)$$

If it is a fixpoint, we declare that the safety property holds. Otherwise, we get more traces by invoking the function $GetTraces$ (successive calls to this function generate new traces) and continue the learning procedure.

4   Correctness of the Verification Procedure

The soundness of the procedure is straightforward. For a learned set of traces L, if $\mathcal{R}(L)$ has an empty intersection with the set of unsafe states, S_u, and is a fixpoint under the transition relation, the safety property holds. Any counterexample is finite and gives a supposed execution of the system leading to an unsafe state which can then be automatically checked for validity by simulation of the system.

We can also show completeness (*i.e.* the procedure terminates with the correct answer) under the condition that $AL(F)$ is regular. Then, given a "fair" method of generating the system traces, in the limit, the learning paradigm will either

---

[3] For $\Sigma = \{a, b\}$, the ordering is $\epsilon, a, b, aa, ab, ba, bb, aaa, \ldots$

prove that the system satisfies the property or find a valid counterexample. By a fair method, we mean one which will eventually generate any given finite trace. There can be many different ways of generating fair traces, one of the simplest being a breadth first traversal of all traces.

Lemma 1. *If $AL(F)$ is regular, then using any fair strategy for generating traces, in the limit, given a sufficiently large sample, the learning procedure outputs a DFA which generates $AL(F)$.*

Theorem 1. *If $AL(F)$ is regular and $\mathcal{R}(AL(F))$ is the set of all reachable states, then the learning to verify procedure will eventually either prove that the system satisfies the property or find a valid counterexample.*

The proofs of the lemma and the theorem are available in the full version of this paper [4]. The running time of the algorithm is dependent on the strategy for getting the traces. For a simple breadth-first strategy, in the worst case, the algorithm might need to explore all traces up to a depth D. Here, D is the length of the longest path starting from the initial state in the minimal DFA representing $AL(F)$ (assuming $AL(F)$ is regular). Thus, the running time can be exponential in the size of the DFA for $AL(F)$. However, as discussed in Section 6, we can use some heuristics to prune down the number of traces needed. In practice, for a number of FIFO systems, the learning procedure is able to converge to the correct answer in a fairly small time period which is comparable to other tools.

Note that the conditions required by Theorem 1 are merely sufficient for termination of the learning procedure and the verification procedure can be successfully used for many systems even if $AL(F)$ is not regular. In fact, an important observation is that for a number of systems with nonregular $AL(F)$, there exists a regular subset $L' \subseteq AL(F)$ such that the traces in L' "cover" all the reachable states, *i.e.* $\mathcal{R}(L') = \mathcal{R}(AL(F))$. In other words, every reachable state in F is witnessed by some trace in L'. For example, the set of annotated traces corresponding to the automaton in Figure 2(a) is not regular but the regular language $L' = \theta_1^*$ covers all the reachable states. Note that $\mathcal{R}(L')$ is not an approximation; we are simply content with finding any regular set of annotated traces that can cover the reachable states. In Section 6, we analyze FIFO systems which have a regular $AL(F)$ as well as systems for which $AL(F)$ is not regular but a "covering" $L' \subseteq AL(F)$ is regular. In all cases, the algorithm terminates with the correct reachable set.

5   Generalization to Other Infinite State Systems

The verification procedure described for FIFO automata can be easily generalized to other infinite state systems. The challenge is to identify the alphabet Σ which provides the "annotation" and the functions $\mathcal{A}$, $RevA$, $\mathcal{R}$ and $\mathcal{W}$ which are used by the verification procedure. Notice that the procedure does not assume anything else about FIFO automata other than the above functions. The key properties of Σ needed to make the procedure work are summarized below.

- There exists an *injective* function $\mathcal{A} : L(F) \mapsto \Sigma^*$ which maps a system execution to a sequence of labels in Σ. Recall that $L(F)$ is the language of traces that can be executed by the system F. Let $AL(F) \in \Sigma^*$ be the language $\{\mathcal{A}(t) \mid t \in L(F)\}$.
- There exists a substitution $RevA : \Sigma \mapsto \Theta^*$ which "reverses" the operation $\mathcal{A}$. Extending $RevA$ to strings in the usual way, it must be true that $RevA(\mathcal{A}(t)) = t$. In FIFOs, $RevA$ simply removes the "bars".
- There exists a (computable) function $\mathcal{R}$ such that for a set $L \in \Sigma^*$, $\mathcal{R}(L)$ gives a set of states (supposedly) reached during the execution of the traces in L. It is required that $\mathcal{R}(AL(F))$ must be the exact reachable region of F.
- There exists a (computable) function $\mathcal{W}$ such that for $L \in \Sigma^*$, and a set of "unsafe" states S_u, if $\mathcal{R}(L) \cap S_u \neq \emptyset$ then $\mathcal{W}(L, S_u)$ gives a finite trace $l_c \in L$ which witnesses the reachability of some state in S_u.

It can be easily seen that the proof of correctness of the learning algorithm in Section 4 generalizes to other systems if Σ satisfies the above properties. Thus, we can think of this approach as a "paradigm" for the verification of safety properties of infinite systems.

6   Implementation

We have implemented the verification framework for FIFO automata as part of the LEVER (LEarning to VERify) tool suite available from [10]. The tool is written in Java and implements the *learning to verify* procedure shown in Figure 3. For general automata related decision procedures, we use the Java package `dk.brics.automata` available from [11]. Currently, the incremental learning approach is not implemented in LEVER, so if an answer to the verification problem is not solved in a particular run, we restart the procedure with more positive samples.

For generating the annotated traces that are used for the positive and negative examples, we use the following strategy. Starting from the initial state, we explore the system states (cross product of the control state and channel contents) in a breadth-first manner. To limit the number of traces generated, we do not distinguish between FIFO states if they have the same control state and same channel contents up to a position d from the start of the channel. We start with $d = 1$ and keep increasing d if more traces are needed. We have seen that this heuristic works quite well in practice to generate sufficient traces for the learning procedure.

We have used LEVER to analyze some canonical FIFO automata verification problems described below.

[**Producer Consumer**] A simple producer consumer problem with one FIFO channel. The producer can either be in an "idle" or in a "send" state in which it transmits either 0 or 1 to the FIFO channel.

[**Data with Parity**] A simple data communication protocol in which the sender sends data and a parity bit for the number of 1's sent. The receiver uses the parity bit as a simple check for data integrity.

[**Resource Arbitrator**] In this example, two senders wish to broadcast over a shared channel and use a resource manager to arbitrate which one is allowed to use it at any time.

[**Alternating Bit Protocol (ABP)**] This consists of a sender and receiver communicating over a data and an acknowledgment channel. We consider a non-lossy version of ABP.

[**Sliding Window Protocol**] This is similar to ABP except that the sender can keep multiple data messages in flight. We use a window size of 2 and maximum sequence number also of 2.

"Producer Consumer", "Alternating bit protocol" and "Sliding window protocol" are fairly well-known in the FIFO research community, see for example [12]. For the other two systems, a detailed description is available in the full version of this paper [4].

Table 1 shows the results obtained. Here "Samples" is the number of positive samples generated, T is the running time on a 1594 MHz notebook computer with 512 MB of RAM using Java virtual machine version 1.4.1 from Sun Microsystems. In all cases, LEVER terminates with the correct reachable region. We also report the time taken (T_{rmc}) by the regular model checking tool [13] on the same examples. Although a complete comparative analysis with all available tools remains to be done, it can be seen the running time of LEVER is comparable to the regular model checking tool and in fact better for all examples except "Sliding window protocol".[4]

Table 1. Samples and running time

	Samples	T	T_{rmc}
Producer Consumer	42	0.4s	3.3s
Data with parity	42	0.5s	12.7s
Resource arbitrator	146	0.7s	33.2
Alternating Bit	1122	4.1s	24.7
Sliding Window	2535	81.2s	78.4

LEVER is still in the prototype stage and we see the current version as a proof of concept of the *learning to verify* approach. We plan to introduce various optimizations and features which should enable LEVER to handle larger and more complex examples.

---

[4] The encoding of sliding window protocol in the regular model checking tool is slightly different; instead of limiting the window size, the size of the queue is bounded.

7   Related Work

Verification of Infinite State Systems: For automatic verification of infinite state FIFO systems, the state space has to be represented by symbolic means. Some common representations are: regular sets [1, 14], Queue Decision Diagrams [15], semi-linear regular expressions [9] and constrained QDDs [16]. Since an iterative approach of computing the fixpoint for reachability does not terminate for most cases, various mechanisms are used for finding the reachable set. We now discuss some of these techniques and show their relation to our learning approach.

In the approach using *meta-transitions* and *acceleration* [15, 16, 9], a sequence of transitions, referred to as a *meta-transition*, is selected and the effect of its infinite iteration calculated. This is complementary to our learning approach, since meta-transitions can be also be incorporated into our learning algorithm. Another popular approach for FIFO, parametric, integer and stack systems is *regular model checking* [1, 14]. A regular set is used to represent the states and a transducer is used to represent the transition relation. The problem is reduced to finding a finite transducer representing the infinite composition of this relation. However, there are some examples in which even if such a finite transducer exists, the procedure may not be able to converge to it. One such example of a FIFO automaton is shown in Figure 2(b) in Section 3. We used the regular model checking tool from [13] to analyze this example, but the tool failed to terminate even after two hours. On the other hand, our learning-based tool is able to automatically find the reachable set in about fifty milliseconds. It is certainly possible that in other examples, transducer construction may be able to find the reachable region faster. Thus, our approach can be seen as complementary and seen to extend the range of systems that can be automatically analyzed.

An approach for computing the reachable region that is closely related to ours is *widening*. In this approach, the transition relation is applied to the initial configuration some number of times and then by comparing the sets thus obtained, the limit of the iteration is guessed. A simple widening principle in the context of regular model checking is given in [1] which is extended in [17] for parametric systems. Bultan [18] uses a widening technique for Presburger formulas to enable faster convergence for fixpoint. Bartzis *et al.* [19] present a widening technique for arithmetic automata. At a very high level, both *widening* and our approach use similar ideas. In both methods, based on certain sample points obtained using the transitions, a guess is made for the fixpoint being searched for. One important difference between widening and our approach is that widening (except for certain special contexts where it can be shown to be exact) is a mechanism to prove the correctness of a system and cannot be used to prove a system to be incorrect. On the other hand, the approach presented here allows one to both prove a system to be correct and to detect bugs.

Use of Machine Learning for Verification: The application of techniques from *machine learning* for verification is relatively new. Peled *et al.* [20] give a method called "Black Box Checking" which is extended by Groce *et al.* [21] as *Adaptive*

Model Checking. Briefly, in this method, one starts with a possibly inaccurate model and incrementally updates it using Angluin's [7] query based learning of regular sets. Cobleigh *et al.* [22] also use a variant of Angluin's algorithm to learn the assumptions about the environment to aid compositional verification. Boigelot *et al.* [23] present a technique for constructing a finite state machine that simulates all observable operations of a given reactive program. Ammons *et al.* [24] use machine learning to discover formal specifications of the protocols that a client of an application program interface must observe. Edelkamp *et al.* [25] consider the problem of finding "bad" states in a model as a directed search problem and use AI heuristic search methods to attempt to find these states. Ernst *et al.* [26] have developed a system called *Daikon* which attempts to discover likely invariants in a program by analyzing the values taken by its variables while the program is exercised in a test suite.

Our approach in using the machine learning techniques for verification is unique in that we are not trying to learn an unknown system model but rather the behavior of a system which is already fully described. This is closest in spirit to Ernst *et al.* [26], although the domain of application and objective are completely different. Another difference with other learning methods is that we do not use Angluin's algorithm. Angluin's algorithm needs a teacher which can answer equivalence queries; answering such queries is typically hard to achieve. Instead, we use an algorithm called RPNI [2, 3] which simply needs positive and negative samples of the concept to be learned.

8   Conclusion and Future Work

We have presented a novel approach based on machine learning to verify finite state machines communicating over unbounded FIFO channels. A prototype implementation, called LEVER, has been developed and the approach has been shown to be feasible in analyzing practical networks protocols like alternating bit and sliding window. We have also shown how this approach can be generalized to analyze infinite state systems other than FIFO automata.

The learning to verify procedure can be applied to other systems such as: automata with unbounded integers; real-time and hybrid systems; parameterized systems; counter automata; and push-down automata with multiple stacks. The approach could be extended to handle not only safety properties but also liveness and more general temporal properties. Other avenues for future work include research for getting better execution traces and practical optimizations and engineering for the LEVER tool.

References

1. A. Bouajjani, B. Jonsson, M. Nilsson, and T. Touili, "Regular model checking," in *Proceedings of the 12th International Conference on Computer-Aided Verification (CAV'00)*, E. A. Emerson and A. P. Sistla, Eds. 2000, vol. 1855 of *LNCS*, pp. 403–418, Springer.

2. J. Oncina and P. Garcia, "Inferring regular languages in polynomial update time," in *Pattern Recognition and Image Analysis*, vol. 1 of *Series in Machine Perception and Artificial Intelligence*, pp. 49–61. World Scientific, Singapore, 1992.

3. P. Dupont, "Incremental regular inference.," in *Proceedings of the 3rd International Colloquium on Grammatical Inference (ICGI-96): Learning Syntax from Sentences*, Berlin, September 1996, vol. 1147 of *LNAI*, pp. 222–237, Springer.

4. Abhay Vardhan, Koushik Sen, Mahesh Viswanathan, and Gul Agha, "Learning to verify safety properties,"   Tech. Rep. UIUCDCS-R-2004-2445, `http://osl.cs.uiuc.edu/docs/sub2004vardhan/cfsmLearn.pdf`, University of Illinois, 2004.

5. John E. Hopcroft, Rajeev Motwani, Rotwani, and Jeffrey D. Ullman, *Introduction to Automata Theory, Languages and Computability*, Addison-Wesley Longman Publishing Co. Inc., 2000.

6. J. Berstel, *Transductions and Context-Free-Languages*, B.G. Teubner, Stuttgart, 1979.

7. D. Angluin, "Learning regular sets from queries and counterexamples," *Inform. Comput.*, vol. 75, no. 2, pp. 87–106, Nov. 1987.

8. E. M. Gold, "Language indentification in the limit," *Inform. Control*, vol. 10, pp. 447–474, 1967.

9. A. Finkel, S. Purushothaman Iyer, and G. Sutre, "Well-abstracted transition systems: Application to FIFO automata," *Information and Computation*, vol. 181, no. 1, pp. 1–31, 2003.

10. LEVER, "Learning to verify tool," `http://osl.cs.uiuc.edu/~vardhan/lever.html`, 2004.

11. Anders Møller, "`http://www.brics.dk/~amoeller/automaton/`," 2004.

12. A. S. Tanenbaum, *Computer Networks, 2nd Ed.*, Prentice-Hall, Englewood Cliffs, NJ, 1989.

13. Marcus Nilsson, "`http://www.regulalrmodelchecking.com`," 2004.

14. P. A. Abdulla, B. Jonsson, M. Nilsson, and J. d'Orso, "Algorithmic improvements in regular model checking," in *Computer-Aided Verification (CAV'03)*. 2003, vol. 2725 of *LNCS*, pp. 236–248, Springer.

15. B. Boigelot, *Symbolic Methods for Exploring Infinite State Spaces*, Ph.D. thesis, Collection des Publications de la Faculté des Sciences Appliquées de l'Université de Liége, 1999.

16. A. Bouajjani and P. Habermehl, "Symbolic reachability analysis of FIFO-channel systems with nonregular sets of configurations," *Theoretical Computer Science*, vol. 221, no. 1–2, pp. 211–250, June 1999.

17. T. Touili, "Regular model checking using widening techniques," in *ENTCS*. 2001, vol. 50, Elsevier.

18. T. Bultan, *Automated symbolic analysis of reactive systems*, Ph.D. thesis, Dept. of Computer Science, University of Maryland, College Park, Md., 1998.

19. C. Bartzis and T. Bultan, "Widening arithmetic automata," in *Computer Aided Verification'04 (to appear)*, 2004.

20. D. Peled, M. Y. Vardi, and M. Yannakakis,   "Black box checking,"   in *FORTE/PSTV, Beijing, China*, 1999.

21. A. Groce, D. Peled, and M. Yannakakis, "Adaptive model checking," in *Tools and Algorithms for the Construction and Analysis of Systems (TACAS'02)*, 2002, vol. 2280 of *LNCS*, pp. 357–371.

22. J. M. Cobleigh, D. Giannakopoulou, and C. S. Pasareanu, "Learning assumptions for compositional verification," in *Proceedings of the 9th International Conference on Tools and Algorithms for the Construction and Analysis of Systems (TACAS)*, 2003, pp. 331–346.

23. B. Boigelot and P. Godefroid, "Automatic synthesis of specifications from the dynamic observation of reactive programs," in *Tools and Algorithms for the Construction and Analysis of Systems*, E. Brinksma, Ed., Enschede, The Netherlands, 1997, pp. 321–334, Springer Verlag, LNCS 1217.

24. Glenn Ammons, Rastislav Bodík, and James R. Larus, "Mining specifications," *ACM SIGPLAN Notices*, vol. 37, no. 1, pp. 4–16, Jan. 2002.

25. S. Edelkamp, A. Lafuente, and S. Leue, "Protocol verification with heuristic search," in *AAAI Symposium on Model-based Validation of Intelligence*, 2001.

26. M. D. Ernst, J. Cockrell, W. G. Griswold, and D. Notkin, "Dynamically discovering likely program invariants to support program evolution," in *International Conference on Software Engineering (ICSE'99)*, 1999, pp. 213–224.

Automatic Extraction of Object-Oriented Observer Abstractions from Unit-Test Executions

Tao Xie and David Notkin

Department of Computer Science & Engineering,
University of Washington,
Seattle, WA 98195, USA
{taoxie,notkin}@cs.washington.edu

Abstract. Unit testing has become a common step in software development. Although manually created unit tests are valuable, they are often insufficient; therefore, programmers can use an automatic unit-test-generation tool to produce a large number of additional tests for a class. However, without a priori specifications, programmers cannot practically inspect the execution of each automatically generated test. In this paper, we develop the observer abstraction approach for automatically extracting object-state-transition information of a class from unit-test executions, without requiring a priori specifications. Given a class and a set of its initial tests generated by a third-party tool, we generate new tests to augment the initial tests and produce the abstract state of an object based on the return values of a set of observers (public methods with non-void returns) invoked on the object. From the executions of both the new and initial tests, we automatically extract observer abstractions, each of which is an object state machine (OSM): a state in the OSM represents an abstract state and a transition in the OSM represents method calls. We have implemented the Obstra tool for the approach and have applied the approach on complex data structures; our experiences suggest that this approach provides useful object-state-transition information for programmers to inspect unit-test executions effectively.

1 Introduction

Automatic test-generation tools are powerful; given a class, these tools can generate a large number of tests, including some valuable corner cases or special inputs that programmers often forget to include in their manual tests. When programmers write specifications, some specification-based test generation tools [4, 10, 18] automatically generate tests and check execution correctness against the written specifications. Without a prior specifications, some automatic test-generation tools [11] perform structural testing by generating tests to increase structural coverage. Some other tools [5] perform random testing by generating random inputs. Without a prior specifications, programmers rely on uncaught exceptions or inspect the executions of generated tests for determining whether the program behaves as expected. However, relying on only uncaught exceptions for catching bugs is limited and inspecting the executions of a large number of generated tests is impractical.

J. Davies et al. (Eds.): ICFEM 2004, LNCS 3308, pp. 290–305, 2004.

To help programmers to inspect unit-test executions effectively, we develop the *observer abstraction* approach, a novel black-box approach for summarizing and presenting object-state-transition information from unit-test executions. The approach is automated and does not require a priori specifications. Instead of inspecting the execution of each single test, programmers can inspect the summarized object-state-transition information for various purposes. For example, programmers can inspect the information to determine whether the class under test exhibits expected behavior. Programmers can also inspect the information to investigate causes of the failures exhibited by uncaught exceptions. Programmers can inspect the information for achieving better understanding of the class under test or even its tests.

A *concrete object state* of an object is characterized by the values of all the fields reachable from the object. An *observer* is a public method with a non-void return.[1] The observer abstraction approach abstracts a concrete object state exercised by a test suite based on the return values of a set of observers that are invoked on the concrete object state. An *observer abstraction* is an object state machine (OSM): a state in the OSM represents an abstract state and a transition in the OSM represents method calls. We have implemented a tool, called Obstra, for the observer abstraction approach. Given a Java class and its initial unit test, Obstra identifies concrete object states exercised by the tests and generates new tests to augment these initial tests. Based on the return values of a set of observers, Obstra maps each concrete object state to an abstract state and constructs an OSM.

This paper makes the following main contributions:

- We propose a new program abstraction, called observer abstraction.
- We present and implement an automatic approach for dynamically extracting observer abstractions from unit-test executions.
- We apply the approach on complex data structures and their automatically generated tests; our experiences show that extracted observer abstractions provide useful object-state-transition information for programmers to inspect.

2 Observer Abstraction Approach

We first discuss two techniques (developed in our previous work [22, 23]) that enable the dynamic extraction of observer abstractions. We next describe object state machines, being the representations of observer abstractions. We then define observer abstractions and illustrate dynamic extraction of them. We finally describe the implementation and present an example of dynamically extracted observer abstractions.

2.1 Concrete-State Representation and Test Augmentation

In previous work, we have developed the Rostra framework and five automatic techniques to represent and detect equivalent object states [23]. This work focuses on using one of the

---

[1] We follow the definition by Henkel and Diwan [12]. The definition differs from the more common definition that limits an observer to methods that do not change any state. We have found that state-modifying observers also provide value in our technique and state modification does not harm our technique.

techniques for state representation: the WholeState technique. The technique represents a *concrete object state* of an object as a sequence of the values of the fields reachable from the object. We use a linearization algorithm [23] to avoid putting those field values with reference addresses in the sequence[2] but still keep the referencing relationship among fields. A set of *nonequivalent concrete object states* contain those concrete object states any two of which do not have the same state representation.

A unit test suite consists of a set of unit tests. Each execution of a unit test creates several objects and invokes methods on these objects. Behavior of a method invocation depends on the state of the receiver object and method arguments at the beginning of the invocation. A *method call* is characterized by the actual class of the receiver object, the method name, the method signature, and the method-argument values. When argument values are not primitive values, we represent them using their state representations. We determine whether two method calls are equivalent by checking the equivalence of their corresponding characteristic entities, including the receiver-object class, method name, method signature, and method-argument values. A set of *nonequivalent method calls* contain those method calls any two of which are not equivalent.

After we execute an initial test suite, the concrete-state representation technique identifies all nonequivalent object states and nonequivalent method calls that were exercised by the test suite. The test augmentation technique generates new tests to exercise each possible combination of nonequivalent object states and nonequivalent non-constructor method calls [22]. We augment an initial test suite because the test suite might not invoke each observer on all nonequivalent object states; invoking observers on a concrete object state is necessary for us to know the abstract state enclosing the concrete object state. The augmented test suite guarantees that each nonequivalent object state is exercised by each nonequivalent non-constructor method call at least once. In addition, the observer abstractions extracted from the augmented test suite can better help programmers to inspect object-state-transition behavior. The complexity of the test augmentation algorithm is $O(|CS| \times |MC|)$, where CS is the set of the nonequivalent concrete states exercised by an initial test suite T for the class under test and MC is the set of the nonequivalent method calls exercised by T.

2.2   Object State Machine

We define an object state machine for a class:[3]

Definition 1. *An* object state machine *(OSM) M of a class c is a sextuple* $M = (I, O, S, \delta, \lambda, INIT)$ *where I, O, and S are nonempty sets of method calls in c's interface, returns of these method calls, and states of c's objects, respectively. $INIT \in S$ is the initial state that the machine is in before calling any constructor method of c. $\delta : S \times I \rightarrow P(S)$ is the state transition function and $\lambda : S \times I \rightarrow P(O)$ is the output function where $P(S)$ and $P(O)$ are the power sets of S and O, respectively. When the machine is in a current*

---

[2] Running the same test twice might produce different reference addresses for those fields of non-primitive types.

[3] The definition is adapted from the definition of finite state machine [15]; however, an object state machine is not necessarily finite.

state s and receives a method call i from I, it moves to one of the next states specified by $\delta(s, i)$ and produces one of the method returns given by $\lambda(s, i)$.

An OSM can be deterministic or nondeterministic.

2.3   Observer Abstractions

The object states in an OSM can be concrete or abstract. An *abstract state* of an object is defined by an *abstraction function* [16]; the abstraction function maps each concrete state to an abstract state. The observer abstraction approach constructs abstraction functions to map concrete states to abstract states in an OSM.

We first define an observer following previous work on specifying algebraic specifications for a class [12]:

Definition 2. *An* observer *of a class c is a method ob in c's interface such that the return type of ob is not void.*

Given a class c and a set of observers $OB = \{ob_1, ob_2, ..., ob_n\}$ of c, the observer abstraction approach constructs an abstraction of c with respect to OB. In particular, a concrete state cs is mapped to an abstract state as defined by n values $OBR = \{obr_1, obr_2, ..., obr_n\}$, where each value obr_i represents the return value of method call ob_i invoked on cs.

Definition 3. *Given a class c and a set of observers $OB = \{ob_1, ob_2, ..., ob_n\}$ of c, an* observer abstraction *with respect to OB is an OSM M of c such that the states in M are abstract states defined by OB.*

2.4   Dynamic Extraction of Observer Abstractions

We dynamically extract observer abstractions of a class from unit-test executions. The number of the concrete states exercised by an augmented test suite is finite and the execution of the test suite is assumed to terminate; therefore, the dynamically extracted observer abstractions are also finite.

In a dynamically extracted observer abstraction M, we add additional statistical information: the transition count and the emission count. The *transition count* for a nonequivalent method call mc transiting from a state s to a state s' is the number of nonequivalent concrete object states in s that transit to s' after mc is invoked. The *emission count* for s and mc is the number of nonequivalent concrete object states in s where mc is invoked.

Given an initial test suite T for a class c, we first identify the nonequivalent concrete states CS and method calls MC exercised by T. We then augment T with new tests to exercise CS with MC exhaustively, producing an augmented test suite T'. We have described these steps in Section 2.1. T' exercises each nonequivalent concrete state in CS with each method call in MC; therefore, each nonequivalent observer call in MC is guaranteed to be invoked on each nonequivalent concrete state in CS at least once. We then collect the return values of observer calls in MC for each nonequivalent concrete state in CS. We use this test-generation mechanism to collect return values of observers, instead of inserting observer method calls before and after any call site to c in T, because the latter does not work for state-modifying observers, which change the functional behavior of T.

Given an augmented test suite T' and a set of observers $OB = \{ob_1, ob_2, ..., ob_n\}$, we go through the following steps to produce an observer abstraction M in the form of OSM. Initially M is empty. During the execution of T', we collect the following tuple for each method execution in c's interface: (cs_s, m, mr, cs_e), where cs_s, m, mr, and cs_e are the concrete object state at the method entry, method call, return value, and concrete object state at the method exit, respectively. If m's return type is void, we assign " $-$ " to mr. If m's execution throws an uncaught exception, we also assign " $-$ " to mr and assign the name of the exception type to cs_e, called an *exception state*. The concrete object state at a constructor's entry is $INIT$, called an *initial state*.

After the test executions terminate, we iterate on each distinct tuple (cs_s, m, mr, cs_e) to produce a new tuple (as_s, m, mr, as_e), where as_s and as_e are the abstract states mapped from cs_s and cs_e based on OB, respectively. If cs_e is an exception state, its mapped abstract state is the same as cs_e, whose value is the name of the thrown-exception type. If cs_s is an initial state, its mapped abstract state is still $INIT$. If cs_e is not exercised by the initial tests before test augmentation but exercised by new tests, we map cs_e to a special abstract state denoted as N/A, because we have not invoked OB on cs_e yet and do not have a known abstract state for cs_e.

After we produce (as_s, m, mr, as_e) from (cs_s, m, mr, cs_e), we then add as_s and as_e to M as states, and put a transition from as_s to as_e in M. The transition is denoted by a triple $(as_s, m?/mr!, as_e)$. If as_s, as_e, or $(as_s, m?/mr!, as_e)$ is already present in M, we do not add it. In addition, we increase the transition count for $(as_s, m?/mr!, as_e)$, denoted as $C_{(as_s, m?/mr!, as_e)}$, which is initialized to one when $(as_s, m?/mr!, as_e)$ is added to M at the first time. We also increase the emission count for as_s and m, denoted as $C_{(as_s, m)}$. After we finish processing all distinct tuples (cs_s, m, mr, cs_e), we postfix the label of each transition $(as_s, m?/mr!, as_e)$ with $[C_{(as_s, m?/mr!, as_e)}/C_{(as_s, m)}]$. The complexity of the extraction algorithm for an observer abstraction is $O(|CS| \times |OB|)$, where CS is the set of the nonequivalent concrete states exercised by an initial test suite T and OB is the given set of observers.

2.5   Implementation

We have developed a tool, called Obstra, for the observer abstraction approach. Obstra is implemented based on the Rostra framework developed in our previous work [23]. We use the Byte Code Engineering Library (BCEL) [6] to rewrite the bytecodes of a class at class-loading time. Objects of the class under test are referred as *candidate objects*. We collect concrete object states at the entry and exit of each method call invoked from a test suite to a candidate object; these method calls are referred as *candidate method calls*. We do not collect object states for those method calls that are internal to candidate objects.

To collect concrete object states, we use Java reflection mechanisms [2] to recursively collect all the fields that are reachable from a candidate object, an argument object, or a return object of candidate method calls. We also instrument test classes to collect method call information that is used to reproduce object states in test augmentation. We also use Java reflection mechanisms [2] to generate and execute new tests online. We export a selected subset of tests in the augmented test suite to a JUnit [13] test class using JCrasher's functionality of test-code generation [5]; we select and export a test if it exercises at least one previously uncovered transition in an observer abstraction. Each exported test is annotated with its exercised transitions as comments. We display extracted observer abstractions by using the Grappa package, which is part of graphviz [8].

By default, Obstra generates one OSM for each observer (in addition to one OSM for all observers) and outputs a default grouping configuration file; programmers can manipulate the configurations in the file to generate OSM's based on multiple observers.

2.6   Example

We use a class of Binary Search Tree (named as `BSTree`) as an example of illustrating observer abstractions. This class was used in evaluating Korat [4] and the Rostra framework in our previous work [23]. Parasoft Jtest (a commercial tool for Java) [18] generates 277 tests for the class. The class has 246 non-comment, non-blank lines of code and its interface includes eight public methods (five observers), some of which are a constructor (denoted as `[init]()`), `boolean contains(MyInput info)`, `void add(MyInput info)`, and `boolean remove (MyInput info)` where `MyInput`[4] is a class that contains an integer field `v`.

Figure 1 shows the observer abstraction of BSTree with respect to an observer `contains(MyInput info)` (including two observer instances: `add(a0.v:7;)`[5] and `add(a0:null;)`) and augmented Jtest-generated tests. The top state in the figure is marked with `INIT`, indicating the object state before invoking a constructor. The second-to-top state is marked with the observer instances and their `false` return values. This abstract state encloses those concrete states such that when we invoke these two observer instances on those concrete states, their return values are `false`. In the central state, the observers throw uncaught exceptions and we put the exception-type name `NullPointerException` in the positions of their return values. The bottom state is marked with the exception-type name `NullPointerException`. An object is in such a state after a method call on the object throws the `NullPointerException`.

Each transition from a starting abstract state to an ending abstract state is marked with method calls, their return values, and some statistics. For example, the generated test suite contains two tests:

```
Test 1 (T1):                    Test 2 (T2):
    BSTree b1 = new BSTree();       BSTree b1 = new BSTree();
    MyInput m1 = new MyInput(0);    b1.remove(null);
    b1.add(m1);
    b1.remove(null);
```

---

[4] The original argument type is `Object`; we change the type to `MyInput` so that Jtest can be guided to generate better arguments.

[5] ai represents the $(i+1)$th argument and $ai.v$ represents the v field of the $(i+1)$th argument. Argument values are specified following their argument names separated by : and different arguments are separated by ; .

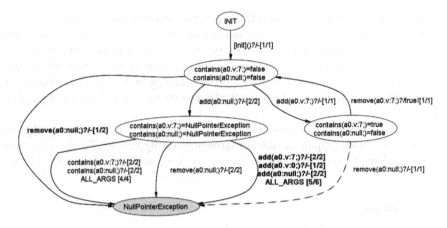

Fig. 1. contains observer abstraction of BSTree

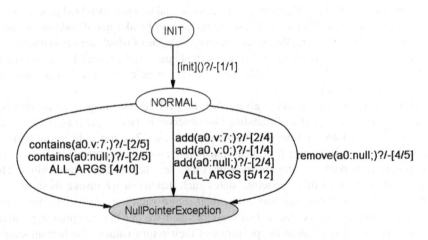

Fig. 2. exception observer abstraction of BSTree

The execution of b1.remove(null) in T1 does not throw any exception. Both before and after invoking b1.remove(null) in T1, if we invoke the two observer instances, their return values are false; therefore, there is a state-preserving transition on the second-to-top state. (To present a succinct view, by default we do not show state-preserving transitions.) The execution of b1.remove(null) in T2 throws a NullPointerException. If we invoke the two observer instances before invoking b1.remove(null) in T2, their return values are false; therefore, given the method execution of b1.remove(null) in T2, we extract the transition from the second-to-top state to the bottom state and the transition is marked with remove(a0:null;)?/-. In the mark of a transition, when return values are void or method calls throw uncaught exceptions, we put – in the position of their return values. We put ? after the method calls and ! after return values if return values are not –. We also attach two numbers for each transition in the form of [N/M], where N is the transition count and M is the emission count. If these two numbers are equal, the transition is deterministic, and is indeterministic otherwise. Because there are two different transitions from the second-to-top state with the same method call remove(a0:null;) (one transition is state-preserving being extracted from T1), the transition remove(a0:null;) from the second-to-top state to the bottom state is indeterministic, being attached with [1/2]. We display thicker edges and bold-font texts for nondeterministic transitions so that programmers can easily identify them based on visual effect.

To present a succinct view, we do not display N/A states and the transitions leading to N/A states. In addition, we combine multiple transitions that have the same starting and ending abstract states, and whose method calls have the same method names and signatures. When we combine multiple transitions, we calculate the transition count and emission count of the combined transitions and show them in the bottom line of the transition label. When a combined transition contains all nonequivalent method calls of the same method name and signature, we add ALL_ARGS in the bottom line of the transition label. When a transition contains only method calls that are exercised by new generated tests but not exercised by the initial tests, we display a dotted edge for the transition.

To focus on understanding uncaught exceptions, we create a special *exception observer* and construct an observer abstraction based on it. Figure 2 shows the exception-observer abstraction of BSTree extracted from augmented Jtest-generated tests. The exception observer maps all concrete states except for $INIT$ and exception states to an abstract state called NORMAL. The mapped abstract state of an initial state is still $INIT$ and the mapped abstract state of an exception state is still the same as the exception-type name.

3   Experiences

We have used Obstra to extract observer abstractions from a variety of programs, most of which were used to evaluate our previous work in test selection [25], test minimization [23], and test generation [22]. Many of these programs manipulate nontrivial data structures. Because of the space limit, in this section, we illustrate how we applied Obstra on two complex data structures and their automatically generated tests. We applied Obstra on these examples on a MS Windows machine with a Pentium IV 2.8 GHz processor using Sun's Java 2 SDK 1.4.2 JVM with 512 Mb allocated memory.

3.1   Binary Search Tree Example

We have described the BSTree in Section 2.6 and two of its extracted observer abstractions in Figure 1 and 2. Jtest generates 277 tests for BSTree. These tests exercise five nonequivalent concrete object states in addition to the initial state and one exception state, 12 nonequivalent non-constructor method calls in addition to one constructor call, and 33 nonequivalent method executions. Obstra augments the test suite to exercise

61 nonequivalent method executions. The elapsed real time for test augmentation and abstraction extraction is 0.4 and 4.9 seconds, respectively.

Figure 2 shows that `NullPointerException` is thrown by three nondeterministic transitions. During test inspection, we want to know in what conditions the exception is thrown. If the exception is thrown because of illegal inputs, we can add necessary preconditions to guard against the illegal inputs. Alternatively, we can perform defensive programming: we can add input checking at method entries and throw more informative exceptions if the checking fails. However, we do not want to add over-constrained preconditions, which prevent legal inputs from being processed. For example, after inspecting the exception OSM in Figure 2, we should not consider all arguments for `add`, the `null` argument for `remove`, or all arguments for `contains` as illegal arguments, although doing so indeed prevents the exceptions from being thrown. After we inspected the `contains` OSM in Figure 1, we gained more information about the exceptions and found that calling `add(a0:null;)` after calling the constructor leads to an undesirable state: calling `contains` on this state deterministically throws the exception. In addition, calling `remove(a0:null;)` also deterministically throws the exception and calling `add` throws the exception with a high probability of 5/6. Therefore, we had more confidence on considering `null` as an illegal argument for `add` and preventing it from being processed. After we prevented `add(a0:null;)`, two `remove(a0:null;)` transitions still throw the exception: one is deterministic and the other is with 1/2 probability. We then considered `null` as an illegal argument for `remove` and prevented it from being processed. We did not need to impose any restriction on the argument of `contains`.

We found that there are three different arguments for `add` but only two different arguments for `contains`, although these two methods have the same signatures. We could add a method call of `contain(a0.v:0;)` to the Jtest-generated test suite; therefore, we could have three observer instances for the `contains` OSM in Figure 1. In the new OSM, the second-to-top state includes one more observer instance `contains(a0.v:0)=false` and the indeterministic transition of `remove(a0:null;)` `?/-[1/2]` from the second-to-top state to the bottom state is turned into a deterministic transition `remove(a0:null;)?/-[1/1]`. In general, when we add new tests to a test suite and these new tests exercise new observer instances in an OSM, the states in the OSM can be refined, thus possibly turning some indeterministic transitions into deterministic ones. On the other hand, adding new tests can possibly turn some deterministic transitions into indeterministic ones.

3.2   Hash Map Example

A HashMap class was given in `java.util.HashMap` from the standard Java libraries [19]. A `repOK` and some helper methods were added to this class for evaluating Korat [4]. We also used this class in our previous work for evaluating Rostra [23]. The class has 597 non-comment, non-blank lines of code and its interface includes 19 public methods (13 observers), some of which are `[init]()`, `void setLoadFactor(float f)`, `void putAll(Map t)`, `Object remove(MyInput key)`, `Object put(MyInput key, MyInput value)`, and `void clear()`. Jtest generates 5186 tests for HashMap. These tests exercise 58 nonequivalent concrete object states in addition to the initial state and

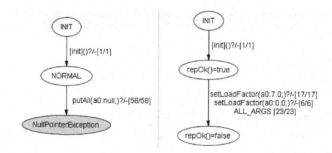

Fig. 3. exception observer abstraction and repOk observer abstraction of HashMap

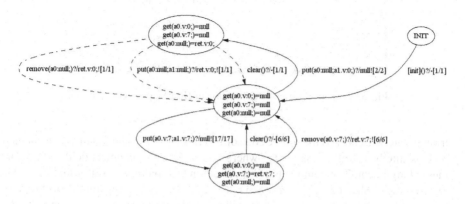

Fig. 4. get observer abstraction of HashMap

one exception state, 29 nonequivalent non-constructor method calls in addition to one constructor call, and 416 nonequivalent method executions. Obstra augments the test suite to exercise 1683 nonequivalent method executions. The elapsed real time for test augmentation and abstraction extraction is 10 and 15 seconds, respectively.

We found that the exception OSM of HashMap contains one deterministic transition putAll(a0:null;) from NORMAL to NullPointerException, as is shown in the left part of Figure 3. Therefore, we considered null as an illegal argument for putAll. We checked the Java API documentation for HashMap [19] and the documentation states that putAll throws NullPointerException if the specified map is null. This description confirmed our judgement. In other observer abstractions, to provide a more succinct view, by default Obstra does not display any deterministic transitions leading to an exception state in the exception OSM.

We found an error in setLoadFactor(float f), a method that was later added to facilitate Korat's test generation [4]. The right part of Figure 3 shows the repOk OSM of HashMap. repOk is a predicate used to check class invariants [16]. If calling repOk on an object state returns false, the object state is invalid. By inspecting the repOK OSM, we found that calling setLoadFactor with all arguments deterministically leads to an

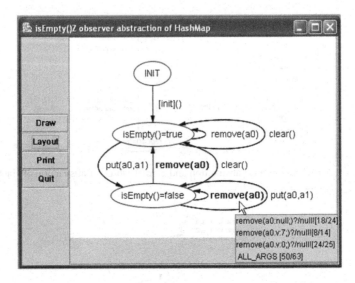

Fig. 5. isEmpty observer abstraction of HashMap (screen snapshot)

invalid state. We checked the source code of setLoadFactor and found that its method body is simply loadFactor = f;, where loadFactor is an object field and f is the method argument. The comments for a private field threshold states that the value of threshold shall be (int)(capacity * loadFactor). Apparently this property is violated when setting loadFactor without updating threshold accordingly. We fixed this error by appending a call to an existing private method void rehash() in the end of setLoadFactor's method body; rehash updates threshold using the new loadFactor.

Figure 4 shows the get OSM of HashMap. In the representation of method returns on a transition or in a state, ret represents the non-primitive return value and ret.v represents the v field of the non-primitive return value. Recall that a transition with a dotted edge is exercised only by new generated tests but not by the initial tests. We next walk through the scenario in which programmers could inspect Figure 4. During inspection, programmers might focus their exploration of an OSM on transitions. Three such transitions are clear, remove, and put. Programmers are not surprised to see that clear or remove transitions cause a nonempty HashMap to be empty, as is shown by the transitions from the top or bottom state to the central state. But programmers are surprised to see the transition of put(a0:null;a1:null) from the top state to the central state, indicating that put can cause a nonempty HashMap to be empty. By browsing the Java API documentation for HashMap [19], programmers can find that HashMap allows either a key or a value to be null; therefore, the null return of get does not necessarily indicate that the map contains no mapping for the key. However, in the documentation, the description for the returns of get states: "the value to which this map maps the specified key, or null if the map contains no mapping for this key." After reading the documentation more carefully, they can find that the description for get (but not the description for the returns of get) does specify the accurate behavior. This finding shows that the informal description for the returns of get is not accurate or consistent with the description of get even in such widely published Java API documentation [19].

Figure 5 shows a screen snapshot of the isEmpty OSM of HashMap. We configured Obstra to additionally show each state-preserving transition that has the same method name as another state-modifying transition. We also configured Obstra to display on each edge only the method name associated with the transition. When programmers want to see the details of a transition, they can move the mouse cursor over the method name associated with the transition and then the details are displayed. We have searched the Internet for manually created state machines for common data structures but few could be found. One manually created state machine for a container structure [17] is almost the same as the isEmpty OSM of HashMap shown in Figure 5. There are two major differences. The $INIT$ state and the [init]() transition are shown in Figure 5 but not in the manually created state machine. The manually created state machine annotates "not last element" for the state-preserving transition remove(a0) (pointed by the mouse cursor in Figure 5) on the isEmpty()=false state and "last element" for the state-modifying transition remove(a0) (shown in the middle of Figure 5) starting from the isEmpty()=false state; Figure 5 shows these two transition names in bold font, indicating them to be indeterministic.

3.3 Discussion

Our experiences have shown that extracted observer abstractions can help investigate causes of uncaught exceptions, identify weakness of an initial test suite, find bugs in a class implementation or its documentation, and understand class behavior. Although many observer abstractions extracted for the class under test are succinct, some observer abstractions are still complex, containing too much information for inspection. For example, three observers of HashMap, such as Collection values(), have 43 abstract states. The complexity of an extracted observer abstraction depends on both the characteristics of its observers and the initial tests. In future work, we plan to display a portion of a complex observer abstraction based on user-specified filtering criteria or extract observer abstractions from the executions of a user-specified subset of the initial tests.

Although the isEmpty OSM of HashMap is almost the same as a manually created state machine [17], our approach does not guarantee the completeness of the resulting observer abstractions — our approach does not guarantee that the observer abstractions contain all possible legal states or legal transitions. Our approach also does not guarantee that the observer abstractions contain no illegal transitions. Instead, the observer abstractions faithfully reflect behavior exercised by the executed tests; inspecting observer abstractions could help identify weakness of the executed tests. This characteristic of our approach is shared by other dynamic inference techniques [1, 7, 12, 21] discussed in the next section.

4   Related Work

Ernst et al. use Daikon to dynamically infer likely invariants from test executions [7]. Invariants are in the form of axiomatic specifications. These invariants describe the observed relationships among the values of object fields, arguments, and returns of a single method in a class interface, whereas observer abstractions describe the observed state-transition relationships among multiple methods in a class interface and use the return values of observers to represent object states, without explicitly referring to object fields. Henkel and Diwan discover algebraic specifications from the execution of automatically generated unit tests [12]. Their discovered algebraic specifications present a local view of relationships between two methods, whereas observer abstractions present a global view of relationships among multiple methods. In addition, Henkel and Diwan's approach cannot infer local properties that are related to indeterministic transitions in observer abstractions; our experiences show that these indeterministic transitions are useful for inspection. In summary, observer abstractions are a useful form of property inference, complementing invariants or algebraic specifications inferred from unit-test executions.

Whaley et al. extract Java component interfaces from system-test executions [21]. The extracted interfaces are in the form of multiple finite state machines, each of which contains the methods that modify or read the same object field. Observer abstractions are also in the form of multiple finite state machines, each of which is with respect to a set of observers (containing one observer by default). Whaley et al. map all concrete states that are at the same state-modifying method's exits to the same abstract state. Our approach maps all concrete states on which observers' return values are the same to the same abstract state. Although Whaley et al.'s approach is applicable on system-test executions, it is not applicable on the executions of automatically generated unit tests, because their resulting finite state machine would be a complete graph of methods that modify the same object field. Ammons et al. mine protocol specifications in the form of a finite state machine from system-test executions [1]. Their approach faces the same problem as Whaley et al.'s approach when being applied on the executions of automatically generated unit tests. In summary, neither Whaley et al. nor Ammons et al.'s approaches capture object states as accurate as our approach and neither of them can be applied on the executions of automatically generated unit tests.

Given a set of predicates, predicate abstraction [3, 9] maps a concrete state to an abstract state that is defined by the boolean values of these predicates on the concrete state. Given a set of observers, observer abstraction maps a concrete state to an abstract state that is defined by the return values (not limited to boolean values) of these observers on the concrete state. Concrete states considered by predicate abstractions are usually those program states between program statements, whereas concrete states considered by observer abstractions are those object states between method calls. Predicate abstraction is mainly used in software model checking, whereas observer abstraction in our approach is mainly used in helping inspection of test executions.

Turner and Robson use finite state machines to specify the behavior of a class [20]. The states in a state machine are defined by the values of a subset or complete set of object fields. The transitions are method names. Their approach specifies specifications in the form of finite state machines and generates tests based on the specifications, whereas our approach extracts observer abstractions in the form of finite state machines without requiring a priori specifications. In future work, we plan to use extracted observer abstractions to guide test generation using existing finite-state-machine-based testing techniques [15] and use new generated tests to further improve observer abstractions. This future work fits into the feedback loop between test generation and specification inference proposed in our previous work [24].

Kung et al. statically extract object state models from class source code and use them to guide test generation [14]. An object state model is in the form of a finite state machine: the states are defined by value intervals over object fields, which are derived from path conditions of method source; the transitions are derived by symbolically executing methods. Our approach dynamically extracts finite state machines based on observers during test executions. Grieskamp et al. generate finite state machines from executable abstract state machines [10]. Manually specified predicates are used to group states in abstract state machines to hyperstates during the execution of abstract state machine. Finite state machines, abstract state machines, and manually specified predicates in their approach correspond to observer abstractions, concrete object state machines, and observers in our approach, respectively. However, our approach is totally automatic and does not require programmers to specify any specifications or predicates.

5   Conclusion

It is important to provide tool support for programmers as they inspect the executions of automatically generated unit tests. We have proposed the observer abstraction approach to aid inspection of test executions. We have developed a tool, called Obstra, to extract observer abstractions from unit-test executions automatically. We have applied the approach on a variety of programs, including complex data structures; our experiences show that extracted observer abstractions provide useful object-state-transition information for programmers to inspect.

Acknowledgments

We thank Arnaud Gotlieb, Amir Michail, Andrew Peterson, Vibha Sazawal and the anonymous reviewers for their valuable feedback on an earlier version of this paper. We thank Darko Marinov for providing Korat subjects. This work was supported in part by the National Science Foundation under grant ITR 0086003. We acknowledge support through the High Dependability Computing Program from NASA Ames cooperative agreement NCC-2-1298.

References

1. G. Ammons, R. Bodik, and J. R. Larus. Mining specifications. In *Proc. the 29th ACM SIGPLAN-SIGACT Symposium on Principles of Programming Languages*, pages 4–16, 2002.

2. K. Arnold, J. Gosling, and D. Holmes. *The Java Programming Language*. Addison-Wesley Longman Publishing Co., Inc., 2000.
3. T. Ball, R. Majumdar, T. Millstein, and S. K. Rajamani. Automatic predicate abstraction of C programs. In *Proc. the ACM SIGPLAN 2001 Conference on Programming Language Design and Implementation*, pages 203–213, 2001.
4. C. Boyapati, S. Khurshid, and D. Marinov. Korat: automated testing based on Java predicates. In *Proc. the International Symposium on Software Testing and Analysis*, pages 123–133, 2002.
5. C. Csallner and Y. Smaragdakis. JCrasher documents. Online manual, December 2003.
6. M. Dahm and J. van Zyl. Byte Code Engineering Library, April 2003. `http://jakarta.apache.org/bcel/`.
7. M. D. Ernst, J. Cockrell, W. G. Griswold, and D. Notkin. Dynamically discovering likely program invariants to support program evolution. *IEEE Trans. Softw. Eng.*, 27(2):99–123, 2001.
8. E. R. Gansner and S. C. North. An open graph visualization system and its applications to software engineering. *Software: Practice and Experience*, 30(11):1203–1233, Sept. 2000.
9. S. Graf and H. Saidi. Construction of abstract state graphs with PVS. In *Proc. the 9th International Conference on Computer Aided Verification*, pages 72–83, 1997.
10. W. Grieskamp, Y. Gurevich, W. Schulte, and M. Veanes. Generating finite state machines from abstract state machines. In *Proc. the International Symposium on Software Testing and Analysis*, pages 112–122, 2002.
11. N. Gupta, A. P. Mathur, and M. L. Soffa. Automated test data generation using an iterative relaxation method. In *Proc. the 6th ACM SIGSOFT International Symposium on Foundations of Software Engineering*, pages 231–244, 1998.
12. J. Henkel and A. Diwan. Discovering algebraic specifications from Java classes. In *Proc. the 17th European Conference on Object-Oriented Programming*, pages 431–456, 2003.
13. JUnit, 2003. `http://www.junit.org`.
14. D. Kung, N. Suchak, J. Gao, and P. Hsia. On object state testing. In *Proc. the 18th Annual International Computer Software and Applications Conference*, pages 222–227, 1994.
15. D. Lee and M. Yannakakis. Principles and methods of testing finite state machines - A survey. In *Proc. The IEEE*, volume 84, pages 1090–1123, Aug. 1996.
16. B. Liskov and J. Guttag. *Program Development in Java: Abstraction, Specification, and Object-Oriented Design*. Addison-Wesley, 2000.
17. D. Nguyen. Design patterns for data structures. In *Proc. the 29th SIGCSE Technical Symposium on Computer Science Education*, pages 336–340, 1998.
18. Parasoft. Jtest manuals version 4.5. Online manual, April 2003. `http://www.parasoft.com/`.
19. Sun Microsystems. Java 2 Platform, Standard Edition, v 1.4.2, API Specification. Online documentation, Nov. 2003. `http://java.sun.com/j2se/1.4.2/docs/api/`.
20. C. D. Turner and D. J. Robson. The state-based testing of object-oriented programs. In *Proc. the Conference on Software Maintenance*, pages 302–310, 1993.
21. J. Whaley, M. C. Martin, and M. S. Lam. Automatic extraction of object-oriented component interfaces. In *Proc. the International Symposium on Software Testing and Analysis*, pages 218–228, 2002.
22. T. Xie, D. Marinov, and D. Notkin. Improving generation of object-oriented test suites by avoiding redundant tests. Technical Report UW-CSE-04-01-05, University of Washington Department of Computer Science and Engineering, Seattle, WA, January 2004.

23. T. Xie, D. Marinov, and D. Notkin. Rostra: A framework for detecting redundant object-oriented unit tests. In *Proc. 19th IEEE International Conference on Automated Software Engineering*, 2004.
24. T. Xie and D. Notkin. Mutually enhancing test generation and specification inference. In *Proc. 3rd International Workshop on Formal Approaches to Testing of Software*, volume 2931 of *LNCS*, pages 60–69, 2003.
25. T. Xie and D. Notkin. Tool-assisted unit test selection based on operational violations. In *Proc. 18th IEEE International Conference on Automated Software Engineering*, pages 40–48, 2003.

A Specification-Based Approach to Testing Polymorphic Attributes*

Ling Liu and Huaikou Miao

School of Computer Engineering and Science, Shanghai University,
Shanghai, 200072, China
liuling@staff.shu.edu.cn, hkmiao@mail.shu.edu.cn

Abstract. The object-oriented features, such as aggregation, inheritance and polymorphism, facilitate software reuse and improve software quality. But those features also cause new problems that traditional testing techniques cannot resolve effectively. Existing researches on object-oriented software testing are mainly based on some graph representations and seldom consider the combinational effect of aggregation, inheritance and polymorphism. For some model-based specifications that do not include graph representations, it is difficult to use the graph based testing techniques to derive test cases. This paper provides an approach to deriving test cases for testing the combinational effect of aggregation, inheritance and polymorphism from a model-based class specification. This approach contains two techniques at intra-class and inter-class testing levels and is mechanized using the algorithms presented in this paper. Finally, through the experimental analysis, we present the effectiveness and applicability of our testing approach.

1 Introduction

A procedure-oriented software is composed of functions and procedures. Each function or procedure has a clear control structure, which can be used by traditional testing techniques (such as control or data flow testing criteria) to generate effective test cases. While in object-oriented software development, we shift our emphasis to defining data abstraction. These abstractions normally appear in the language as user-defined types (classes) that have both attributes and methods. An object-oriented software consists of classes and their instances (objects). As the data objects are relatively stable elements in the world, object-oriented techniques can help developers to achieve the high quality software. However, the object-oriented features such as inheritance, aggregation and polymorphism do not have their counterparts in procedure-oriented software. That makes traditional testing techniques ineffective for the object-oriented software.

In object-oriented programming, class is the fundamental building block, which is used to define new type. Inheritance and aggregation bring two ways of composing classes to form new types. Inheritance can be used to define a new

---

* This work is supported by the Natural Science Foundation of China (60173030) and National 973 Program (2002CB312001).

class with a set of existing classes. Through inheritance, the new class can get the attributes and methods from those existing classes. Aggregation enables a class to contain the instances of another class. Polymorphism allows an object to have any type in a class hierarchy. Polymorphism combined with dynamic binding allows the same method call to execute different method bodies; which one is executed depends on the current type of the object that is used in the method call. Aggregation, inheritance and polymorphism bring great flexibility in integrating objects and classes. But they also cause new problems that the traditional software testing techniques cannot resolve effectively. For example, polymorphism and aggregation make it impossible to extract the exact control flow or data flow information. Inheritance brings the question of test case reuse. Aiming at solving these problems, the researchers provided some methods of extending control-flow and data-flow graphs to represent the relations among classes. Based on the extended graph representations, they also present some new testing criteria to guide the generation or evaluate the quality of test cases [1, 2, 3]. Moreover, some rules of reusing parent classes' test cases are also given [4]. In these rules, we find that most of the parent classes' specification based test cases can be reused in the testing process of their subclasses. Thus how to derive effective specification based test cases becomes our concern. Since the model-based specification (such as Object-Z, VDM++) does not include the graph representations, and from this kind of specification it is difficult and error prone to extract the graphs, some specification based testing techniques are presented [5, 6, 7, 8]. However, these specification based testing techniques do not pay enough attention to the object-oriented features, especially the inheritance, polymorphism and aggregation.

To address above issues, this paper presents an approach to testing the polymorphic attributes defined in a class specification. This approach is essentially a technique that is used to generate test cases from a model-based class specification. The technique first constructs test cases to test the interacting relation among the methods in a class, then extends these tests according to the possible type values of the polymorphic attributes. In the whole tests constructing process, our technique does not need to extract extra graph representation; all results are derived directly from the model-based class specification. Thus, the main contributions of this paper are providing an approach to directly deriving class tests from model-based class specification; giving a method of testing combinational relationship of aggregation, inheritance and polymorphism; making it possible to automate generating tests from model-based specification.

The next section presents our testing approach. Section 3 gives the results from a case study of applying our testing approach and analyzes the capability of the resulted test cases. Section 4 gives some conclusions.

2 Testing Polymorphical Attributes

For object-oriented software, Harrold and Rothermel gave three levels of testing classes [9]: intra-method testing, inter-method testing and intra-class testing.

Intra-method testing tests individual methods, inter-method testing tests public methods together with other methods that is called directly or indirectly, and intra-class testing tests the interactions of public methods when they are called in various sequences. This way was extended to the fourth level by Gallagher and Offutt[10]: inter-class testing that is testing the integration relationships among different classes through public method calls and references to public data members.

The testing approach presented in this paper includes some techniques at two object-oriented testing levels: intra-class level and inter-class level. At intra-class level, we define the intra-class tests as a sequence of intra-method tests, and give a technique used to construct intra-class tests from intra-method tests. This technique is essentially a method of deriving intra-class tests from a formal class specification, which uses predicates to depict its states and operations. Through our intra-class testing technique, testers can get tests from a model-based class specification directly. Thus this technique reduces the test costs and makes the automatic tests generation possible. At inter-class level, our testing approach provides a method of reusing intra-class tests to test the polymorphic attributes.

2.1   Intra-method Testing

At intra-method testing level, the specification-based approach often takes the category partition testing criteria [11] to derive test cases for each method in a class. This section presents the results of applying the category partition testing criteria to an Object-Z[12, 13] class specification.

Object-Z is an extension of the model-based formal specification language Z to accommodate object orientated language features. In Object-Z, a class is defined with a state schema, which defines the attributes and the state invariants of the class, and its associated operations. The syntax of Object-Z class is presented in Figure 1.

```
┌─ClassName[FormalParameters]──────────┐
│ [VisibilityLists]                     │
│ [InheritedClasses]                    │
│ [LocalDefinitions]                    │
│ [StateSchemas]                        │
│ [InitialStateSchemas]                 │
│ [OperationSchemas]                    │
└───────────────────────────────────────┘
```

Fig. 1. The Class Schema in Object-Z

FormalParameters is frequently used to represent the types of the variables in a class. This part is analogous to the type declaration in a C++ template class. VisibilityLists defines the class's interface. It is analogous to the public definitions in a C++ class. InheritedClasses specifies the classes, from which the current class inherits the state space and operations. LocalDefinitions defines the types and constants that may be used within the class. StateSchemas defines the sate variables of the class. StateSchema and some local axiomatic definitions define possible states of the class. InitialStateSchemas defines the initial state of the class. OperationSchemas defines all operations that can be applied to the objects of the class.

Figure 2 gives the Object-Z specification of class List. "List[T]" denotes that the name of the class is "List" and the variables have the generic type T. When an object of the class is defined, T can be substituted with a concrete type. "|max:N" defines a constant "max", which has the type N. After the constant definition, the state schema of class List defines a state variable *items* as a sequence of elements to represent a list. The maximus size of items is "max" (represented by the predicate "#*items*≤max"). Moreover, class List defines three public methods: *INIT*, *add* and *remove*. The method *INIT* specifies that the list is empty initially. The method *add* adds an element to the list as a last element when the list is not full. The method *remove* removes the first element out of the list when the list is not empty, where *items'* represents the value of state variable *items* after executing an operation; notation "⌢" represents the concatenating operation of two sequences. For sequences s and t, s ⌢ t is the concatenation of s and t. It contains the elements of s followed by the elements of t.

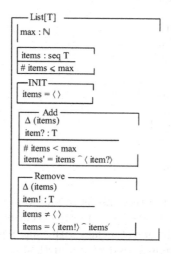

Fig. 2. The Specification of Class List

Applying the category partition testing criteria to each method of the List class, we can get following six intra-method test cases.

1. Test Specification INIT

Preconditions:	NULL
Test case values:	NULL
Expected outputs:	NULL
Postconditions:	#items'=0

2. Test Specification add.1
   Preconditions: #items = 0
   Test case values: item : T
   Expected outputs: NULL
   Postconditions: #items' = 1

3. Test Specification add.2
   Preconditions: $1 \leq$ #items$\leq$max-1
   Test case values: item : T
   Expected outputs: NULL
   Postconditions: $2 \leq$items'$\leq$max

4. Test Specification add.3
   Preconditions: #items=max
   Test case values: item : T
   Expected outputs: NULL
   Postconditions: #items'=max

5. Test Specification remove.1
   Preconditions: #items=0
   Test case values: NULL
   Expected outputs: NULL
   Postconditions: #items'=0

6. Test Specification remove.2
   Preconditions: #items>0
   Test case values: NULL
   Expected outputs: item : T
   Postconditions: #items'$\geq$0

2.2   Intra-class Testing

At the intra-class testing level, a test case is usually represented as a sequence of method calls. These method calls are actually executing the public methods under some special state conditions of a class with some representative. Thus, if an intra-method test case is represented with a method call that contains input data, preconditions, expected outputs and postconditions, as the form in section 2.1, the intra-class test cases can be seen as the sequences of intra-method test cases. Based on this observation, this paper gives some techniques of reusing intra-method test cases to construct intra-class test cases.

The first step in addressing incorrect interactions among methods is to recognize that certain intra-method tests are related to others in terms of method postconditions satisfying the preconditions of other methods. This allows the intra-method test cases in a sequence to be run one after another. The relation among test cases is captured in the **connected** relation.

Connected:	If the postconditions of a test case t_1 imply the preconditions of a test case t_2, then t_1 and t_2 are called **connected** and t_1 can be said to be **connected** with t_2.

For example, if the postcondition of test case t_1 is $x>5 \wedge y>10$, and the precondition for test case t_2 is $y>5$, then the postcondition of t_1 implies the precondition of t_2. So, t_1 and t_2 are connected. However, if the postcondition of t_1 is $x>5 \vee y>10$, then t_1 and t_2 are not connected because the precondition of t_2 will not always be satisfied.

The connected relation does not address the possibility that the same intra-method test is used more than once in a test case sequence, but sometimes it is necessary to include this instance in a test set. For example, the intra-method test set for operation *add* includes three test cases: (1) adding an element to an empty list (test case add.1), (2) adding an element to a non-empty and non-full list(test case add.2) and (3) adding an element to a full list(test case add.3). When a tester tests the class List, he or she usually run add.2 several times until the list is full and then run add.3. Here, the test sequence is represented as <<u>add.2</u>, add.3>. Where the underline denotes that the first test case in this test sequence needs to be executed several times. Through observation, we find that the two test cases in above test sequence satisfy the following properties.

- Test cases add.2 and add.3 belong to the same operation
- The precondition (#items=max) of add.3 implies the postcondition ($2 \leq$ #items $\leq$ max) of add.2
- The intersection of the domain defined by the precondition (#items=max) in add.3 and the domain defined by the precondition ($1 \leq$ #items $\leq$ max-1) of add.2 is empty

This relation between above two test cases can be expressed with the **broad connected** relation.

Broad Connected:	If test cases t_1 and t_2 are used to test the same operation, the preconditions of t_2 imply the postconditions of t_1 and the intersection of the domain defined by the preconditions of test case t_1 and the domain defined by the preconditions of test case t_2 is empty, then t_1 and t_2 are called **broad connected** and t_1 can be said to be broadly connected with t_2.

For the class List, test cases add.2 and add.3 are broad connected. When executing a test sequence, each pair of broad connected test cases needs to be refined further to specify the exact number of times that the first test case in the pair should be executed. But this refinement is obvious and easy when the test engineers have an existing implementation. For example, in the test sequence

<INIT, add.1, add.2, add.3>, the test case add.2 should be executed max-1 times then the test case add.3 can be executed.

A **connected test sequence** is a sequence of test cases in which every pair of contiguous test cases are **connected** or **broad connected**.

A connected test sequence of intra-method test cases starting with a test case of the INIT operation can be taken as an intra-class test. Here, the INIT operation corresponds to a constructor of a class. But taking all possible test sequences starting with INIT test as the intra-class test set will result in very expensive tests and lots of redundancy. For example, consider the test sequence $< t_{INIT}, t_2, ..., t_i, ...,t_n >$ where t_{INIT} is a test case of INIT operation. If t_n satisfies following properties, appending t_n with other method tests will bring redundancy.

- The postconditions of t_n are the same as that of t_{INIT}.
  In this instance, the test cases appended to the test sequence will check the same state transitions that follow t_{INIT}. For the class List, test sequence <INIT, remove.1> cannot be extended because the postconditions of remove.1 is the same as that of INIT.
- The postconditions of t_n are same as t_i, and t_i and t_n belong to different methods.
  In this instance, the tests appended to the test sequence will check the same state transitions that follows t_i.

In order to avoid above two kinds of redundant test sequences in the intra-class test cases defined above, an effective test sequence is defined as follows.

An **effective test sequence** is a connected test sequence $<t_1, t_2, ..., t_i, ..., t_n>$ where t_1 is a test case for the operation INIT; t_n cannot be connected or broad connected with any other test cases; or t_n has the same postconditions with $t_i(1 \leq i < n)$ that test different method from that tested by t_n.

A **loop-free effective test sequence** is an effective test sequence in which no intra-method test case can appear more than once.

A **maximum loop-free effective test sequence** is a loop-free effective test sequence that cannot be a subsequence of any other test sequence.

The following algorithm, here we call it **intra-class testing algorithm**, gives the detailed steps to obtain all maximum loop-free effective test sequences from the intra-method tests. T represents an intra-class test set and S represents an existing intra-method test sequence$<t_1, t_2, ..., t_i, ..., t_n>$, where t_1 is a test case for an operation INIT; t_n cannot be connected or broad connected with any other test cases; or t_n has the same postconditions with $t_i(1 \leq i < n)$ that test different method from that tested by t_n.

a) Initially, let S_1 = <INIT.1>, S_2 = <INIT.2>, ... S_n = <INIT.n>, where, INIT.1, INIT.2 ... INIT.n are all intra-method test cases for the INIT operation. The intra-class set T is initialized as T = $\{S_1, S_2, ..., S_n\}$, where each $S_i, 1 \leq i \leq n$, is assigned the flag "unfinished".

b) Select an "unfinished" test sequence S in T.

c) Remove S from T. Find all intra-method test cases that can be connected or broad connected with the last element of S. If these test cases **do not appear** in S, then, append each of these test cases to S to form several new test sequences. For example, if S = $<s_1, s_2, \ldots, s_n>$, and intra-method tests $t_1, t_2, \ldots, t_m$ can be connected or broad connected with the last element s_n in S, and they do not appear in S, then, we can form the appended test sequences, $< s_1, s_2, \ldots, s_n , t_1>$, $< s_1, s_2, \ldots, s_n , t_2>$, $\ldots$, $< s_1, s_2, \ldots, s_n , t_m>$.

d) Check each new test sequence. If it is an effective test sequence, then assign it the flag "finished," else assign it the flag "unfinished".

e) Add these new test sequences to T.

f) Repeat steps b, c, d, and e until all test sequences in T have the flag "finished".

For the class List, following intra-class test sequences are maximum loop-free effective test sequences.

{ <INIT, remove.1>,
<INIT, add.1, remove.2, remove.1>,
<INIT, add.1, add.2, remove.2, remove.1>
<INIT, add.1, add.2, add.3, remove.2, remove.1>
}

All maximum loop-free effective test sequences got through this algorithm can be used as the intra-class tests. For the class List, above four test sequences are its intra-class tests.

2.3   Testing Polymorphic Attributes

A polymorphic attribute defined in a class is essentially an instance of some class family. When some method of a polymorphic attribute is called by a method in the class, the interaction between that class and a class family occurs. The aim of testing polymorphic attributes is verifying these interactions. Here, suppose the class that contains polymorphic attributes is called A, the class family defining the type of the polymorphic attributes is called B. If we want to verify the interactions between A and B, we must check all A's methods that call methods of B, and the interactions between those callers and other methods in A. Section 2.2 gives an approach to automatically deriving the intra-class test cases for testing the interactions among the methods in a class. Through this approach, we can construct the intra-class test cases of A, which may contain some method calls of B. When we check the method calls in all classes of B, we can verify the interactions between A and each class in B completely. For checking these polymorphic method calls, our intra-class testing approach can be extended to the inter-class level to include following definitions.

Assume $v_1, v_2, \ldots, v_n$ are the polymorphic attributes defined in class A, for each possible class type $o_1, o_2, \ldots, o_n$ of $v_1, v_2, \ldots, v_n$, **Context($A_{o1,o2,\ldots,on}$)** represents the class definition of A that the polymorphic variables $v_1, v_2, \ldots, v_n$ are bound to $o_1, o_2, \ldots, o_n$. **Context(A)** represents the set of all these class definitions.

Consider Figure 3, class D includes a polymorphic attribute p. The declared type of p is A, but the actual type of p may be A, B or C. Context(D_A) represents the definition of D that bind p to A. Context(D) represents the set of Context(D_A), Context(D_B) and Context(D_C).

When the method m() or n() calls p.i(), the interaction between class D and class A, B or C occurs. For verifying this interaction, we present the maximum polymorphism loop-free effective sequence coverage criterion, which absorbs the all polymorphic set concept in [2]. This criterion is defined as follows (assume A is the class includings polymorphic attributes).

Maximum Polymorphis Loop-Free Effective Sequence Coverage (MPLES): For each Context($A_{o1,o2,...,on}$) in Context(A), the test case set CT must includes all maximum loop-free effective test sequences.

Using intra-class testing algorithm we can get following algorithm that implement above testing criterion.

a) For each Context($A_{o1,o2,...,on}$) in Context(A) call intra-class testing algorithm to obtain its intra-class tests
b) All these resulted intra-class tests construct the tests for testing the polymorphic attributes in A.

We can see that the above algorithm is essentially a mechanical way of constructing some inter-class test cases from the intra-method test cases. For the class D in Figure 3, According to this algorithm, we need to construct the intra-method tests in Context(D_A), Context(D_B) and Context(D_C) first, then construct the intra-class test cases in each Context, finally use all these intra-class test cases to check the problems brought by the polymorphic attribute p. Usually, we use following format to represent these inter-class tests.

$$<INIT, m, n>_{p=A}$$

Here subscript $p = A$ means the polymorphic attribute p is bound to class A.

3   Empirical Evaluation

A preliminary experiment has been carried out to demonstrate the feasibility and applicability of the MPLES criterion. In this experiment, an Object-Z class specification was used as the source of intra-class and inter-class test cases. The intra-method test cases are the methods themselves. Inter-class test cases were then constructed from intra-method test cases by applying the algorithms given in section 2.3.

The inter-class test cases were executed on a C++ program that was implemented to satisfy its corresponding Object-Z specification. In the program, the names of variables are same as the names of variables in its specification. That allows test specifications to conveniently act as test scripts.

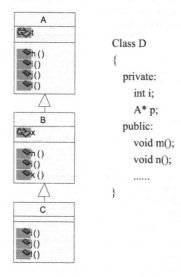

Class D
{
    private:
        int i;
        A* p;
    public:
        void m();
        void n();
        ......
}

Fig. 3. A Class with A Polymorphic Attribute

3.1   Object-Z Specification of Class Tetris

Figure 4 gives the Object-Z specification of class Tetris [13], which is used for the empirical evaluation in this paper. Class Tetris specifies a game. The goal of the player of Tetris is to position falling blocks of various shapes so that entire rows of the playing screen are filled. When a row is filled, it disappears from the screen, the rows above it move down and the player's score is advanced. The game continues until the fallen blocks pile up to the top of the playing screen.

The first statement in the class schema defines the interface of class Tetris. The interface of class Tetris includes three attributes and seven operations. Where three operations – *MoveRight*, *MoveLeft* and *Rotate* – model the player's options of moving the falling block left, right or rotating it respectively. Another three operations – *MoveDown*, *AddBlock* and *RemoveRow* – modeling a block moving down one row, a block being added to the screen, and a row being removed.

The state schema of class Tetris defines three attributes: *screen*, *block* and *score*. The attribute *screen* is an object of class Screen and used to represent the playing screen. The attribute *block* is an object of class family Block and used to represent the falling block. The attribut *score* has type N and represents the player's score. The staement "block∉Block∧Block∉Polygon" in the predicate part of the state schema denotes that the actual type of the attribute *block* cannot be class Block and Polygon. Figure 5 gives the class hierarchy of Tetris system. From this figure, we can see that there are nine classes in class family Block. According to above constraint the actual type of the attribute *block* can

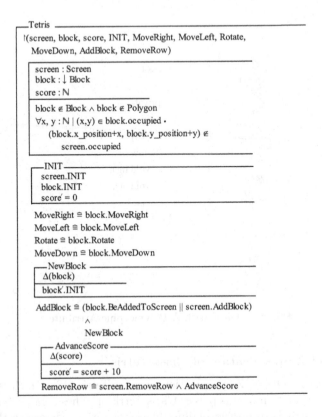

Fig. 4. The Tetris Class

only be one of seven class. The other statement in the predicate part denotes that the position of a falling block cannot exceed the boundary of the playing screen.

The *INIT* schema defines the initial state of class Tetris. Initially, at the beginning of a game of Tetris, the screen has no occupied positions; a new block is prepared to fall and the player's score is zero.

3.2   Test Generation

According to MPLES criterion, there are three steps of generating inter-class tests for testing the polymorphic attributes. First, binding the polymorphic attributes to some class in a class family; then, deriving intra-methods tests for the class; finally, constructing the inter-class tests using the algorithm presented in section 2.3.

Following these three steps, the polymorphic attribute *block* in Tetris needs to be bound to a class first. According to the state schema, the attribute *block* can be bound to class Square, Rectangle, T, S, Z, L or ReverseL. Here, assume

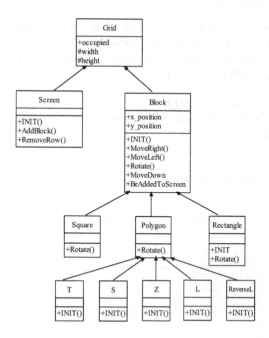

Fig. 5. The Class Hierarchy of Tetris System

block is bound to class Square. As a result, the Rotate method of Tetris will not change its state space.

Then, for each interface of the Tetris whose polymorphic attribute is already bound to class Square, the intra-method tests should be derived. Because each interface of Tetris is very simply, we take each interface method as its intra-method test. For example, method MoveRight is also its intra-method test.

Finally, applying the inter-class tests generating algorithm, we got 1589 inter-class tests. Where 89 tests are derived when block is bound to class Square. Consider test case <INIT, MoveLeft, MoveRight>$_{block=square}$, initially, screen is not occupied by any block, then a square is produced (denoted by INIT method). That square is moved left (denoted by MoveLeft method), This method changes the state of Tetris through changing the value of state variable block. Then that square is move right (denoted by MoveRight method). After executing this method, the state of Tetris is the same as the state of executing INIT. Thus, during this test sequence, the postconditions of MoveRight is the same as the postconditions of INIT, and INIT and MoveRight are different method. These conditions mean test case 1 is a maximum loop-free effective test sequence, and can be taken as an inter-class test according to the maximum polymorphism loop-free effective sequence coverage.

3.3   Results Analysis

In order to demonstrate the feasibility and applicability of our testing approach, we first used C++ to implement the Tetris system, then, seeded 49 faults in the system. These seeded faults can be classified into following four categories, which are given by Offutt et al [14].

- State definition anomaly (SDA)
- State definition inconsistency due to state variable hiding (SDIH)
- State defined incorrectly (SDI)
- Incomplete (failed) construction (IC)

The testing results for our 1589 tests are shown in Table 1.

Table 1. Faults Detected

	MPLES
Number of test cases	1589
Faults found	46
Faults missed	3
Percentage of fault detection	94%

Through table 1, we can conclude that our testing approach can detect the normal faults caused by inheritance and polymorphism.

4   Conclusions

This paper presents a testing approach to detecting the faults caused by the polymorphic attributes that embody the combining results of aggregation, inheritance and polymorphism. Our testing approach includes an intra-class testing method and an inter-class testing criterion. The algorithms that are used to implement our testing approach are also given. These algorithms make it possible to automate generating some inter-class test cases from a model-based formal specification. Moreover, through a case study we preliminarily verify the applicability and feasibility of our testing approach.

Now the intra-class testing algorithm has been preliminarily implemented with Java and verified with some classes. In the future, our work will focus on the tool supports and application of the testing approach for polymorphic attributes. Furthermore, the evaluation of testing criterion needs more research.

References

1. Mei, H. Chen, H.M. Kao: Testing Object-Oriented Programs - An Integrated Approach. In: Proceedings of International Symposium on Software Reliability Engineering, Boca Raton, Florida(Nov. 1999), 73-82

2. Roger T. Alexander, A. Jefferson Offutt: Criteria for Testing Polymorphic Relationship. In: Proceedings of International Symposium on Software Reliability Engineering, California, USA(Oct. 2000), 8-11
3. V. Martena, A. Orso, M. Pezze: Interclass Testing of Object Oriented Software. In: Proceedings of the Conference on Engineering of Complex Computer Systems, MD, USA(Dec. 2002), 135-144
4. Mary J. Harrold, John D. McGregor, Kevin Fitzpatrick: Incremmental Testing of Object-Oriented Class Inheritance Structures. In: Proceedings of the International Conference on Software Engineering, Melborne, Australia(May 1992), 68-80
5. P. Stocks, D. Carrington: A Framework for Specification-Based Testing. IEEE Transaction on Software Engineering. **22(11)** (1996) 777-793
6. Leesa Murray, David A. Carrington, Ian MacColl, Paul A. Strooper:Extending Testing Templates with Inheritance. Autralian Software Engineering Conference, Australia(Oct. 1997), 80-87
7. Ling Liu, Huaikou Miao, Xuede Zhan: A Framework for Specification-Based Class Testing. In: Proceedings of the Conference on Engineering of Complex Computer Systems, MD, USA(Dec. 2002), 153-162
8. Ling Liu: Object-Oriented Formal Specification Based Test Generation. Ph.D. thesis, Shanghai University, 2004
9. M. Harrold, G. Rothermel: Performing Data Flow Testing on Classes. In: Symposium on Foundations of Software Engineering, New Orleans(April, 1994), 200-207
10. L. Gallagher, J. Offutt: Integration Testing of Object-Oriented Components Using Finite State Machines. Submitted for publication, 2002
11. T. Ostrand, M. Balcer: The Category-Partition Method for Specifying and Generating Functional Tests. Communications of the ACM. **31(6)** (1988) 676-686
12. G. Smith: An Object-Oriented Approach to Formal Specifications. Ph.D. Thesis, University of Queensland, 1992
13. G. Smith: The Object-Z Specification Language. Kluwer Academic Publishers, 2000
14. Jeff Offutt, Roger Alexander, Ye Wu, Wuangsheng Xiao, Chunk Hutchinson: A Fault Model for Subtype Inheritance and Polymorphism. In: Symposium on Software Reliability Engineering, Hong Kong, PRC(Nov. 2001) 84-93

From *Circus* to JCSP

Marcel Oliveira and Ana Cavalcanti

Department of Computer Science – The University of York
York, YO10 5DD, England

Abstract. *Circus* is a combination of Z, CSP, and Morgan's refinement calculus; it has an associated refinement strategy that supports the development of reactive programs. In this work, we present rules to translate *Circus* programs to Java programs that use JCSP, a library that implements CSP constructs. These rules can be used as a complement to the *Circus* algebraic refinement technique, or as a guideline for implementation. They are a link between the results on refinement in the context of *Circus* and a practical programming language in current use. The rules can also be used as the basis for a tool that mechanises the translation.

Keywords: concurrency, object-orientation, program development.

1 Introduction

Languages like Z, VDM, Abstract State Machines, and B, use a model-based approach to specification, based on mathematical objects from set theory. Although possible, modelling behavioural aspects such as choice, sequence, parallelism, and others, using these languages, is difficult and needs to be done in an implicit fashion. On the other hand, process algebras like CSP and CCS provide constructs that can be used to describe the behaviour of the system. However, they do not support a concise and elegant way to describe complex data aspects.

Many attempts to join these two kinds of formalism have been made. Combinations of Z with CCS [5,18], Z with CSP [16], and Object-Z with CSP [3] are some examples. Our work is based on *Circus* [20], which combines Z [21] and CSP [7,15] and, distinctively, includes refinement calculi constructs and provides support for refinement in a calculational style, as that presented in [10].

Circus characterises systems as processes, which group constructs to describe data and behaviour. Z is used to define the data aspects, and CSP, Z schemas, and guarded commands are used to define behaviour. The semantics of *Circus* is based on the unifying theories of programming [8], a relational framework that unifies the programming theory across many different computational paradigms.

The main objective of this work is to provide a strategy for implementing *Circus* programs in Java. The strategy is based on a number of translation rules, which, if applied exhaustively, transforms a *Circus* program into a Java program that uses the JCSP [14] library. These rules capture and generalise the approach that we took in the implementation of a large case-study in *Circus*.

J. Davies et al. (Eds.): ICFEM 2004, LNCS 3308, pp. 320–340, 2004.

The result of refining a *Circus* specification is a program written in a combination of CSP and guarded commands. In order to implement this program, we need a link between *Circus* and a practical programming language. The transformation rules presented in this paper create this link. The existence of tool support for refinement and automated translation to Java makes formal development based on *Circus* relevant in practice. Our rules can be used as a basis in the implementation of a translation tool.

We assume that, before applying the translation strategy, the specification of the system we want to implement has been already refined, using the *Circus* refinement strategy presented in [2]. The translation strategy is applicable to programs written in the executable subset of *Circus*.

In Section 2, we use an example to introduce the main constructs of *Circus*. Section 3 presents JCSP with some examples. The strategy to implement *Circus* programs using JCSP is presented in Section 4. Finally, in Section 5 we conclude with some considerations about the strategy, and describe some future work.

2   *Circus*

Circus programs are formed by a sequence of paragraphs, which can either be a Z paragraph, a declaration of channels, a channel set declaration, or a process declaration. In Figure 1, the syntactic categories N, Exp, Pred, SchemaExp, Par, and Decl are those of valid Z identifiers, expressions, predicates, Z schemas, paragraphs in general, and declarations, respectively, as defined in [17].

We illustrate the main constructs of *Circus* using the specification of a simple register (Figure 2). It is initialised with zero, and can store or add a given value to its current value. It can also output or reset its current value.

All the channels must be declared; we give their names and the types of the values they can communicate. If a channel is used only for synchronisation, its declaration contains only its name. For example, *Register* outputs the current value through the channel *out*; it may also be reset through channel *reset*.

The declaration of a process is composed by its name and by its specification. A process may be explicitly defined or compound: defined in terms of other processes. An explicit process specification is formed by a sequence of process paragraphs and a distinguished nameless main action, which defines the process behaviour. We use Z to define the state; in our example, *RegSt* describes the state of the process *Register*: it contains the current *value* stored in the register.

Process paragraphs include Z paragraphs and declarations of (parametrised) actions. An action can be a schema, a guarded command, an invocation to another action, or a combination of these constructs using CSP operators.

The primitive action *Skip* does not communicate any value or changes the state: it terminates immediately. The action *Stop* deadlocks, and *Chaos* diverges; the only guarantee in both cases is that the state invariant is maintained.

The prefixing operator is standard. However, a guard construction is also available. For instance, if the condition p is *true*, the action p & $c?x \rightarrow A$

Program	::=	Par* CDecls* ProcDecl*
CDecls	::=	**channel** CDecl
CDecl	::=	SimpleCDecl |SimpleCDecl; CDecl
SimpleCDecl	::=	N^+ | N^+ : Exp
CSExp	::=	{⎨⎬} | {⎨ N^+ ⎬} | N | CSExp $\cup$ CSExp | CSExp $\cap$ CSExp
	|	CSExp \ CSExp
ProcDecl	::=	**process** N $\widehat{=}$ ParProc
ParProc	::=	Decl • Proc | Proc
Proc	::=	**begin** PPar* **state** SchemaExp PPar* • Action **end** | N
	|	Proc; Proc | Proc □ Proc | Proc ⊓ Proc
	|	Proc ⟦ CSExp ⟧ Proc | Proc ⫴ Proc | Proc \ CSExp
	|	Proc[N^+ := N^+] | ParProc(Exp$^+$)
	|	$\overset{\circ}{\circ}$ Decl • Proc | ⊓ Decl • Proc
	|	∥ Decl ⟦ CSExp⟧ • Proc | ⫴ Decl • Proc
NSExp	::=	{} | {N^+} | N | NSExp $\cup$ NSExp | NSExp $\cap$ NSExp
	|	NSExp \ NSExp
PPar	::=	Par | N $\widehat{=}$ ParAction
ParAction	::=	Decl • Action | Action
Action	::=	SchemaExp | CSPAction | Command | N
CSPAction	::=	*Skip* | *Stop* | *Chaos* | Comm → Action | Pred & Action
	|	Action; Action | Action □ Action | Action ⊓ Action
	|	Action ⟦ NSExp | CSExp | NSExp ⟧ Action
	|	Action ⟦NSExp | NSExp⟧ Action
	|	Action \ CSExp | μ N • Action | ParAction(Exp$^+$)
	|	$\overset{\circ}{\circ}$ Decl • Action | ⊓ Decl • Action
Comm	::=	N?N | N!Expression | N
Command	::=	N := Exp | **if** GActions **fi** | **var** Decl • Action
GActions	::=	Pred → Action | Pred → Action □ GActions

Fig. 1. Executable *Circus* Syntax

inputs a value through channel c and assigns it to x, and then behaves like A, which has the variable x in scope. If, however, p is *false*, the same action blocks.

The CSP operators of sequence, external and internal choice, parallelism, interleaving, hiding may also be used to compose actions. Communications and recursive definitions are also available. The process *Register* has a recursive behaviour: after its initialisation, it behaves like *RegCycle*, and then recurses. The action *RegCycle* is an external choice: values may be stored or accumulated, using channels *store* and *add*; the result may be requested using channel *result*, and output through *out*; finally, the register may be reset through channel *reset*.

channel *store, add, out* : $\mathbb{N}$
channel *result, reset*
process *Register* $\widehat{=}$ **begin state** *RegSt* $\widehat{=}$ [*value* : $\mathbb{N}$]
$\quad$ *RegCycle* $\widehat{=}$ *store?newValue* $\rightarrow$ *value* := *newValue*
$\qquad\qquad\qquad$ $\square$ *add?newValue* $\rightarrow$ *value* := *value* + *newValue*
$\qquad\qquad\qquad$ $\square$ *result* $\rightarrow$ *out!value* $\rightarrow$ *Skip*
$\qquad\qquad\qquad$ $\square$ *reset* $\rightarrow$ *value* := 0
$\quad$ • *value* := 0; (μX • *RegCycle*; X) **end**

channel *read, write* : $\mathbb{N}$
process *SumClient* $\widehat{=}$
$\quad$ **begin** *ReadValue* $\widehat{=}$ *read?n* $\rightarrow$ *reset* $\rightarrow$ *Sum*(*n*)
$\qquad\quad$ *Sum* $\widehat{=}$ $n : \mathbb{N}$ • ($n = 0$) & *result* $\rightarrow$ *out?r* $\rightarrow$ *write!r* $\rightarrow$ *Skip*
$\qquad\qquad\qquad\qquad$ $\square$ ($n \neq 0$) & *add!n* $\rightarrow$ *Sum*($n - 1$)
$\quad$ • μX • *ReadValue*; X **end**
chanset *RegAlphabet* == $\{\!|$ *store, add, out, result, reset* $|\!\}$
process *Summation* $\widehat{=}$ (*SumClient* $[\!|$ *RegAlphabet* $|\!]$ *Register*) \ *RegAlphabet*

Fig. 2. A simple register

The parallelism and interleaving operators are different from those of CSP. We must declare a synchronisation channel set, and, to avoid conflicts, two sets that partition the variables in scope: state components, and input and local variables. In a parallelism $A_1 [\![ns_1 \mid cs \mid ns_2]\!] A_2$, the actions A_1 and A_2 synchronise on the channels in the set cs. Both A_1 and A_2 have access to the initial values of all variables in ns_1 and ns_2, but A_1 may modify only the values of the variables in ns_1, and A_2, the values of the variables in ns_2.

References to parametrised actions need to be instantiated. Actions may also be defined using assignment, guarded alternation, or variable blocks. Finally, in the interest of supporting a calculational approach to development, an action can be a Morgan's specification statement [10].

The CSP operators of sequence, external and internal choice, parallelism, interleaving, and hiding may also be used to compose processes. Furthermore, the renaming $P[oldc := newc]$ replaces all the references to channels $oldc$ by the corresponding channels in $newc$, which are implicitly declared. Parametrised processes may also be instantiated.

In Figure 2, the process *SumClient* repeatedly receives a value n through channel *read*, interacts with *Register* to calculate the sum $\sum_{i=0}^{n} i$, and finally outputs this value through *write*. The process *Summation* is the parallel composition of *Register* and *SumClient*. They synchronise on the set of channels *RegAlphabet*, which is hidden from the environment: iterations with *Summation* can only be made through *read* and *write*.

Some other operators are available in *Circus*, but are omitted here for conciseness. The translation of these operators is either trivial or left as future work. They are discussed in Section 5.

3   JCSP

Since the facilities for concurrency in Java do not directly correspond with the idea of processes in CSP and *Circus*, we use JCSP, a library that provides a model for processes and channels. This allows us to abstract from basic monitor constructs provided by Java. In JCSP, a process is a class that implements the interface CSProcess{public void run();}, where the method run encodes its behaviour. We present an Example process below.

```
import jcsp.lang.*; // further imports
class Example implements CSProcess {
    // state information, constructors, and auxiliary methods
    public void run { /* execution of the process */ } }
```

After importing the basic JCSP classes and any other relevant classes, we declare Example, which may have private attributes, constructors, and auxiliary methods. Finally, we must give the implementation of the method run.

Some JCSP interfaces represent channels: ChannelInput is the type of channels used to read objects; ChannelOutput is for channels used to write objects; and AltingChannel is for channels used in choices. Other interfaces are available, but these are the only ones used in our work.

The simplest implementation of a channel interface is that provided by the class One2OneChannel, which represents a point-to-point channel; multiple readers and writers are not allowed. On the other hand, Any2OneChannel channels allow many writers to communicate with one reader. For any type of channel, a communication happens between one writer and one reader only.

Mostly, JCSP channels communicate Java objects. For instance, in order to communicate an object o through a channel c, a writer process may declare c as a ChannelOutput, and invoke c.write(o); a reader process that declares c as a ChannelInput invokes c.read().

The class Alternative implements the choice operator. Although other types of choice are available, we use a fair choice. Only AltingChannelInput channels may be involved in choices. The code below reads from either channel l or r.

```
AltingChannelInput[] chs = new AltingChannelInput[]{l,r};
final Alternative alt = new Alternative(chs);
chs[alt.select()].read();
```

The channels l and r are declared in an array of channels chs, which is given to the constructor of the Alternative. The method select waits for one or more channels to become ready, makes an arbitrary choice between them, and returns an int that corresponds to the index of the chosen channel in chs. Finally, we read from the channel located at the chosen position of chs.

Parallel processes are implemented using the class Parallel. Its constructor takes an array of CSProcesses and returns a CSProcess that is the parallel composition of its process arguments. A run of a Parallel process

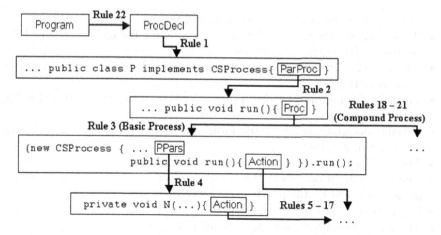

Fig. 3. Translation Strategy Overview

terminates when all its component processes terminate. For instance, the code
`(new Parallel(new CSProcess[]{P_1,P_2})).run();` runs two processes `P_1`
and `P_2` in parallel. It creates the array of processes which will run in parallel,
gives it to the constructor of `Parallel`, and finally, runs the parallelism.

The CSP constructors *Skip* and *Stop* are implemented by the classes `Skip`
and `Stop`. JCSP includes other facilities beyond those available in CSP; here we
concentrate on those that are relevant for our work.

4   From Circus to JCSP

Our strategy for translating *Circus* programs considers each paragraph individually, and in sequence. In Figure 3, we present an overview of the translation
strategy. First, for a given Program, we use a rule (Rule 22) that deals with the Z
paragraphs and channel declarations. Each process declaration ProcDecl in the
program is transformed into a new Java class (Rule 1). The next step (Rule 2)
declares the class attributes, constructor, and its run method. Basic process
definitions are translated (Rule 3) to the execution of a process whose private methods correspond to the translation (Rule 4) of actions of the original *Circus* process; the translation (Rules 5-17) of the main Action, which determines the body of the method run, and of the Action bodies conclude the
translation of basic processes. Compound processes are translated using a
separate set of rules (Rules 18-21) that combines the translations of the basic
processes.

Only executable *Circus* programs can be translated: the technique in [2, 19]
can be used to refine specifications. Other restrictions are syntactic and can be
enforced by a (mechanised) pre-processing; they are listed below.

- The *Circus* program is well-typed and well-formed.
- Paragraphs are grouped in the following order: Z paragraphs, channel declarations, and process declarations.
- Z paragraphs are axiomatic definitions of the form $v : T \mid v = e_1$, free types, or abbreviations.
- The only Z paragraphs inside a process declaration are axiomatic definitions of the above form.
- Variable declarations are of the form $x_1 : T_1;\ x_2 : T_2;\ \ldots;\ x_n : T_n$, and names are not reused.
- There are no nested external choices or nested guards.
- The synchronisation sets in the parallelisms are the intersection of the sets of channels used by the parallel actions or processes.
- No channel is used by two interleaved actions or processes.
- The types used are already implemented in Java.
- Only free types, abbreviations, and finite subsets of $\mathbb{N}$ and $\mathbb{Z}$ with equally spaced elements, are used for typing indexing variables of iterated operators.
- There are no multi-synchronisations or guarded outputs.

Axiomatic definitions can be used to define only constants. All types, abbreviations and free types, need a corresponding Java implementation. If necessary, the *Circus* data refinement technique should be used. In [11] we present rules to translate some forms of abbreviations and free types. Nested external choices and guarded actions can be eliminated with simple refinement laws.

The JCSP parallel construct does not allow the definition of a synchronisation channel set. For this reason, the intersection of the alphabets determines this set: if it is not empty, we have a parallelism; otherwise, we have actually an interleaving. JCSP does not have an interleaving construct; when possible we use the parallel construct instead.

Multi-synchronisation channels and guarded outputs are not implementable in JCSP. Before applying the translation strategy they must be removed applying refinement strategies as those presented in [19, 9].

The types of indexing variables in iterated operators are considered to be finite, because their translation uses loops. A different approach in the translation could make it possible to remove this restriction.

The output of the translation is Java code composed of several class declarations that can be split into different files and allocated in packages. For each program, we require a project name `proj`. The translation generates six packages: `proj` contains the main class, which is used to execute the system; `proj.axiomaticDefinitions` contains the class that encapsulates the translation of all axiomatic definitions; the processes are declared in the package `proj.processes`; `proj.typing` contains all the classes that implement types; and `proj.util` contains all the utility classes used by the generated code. For example, class `RandomGenerator` is used to generate random numbers; it is used in the implementation of internal choice.

The translation uses a channel environment δ. For each channel c, it maps c to its type, or to *sync*, if c is a synchronisation channel. We consider δ to be available throughout the translation.

For each process, two environments store information about channels: ν and ι for visible and hidden channels. They both map channel names to an element of *ChanUse* $::= I \mid O \mid A$. The constant I is used for input channels, O for output channels, and A for input channels that take part in external choices. Synchronisation channels must also be associated to one of these constants, since every JCSP channel is either an input or an output channel. If a channel c is regarded as an input channel in a process P, then it must be regarded as an output channel in any process parallel to P, and vice-versa.

The function *JType* defines the Java type corresponding to each of the used *Circus* types; and *JExp* translates expressions. The definitions of these functions are simple; for conciseness, we omit them. For example, we have that $JType(\mathbb{N})$ =Integer, and $JExp(x > y) = $ x.intValue() > y.intValue().

This section is organised as follows: the rules of translation of processes declarations are presented in Section 4.1. Section 4.2 presents the translation of the body of basic processes, which is followed by the translation of the CSP actions (Section 4.3), and commands (Section 4.4). The translation of compound processes is presented in Section 4.5. Finally, Section 4.6 presents how to run the program. For conciseness, we omit some of the formal definitions of our translation strategy. They can be found in [11].

4.1   Processes Declarations

Each process declaration is translated to a Java class that implements the JCSP interface jcsp.lang.CSProcess. For a process P in a project named *proj*, we declare a Java class P that imports the Java utilities package, the basic JCSP package, and all the project packages.

Rule 1. $\| \mathbf{process}\ P \mathrel{\widehat{=}} ParProc \|^{ProcDecl}\ proj =$

> package *proj*.processes; import java.util.*;
> import jcsp.lang.*; import *proj*.axiomaticDefinitions.*;
> import *proj*.typing.*; import *proj*.util.*;
> public class P implements CSProcess { $\| ParProc \|^{ParProc}$ P }

The function $\|\_\|^{ProcDecl}$ takes a *Circus* process declaration and a project name to yield an Java class definition; our rule defines this function. The body of the class is determined by the translation of the paragraphs of P.

As an example, we translate *Register*, *SumClient*, and *Summation* (Figure 2); the resulting code is in [12]. The translation of *Register* is shown below; we omit package and import declarations.

> public class Register implements CSProcess
> $\{ \| \ \mathbf{begin} \ \ldots \bullet value := 0; (\mu X \bullet \ldots) \ \mathbf{end} \ \|^{ParProc} $ Register $\}$

The translation the body of a parametrised process is captured by the function $\|\_\|^{ParProc}$: ParProc $\twoheadrightarrow$ N $\twoheadrightarrow$ JCode.

Rule 2. $\|[D \bullet P]\|^{ParProc}$ $N = (ParDecl\ D)\ (VisCDecl\ \nu)\ (HidCDecl\ \iota)$
$$\text{public } N(ParArgs\ D, VisCArgs\ \nu)\ \{$$
$$(MAss\ (ParDecl\ D)\ (ParArgs\ D))$$
$$(MAss\ (VisCDecl\ \nu)\ (VisCArgs\ \nu))$$
$$HidCC\ \iota\ \}$$
$$\text{public void run()\{ } \|[P]\|^{Proc}\ \}$$

The process parameters D are declared as attributes: for each $x : T$, the function *ParDecl* yields a declaration `private` $(JType\ T)$ `x;`. The visible channels are also declared as attributes: for each channel c, with use t, *VisCDecl* gives `private` $(TypeChan\ t)$ `c;`, where *TypeChan* t gives `ChannelInput` for $t = I$, `ChannelOutput` for $t = O$, and `AltingChannelInput` for $t = A$. For *Register*, we have declarations for the channels in the set *RegAlphabet*.

```
private AltingChannelInput store;...; ChannelOutput out; ...;
```

Hidden channels are also declared as attributes, but they are instantiated within the class. We declare them as `Any2OneChannel`, which can be instantiated. The process *Summation* hides all the channels in the set *RegAlphabet*. For this reason, within `Summation` they are declared to be of type `Any2OneChannel`.

The constructor receives the processes parameters and visible channels as arguments (*ParArgs* D and *VisCArgs* ν generates fresh names). The arguments are used to initialise the corresponding attributes (*MAss* (*ParDecl* D) (*ParArgs* D) and *MAss* (*VisCDecl* ν) (*VisCArgs* ν)), and hidden channels are instantiated locally (*HidCC* ι). In our example, we have the result below.

```
public Register (AltingChannelInput newstore, ...)
    { this.store = newstore; ... }
```

For *Summation*, we have the instantiation of all channels in the set *RegAlphabet*. For instance, `this.store = new Any2OneChannel();` instantiates *store*.

Finally, the method `run` implements the process body translated by $\|\_\|^{Proc}$. In our example, we have `public void run(){`$\|[$**begin** ... **end**$]\|^{Proc}$ `}`. For a non-parametrised process, like *Register*, we actually do not use Rule 1, but a simpler rule. The difference between the translation of parametrised and non-parametrised processes are the attributes corresponding to parameters.

4.2   Basic Processes

Each process body is translated by $\|\_\|^{Proc}$: Proc $\twoheadrightarrow$ JCode to an execution of an anonymous inner class that implements `CSProcess`. Inner classes are a Java feature that allows classes to be defined inside classes. The use of inner classes allows the compositional translation even in the presence of nameless processes.

Basic processes are translated as follows.

Rule 3. $\llbracket \textbf{begin } PPars_1 \textbf{ state } PSt \; PPars_2 \bullet A \rrbracket^{Proc} =$
$\qquad$ (new CSProcess(){ $(StateDecl \; PSt)$ $(\llbracket PPars_1 \; PPars_2 \rrbracket^{PPars})$
$\qquad\qquad$ public void run(){ $\llbracket A \rrbracket^{Action}$ }}).run();

The inner class declares the state components as attributes ($StateDecl \; PSt$). Each action gives rise to a private method ($\llbracket PPars_1 \; PPars_2 \rrbracket^{PPars}$). The body of run is the the translation of the main action A. Our strategy ignores any existing state invariants, since they have already been considered in the refinement of the process. It is kept in a *Circus* program just for documentation purposes.

As an example, we present the translation of the body of *Register*. For conciseness, we name its paragraphs *PPars*, and its main action *Main*.

$\qquad$ (new CSProcess(){ private Integer value; $\llbracket PPars \rrbracket^{PPars}$
$\qquad\qquad$ public void run() { $\llbracket Main \rrbracket^{Action}$ } }).run();

The function $\llbracket \_ \rrbracket^{PPars}$: PPar* $\nrightarrow$ JCode translates the paragraphs within a *Circus* process, which can either be axiomatic definitions, or (parametrised) actions. The translation of an axiomatic definition $v : T \mid v = e_1$ is a method private $(JType \; T)$ v(){return $(JExp \; e_1)$;}. Since the paragraphs of a process p can only be referenced within p, the method is declared private. We omit the relevant rule, and a few others in the sequel, for conciseness.

Both parametrised actions and non-parametrised actions are translated into private methods. However, the former requires that the parameters are declared as arguments of the new method. The reason for the method to be declared private is the same as that for the axiomatic definitions above.

Rule 4. $\llbracket N \mathrel{\widehat{=}} (D \bullet A) \; PPars \rrbracket^{PPars} =$
$\qquad$ private void N($ParArgs \; D$){ $\llbracket A \rrbracket^{Action}$ } $\llbracket PPars \rrbracket^{PPars}$

The function *ParArgs* declares an argument for each of the process parameters. The body of the method is defined by the translation of the action body.

For instance, the translation of action *RegCycle* generates the following Java code. We use *body* to denote the body of the action.

$\qquad \llbracket RegCycle \mathrel{\widehat{=}} body \rrbracket^{PPars} =$ private void RegCycle(){ $\llbracket body \rrbracket^{Action}$ }

The function $\llbracket \_ \rrbracket^{Action}$: Action $\nrightarrow$ JCode translates CSP actions and commands.

4.3 CSP Actions

In the translation of each action, the environment λ is used to record the local variables in scope in the translation of parallel and recursive actions. For each variable, λ maps its name to its type. Besides, as for processes, we have channel environments ν and ι to store information about how each channel is used.

The translations of *Skip* and *Stop* use basic JCSP classes: *Skip* is translated to
`(new Skip()).run();`, and *Stop* is translated to `(new Stop()).run();`. *Chaos*
is translated to an infinite loop `while(true){};`, which is a valid refinement of
Chaos. For input communications, we declare a new variable whose value is read
from the channel. A cast is needed, since the type of the objects transmitted
through the channels is `Object`; we use the channel environment δ.

Rule 5. $[\![c?x \rightarrow Act]\!]^{Action} = \{ \ t \ x \ = \ (t)c.\texttt{read}(); \ \ [\![Act]\!]^{Action} \ \}$

   where $t = JType(\delta \ c)$.   □

For instance, the communication *add?newValue* used in the action *RegCycle*
is translated to `Integer newValue = (Integer)add.read();`
   An output communication is easily translated as follows.

Rule 6. $[\![c!x \rightarrow Act]\!]^{Action} = \texttt{c.write(x)}; \ \ [\![Act]\!]^{Action}$

For synchronisation channels, we need to know whether it is regarded as an
input or output channel; this information is retrieved either from ν or ι.

Rule 7. $[\![c \rightarrow Act]\!]^{Action} = \texttt{c.read()};$

   provided $\nu \ c \in \{ I, A \} \vee \iota \ c \in \{ I, A \}$ □

Rule 8. $[\![c \rightarrow Act]\!]^{Action} = \texttt{c.write(null)};$

   provided $\nu \ c = O \vee \iota \ c = O$ □

For example, in the process *SumClient*, the action *reset* $\rightarrow$ *Sum(n)* is translated to `reset.write(null);`, followed by the translation of *Sum(n)*. Within
Register, the translation of *reset* is `reset.read();`. The difference is because
reset is an output channel for *SumClient*, and an input channel for *Register*.
   Sequential compositions are translated to a Java sequential composition.

Rule 9. $[\![A_1; \ \ldots \ ; \ A_n]\!]^{Action} = [\![A_1 \ ]\!]^{Action} ; \ \ldots \ ; \ \ [\![A_n]\!]^{Action}$

The translation of external choice uses the corresponding `Alternative` JCSP
class; all the initial visible channels involved take part.

Rule 10. $[\![A_1 \ \square \ \ldots \ \square \ A_n]\!]^{Action} =$
```
          Guard[] g = new Guard[]{ICAtt A₁,...,ICAtt Aₙ};
          final Alternative alt = new Alternative(g);
          (DeclCs (ExIC A₁) 0) ... (DeclCs (ExIC Aₙ) (#(ExIC Aₙ₋₁)))
          switch(alt.select())
                  { Cases (ExIC A₁) A₁... Cases (ExIC Aₙ) Aₙ }
```

   provided $A_1, \ldots, A_n$ are not guarded actions $g_i \ \& \ A_i$.   □

In Figure 4 we present the translation of the body of *RegCycle*. It declares an array containing all initial visible channels of the choice (1). The function *ICAtt* returns a ,-separated list of all initial visible channels of an action; informally, these are the first channels through which the action is prepared to communicate. The array is used in the instantiation of the `Alternative` process (2). Next, an `int` constant is declared for each channel (3). The function *DeclCs* returns a ;-separated list of `int` constant declarations. The first constant is initialised with 0, and each subsequent constant with the previous constant incremented by one. Finally, a choice is made, and the chosen action executed. We use a `switch` block (4); the body of each `case` is the translation of the corresponding action (5); the function *Cases* takes the initial visible channel as argument (*ExIC*).

```
Guard[] guards = new Guard[]{store,add,result,reset};       (1)
final Alternative alt = new Alternative(guards);            (2)
final int C_STORE = 0; ... ; final int C_RESET = 3;         (3)
switch(alt.select())                                        (4)
    { case C_STORE:{...} break; ...; case C_RESET:{...} break; } (5)
```

Fig. 4. Example of External Choice Translation

For guarded actions $\square_i \, g_i \, \& \, A_i$, we have to declare an array `g` of boolean *JExp* g_i. We use this array in the selection `alt.select(g)`. Each unguarded action A_i can be easily refined to *true* $\& \, A_i$.

If the guards are mutually exclusive, we can apply a different rule to obtain an `if-then-else`. This simplifies the generated code, and does not require the guarded actions to be explored in the translation of the external choice.

The translation of an internal choice chooses a random number between 1 and n. It uses the static method `generateNumber` of class `RandomGenerator`. Finally, it uses a `switch` block to choose and run the chosen action.

Rule 11. $[\![A_1 \sqcap \ldots \sqcap A_n]\!]^{Action} =$

       `switch(RandomGenerator.generateNumber(1,n))`
        `{case 1:{` $[\![A_1]\!]^{Action}$ `}break; ...case n:{` $[\![A_n]\!]^{Action}$ `}break;}`

To translate a parallelism, we define an inner class for each parallel action, because the JCSP `Parallel` constructor takes an array of processes as argument. To deal with the partition of the variables, we use auxiliary variables to make copies of each state component. The body of each branch is translated and each reference to a state component is replaced with its copy. After the parallelism, we merge the values of the variables in each partition.

Local variables need to be copied as well, but since they are not translated to attributes, as state components are, they cannot be directly accessed in the inner classes created for each parallel action. For this reason, their copies are not initialised when declared; they are initialised in the constructor of each parallel action. Their initial values are given to the constructor as arguments.

The names of the inner classes are defined in the translation. To avoid clashes, we use a fresh index *ind* in the name of inner classes and local variables copies. In the following rule, *LName* and *RName* stand for the names of the classes that implement A_1 and A_2. We omit *RName*, which is similar to *LName*.

The function *IAuxVars* declares and initialises an auxiliary variable for each state component in the partition of A_1. Next, *DeclLcVars* declares one copy of each local variable; the initial values are taken by the constructor (*LcVarsArgs*). In the body of the constructor, the function *ILcVars* initialises each local variable with the corresponding value received as argument. The body of the method **run** is the translation of the action. The function *RenVars* is used to replace occurrences of the state components and variables in scope with their copies.

After the conclusion of the declaration of the inner class *LName*, we create an object of *LName*. A similar approach is taken in the translation of A_2 to *RName* and an object creation. The next step is to run the parallelism. Afterwards, a merge retrieves the final values of the state components and the variables in scope from their copies (*MergeVars*).

Rule 12. $\| A_1 \| [\, ns_1 \mid cs \mid ns_2 \,] \| A_2 \|^{Action} =$

        class *LName* **implements CSProcess {**
            (*IAuxVars* $(ns_1 \setminus (\text{dom } \lambda))$ *ind L*) (*DeclLcVars* λ *ind L*)
            public *LName*((*LcVarsArg* λ)) **{** *ILcVars* λ *ind L* **}**
            public void run()
                { *RenVars* $\| A_1 \|^{Action}$ $(ns_1 \cup (\text{dom } \lambda))$ *ind L* **}}**
        CSProcess l_*ind* = **new** *LName*(*JList* (*ListFirst* λ));
        class *RName* **declaration, process** r_*ind* **instantiation**
        CSProcess[] procs_*ind* = **new CSProcess[]{** l_*ind*,r_*ind* **};**
        (**new Parallel**(procs_*ind*)).**run();**
        (*MergeVars LName* ns_1 *ind L*) (*MergeVars RName* ns_2 *ind R*)

    where *LName* = ParLBranch_*ind* and *RName* = ParRBranch_*ind*

For instance, we present the translation of $x := 0 \| [\, \{x\} \mid \emptyset \mid \{y\} \,] \| y := 1$ in Figure 5. We consider that the action occurs within a process with one state component $x : \mathbb{N}$, and that there is one local variable $y : \mathbb{N}$ in scope.

The state component x is declared in the left partition of the parallelism. For this reason, the class ParLBranch_0 has two attributes: one corresponding to the state component x (2) and one corresponding to the local variable y (3), whose initial value is received in the constructor (4). The body of the method **run** (5) replaces all the occurrences of x by its copy aux_1_x_0. This concludes the declaration of the class ParLBranch_0, which is followed by the creation of an object 1_0 of this class (6). For conciseness, we omit the declaration of the class related to the right-hand side of the parallelism (7). Its declaration, however, is very similar to the left-hand side: its only auxiliary variable aux_1_y_0 is declared and initialised as in class ParLBranch_0; the body of method **run** is the assignment aux_r_y_0 = new Integer(1);. Finally, after running the par-

```
class ParLBranch_0 implements CSProcess {                        (1)
    public Integer aux_l_x_0 = x;                                (2)
    public Integer aux_l_y_0;                                    (3)
    public ParLBranch_0(Integer y) { this.aux_l_y_0 = y; }  (4)
    public void run() { aux_l_x_0 = new Integer(0); } }      (5)
CSProcess l_0 = new ParLBranch_0(y);                             (6)
\* Right-hand side of the parallelism*\                          (7)
CSProcess[] procs_0 = new CSProcess[]{l_0,r_0};                  (8)
(new Parallel(procs_0)).run ();                                  (9)
x = ((ParLBranch_0)procs_0[0]).aux_l_x_0;                       (10)
y = ((ParRBranch_0)procs_0[1]).aux_r_y_0;                       (11)
```

Fig. 5. Example of Parallelism Translation

allelism (8,9), the final value of x is that of its left branch copy (10), and the final value of y is that of its right branch copy (11).

If we have a *Circus* action invocation, all we have to do is to translate it to a method call. If no parameter is given, the method invocation has no parameters. However, if any parameter is given, we use a Java expression corresponding to each parameter in the method invocation. In our example, $Sum(n)$ and $Sum(n-1)$ translate to `Sum(n);` and `Sum(new Integer(n.intValue()-1));`.

In order to avoid the need of indexing recursion variables, we also use inner classes to declare the body of recursions. As for parallelism, this requires the use of copies of local variables, which are declared as attributes of the inner class, and initialised in its constructor with the values given as arguments. The `run` method of this new inner class executes the body of the recursion, instantiates a new object of this class, where the recursion occurs, and executes it.

Rule 13. $\|[\mu X \bullet A(X)]\|^{Action} =$

> class I_*ind* implements CSProcess {
>   *DeclLcVars* λ *ind L*
>   public I_*ind*(*LcVarsArg* λ) { *ILcVars* λ *ind L* }
>   public void run(){
>   *RenVars* $\|[A(RunRec\ ind)]\|^{Action}$ (dom λ) *ind L*}};
> (*RunRec ind*)

The function *RunRec* instantiates a recursion process, invokes its `run` method, and finally collects the values of the auxiliary variables. For the same reason as for the translation of parallelism, we use a fresh index in the name of the inner class created for the recursion. Besides, since we are also using a inner class to express the recursion, the local variables must be given to the constructor of this inner class, and their final values retrieved after the execution of the recursion.

For instance, in Figure 6, we present the translation of the main action of process *Register*. First, we initialise `value` with 0 (1). Next, we declare the class I_0, which implements the recursion. It has a copy of the state component `value` as its attribute (3), which is initialised in the constructor (4). The method `run`

```
value:=new Integer(0);                                           (1)
class I_0 implements CSProcess {                                 (2)
    public Integer aux_1_value_0;                                (3)
    public I_0(Integer value){ this.aux_1_value_0 = value; }     (4)
    public void run() {                                          (5)
        RegCycle();                                              (6)
        I_0 i_0_1 = new I_0(aux_1_value_0); i_0_1.run();         (7)
        aux_1_value_0 = i_0_1.aux_1_value_0; } };                (8)
I_0 i_0_2 = new I_0(value); i_0_2.run();                         (9)
value = i_0_2.aux_1_value_0;                                    (10)
```

Fig. 6. Example of Recursion Translation

calls the method RegCycle (6), instantiates a new recursion (7), and executes it (8); this concludes the declaration of the recursion class. Next, we instantiate an object of this class, and execute it (9). Finally, we retrieve the final value.

The translation of parametrised action invocations also makes use of inner classes. Each of the local variables in scope has a corresponding copy as an attribute of the new class; the action parameters are also declared as attributes of the new class; both local variable copies attributes and parameters are initialised within the class constructor with the corresponding values given as arguments. The run method of the new class executes the parametrised action. However, the references to the local variables are replaced by references to their copies. Next, the translation creates an object of the class with the given arguments, and calls its run method. Finally, it restores the values of the local variables.

The translation of iterated sequential composition is presented below.

Rule 14. $\| [\S \; x_1 : T_1; \; \ldots; \; x_n : T_n \bullet Act] \|^{Action} =$

$\qquad InstActions \; pV\_ind \; (x_1 : T_1; \; \ldots; \; x_n : T_n) \; Act \; ind$
$\qquad$ for(int i = 0; i < pV_ind.size(); i++)
$\qquad\qquad$ { ((CSProcess)pV_ind.elementAt(i)).run(); }

The function *InstActions* declares an inner class I_ind that implements the action *Act* parametrised by the indexing variables. Then, it creates a vector pV_ind of actions using a nested loop over the possible values of each indexing variable: for each iteration, an object of I_ind is created using the current values of the indexing variables, and stored in pV_ind. Finally, each action within pV_ind is executed in sequence.

The translation of iterated internal choice uses the RandomGenerator to choose a value for each indexing variable. Then, it instantiates an action using the chosen values, and runs it.

4.4   Commands

Single assignments are directly translated to Java assignments.

```
// Package declaration and imports (Rule 1)
public class Register implements CSProcess {
    private AltingChannelInput store; ...
    public Register (AltingChannelInput newstore, ...) { ... }
    public void run(){
        (new CSProcess(){
            private Integer value;
            private void RegCycle(){
                Guard[] guards = new Guard[]{store,add,result,reset};
                final Alternative alt = new Alternative(guards);
                final int C_STORE = 0; ...; final int C_RESET = 3;
                switch(alt.select()) { case C_STORE: { ... } break;
                                       case C_ADD: { ... } break;
                                       case C_RESULT: { ... } break;
                                       case C_RESET: { ... } break; } }
            public void run() { /* Figure 6 */ } }).run(); } }
```

Fig. 7. Translation of Process Register

Rule 15. $\llbracket x := e \rrbracket^{Action} = $ x = (*JExp e*);

Variable declarations only introduce the declared variables in scope.

Rule 16. $\llbracket \text{var } x_1 : T_1; \ldots ; x_n : T_n \bullet Act \rrbracket^{Action} =$
$\quad$ { (*JType T_1*) x_1; ...; (*JType T_n*) x_n; $\llbracket Act \rrbracket^{Action}$ }

Alternations(**if_fi**) are translated to if-then-else blocks. The possible non-determinism is removed by choosing the first *true* guard. If none of the guards is *true*, the action behaves like *Chaos* (while(true){}).

Rule 17. $\llbracket \text{if } g_1 \rightarrow A_1 \; \square \; \ldots \; \square \; g_n \rightarrow A_n \; \text{fi} \rrbracket^{Action} =$

$\quad$ if(*JExp g_1*){ $\llbracket A_1 \rrbracket^{Action}$ }...else if(*JExp g_n*){ $\llbracket A_n \rrbracket^{Action}$ }
$\quad$ else { while(true){} }

At this point, we are able to translate basic process. By way of illustration, Figure 7 presents a skeleton of the complete translation of process *Register*.

4.5 Compound Processes

We now concentrate in the translation of the processes that are defined in terms of other processes. At this stage, we are actually translating the body of some process (Figure 3). This means, we are translating the body of its method run.

For a single process name N, we must instantiate the process N, and then, invoke its run method. The visible channels of the process are given as arguments to the process constructor. The function *ExtChans* returns a list of all channel names in the domain of the environment ν.

Rule 18. $\llbracket N \rrbracket^{Proc} =$ (new CSProcess(){
             public void run(){(new N(*ExtChans* ν)).run();}
             }).run();

The invocation of (parametrised) processes is translated to a new inner class. It runs the parametrised process instantiated with the given arguments. The new classes names are also indexed by a fresh *ind* to avoid clashes.

The sequential composition of processes is also easily translated to the sequential execution of each process.

Rule 19. $\llbracket P_1; \ldots; P_n \rrbracket^{Proc} = \llbracket P_1 \rrbracket^{Proc}; \ldots; \llbracket P_n \rrbracket^{Proc}$

External choice has a similar solution to that presented for actions. The idea is to create an alternative in which all the initial channels of both processes, that are not hidden, take part. However, all auxiliary functions used in the previous definitions take actions into account. All we have to do is use similar functions that take processes into account.

As the internal choice for actions, the internal choice $P_1 \sqcap \ldots \sqcap P_n$ for processes randomly chooses a process, and then, starts to behave as such. Its definition is very similar to the corresponding one for actions.

The translation of parallelism executes a **Parallel** process. This process executes all the processes that are elements of the array given as argument to its constructor in parallel. In our case, this array has only two elements: each one corresponds to a process of the parallelism. Furthermore, the translation of parallelism of processes does not have to take into account variable partitions.

Rule 20. $\llbracket P_1 \llbracket cs \rrbracket P_2 \rrbracket^{Proc} =$
           (new CSProcess(){ public void run() {   new Parallel(
               new CSProcess[]{ $\llbracket P_1 \rrbracket^{Proc}$, $\llbracket P_2 \rrbracket^{Proc}$ }).run();}}).run();

It is important to notice that, when using JCSP, the intersection of the alphabets determines the synchronisation channels set. For this reason, *cs* may be ignored.

The renaming operation $P[x_1, \ldots, x_n := y_1, \ldots, y_n]$ is translated by replacing all the x_is by the corresponding y_is in the translated Java code of P.

As for actions, the iterated operators are translated using **for** loops. The same restrictions apply for processes. The first iterated operator on processes is the sequential composition $\S$. As for actions, we use an auxiliary function to create a vector of processes, and execute in sequence each process within this vector. The iterated internal choice chooses a value for each indexing variable, and runs the process with the randomly chosen values for the indexing variables.

The translation of iterated parallelism of processes are simpler than that of actions, since we do not need to deal with partitions of variables in scope.

Rule 21. $\|[\ \| \ x_1 : T_1; \ \ldots; \ x_n : T_n \ \|[\ cs]\| \bullet P]\|^{Proc} =$

```
(new CSProcess(){
    public void run(){
        InstProcs pV_ind (x_1 : T_1; ...; x_n : T_n) P ind
        CSProcess[] pA_ind = new CSProcess[pV_ind.size()];
        for (int i = 0; i < pV_ind.size(); i++)
            { pA_ind[i] = (CSProcess)pV_ind.get(i); }
        (new Parallel(pA_ind)).run(); } }).run();
```

It uses the function *InstProcs* to instantiate a vector pV_*ind* containing each of the processes obtained by considering each possible value of the indexing variables. Then, it transforms this pV_*ind* in an array pA_*ind*, which is given to the constructor of a `Parallel` process. Finally, we run the `Parallel` process.

The indexed operator translation uses array of channels. Its definition can be found in [11]. Furthermore, the translation of free types, abbreviations, generic channels, and further types of communications are also present in [11].

4.6   Running the Program

The function $\|[\_]\|^{Program}$ summarises our translation strategy. Besides the *Circus* program, this function also receives a project name, which is used to declare the package for each new class. It declares the class that encapsulates all the axiomatic definitions (*DeclAxDefCls*), and translates all the declared processes.

Rule 22. $\|[Types\ AxDefs\ ChanDecls\ ProcDecls]\|^{Program}\ proj =$
$$(DeclAxDefCls\ proj\ AxDefs)\ (\|[ProcDecls]\|^{ProcDecls}\ proj)$$

In order to generate a class with a `main` method, which can be used to execute a given process, we use the function $\|[\_]\|^{Run}$. This function is applied to a *Circus* process, and a project name. It creates a Java class named `Main`, which is created in the package *proj*. After the package declaration, the class imports the packages `java.util`, `jcsp.lang`, and all the packages within the project. The method `main` is defined as the translation of the given process.

For instance, in order to run the process *Summation*, we have to apply the function $\|[\_]\|^{Run}$ to this process and give the project name `sum` as argument. This application results in the following Java code.

```
(new CSProcess() {
    public void run(){(new Summation()).run();} }).run();
```

For conciseness, we present only the body of the `main` method, and omit the package, import, class, and `main` method declarations.

5   Conclusion

The translation strategy presented in this work has been used to implement several programs, including a quite complex fire control system developed from its abstract centralised specification [11]. The application of the translation rules was straightforward; only human errors, which could be avoided if a translation tool were available, raised problems. The choice of JCSP was motivated by the local support of the JCSP implementors. Furthermore, the direct correspondence between many CSP and *Circus* constructs is a motivation for extending JCSP to support *Circus*, instead of creating another library from scratch.

Certainly, code generated by hand could be simpler. For instance, the translation of compound processes do not always need anonymous inner classes; they are used in the rules for generalisation purposes. However, our experiments have shown no significant improvement in performance after simplification.

In [4], Fischer formalises a translation from CSP-OZ to annotations of Java programs. A CSP-OZ specification is composed mostly by class definitions that model processes. They contain Z schemas that describe the internal state and its initialisation, and CSP processes that model the behaviour of the class. For each channel, an enable schema specifies when communication is possible, and an effect schema specifies the state changes caused by the communication.

In the translation, enable and effect schemas become pre and postconditions; the CSP part becomes trace assertions, which specify the allowed sequences of method calls; finally, state invariants become class invariants. The result is not an implementation of a CSP-OZ class, but annotations that support the verification of a given implementation. The treatment of class composition is left as future work. Differently, our work supports the translation from *Circus* specifications, possibly describing the interaction between many processes, to correct Java code.

The translation from a subset of CSP-OZ to Java is also considered in [1], where a language called COZJava, which includes CSP-OZ and Java, is used. A CSP-OZ specification is first translated to a description of the structure of the final Java program, which still contains the original CSP processes and Z schemas; these are translated afterwards. The library that they use to implement processes is called CTJ [6], which is in many ways similar to JCSP. The architecture of the resulting Java program is determined by the architecture of CSP-OZ specifications, which keep communications and state update separate. As a consequence, the code is usually inefficient and complicated. It was this difficulty that motivated the design of *Circus*.

In *Circus*, communications are not attached to state changes, but are freely mixed as exemplified by the action *RegCycle* of process *Register*. As a consequence, the reuse of Z and CSP tools is not straightforward. On the other hand, *Circus* specifications can be refined to code that follow the usual style of programming in languages like occam, or JCSP, and are more efficient.

Due to JCSP limitations, we consider a restrict set of communications: non-typed inputs, outputs, and synchronisations. In [11], we treat generic channels and synchronisations $c.e$ over a channel c with expression e. Strategies to refine out the remaining forms of communication, multi-synchronisation, and guarded outputs are left as future work. A strategy to remove a special case of multi-synchronisation, in which it is not part of an external choice, is presented in [19].

JCSP itself restricts our strategy in the translation of parallelism. It does not support the definition of a synchronisation channel set: the intersection of the alphabets determines the synchronisation channels set.

We have considered the type of indexing variables of iterated operators to be finite. Furthermore, not all iterated operators are treated directly. The translation of iterated parallelism and interleaving of actions requires their expansion. For external choice, expansion is required for both the action and the process operator, due to the need to determine their initials. For conciseness, we omitted the *Circus* indexing operator, which expands the types of values communicated through the channels used in an action (or process) to include an index. Its simple translation involves arrays of channels; the rules can be found in [11].

The most important piece of future work is the implementation of a tool to support the translation strategy. In order to prove the soundness of such a tool, the proof of the translation rules presented here would be necessary. This, however, is a very complex task, as it involves the semantics of Java and *Circus*. We currently rely on the validation of the implementation of our industrial-scale case study [13] and on the fairly direct correspondence of JCSP and *Circus*.

References

1. A. L. C. Cavalcanti and A. C. A. Sampaio. From CSP-OZ to Java with Processes (Extended Version). Technical report, Centro de Informática/UFPE, 2000. Available at http://www.cin.ufpe.br/~lmf.
2. A. L. C. Cavalcanti, A. C. A. Sampaio, and J. C. P. Woodcock. A Refinement Strategy for Circus. *Formal Aspects of Computing*, 15(2-3):146–181, 2003.
3. C. Fischer. CSP-OZ: A combination of Object-Z and CSP. In H. Bowmann and J. Derrick, editors, *Formal Methods for Open Object-Based Distributed Systems (FMOODS'97)*, volume 2, pages 423 – 438. Chapman & Hall, 1997.
4. C. Fischer. *Combination and Implementation of Processes and Data: from CSP-OZ to Java*. PhD thesis, Fachbereich Informatik, Universität Oldenburg, Oldenburg - Germany, 2000.
5. A. J. Galloway. *Integrated Formal Methods with Richer Methodological Profiles for the Development of Multi-perspective Systems*. PhD thesis, University of Teeside, School of Computing and Mathematics, 1996.
6. G. Hilderink, J. Broenink, W. Vervoort, and A. Bakkers. Communicating Java Threads. In *Parallel Programming and Java Conference*, 1997.
7. C. A. R. Hoare. *Communicating Sequential Processes*. Prentice-Hall International, 1985.
8. C. A. R. Hoare and J. He. *Unifying Theories of Programming*. Prentice-Hall, 1998.
9. A. A. McEwan. *Concurrent Program Development*. PhD thesis, Oxford University Computing Laboratory, Oxford - UK, 2000. To appear.
10. Carroll Morgan. *Programming from Specifications*. Prentice-Hall, 2nd edition, 1994.
11. M. V. M. Oliveira. A Refinement Calculus for Circus - Mini-thesis. Mini-thesis 8-04, University of Kent, Canterbury, CT2 7NF, UK, April 2004.
12. M. V. M. Oliveira. From Circus to JCSP - Summation Example Source Code, 2004. At http://www.cs.kent.ac.uk/~mvmo2/circus/summation.pdf.

13. M. V. M. Oliveira, A. L. C. Cavalcanti, and J. C. P. Woodcock. Refining Industrial Scale Systems in Circus. In Ian East, Jeremy Martin, Peter Welch, David Duce, and Mark Green, editors, *Communicating Process Architectures*. IOS Press, September 2004. To Appear.

14. P.H.Welch, G.S.Stiles, G.H.Hilderink, and A.P.Bakkers. CSP for Java : Multithreading for All. In B.M.Cook, editor, *Architectures, Languages and Techniques for Concurrent Systems*, volume 57 of *Concurrent Systems Engineering Series*, Amsterdam, the Netherlands, April 1999. WoTUG, IOS Press.

15. A. W. Roscoe. *The Theory and Practice of Concurrency*. Prentice-Hall Series in Computer Science. Prentice-Hall, 1998.

16. A. W. Roscoe, J. C. P. Woodcock, and L. Wulf. Non-interference through Determinism. In D. Gollmann, editor, *ESORICS 94*, volume 1214 of *Lecture Notes in Computer Science*, pages 33 – 54. Springer-Verlag, 1994.

17. J. M. Spivey. *The Z Notation: A Reference Manual*. Prentice-Hall, 2nd edition, 1992.

18. K. Taguchi and K. Araki. The State-based CCS Semantics for Concurrent Z Specification. In M. Hinchey and Shaoying Liu, editors, *International Conference on Formal Engineering Methods*, pages 283 – 292. IEEE, 1997.

19. J. C. P. Woodcock. Using Circus for Safety-Critical Applications. In *VI Brazilian Workshop on Formal Methods*, pages 1–15, Campina Grande, Brazil, 12th–14st October 2003.

20. J. C. P. Woodcock and A. L. C. Cavancanti. Circus: a concurrent refinement language. Technical report, Oxford University Computing Laboratory, Wolfson Building, Parks Road, Oxford OX1 3QD UK, July 2001.

21. J. C. P. Woodcock and J. Davies. *Using Z – Specification, Refinement, and Proof*. Prentice-Hall, 1996.

An Approach to Preserve Protocol Consistency and Executability Across Updates

Mahadevan Subramaniam and Parvathi Chundi

Computer Science Department,
University of Nebraska at Omaha,
Omaha, NE 68182
{msubramaniam, pchundi}@mail.unomaha.edu

Abstract. An approach to systematically update finite state protocols while preserving application independent properties such as consistency and executability is described. Protocols are modelled as a network of communicating finite state machines with each machine denoting the behavior of a single protocol controller. Updates to protocols are specified as a finite set of rules that may add, delete and/or replace one or more transitions in one or more controllers. Conditions on updates are identified under which a single transition in a single controller or multiple transitions in one or more controllers can be changed to produce an executable protocol with a consistent global transition relation. The effectiveness of the proposed approach is illustrated on a large class of cache coherence protocols. It is shown how several common design choices can be consistently incorporated into these protocols by specifying them as updates. Many changes to verified protocols are non-monotonic in the sense that they do not preserve all of the verified protocol invariants. The proposed approach enables incremental verification of application independent properties that need to be preserved by any update and are a precursor to verification of the application specific properties.

1 Introduction

Design and verification of protocols is an evolutionary and iterative process. Verified protocols are updated several times during a design cycle to optimize various system parameters that can often be accurately measured only based on an executable implementation. The updated protocols are re-verified, resulting implementation is analyzed, and the process repeats until the desired system parameter values are obtained.

Protocols in practice tend to be quite elaborate with several distributed and interacting components (*controllers*). Changing these protocols in an ad hoc manner, as usually done in practice, is highly error prone. Even apparently trivial changes frequently result in non-executable protocols containing unspecified message receptions, unreachable states, and introduce deadlocks. Consequently, each update is typically followed by extensive debugging, a tedious and time consuming activity that does not provide any additional insight about the protocol

J. Davies et al. (Eds.): ICFEM 2004, LNCS 3308, pp. 341–356, 2004.

and the changes. More importantly, properties such as protocol being executable, absence of unspecified and non-executable message receptions, and absence of deadlocks are application independent properties that must hold for any protocol. Preservation of such properties by any update is a pre-requisite for the re-verification of any application specific protocol invariants.

The main objective of this paper is to develop an approach to systematically specify updates to protocols that can be automatically applied while guaranteeing that the updated protocol is consistent and executable. We identify conditions on update specifications such that the updated protocol is guaranteed to be executable and consistent whenever these conditions are met and the original protocol is consistent and executable.

Protocols are modelled as a network of communicating finite state machines (*CFSMs*) [1] that exchange messages with each other over dedicated, bounded, FIFO channels. Each *CFSM* describes the behavior of a single protocol controller. The transition relation of a *CFSM* describes the outputs generated by the controller for each legal input combination to the controller. Each transition takes a message and a controller state as its inputs and outputs a set of messages and the next controller state. The global transition relation based on asynchronous composition of these machines with message exchanges describes the overall protocol behavior.

A protocol is said to be *executable* if it is possible to reach any initial global state from another using the global transition relation. A protocol is said to be *consistent* if its global transition relation is deterministic, every transition appears in a path between a pair of initial global states, and every path reaching any transition in the relation can be extended to an initial global state.

Updates to protocols are specified as a finite set of rules, *update rules*, that may add, delete or replace one or more transitions in one or more controllers. Updates with single as well multiple rules involving multiple controllers are considered. Updates with a single rule affect only single controller. They may either add a transition with a new legal input combination to the controller or they may replace an existing transition by another that produces different outputs. We show that a transition with a new input combination can be added while preserving executability if the messages and states in the transition already appear in the original protocol. Consistency is preserved if the input state is an initial state and every path from any initial global state reaching the newly added transition can be extended to reach an initial global state. For updates that replace transitions, the requirement that the input state be initial can be relaxed; it can be any state appearing in the original protocol. However, when we replace a transition, to preserve consistency, every transition following the replaced transition in any path between a pair of initial global states must appear in another such path not involving the replaced transition.

Updates with single rule may seem limited. However, several changes to industrial-strength protocols such as cache coherence protocols can be specified using single rule updates. This is illustrated in detail in section 7.

Updates with a single rule however, cannot introduce new states and/or new messages while preserving consistency and executability. Simultaneous updates to multiple controllers each with multiple update rules are needed to specify such changes. Rules in such updates can be classified as *addition*, *replacement* or *deletion* rules. Updates with multiple rules preserve executability and consistency if each rule in the update preserve these properties. Each addition and replacement rule can be viewed as a single rule update and the conditions required for these rules to preserve these properties can be checked. For deletion rules it needs to be additionally ensured that every transition appearing in a path between initial global states with the transition being deleted is also either deleted or appears in some other path not involving the nodes that are deleted.

The proposed approach is largely motivated by the industrial experience of one of the authors in design and verification of hardware-based cache coherence protocols for shared memory multiprocessors. The effectiveness of the proposed approach is illustrated by showing how common design choices for these protocols [2] can be incorporated by specifying them as updates. However, we believe that the proposed approach is general and is applicable to other protocols that can be modelled using *CFSM*s with bounded channels.

2   Related Work

CFSMs based on both bounded and unbounded channels have been extensively used to specify, synthesize and verify protocols [1, 3, 5, 6, 11, 10]. Protocols modelled using CFSMs been analyzed to verify application independent properties such as the absence of unspecified and unxecutable message receptions [1, 11] as well as the absence of deadlocks [6, 10, 11]. However, approaches to systematically update protocols modelled using CFSMs do not seem to have been considered earlier. To the best of our knowledge, this is also the first attempt identifying conditions on updates so that these application independent properties are preserved. However, our model of CFSMs is more constrained than those considered earlier since we consider only bounded channels and constrain the transition relations to be deterministic both of which are common for several protocols in practice, especially those realized in hardware.

Preservation of protocol properties with respect to updates have also been considered in the context of incremental model checking [13, 8] as well as in terms of correctness preserving refinements and abstractions [9, 7]. Olga and Smolka in [8, 13] also model updates as changes to transitions as done here. However, the focus in [8, 13] is to efficiently re-verify properties and no attempt is made to relate preservation of properties to constraints on update specifications. Further, the updates described in this paper can be non-monotonic with respect to the established protocol invariants and hence do not strictly correspond to correctness preserving refinements or abstractions of protocols.

3   Modelling Protocols by CFSMs

In this section a brief overview of (*CFSMs*) is given. Most of the section is based on [1, 10].

Typically, a protocol is modelled as network of CFSMs, $P = (P_1, \cdots, P_n, \mathcal{E})$ where each P_i is a *CFSM* representing a protocol controller and $\mathcal{E}$ denotes the environment. The protocol controllers communicate with each other and the environment by exchanging messages over a network of bounded FIFO channels. Each *CFSM* P_i is a 4-tuple (S_i, I_i, M_i, T_i) where S_i is a finite set of states, $I_i \subseteq S_i$ is a finite set of initial states, M_i are the messages sent and received by P_i and $T_i \subseteq S_i \times M_i \times S_i \times 2^{M_i}$ is the transition relation.

Each set $M_i = M_{i,j} \cup M_{j,i}$, for $1 \leq i, j \leq n$, $i \neq j$, where $M_{i,j}$ denotes the messages sent by the machine P_i to the machine P_j and $M_{j,i}$ denotes the messages received by P_i from P_j. Each message in $M_{i,j}$ is written as $m(i, j)$ where m is the message label. The set $M_{i,i}$ is empty for all i since we assume that no P_i exchanges messages with itself.

Each transition t in T_i is a 4-tuple $\langle m_0(j, i), s_i, s_i', \{m_1(i, k_1), \cdots, m_l(i, k_l)\}\rangle$ where m_0 is the input message, s_i and s_i' are respectively the input and output states, and $m_1, \cdots, m_l$ are respectively the output messages to the controllers $k_1 \cdots k_l$, $1 \leq l \leq n$, $l \neq i$. Let $im[t]$, $is[t]$, $os[t]$ and $om[t]$ respectively stand for the input message, input state, output state and the set of output messages of t. The set $om[t]$ could be empty and means that no output messages are sent by the transition t. Allowing $om[t]$ to contain multiple elements allows t to send out multiple different messages to different controllers on processing the input message. A transition with multiple identical output messages models multi-casting and is used to model cache coherence protocols in section 7.

Let (i, j), $i \neq j$, denote the channel on which a message in $M_{i,j}$ is transmitted. We slightly abuse the notation and use the channel (i, j) to denote the contents of the channel (i, j) as well. We assume in this paper that all channels are bounded and have length 1. Further, $(i, i) = \{\}$ for all i since no controller P_i exchanges messages with itself.

The *global state* of P is a pair $[\vec{u}, \vec{v}]$ where $\vec{u} = \langle s_i \rangle$, $s_i \in S_i$ and $\vec{v} = \langle (i, j) \rangle$, $1 \leq i, j \leq n$, $i \neq j$. We use $\vec{u}[j]$ to denote the jth element of $\vec{u}$ and $\vec{v}[i, j]$ to denote the contents of channel (i, j). The *initial global state* is a tuple $[\vec{u_0}, \vec{v_0}]$ where $\vec{u}[i] \in I_i$ for all i, and $\vec{v_0}[i, j] = \{\}$ if $i \neq \mathcal{E}$ and $j \neq \mathcal{E}$. So, the only channel messages in an initial global states are messages from/to $\mathcal{E}$.

Given a transition $t_i = \langle m_0(j, i), s_i, s_i', \{m_1(i, k_1), \cdots, m_l(i, k_l)\}\rangle$, an *execution step* $\rightarrow$ of P is a binary relation on global states: $[\vec{u1}, \vec{v1}] \rightarrow [\vec{u2}, \vec{v2}]$ where the input message m_0 from controller P_j to P_i in the channel (j, i) is dequeued and processed by controller P_i in state s_i and the output messages $m_1 \cdots m_l$ to controllers $P_{k_1} \cdots P_{k_l}$ are enqueued to the channels $(i, k_1), \cdots, (i, k_l)$. After m_0 is dequeued, channel (j, i) is empty in $\vec{v2}$. Similarly, before $m_1, \cdots, m_l$ are enqueued, channels $(i, k1), \cdots, (i, kl)$ are empty in $\vec{v1}$. The controller P_i transitions to the next state s_i' while all other controller states remain unchanged.

The relation $\rightarrow^*$, the reflexive, transitive closure of $\rightarrow$ is used to define the notion of reachability among global states. A global state $[\overrightarrow{u_2}, \overrightarrow{v_2}]$ is *reachable* from $[\overrightarrow{u_1}, \overrightarrow{v_1}]$ if $[\overrightarrow{u_1}, \overrightarrow{v_1}] \rightarrow^* [\overrightarrow{u_2}, \overrightarrow{v_2}]$.

A path $[\overrightarrow{u_0}, \overrightarrow{v_0}] \rightarrow^* [\overrightarrow{u_1}, \overrightarrow{v_1}]$ is *valid* if $[\overrightarrow{u_0}, \overrightarrow{v_0}]$ and $[\overrightarrow{u_1}, \overrightarrow{v_1}]$ are initial global states.

We say that protocol P *executable* if there is a valid path between every pair of initial global states of P. If P has a single initial global state then there must be a valid path from the initial global state to itself.

3.1   Transition Dependency Graph

Updates modify the protocol at the transition level. To produce a consistent updated protocol it is necessary to understand the effects of modifying one transition on other dependent transitions. To explicate transition dependencies the global transition relation is modelled as a *transition dependency graph(TDG)*.

The TDG is a directed graph whose nodes are the transitions of controllers P_i along with the node $\mathcal{E}$. A node u is *initial* if $is[u]$ belongs to I_i.

Edges in TDG are labelled either as a *message edges* or *state edges*. There is a state edge from node u to v, (u, v, s_i), whenever $os[u] = is[v] = s_i$. There is a message edge from u to v, (u, v, m_1) whenever $om[u] = im[v] = m_1$. State edges are always among nodes of the same controller and message edges are always among nodes of different controllers. So, between u and v there is at most one edge. There are no state edges from/to $\mathcal{E}$. There may be no outgoing message edges from a node if it does not issue an output message.

Node u is an immediate message predecessor of node v, $mpre[v] = u$, if (u, v, m) belongs to TDG. Then, node v is the immediate message successor of u, $mpos[u] = v$. The immediate state predecessor $spre[u]$ and successor $spos[u]$ of a node u are similarly defined. Note that in general $mpos[]$, $mpre[]$, $spre[]$ and $spos[]$ are sets of nodes since nodes may have several immediate successors and predecessors. If u is an initial node then $spre[u] = \{\}$.

A *message path* in TDG is a sequence of nodes $u_1, \cdots, u_n$ such that each u_i is a immediate message predecessor of u_{i+1}. A node u is a message predecessor for a node v if there is a message path starting at u and ending in v. Then, node v is the message successor of u. A *state path* in TDG is similarly defined based on state edges. State predecessor and successor are similarly defined based on state paths.

Two transitions *match* if their inputs are the same.

Two nodes in TDG *match* if the corresponding transitions match. The graph TDG is *deterministic* if it does not contain matching nodes with different outputs.

Definition 1. *A TDG is* consistent *if and only if for each node n*

- *No other node in TDG matches n and*
- *n appears in a valid path and*
- *each path $[\overrightarrow{u_0}, \overrightarrow{v_0}] \rightarrow^* \cdots \rightarrow^n [\overrightarrow{u}, \overrightarrow{v}]$ for a global initial state $[\overrightarrow{u_0}, \overrightarrow{v_0}]$, is a prefix of a valid path*

Note that consistency of TDG does not imply that the corresponding protocol P is executable. For instance, consider protocol P with a single controller P_i with the transition relation TDG with three initial nodes $n_0 = \langle m_1(\mathcal{E}, i), s_0, s_1, m_1(i, \mathcal{E}) \rangle$, $n_1 = \langle m_1(\mathcal{E}, i), s_1, s_0, m_1(i, \mathcal{E}) \rangle$ and $n_2 = \langle m_1(\mathcal{E}, i), s_2, s_0, m_1(i, \mathcal{E}) \rangle$. The TDG is consistent since it is deterministic, every node appears in a valid path and every path containing these nodes is a prefix of a valid path since all nodes are initial nodes. However, P is not executable since there is no valid path from between the global initial states $[\langle s_0 \rangle, \langle m_1(\mathcal{E}, i) \rangle]$ and $[\langle s_0 \rangle, \langle m_1(i, \mathcal{E}) \rangle]$. One can construct a similar example to observe that the executability of a protocol does not imply the consistency of the corresponding TDG.

4 Specifying Updates

Updates add and/or replace one or more nodes of a given TDG. An update specification δ of a protocol P is a set of updates $\delta_1, \cdots, \delta_n$ where each δ_i updates the controller P_i. An update δ_i is specified as a set of update rules of the form $ur_i : mt_i \rightarrow ct_i$. The rule denotes replacement of a TDG node matching mt_i by the node ct_i. The node mt_i is called the *match node* and ct_i is the *change node*. If the match node of the rule ur_i does not belong to TDG then the update simply adds the change node ct_i to TDG. If there is no update for a controller P_k in δ its transitions remain unchanged.

Let $UTDG$ stand for the updated transition dependency graph.

Many common updates to protocols require that each δ_i have multiple rules. For example, an update that introduces a new non-initial state s in a controller must include at least two rules – a rule that specifies the predecessor of s and another that specifies its successor. In general, if δ_i contains multiple rules, then it is possible that different updated transition graphs are produced based on the order of application of rules. For instance, if a match node mt_k in a rule ur_k matches a change node ct_l of another rule ur_l, then the updated graph will include node ct_l if ur_k is applied before ur_l. Otherwise, the change node ct_l added by the rule ur_l will be deleted by the application of the rule ur_k.

To avoid this we require that for any two rules ur_k and ur_l, either mt_k does not match ct_l, and mt_l does not match ct_k or $ct_k = ct_l$. Then, the rules ur_k and ur_l are said to be *order-independent*. An update δ_i with multiple-rules is order-independent if its rules are pairwise order-independent. The update δ is order-independent if each δ_i is order-independent. Henceforth, we assume updates with multiple rules to be order-independent.

An update δ may also represented using the transition dependency graph $TDG(\delta)$ whose nodes are all the change nodes of δ. For instance, the $TDG(\delta_i)$ for an update with a single update rule ur_i, is a single node ct_i and has a single state edge $(ct_i, ct_i, is[ct_i])$ if $is[ct_i] = os[ct_i]$ and no edges otherwise.

An update δ is deterministic if the corresponding $TDG(\delta)$ is deterministic.

4.1   Preserving Determinism

Now we describe the conditions on updates to preserve determinism. A notion of *match-complete* updates is introduced and it is shown that the updated graph $UTDG$ obtained from a given a deterministic TDG and a match-complete update is deterministic.

Determinism can be preserved if $TDG(\delta_i)$ is deterministic and it is guaranteed that all nodes of TDG matching a change node in $TDG(\delta_i)$ will be deleted by the update operation. An update δ_i with a single rule $mt_i \rightarrow ct_i$ will delete a TDG node matching the change node ct_i if ct_i matches the node mt_i. Such updates are said to be *match-complete*.

An update δ_i with multiple rules is match-complete if for each rule ur_k there is a rule ur_l such that the change node ct_k of the rule ur_k matches the match node mt_l of the rule ur_l.

Update $\delta = (\delta_1, \cdots, \delta_k)$ is match-complete if each δ_i is match-complete. Henceforth, we will assume that updates δ are match-complete and consistent.

Proposition 1. *A deterministic, match-complete update δ preserves determinism.*

5   Updating with a Single Rule

Consider updating a single controller P_i in an executable protocol P by a single update rule ur_i: $mt_i \rightarrow ct_i$. If none of the nodes of TDG matches mt_i then the updated protocol is obtained by simply adding the change node ct_i to TDG. In this case, the update is referred to as an **add update**. Otherwise, ct_i replaces the matching node to produce the updated protocol and is a **replacement update**. Below, add updates are considered first. Then, replacement updates are discussed.

In updates with a single rule, the match node mt_i and the change node ct_i must have identical input states and messages to be match-complete.

5.1   Add Updates

In this case, the updated protocol is obtained by adding a new message and state input combination specified by the change node ct_i to the controller P_i.

Consider the following protocol P with two controllers P_1 and P_2 with initial states $\{s_0, s_0'\}$ and $\{t_0\}$ respectively. It can be verified that P is executable and has a consistent TDG.

P_1 :   1. $\langle m_1(2,1), s_0, s_1, m_2(1,2)\rangle$,   2. $\langle m_3(2,1), s_1, s_2, m_4(1,2)\rangle$,
        3. $\langle m_5(2,1), s_2, s_0', m_6(1,\mathcal{E})\rangle$,   4. $\langle m_0(\mathcal{E},1), s_0', s_0, m_0(1,\mathcal{E})\rangle$,
P_2 :   5. $\langle m_0(\mathcal{E},2), t_0, t_0, m_1(2,1)\rangle$,   6. $\langle m_2(1,2), t_0, t_0, m_3(2,1)\rangle$,
        7. $\langle m_4(1,2), t_0, t_0, m_5(2,1)\rangle$.

Consider the following add update mt_i: $\langle m_7(\mathcal{E},1), s_0, s_0', m_8(1,\mathcal{E})\rangle \rightarrow ct_i$: $\langle m_7(\mathcal{E},1), s_0, s_0', m_8(1,\mathcal{E})\rangle$. The change node ct_i appears in a valid path by itself and this is the only valid path containing ct_i. Further, all valid paths of the original protocol are preserved since all TDG nodes are retained. Hence $UTDG$ is consistent. Moreover, since no new initial states are introduced by ct_i this also implies that there is valid path between every pair of initial global states in the updated protocol as well. Therefore, the updated protocol is executable.

It is not necessary that messages in ct_i be exchanged only with $\mathcal{E}$. For instance, we can add ct_i: $\langle m_1(2, 1), s_0', s_1, m_2(1, 2) \rangle$ to P_1 while preserving consistency and executability. A valid path including ct_i can be constructed by starting in the input state of ct_i to reach $[\langle s_1, t_0 \rangle, \langle m_2(1, 2) \rangle]$, a state in the original protocol P, that reaches the global initial state $[\langle s_0', t_0 \rangle, \langle \rangle]$. Since this is the only path from an initial global state in which ct_i appears, every path involving ct_i is a prefix of a valid path. Paths in $UTDG$ without ct_i are all valid since TDG is consistent.

Also, for any ct_i to appear in a valid path its input state must be an initial state. Suppose ct_i: $\langle m_1(2, 1), s_1, s_1, m_2(1, 2) \rangle$, it can be verified that ct_i cannot appear in a valid path in the updated protocol obtained from the protocol above.

In general, when a ct_i is being added, to preserve the consistency of $UTDG$, all global states $[\vec{u_1}, \vec{v_1}]$ from which ct_i can be executed and all global states $[\vec{u_2}, \vec{v_2}]$ resulting after executing ct_i are considered. The node ct_i is added to $UTDG$ only if there is a path p_m from an initial global state to $[\vec{u_1}, \vec{v_1}]$ and there is a path p_n from some initial global state (not necessarily the same as that of p_m) to $[\vec{u_2}, \vec{v_2}]$ such that $\vec{u_1}[j] = \vec{u_2}[j]$ for all $j \neq i$ and $\vec{v_1} = \vec{v_2}$ for all channels except (j, i) and (i, k). Further, for each path p_m we must be able to find a path p_n such that the above conditions hold. This ensures that ct_i appears in a valid path and all paths from initial states to ct_i are prefixes of a valid path in the updated protocol.

The transition graph $UTDG$ will not be consistent if we cannot find paths p_m and p_n that meet the above conditions. For example, consider adding the change node ct_i: $\langle m_7(\mathcal{E}, 1), s_0, s_2, m_2(1, 2) \rangle$ to the controller P_1 above. The global state where ct_i is executable is the initial state $[\langle s_0, t_0 \rangle, \langle m_7(\mathcal{E}, 1) \rangle]$, which is trivially reachable from an initial state ($p_m = \{\}$). However, the $UTDG$ with ct_i is not consistent since we cannot find a path p_n from the global state $[\langle s_2, t_0 \rangle \langle m_2(1, 2) \rangle$ to any initial global state.

Further, it is clear that ct_i cannot introduce new states because we are adding only one node which cannot create the valid paths required to make $UTDG$ consistent. Similarly, ct_i cannot contain a new input (output) message as there is no node in $UTDG$ to send (receive) the message.

The following lemma establishes the requirements on updates with a single rule for preserving consistency and executability when there is no matching node in TDG. Recall that any update specification δ is match-complete.

Lemma 1. *An add update* $\delta_i = \langle mt_i, ct_i \rangle$ *preserves executability and consistency of a protocol* P *if all of the following conditions hold. Let* $ct_i = \langle m_1(j, i), s, s', m_2(i, k) \rangle$.

1. $s, s' \in S_i$ *and* $s \in I_i$ *and* $m_1(j, i) \in M_{j,i}$ *or* $j = \mathcal{E}$ *and* $m_2(i, k) \in M_{i,k}$ *or* $k = \mathcal{E}$ *and*

2. ct_i is reachable from an initial global state and for each path $p_m = [\overrightarrow{u_0}, \overrightarrow{v_0}]$
$\rightarrow^{p_m} [\overrightarrow{u_1}, \overrightarrow{v_1}]$ in the updated protocol where $\overrightarrow{u_1}[i] = s$ and $\overrightarrow{v_1}[j, i] = m_1$, and
$[\overrightarrow{u_0}, \overrightarrow{v_0}]$ is an initial global state, there exists a path $p_n = [\overrightarrow{u_2}, \overrightarrow{v_2}] \rightarrow^{p_n} [\overrightarrow{u_3}, \overrightarrow{v_3}]$
for an initial global state $[\overrightarrow{u_2}, \overrightarrow{v_2}]$ such that $\overrightarrow{u_3}[i] = s'$ and $\overrightarrow{v_3}[i, k] = m_2$ and
$\overrightarrow{u_1}[j] = \overrightarrow{u_3}[j]$, $j \neq i$, and $\overrightarrow{v_1} = \overrightarrow{v_3}$ for all channels but (j, i) and (i, k).

5.2   Replacement Updates

Replacement unlike addition does not introduce a new message, state input combination for a controller but changes the outputs for a given input combination by a different one. The requirements on the messages and the states in the change node are the same as that of addition except that it can have a non-initial state as an input state.

For example, in the executable protocol,

P_1 :   1. $\langle m_0(\mathcal{E}, 1),\ s_0,\ s_1,\ m_1(1, 2) \rangle$,   2. $\langle m_2(2, 1),\ s_1,\ s_2,\ m_3(1, 2) \rangle$,
3. $\langle m_4(2, 1),\ s_2,\ s_0, m_5(1, \mathcal{E}) \rangle$,
P_2 :   4. $\langle m_1(1, 2),\ t_0,\ t_0,\ m_2(2, 1) \rangle$,   5. $\langle m_3(1, 2),\ t_0,\ t_0,\ m_4(2, 1) \rangle$,

we can replace the node mt_i: $\langle m_4(2, 1), s_2, s_1, m_5(1, \mathcal{E}) \rangle$ by ct_i: $\langle m_4(2, 1), s_2, s_0, m_0(1, \mathcal{E}) \rangle$ to produce an executable protocol with a consistent updated transition relation where the change node has a non-initial state.

In general, replacing a node n may make other nodes that follow n in a valid path in the original protocol unreachable in the updated protocol. For example, consider replacing the node mt_i: $\langle m_2(2, 1),\ s_1,\ s_2,\ m_3(1, 2) \rangle$ by the node ct_i: $\langle m_2(2, 1),\ s_1,\ s_0,\ m_3(1, 2) \rangle$. The change node ct_i appears in a valid path which is also the only valid path in the protocol. However, the nodes $\langle m_3(1, 2), t_0, t_0, m_4(2, 1) \rangle$ and $\langle m_4(2, 1), s_2, s_0, m_5(1, \mathcal{E}) \rangle$ no longer appear in a valid path. This can be determined a priori by identifying all nodes that may appear in any valid path following a node n that matches the node mt_i and ensuring that each node either appears in some valid path in the original protocol not involving the node n or it appears in the updated protocol in a valid path involving ct_i.

For example, it can be verified that the same update of the following slightly modified protocol,

P_1 :   1. $\langle m_0(\mathcal{E}, 1),\ s_0,\ s_1,\ m_1(1, 2) \rangle$,   2. $\langle m_2(2, 1),\ s_1,\ s_2,\ m_3(1, 2) \rangle$,
3. $\langle m_4(2, 1),\ s_2,\ s_0, m_5(1, \mathcal{E}) \rangle$,
4. $m_1(\mathcal{E}, 1), s_0, s_{11}, m_1(1, 2) \rangle$,   5. $m_2(2, 1), s_{11}, s_2, m_3(1, 2) \rangle$
P_2 :   6. $\langle m_1(1, 2),\ t_0,\ t_0,\ m_2(2, 1) \rangle$,   7. $\langle m_3(1, 2),\ t_0,\ t_0,\ m_4(2, 1) \rangle$,

with an additional initial state s_{11} in controller P_1, will produce an executable protocol with a consistent $UTDG$. In this case, the nodes $\langle m_3(1, 2), t_0, t_0, m_4(2, 1) \rangle$ and $\langle m_4(2, 1), s_2, s_0, m_5(1, \mathcal{E}) \rangle$ both appear in valid paths not involving the node $\langle m_2(2, 1),\ s_1,\ s_2\ m_3(1, 2) \rangle$. Hence this node can be replaced with a different outputs that reach an initial state without involving these nodes.

Lemma 2. *A replacement update $\delta_i = \langle mt_i, ct_i \rangle$ preserves executability and consistency of a protocol P if all of the following conditions hold. Let $ct_i = \langle m_1(j, i), s, s', m_2(i, k) \rangle$.*

1. *$s, s' \in S_i$ and $m_1(j, i) \in M_{j,i}$ or $j = \mathcal{E}$ and $m_2(i, k) \in M_{i,k}$ or $k = \mathcal{E}$ and*
2. *ct_i is reachable from an initial global state and for each path $p_m = [\overrightarrow{u_0}, \overrightarrow{v_0}]$ $\rightarrow^{p_m} [\overrightarrow{u_1}, \overrightarrow{v_1}]$ in the updated protocol where $\overrightarrow{u_1}[i] = s$ and $\overrightarrow{v_1}[j, i] = m_1$, and $[\overrightarrow{u_0}, \overrightarrow{v_0}]$ is an initial global state, there exists a path $p_n = [\overrightarrow{u_2}, \overrightarrow{v_2}] \rightarrow^{p_n} [\overrightarrow{u_3}, \overrightarrow{v_3}]$ for an initial global state $[\overrightarrow{u_2}, \overrightarrow{v_2}]$ such that $\overrightarrow{u_3}[i] = s'$ and $\overrightarrow{v_3}[i, k] = m_2$ and $\overrightarrow{u_1}[j] = \overrightarrow{u_3}[j]$, $j \neq i$, and $\overrightarrow{v_1} = \overrightarrow{v_3}$ for all channels but (j, i) and (i, k) and*
3. *each node n' following the node n in a valid path in P either appears in a valid path in P not involving n or appears in a valid path in the updated protocol with ct_i.*

6 Updating with Multiple Rules

As discussed earlier in section 4, more general changes to protocols that introduce new states and/or new messages cannot be specified by updates with a single rule. Updates to a controller with multiple rules are needed to introduce new states and it is necessary to simultaneously update multiple controllers to introduce new messages. Due to the dependency among the rules, often, the intermediate protocol produced by application of any individual rule may not preserve executability and consistency.

Consider an update $\delta = \{ur_1, \cdots, ur_k\}$ with multiple rules.

A rule ur_i is called an *addition rule* if its match node mt_i does not match any TDG node. A rule ur_i is called a *deletion rule* if its match node mt_i matches some TDG node but does not match the change node of any rule ur_j. A rule ur_i is called a *replacement rule* if its match node mt_i matches some TDG node and matches the change node of some rule ur_j. Each rule in δ is either an addition, deletion or a replacement rule. An update δ can be made of only addition and/or replacement rules. However, it cannot be made only of deletion rules since it will not be match-complete.

Consider updating the protocol P with a single controller P_1 with initial state $\{s_0\}$ and non-initial states $\{s_1, s_2\}$,

$$P_1: \quad 1.\ \langle m_0(\mathcal{E}, 1), s_0, s_0, m_1(1, \mathcal{E}) \rangle, \quad 2.\ \langle m_1(\mathcal{E}, 1), s_0, s_1, m_2(1, \mathcal{E}) \rangle,$$
$$3.\ \langle m_3(\mathcal{E}, 1), s_1, s_2, m_4(1, \mathcal{E}) \rangle, \quad 4.\ \langle m_5(\mathcal{E}, 1), s_2, s_0, m_6(1, \mathcal{E}) \rangle,$$

using an update δ with two addition rules with change nodes $ct_1 = \langle m_1(\mathcal{E}, 1), s_0, s_3, m_2(1, \mathcal{E}) \rangle$ and $ct_2 = \langle m_3(\mathcal{E}, 1), s_3, s_0, m_4(1, \mathcal{E}) \rangle$ where s_3, is a new non-initial state. Let $mt_1 = ct_1$ and $mt_2 = ct_2$. It is easy to see that the intermediate protocol obtained by adding either of these change nodes does not have a consistent transition relation since neither ct_1 nor ct_2 can appear in a valid path without the other. Similar cyclic dependencies are evident among change nodes in updates that introduce new messages.

To handle such cyclic dependencies, all the rules in an update are applied to the transition relation TDG to produce an $UTDG$. Then, for each rule, depending on whether it is an addition, deletion or replacement rule, conditions to guarantee an executable updated protocol with a consistent transition relation are identified and checked with respect to $UTDG$. If each rule satisfies the conditions then the updated protocol is executable with the consistent transition relation being $UTDG$. Otherwise, it is concluded that δ cannot be applied while preserving executability and consistency.

The conditions for an addition and a replacement rules are the same as those for the corresponding single rule updates except that the constraints on the messages and states in the change nodes are no longer needed (condition 1 of Lemmas 1 and 2 can be dropped).

In the above example, nodes ct_1 and ct_2 are added to the nodes 1-4 to produce an updated transition relation. Since ur_1 and ur_2 both satisfy the condition 2 of Lemma 1 the update can be applied and the updated protocol is guaranteed to be executable with a consistent transition relation as can be verified.

However, additional conditions are necessary to guarantee an executable protocol with a consistent transition relation when δ has deletion rules. For example, consider updating the protocol P above using δ with rules ur_1: $mt_1 : 3 \rightarrow \langle m_7(\mathcal{E}, 1), s_0, s_0, m_8(1, \mathcal{E}) \rangle$, ur_2: $\langle m_7(\mathcal{E}, 1), s_0, s_0, m_8(1, \mathcal{E}) \rangle, \rightarrow \langle m_7(\mathcal{E}, 1), s_0, s_0, m_8(1, \mathcal{E}) \rangle$. The rule ur_1 is a deletion rule and the rule ur_2 is an addition rule. Note that rule ur_2 is needed to ensure that the update δ is match-complete as mentioned above. It can also be verified that the update δ is order-independent.

In the protocol P, the node 1 appears in a valid path by itself and the nodes 2, 3 and 4 form another valid path. Applying δ deletes the node 3 and adds the change node $\langle m_7(\mathcal{E}, 1), s_0, s_0, m_8(1, \mathcal{E}) \rangle$. In the updated protocol, there is no node that can process the message $m_3(\mathcal{E}, 1)$ in state s_2 and hence the nodes 2 and 4 do not appear in a valid path and must be deleted as well to get a consistent transition relation. Further, suppose node 1 were not be present in the protocol above, then node 2 is the only node with the initial state s_0 then update δ cannot delete 3. Otherwise, there is no path from initial global state s_0 to itself in the updated protocol which makes the protocol unexecutable.

Let $mt_i = \langle m_1, s_1, s_2, m_2 \rangle$ be a match node of a deletion rule. Let $p_m = [\overrightarrow{u_0}, \overrightarrow{v_0}] \rightarrow^* [\overrightarrow{u_1}, \overrightarrow{v_1}] \cdots \rightarrow^n [\overrightarrow{u}, \overrightarrow{v}]$ be a prefix of a valid path in which a TDG node n that matches mt_i appears. Since after deleting n, the updated graph does not have any node with the same inputs as n, none of the nodes in the prefix of p_m, $[\overrightarrow{u_0}, \overrightarrow{v_0}] \rightarrow^* [\overrightarrow{u_1}, \overrightarrow{v_1}]$ can appear in a valid path in the updated protocol. Therefore, all these nodes must also deleted for the updated protocol to have a consistent transition relation. This implies that all the nodes that appear in a path from an initial global state to n must also match the match node of some delete only rule in δ. Additionally, to make sure that every node in the updated protocol continues to appear in a valid path after deleting the node n and other associated nodes, each node that appears in a valid path with any of the nodes being deleted must either also be deleted by the update or the node must appear in a valid path involving none of these nodes.

If p_m is the only path from an initial global state then there is no way to reach any other initial state from that initial state. Hence in such cases, it is not possible to get an executable updated protocol using the update δ.

Theorem 1. *An update* $\delta = \{ur_1, \cdots, ur_k\}$ *preserves executability and consistency of a protocol P if all of the following conditions hold. Let UTDG be the transition relation obtained by applying all the rules in δ to TDG.*

1. *Condition 2 of Lemma 1 holds with respect to UTDG for each addition rule in δ and*
2. *conditions 2 and 3 of Lemma 2 hold with respect to UTDG for each replacement rule of δ and*
3. *For each deletion rule with match node mt_i,*
   (a) *every node in every path from an initial global state to n is deleted by δ and*
   (b) *each initial state of the updated protocol appears in UTDG and*
   (c) *Let n be a node that matches mt_i. For each node n' of TDG that follows n in any valid path in P, the node n' is either deleted by δ or appears in a valid path with nodes that are not deleted by δ.*

7   An Application – Snoop-Based MSI Protocol

The snoop-based *MSI* protocol provides a coherent view of the memory subsystem to all processors by serializing accesses to memory locations. Memory accesses are broadcast over a bus to all processors and the main memory, which then provide the appropriate responses. Each memory location is stored in a processor's cache in one of M (modified), S (shared) or I (invalid) states. The cache state M means that the most recent copy is with cache and the corresponding cache has both read and write permissions. The cache state S means that both memory and cache have the most recent copy and cache has only read permission. The cache state I means that the location is not present in cache. In the *MSI* protocol, at most one cache can have the cache state as M for a location; however the location can be cached in S state in many caches. Further, all other cached copies must be invalidated before granting write permission for a location to a cache.

The protocol is abstractly modelled using three controllers – *request*(Rq), *reply* (Rp) cache controllers and a *memory* (Mm) controller. The processors constitute the environment $\mathcal{E}$. The controller Rq processes each access request from $\mathcal{E}$, communicates with the controllers Rp in other caches and the memory controller Mm, if needed, to get the most recent copy, and responds back to $\mathcal{E}$. The two primary protocol transactions are as follows.

Read Transaction: is initiated by a *Read* request from $\mathcal{E}$ to the controller Rq. If Rq has read permission (state is M or S) for the location, then Rq sends *Data* to $\mathcal{E}$. Otherwise, Rq multi-casts a *Busrd* (Bus Read) request to the controllers Rp and Mm. Receipt of a *Busrd* is acknowledged by Rp with data, *Ackd*, if it has the most recent copy[1]. Otherwise, Rp merely acknowledges with an Ack, and Mm supplies the $Data$. The response from Rp determines whether Mm should send the data. The $Data$ is forwarded to $\mathcal{E}$ by Rq to end the transaction.

Write Transaction: is initiated by the $Readex$ (Read for exclusive) request from $\mathcal{E}$ to Rq. If the Rq has write permission then it sends a $Done$ message to $\mathcal{E}$. Otherwise, (state is either S or I) Rq multi-casts a $Breadex$ (Bus Read Exclusive) request to Rp and Mm. The controller Rp invalidates cached copies on receipt of $Breadex$ and sends acknowledgement with data to Rq, $Ackd$, if the cache state M; it sends Ack to Rq otherwise. In the latter case, Mm supplies $Data$ to Rq. The controller performs write on receipt of both Ack and $Data$ and sends $Done$ to $\mathcal{E}$ to end the transaction.

The TDG for the MSI protocol is given below. The nodes pertaining to the read transaction appear on the left and those for the write transaction appear on the right. The initial states of controllers Rq and Rp are the states M, S and I and that of Mm is $free$. All other states are non-initial. For brevity we indicate channels with messages only for multi-casting.

Rq_1 : $\langle Read, M, M, \{Data\}\rangle$,

Rq_2 : $\langle Read, I, Brad,$
$\{Busrd(Rq, Mm), Busrd(Rq, Rp)\}\rangle$,

Rq_3 : $\langle Ack, Brad, Brd, \{\}\rangle$

Rq_4 : $\langle Ackd, Brad, S, \{Data\}\rangle$,

Rq_5 : $\langle Data, Brd, S, \{Data\}\rangle$

Rq_6 : $\langle Read, S, S, \{Data\}\rangle$.

Mm_1 : $\langle Busrd, free, Waitackdr, \{\}\rangle$,

Mm_2 : $\langle Ack, Waitackdr, free, \{Data\}\rangle$,

Mm_3 : $\langle Ackd, Waitackdr, free, \{\}\rangle$,

Rp_1 : $\langle Busrd, S, S, \{Ack(Rp, Rq\text{-}Mm)\}\rangle$,

Rp_2 : $\langle Busrd, M, S, \{Ackd(Rp, Rq\text{-}Mm)\}\rangle$,

Rp_3 : $\langle Busrd, I, I, \{Ack(Rp, Rq\text{-}Mm)\}\rangle$.

Rq_7 : $\langle Readex, M, M, \{Done\}\rangle$,

Rq_8 : $\langle Readex, S, Bradx, \{Busrdx(Rq, Mm),$
$Busrdx(Rq, Rp)\}\rangle$,

Rq_9 : $\langle Readex, I, Bradx, \{Busrdx(Rq, Mm),$
$Busrdx(Rq, Rp)\}\rangle$,

Rq_{10} : $\langle Ack, Bradx, Brdx, \{\}\rangle$,

Rq_{11} : $\langle Ackd, Bradx, M, \{Done\}\rangle$,

Rq_{12} : $\langle Data, Brdx, M, \{Done\}\rangle$,

Rp_4 : $\langle Busrdx, I, I, \{Ack(Rp, Rq),$
$Ack(Rp, Mm)\}\rangle$,

Rp_5 : $\langle Busrdx, S, I, \{Ack(Rp, Rq),$
$Ack(Rp, Mm)\}\rangle$,

Rp_6 : $\langle Busrdx, M, I, \{Ackd(Rp, Rq),$
$Ackd(Rp, Mm)\}\rangle$,

Mm_4 : $\langle Busrdx, free, Waitackdw, \{\}\rangle$,

Mm_5 : $\langle Ack, Waitackdw, free, \{Data\}\rangle$,

Mm_6 : $\langle Ackd, Waitackdw, free, \{\}\rangle$,

Below we describe two common updates to the MSI protocol from Chapter 5 of [2]. The first update has a single rule and involves the read transaction. The second one has multiple rules and deals with write transaction.

7.1   Cache-Cache Transfers

To alleviate memory bandwidth and access latency requirements, the read transaction in the protocol in the above protocol may be changed so that the reply

---

[1] Typically, in practice, acknowledgements do not appear in the bus in a snoop-based protocol and additional hardware such as wired-or signals are used to report these results [2] (pp: 384). In this paper, for simplicity, we assume that the bus is used for these as well.

controller Rp at a cache supplies data instead of Mm whenever both of them have the most recent copy (i.e., cache state is S). This change can be specified using the update with a single replacement rule mt : $\langle Busrd, S, S, \{Ack(Rp, Rq), Ack(Rp, Mm)\}\rangle$, $\rightarrow ct$: $\langle Busrd, S, S, \{Ackd(Rp, Rq), Ackd(Rp, Mm)\}\rangle$ that replaces the node Rp_1 by the node ct.

It can be easily verified that Proposition 1 and Lemma 2 is satisfied primarily because there is a path from the initial global state $S_0 = [\langle I, S, free\rangle, \langle Read\rangle]$ is p_m: $S_0 \rightarrow^{Rq_2} [\langle Brad, S, free\rangle, \langle Busrd(Rq, Rp), Busrd(Rq, Mm)\rangle] \rightarrow^{ct} [\langle Brad,$ $S, free\rangle, \langle Busrd(Rq, Mm), Ackd(Rp, Rq), Ackd(Rp, Mm)\rangle]$. This path extends to the valid path reaching the initial state $[\langle S, S, free\rangle, \langle\rangle]$ with nodes Mm_1, Mm_3, and Rq_4. Hence the updated protocol is executable with a consistent transition relation, which can be verified.

7.2   Multi-controller Update - Upgrade Transaction

In the write transaction of the MSI protocol, the controller Rq does not distinguish between the states I and S; in both cases a $Busrdx$ request is multi-cast leading to data transfer. If the state is S then the requestor only needs write-permission and data transfer can be avoided. This change can be specified by the update δ, given below, that simultaneously updates all the three controllers while introducing a new message $Busupgr$ (Bus Upgrade) indicating request for write-permission but not data. The update also introduces a new non-initial state Bup in the request controller to handle responses to the request $Busupgr$.

urq_1: $mt_1 :Rq_8 \rightarrow ct_1$: $\langle Readex, S, Bup, \{Busupgr(Rq, Mm), Busupgr(Rq, Rp)\}\rangle$,

urq_2: $mt_2 :\langle Ack, Bup, M, \{Done\}\rangle \rightarrow ct_2$: $\langle Ack, Bup, M, \{Done\}\rangle$,

urp_1: mt_3 : $\langle Busupgr, I, I, \{Ack(Rp, Rq), Ack(Rp, Mm)\}\rangle \rightarrow$
   ct_3 : $\langle Busupgr, I, I, \{Ack(Rp, Rq), Ack(Rp, Mm)\}\rangle$,

urp_1: mt_4 : $\langle Busupgr, S, I, \{Ack(Rp, Rq), Ack(Rp, Mm)\}\rangle \rightarrow$
   ct_4 : $\langle Busupgr, I, I, \{Ack(Rp, Rq), Ack(Rp, Mm)\}\rangle$,

urm_1: mt_5 : $\langle Busupgr, free, free, \{\}\rangle \rightarrow ct_5$: $\langle Busupgr, free, free, \{\}\rangle$.

The rule urq_1 is a replacement rule that replaces Rq_8 by the corresponding change node; all the other rules are addition rules. It can be verified that the update δ is order-independent. It is also match-complete and hence by Proposition 1, the updated protocol is deterministic.

According to Theorem 1, each of the addition rules must satisfy the condition 2 of Lemma 1 with respect to the updated graph $UTDG$ and the replacement rule urq_1 must satisfy the conditions 2 and 3 of Lemma 2 with respect to $UTDG$ to guarantee an executable updated protocol with a consistent transition relation.

Consider the addition rule urq_2 with the change node ct_2. It is reachable from the initial global state $S_0 = [\langle S, S, free\rangle, \langle Readex\rangle]$ through the path p_m $= S_0 \rightarrow^{ct_1} [\langle Bup, S, free\rangle, \langle Busupgr(Rq, Rp), Busupgr(Rq, Mm)\rangle] \rightarrow^{ct_3}$ $\langle Bup, I, free\rangle, \langle Busupgr(Rq, Mm), Ack(Rp, Rq), Ack(Rp, Mm)\rangle]$. Note that unlike single rule update, the path p_m in this case can involve change nodes from δ since conditions are checked with respect to the updated graph $UTDG$. The path p_m can be extended to an initial state $[\langle M, I, free\rangle, \langle\rangle]$ using the node ct_2 and ct_5. The other valid path to ct_2 from the initial state $[\langle S, I, free\rangle, \langle Readex\rangle]$

can be similarly extended to a valid path. Hence the condition 2 of Lemma 1 holds for the addition rule urq_2. It can be similarly verified that all the other addition rules also satisfy the condition 2 of Lemma 1 with respect to $UTDG$.

The change node ct_1 in the replacement rule ur_1 is reachable from the same initial states as the addition rules and all the valid paths containing ct_1 are those that contain the change nodes of the addition rules. Hence, ct_1 appears in a valid path and every path from an initial global state to ct_1 is a prefix of a valid path in the updated protocol. Therefore, condition 2 of Lemma 2 is met with respect to $UTDG$. The nodes that can appear in any valid path following Rq_8 in the original protocol are Rq_{10}, Rq_{12}, Rp_4, Rp_5, Mm_4 and Mm_5. Since all of these nodes also appear in a valid path involving Rp_9 which does not involve Rp_{10}, the condition 3 of Lemma 2 is also satisfied. Hence all conditions of Theorem 1 are met by δ and hence the updated protocol is executable and has a consistent relation, which can be verified.

8   Conclusion and Future Work

An approach to systematically update protocols specified as a network of deterministic $CFSMs$ is proposed. Updates are specified as a finite set of rules that add, delete, and/or replace one more transitions from one or more protocol controllers. Sufficient conditions on updates are identified for preserving the executability and consistency of a given protocol. Conditions under which a single transition can be changed in a single controller as well as conditions for simultaneously updating multiple transitions in multiple controllers are described. The effectiveness of the approach is illustrated by showing how different commonly used design choices for cache coherence protocols can be incorporated by specifying them as updates. The proposed approach is equally applicable to other finite state protocols that can be modelled using a network $CFSMs$ with bounded channels.

References

1. D. Brand and P. Zafiropulo, "On Communicating Finite State Machines", JACM, 30(2), 1983.
2. D. E. Culler, J.P. Singh, A. Gupta, "Parallel Computer Architecture", Morgan Kauffman, 1999.
3. P. Chu and M.T.Liu, "Protocol Synthesis in a state transition model," COMPSAC, 1988.
4. R. Cleaveland and B. Steffen, "A linear-time model checking algorithm for the alternation-free modal mu-calculus,", *Int. Journal of Formal Methods in System Design,*, Vol-2, 1993.
5. R. Gotzhein, G.V. Bochmann, "Deriving protocol specifications from service specifications: an extended algorithm," Tech. Report, Universite de Montreal, 1986.
6. M. Gouda, "Closed Covers: To verify progress for Communicating Finite, State Machines, *IEEE Trans. on Software Engineering*, SE-10, 1995.

7. R. Nalamasu, G. Gopalakrshnan, "Deriving Efficient Cache Coherence Protocols Trhough Refinement,", *Formal Methods in System Design*, Vol-20, 2002.
8. O. Sokolsky, "Efficient Graph-based Algorithms for Model Checking in the Modal Mu-Calculus,", Doctoral Dissertation, State University of New York, Stonybrook, 1996.
9. A. Pardo, G. Hachtel, "Incremental model checking using BDD subsetting,", *Thirtyfifth Annual ACM/IEEE. Design Automation Conference*, 1998.
10. W. Peng, "Deadlock detection in communicating finite state machines by even reachability analyses,", *Mobile Networks and Applications*, 2(3), 1997.
11. W. Peng, S. Purushothaman, "Data Flow Analyses of Communicating Finite State Machines,", *Transactions on Programming Languagaes and Systems, TOPLAS*, Vol. 13, 1991.
12. M. Subramaniam, "Early Validation of Industrial-Strength Cache Coherence Protocols Using SQL", *In Proc. of IEEE Conference on Parallel and Distributed Systems (IPDPS), in Workshop on Testing and Debugging of Parallel and Distributed Systems*, 2003.
13. O.V. Skolovosky and S.A. Smolka, "Incremental Model Checking in the Modal Mu-Calculus", *In Int. Symp. on Computer Aided Verification*, D. Dill (editor), LNCS 818, 1994.

A Formal Monitoring-Based Framework for Software Development and Analysis

Feng Chen, Marcelo D'Amorim, and Grigore Roşu

Department of Computer Science,
University of Illinois at Urbana - Champaign, USA
{fengchen,damorim,grosu}@uiuc.edu

Abstract. A formal framework for software development and analysis is presented, which aims at reducing the gap between formal specification and implementation by integrating the two and allowing them *together* to form a system. It is called *monitoring-oriented programming* (MOP), since runtime monitoring is supported and encouraged as a fundamental principle. Monitors are automatically synthesized from formal specifications and integrated at appropriate places in the program, according to user-configurable attributes. Violations and/or validations of specifications can trigger user-defined code at any points in the program, in particular recovery code, outputting/sending messages, or raising exceptions. The major novelty of MOP is its generality w.r.t. logical formalisms: it allows users to insert their favorite or domain-specific specification formalisms via *logic plug-in* modules. A WWW repository has been created, allowing MOP users to download and upload logic plug-ins. An experimental prototype tool, called JAVA-MOP, is also discussed, which currently supports most but not all of the desired MOP features.

1 Introduction

We present a tool-supported software development and analysis framework, aiming at increasing the quality of software through monitoring of formal specifications against running programs. Based on the belief that specification and implementation should *together* form a system, the presented framework technically allows and methodologically encourages designs in which the two *interact* with each other. For this reason, we call it *monitoring-oriented programming* (MOP). In MOP, runtime violations and validations of specifications result in adding functionality to a system by executing user-defined code at user-defined places in the program; executing recovery code, outputting or sending messages, throwing exceptions, etc., are just special cases. Monitors are automatically synthesized from specifications and integrated appropriately within the system.

Practice has shown that there is no "silver bullet" logic to formally express any software requirements. One of the major design decisions of MOP was to keep it independent from any particular specification formalism. Instead, a specification formalism can be modularly added to the MOP framework, provided that it is coded as a *logic plug-in*, that is, a module whose interface respects some

J. Davies et al. (Eds.): ICFEM 2004, LNCS 3308, pp. 357–372, 2004.

rigorously defined and standardized conventions explained in the paper. A logic plug-in essentially incorporates a *monitor synthesis* algorithm, taking formal specifications to corresponding concrete monitoring code that analyzes program execution traces. No other restrictions are imposed on the MOP-admissible specification formalisms, such as to be "executable" or "declarative"; these can range from highly abstract to very detailed. Once a specification formalism is defined as a logic plug-in, any MOP user can include it into her MOP framework. To facilitate the reuse of logic plug-ins, we created a WWW repository where users can download and upload their favorite, or application-specific, logic plug-ins.

Besides monitor synthesis, another major aspect of MOP is *monitor integration*. This is technically very challenging, because some specifications may need to be checked at various places in a program, some of them hard to detect statically. Monitor integration is highly dependent upon the target programming language(s). We have implemented a prototype MOP framework for JAVA software development and analysis, called JAVA-MOP, which will be also discussed.

In short, one can understand MOP from at least three perspectives:

(1) As a discipline allowing one to *improve reliability of a system by monitoring* its requirements against its implementation at runtime. By generating and integrating the monitors automatically rather than manually, MOP provides several important advantages, including reduced risk of producing wrong monitors due to misunderstanding of specifications, complete integration of monitors at places that may change as the application evolves, software products more amenable to formal verification and validation, and increased separation of concerns.

(2) As an *extension of programming languages with logics*. One can add logical statements anywhere in the program, referring to past or future states. These can be seen at least like any other boolean expressions, so they give the user a maximum of flexibility in using them: to terminate the program, guide its execution, recover from a bad state, add functionality, throw exceptions, etc. In some sense, MOP can be regarded as a framework potentially enabling fault-tolerant software development methodologies.

(3) As a *lightweight formal method*. While firmly based on logical formalisms and mathematical techniques, MOP aims at avoiding verifying an implementation against its specification before operation, by *not letting it go wrong* at runtime.

The idea of MOP was first introduced in [6] at the *Runtime Verification (RV) workshop*, focusing mainly on the logic independence aspect of it and having minimal tool support. The current paper reports significant advances of both ideological and technical nature, such as: (a) an AOP-based instrumentation package allowing more flexible monitors to be generated as aspects, based on which our current prototype can now support JASS annotations and will soon support JML; (b) several novel configuration attributes besides the in-line and out-line ones in [6], such as on-line, off-line, and synchronous; (c) a WWW repository of logic-plug-ins where users can test, download and upload logic plug-ins, containing already four of them: future time and past time temporal logics, extended regular expressions and JASS; and a new and much improved implementation of

JAVA-MOP which can be configured to generate monitoring code using directly the logic plug-ins in the WWW repository. Since RV has a relatively limited audience, in this paper we do *not* assume the reader already familiar to MOP concepts and terminology. All the necessary notions are introduced as needed.

Related Work. There are many approaches related to MOP that were a great source of inspiration for us. What makes MOP different is its generality and modularity with respect to specification languages, allowing it to include other approaches as special cases. It is a major part of our efforts to capture these relationships explicitly, by providing specific logic plug-ins.

Design by Contract (DBC) [20] is a software design methodology particularly well supported in Eiffel [11]. DBC allows specifications to be associated with programs as assertions and invariants, which are compiled into runtime checks. There are DBC extensions proposed for several languages, such as JASS [4] and JCONTRACTOR [1] for JAVA. JAVA 1.4 introduces simple assertions as part of the language, which are then compiled into runtime checks. DBC approaches fall under the uniform format of logic plug-ins, so MOP can naturally support DBC variants as special methodological cases. To strengthen this claim, we have implemented a logic plug-in for JASS. However, MOP also allows monitors to be synthesized *out-line* (See section 2.1 for more details), which is crucial in assuring high reliability of software and is not provided by any DBC approach.

Java Modeling Language (JML) [18] is a behavioral specification language for JAVA. It can be used to specify designs for JAVA classes and interfaces, and provides the basis for further analysis, e.g., runtime debugging [7] and static analysis [12]. JML assertions are presented as special annotations, using a fixed logical formalism, so JML can be easily incorporated into JAVA-MOP.

Runtime Verification (RV) is an area [14, 15, 26] dedicated to providing more rigor in testing. In RV, monitors are automatically synthesized from formal specifications, and can be deployed *off-line* for debugging, i.e., they analyze the execution trace "post-mortem" by potentially random access to states, or *on-line* for dynamically checking properties are not being violated during execution. JAVA-MAC [17], JPAX [24], and TEMPORAL ROVER [9] are examples of such RV systems; however, they also have their requirements logics hardwired, and their generated monitors are synchronous. The MOP paradigm supports both in-line and out-line, both on-line and off-line, as well as both synchronous and asynchronous monitoring; these modes will be explained in Section 2. Although our current JAVA-MOP prototype does not support all these modes yet, as argued in Section 4, it is not hard to incorporate them. MOP also allows any logical specification formalism to be modularly added to the system. It is expected that all the RV systems that we are aware of will fall under the general MOP architecture, provided that appropriate logic plug-ins are defined.

Aspect Oriented Programming (AOP) [16] is a software development technique aiming at separation of concerns [27]. An *aspect* is a module that characterizes the behavior of cross-cutting concerns. AOP provides a means to define behavior that cross-cuts different abstractions of a program, avoiding scattering code that is related to a single concept at different points of the program, thus aiming for maintenance and extensibility of the code. Similarly to AOP, MOP requires instrumentation to integrate monitors into the code; however, instrumentation is a small piece of MOP, namely a subpart of its *monitor integration* capability. MOP's most challenging part is indeed to *synthesize monitors* from user defined logical formulae. In AOP, the behavior of each aspect is left to be defined by the programmer. Actually, MOP and AOP are intended to solve different problems. MOP is tuned and optimized to *merge* specification and implementation via monitoring, while AOP aims at separation of concerns. Our current MOP prototype uses ASPECTJ [2] as an instrumentation infrastructure. However, ASPECTJ does not provide support for several important MOP features, such as asynchronous and/or out-line monitoring, as well as strong runtime support needed to check a property at each change of the state of an object, which is a must in the context of safety critical software.

2   Overview of MOP

The general idea underlying MOP is that specifications are inserted in programs via *annotations*. Actual monitoring code is automatically synthesized from these annotations and integrated at appropriate places in the program, according to user-defined configuration attributes of the monitor. Before we present the general principles of MOP, we first present a simple example. Figure 1 shows a JAVA-MOP annotation, where a traffic light controller is monitored against the safety property "yellow after green" expressed as a future time linear temporal logic (FTLTL) formula. JAVA-MOP takes such an annotated code and generates the corresponding monitor as plain JAVA code, which is shown in Figure 2. More details on the syntax of annotations are given in Section 2.1; [5] presents temporal logic and its corresponding monitor synthesis algorithm.

```
... (Java code A) ...
/*@ FTLTL
    Predicate red : tlc.state.getColor() == 1;
    Predicate green : tlc.state.getColor() == 2;
    Predicate yellow : tlc.state.getColor() == 3;
    // yellow after green
    Formula : [](green -> (! red U yellow));
    Violation handler : ... (Java "recovery" code) ...
@*/
... (Java code B) ...
```

Fig. 1. JAVA-MOP specification

One way to regard MOP is as an extension of programming languages with special statements which can refer to current, past or future states of the program. To effectively handle these special statements, a standardized annotation language is needed. Annotations are automatically converted into monitors,

```
... (Java code A) ...
switch(FTLTL_1_state) {
case 1:
    FTLTL_1_state = (tlc.state.getColor() == 3) ? 1 :
        (tlc.state.getColor() == 2) ? (tlc.state.getColor() == 1) ? -2 : 2 : 1; break;
case 2:
    FTLTL_1_state = (tlc.state.getColor() == 3) ? 1 :
        (tlc.state.getColor() == 1) ? -2 : 2; break ;
}
if (FTLTL_1_state == -2) { ...(Violation Handler)... }
// Validation Handler is empty
... (Java code B) ...
```

Fig. 2. Monitor generated for the MOP specification in Figure 1

which can have several configurable attributes. The monitors may need meta-information about the program's state, such as the name of the current method or class, so a standardized communication interface between the program and annotations is also needed. Logics should be easy to incorporate as modules, called logic plug-ins, so another standardized interface is necessary for these.

2.1 Extending Programming Languages with Logical Annotations

Most works on extending languages with annotations mainly focus on detecting program errors. MOP is built on the belief that logical annotations can play a deeper, active role in the execution of a program. For example, Figure 3 shows how one can use MOP to guarantee authentication before access to protected resources, by simply adding an appropriate safety policy together with an action. The safety policy, expressed in negative form using extended regular expressions (ERE; see [5]), states that "if one accesses a resource, it must be the case that at some moment in the past the end of the authentication process has been seen". This policy is violated iff the ERE formula [^end(a)]* start(m), stating that the end of the authentication has not occurred before the resource started to be managed, is validated. If that is the case then, instead of reporting an error, one simply enforces the authentication. Note that this specification has the attribute class (explained below), so the generated monitor will check the safety policy at each state change of the current object.

```
/*@ ERE {class}
    Event a : authenticate() ;
    Event m : manageResource() ;
    // If the resource is accessed without authentication
    Formula : (^ end(a))* start(m)
    // enforce the authentication
    Validation Handler: authenticate();
@*/
```

Fig. 3. A class monitor to assure authentication

It is often the case that it is easier to express a safety policy by what should *not* happen. This is one of the reasons for which MOP accepts both a violation and a validation handler; another reason comes from the fact that there are situations where one may want to take different actions depending on whether a policy is violated or validated. Note that violation and validation are not complementary properties. Hence, by combining specifications expressed using appropriate underlying logical formalisms and code, and by synthesizing and integrating automatically corresponding monitoring code, critical properties of a program can be expressed and implemented rigorously and compactly. Moreover, the obtained program is more amenable to formal verification and validation, because significant parts of it are directly generated from its specification.

MOP Annotations. Specifications are introduced as comments in the host language, having the structure in Figure 4. They begin with an optional name,

```
/*@ [Annotation Name] <Logic Name> [{attributes}]
    ... Specification Body ...
    [Violation Handler: ... code handling the violation ...]
    [Validation Hander: ... code to trigger when validated ...
@*/
```

Fig. 4. The structure of MOP annotations

followed by a required name of its underlying logic, e.g., FTLTL or ERE in the examples in Figures 1 or 3, respectively, followed by optional monitor configuration attributes (which will be discussed shortly), followed by the main body of the annotation, whose format is logic-specific. In case of FTLTL, e.g., the body of the specification has two parts: one containing declarations of predicates based on program states, and the other containing the FTLTL formula built on these.

The last part of the annotation contains user-defined actions, including a *violation handler* and a *validation handler*. Catching the violation is a programmer's main concern in most cases, and then common actions are to throw exceptions or produce error logs; MOP gives one full freedom in how to continue the execution of the program. One may also want to take an action when the specification is fulfilled at runtime. For example, a requirement "eventually F", which is validated when F first holds, may trigger a certain action. All these suggest a strong sense of programming with logics in MOP.

Monitor Configuration Attributes. Monitors generated from specifications can be used in different ways and can be integrated at different places, depending on specific needs of the application under consideration. For example, some specifications need to be checked at only one point (e.g., pre- or post-conditions), while others must be monitored at any point in the program (e.g., class invariants). In some applications, one may want generated monitors to use the same resources as the rest of the program, in others one may want to run the monitors as different processes. To give the software developers maximum flexibility, MOP allows one to configure the monitors using attributes in annotations.

The **uniqueness** attribute, denoted !. The default monitor configuration behavior is to create a monitor instance for each object of the corresponding class. However, if a monitor is specified as *unique*, it will only have one instance at runtime, regardless of the number of objects of that class.

There are two running mode attributes, stating how the generated monitoring code is executed. One is ***in-line*** versus ***out-line*** monitoring. Under *in-line* monitoring, which is the default, the monitor runs using the same resource space as the program. The monitor is inserted as one or more pieces of code into the monitored program. In the *out-line* mode, the monitoring code is executed as a different process, potentially on a different machine or CPU. The in-line monitor can often be more efficient because it does not need inter-process communication and can take advantage of compiler optimizations. However, an in-line monitor cannot detect whether the program deadlocks or stops unexpectedly. Out-line monitoring has the advantage that it allows, but does not enforce, a centralized computation model, that is, one monitor server can be used to monitor multiple programs. In order to reduce the runtime overhead of out-line monitoring in certain applications, one can define communication strategies; for example, the monitored program can send out the concrete values of the relevant variables and the out-line monitor evaluates the state predicates, or, alternatively, the monitored program sends out directly the boolean values of the state predicates.

The other running mode attribute is ***on-line*** versus ***off-line***. Under *on-line* monitoring, which is the default, specifications are checked against the execution of the program dynamically and run-time actions are taken as the specifications are violated or validated. The *off-line* mode is mostly used for debugging purposes: the program is instrumented to log an appropriate execution trace in a user-specified file and a program is generated which can analyze the execution trace. The advantage of off-line monitoring is that the monitor has random access to the execution trace. Indeed, there are common logics for which on-line monitoring is exponential while off-line monitoring is linear [24].

Note that the two running mode attributes are orthogonal to each other. In particular, an in-line off-line configuration inserts instrumentation code into the original program for generating and logging the relevant states as the program executes. Alternatively, an out-line off-line configuration generates an observer process which receives events from the running program and generates and then logs the states relevant to the corresponding specification. The latter may be desirable, for example, when specifications involve many atomic predicates based on a relatively small number of program variables; in this case, the runtime overhead may be significantly reduced if the program is instrumented to just send those variables to the observer and let the latter evaluate the predicates.

In the case of on-line monitoring, a further attribute, **synchronization**, is possible. This attribute states whether the execution of the monitor should block the execution of the monitored program or not. In in-line monitoring, for example, a synchronized monitor is executed within the same thread as the surrounding code, while an asynchronous one may create a new execution thread and thus reduce the runtime overhead on multi-threaded/multi-processor platforms. Synchronization also plays a role in synthesizing code from logic formulae, because, for some logics, asynchronous monitoring is more efficient than synchronous monitoring. Consider, for example, the formula "next F and next not F" which is obviously not satisfiable: a synchronous monitor must report a violation right away, while an asynchronous one can wait one more event, derive the formula to "F and not F", and then easily detect the violation by boolean simplification. Note that synchronous monitoring requires running a satisfiability test, which for most logics is very expensive (PSPACE-complete or worse).

The **effective scope** attribute, which can be *class, method, block* or *checkpoint*, specifies the points at which the monitoring code is merged with the monitored program. As indicated by name, the class attribute specifies an invariant of a class, so it should be checked whenever the class state changes. The method one refers to a specific method, which can be further divided into three subcategories: pre-method (before the method), post-method (after the method), and exceptional-method (when the method raises exceptions). The annotation can also be associated to a block, e.g., as a loop invariant/variant. Similar to the method annotation, it is divided into three subtypes, namely, pre-block (before the block), post-block (after the block), and exceptional-block (when the block throws exceptions). Finally, the checkpoint attribute, which is the default, states that the monitoring code should be integrated at the exact current place in the program. Section 2.2 describes in more depth the monitor integration problem.

Retrieving Program Information. Since specification and implementation live together in MOP, the specification needs information about the program in order to define and synthesize its runtime behavior. The general principle is to use the elements of the program to construct the elements of the specification, such as the atomic predicates which are defined on the state of the program. Three other pieces of information about the program, besides its state, have turned out to be practically important in MOP to enhance its expressibility and functionality, namely, *positions, results* and *historic references.* Figure 5 shows an example of how a JASS specification in JAVA-MOP can use such information.

```
/*@ JASS {post-method}
   @ ensures x == Old.x ;
   @ ensures Result == a * a ;
   Violation Handler:
   throw new Exception("Method "+@FNCT_NAME_+" violated property "+ @ANNT_Name);
@*/
int square(int a) { ... (Java Code) ... }
```

Fig. 5. Specification retrieving program information

The *position* information is extracted via special variable names, such as @METHOD_NAME_ for the name of the method that contains the current annotation. Position information is useful to generate effective messages to users. Many other special position variables are available, including ones for class and file names, line numbers, etc. The use of predefined variables allows certain specifications to be independent of their position and of changes of names of methods, classes, etc. The *result* and *historic references* are useful to state certain properties, such as pre- and post-conditions of methods. The specification in Figure 5 states that after each execution of the `square` method, the value of the class field x stays unchanged and the result of the method is indeed the square of its input.

2.2   Extensible Logical Framework

To allow specifications using potentially different underlying formalisms, support for attaching new logical frameworks to an MOP environment is needed. The layered MOP architecture in Figure 6 is currently adopted. It is especially tuned to facilitate extending the MOP framework with new logical formalisms added to the system as new components, which we simply call *logic plug-ins*. More specifically, a logic plugin is usually composed of two modules in the architecture, namely a *logic engine* and a *language shell*. By standardizing the protocols between layers, new modules can be easily and independently added, and modules on a lower layer can be reused by those on the adjacent upper layer.

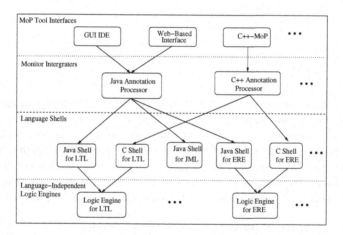

Fig. 6. MOP Architecture

The first layer provides a friendly user interface, via which one can define, process, and debug MOP annotations. The second layer contains *annotation processors*, each specialized on a specific target programming language. It consists essentially of a program scanner, which isolates annotations to be processed by specialized modules and report errors if these do not follow the expected structure. Annotation processors extract the specifications and dispatch them to the corresponding logic plug-ins. Then they collect the generated monitoring code and integrate it within the monitored program according to the configuration attributes. The two upper levels are not expected to change or update frequently.

The two lower levels contain the *logic plug-ins*, which may be added, removed, or updated on a frequent basis. To employ a new specification language, the user needs to develop a new logic plug-in, or obtain one from others or the provided WWW repository (see Section 3), and add it to her MOP framework. Then, annotations using the new formalism can be processed in a "push button" manner. Monitors generated for a specific programming language and specification formalism are generated on the third layer, by modules called *language shells*, acting as intermediaries between annotation processors and logic engines. In some simple cases, such as DBC or JML, the shell can directly generate monitors without the need of a logic engine. Modules on the bottom layer are the *logic engines*, forming a core and distinguished feature of MOP. These are generic translators from logic formulae into efficient monitors. Their output uses abstract pseudocode, which is further translated into specific target code by language shells. Therefore, logic engines can be reused across different languages.

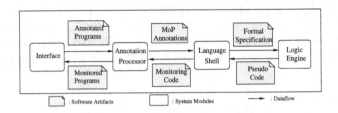

Fig. 7. Program transformation flow in MOP

The protocols between adjacent layers are based exclusively on ASCII text, to achieve maximum flexibility, extensibility, and to ease debugging and testing. Basically, components in this architecture are implemented as individual programs receiving ASCII text from the standard input and outputting ASCII text to the standard output. Hence, the modules can be implemented by different roles using different languages, and can run on different platforms. Figure 7 shows how an MOP supporting tool transforms an annotated program.

Interface of Logic Plug-ins. An important interface is the one between the upper two layers and the lower ones, allowing MOP supporting tools to interact with the logic plug-ins. The input of a logic plug-in is clearly a formal specification, but the format of its output is less obvious. We next discuss five dimensions that the output of any logic plug-in must consider in order to be attachable to an MOP supporting tool, regardless of its internal monitor synthesis technique. Several concrete logic plug-ins that have already been experimentally evaluated using our JAVA-MOP prototype are discussed in [5].

(1) Declarations. Variables storing the state of the monitor. These will be automatically inserted at appropriate places in the program, depending upon the target programming language and the configuration attributes of the monitor.

(2) Initialization. This phase prepares the variables for starting the monitoring and is executed only once, the first time the monitoring breakpoint is encountered during the execution of the program.

(3) Monitoring Body. This is the main part of the monitor, executed whenever the monitor breakpoint is reached.

(4) Success Condition. This gives the condition stating that the monitoring requirement has been fulfilled, so that there is no reason to monitor it anymore. For example, for a formula "eventually F" in future time temporal logic, this condition becomes true when F holds the first time.

(5) Failure Condition. This gives the condition that states when the trace violates the requirements. When this condition becomes true, user-provided recovery code will be executed. "Recovery" should be taken with a grain of salt here, because such code can not only throw an exception or put the system in a safe state, but also attach (any) new functionality to the program.

Logic Plug-ins Development. Designing and implementing a monitoring logic plug-in is a highly nontrivial task, requiring a careful analysis of trade-offs among various existing possibilities, or even developing entirely new algorithms. Two or more logic plug-ins can be possible for a given logic, each with different advantages and disadvantages. One typical situation is for a logic to admit a logic plug-in in which all the states of the monitor are explicitly generated, such as an automaton, and one in which only one current state of the monitor is stored, but a means to generate the next state on-the-fly is provided. A major benefit of the modular MOP architecture is that users are encouraged to develop such logic plug-ins *once and for all*, and then to post them in WWW repositories. We have devised monitor synthesis algorithms for future time, past time, metric and epistemic temporal logics, extended regular expressions and JASS (Section 3); and we are currently developing logic plug-ins for other logics, including real-time logic (RTL) [23] and EAGLE [3]. A logic plug-in contains two sub-modules, a *logic engine* and a *programming language shell.* The former generates monitoring pseudocode from the input specification, and then the later turns that pseudocode into target programming language code. This way, a mathematically skilled developer of the specific logic engine does not need to know the target programming language, and the logic engine can be reused for different programming languages. The language shells are usually straightforward.

Monitor Integration. Once a monitoring code is generated, an MOP supporting tool needs to integrate it into the original program according to the configuration attributes. Specifically, under the in-line mode the monitoring code is placed at proper positions within the monitored program, while under the out-line mode the MOP tool firstly constructs a stand-alone monitor program and then generates corresponding communication code which is placed at proper positions into the monitored program. For the off-line case, code that logs the relevant execution trace is inserted at specific places in the program and a stand-alone analysis program is also generated, but its role is to detect errors in the log rather than to influence the execution of the program at runtime.

The effective scope attribute says where the monitoring, communication or logging code needs to be placed. The method-related monitor is placed at the beginning of the method or at the end of it, and the monitor associated to the block is handled similarly, but with a smaller scope. The checkpoint monitor is easy to integrate by replacing the annotation with the generated code.

Class-scoped monitors, i.e., those generated from annotations with the configuration attribute `class`, are the most difficult to integrate; JAVA-MOP currently supports only a partial integration of these monitors. One approach towards a complete solution would be to insert the monitoring code at all places where relevant events can take place, e.g., before or after method calls, or after variable assignments. However, this simplistic approach can add an unacceptable runtime overhead and may raise some additional technical difficulties because of aliasing. JASS provides a tempting trade-off to reduce the complexity of this problem, by requiring that the specification holds only in those states that can be acknowledged by the client of a library, e.g., before or after the invocation to a method. We are currently adopting this trade-off in our JAVA-MOP prototype, which may admittedly allow safety leaks in critical systems.

Monitor integration gives MOP a flavor of AOP, and indeed, our current prototype uses ASPECTJ to realize the instrumentation. However, MOP's major purpose is to extend programming languages with logics as a means to combine formal specification and implementation, rather than to explicitly address crosscutting concerns. The essential and most challenging parts in the development of a framework supporting MOP are to set up the general logic-extensible infrastructure and to develop the individual logic plug-ins. AOP techniques are only employed to facilitate the final monitoring code integration. Besides, MOP supports local specifications, such as block properties and/or checkpoint, which are not considered in AOP. Moreover, MOP is concerned with the runtime behavior of the program rather than with its static structure. As previously mentioned, our current prototype can not support rigorous class invariants monitoring, because the required runtime support is beyond the current abilities of AOP.

3   Java-MOP

We next present JAVA-MOP, an MOP prototype framework. It consists of an integrated collection of specialized programs, allowing one to easily, naturally and automatically process annotations in JAVA programs, via a user-friendly interface. It is also available for download from the MOP website [21].

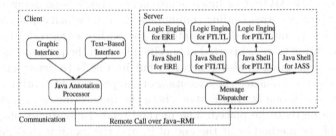

Fig. 8. The Architecture of JAVA-MOP

Overview. JAVA-MOP is essentially a distributed client-server application, whose architecture is shown in Figure 8 and whose implementation is discussed in more depth in [5]. Users of JAVA-MOP only need to download and install the client, which is implemented entirely in JAVA and is platform independent. One can also download and start the server locally and then reconfigure the client to request monitor synthesis services locally, but this is not necessary.

The client provides both a textual and a graphical user interface. The textual one consists of a simple command taking one or more names of annotated JAVA files as input and generating corresponding files in which monitors are synthesized and integrated appropriately. The textual interface is typically used for batch processing, which is recommended when lots of monitors need to be generated and/or when they involve complex logical formulae which need a long time to be processed.

A friendly GUI interface is also implemented and available for download, based on the ECLIPSE platform [10]. The Java-MOP tool provides an editor plug-in for Eclipse, called Annotated Java Editor, which can be used to process MOP annotations in a interactive way.

Logic Plug-ins. We have developed several logic plug-ins so far, which are currently supported by JAVA-MOP. The discussion here is rather informal, but [5] gives formal definitions and monitor synthesis algorithms. The interested reader is encouraged to try all the examples in this paper, as well as many others, at our WWW plug-in repository [21], where one can generate and visualize monitors via an HTML client.

Design by Contract - JASS. Since the various DBC approaches are based on the idea of compiling special annotations into runtime checks, MOP can smoothly include these approaches, provided that appropriate logic plug-ins are developed. To test and evaluate this hypothesis, we have implemented a JAVA logic plug-in for JASS. The original syntax of JASS annotations has been slightly modified to fit the uniform, logic-independent syntactic conventions in JAVA-MOP. JASS supports the following types of assertions: method pre-conditions and post-conditions, loop variants and invariants, and class invariants. Pre-conditions must be satisfied by the caller but the callee is in charge of checking it. Post-conditions need to be satisfied at the exit of a method. Loop variants, used to check termination of loops, are integer expressions that must decrease at every iteration and whose evaluation should never reach 0. Loop invariants are checked at the boundaries of a loop, and class invariants are properties over the fields of an object and are checked on the boundaries of methods. JASS' logic is relatively simple, so its monitor generation is straightforward.

Temporal Logics. Temporal logics have proved to be indispensable expressive formalisms in the field of formal specification and verification of systems [22, 8]. Many practical safety properties can be naturally expressed in temporal logics, so these logics are also useful as specification formalisms in our MOP framework. We implemented plug-ins for both future and past time temporal logics. In future

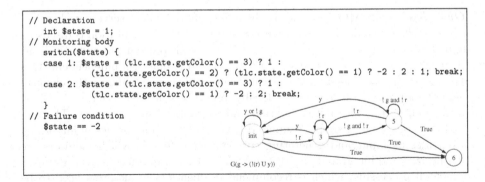

```
// Declaration
   int $state = 1;
// Monitoring body
   switch($state) {
   case 1: $state = (tlc.state.getColor() == 3) ? 1 :
             (tlc.state.getColor() == 2) ? (tlc.state.getColor() == 1) ? -2 : 2 : 1; break;
   case 2: $state = (tlc.state.getColor() == 3) ? 1 :
             (tlc.state.getColor() == 1) ? -2 : 2; break;
   }
// Failure condition
   $state == -2
```

Fig. 9. Generated monitor for Figure 1 and its graphical visualization

time linear temporal logic (FTLTL), one can state properties about the future execution of a system. Consider the example in Figure 1, which formally states in FTLTL a safety property of a traffic light controller: "if the green light is on then the red light should not be turned on until the yellow has been turned on". Figure 2 already showed the final monitoring code monitor generated from this specification. Figure 9 shows the output of the FTLTL logic plug-in, before it is merged within the original code by the annotation processor, as well as the automaton generated by the HTML client to the FTLTL logic plug-in. Note that the additional variables in the generated code have generic names, starting with the $ symbol; the annotation processor will replace these by appropriate fresh names, to avoid conflicts with other variable names already occurring in the program. Dually, in past time linear temporal logic (PTLTL), one can specify properties referring to the past states. PTLTL has been shown to have the same expressiveness as FTLTL [13]. However, it is exponentially more succinct than FTLTL [19] and often more convenient to specify safety policies.

Extended Regular Expressions. Software engineers and programmers understand easily regular patterns, as shown by the interest in and the success of scripting languages like PERL. We believe that regular expressions provide an elegant and powerful specification language also for monitoring requirements, because an execution trace of a program is a string of states. Extended regular expressions (ERE) add complementation to regular expressions, allowing one to specify patterns that must *not* occur. Complementation gives one the power to express patterns on traces non-elementarily more compactly. However, complementation leads to a non-elementary exponential explosion in the number of states of the corresponding automaton, so naive ERE monitoring algorithms may be impractical. Preliminary efforts in [25] show how to generate simply exponential monitoring algorithms for ERE. A logic engine for ERE and a corresponding logic plug-in incorporating these algorithms has been implemented.

Online Logic Plug-in Repository. Due to the standardized interface of MOP components, once a logic plug-in is developed, which in most cases is expected to be a highly nontrivial and time-consuming task, potentially any other MOP user can use it. To facilitate the reuse of logic plug-ins and to encourage users to propose, design, implement, and share them, we set up an online WWW repository of logic plug-ins [21]. The MOP user can try a logic plug-in online, via a provided HTML client, before she decides to download and install it. This repository is also implemented so that it can serve as a remote logic plug-in server, as discussed in Section 3. Thus, it is possible for the user to install few or no logic plug-ins on her machine, but to retrieve them by need from the repository. This facilitates the usage of the MOP framework, because the user does not need to search, download, compile and install all wanted plug-ins on her own server.

4   Conclusion and Future Work

We presented monitoring-oriented programming (MOP) as a general software development and analysis framework, aiming at increasing the quality of software by merging formal specifications into programs via monitors synthesized and integrated automatically. Specification formalisms can be easily added to and removed from an MOP supporting system, due to logic plug-ins. A WWW repository of logic plug-ins allows MOP users to download or upload them, thus avoiding the admittedly heavy task of developing their own logic plug-ins. The logic-independence and the broad spectrum of generated monitor integration capabilities allow MOP to paradigmatically capture other related techniques as special important cases. We also introduced JAVA-MOP, a prototype system supporting most of the desired features of MOP.

There is much future work to be done, part of it already started. We intend to extend our prototype to support all the running modes soon, to incorporate other related approaches, such as JML, and especially to evaluate the MOP paradigm on students and in practical large size applications. Advanced techniques to dynamically "observe" the execution of a program in as much depth as needed are imperiously needed; the current AOP capabilities that we are using are rather static and limited. We believe that MOP may also lead to novel programming techniques, and more work will be dedicated to methodologies for developing MOP-based high quality software.

References

1. P. Abercrombie and M. Karaorman. jContractor: Bytecode Instrumentation Techniques for Implementing DBC in Java. In *ENTCS*, volume 70. Elsevier, 2002.
2. Aspectj project. http://eclipse.org/aspectj/.
3. H. Barringer, A. Goldberg, K. Havelund, and K. Sen. Rule-Based Runtime Verification. In *Intl. Conference on Verification, Model Checking and Abstract Interpretation (VMCAI'04)*, LNCS, 2004.
4. D. Bartetzko, C. Fischer, M. Moller, and H. Wehrheim. Jass - Java with Assertions. In *ENTCS*, volume 55. Elsevier, 2001.

5. F. Chen, M. D'Amorim, and G. Roşu. Monitoring-Oriented Programming. Technical Report UIUCDCS-R-2004-2420, Univ. of Illinois Urbana-Champaign, 2004.
6. F. Chen and G. Roşu. Towards Monitoring-Oriented Programming: A paradigm combining specification and implementation. In *Workshop on Runtime Verification (RV'03)*, volume 89 of *ENTCS*, pages 106–125. Elsevier, 2003.
7. Y. Cheon and G. T. Leavens. A Runtime Assertion Checker for JML. In *Software Engineering Research and Practice (SERP'02)*. CSREA Press, 2002.
8. E. M. Clarke, O. Grumberg, and D. A. Peled. *Model Checking*. The MIT Press, Cambridge, Massachusetts, 1999.
9. D. Drusinsky. The Temporal Rover and the ATG Rover. In *SPIN Model Checking and Software Verification*, volume 1885 of *LCNS*, pages 323–330. Springer, 2000.
10. Eclipse project. http://www.eclipse.org.
11. Eiffel Software. The Eiffel Language. http://www.eiffel.com/.
12. C. Flanagan, K. R. M. Leino, M. Lillibridge, G. Nelson, J. Saxe, and R. Stata. Extended static checking for Java. In *PLDI'02*, pages 234–245, 2002.
13. D. M. Gabbay. The Declarative Past and Imperative Future: Executable Temporal Logic for Interactive Systems. In *Conference on Temporal Logic in Specification*, volume 398 of *LNCS*, pages 409–448. Springer, 1989.
14. K. Havelund and G. Roşu. *Workshops on Runtime Verification (RV'01, RV'02, RV'04)*, volume 55, 70(4), to appear of *ENTCS*. Elsevier, 2001, 2002, 2004.
15. K. Havelund and G. Roşu. Runtime verification. *Formal Methods in System Design*, 24(2), 2004. Special issue dedicated to RV'01.
16. G. Kiczales, J. Lamping, A. Menhdhekar, C. Maeda, C. Lopes, J.-M. Loingtier, and J. Irwin. Aspect-Oriented Programming. In *ECOOP*, volume 1241, pages 220–242. Springer-Verlag, Berlin, Heidelberg, and New York, 1997.
17. M. Kim, S. Kannan, I. Lee, and O. Sokolsky. Java-MaC: a Runtime Assurance Tool for Java. In *Runtime Verification (RV'01)*, ENTCS. Elsevier, 2001. vol. 55.
18. G. T. Leavens, K. R. M. Leino, E. Poll, C. Ruby, and B. Jacobs. JML: notations and tools supporting detailed design in Java. In *OOPSLA'00*, 2000.
19. N. Markey. Temporal Logic with Past is Exponentially more Succinct. *EATCS Bull*, 79:122–128, 2003.
20. B. Meyer. *Object-Oriented Software Construction, 2nd edition*. Prentice Hall, Upper Saddle River, New Jersey, 2000.
21. Mop website. http://fsl.cs.uiuc.edu/mop.
22. A. Pnueli. The Temporal Logic of Programs. In *IEEE Symposium on Foundations of Computer Science*, pages 46–77, 1977.
23. R. Alur and T.A. Henzinger. Real-Time Logics: Complexity and Expressiveness. In *IEEE Symposium on Logic in Computer Science*, pages 390–401. IEEE, 1990.
24. G. Roşu and K. Havelund. Rewriting-based Techniques for Runtime Verification. *Automated Software Engineering*, to appear in 2005.
25. K. Sen and G. Roşu. Generating Optimal Monitors for Extended Regular Expressions. In *Workshop on Runtime Verification (RV'03)*, ENTCS, 2003. vol. 89.
26. O. Sokolsky and M. Viswanathan. *Workshop on Runtime Verification (RV'03)*, volume 89 of *ENTCS*. Elsevier, 2003. Computer Aided Verification (CAV'03).
27. P. L. Tarr, H. Ossher, W. H. Harrison, and S. M. Sutton. N Degrees of Separation: multi-dimensional separation of concerns. In *ICSE'99*, pages 107–119, 1999.

Verifying the On-line Help System of SIEMENS Magnetic Resonance Tomographs

Carsten Sinz and Wolfgang Küchlin

Symbolic Computation Group, WSI for Computer Science,
University of Tübingen and Steinbeis Technology Transfer Center OIT,
72076 Tübingen, Germany
{sinz,kuechlin}@informatik.uni-tuebingen.de
http://www-sr.informatik.uni-tuebingen.de

Abstract. Large-scale medical systems—like magnetic resonance tomographs—are manufactured with a steadily growing number of product options. Different model lines can be equipped with large numbers of supplementary equipment options like (gradient) coils, amplifiers, magnets or imaging devices. The diversity in service and maintenance procedures, which may be different for each of the many product instances, grows accordingly. Therefore, instead of having one common on-line service handbook for all medical devices, SIEMENS parcels out the on-line documentation into small (help) packages, out of which a suitable subset is selected for each individual product instance. Selection of packages is controlled by XML terms. To check whether the existing set of help packages is sufficient for all possible devices and service cases, we developed the *HelpChecker* tool. *HelpChecker* translates the XML input into Boolean logic formulae and employs both SAT- and BDD-based methods to check the consistency and completeness of the on-line documentation. To explain its reasoning and to facilitate error correction, it generates small (counter-)examples for cases where verification conditions are violated. We expect that a wide range of cross-checks between XML documents can be handled in a similar manner using our techniques.

1 Introduction

There is a persistent trend towards products that are individually adaptable to each customer's needs (*mass customization* [Dav87]). This trend, while offering considerable advantages for the customer, at the same time demands special efforts by the manufacturer, as he now must make arrangements to cope with myriads of different product instances. Questions arising in this respect include: How can such a large set of product variants be represented and maintained concisely and uniquely? How can the parts be determined that are required to manufacture a given product instance? Is a certain requested product variant manufacturable at all? And, last but not least, how can the documentation—both for internal purposes and for the customer—be prepared adequately?

Triggered, among other reasons, by an increased product complexity, SIEMENS Medical Solutions recently introduced a formal description for their magnetic resonance tomographs (MR) based on XML. Thus, not only individual product instances, but also the set of all possible (*valid, correct*) product configurations can now be described by an

J. Davies et al. (Eds.): ICFEM 2004, LNCS 3308, pp. 391–402, 2004.

XML term which implicitly encodes the logical configuration constraints. This formal *product documentation* allows for an automated checking of incoming customer orders for compliance with the product specification. Besides checking an individual customer order for correctness, further tests become possible, including those for completeness and consistency of the on-line help system which are the topic of this paper. Similarly, cross-checks between the set of valid product instances and the parts list (in order to find superfluous parts) or other product attributes are within the reach of our method [SKK03].

In order to apply formal verification methods to an industrial process, the following steps are commonly necessary. First, a formal model of the process must be constructed. Second, correctness assertions must be derived in a formal language which is compatible with the model. Third, it must be proved mechanically whether the assertions hold in the model. Finally, those cases where the assertion fail must be explained to the user to make debugging possible. Throughout the formal process, speed is usually an issue, because in practice verification is often applied repeatedly as a formal debugging step embedded in an industrial development cycle.

In this paper we develop a formal semantics of the SIEMENS XML representation of their MR systems using propositional logic. This is accomplished by making the implicit assumptions and constraints of the tree-like XML representation explicit. We then translate different consistency properties of the on-line help system (help package overlaps, missing help packages) into propositional logic formulae, and thus we are able to apply automatic theorem proving methods (like SAT-checkers) in order to find defects in the package assignment of the on-line help system. Situations in which such a defect occurs are computed and simplified using Binary Decision Diagrams (BDDs). This exceeds the possibilities of other previously suggested checking techniques, as e.g. those of the XLinkIt system [NCEF02].

2   Product Documentation Using XML

Product Structure. Many different formalisms have been proposed in the literature to model the structure of complex products [MF89, SW98, STMS98, MW98, KS00]. The method used by SIEMENS for the configuration of their MR systems was developed in collaboration with the first author of this paper and resembles the approach presented by Soininen *et al.* [STMS98]. Structural information is explicitly represented as a tree. This tree serves two purposes: first, it reflects the hierarchical assembly of the device, i.e. it shows the constituent components of larger (sub-)assemblies; and, second, it collects all available, functionally equivalent configuration options for a certain functionality. These two distinct purposes are reflected by two different kinds of nodes in the tree, as can be seen from the example in Fig. 1.

Type Nodes are employed to reflect the hierarchical structure, whereas *Item Nodes* represent possible configuration options with common functionality. From the example tree shown in Fig. 1 we may, e.g., conclude that there are two different possibilities for choosing a *System*: *Harmony* and *Concerto*. A *Harmony* system possesses three configurable (direct) subcomponents, of type *MPCU*, *Receiver*, and *Rx4*, respectively.

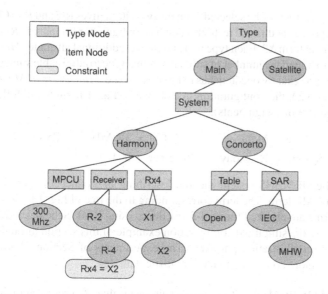

Fig. 1. Product Structure of Magnetic Resonance Tomographs (Simplified Example)

```
<Config auto-ns1:noNamespaceSchemaLocation="Config.xsd"
        xmlns:xsi="http://www.w3.org/2001/XMLSchema-instance">
    <Structure>
        <Type IDREF="INT_ConsoleType" MinOccurs="1" MaxOccurs="1">
            <Item IDREF="INI_ConsoleType_Sat"/>
            <Item IDREF="INI_ConsoleType_Main">
                <SubType IDREF="INT_System" MinOccurs="1" MaxOccurs="1">
                    <!-- Harmony -->
                    <Item IDREF="INI_System024">
                        <SubType IDREF="INT_Comp_MPCU" Default="INI_Comp_MPCU300"
                                 ReadOnly="true" MinOccurs="1" MaxOccurs="1">
                            <Item IDREF="INI_Comp_MPCU300"/>
                        </SubType>
                        <SubType IDREF="INT_Comp_RXNumOf" Default="INI_Comp_RXNumOf1"
                                 MinOccurs="1" MaxOccurs="1">
                            <Item IDREF="INI_Comp_RXNumOf1"/>
                            <Item IDREF="INI_Comp_RXNumOf2"/>
                        </SubType>
                        <SubType IDREF="INT_Comp_ReceiverNumOf" MinOccurs="1"
                                 MaxOccurs="1">
                            <Item IDREF="INI_Comp_ReceiverNumOf2"/>
                            <Item IDREF="INI_Comp_ReceiverNumOf4">
                                <Conditions>
                                    <Condition Type="INT_Comp_RXNumOf" Op="eq"
                                               Value="INI_Comp_RXNumOf2"/>
                                </Conditions>
                            </Item>
                        </SubType>
                    </Item>
                    <!-- Concerto -->  ...
                </SubType>
            </Item>
        </Type>
    </Structure>
</Config>
```

Fig. 2. Product Structure of Fig.1 in XML Representation (Excerpts)s

The receiver, in turn, may be selected from the two alternatives $R-2$ and $R-4$. Choosing the latter option puts an additional restriction on the configurable component $Rx4$: this has to be selected in its form $X2$. Each type node possesses additional attributes *MinOccurs* and *MaxOccurs* to bound the number of subitems of that type to admissible values. Assuming that for each type exactly one item has to be selected (i.e. *MinOccurs* $=$ *MaxOccurs* $= 1$ for all type nodes), the configuration tree shown in Fig. 1 permits the following valid configuration (set of assignments):

$$\text{Type} = \text{Main} \qquad \text{MPCU} = 300\text{MHz} \qquad \text{Rx4} = \text{X2}$$
$$\text{System} = \text{Harmony} \qquad \text{Receiver} = \text{R-4}$$

Within the SIEMENS system, the tree describing all product configurations is represented as an XML term. The term corresponding to the tree of Fig. 1 is shown in Fig. 2. All XML terms are checked for well-formedness using XML Schemas [XML01].

We will use the simplified configuration example of this section throughout the rest of the paper for illustration purposes. The experiments of Section 4, however, were conducted on more complex and more realistic data sets.

Structure of On-line Help. The on-line help pages that are presented to the user of an MR system may depend on the configuration of the system. For example, help pages should only be offered for those components that are in fact present in the system configuration. Moreover, for certain service procedures (e.g., tune up, quality assurance), the pages depend not only on the system configuration at hand, but also on the (workflow) steps that the service personnel already has executed. Thus, the help system is both configuration and workflow state dependent.

To avoid writing the complete on-line help from scratch for each possible system configuration and all possible workflow states, the whole help system is broken down into small *Help Packages* (see Fig. 3). A help package contains documents (texts, pictures, demonstration videos) on a specialized topic. The authors of the help packages decide autonomously about how they break down the whole help into smaller packages. So it is their own decision whether to write a whole bunch of smaller packages, one for each system configuration, or to integrate similar packages into one.

Now, in order to specify the assignment of help packages to system configurations, a list of *dependencies* is attached to each help package, in which the author lists the

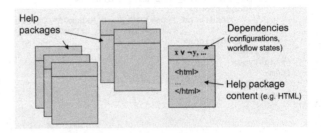

Fig. 3. Illustration of Help Packages: For each system configuration and workflow state a suitable help package has to be selected (controlled by dependencies)

```
<Package ID="HLP_HP-1-181203-01-001" Name="HP-1-181203-01-001">
   <Content> ... </Content>
   <Dependencies>
      <Dependency>
         <RefType IDREF="INT_Workflow">
            <RefItem IDREF="INI_Workflow_TUNEUP"/>
         </RefType>
         <RefType IDREF="INT_System">
            <RefItem IDREF="INI_System_003"/>
         </RefType>
      </Dependency>
   </Dependencies>
</Package>

<Context>
   <RefType IDREF="INT_System">
      <RefItem IDREF="INI_System_003"/>
   </RefType>
   <RefType IDREF="INT_Workflow">
      <RefItem IDREF="INI_Workflow_TUNEUP"/>
   </RefType>
   <RefType IDREF="INT_WorkflowMode">
      <RefItem IDREF="INI_WorkflowMode_General"/>
   </RefType>
   <RefType IDREF="INT_WorkflowSfp">
      <RefItem IDREF="INI_WorkflowSfp_SfpTuncalOpen"/>
   </RefType>
</Context>
```

Fig. 4. Example of a Help Package (with Dependencies) and a Help Context

system configurations and workflow states for which his package is suitable (see Fig. 4 for an example): all of a dependency's RefType/RefItem assignments must match in order to activate the package and to include it into the set of on-line help pages for that system. Multiple matching situations may be specified by associating further Dependency-elements to the package.

The situations for which help packages must be available are specified by the engineering department using so-called *Help Contexts*. A help context determines system parameters and workflow steps for which a help package must be present. Examples for both a help package and a context (in XML representation) can be found in Fig. 4. The help package of this example fits any state of workflow *tune up* and all configurations of *System_003*. The example's context specifies that for step *TuncalOpen* in the *tune up* procedure of *System_003* a help package is required.

Currently, almost a thousand help contexts are defined for eleven MR systems, each with millions of different configuration possibilities. So, in spite of in-depth product knowledge, it is a difficult and time consuming task for the authors of help packages to find gaps (missing packages) or overlaps (ambiguities in package assignment) in the help system. To assist the authors, we therefore developed the *HelpChecker* tool, which is able to perform cross-checks between the set of valid system configurations, the situations for which help may be requested (determined by the contexts) and the situations for which help packages are available (determined by the packages' dependencies).

3   Logical Translation of Product Structure and Help System

To check the completeness and consistency of the on-line help system we need a translation into a logical formalism. We have chosen propositional logic for this purpose because of its relative simplicity and the presence of fast and elaborate decision procedures (SAT, BDD). We now lay down precisely what constitutes a consistent help system. Informally speaking, for each situation in which help may be requested for an existing system (and therefore a valid system configuration) there should be a matching help package. This means, help should be *complete*. Furthermore, to avoid possible ambiguities or even contradictions, there should be exactly one unique help package. This means, help should be *consistent*.

Therefore, we first have to find out which situations and product configurations can actually occur. We therefore develop a formalization of the product structure by building a configuration validity formula (ValidConf) describing the set of all valid configurations. The validity formula can automatically be derived from the XML data of the product structure and consists of consistency criteria for each of the structure's tree nodes. For a type node the following three validity conditions have to hold:

T1. The number of sub-items of the node must match the number restrictions given by the MinOccurs and MaxOccurs attributes.

T2. All selected sub-items must fulfill the validity conditions for item nodes.

T3. No sub-items may be selected that were not explicitly listed as admissible for this type.

For an item node the following three validity conditions have to hold:

I1. All sub-type nodes must fulfill the validity conditions for type nodes.

I2. The item's constraint, if present, has to be fulfilled.

I3. Unreferenced types and their items must not be used in the configuration. Types are considered unreferenced, if they do not appear as a subnode of the item.

We now informally define completeness and consistency of the on-line help system.

Definition 1. *The on-line help system is complete if, for each context, a matching help package exists. Only valid system configurations have to be considered.*

Remember that contexts specify situations (system configuration plus workflow state) for which help may be requested by the user. Thus the system has to make sure that for each such situation a help package is available.

To define consistency, we first need the notion of overlapping help packages:

Definition 2. *There is an overlap between two help packages ("ambiguity"), if there is a context and a valid system configuration for which both help packages' dependencies match (i.e., evaluate to true).*

Definition 3. *An on-line help system is consistent if there are no overlaps between help packages.*

In the next section we will give propositional criteria for these two properties. To build the link between XML terms and propositional logic, we will have to select sub-elements and attributes from an XML term. For this purpose we will use XPath [XPa02] expressions as shown in Table 1. The result of an XPath selection is always a set of XML nodes or a set of attributes. In Table 1, a stands for an arbitrary XML attribute and p for an arbitrary path, i.e. a list of XML elements separated by slashes (/).

Table 1. XPath Examples

expression	denotation	example(s)
/p	absolute path	/Config/Structure
p/..	parent element	Type/Item/.. (= Type)
p@a	attribute selection	Item@MaxOccurs, SubType@IDREF

3.1 Formalization of the Product Structure

In this subsection we derive a propositional logic formula describing all valid system configurations. The variables of this formula stem from the XML specification's unique identifiers (ID and IDREF attributes) for types (InvType) and items (InvItem). A propositional variable is true for a given configuration if and only if the respective type or item is actually present in the configuration, i.e. is selected for the present product instance. Thus, the item-variables uniquely describe the system configuration, and a type variable is true if and only if at least one of its items occurs in the configuration.

Validity of a Configuration:

$$\text{ValidConf} = \text{TypeDefs} \wedge \bigvee_{\substack{t \in /\text{Config}/ \\ \text{Structure}/\text{Type}}} \text{ValConfT}(t) \tag{$\ddagger$}$$

$$\text{TypeDefs} = \bigwedge_{\substack{t \in /\text{Inventory}/ \\ \text{InvTypes}/\text{InvType}}} \left(t@\text{ID} \Longleftarrow \bigvee_{i \in t/\text{InvItem}} i@\text{ID} \right)$$

Formula ValidConf describes the set of all valid system configurations. A configuration is valid, if and only if it respects the type definitions (TypeDefs) and if it matches at least one configuration structure of the XML document, which is assured by the formula part around ValConfT(t). Whether a configuration matches a structure depends on the items of the configuration, on the tree-like assembly of the structure nodes as well as the constraints given in the item nodes. The type definitions are collected in a subformula (TypeDefs) that is responsible for a type variable to be set, as soon as at least one of its items is selected. As the MR system structure is recursively defined over tree nodes, the validity formulae are also recursive. In the same way, the distinction between type and item nodes is carried over to a distinction between validity formulae for type and item nodes. The overall validity of a configuration is determined by its top node in the tree, as can be seen from Formula ($\ddagger$).

Validity of a Type Node:

$$\text{ValConfT}(t) = \text{CardinalityOK}(t) \wedge \text{SubItemsValid}(t)$$
$$\wedge \text{ForbidUnrefItems}(t)$$
$$\text{CardinalityOK}(t) = S^{t@\text{MaxOccurs}}_{t@\text{MinOccurs}}(\{i@\text{IDREF} \mid i \in t/\text{Item}\})$$
$$\text{SubItemsValid}(t) = \bigwedge_{i \in t/\text{Item}} \left(i@\text{IDREF} \Rightarrow \text{ValConfI}(i)\right)$$
$$\text{ForbidUnrefItems}(t) = \bigwedge_{i \in \text{unrefItems}(t)} \neg i@\text{IDREF}$$

A type node t is valid if and only if the three conditions (corresponding to T1-T3) of ValConfT(t) hold. First, the number of selected items must match the MinOccurs and MaxOccurs attributes (CardinalityOK(t)). To express number restrictions, we use the selection operator S introduced by Kaiser [Kai01, SKK03]. $S^a_b(M)$ is true if and only if between a and b formulae in M are true. Second, the validity of all selected subitems of type t, i.e. those items i, for which $i@\text{IDREF}$ is true, must be guaranteed (SubItemsValid(t)). And, third, items that are not explicitly specified as sub-items of type node t are not allowed (ForbidUnrefItems(t)).

Validity of an Item Node:

$$\text{ValConfI}(i) = \text{SubTypesValid}(i) \wedge \text{ConditionValid}(i)$$
$$\wedge \text{ForbidUnrefTypes}(i)$$
$$\text{SubTypesValid}(i) = \bigwedge_{t \in i/\text{SubType}} \text{ValConfT}(t)$$
$$\text{ConditionValid}(i) = \begin{cases} \top & \text{if } i/\text{Conditions} = \emptyset, \\ \bigvee_{c \in i/\text{Conditions}} \bigwedge_{d \in c/\text{Condition}} \text{DecodeOp}(d) & \text{otherwise} \end{cases}$$
$$\text{ForbidUnrefTypes}(i) = \bigwedge_{t \in \text{unrefTypes}(i)} \neg t@\text{IDREF}$$

The validity of item nodes is defined in an analogous way. Again, three conditions (according to I1-I3) have to be fulfilled for an item node i to be valid. First, all sub-type nodes of item i have to be valid. Second, the item node's *Condition* XML-elements, if present, have to be fulfilled (ConditionValid(i)), where each *Condition* is a disjunction of conjunctions (DNF) of atomic equality or disequality expressions, as delivered by DecodeOp. And, third, unreferenced types, i.e. types that are not used beyond item node i, may not be used (ForbidUnrefTypes(i)).

Definitions of auxiliary expressions used in these formulae can be found in Appendix A.

3.2   Formalization of Help Package Assignment

To formalize the help package assignment we first need three basic formula definitions. Here, c and p are XML help context and help package elements, respectively.

Assignment of Help Packages:

$$\text{HelpReq}(c) = \bigwedge_{t \in c/\text{RefType}} \text{HelpTypeCond}(t)$$

$$\text{HelpProv}(p) = \bigvee_{d \in p/\text{Dependencies}} \bigwedge_{t \in d/\text{Dependency}} \text{HelpTypeCond}(t)$$

$$\text{HelpTypeCond}(t) = \begin{cases} \bigvee_{i \in t/\text{RefItem}} i@\text{IDREF} & \text{if } t/\text{RefItem} \neq \emptyset, \\ \bigvee_{\substack{i \in /\text{Inventory}/ \\ \text{InvTypes}/t/\text{InvItem}}} i@\text{ID} & \text{otherwise} \end{cases}$$

HelpReq(c) defines for which situations, i.e. configurations and workflows, context c requires a help package, whereas HelpProv(p) determines the situations for which help package p provides help. Now, completeness of the help system is equivalent to the validity of

$$\bigwedge_{c \in /\text{Help/Contexts}} \left(\text{HelpReq}(c) \wedge \text{ValidConf} \Rightarrow \bigvee_{p \in /\text{Help/Packages}} \text{HelpProv}(p) \right) . \qquad (*)$$

All cases which satisfy the negation of this formula are error conditions. Moreover, there is an overlap between help packages p_1 and p_2 if and only if

$$\bigvee_{c \in /\text{Help/Contexts}} \left(\text{HelpReq}(c) \wedge \text{ValidConf} \wedge \text{HelpProv}(p_1) \wedge \text{HelpProv}(p_2) \right) \qquad (**)$$

is satisfiable. Thus, the help system is consistent, if the latter formula is unsatisfiable for all help packages p_1 and p_2 with $p_1 \neq p_2$. All cases which satisfy this formula are thus error conditions.

4   Technical Realization and Experimental Results

Our implementation *HelpChecker* is a C++ program that builds on Apache's Xerces XML parser to read the SIEMENS product and help system descriptions. From these data, it generates Formulae (*) and (**). After having generated these formulae, it checks their satisfiability (in case of (*), it checks satisfiability of the negation). The intermediate conversion to conjunctive normal form (CNF) required by the SAT-checker is done using the well-known technique due to Tseitin [Tse70]. In case of an error condition, a formula is generated describing the set of situations in which this error occurs. This formula, call it F, is simplified by existential abstraction over irrelevant variables using standard BDD techniques (i.e. by replacing F by $\exists x F$ or, equivalently, by $F|_{x=0} \vee F|_{x=1}$ for an irrelevant propositional variable x).

HelpChecker is embedded into a larger interactive authoring system for the authors of help packages at SIEMENS. The system is not yet in everyday use, but still in the evaluation phase. Production use of the system is planned for the end of 2004. Thus, we do not have user feedback yet, and can only report on manually created (and thus possibly artificial) tests. All test cases were generated by SIEMENS documentation experts, though.

First experiments and timing measurements with the *HelpChecker* were conducted on a data set containing eleven lines of basic MR systems, 964 help contexts and twelve (dummy) help packages. To check the completeness and consistency of this data set, 35 SAT instances were generated (we use a fast approximative pre-test for package overlaps that filters out trivial cases). These SAT instances contained 1425 different propositional variables and between 11008 and 11018 clauses. Ten of them were satisfiable, corresponding to error cases (as can be seen from Equations (*) and (**) above), 25 unsatisfiable. One satisfiable instance corresponded to a missing help package, the other nine were due to package overlaps.

Initially, to check satisfiability we used a sequential version of our parallel SAT-checker PaSAT [SBK01]. Unsatisfiability could always be determined by unit propagation alone, the maximal search time for a satisfiable instance amounted to 15.90 ms on a 1.2 GHz Athlon running under Windows XP (80 branches in the Davis-Putnam algorithm, search heuristics MAX OCC). The current version of *HelpChecker* makes use of a BDD-based satisfiability checker developed at our department, and refrains from using a Davis-Putnam-style SAT-checker. The resulting BDDs contained up to 9715 nodes and 458 variables (with intermediate BDD sizes of over 100,000 nodes). A complete check of our experimental XML help—including computation of error situations—with eleven model lines, 964 help contexts and twelve help packages took 6.96 seconds. These input data already contain the complete configuration structure for all of SIEMENS' current MR model lines. However, the number of help packages is much lower than what we expect during production use.

In our context, speed is an important issue, because the authoring system will not allow a new help package to be checked in unless the *HelpChecker* reports an absence of all error conditions.

5   Related Work and Conclusion

Related Work. On the syntactic level, consistency checking of XML documents can be accomplished for the most part by XML Schema [XML01]. The appropriateness (i.e. consistency) of the semantic content, however, can not—or at most partially—be checked using these techniques. Among the different approaches to check the semantical consistency of XML documents are work on Java-based XML document evaluation by Bühler and Küchlin [BK01], the XLinkIt system by Nentwich *et al.* [NCEF02] and work on consistency checking of CIM models by Sinz *et al.* [SKKM03]. All these approaches differ considerably in the extent of expressible formulae and practically checkable conditions. From a logical point of view, none of these techniques exceeds an evaluation of first-order formulae in a fixed structure, which is not sufficient for our application. In this respect, our method opens up new application areas for the discipline of XML checking.

For work on consistency checking of Boolean configuration constraints in the automotive industry see [KS00] and [SKK03].

Conclusion. In this paper we presented an encoding of the configuration and on-line help system of SIEMENS MR devices in propositional logic. Consistency properties of the on-line help system are expressed as Boolean logic formulae, checked by a SAT-solver, and simplified using BDD techniques. By using a Boolean encoding we are able to employ advanced SAT-solvers as they are also used, e.g., in hardware verification to efficiently check formulae with hundreds of thousands of variables.

Although we demonstrated the feasibility of our method only for the MR systems of SIEMENS Medical Solutions, we suppose that the presented techniques are also usable for other complex products. More generally, we expect that a wide range of cross-checks between XML documents can be computed efficiently using SAT-solvers.

References

[BK01]   D. Bühler and W. Küchlin. A flexible similarity assessment framework for XML documents based on XQL and Java Reflection. In *Proc. 14th Intl. Conf. on Industrial and Engineering Applications of Artificial Intelligence and Expert Systems (IEA/AIE 2001)*, LNAI, Budapest, Hungary, June 2001. Springer-Verlag.

[Dav87]   S. M. Davis. *Future Perfect*. Addison-Wesley, 1987.

[Kai01]   A. Kaiser. A SAT-based propositional prover for consistency checking of automotive product data. Technical report, WSI-2001-16, University of Tübingen, 2001.

[KS00]   W. Küchlin and C. Sinz. Proving consistency assertions for automotive product data management. *J. Automated Reasoning*, 24(1–2):145–163, February 2000.

[MF89]   S. Mittal and F. Frayman. Towards a generic model of configuration tasks. In *Proc. of the 11th Intl. Joint Conf. on Artificial Intelligence*, pages 1395–1401, Detroit, MI, August 1989.

[MW98]   D.L. McGuiness and J.R. Wright. Conceptual modelling for configuration: A description logic-based approach. *AI EDAM*, 12(4):333–344, 1998.

[NCEF02] C. Nentwich, L. Capra, W. Emmerich, and A. Finkelstein. XLinkIt: A consistency checking and smart link generation service. *ACM Transactions on Internet Technology*, 2(2):151–185, May 2002.

[SBK01]   C. Sinz, W. Blochinger, and W. Küchlin. PaSAT - parallel SAT-checking with lemma exchange: Implementation and applications. In H. Kautz and B. Selman, editors, *LICS'2001 Workshop on Theory and Applications of Satisfiability Testing (SAT'2001)*, volume 9 of *Electronic Notes in Discrete Mathematics*, Boston, MA, June 2001. Elsevier Science Publishers.

[SKK03]   C. Sinz, A. Kaiser, and W. Küchlin. Formal methods for the validation of automotive product configuration data. *Artificial Intelligence for Engineering Design, Analysis and Manufacturing*, 17(1):75–97, January 2003. Special issue on configuration.

[SKKM03] C. Sinz, A. Khosravizadeh, W. Küchlin, and V. Mihajlovski. Verifying CIM models of Apache web server configurations. In *Proc. of the 3rd International Conference on Quality Software (QSIC 2003)*, pages 290–297, Dallas, TX, November 2003. IEEE Computer Society.

[STMS98] T. Soininen, J. Tiihonen, T. Männistö, and R. Sulonen. Towards a general ontology of configuration. *AI EDAM*, 12(4):357–372, 1998.

[SW98]   D. Sabin and R. Weigel. Product configuration frameworks – a survey. *IEEE Intelligent Systems*, 13(4):42–49, July/August 1998.

[Tse70]   G. S. Tseitin. On the complexity of derivation in propositional calculus. In A. O. Silenko, editor, *Studies in Constructive Mathematics and Mathematical Logic*, pages 115–125, 1970.

[XML01]   *XML Schema Parts 0–2: Primer, Structures, Datatypes. W3C Recommendation*, May 2001.

[XPa02]   *XML Path Language 2.0. W3C Working Draft*, April 2002.

A   Appendix: Auxiliary Definitions

$$\text{DecodeOp}(d) = \begin{cases} d@\text{Value} & \text{if } d@\text{Op} = \text{``eq''}, \\ \neg d@\text{Value} & \text{if } d@\text{Op} = \text{``ne''} \end{cases}$$

$$\text{unrefItems}(t) = \text{allItems}(t) \setminus t/\text{Item}$$

$$\text{allItems}(t) = \bigcup_{t'@\text{ID}=t@\text{IDREF}} /\text{Inventory}/\text{InvTypes}/t'/\text{InvItem}$$

$$\text{unrefTypes}(i) = (\text{refTypesT}(i/..) \setminus \{i/..\}) \setminus \text{refTypesI}(i)$$

$$\text{refTypesT}(t) = \{t\} \cup \bigcup_{i \in t/\text{Item}} \text{refTypesI}(i)$$

$$\text{refTypesI}(i) = \bigcup_{t \in i/\text{RefType}} \text{refTypesT}(t)$$

$$S_a^b(M) = \begin{cases} S^b(M) & \text{if } a = 0, \\ S^b(M) \wedge \neg S^{a-1}(M) & \text{otherwise} \end{cases}$$

$$S^b(M) = \bigwedge_{\substack{K \subseteq M \\ |K|=b+1}} \bigvee_{f \in K} \neg f$$

Implementing Dynamic Aggregations of Abstract Machines in the B Method

Nazareno Aguirre[1], Juan Bicarregui[2], Lucio Guzmán[1], and Tom Maibaum[3]

[1] Departamento de Computación, FCEFQyN, Universidad Nacional de Río Cuarto,
Enlace Rutas 8 y 36 Km. 601, Río Cuarto, Córdoba, Argentina
{naguirre, lucio}@dc.exa.unrc.edu.ar
[2] Rutherford Appleton Laboratory, Chilton, Didcot,
OXON, OX11 0QX, United Kingdom
J.C.Bicarregui@rl.ac.uk
[3] Department of Computing & Software, McMaster University,
1280 Main St. West, Hamilton, Ontario, Canada L8S 4K1
tom@maibaum.org

Abstract. We previously defined an extension to the B method to be able to dynamically aggregate components. The proposed extension allowed one to build specifications which can create and delete instances of machines at run time, a feature often associated with object oriented languages and not directly supported in the B method. In this paper, we study the refinement of specifications written using this extension.

We define a procedure that, given a valid implementation of an abstract machine M, systematically generates an implementation for a machine representing a dynamic aggregation of "instances" of M. Moreover, the generated implementation is guaranteed to be correct *by construction*.

Following the approach initiated in our previous work, the refinement process is defined in a way that is fully compatible with the standard B method.

1 Introduction

The B formal specification language is one of the most successful model based formalisms for software specification. It has an associated method, the B Method [1], and commercial tool support, including proof assistance [3][4]. As all formal methods, the B method provides a formal language to describe systems, allowing for analysis and verification of certain system properties prior to implementation. An important characteristic of B is that it covers the whole development process, from specification to implementation.

Various facilities for structuring specifications are provided in B, helping to make the specification and refinement activities scalable. However, the B method has an important restriction regarding structuring mechanisms, namely, it does not provide dynamic creation and deletion of modules or components. All structuring mechanisms of B are *static*; they allow one to define *abstract machines*

J. Davies et al. (Eds.): ICFEM 2004, LNCS 3308, pp. 403–417, 2004.

(the specification components of B) whose architectural structure in terms of other components is fixed, i.e., it does not change at run time [5]. Dynamic management of the population of components is a feature often associated with object oriented languages, since the replication of *objects* is intrinsic to these languages [9]. Indeed, dynamic management of "objects" appears frequently and naturally when modelling software, perhaps due to the success of object oriented methodologies and programming languages. However, fully fledged object oriented extensions of B would imply a significant change to B's (rather neat) syntax and semantics, and would excessively complicate the tool support implementation (especially in relation to proof support).

In [2], an extension of the syntax of B is proposed for supporting dynamic population management of components. This extension, in contrast with other proposed extensions to model based specification languages with this feature, such as some of the object oriented extensions to Z [11] or VDM [7], is not object oriented. Moreover, it does not imply any changes to the standard semantics of B, since it can be mapped into the standard language constructs [2]. The extension is essentially the provision of an extra structuring mechanism, the AGGREGATES clause, which intuitively allows us to dynamically "link" a set of abstract machines to a certain including machine.

The aggregation relies on the generation of a *population manager* of the aggregated machines. A population manager of an abstract machine M puts together the relativisation of the operations of M (so they work for multiple instances) with operations that mimic the creation and deletion of machine instances. However, these population managers are meant to be hidden from the specifier, who can use aggregation without worrying or knowing about the managers, via the "dot notation", borrowed from object orientation, and an extra combinator of substitutions, the *interleaving parallel composition*. In fact, AGGREGATES works as other conventional structuring mechanisms of B: the internal consistency[1] of machines aggregating other machines can be reduced to the consistency of the aggregate, and a number of further conditions on the aggregating machine. This is the case thanks to the fact that the population manager of a machine M is internally consistent *by construction*, provided that M is internally consistent [2].

In this paper, we complement the work of [2] by showing how the new AGGREGATES clause can be refined. Since we want to keep the managers hidden from the software engineer, the refinement process consists of the systematic generation of implementations for the managers introduced by a specification using AGGREGATES. More precisely, if a machine M' "aggregates" a machine M, then, given a valid implementation of M, we generate an implementation

---

[1] An abstract machine is *internally consistent* if it satisfies its *proof obligations*, i.e., if it satisfies the requirements imposed in the B method for considering a machine *correct*. Proof obligations for the correctness of abstract machines include conditions such as non-emptiness of the state space determined by the machine, or the preservation of the machine's invariant by the machine's operations [1].

```
MACHINE
    MinMax
VARIABLES
    y
INVARIANT
    y ∈ F(NAT₁)
INITIALIZATION
    y := ∅
OPERATIONS
    ins(x)  ≙  PRE   x ∈ NAT₁   THEN   y := y ∪ {x}   END;
    x ⟵ getMin  ≙  PRE   y ≠ ∅   THEN   x := min(y)   END;
    x ⟵ getMax  ≙  PRE   y ≠ ∅   THEN   x := max(y)   END
END
```

Fig. 1. Abstract machine *MinMax*

of *MManager*, which is guaranteed to be internally consistent *by construction*. The generated implementation of *MManager* can then be used as part of an implementation for *M'*.

2   Aggregating Abstract Machines

Consider the abstract machine *MinMax* shown in Fig. 1. This is a simple variant of machine *Little_Example*, from page 508 of [1]. To illustrate the use of AG-GREGATES, suppose we want a dynamic set of "instances" of machine *MinMax*, together with extra operations, to somehow "synchronise" the "min" or "max" values of two instances. This can be defined easily, by exploiting AGGREGATES and *interleaving parallel composition*, as shown in Fig. 2. The AGGREGATES *M* clause within a machine *M'* can be understood as the inclusion of a dynamic set of "instances" of *M* in *M'*, in the style of EXTENDS, i.e., *promoting the*

```
MACHINE
    MultipleMinMax
AGGREGATES
    MinMax
OPERATIONS
    syncMin(m₁, m₂)   ≙
        PRE   m₁, m₂ ∈ MinMaxSet ∧ (m₁.y ∪ m₂.y ≠ ∅)
        THEN
            ANY   x
            WHERE   x = min(m₁.y ∪ m₂.y)
            THEN   m₁.ins(x) ||| m₂.ins(x)
            END
        END;
    syncMax(m₁, m₂)   ≙
        PRE   m₁, m₂ ∈ MinMaxSet ∧ (m₁.y ∪ m₂.y ≠ ∅)
        THEN
            ANY   x
            WHERE   x = max(m₁.y ∪ m₂.y)
            THEN   m₁.ins(x) ||| m₂.ins(x)
            END
        END
END
```

Fig. 2. Abstract machine *MultipleMinMax*, a dynamic aggregation of *MinMax* machines

operations of the included machine as part of the "interface" of the including machine.

$MSet$ represents the set of "live instances" of M within an aggregating machine. In our case, $MinMaxSet$ represents the live $MinMax$ instances (see the preconditions of operations $syncMin$ and $syncMax$).

Note that we employ the "dot notation" to access the variables and operations of the aggregated machines. For instance, the expression $m_1.y$ intuitively represents the value of variable y corresponding to instance m_1; analogously, the expression $m_1.ins(x)$ represents a "call" to operation ins, with argument x, corresponding to instance m_1 (see the definitions of operations $syncMin$ and $syncMax$). As we said, the operations of the aggregated machines are promoted by the aggregating machine. For our example, this means that the operations ins, $getMin$ and $getMax$ of the live instances are accessible from the interface of $MultipleMinMax$.

Besides the operations explicitly defined in the aggregating machine M', we have available the operations originating in the aggregated machine M and two further (implicitly defined) operations. These further operations are add_M and del_M, and correspond to the population management of M, allowing for the creation and deletion of instances of machine M within M'.

2.1   The Population Managers

The AGGREGATES structuring mechanism relies on the generation of a *population manager* of the aggregated machines. A population manager of an abstract machine M puts together the relativisation of the operations of M with operations that mimic the creation and deletion of machine instances. The relativisation of the operations is a process that transforms the definitions of the operations of a basic machine so they work for multiple instances. An extra parameter is given for the relativised operations. This extra parameter represents the name of the "instance" on which the operation performs. When "calling" relativised operations, we simply put the extra parameter as a prefix, using the dot notation from object orientation.

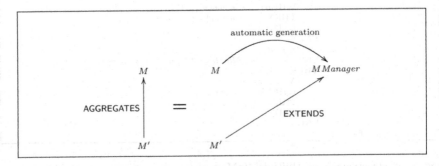

Fig. 3. The meaning of AGGREGATES in terms of EXTENDS

As the reader might imagine, **AGGREGATES** M within a machine definition is simply interpreted as **EXTENDS** $MManager$. Figure 3 illustrates this. The population manager for the $MinMax$ machine is shown in Fig. 4. Note how the operations ins, $getMin$ and $getMax$ have changed.

```
MACHINE
    MinMaxManager
VARIABLES
    y, MinMaxSet
INVARIANT
    (∀n · n ∈ MinMaxSet ⇒ y(n) ∈ F(NAT₁)) ∧
    (MinMaxSet ⊆ NAME) ∧ (y ∈ MinMaxSet → F(NAT₁))
INITIALIZATION
    y, MinMaxSet := ∅, ∅
OPERATIONS
    ins(x, n)   ≙
        PRE   n ∈ MinMaxSet ∧ x ∈ NAT₁
        THEN   y(n) := y(n) ∪ {x}
        END;
    x ⟵ getMin(n)   ≙
        PRE   n ∈ MinMaxSet ∧ y(n) ≠ ∅
        THEN   x := min(y(n))
        END;
    x ⟵ getMax(n)   ≙
        PRE   n ∈ MinMaxSet ∧ y(n) ≠ ∅
        THEN   x := max(y(n))
        END;
    add_MinMax(n)   ≙
        PRE   n ∈ NAME − MinMaxSet
        THEN
            MinMaxSet := MinMaxSet ∪ {n} || y := y ∪ {n, ∅}
        END;
    del_MinMax(n)   ≙
        PRE   n ∈ MinMaxSet
        THEN
            y := {n} ⩤ y ||
            MinMaxSet := MinMaxSet − {n}
        END;
END
```

Fig. 4. $MinMaxManager$: Population manager of abstract machine $MinMax$

The population manager of a basic machine M is *automatically constructed*. Moreover, the population manager of a machine M is internally consistent *by construction*, provided that M is internally consistent [2]. Thus, population managers can be hidden from the specifier, who can use **AGGREGATES** as other conventional structuring mechanisms of B.

2.2 Interleaving Parallel Composition

Note that, in machine $MultipleMinMax$ (see Fig. 2), we have used a new combination of substitutions, denoted by $|||$. The reason for the use of this operator has to do with the conditions under which parallel composition is well formed. In B, a (reasonable) restriction on the parallel composition $S||T$ of two substitutions S and T is that these substitutions must not write on the same variables.

In order to understand the need for the triple bar, consider the operations $m_1.ins$ and $m_2.ins$ within a machine aggregating *MinMax* (*MultipleMinMax*, for instance). When m_1 and m_2 are different, $m_1.ins$ and $m_2.ins$ *seem* to update different variables, namely $m_1.y$ and $m_2.y$. Thus, we would like to be able to combine these substitutions in parallel, using ||. However, what actually happens is that $m_1.ins$ and $m_2.ins$ are the same operation, called with different parameters; so, $m_1.ins$ and $m_2.ins$ modify the same variable, namely, the mapping y. For defining operations such as $syncMin(m_1, m_2)$ and $syncMax(m_1, m_2)$, we still want to somehow obtain the joint "behaviour" of $m_1.ins$ and $m_2.ins$; we could use sequential composition, but this is not allowed in B at the specification stage, for very good reasons. Hence, we decided to introduce a new combinator of substitutions, called *interleaving parallel composition*. This is a derived combinator of substitutions, whose semantics, in terms of weakest precondition, is:

$$[S|||T]P \equiv [S][T]P \wedge [T][S]P$$

Note that there are no syntactic restrictions on S and T for the well-formedness of $S|||T$. In particular, S and T can write on the same variables. Also, triple bar maintains the abstraction required at the specification stage, not allowing us to enforce sequentiality on substitutions.

We refer the reader to [2] for more details on this combinator, as well as its relationship with parallel composition.

3   The Refinement Process in the Presence of Aggregation

Our promise with aggregation during specification is that the specifier will not need to see or know about the managers, and should just use them abstractly, via the dot notation and interleaving parallel composition. However, AGGREGATES exists only at the specification stage. So, the specifier cannot, in principle, escape from the managers when considering refinements and implementations of machines with aggregation.

As explained in [1][3], the purposes of structuring a development at specification stage are different from the purposes of structuring it in the implementation. When decomposing a specification, one primarily seeks to alleviate the effort of proving consistency and to make specifications more understandable. On the other hand, the main motivations for structuring an implementation are to allow separate implementability and to promote reuse (of both library implementations and subsystems of the development). Thus, the architectural shape of a development at specification stage might be completely different from its architectural structure at implementation.

An extreme case of "architectural refactoring" during a development would be to flatten the top level machine of a specification (after proving its consistency) and then refine the resulting flat machine, introducing a new structure during the refinement process. However, in practice, both the purposes of structuring at specification and the purposes of structuring at implementation concern us throughout the whole development process (e.g., we factor implementations to make them more understandable, we decompose specifications to reuse common substructures, etc). So, one usually prefers to preserve, perhaps partially, the decomposition of the specification when refining.

Indeed, this last approach is an alternative available in the B method. In particular, the INCLUDES structure of a specification can be preserved when refining or implementing:

"if a specification component **B** INCLUDES a machine **A** then we can use an IMPORTS **A** clause in the implementation **B_1** of **B** to carry out the functionality supplied by **A** in the specification" (cf. pp. 148-149 of [8]).

A diagrammatic presentation of the above situation is shown in Fig. 5. We refer the reader to [8] for details on the exact process needed for translating the INCLUDES into IMPORTS at implementation.

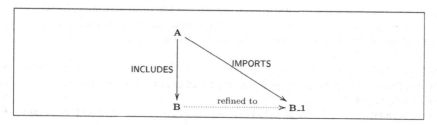

Fig. 5. The INCLUDES structure being preserved by implementations

We would like to provide the same result for our AGGREGATES clause, i.e., to somehow translate the AGGREGATES structure into a corresponding structure at implementation. For that purpose, we need to keep the managers hidden. Our intention is to make the process of refining the managers fully automated, making the use of aggregations completely transparent. Essentially, we propose the following procedure: Let M be a basic machine, and M' a machine aggregating M. M' then relies on a manager $MManager$ of M. If M is refined and eventually implemented by an implementation I_M, then we can automatically produce an implementation $I_{MManager}$ for the manager $MManager$ of M. We can then exploit the above cited result, relating INCLUDES to IMPORTS, to construct an implementation of M' based on $I_{MManager}$. Finally, what keeps the manager hidden is the fact that we generate the implementation $I_{MManager}$ of $MManager$ in such a way that its consistency is ensured, provided that I_M is a valid implementation of M. Therefore, the specifier will be able to use abstractly the dynamic aggregation of M within M', and will just need to deal with M and M' and their implementations.

3.1   Refining the Machine Managers

During a development in standard B, the whole state in implementations of abstract machines (i.e., the variables) must be imported from the state of other machines [1]. These imported (simpler) machines either (i) have already been refined and implemented, or (ii) will need to be subsequently refined and implemented, to obtain an implementation of the whole system. So, we can always assume that if a machine M is imported in some implementation, we count (or will eventually count) on an implementation of it. A set of *library machines*, for which there exist (proved correct) implementations, constitutes the *base case* of this recursive process of implementation.

Our main requirement for automatically implementing managers of arbitrary machines is the following: For every library machine M_l, there exists a provably correct implementation of its corresponding *manager* $M_l Manager$. Note that machine $M_l Manager$ is systematically produced from M_l, and is consistent provided that M_l is consistent; but the implementation of $M_l Manager$ will have to be provided. These managers, and their implementations, will constitute the base case for the implementations of managers for arbitrary machines.

For every machine M with a corresponding implementation I_M, an implementation of $M Manager$ is built via the following procedure:

```
/* ------------------------------------------------------------------- */
/* implManager(M, I_M): builds an implementation for the manager       */
/* MManager of M.                                                       */
/* Precondition: I_M is a valid implementation of M, and all machines   */
/* imported in I_M are already implemented.                             */
/* Postcondition: A valid implementation of MManager is returned. The   */
/* implementation of the manager is constructed from the               */
/* implementation I_M of M.                                             */
/* ------------------------------------------------------------------- */
implManager(Machine M, Implementation I_M) returns Implementation
begin
    create an "Empty Implementation" I_MManager
    add "REFINES MManager" to I_MManager
    let N1, ..., Nk be the machines imported by I_M
    for every Ni do
    begin
        let NiManager be the manager of Ni
        if (Ni is not a library machine and
            NiManager is not implemented) then
                create an impl. of NiManager via implManager(Ni, I_Ni)
        add "IMPORTS NiManager" to I_MManager
    end
    relativise the invariant in I_M and add it to I_MManager
    relativise the operations defs. in I_M and add them to I_MManager
    add operations for creation/deletion of instances, with standard
                                                implementations
    return I_MManager
end
```

Note that the above process is recursive. Each "IMPORTS N_i" is translated into "IMPORTS N_iManager", and incorporated as part of the implementation being built. In case these imported managers do not have corresponding implementations, we recursively employ the procedure to obtain implementations for them. The process is **guaranteed to terminate**, since the recursive calls will eventually reach library machines, for which, as we assume, there exist implemented managers. An important point to note is that the decision on how the deferred set NAME is implemented will have to be made only in the implementation of the managers of library machines (then it will be simply used by the rest of the implementations for managers).

The relativisation of the invariant and the operations is similar to the relativisation involved in the creation of a machine manager from an abstract machine. We will describe in detail the relativisation in implementations later on in this paper.

In order to get an intuition of the process for implementing managers, consider the following example.

Example 1. Let us consider the abstract machine *MinMax* (Fig. 1), previously introduced, and an implementation of it, shown in Fig. 6. This implementation is based on another machine, called *Pair* and shown in Fig. 7. Machine *Pair* is also implemented, as shown in Fig. 8, this time by using the library machine *Scalar*. Note that, strictly speaking, the implementation in Fig. 8 is not a proper B implementation: we are not allowed to use the suffix dot mechanism in order to import multiple instances of a machine in an implementation. However, this mechanism can be easily implemented in B, by replicating the machine specifications we need to import.

```
IMPLEMENTATION
    I_MinMax
REFINES
    MinMax
IMPORTS
    Pair(maxint, 0)
INVARIANT
    first = min({maxint} ∪ y) ∧ second = max({0} ∪ y)
OPERATIONS
    ins(x)  ≙
        VAR  v, w  IN
            v ⟵ getFirst;
            w ⟵ getSecond;
            IF   x < v   THEN   setFirst(x)   END;
            IF   w < x   THEN   setSecond(x)   END
        END;
    x ⟵ getMin  ≙  BEGIN  x ⟵ getFirst  END;
    x ⟵ getMax  ≙  BEGIN  x ⟵ getSecond  END
END
```

Fig. 6. An implementation of abstract machine *MinMax*

Let us apply the previous algorithm to obtain an implementation of the manager *MinMaxManager*. The resulting implementation is shown in Fig. 9.

Note how the operations and the invariant have been relativised. Also, standard implementations for the operations for creation and deletion of instances are incorporated. The exact process of relativisation will be described later on.

Since I_{MinMax} is defined in terms of $Pair$, the algorithm recursively generates an implementation for $PairManager$. Again, the generation of $PairManager$ from $Pair$ is systematic (and is left as an exercise for the interested reader). The obtained implementation of $PairManager$, generated from I_{Pair}, is shown in Fig. 10. The implementation I_{Pair} is based on $Scalar$, which is a library machine; $I_{PairManager}$ is then based on $ScalarManager$, for which, as we assumed, there exists a proved correct implementation.

3.2   Relativisation of Invariant and Operations of an Implementation

The algorithm for the generation of implementations for managers involves the relativisation of invariants and operations. We already had examples of these relativisations, for the implementations of $MinMaxManager$ and $PairManager$. Here, we define precisely how operations and invariants are relativised.

Relativisation of Invariants. Let M be an abstract machine, with a valid implementation I_M. The invariant of I_M is an expression that relates the "state space" of M (i.e., its variables) with the "state space" of I_M (composed of the variables of the machines imported by I_M). Thus, if v are the variables of M, and $M_1, \ldots, M_k$ are machines imported in I_M, with variables $M_1.v, \ldots, M_k.v$ respectively, then the invariant of I_M has the form:

$$INV(v, M_1.v, \ldots, M_k.v)$$

The relativisation of this invariant has the purpose of relating the state space of $MManager$ with the implementation for it that we generate from I_M. It has the following form:

$$(MSet = M_1Set \wedge \ldots \wedge MSet = M_kSet) \quad \wedge$$
$$[\forall n \cdot n \in MSet \Rightarrow INV(v(n), M_1.v(n), \ldots, M_k.v(n))]$$

```
MACHINE
    Pair(x, y)
VARIABLES
    first, second
INITIALIZATION
    first := x  ||  second := y
OPERATIONS
    setFirst(fst)  ≙  BEGIN  first := fst  END;
    setSecond(snd)  ≙  BEGIN  second := snd  END;
    fst ⟵ getFirst  ≙  BEGIN  fst := first  END;
    snd ⟵ getSecond  ≙  BEGIN  snd := second  END
END
```

Fig. 7. Abstract machine $Pair$

```
IMPLEMENTATION
    I_Pair(x, y)
REFINES
    Pair
IMPORTS
    xx.Scalar(x), yy.Scalar(y)
INVARIANT
    xx.var = first ∧ yy.var = second
OPERATIONS
    setFirst(fst)   ≙  BEGIN  xx.chg(fst)  END;
    setSecond(snd)  ≙  BEGIN  yy.chg(snd)  END;
    fst ⟵ getFirst  ≙  BEGIN  fst ⟵ xx.val  END;
    snd ⟵ getSecond ≙  BEGIN  snd ⟵ yy.val  END
END
```

Fig. 8. An implementation of abstract machine *Pair*

```
IMPLEMENTATION
    I_MinMaxManager
REFINES
    MinMax Manager
IMPORTS
    PairManager(maxint, 0)
INVARIANT
    (MinMaxSet = PairSet)   ∧
    [∀n · n ∈ MinMaxSet ⟹
        (n.first = min({maxint} ∪ n.y) ∧ n.second = max({0} ∪ n.y))]
OPERATIONS
    ins(x, n)  ≙
        VAR  v, w  IN
            v ⟵ n.getFirst;
            w ⟵ n.getSecond;
            IF  x < v  THEN  n.setFirst(x)  END;
            IF  w < x  THEN  n.setSecond(x)  END
        END;
    x ⟵ getMin(n)  ≙  BEGIN  x ⟵ n.getFirst   END;
    x ⟵ getMax(n)  ≙  BEGIN  x ⟵ n.getSecond  END;
    add_MinMax(n)  ≙  BEGIN  add_Pair(n)  END;
    del_MinMax(n)  ≙  BEGIN  del_Pair(n)  END
END
```

Fig. 9. The implementation of *MinMaxManager* obtained from I_{MinMax}

The first conjunct indicates how *MSet* is represented in the implementation of *MManager*, by identifying it with each of the instance sets of the imported managers. The second conjunct shows how the variables of *MManager* are represented by using the representation of *M*'s variables introduced by I_M.

Example 2. Consider the following expression:

$$first = \min(\{\mathsf{maxint}\} \cup y) \wedge second = \max(\{0\} \cup y)$$

This is the invariant of the implementation I_{MinMax}. The relativisation of this is the following:

$$(MinMaxSet = PairSet) \wedge$$
$$[\forall n \cdot n \in MinMaxSet \Rightarrow$$
$$(first(n) = \min(\{\mathsf{maxint}\} \cup y(n)) \wedge second(n) = \max(\{0\} \cup y(n)))]$$

```
    IMPLEMENTATION
        I_PairManager(x, y)
    REFINES
        PairManager
    IMPORTS
        xx.ScalarManager(x), yy.ScalarManager(y)
    INVARIANT
        (PairSet = xx.ScalarSet ∪ yy.ScalarSet)   ∧
        [∀n · n ∈ PairSet ⇒ (xx.var(n) = n.first ∧ yy.var(n) = n.second)]
    OPERATIONS
        setFirst(fst, n)   ≘   BEGIN  xx.chg(fst, n)  END;
        setSecond(snd, n)  ≘   BEGIN  yy.chg(snd, n)  END;
        fst ⟵ getFirst(n)  ≘   BEGIN  fst ⟵ xx.val(n)  END;
        snd ⟵ getSecond(n) ≘   BEGIN  snd ⟵ yy.val(n)  END;
        add_Pair(n)   ≘   BEGIN  xx.add_Scalar(n); yy.add_Scalar(n)   END;
        del_Pair(n)   ≘   BEGIN  xx.del_Scalar(n); yy.del_Scalar(n)   END
    END
```

Fig. 10. The implementation of machine $PairManager$ generated from I_Pair

Relativisation of Operations. Let M be an abstract machine, with a valid implementation I_M. Let op be an operation of M, implemented in I_M. The implementation of op is a substitution with certain restrictions, that can be, as any substitution, reduced to the normal form as described in page 284 of [1]. So, we can say that the implementation of op in I_M has the following form:

$$r \leftarrow op(\overline{p}) \quad \triangleq \quad P'(\overline{p}, M_i.v) \,|\, @\overline{x}'.(Q'(\overline{x}', \overline{p}, M_i.v) \implies M_i.v, r := \overline{x}')$$

The relativisation of this operation has the following form:

$$
\begin{aligned}
r \leftarrow op(\overline{p}, n) \quad &\triangleq \\
P'(\overline{p}, M_i & Manager.v(n)) \,| \\
& @\overline{x}'.(Q'(\overline{x}', \overline{p}, M_i Manager.v(n)) \implies M_i Manager.v(n), r := \overline{x}')
\end{aligned}
$$

Example 3. Consider the following operation:

```
ins(x)   ≘
    VAR  v, w  IN
        v ⟵ getFirst;
        w ⟵ getSecond;
        IF  x < v  THEN  setFirst(x)  END;
        IF  w < x  THEN  setSecond(x)  END
    END
```

This is the implementation of ins provided by I_{MinMax}. Its relativisation, which corresponds to an implementation of ins as an operation of $MinMaxManager$ is the following:

```
ins(x, n)   ≘
    VAR  v, w  IN
        v ⟵ getFirst(n);
        w ⟵ getSecond(n);
        IF  x < v  THEN  setFirst(x, n)  END;
        IF  w < x  THEN  setSecond(x, n)  END
    END
```

Note that, in Fig. 9, we denoted this operation by using the dot notation, i.e., denoting the extra parameter n as a prefix of the corresponding expressions.

3.3 Refining Interleaving Parallel Composition

The implementation of interleaving parallel composition does not present any difficulties, since this combinator of substitutions is a *derived* one. In fact, refining $S|||T$ is equivalent to refining:

$$S; T \ [] \ T; S$$

4   Proving Consistency of Automatically Generated Implementations

Unfortunately, due to space restrictions we are unable to reproduce the proof of the fact that the implementations that we generate are correct by construction. We restrict ourselves to giving a sketch of the proof in this section.

The proof proceeds as follows. We first consider a generic abstract machine M which has a valid implementation I_M. Then, the following proof obligations indicating that I_M is a correct implementation of M are fulfilled:

a1 Correct instantiation of the parameters of imported machines in I_M,
a2 Non-emptiness of the joint state space of M and I_M,
a3 refinement of the initialisation of M by I_M,
a4 Refinement of the operations of M by I_M.

Assuming that M is internally consistent, we automatically generate the manager $M\,Manager$ of M, which, as proved in [2], is consistent by construction; moreover, we apply the algorithm presented previously in this paper to produce an implementation for $M\,Manager$. We then prove that the following proof obligations, indicating that $I\_M\,Manager$ is a correct implementation of $M\,Manager$, are satisfied as a consequence of our hypotheses:

b1 Correct instantiation of the parameters of imported machines in $I\_M\,Manager$,
b2 Non-emptiness of the joint state space of $M\,Manager$ and $I\_M\,Manager$,
b3 refinement of the initialisation of $M\,Manager$ by $I\_M\,Manager$,
b4 Refinement of the operations of $M\,Manager$ by $I\_M\,Manager$.

Proof obligation b1 follows immediately from a1, since the constraints and properties of M and I_M are preserved by $M\,Manager$ and $I\_M\,Manager$, respectively. The non-emptiness of the joint state space of machine $M\,Manager$ and its implementation $I\_M\,Manager$, i.e. proof obligation b2, is easily proved by taking the instance sets $M\,Set, M_1\,Set, \ldots, M_k\,Set$ as empty sets. Proof obligation b3 is proved by relatively simple calculations, using the form of the initialisation of $M\,Manager$ and its refinement in $I\_M\,Manager$. Finally, proof obligation b4 is actually split into two parts: *(i)* refinement of the population management operations add_M and del_M, and *(ii)* refinement of the operations originating in

M. The correctness of the refinement of the population management operations requires some calculations, and concerns the general forms of these operations and their implementations. The correctness of the refinement of the operations originating in M requires more complex calculations, and uses the fact that the refinements of the operations of M by I_M are correct, i.e., proof obligation a4.

5   Conclusions

We have defined a procedure that, given an abstract machine M correctly implemented, automatically generates an implementation for a machine representing a dynamic aggregation of "instances" of M. The implementation is generated in such a way that its consistency is guaranteed by construction.

This work complements the work initiated in [2], where we proposed an extension to the B language to support dynamic creation or deletion of instances of abstract machines. The extension was based on the provision of a new structuring mechanism, AGGREGATES. Now the specifications written using the AGGREGATES clause can be implemented in a way that is fully transparent to the specifier.

The semantics of standard B is preserved by the defined extensions (including the conditions for the generation of implementations). Only some basic machinery has to be built on top of standard B.

There is some evidence of the need for complementing model oriented formal specification languages with support for some of the current systems engineering practices. The work in [12] and the various object oriented extensions to model oriented specification languages (e.g., [13], [10]), for instance, are cases in which this need becomes manifest. The proposed extension, although preliminary, builds into B support for some common activities of the current systems design practice (highly influenced by object orientation), and avoids the complexities often associated with the semantics of fully-fledged object oriented languages.

As work in progress, we are currently studying some further properties of the interleaving parallel composition operator, in particular, trying to find a stronger relationship between the standard parallel composition and triple bar. We are doing so in the context of Dunne's theory of generalised substitutions [6], which has so far simplified our proof efforts. We are also exploring ways of incorporating support for associations between dynamic instances of abstract machines, trying not to fall into the complexities of object orientation, i.e., keeping the structural organisation of machines hierarchical. Also, we are currently studying how our AGGREGATES structuring mechanism combines with other structuring mechanisms of B when the architectural organisation of a specification involves various layers of abstract machines. We believe there will be no difficulties in applying our aggregation approach to abstract machines with complex architectural organisations.

Acknowledgments

Nazareno Aguirre wishes to thank the Z User Group for supporting him and other students for their participation in the ZB2003 Conference, where some of the ideas presented in this paper evolved. The authors wish to thank Steve Dunne, Kevin Lano and the anonymous referees for their useful comments on a preliminary version of this paper.

References

1. J.-R. Abrial, *The B-Book, Assigning Programs to Meanings*, Cambridge University Press, 1996.
2. N. Aguirre, J. Bicarregui, T. Dimitrakos and T. Maibaum, *Towards Dynamic Population Management of Components in the B Method*, in Proceedings of the 3rd International Conference of B and Z Users ZB2003, Turku, Finland, Springer-Verlag, June 2003.
3. *The B-Toolkit User's Manual*, version 3.2, B-Core (UK) Limited, 1996.
4. Digilog, *Atelier B - Générateur d'Obligation de Preuve, Spécifications*, Technical Report, RATP SNCF INRETS, 1994.
5. T. Dimitrakos, J. Bicarregui, B. Matthews and T. Maibaum, *Compositional Structuring in the B-Method: A Logical Viewpoint of the Static Context*, in Proceedings of the International Conference of B and Z Users ZB2000, York, United Kingdom, LNCS, Springer-Verlag, 2000.
6. S. Dunne, *A Theory of Generalised Substitutions*, in Proceedings of the International Conference of B and Z Users ZB2002, Grenoble, France, LNCS, Springer-Verlag, 2002.
7. C. Jones, *Systematic Software Development Using VDM*, 2nd edition, Prentice Hall International,1990.
8. K. Lano, *The B Language and Method, A Guide to Practical Formal Development*, Fundamental Approaches to Computing and Information Technology, Springer, 1996.
9. B. Meyer, *Object-Oriented Software Construction*, Second Edition, Prentice-Hall International, 2000.
10. G Smith, *The Object-Z Specification Language*, Advances in Formal Methods, Kluwer Academic Publishers, 2000.
11. M. Spivey, *The Z Notation: A Reference Manual*, 2nd edition, Prentice Hall International, 1992.
12. H. Treharne, *Supplementing a UML Development Process with B*, in Proceedings of FME 2002: Formal Methods– Getting IT Right, Denmark, LNCS 2391, Springer, 2002.
13. R. Holzapfel and G. Winterstein, *VDM++ – A Formal Specification Language for Object-oriented Designs*, in Proceedings of Ada-Europe Conference 1988, Ada in Industry, Cambridge University Press, 1989.

Formal Proof from UML Models

Nuno Amálio, Susan Stepney, and Fiona Polack

Department of Computer Science, University of York, York, YO10 5DD, UK
{namalio,susan,fiona}@cs.york.ac.uk

Abstract. We present a practical approach to a formal analysis of UML-based models. This is achieved by an underlying formal representation in Z, which allows us to pose and discharge conjectures to analyse models. We show how our approach allows us to consistency-check UML models, and model analysis by simply drawing snapshot diagrams.

Keywords: UML, Z, model analysis, formal proof, consistency checking.

1   Introduction

This paper describes a practical approach to the formal analysis of models of sequential systems. Our models are UML-based, yet they are amenable to formal analysis. This is achieved by an underlying formal representation in Z, which allows us to pose and discharge conjectures to analyse models. This formal analysis is supported by the Z/Eves theorem prover [1].

UML is the *defacto* standard modelling notation among software engineers. One feature of UML often forgotten (or perhaps unknown in some circles) is that the language has a multi-interpretation nature; the semantics of the language's constructs vary with the application domain. When using UML, modellers ought to make explicit the interpretation being followed, but this is seldom done.

Moreover, UML has many limitations that preclude rigorous (or sound) development. UML models are imprecise and cannot be formally analysed in the UML context. This brings the following consequences: (a) UML models result in ambiguous descriptions of software systems; (b) UML models cannot be checked for consistency, which means that one may produce unsatisfiable models for which no implementation may possibly exist; and (c) there are no means for checking whether certain desired system properties hold in a UML model.

Formal specification languages (FSLs), on the other hand, allow sound development. They yield precise descriptions of software systems that are amenable to formal analysis. However, these languages require substantial expertise from developers, and they are criticised for being *unpractical*, as substantial effort is involved in formally model and analyse systems.

In our modelling approach we aim at addressing these issues. We want (a) to deal with the multi-interpretation nature of UML, (b) to introduce soundness into UML-based development, and (c) to make sound development more approachable to developers and substantial more practical for use in wide engineering domains.

J. Davies et al. (Eds.): ICFEM 2004, LNCS 3308, pp. 418–433, 2004.
© Springer-Verlag Berlin Heidelberg 2004

To address these issues we propose *modelling frameworks*. Modelling frameworks are environments for building and analysing models that are tailored to problem domains. Each modelling framework comprises a set of UML notations, a semantics for those notations and an analysis approach for models built using the framework. The semantics of the UML notations is expressed by using a FSL; the analysis approach is based on the analysis means of the FSL being used. The components that make-up the framework (definitions and FSL) are appropriate to the problem domain being targeted by the framework.

We use *templates* to define modelling frameworks. Templates are used to describe meta-level properties, such as, the formal representation (or semantics) of UML modelling elements (e.g. class), and proof-obligations (or meta-conjectures). Our templates are parametric descriptions of phrases in a FSL (here Z), describing the essential structure of a phrase. A template instantiation involves providing names for the template's parameters; when properly instantiated a template yields a FSL phrase.

By using the templates of a framework, we can generate conjectures to formally analyse a UML-based model. Some of these conjectures are simply *true by construction* because our meta-level representations based on templates allows us to do *meta-proofs* of properties (i.e., the property is proved at the meta-level), which, once proved, are true for many instantiations of a particular form. Other conjectures can be automatically generated just by drawing diagrams; this allows formal model analysis by simply drawing simple and intuitive diagrams.

The following terminology is used to refer to the results of proving conjectures:

- *true by construction* — it is guaranteed to be true, so there is no need to do a proof, essentially, a meta-proof has been done;
- *trivially true* – Z/Eves can do it automatically;
- and *provable* – can be proved but Z/Eves needs some help: we are working on patterns/tactics for this class, to make them *trivial*.

Here we present and illustrate the use of a modelling framework for sequential systems based on UML and Z. The illustration is a simplified library system, comprising a library catalogue, copies of catalogued books for borrowing, tracking and renewal of loaned copies, and recalling of books. Section 2 presents the framework. Sections 3 to 6 construct and analyse the model of the library system.

2   A Modelling Framework for Sequential Systems

We have developed a modelling framework to construct and analyse models of sequential systems by using Z as the FSL [2]. Models and associated analysis conjectures are built by instantiating templates of the framework [3].

The models of our framework comprise UML class, state and snapshot diagrams with an underlying Z representation. Snapshot diagrams are a feature of Catalysis [4]; they are essentially object diagrams, illustrating either one system state or one system state transition. In the framework, most properties are expressed diagrammatically, but the modeller needs to resort to Z to express: invariants (or model constraints), and operation specifications. These properties would be expressed in OCL in a UML-only development.

Z has proved to be an appropriate language to represent abstract UML models. Z has semantics that is mathematical rather than computational. This makes the language flexible, powerful and extensible, and allows structuring based on different computational models. We have developed a model for Z based on the OO paradigm to represent abstract UML models. This results in well-structured and natural Z specifications. Another Z feature that is important in our approach is Z conjunction, which allows us to assemble the local pieces of state and behaviour into global ones. This gives us modular and conceptually clear Z.

In the following subsections, we discuss the semantic model used to represent UML diagrams, and the analysis strategy of the framework.

2.1 The Semantic Model

A semantic model is required to formally represent UML models. This is defined by using our OO Z structuring [2], which can be used to represent UML-based models and to construct Z specifications in a OO style.

Our OO structuring extends those reviewed in [5]. One of the novel features of our structuring is that it is views based, following a views structuring approach for Z [6]. The need for a views structuring approach came from the observation that not all properties of class models would fit elegantly into a single view.

In our structuring, a class has a dual meaning. *Class intension* defines the properties shared by the objects of that class (e.g, *Member* of figure 1 has properties *name*, *address*, and *category*). *Class extension* defines the class in terms of currently existing objects (e.g., *Member* is {*oRalph, oJohn, oAlan*}).

The main modelling entities are represented in Z in a state and operations style. Each class intension, class extension, association, subsystem and ultimately the whole system is represented as a Z abstract data type (ADT), consisting of a state description, an initialisation, and operations upon the state.

2.2 Analysis Strategy

The models of our framework are analysed through proof in Z. Our OO structuring based on ADTs across views, makes the task of demonstrating the consistency of our modelling entities easier, we just have to follow Z's consistency checking approach (proving initialisation theorems and calculating preconditions of operations). We also generate conjectures from diagrams, either to check the consistency of a diagram or to validate the system model. It is important to emphasise our approach to model validation, which is based on drawing snapshot diagrams; once we have these diagrams we can then generate conjectures, by instantiating templates, which are either trivially true or provable.

3   Modelling State

Modelling of state involves: building class models, describing the main entities of the system and the relationships between them; formally representing the class model and adding the model's static constraints (or invariants); and drawing snapshots of system state to validate the overall model of state.

3.1   UML Class Model

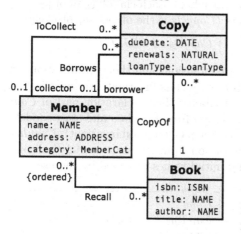

Fig. 1. Class diagram of library system

Figure 1 is the abstract UML class model of the library system. *Book* represents the entries in the library catalogue, comprising an *isbn*, the *title* and *author* of the book. *Copy* represents the actual instances of book; the attributes record the *dueDate* of a loaned copy, the number of *renewals* that have been made, where each renewal would set a later due date, and the *loanType*. *Member* represents the library members that are entitled to borrow and recall copies of books; the attributes record the *name* of a member, the *address* and the member *category*.

Structurally, *CopyOf* associates each Copy object with one Book object; there may be many copies of each book. A Member object *Borrows* zero, one or many copies; at any time each Copy object may or may not be borrowed. Members may issue a *Recall* against a catalogued Book object for which no copy is available; a Book object may have many unserved recalls at a time. The *Recall* association is subject to an *ordering* constraint, because, when a copy of a book for which there is a recall is returned to the library, the copy is offered to the member who made the earliest unmet recall. There is inevitably a period of time between the copy of the recalled book becoming available and the recalling member collecting the copy; *ToCollect* expresses the association between the recalling member and the copy whilst the book is awaiting collection.

3.2   Formal Representation of UML Class Model and Constraints

Here we show how the class diagram is formally represented by instantiating templates. We also show how we can add model constraints that do not have a diagrammatic representation. In representing the different modelling elements we follow systematic naming conventions; extensional definitions are preceeded by $\mathbb{S}$, and association-related ones by $\mathbb{A}$.

The formal representation is illustrated for each view of our structuring, namely, *structural, intensional, extensional, relational* and *global*. In the structural view we represent objects. In the intensional and extensional views we represent the intensional and extensional meaning of classes, respectively. In the relational view we represent associations. The global view groups classes and associations into subsystems and ultimately the system.

Structural View. Objects are represented as atoms. There is a given set of all objects ($OBJECT$), of which objects are members. Each class has an object set, which is a subset of the set of all objects ($CopyOs$ is the object set of $Copy$).

$$[OBJECT] \qquad\qquad | \; CopyOs : \mathbb{P}\,OBJECT$$

Intensional View. Here we represent state intensions and their initialisations. A state intension comprises class attributes and a class invariant. An initialisation makes an assignment of values to class attributes. The declaration part of $Copy$ (below) is generated by template instantiation from the class and state models; the user provides the predicate part of the schema (intension invariant). $CopyInit$ (below) is generated by template instantiation from the state model (indicates the initial value of *state*, see Fig. 4) and initial values provided by the user.

$$
\begin{array}{|l}
\_\,Copy \rule{3cm}{0pt} \\
\quad dueDate : DATE \\
\quad loanType : LoanType \\
\quad renewals : \mathbb{N} \\
\quad state : CopyState \\
\hline
\quad renewals \le renewalLimit \\
\end{array}
\qquad
\begin{array}{|l}
\_\,CopyInit \rule{2.5cm}{0pt} \\
\quad Copy' \\
\quad loanType? : LoanType \\
\hline
\quad dueDate' = nullDate \\
\quad renewals' = 0 \\
\quad loanType' = loanType? \\
\quad state' = shelved \\
\end{array}
$$

Extensional View. Class state extension defines the set of all existing class objects (a subset of the class' object set), and a mapping between object atoms and their state intensions. We represent state extension as a Z generic ($\mathbb{S}\,Class$ below), actual state extensions are instantiations of this generic. The $\mathbb{S}\,Copy$ state extension (below) and its initialisation are generated from the class model by instantiating their corresponding templates [1]; if there were extension invariants they would have to be provided by the user.

$$
\begin{array}{|l}
\_\,\mathbb{S}Class\,[OSET, OSTATE] \rule{5cm}{0pt} \\
\quad objs : \mathbb{P}\,OSET \\
\quad objSt : OSET \nrightarrow OSTATE \\
\hline
\quad \mathrm{dom}\; objSt = objs \\
\end{array}
$$

$$\mathbb{S}\,Copy == \mathbb{S}Class[CopyOs, Copy][copys/objs, copySt/objSt]$$

---

[1] The renaming in the definition of $\mathbb{S}\,Copy$ is done to avoid name clashing when component schemas are composed to make the system schema.

Relational View. An association denotes a set of tuple pairs, where each tuple describes the pair of objects being linked. Association state defines a mathematical relation between the object sets of the classes being associated (e.g. association *Borrows* is defined as *borrows* : $MemberOs \leftrightarrow CopyOs$). Association static representations (state and initialisation) in Z are mostly generated from the class diagram information by instantiating proper templates; again only association invariants, if they exist, need to be added by the user. We have templates to handle special kinds of associations, such as those with the *ordered* constraint.

Global View. Subsystem state groups classes and association of the subsystem, includes consistency constraints between classes and associations, and system constraints that cross modelling elements. The system state of the library problem is given below, with its three classes and four associations. In the predicate, each name refers to another Z schema – *Consistency* predicates refer to consistency constraints on associations, and *Constraint* predicates to system-wide constraints. The initialisation of system state (*SysInit* below) consists of initialising each system component (class or association); this is defined by conjoining the initialisations of class extensions and associations. Both state and initialisation schemas are generated from templates, where most information comes from the class model; the user adds the *Constraint* schemas.

$$
\begin{array}{l}
\underline{\quad System \underline{\hspace{6cm}}} \\
SMember;\ SCopy;\ SBook;\ ABorrows;\ AToCollect;\ ACopyOf;\ ARecall \\
\underline{\hspace{11cm}} \\
ConsistencyABorrows \wedge ConsistencyAToCollect \\
ConsistencyACopyOf \wedge ConsistencyARecall \\
ConstraintNoCommonCopiesBorrowsToCollect \\
ConstraintBorrowingLimit \\
\end{array}
$$

$$
\begin{array}{l}
SysInit == System' \wedge SMemberInit \wedge SCopyInit \wedge SBookInit \\
\qquad \wedge ABorrowsInit \wedge AToCollectInit \wedge ACopyOfInit \wedge ARecallInit
\end{array}
$$

3.3 State Snapshots

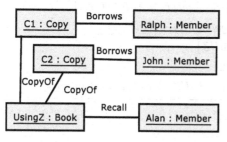

Fig. 2. Snapshot of a desired system state

State snapshots are UML object diagrams describing one specific state of the system.

Figure 2 is a valid snapshot of the system state, comprising a book, *UsingZ*, with two copies, *C*1 and *C*2. There are three library members, two of whom are borrowing the copies of *UsingZ*; and the third of whom has issued a recall. Informally, one can see that this snapshot illustrates a valid state of our class model.

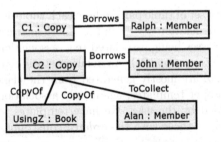

Fig. 3. Snapshot of an undesired system state

Figure 3 is an invalid state snapshot. Here, copy $c2$ is being borrowed by *John* but also being kept awaiting collection for *Alan*. We want the system to disallow this – as soon as a copy of a recalled book is returned, its *Borrows* link should be replaced by a *ToCollect* link with a recalling member.

We considered placing a *disjoint* constraint between *Borrows* and *ToCollect*, with the intention of making the snapshot in Figure 3 invalid. Formal analysis shows that such a constraint would leave the snapshot valid, as the tuples in the snapshot are disjoint: *Borrows* comprises $\{(Ralph, C1), (John, C2)\}$ and *ToCollect* comprises $\{(Alan, C2)\}$. We express this in a Z constraint schema (included in the *System* schema, above), by stating that the tuples of those associations may not have copies in common (the *ranges* of relations *Borrows* and *ToCollect* must be disjoint).

$$
\begin{array}{l}
\hline
\; ConstraintNoCommonCopiesBorrowsToCollect \underline{\qquad\qquad} \\
\; \Delta Borrows; \; \Delta ToCollect \\
\hline
\; \text{disjoint}\langle \text{ran } borrows, \text{ran } toCollect\rangle \\
\hline
\end{array}
$$

3.4   Formally Representing Snapshots

Each snapshot is formalised as a specific instance of the system, by equating each general concept to a specific set of instances. The representation of the snapshot of Fig. 2 is given below; this is fully generated from the snapshot diagram by instantiating templates (names are declared axiomatically).

$$
\begin{array}{l}
\hline
\; LibrarySnapshot1 \underline{\qquad\qquad} \\
\; System \\
\hline
\; books = \{oUZ\} \wedge bookSt = \{oUZ \mapsto uz\} \wedge copys = \{oC1, oC2\} \\
\; copySt = \{oC1 \mapsto c1, oC2 \mapsto c2\} \wedge members = \{oR, oJ, oA\} \\
\; memberSt = \{oR \mapsto ralph, oJ \mapsto john, oA \mapsto alan\} \\
\; copyOf = \{oC1 \mapsto oUZ, oC2 \mapsto oUZ\} \\
\; borrows = \{oR \mapsto oC1, oJ \mapsto oC2\} \\
\; recall = \{oA \mapsto oUZ\} \wedge ordRecall = \{oUZ \mapsto \langle oA\rangle\} \wedge toCollect = \varnothing \\
\hline
\end{array}
$$

4   Analysing State

State analysis involves: checking the consistency of the class model; and checking the class model against state snapshots.

4.1   Class Model

To demonstrate the consistency of state, we prove *initialisation* theorems. An initialisation theorem is of the form, $\vdash \exists State' \bullet StateInit$. This says that there is some valid instance of *State* satisfying its initialisation (hence the model of state is satisfiable). We need to prove initialisation theorems for the various system components, including, class intensions and extensions, associations, and the whole system.

For the example (and most that we studied), with correctly-instantiated templates,

- the initialisation theorem on class extensions and associations are true by construction;
- the initialisation theorem on the class intensions are trivially true;
- the initialisation theorem on the whole system, which ensures that all the constraints hold in the initial state, is (easily) provable[2].

In our example, the *Copy* intension initialisation, $\vdash \exists Copy' \bullet CopyInit$, is automatically discharged (proved true) by Z/Eves. Since *Copy* has an invariant stating that the number of renewals of a copy loan must be no more than the maximum number of renewals allowed (*renewals* $\leq$ *renewalLimit*), the proof confirms that this constraint is satisfiable. Suppose that *Copy* state has the contradictory invariant, *renewals* $< 5 \wedge$ *renewals* > 10. Z/Eves would now reduce the initialisation conjecture to *false*; no initialisation can be made in which this invariant is satisfied.

For the example, we proved the initialisation theorem for the whole system, $\vdash \exists System' \bullet SysInit$. This means that the overall system constraints are consistent, and that the specification is a satisfiable model.

4.2   State Snapshots

A state snapshot is a witness of the system model. Analysis demonstrates whether the snapshot is a valid witness or not. This involves proving an *existence conjecture*. As for the initialisation, if this conjecture is true then there is a state of the specified system that satisfies the state described in the snapshot. One can also perform negative model validation by using deliberately invalid snapshots (see section 6.3).

The instantiated template conjectures that validate the two state snapshots in Figures 2 and 3 are, respectively,

$$\vdash \exists System \bullet LibrarySnapshot1 \qquad\qquad \vdash \exists System \bullet LibrarySnapshot2$$

The first is provable in Z/Eves, confirming the validity of the snapshot; the second reduces to *false*, so is an invalid state of the whole system (as required), and we can conclude that our model disallows this state.

---

[2] By using meta-proof we could substantially simplify the system initialisation conjecture. The simplified conjecture, for this system, is easily provable in Z/Eves.

5   Modelling Behaviour

Modelling behaviour in our framework involves: describing the reactive behaviour of relevant classes with *state diagrams*; describing changes of system state in the context of system operations with *operation snapshots*; specifying operations in Z based on operation snapshot diagrams.

5.1   UML State Diagrams

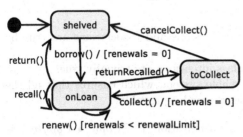

Fig. 4. State diagram of *Copy*

UML state diagrams describe the permitted state transitions of objects of each class. Figure 4 is the state diagram of the *Copy* class. We follow a Catalysis [4] convention, that each event is described in the form, *event*[*guard*]/[*postcondition*], where *event*, the name of the event, equates to the name of a class operation; *guard* is an optional predicate stating the precondition for the transition; *postcondition* is an optional predicate to express what the transition is required to establish.

Here, the initial state of a copy is *shelved*. The loan of a copy by a member, *borrow*(), results in a transition from *shelved* to *onLoan*. When in the *onLoan* state, copies may be renewed, *renew*(), and recalled, *recall*(). The return of a copy, *return*(), results in a transition either back to *shelved*, or, if there is a recall on the copy's book, *returnRecalled*(), to *toCollect*. When the relevant member collects the copy, *collect*(), there is a transition from *toCollect* to *onLoan*. If the recalling member indicates that they no longer require the copy awaiting collection, *cancelCollect*(), there is a transition from *toCollect* to *shelved*. We might expect a fourth state, for copies which are being borrowed but which are subject to a recall; such a state would not allow *renew*() operations. However, in our domain recalls are made upon books, not copies; a recall is active until one of the copies of the recalled book is returned; as copies are not aware of the state of other copies, such a state would require a message to each copy on loan to unset the recall. Instead, in our model, there is a system level renewal operation which takes as input a copy instance, and checks whether there are any *Recall* links from the *Book* to which the copy is linked; only if there are no *Recall* links can the *copy.renew*() operation be executed.

5.2   Formal Representation of UML State Diagrams

State diagrams are represented in the intensional view, as part of the intensional definition of the class to which they associated. Such a representation involves defining the class' state (to indicate the current state an object is in according to the state model), initialisation and operations, according to the contents of the state model. This is achieved by instantiating templates.

In our example, *Copy*'s state schema includes a component *state* of type {*shelved, onloan, toCollect*} (the possible states of *Copy* objects); the initialisation sets *state* to *shelved*, the initial state of the state model (see section 3.2 for schemas *Copy* and *CopyInit*); the operations establish the state transitions of the state model, for example, the operation *CopyBorrow* (see below) is associated with the state transition *shelved* to *onLoan*, the specification has a precondition stating that *state* is *shelved*, and a post-condition stating that *state* is *onLoan* and *renewals* is 0 (post-condition of transition).

5.3   Operation Snapshots

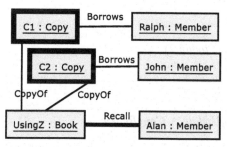

Fig. 5. Operation snapshot in the context of *Recall*

Operation Snapshots describe one system state transition in the context of an operation. These are valuable in understanding and describing operations, and in validating their specifications.

Figure 5 is a valid snapshot in the context of the *Recall* operation, invoked when *Alan* issues a recall on *UsingZ*. Highlighting denotes the change of state after execution – a link between the member that issued the recall and the recalled book is formed. The changes to *c1* and *c2* represent the resetting of due dates imposed when a recall is received.

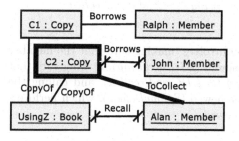

Fig. 6. Operation snapshot in the context of *Return*

Figure 6 is a snapshot in the context of the *Return* operation, invoked when *John* returns *C2*. Since *UsingZ* has an active recall, a link is formed between *Alan* and *C2*; as the recall is satisfied, the *Recall* link is deleted.

The snapshots increase confidence that the class and state diagrams and operation specifications are sensible. Later we see how we can use them to validate the model.

5.4   Operation Specifications

Operations are specified in Z from operation snapshot diagrams.

Class operations have intensional and extensional definitions. The intension specifies the required state changes of one class object. The extension *promotes* the intensional operation to all existing objects of a class. Below,

CopyRenew is the intensional definition of *Copy.renew()* and $\mathbb{S}CopyRenew$ the extensional one (each defined in intensional and extensional views respectively); $\mathbb{S}CopyRenew$ is defined by using Z promotion [7], where $\Phi\mathbb{S}CopyUpdate$ is the update promotion framing schema, and *CopyRenew* the intensional operation being promoted. These definitions have templates that capture their structure; *CopyRenew* is generated with information coming from the state diagram (*state* predicates), and provided by the user; $\mathbb{S}CopyRenew$ can be automatically generated.

$$
\begin{array}{l}
\underline{\;CopyRenew\;}\\
\Delta Copy\\
\hline
state = onLoan\\
state' = onLoan\\
renewals' = renewals + 1\\
dueDate' = nextDueDate\,(loanType, todayD)\\
loanType' = loanType
\end{array}
$$

$$\mathbb{S}CopyRenew == \exists\,\Delta Copy \bullet \Phi\mathbb{S}CopyUpdate \wedge CopyRenew$$

System operations are defined in the global view by conjoining a framing schema[3], class extensional operations, association operations, and predicates. This structure is captured by a template. The system operation *Renew()* is generated from this template with parameters provided by the user to yield,

$$
\begin{aligned}
SysRenew == {}& \Psi SysRenew \wedge \mathbb{A}IsBorrowing \wedge \neg\, \mathbb{A}IsCopyRecalled\\
& \wedge \mathbb{S}CopyRenew
\end{aligned}
$$

which states that the renewal of a *Copy* involves: making sure that the member is indeed borrowing the *Copy* being renewed ($\mathbb{A}IsBorrowing$), making sure that there is no active recall upon the *Copy* ($\neg\,\mathbb{A}IsCopyRecalled$), and calling the renew operation upon the *Copy* being renewed ($\mathbb{S}CopyRenew$), which performs a change of state in the *Copy* being renewed.

6   Analysing Behaviour

Analysis of behaviour consists of: checking the consistency of state diagrams against class models and operation specifications; pre-condition investigation of operations; and using operation snapshots to validate the model.

---

[3] Indicates what parts of system state change with the operation; this kind of framing schemas are preceeded by Ψ, to distinguish them from Φ promotion framing schemas.

6.1   State Diagrams

A state diagram sets requirements upon the initialisation and operations of a class intension. To check the consistency of a state diagram against initialisation and operation specifications, we state and try to prove conjectures expressing what we wish to hold. This gives us one conjecture for the initial state, and two conjectures per state transition: one for the pre-condition of the operation associated with the transition and one for the post-condition. These conjectures are captured by templates that can be fully generated from the state diagram.

In our example, the initialisation conjecture:

$$CopyInit \vdash state' = shelved$$

assumes the initialisation to show that the initial value of state is set as described by the state model. This conjecture is true by construction.

The approach to check pre- and post-conditions of operations is similar. The precondition conjecture for $Copy.renew()$:

$$\text{pre } CopyRenew \vdash state = onLoan \wedge renewals < renewalLimit$$

assumes the precondition of the operation to show that the before-state ($state = onLoan$) and the guard of the $Renew$ state transition ($renewals < renewalLimit$) are satisfied by the operation's precondition. This is trivially true. However, if we had made the common mistake of simply using the relevant class invariant ($renewals \leq renewalLimit$) as the guard, the calculated precondition would no longer establish the consequent, and the conjecture would be *false* – in some cases, a further renewal would exceed the limit set in the state constraint.

The postcondition conjecture for $Copy.renew()$:

$$CopyRenew \vdash state' = onLoan$$

assumes the operation to show that the $Copy$ is left in the after-state of the $Renew$ state transition ($state' = onLoan$). This is true by construction in this example, as there is no explicit postcondition in the state model for this transition.

6.2   Precondition Investigation

The precondition of an operation describes the sets of states for which the outcome of the operation is properly defined. Precondition calculation is routine in formal analysis. Systematic precondition analysis of class-level operations can reveal flaws in the specification. For example, consider a specification of *Recall* that has a precondition that (a) the recall must must be done by a member, (b) the requested book must be a book in the library catalogue, and (c) there are no copies of the book available in shelves. Pre-condition analysis reveals that this is too weak, in that it allows the recall of a book that have no copies (the multiplicity of the *Copy* end of *CopyOf* is $0 .. *$), the placing of two or more active recalls by the same member, and recall by a member who already has a copy of the book on loan or awaiting collection. Analysis allows the precondition to be strengthened to disallow such behaviour.

6.3   Operation Snapshots

Snapshots of system-level operations result in a dual formal representation: the before-state, and the after-state. Both are generated by instantiating templates with information coming from the diagram, and both need to be challenged.

The before-state of the snapshot is required to satisfy the operation's precondition. This results in a conjecture that assumes the formal representation of the snapshot's before-state, and establishes the precondition of the system operation. For instance, the snapshot in Fig. 5, representing the system-wide effect of a recall, would result in the following instantiated template conjecture:

$$LibraryBeforeRecallSnp \vdash \text{pre } SysRecall$$

This is provable in Z/Eves.

For the after-state, we require that from the snapshot's before-state, the system-level operations establish the snapshot's after-state. The conjecture assumes the formal representation of the snapshot's before-state and the system operation, and establishes the snapshot's after-state. For the snapshot in Figure 5, the instantiated template conjecture is:

$$LibraryBeforeRecallSnp; \; SysRecall \vdash LibraryAfterRecallSnp$$

This is provable in Z/Eves. The pre- and post- conjectures for the snapshot in Figure 6 are similarly constructed and proved.

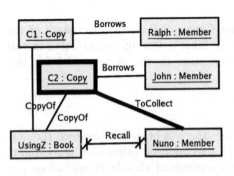

Fig. 7. State snapshot of an undesired behaviour in the context of *Return*

We can also perform negative validation. Figure 7 illustrates a state transition, in the context of operation *Return*, that our model should disallow. The snapshot differs from that in Figure 6 in that the *Borrows* link between *John* and *C2* is not deleted, violating the constraint added to the system state to prevent simultaneous *Borrows* and *ToCollect* links on the same copy.

If the post-condition conjecture on the formalised snapshot does not reduce to *false*, this indicates there may be missing preconditions or other constraints. Once determined, these can be added to the specification, and the conjecture reinvestigated, until it does reduce to *false*. (Clearly, other conjectures involving the same operation will also need to be reproved as part of this process).

7   Discussion

Our template approach provides a Z formalisation of class, state, and snapshot diagrams, and, in addition, provides an analysis strategy for models composed of these diagrams. Currently, our approach allows rigorous hand-generation of Z from diagrams by instantiating templates. Future work should address automation (tool development).

By using the templates of our framework, we can challenge a model by drawing snapshot diagrams; the associated formal representations and conjectures are generated by template instantiation (hence potentially automatable). The discharging of snapshot conjectures can also be partially automated; snapshots deal with model instances, which are more tractable by theorem provers. We can see snapshots as giving life to a model. Snapshot-based validation is a useful technique even if one builds Z-only specifications in a OO style.

The current drawback of our approach is that the discharging of some of the proofs in Z/Eves requires expertise in using the prover (mainly proofs dealing with system operations). We are looking at ways to mitigate this problem by using proof tactics and patterns that, potentially, could substantially simplify and perhaps fully automate some of the proofs.

Our approach of formalising UML class and state diagrams in Z with a state and operations style, using the schema calculus, enhances the analysis capabilities of our approach. Analysis in Z is tied to the state and operations style, where one is required to prove initialisation theorems and calculate pre-conditions.

Moreover, templates allow us to minimise the proof effort. We can prove properties at the meta-level that are applicable to all instantiations of a template, or to instantiations of particular form. We try to make as much proof as possible at the meta-level – a property is proved once, and then it becomes true when an instantiation relevant to the property occurs (true by construction).

The modelling framework presented here requires modellers that know both UML and Z. Our aim is to allow UML-only modellers to use our framework, hence, we need to make the underlying Z completely transparent to the user. This involves devising new notations (or using existing ones like OCL), for the expression of constraints and operation specifications, that can be easily represented in Z.

Modelling frameworks would greatly benefit from tool support. Currently we are working on the theoretical foundations. However, we envisage a tool that generates a formal representation of a UML model, checks that model for well formedness (through type-checking and other means), generates the associated conjectures (proof obligations) associated with the model, and then interacts with a prover to discharge those conjectures.

8   Conclusions and Future Work

Modelling frameworks and the associated template mechanism give us:

- Means to introduce soundness in UML-based development. We define interpretations of UML concepts in a FSL that has a formal semantics with analysis means. This allows us to build UML models that are precise and analysable.
- Means to make sound development more usable. Most Z of our framework's models is generated by template instantiation, hence potentially automatable. This may allow the construction of sound models composed of diagrams, opening sound development to UML-only modellers.
- Means to make sound development more practical. Our representations in the template form allows us to prove properties at the meta-level so that users don't have to actually do it.

We are looking at generalising conjectures coming from snapshot diagrams. This will allow us to prove properties that hold in our model for any model-instance, rather than a specific one.

Having generated an underlying formal model, we can exploit other forms of formal analysis. For example, the Alloy tool [8] uses a subset of Z; after some manipulation, we can use Alloy's Alcoa model checker. We have initial results verifying properties of class models [2], and we will also explore reachability analysis on state diagrams. We are also looking at other aspects of development within the formal transformational framework – Catalysis has an informal notion of model refinement based on diagrams, inspired by formal refinement. We want to combine the diagram refinement with the conventional formal refinement calculus, whilst retaining the developer-friendly approach.

Acknowledgements. This research was supported for Amálio by the Portuguese Foundation for Science and Technology under grant 6904/2001.

References

1. Saaltink, M. The Z/EVES system. In *ZUM'97: The Z Formal Specification Notation*, volume 1212 of *LNCS*. Springer-Verlag (1997)
2. Amálio, N., Polack, F., Stepney, S. A sound modelling framework for sequential systems I: Modelling. Technical Report YCS-2004, Department of Computer Science, University of York (2004)
3. Amálio, N., Stepney, S., Polack, F. Modular UML semantics: Interpretations in Z based on templates and generics. In Van, H. D., Liu, Z., eds., *FACS'03: Formal Aspects of Component Software, Int. Workshop, Pisa, Italy*, 284, pp. 81–100. UNU/IIST Technical Report (2003)
4. D'Sousa, D., Wills, A. C. *Object Components and Frameworks with UML: the Catalysis approach*. Addison-Wesley (1998)
5. Amálio, N., Polack, F. Comparison of formalisation approaches of UML class constructs in Z and Object-Z. In Bert et al. [9], pp. 339–358
6. Jackson, D. Structuring Z specifications with views. *ACM Transactions on Software Engineering and Methodology (TOSEM)*, 4(4):365–389 (1995)

7. Stepney, S., Polack, F., Toyn, I. Patterns to guide practical refactoring: examples targetting promotion in Z. In Bert et al. [9], pp. 20–39
8. Jackson, D. Alloy: A lightweight object modelling notation. *ACM Transactions on Software Engineering and Methodology*, 11(2):256–290 (2002)
9. Bert, D., et al., eds. *ZB 2003: Formal Specification and Development in Z and B, Int. Conference, Turku, Finland*, volume 2651 of *LNCS*. Springer-Verlag (2003)

Interactive Verification of UML State Machines

Michael Balser[1], Simon Bäumler[1], Alexander Knapp[2],
Wolfgang Reif[1], and Andreas Thums[1]

[1] Institut für Informatik, Universität Augsburg
{balser,baeumler,reif,thums}@informatik.uni-augsburg.de
[2] Institut für Informatik, Ludwig-Maximilians-Universität München
knapp@pst.ifi.lmu.de

Abstract. We propose a new technique for interactive formal verification of temporal properties of UML state machines. We introduce a formal, operational semantics of UML state machines and give an overview of the proof method which is based on symbolic execution with induction. Usefulness of the approach is demonstrated by example of an automatic teller machine. The approach is implemented in the KIV system.

1 Introduction

The "Unified Modeling Language" (UML [14]), the de facto standard notation for specifying object-oriented software systems, offers state machine diagrams as an operational view of the dynamic aspects of a system, which are a variant of the statechart notations introduced by Harel [5]. Most attempts to verify properties of UML state machines use model checking (see e.g. [11, 10, 16]). Model checking allows a fast and simple way to check, whether a property holds or not. However, the major disadvantage of model checking is that it needs to search the whole state space of the state machine for a violation of the property and thus the verification success highly depends on the size of the state space. If the state space of a state machine is unlimited, e.g. by using an unbounded integer variable, verification of true properties normally fails.

We pursue another approach to the verification of UML state machines. In contrast to model checking, interactive verifiers such as KIV [3] are designed for systems with an infinite state space. Our goal is to provide a uniform, interactive, intuitive and efficient proof method for verifying properties of UML state machines. We have chosen symbolic execution with induction as proof method, because this method has been successfully applied to the verification of sequential programs (e.g. [7, 17]) and gives very intuitive proofs. Furthermore, symbolic execution can be automated to a very large extent. We have also shown how to carry over the proof method to the verification of parallel programs [2]. Here, we demonstrate how to apply the method to the verification of UML state machines.

To our knowledge, this is the first such approach to interactive verification of UML state machines. In contrast to other approaches, we do not formalise the semantics of UML in the existing logic, but derive a calculus to directly execute state machines. We have been able to efficiently support not only a subset but all of the main features of

J. Davies et al. (Eds.): ICFEM 2004, LNCS 3308, pp. 434–448, 2004.

UML state machines such as hierarchical and concurrent states, compound transitions, and a rich action language. Thus, our approach is more complete than e.g. the Omega project [15]. Compared to other interactive calculi for the verification of similar concurrent systems (e.g. [12, 4]), the proof method of symbolic execution promises a higher degree of automation, a uniform treatment of safety and liveness properties, and the use of invariants which are easier to come up with.

We assume the reader to be familiar with UML state machines and to have at least basic knowledge in temporal logic and sequent calculus. The remainder of this paper is structured as follows: In Sect. 2, we give a short introduction to constructing temporal proofs with symbolic execution and induction. Section 3 describes UML state machines and introduces an example. Section 4 formally defines an operational semantics of UML state machines. How to turn the operational semantics of UML into a calculus rule for symbolic execution is sketched in Sect. 5. A safety property of the example is verified in Sect. 6. Section 7 summarizes the results and outlines future work.

2   Temporal Logic Framework

The logical formalism is a variant of ITL (Interval Temporal Logic [13]). It is based on (finite or infinite) linear sequences π of valuations which we call *intervals*. A single valuation (which we also call state) is described by first-order predicate logic formulae over static variables v and dynamic variables V. Different valuations of an interval π may assign different values to the dynamic variables V. In addition, a valuation gives values to primed variables V' and double-primed variables V''; the relation between unprimed and primed variables is interpreted as *system transitions*, the relation between primed and double-primed variables as *environment transitions*. System and environment transitions alternate, the value of V'' being equal to V in the next valuation. Temporal operators, we support, include $\Box\varphi$ (φ always holds), $\Diamond\varphi$ (eventually φ holds), φ **until** ψ, φ **unless** ψ, $\circ\varphi$ (there is a next state which satisfies φ), $\bullet\varphi$ (if there is a next state, it satisfies φ), and **last** (the current state is the last) with their standard semantics. The proof method is based on a sequent calculus.

We focus on a subset of proof obligations, here: Our goal is to take an initial variable condition I, a system S, a configuration C, and a temporal property φ and to prove that $S, C, I \vdash \varphi$. In other words, all runs of system S which satisfy C and I in its initial state must satisfy φ. The proof method is symbolic execution with induction. In the following, we show how to symbolically execute a temporal formula φ, how to execute an arbitrary system description S, and how to use induction to prove properties for infinite system runs. In Sect. 5 we show how to apply this general proof method to the verification of UML state machines.

2.1   Symbolic Execution

Our principle of symbolic execution is to rewrite an arbitrary temporal formula φ to an equivalent formula

$$\varphi \leftrightarrow \tau_0 \wedge \mathbf{last} \vee \bigvee_{1 \leq i \leq n} (\tau_i \wedge \circ \varphi_i)$$

where τ_i are formulae in first-order predicate logic. Either the system represented by φ terminates with condition τ_0, or one of n possible transitions τ_i is executed and execution continues with φ_i in the next step. As an example, consider rewrite rule

(alw) $\Box\varphi \leftrightarrow \varphi \wedge \bullet \Box\varphi$

which unwinds an always operator such that φ must hold now and always in the future. Our calculus provides rewrite rules to similarly unwind all of the temporal operators. By unwinding the single temporal operators with these rules, it is possible to rewrite arbitrary temporal formulae to receive an equivalent formula of the form stated above. Details can be found in [2].

2.2   Executing System Descriptions

We apply the same strategy of symbolic execution to almost arbitrary system descriptions S which describe the operational behaviour of systems as follows: a function $exec(S, C)$ is implemented which returns the possible transitions τ with configurations C_0 for the next state. This function can be used in the rule (to be read bottom-up)

$$\text{(execute)}\quad \frac{\{\tau \wedge \circ(S \wedge C_0), I \vdash \varphi \mid \langle \tau, C_0 \rangle \in exec(S, C)\}}{S, C, I \vdash \varphi}$$

to execute a system S in configuration C. The transition τ relates variable condition I to the variable condition in the next state. We use the *execute* rule to integrate UML state machines into our formalism (see Sect. 5). An implementation for $exec(S, C)$ is rather straightforward if the operational semantics of S is formally defined. The rule (execute) is sound if implementation of $exec(S, C)$ is sound.

This approach avoids the overhead in proof size, which would result if we specify the semantics of UML within our logic. In this case, we would need several basic rules to execute a single state machine step. In our experience, application of rule (execute) is very efficient.

2.3   Taking a Step

After system and temporal formula have been rewritten and execution does not terminate, rule (step) can be applied.

$$\text{(step)}\quad \frac{S, C, I_0 \vdash \varphi}{\tau, \circ(S \wedge C), I \vdash \bullet\varphi} \qquad \text{where } I_0 := (I \wedge \tau)[V, V', V''/v_0, v_1, V]$$

Condition I_0 in the next state is received by replacing in the original I and transition τ all unprimed and primed dynamic variables V and V' with fresh static variables v_0 and v_1, the double-primed variables V'' correspond to the unprimed variables in the next state. In addition, the leading operators $\circ$ and $\bullet$ are eliminated. Symbolic execution continues in the next state.

2.4   Induction

Symbolic execution needs not to terminate. Therefore, we use noetherian induction over a supplied induction term T

$$\text{(ind)} \quad \frac{\Gamma, T = n, \Box(T < n \rightarrow (\bigwedge \Gamma \rightarrow \bigvee \Delta)) \vdash \Delta}{\Gamma \vdash \Delta}$$

The fresh static variable n is assigned to the initial value of T. Always, if the value of T is less than the initial value n, the induction hypothesis $\bigwedge \Gamma \rightarrow \bigvee \Delta$ can be applied. This general induction principle can be applied to prove arbitrary temporal properties. Special derived rules are defined to prove certain temporal properties without induction term. A derived rule for proving safety properties is as follows.

$$\text{(ind alw)} \quad \frac{\Gamma, \bullet(\bigwedge \Gamma \rightarrow \bigvee \Delta) \text{ until } \neg\varphi \vdash \Delta}{\Gamma \vdash \Box\varphi, \Delta}$$

Formula $\Box\varphi$ in the succedent corresponds to a liveness condition $\Diamond\neg\varphi$ in the antecedent and therefore the induction is performed over the number of steps it takes to satisfy $\neg\varphi$. Special rules without induction terms can be given for all safety properties; a term T must only be provided to establish liveness conditions.

2.5   Sequencing

Executing concurrent systems is costly, because in every step typically a number of nondeterministic transitions can be executed leading to large proofs. However, executing several transitions often leads to the same state, no matter in which order they are executed. In this case, an extended sequent rule

$$\text{(seq)} \quad \frac{\Gamma, \rho_1 \vee \rho_2 \vdash \Delta}{\Gamma, \rho_1 \vdash \Delta \qquad \Gamma, \rho_2 \vdash \Delta}$$

can be applied which contains two conclusions to contract two proof obligations with the same temporal formulae. Additional predicate logical formulae ρ_1 and ρ_2 are combined as disjunction. This approach leads to proof graphs instead of proof trees and works best, if automatic simplification is able to significantly reduce $\rho_1 \vee \rho_2$. An example proof graph can be found in Fig. 4.

3   UML State Machines: An Example

We use a simple UML model of an automatic teller machine (ATM), shown in Fig. 1, as our running example: The class diagram in Fig. 1(a) specifies an (active) class Bank. Classes define *attributes*, i.e., local variables of its instances, and *operations* and *signals* that may be invoked on instances by call and send actions, respectively. Additionally, *invariants* restrict the state space of class instances.

The state machine for class Bank is shown in Fig. 1(b), consisting of *states* and *transitions* between states (we number the states for short reference later on). States can be *simple* (such as Idle and PINCorrect) or *composite* (such as Verifying); a *concurrent* composite state contains several *orthogonal regions*, separated by dashed lines. Moreover, *fork* and *join* (pseudo-)states, shown as bars, synchronize several transitions to and from orthogonal regions; *junction* (pseudo-)states, represented as filled circles, chain together multiple transitions. Transitions between states are triggered by *events*. Transitions may also be guarded by conditions and specify actions to be executed or events to be emitted when the transition is fired. For example, the transition leading from state Idle to the fork pseudostate requires signal verifyPIN to be present; the transition branch from VerifyingCard to CardValid requires the guard cardValid to be true; the transition branches from CardValid to Idle set the Bank attributes tries and cardValid. Events may also be emitted by *entry* and *exit* actions that are executed when a state is activated or deactivated. Transitions without an explicit trigger (e.g. the transition leaving DispenseMoney), are called *completion transitions* and are triggered by *completion events* which are emitted when a state completes all its internal activities.

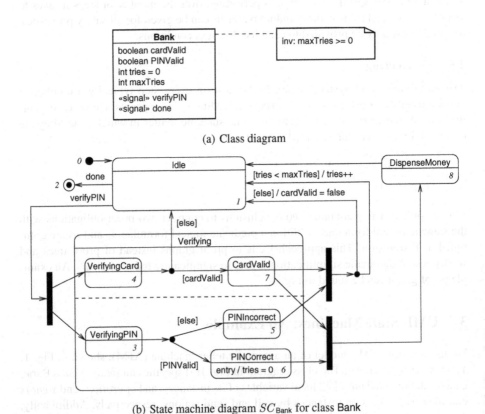

(a) Class diagram

(b) State machine diagram SC_{Bank} for class Bank

Fig. 1. UML model of an ATM

The actual state of a state machine is given by its *active state configuration* and by the contents of its *event queue*. The active state configuration is the tree of active states; in particular, for every active concurrent composite state each of its orthogonal regions is active. The event queue holds the events that have not yet been handled. The *event dispatcher* dequeues the first event from the queue; the event is then processed in a *run-to-completion* (RTC) step. First, a maximally consistent set of enabled transitions is chosen: a transition is *enabled* if all of its source states are contained in the active state configuration, if its trigger is matched by the current event, and if its guard is true; two enabled transitions are *consistent* if they do not share a source state. For each transition in the set, its *least common ancestor* (LCA) is determined, i.e. the lowest composite state that contains all the transition's source and target states. The transition's main source state, that is the direct substate of the LCA containing the source states, is deactivated, the transition's actions are executed, and its target states are activated.

The example state machine simulates card and PIN validation of a bank computer. After initialization the bank computer is in state Idle. The reception of signal done leads to finalizing the state machine, whereas on reception of signal verifyPIN the verification process is started in state Verifying. If the card is invalid, the bank computer immediately returns to state Idle. If the PIN is invalid, it is checked whether the maximum number of trials is exceeded. If this is the case, the card is marked invalid; otherwise the number of trials is incremented by one. In both cases, the bank computer returns to state Idle. If the PIN is valid, the number of trials is reset to zero. If both the PIN and the card are valid, state DispenseMoney is entered from which the bank computer returns to state Idle.

4   Semantics of UML State Machines

The semantics of UML state machines is defined by an execution algorithm. This algorithm forms the basis for embedding UML state machines into temporal logic and, in particular, the symbolic execution technique. Our semantical account of UML state machines follows the semantics definition of the UML 1.5 specification [14] as closely as possible, but fills in some of the gaps of the specification. We take up the ideas presented by Lilius and Porres [11]; however, we use a simplified notion of compound transitions and correct the definition of maximally consistent sets of compound transitions.

We first define the abstract syntax of the sublanguage of UML state machines from the UML specification [14] for which our semantics is valid. Apart from those language constructs which we do not discuss here (i.e. history, sync, and choice pseudostates, call and deferred events, and internal transitions), this definition introduces the following restriction: A transition from an initial pseudostate must target a non-pseudostate contained in the same composite state as the initial pseudostate. Abandoning this restriction would lead to a more intricate definition of compound transitions, which, however, has no relevance in most practical applications.

The semantics of UML state machines is defined in two steps: First, we describe a procedure for statically computing the configurations and the compound transitions of a state machine. Due to our syntactical restriction, compound transitions are trees of state machine transitions (describing the chaining of junctions, forks, and entries of states) with a possible fan-in prefix (describing joins) that represent a move from a configuration into another configuration. Second, we define an algorithm for run-to-completion steps which first computes a maximally consistent set of compound transitions for a given event and then executes the set of compound transitions.

4.1   Abstract Syntax of UML State Machines

We assume an expression language Exp that at least includes boolean expressions (like true, false, $e_1 \wedge e_2$, etc.) and an action language Act that at least includes a skip statement, and sequential (;) and parallel ($\|$) composition of statements. Furthermore, we assume a set of events $Event$ which includes $*$ denoting a completion event.

A *state* s has a kind $kind(s) \in \{$initial, final, simple, composite, concurrent, junction, join, fork$\}$, an entry action $entry(s) \in Act$, and an exit action $exit(s) \in Act$. A *pseudostate* is a state s with $kind(s) \in \{$initial, junction, join, fork$\}$; we require that $entry(s) =$ skip and $exit(s) =$ skip for each pseudostate s. A *composite* state is a state s with $kind(s) \in \{$composite, concurrent$\}$.

A *state hierarchy* is given by a tree (S, E) where S is a finite set of states and $E \subseteq S \times S$ a non-empty substate relation such that the constraints below are satisfied. We write $substates(s) = \{s' \in S \mid (s, s') \in E\}$ for the substates of state s:

1. If $substates(s) \neq \emptyset$ then $kind(s) \in \{$composite, concurrent$\}$.
2. If $kind(s) =$ concurrent then $\#substates(s) \geq 2$ and $kind(s') =$ composite for all $s' \in substates(s)$.
3. If $kind(s) =$ composite then $\#\{s \in substates(s) \mid kind(s') =$ initial$\} \leq 1$.

We further write $container(s)$ for the container state of state s if s is not the root state; $substates^+(s) = \{s' \in S \mid (s, s') \in E^+\}$ and $substates^*(s) = substates^+(s) \cup \{s\}$ denote the set of (reflexive) transitive substates of s; and $initial(s)$ is the initial state contained in the composite state s if it exists. The *least common ancestor* of a set of states $M \subseteq S$ not containing the root state, denoted by $lca(M)$, is the least composite state c w.r.t. E such that $M \subseteq substates^+(c)$; the *least common reflexive ancestor* of $M \subseteq S$, written $lca^=(M)$, is the least state s w.r.t. E such that $M \subseteq substates^*(s)$.

Given a state hierarchy $H = (S, E)$, a *transition* t over H has a source state $source(t) \in S$, a target state $target(t) \in S$, a triggering event $trigger(t) \in Event$, a guard expression $guard(t) \in Exp$, and an effect action $effect(t) \in Act$, such that the following constraints are satisfied:

1. $kind(source(t)) \neq$ final and $kind(target(t)) \neq$ initial.
2. If $kind(source(t)) \in \{$initial, fork$\}$ then $target(t)$ is not a pseudostate.
3. If $kind(source(t)) =$ initial then $container(target(t)) = container(source(t))$.
4. If $kind(target(t)) =$ join then $source(t)$ is not a pseudostate.
5. If $kind(source(t)) =$ composite then $kind(container(source(t))) \neq$ concurrent.
6. If $kind(target(t)) =$ composite then $kind(container(target(t))) \neq$ concurrent.
7. If $kind(source(t)) \in \{$initial, fork, join$\}$ then $guard(t) =$ true.
8. If $kind(target(t)) =$ join then $guard(t) =$ true.
9. If $kind(source(t)) \cdot =$ initial then $effect(t) =$ skip.
10. If $source(t)$ is a pseudostate, then $trigger(t) = *$.

A *state machine* (for a class C) is given by a pair (H, T) where $H = (S, E)$ is a state hierarchy and T a finite set of transitions over H such that the constraints below are satisfied for all $t \in T$. We write $outgoings(s)$ for the set $\{t \in T \mid source(t) = s\}$; $incomings(s)$ for the set $\{t \in T \mid target(t) = s\}$; $sources(M)$ for the set $\{source(t) \mid t \in M\}$; and $targets(M)$ for the set $\{target(t) \mid t \in M\}$:

1. If $kind(s) = $ initial then $\#outgoings(s) = 1$.
2. If $kind(s) = $ junction then $\#incomings(s) = 1$ and $\#outgoings(s) \geq 1$.
3. If $kind(s) = $ fork then $\#incomings(s) = 1$ and $\#outgoings(s) \geq 2$.
4. If $kind(s) = $ fork then there is an $s' \in S$ with $kind(s') = $ concurrent such that $targets(outgoings(s)) \subseteq substates^+(s') \setminus substates(s')$ and the following holds: if $t, t' \in outgoings(s)$ such that $\{target(t), target(t')\} \subseteq substates^+(s'')$ for some $s'' \in substates^+(s')$ then $t = t'$.
5. If $kind(s) = $ join then conditions (3) and (4) hold likewise with replacing $target$ by $source$ and $outgoings$ by $incomings$.

Conditions (4) and (5) require forks and joins to come from and go to different orthogonal regions of a concurrent composite state.

4.2   Configurations and Compound Transitions

The *configurations* of a state machine $((S, E), T)$ are given by the smallest subsets C of S that satisfy the following conditions:

1. The root state of S is in C.
2. No state $s \in C$ is a pseudostate.
3. If $kind(s) = $ composite then there is a single $s' \in C$ such that $container(s') = s$.
4. If $kind(s) = $ concurrent then all states $s' \in S$ with $container(s') = s$ are in C.

In particular, composite states are or-states, concurrent states are and-states.

The *compound transitions* of a state machine $((S, E), T)$ represent semantically complete transition paths that originate from a set of non-pseudostates and target a set of simple states. More precisely, a compound transition consists of three parts: The optional tail part of a compound transition may have multiple transitions in T originating from a set of mutually orthogonal regions that are joined by a join pseudostate. The middle part of a compound transition is a finite chain of transitions in T joined via junction pseudostates. Finally, the optional head part of a compound transition is a tree of transitions in T: If a transition in the middle part of a compound transition or in its head part itself targets a composite state the head part continues at the initial state of this composite transition; if a transition targets a concurrent composite state the head part continues at all initial states of the orthogonal regions of the concurrent composite state; if a transition targets a fork pseudostate the head part continues with the transitions outgoing from the fork pseudostate which target mutually orthogonal regions and simultaneously continues at the initial states of all those orthogonal regions that are not targeted by transitions outgoing from the fork pseudostate.

In the ATM example, the compound transitions outgoing from VerifyingCard just consist of middle parts:

$\langle \{\}, \langle \mathsf{VerifyingCard} \rightarrow \mathsf{junction}, \mathsf{junction} \rightarrow \mathsf{Idle} \rangle, \{\} \rangle,$

$\langle \{\}, \langle \mathsf{VerifyingCard} \rightarrow \mathsf{junction}, \mathsf{junction} \rightarrow \mathsf{CardValid} \rangle, \{\} \rangle.$

The fork transition from Idle consists of a middle part and a tail part:

$\langle \{\}, \langle \mathsf{Idle} \rightarrow \mathsf{fork} \rangle, \{\langle \mathsf{fork} \rightarrow \mathsf{VerifyingCard} \rangle, \langle \mathsf{fork} \rightarrow \mathsf{VerifyingPIN} \rangle\} \rangle.$

The join transition to DispenseMoney consists of a head part and a middle part:

$\langle \{\langle \mathsf{CardValid} \rightarrow \mathsf{join} \rangle, \langle \mathsf{PINCorrect} \rightarrow \mathsf{join} \rangle\}, \langle \mathsf{join} \rightarrow \mathsf{DispenseMoney} \rangle, \{\} \rangle.$

The algorithm for computing the compound transitions outgoing from a non-pseudostate in S of a state machine $((S, E), T)$ relies on a procedure that computes the middle and head parts of compound transitions, also called *forward trees*, outgoing from an arbitrary state in S; the details of the algorithms can be found in [8]. Note that our definition of compound transitions deviates from the explanations in the UML specification [14]. There, compound transitions are not required to target simple states only, but may as well stop at composite states. The proper initialization of composite and concurrent composite states is left to the entry procedure for composite states.

The notions of source states, target states, trigger, guard, and effect are transferred from transitions to compound transitions in the following way: The *source states* of a compound transition τ, written $sources(\tau)$, are the source states of the transitions in the tail part of τ, if τ shows a tail part, and the source state of the middle part, otherwise. Analogously, the target states of τ, written $targets(\tau)$, are the target states of the transitions in the head part of τ, if τ shows a head part, and the target state of the middle part, otherwise. The *trigger* of τ is the set of triggers of the transitions in the tail part of τ, if τ shows a tail part, and the trigger of the first transition in the middle part otherwise. The *guard* of τ is the conjunction of all guards of transitions in τ. Finally, the *effect* of τ is the sequential composition of the effects of the tail, the middle, and the head part of τ, where the effects in the tail and the head are conjoined in parallel whereas the effects in the middle part are composed sequentially. These definitions are naturally extended to sets of compound transitions which show the same trigger.

We recall some notions on compound transitions τ from the UML specification that will be used for the definition of the execution semantics of state machines, in particular, when computing maximally conflict free sets of compound transitions in a given configuration C: The *main source state* of τ, $mainSource(\tau)$, is given by the state $s = lca(lca^=(sources(\tau)), lca^=(targets(\tau)))$ if $kind(s) = $ concurrent, and it is given by the state $s' \in substates(s)$ with $lca^=(sources(\tau)) \in substates^*(s')$, otherwise. The *main target state* of τ, $mainTarget(\tau)$ is defined analogously, but exchanging $sources(\tau)$ and $targets(\tau)$. The set of states *exited* by τ in configuration C, $exited(C, \tau)$, consists of $substates^*(mainSource(\tau)) \cap C$. The set of states *entered* by τ in configuration C, $entered(\tau)$, is $substates^*(mainTarget(\tau)) \cap C$. Again, the definitions for *entered* and *exited* are naturally extended to sets of compound transitions.

Two compound transitions τ_1 and τ_2 are *in conflict* in configuration C, written $\tau_1 \#_C \tau_2$, if $exited(C, \tau_1) \cap exited(C, \tau_2) \neq \emptyset$; more generally, a compound transition τ is in conflict with a set of compound transitions T in configuration C, written $\tau \#_C T$, if

$\tau \natural_C \tau'$ for some $\tau' \in T$. If $\tau_1 \natural_C \tau_2$ let S_1 and S_2 be the sets of states in $sources(\tau_1)$ and $sources(\tau_2)$, resp., that show the maximal numerical distance from the root state of (S, E); τ_1 is *prioritized* over τ_2 in configuration C, written $\tau_1 \prec_C \tau_2$, if $S_1 \subseteq substates^+(S_2)$. Again, $\tau \prec_C T$ for a compound transition τ and a set of compound transitions T in configuration C if $\tau \prec_C \tau'$ for some $\tau' \in T$.

4.3   Run-to-Completion Semantics

The execution semantics of a UML state machine is described in the UML specification as a sequence of *run-to-completion steps*. Each such step is a move from a configuration of the state machine to another configuration. The sequence of steps starts in the *initial configuration* of the state machine, i.e., the configuration that is targeted by the forward tree outgoing from the initial state of the root state of the state hierarchy. In a run-to-completion step from some configuration, first, an event is fetched from the event queue. Second, a maximally consistent set of enabled compound transitions outgoing from the states of the current configuration and whose guards are satisfied is chosen. If such a set, called a *step*, exists, all its compound transitions are fired simultaneously: First, all states that are exited by the step are deactivated in an inside-out manner, executing the exit actions of these states; each such that is marked to be not completed, as it is not part of the configuration any more. Second, the gathered effect of the step is executed. Third, all states entered by the step are activated in an outside-in manner, executing the entry actions of these states. Furthermore, after executing the entry action of a state this state is marked as complete, i.e. a completion event for this state is generated.

More formally, let $((S, E), T)$ be a state machine. We assume a structure of *environments* η for state machines that provides the following primitive operations: An event can be fetched by `fetch`(η); the completion of a state s can be recorded by `complete`(η, s); the revocation of a state s from being completed can be recorded by `uncomplete`(η, s); a statement a can be executed by `exec`(η, a); given a configuration C and an event e all compound transitions of $((S, E), T)$ that are triggered by e can be computed by `enabled`(η, C, e); and, finally, the validity of an expression g can be checked by $\eta \models g$. The enabledness of compound transitions in a configuration C by an event e is indeed solely defined on the basis of the triggers of compound transitions and thus only involves the completed states that have been previously recorded with the environment. The fireable sets of compound transitions, which are maximally consistent sets of enabled compound transitions are computed by the steps algorithm in Fig. 2(a). The execution of a state machine in some configuration and some environment is defined by the RTC algorithm in Fig. 2(b) which uses the algorithm for firing a compound transitions step in Fig. 2(c).

5   Embedding of UML State Machines

Our goal is to make use of symbolic execution as interactive proof method for UML state machines. Embedding state machines into our temporal framework of Sect. 2 requires first to define state machines as temporal formulae and to extend our calculus with rules for their symbolic execution.

$\text{steps}(\textit{env}, \textit{conf}, \textit{event}) \equiv$
$\quad \lceil \textit{transitions} \leftarrow \texttt{enabled}(\textit{env}, \textit{conf}, \textit{event})$
$\quad \{\textit{step} \mid \langle \textit{guard}, \textit{step} \rangle \in \text{steps}(\textit{conf}, \textit{transitions}) \wedge \textit{env} \models \textit{guard}\} \rfloor$

$\text{steps}(\textit{conf}, \textit{transitions}) \equiv$
$\quad \lceil \textit{steps} \leftarrow \{\langle \textsf{false}, \emptyset \rangle\}$
$\quad \textbf{for } \textit{transition} \in \textit{transitions} \textbf{ do}$
$\quad\quad \textbf{for } \langle \textit{guard}, \textit{step} \rangle \in \text{steps}(\textit{transitions} \setminus \{\textit{transition}\}) \textbf{ do}$
$\quad\quad\quad \textbf{if } \textit{transition} \;\sharp_{\textit{conf}}\; \textit{step}$
$\quad\quad\quad \textbf{then if } \textit{transition} \prec_{\textit{conf}} \textit{step}$
$\quad\quad\quad\quad \textbf{then } \textit{guard} \leftarrow \textit{guard} \wedge \neg \, \textit{guard}(\textit{transition}) \textbf{ fi}$
$\quad\quad\quad \textbf{else } \textit{step} \leftarrow \textit{step} \cup \{\textit{transition}\}$
$\quad\quad\quad\quad \textit{guard} \leftarrow \textit{guard} \wedge \textit{guard}(\textit{transition}) \textbf{ fi}$
$\quad\quad\quad \textit{steps} \leftarrow \textit{steps} \cup \{\langle \textit{guard}, \textit{step} \rangle\} \textbf{ od od}$
$\quad \textit{steps} \rfloor$

(a) Transition selection algorithm

$\text{RTC}(\textit{env}, \textit{conf}) \equiv$
$\quad \lceil \langle \textit{event}, \textit{env} \rangle \leftarrow \texttt{fetch}(\textit{env})$
$\quad \textit{steps} \leftarrow \text{steps}(\textit{env}, \textit{conf}, \textit{event})$
$\quad \textbf{if } \textit{steps} \neq \emptyset$
$\quad \textbf{then choose } \textit{step} \in \textit{steps}$
$\quad\quad \langle \textit{env}, \textit{conf} \rangle \leftarrow \text{fire}(\textit{env}, \textit{conf}, \textit{step}) \textbf{ fi}$
$\quad \langle \textit{env}, \textit{conf} \rangle \rfloor$

(b) Run-to-completion step algorithm

$\text{fire}(\textit{env}, \textit{conf}, \textit{step}) \equiv$
$\quad \lceil \textbf{for } \textit{state} \in \text{insideOut}(\text{exited}(\textit{conf}, \textit{step})) \textbf{ do}$
$\quad\quad \textit{env} \leftarrow \texttt{exec}(\textit{env}, \text{exit}(\textit{state}))$
$\quad\quad \textit{conf} \leftarrow \textit{conf} \setminus \{\textit{state}\}$
$\quad\quad \textit{env} \leftarrow \texttt{uncomplete}(\textit{env}, \textit{state}) \textbf{ od}$
$\quad \textit{env} \leftarrow \texttt{exec}(\textit{env}, \text{effect}(\textit{step}))$
$\quad \textbf{for } \textit{state} \in \text{outsideIn}(\text{entered}(\textit{conf}, \textit{step})) \textbf{ do}$
$\quad\quad \textit{env} \leftarrow \texttt{exec}(\textit{env}, \text{entry}(\textit{state}))$
$\quad\quad \textit{conf} \leftarrow \textit{conf} \cup \{\textit{state}\}$
$\quad\quad \textit{env} \leftarrow \texttt{complete}(\textit{env}, \textit{state}) \textbf{ od}$
$\quad \langle \textit{env}, \textit{conf} \rangle \rfloor$

(c) Transition firing algorithm

Fig. 2. State machine execution algorithms

State machines $((S, E), T)$ are embedded into the temporal logic as a special formula $[((S, E), T)]$ with the following semantics:

$$\pi \models [((S, E), T)] \quad \text{iff} \quad \pi \text{ is a valid trace of } ((S, E), T)$$

for sequences of valuations π. The definition of a valid trace is not given here, as it is straightforward to derive from the definition of a single step as was defined in Sect. 4. A state machine configuration is a formula *conf* which represents the active states: for each state, a corresponding dynamic boolean variable is true if and only if the state is part of the current active state configuration of the state machine. Attributes and the event queue are represented as algebraic datatypes.

To define the calculus, we implement the function *exec* of rule (execute), which we described in Sect. 2.2, by setting

$$\textit{exec}([((S, E), T)], \textit{conf}) = \{\langle \textit{guard} \wedge \langle \textit{action} \rangle_{\text{DL}} V' = V, [((S, E), T)] \wedge \textit{conf}_0 \rangle \mid$$
$$\langle \textit{guard}, \textit{step} \rangle \in \text{steps}(\textit{conf}, \text{enabled}(T)),$$
$$\langle \textit{action}, \textit{conf}_0 \rangle = \text{fireaction}(\textit{conf}, \textit{step})\} \, .$$

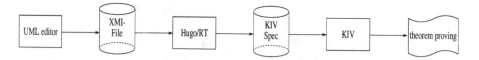

Fig. 3. Tool chain to translate UML models into KIV

Function *exec* provides configuration *conf* and the enabled transitions in T to the function steps of Fig. 2(a) which returns pairs of possible steps *step* and their corresponding guards *guard*. The function *enabled* uses the head element of the event queue as the current triggering event. We cannot use function fire of Fig. 2(c) to execute *step* as we cannot provide an explicit environment *env*. Therefore, we define a similar function fireaction which returns instead of a modified environment an action *action* which combines all of the environment updates as a sequential program. The guard, the action and the modified configuration $conf_0$ are combined to form the result of *exec*. (The special formula $\langle action \rangle_{DL} V' = V$ of Dynamic Logic (DL [6]) takes the unprimed values of variables V as input to *action*, modifies the unprimed variables according to the sequential program and uses the modified variables to evaluate formula $V' = V$. This formula is used to "copy" the new values of the unprimed variables to the primed variables V'.)

This algorithm can be further optimized to ensure that the number of steps which are returned by steps is as small as possible: the context formulae which represent the symbolic environment can be used to automatically simplify guards, and the state hierarchy is exploited to faster detect transition priorities.

We implemented the calculus described above in the interactive verifier KIV. To complete the integration, we use a standard UML modelling tool (e.g. ArgoUML [1]) to draw state machines, and translate the resulting XMI-files to KIV with the model translator Hugo/RT [9]. The complete tool chain is shown in Fig. 3. This translation is fully automatic.

6 An Example Proof

The proof method for UML state machines is very simple: we repeatedly execute steps and test whether we have already encountered the current active state configuration earlier in the proof; in this case, we have executed a cycle and the current goal can be closed with an inductive argument.

As example proof we show for state machine SC_{Bank} that the state DispenseMoney can only be entered, if tries $\leq$ max-tries and PINValid is true. So the property to show is

(prop) $\Box$(DispenseMoney $\rightarrow$ tries $\leq$ maxTries $\wedge$ PINValid) .

With initial state machine configuration $C \equiv$ Idle and variable condition $I \equiv$ tries $= 0 \wedge$ maxTries ≥ 0 the proof obligation is

(init) $[SC_{Bank}]$, Idle, tries $= 0 \wedge$ maxTries $\geq 0 \vdash$ (prop) .

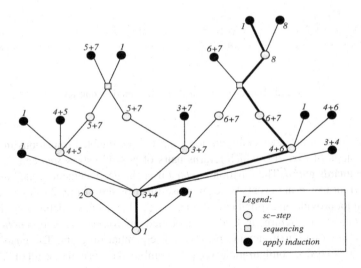

Fig. 4. Proof graph for the example proof

As precondition, we assume that the state machine SC_{Bank} of Fig. 1 is in state Idle and the initial conditions of the class diagram hold. The event queue is unspecified; we make no demands on the events in the initial queue and the queue of the following steps. In other words, the environment behaves arbitrarily. Note that the safety property of (prop) is trivially true for all states with ¬DispenseMoney.

The complete proof is shown in Fig. 4. To demonstrate our proof scheme we explain only the highlighted path. This exemplary run corresponds to the main use case scenario of the automatic teller machine. All other runs of the state machine can be shown following the same pattern. For better understanding of the proof graph, we denoted the nodes with the numbers of the actual states. The state numbers can be found in the state machine diagram (see Fig. 1).

The state machine will always return to state Idle (1). To apply our induction scheme, we must choose an appropriate invariant, because the variable tries may increase in each cycle. We use

(inv) CardValid → tries ≤ maxTries

which can be easily shown with (init). This invariant is preserved in each cycle. Then, to use the current sequent later as induction hypothesis, the rule (ind alw) is applied.

Now we can apply the rule *execute* to advance one step in our state machine:

(a) done ∧ $\langle$**skip**$\rangle_{\text{DL}}$ ⋯ ∧ ○($[SC_{\text{Bank}}]$ ∧ Finalized), (inv) ⊢ (prop)
(b) verifyPIN ∧ $\langle$**skip**$\rangle_{\text{DL}}$ ⋯ ∧ ○($[SC_{\text{Bank}}]$∧
     Verifying ∧ VerifyingCard ∧ VerifyingPIN), (inv) ⊢ (prop)
(c) ¬(verifyPIN ∧ done) ∧ $\langle$**skip**$\rangle_{\text{DL}}$ ⋯ ∧ ○($[SC_{\text{Bank}}]$ ∧ Idle), (inv) ⊢ (prop)

$[SC_{\text{Bank}}]$, Idle, (inv) ⊢ (prop)

The lowest node in the proof graph (Fig. 4) depicts the application of this rule. As expected from the state machine diagram, we get three premises: Either the state machine is finalized (2) with the event done (premise (a)) or the transition to state Verifying $(3+4)$ is taken with event verifyPIN (premise (b)) or the state machine remains in state Idle (1) with any other event (premise (c)). In all cases the action is **skip** and a special formula (omitted) assigns the values of all unprimed variables to their primed complement. Premise (a) terminates and the proof is complete, premise (c) loops and induction is applied. The only nontrivial case is premise (b). After simplification and application of rule (step) we receive

$$[SC_{Bank}], \text{Verifying} \land \text{VerifyingCard} \land \text{VerifyingPIN}, (\text{inv}) \vdash (\text{prop}) .$$

The new active states are Verifying and its substates VerifyingCard (4) and VerifyingPIN (3) and (inv) is preserved. Symbolic execution continues with the next step where we receive four different states for each possible transition and one state if no transition is enabled. We focus on the state Verifying, VerifyingCard (4) and PINCorrect (6). This transition is only taken, if the attribute PINValid is true, so we can assume PINValid to be true for the following steps. Like before, we invoke the next step. One of the next states is Verifying, CardValid (7) and PINCorrect (6). This transition is only possible if the attribute CardValid is true and due to the invariant we can conclude that tries $\leq$ maxTries. The same state is also reachable by first entering CardValid (7) and then entering PINCorrect (6). Both cases can be merged by sequencing, so there is only one open goal. From this state we reach DispenseMoney (8). Because we have shown PINValid and tries $\leq$ maxTries in the previous two steps property (prop) holds in this state. The next step leads again to the state Idle (1), where we use the induction hypothesis and close the current goal.

This proof scheme can be further automated. Our goal is to adapt the heuristics, so that the only user interaction is the specification of an adequate invariant.

7   Conclusion

We have demonstrated how to integrate UML state machines into a proof method to interactively verify temporal properties of state machines. As a first step, we have defined a formal semantics of UML state machines and derived a proof rule for their symbolic execution. As can be seen in the example, the resulting proofs are very intuitive as they follow the different possible system runs. However, only small examples have been tackled so far.

Symbolic execution in general turns out to be a very intuitive approach not only to the verification of sequential programs but also to the construction of proofs for concurrent systems, with the potential to dispel the prejudice that interactive proofs in temporal logic are difficult. Proof rules for the execution of (most of) the temporal operators are invertible ensuring that the calculus can be automated to a large extent. A generic induction principle can be used to establish both safety and liveness properties. Sequencing is used to avoid exponential growth of proof trees for nondeterministic systems. A strategy to automatically apply sequencing is the key to efficiently use the approach for larger case studies. As has been demonstrated with the integration of UML state machines, proof rules for the symbolic execution of different formalisms can be implemented, provided that a formal operational semantics is defined.

Next steps are to further automate proofs, especially to automate sequencing, and to look into compositional proofs. We expect that proofs like the one in Sect. 6 require the invariant as the only user interaction. Very important for the future is to gain more experience in larger case studies.

References

1. ArgoUML homepage. argouml.tigris.org.
2. M. Balser, C. Duelli, W. Reif, and G. Schellhorn. Verifying Concurrent Systems with Symbolic Execution. *J. Logic Computat.*, 12(4):549–560, 2002.
3. M. Balser, W. Reif, G. Schellhorn, and K. Stenzel. KIV 3.0 for Provably Correct Systems. In D. Hutter, W. Stephan, P. Traverso, and M. Ullmann, editors, *Proc. Int. Wsh. Applied Formal Methods (FM-Trends'98)*, volume 1641 of *Lect. Notes Comp. Sci.*, pages 330–337. Springer, Berlin, 1999.
4. Dove homepage. http://www.dsto.defence.gov.au/isl/dove/dove.html.
5. D. Harel. Statecharts: A Visual Formalism for Complex Systems. *Sci. Comp. Program.*, 8(3):231–274, 1987.
6. D. Harel, D. Kozen, and J. Tiuryn. *Dynamic Logic*. Foundations of Computing. The MIT Press, Cambridge, Mass.–London, 2000.
7. M. Heisel, W. Reif, and W. Stephan. A Dynamic Logic for Program Verification. In A. R. Meyer and M. A. Taitslin, editors, *Proc. Symp. Logical Foundations of Computer Science (Logic at Botik '89)*, volume 363 of *Lect. Notes Comp. Sci.*, pages 134–145. Springer, Berlin, 1989.
8. A. Knapp. Semantics of UML State Machines. Technical Report 0408, Institut für Informatik, Ludwig-Maximilians-Universität München, 2004.
9. A. Knapp and S. Merz. Model Checking and Code Generation for UML State Machines and Collaborations. In D. Haneberg, G. Schellhorn, and W. Reif, editors, *Proc. 5th Wsh. Tools for System Design and Verification*, pages 59–64. Technical Report 2002-11, Institut für Informatik, Universität Augsburg, 2002.
10. D. Latella, I. Majzik, and M. Massink. Automatic Verification of a Behavioural Subset of UML Statechart Diagrams Using the SPIN Model-Checker. *Formal Asp. Comput.*, 11(6):637–664, 1999.
11. J. Lilius and I. P. Paltor. Formalising UML State Machines for Model Checking. In R. France and B. Rumpe, editors, *Proc. 2nd Int. Conf. Unified Modeling Language (UML'99)*, volume 1723 of *Lect. Notes Comp. Sci.*, pages 430–445. Springer, Berlin, 1999.
12. Z. Manna and A. Pnueli. *Temporal Verification of Reactive Systems — Safety*. Springer, Berlin—&c., 1995.
13. B. Moszkowski. A Temporal Logic for Multilevel Reasoning about Hardware. *IEEE Computer*, 18(2):10–19, 1985.
14. Object Management Group. Unified Modeling Language Specification, Version 1.5. Specification, OMG, 2003. http://www.omg.org/cgi-bin/doc?formal/03-03-01.
15. Omega homepage. www-omega.imag.fr.
16. T. Schäfer, A. Knapp, and S. Merz. Model Checking UML State Machines and Collaborations. In S. Stoller and W. Visser, editors, *Proc. Wsh. Software Model Checking*, volume 55(3) of *Elect. Notes Theo. Comp. Sci.*, Paris, 2001. 13 pages.
17. K. Stenzel. A Formally Verified Calculus for Full Java Card. In C. Rattray, S. Maharaj, and C. Shankland, editors, *Proc. 10th Int. Conf. Algebraic Methodology and Software Technology (AMAST'04)*, volume 3116 of *Lect. Notes Comp. Sci.* Springer, Berlin, 2004.

Refinement of Actions for Real-Time Concurrent Systems with Causal Ambiguity

Mila Majster-Cederbaum[1], Jinzhao Wu[1,2,*],
Houguang Yue[2], and Naijun Zhan[1]

[1] Fakultät für Mathematik und Informatik,
Universität Mannheim, D7, 27, 68131 Mannheim,
Germany
[2] Chengdu Institute of Computer Applications,
Chinese Academy of Sciences,
Chengdu 610041, China

Abstract. We develop an approach of action refinement for concurrent systems with not only the notation of real-time but also with causal ambiguity, which often exists in real application areas. The systems are modeled in terms of a timed extension of event structures with causal ambiguity. Under a certain partial order semantics, the behavior of the refined system can be inferred compositionally from the behavior of the original system and from the behavior of the systems used to refine actions with explicitly represented start points. A variant of a linear-time equivalence termed pomset trace equivalence and a variant of a branching-time equivalence termed history preserving bisimulation equivalence based on the partial order semantics are both congruences under the refinement. The refinement operation behaves thus well and meets the commonly expected properties.

Keywords: Concurrency, action refinement, causal ambiguity, timed event structure with causal ambiguity.

1 Introduction

We consider the design of concurrent systems in the framework of approaches where the basic building blocks are actions. Refinement of actions is a core concept in the methodology of hierarchical design for concurrent systems, real-time or not. It amounts to introducing a mechanism for transforming high level actions into lower level processes until the implementation level is reached [6, 8, 16].

Refinement of actions for concurrent systems without time constraints has been thoroughly studied in the literature [6, 7, 8]. For real-time concurrent

---

* Partially supported by National Natural Science Foundation of China(60373113).

J. Davies et al. (Eds.): ICFEM 2004, LNCS 3308, pp. 449–463, 2004.

systems it has been discussed recently by us in [4, 15, 16]. In all the previous work, the system models adopted are always under the constraint of unambiguous causality. That is, if an event has happened there must not exist ambiguity in deciding which are the causes of the event. However, causal ambiguity often exists in real application areas. Prominent examples are e.g. the design of distributed systems [20], the design and analysis of speed-independent circuits [23], and the specification of business processes like workflow management systems [21].

In this paper, we investigate how to carry out refinement of actions in concurrent systems with the notions of not only real-time but also causal ambiguity, and analyse its characteristic properties. The main practical benefit from our work is that hierarchical specification of such systems is then made possible, furthering thus the work of [4, 6, 15, 16].

The functional framework of systems is modeled in terms of event structures with causal ambiguity [13, 14], and the approach proposed in [1, 9, 10, 11, 12] to tackling time is taken, where a method to deal with urgent interaction can be incorporated. This approach is very powerful. We are unaware of any other proposal to incorporate time and timeout in a causality based setting.

Let us look at a running example to concretely motivate our paper. Figure 1 (a) shows a timed industrial inspection system observing faults, and Figure 1 (b) is a timed system used to implement action *inspect* in a more detailed level. They are both represented in timed event structures with causal ambiguity.

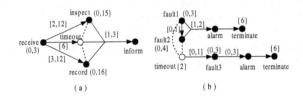

Fig. 1. Two timed systems with causal ambiguity

Solid dots stand for events, performing the action by which they are labeled, open dots represent timeout events, arrows from sets of events to events denote causality relations and are usually called bundles, and dashed lines denote conflict relations on the events. Two events that are in conflict cannot appear in a single system run.

Events and bundles are labeled with intervals (sets of non-negative reals). The intuitive interpretation of an interval associated to an event is that the time at which this event begins to happen is located in this interval, whereas an interval associated to a bundle has the meaning that the transition delay from the end of the causal event to the start of the result event is located in this interval. A timeout event restricts the happening time of the events in conflict with it.

It is unknown which exactly causes *inform* when both *inspect* and *record* occur. So causal ambiguity of *inform* exists in the timed system of Figure 1 (a). Similarly, causal ambiguity of *alarm* exists in the timed system of Figure 1 (b).

The following questions arise. How can action *inspect* in the timed system of Figure 1 (a) be refined by the timed system of Figure 1 (b)? How does the newly derived timed system, when obtained, behave?

The previous approach of action refinement [6, 7, 8] works for the untimed case when causal ambiguity exists [22]. However, this approach no longer applies to timed systems because the property of timeout events is violated, as shown in e.g. [4, 15], and therefore do not provide answers to the questions. To solve this, we present in this paper a new approach. Its characteristic properties are also analyzed. We consider two common problems of interest, the correctness and congruence problems.

The paper is arranged as follows. Section 2 introduces the system model timed event structures with causal ambiguity, describes partial order semantics for their behavior, and defines equivalence notions based on the semantics. Section 3 presents the approach of action refinement in the framework of this model. The correctness and the congruence results are given in Section 4. Section 5 concludes the paper.

2   System Model

We use event structures with causal ambiguity [3, 9, 13, 14] as the system model, and take the way of [1, 9, 10, 11, 12, 15, 16] to include time.

Assume a given set *Obs* of observable actions ranged over by $a, b, c, \ldots$, and an invisible internal action τ ($\tau \notin Obs$). Action $\sqrt{}$ ($\sqrt{} \notin Obs \cup \{\tau\}$) indicates the successful termination of a process. $Act = Obs \cup \{\tau, \sqrt{}\}$. Unlike [1, 9, 10, 11, 12], actions are viewed here as compound happenings having durations in order to have a clean notion of action refinement. Let function $k : Act \to \mathbb{R}^+$ with $k(\tau) = k(\sqrt{}) = 0$ assign durations to actions. Here, $\mathbb{R}^+ = [0, \infty)$, the set of non-negative reals, denotes the domain of time. Note that action durations defined through the function k embody the intrinsic meaning of actions, and the treatment of the function k as a component of a system model may result in conceptual confusion.

2.1   Timed Event Structures with Causal Ambiguity

A *timed event structure with causal ambiguity* (*taes* for short) $\mathcal{E}$ is a tuple $(E, \sharp, \vdash, l, \mathcal{D}, \mathcal{R}, \mathcal{U})$ with

E, a set of *events*;

$\sharp \subseteq E \times E$, the irreflexive and symmetric *conflict relation*;

$\vdash \subseteq 2^E \times E$, the *bundle relation*;

$l : E \longrightarrow Act$, the *action-labeling function*;

$\mathcal{D} : E \to 2^{\mathbb{R}^+}$, the *event delay function*;

$\mathcal{R} : \vdash \to 2^{\mathbb{R}^+}$, the *bundle delay function*; and

$\mathcal{U} \subseteq \{e \in E \mid l(e) = \tau\}$, the set of *urgent events*,

such that for any $X \subseteq E$, events $e \in \mathcal{U}$ and $e' \in E$,

(1) $(X \vdash e) \wedge (e \sharp e') \Rightarrow (X \vdash e') \vee (X \sharp e')$, and

(2) $\exists t \in \mathbb{R}^+ : (\mathcal{D}(e) \subseteq \{t\}) \vee (\exists Y \vdash e : (\mathcal{R}(Y, e) \subseteq \{t\}))$.

Here $2^\bullet$ denotes the power-set function, and $(X \sharp e')$ stands for $(\forall e \in X : e \sharp e')$.

The first constraint specifies a property of timeouts that are modeled by urgent events. The second constraint ensures that timeouts are enabled at a single time instant only. Notice that crucial for a taes is that for each bundle $X \vdash e$, opposite to classical event structures without causal ambiguity, the events in X are not required to be in pairwise conflict as usual. Causal ambiguity thus exists in the system behavior, i.e., if an event e occurs, there are alternative causes for this event.

A taes is depicted as the example shown in the introduction, where event names and delays $[0, \infty)$ are usually omitted.

Example 2.1.1 Figure 1 (a) and (b) are two taes's. In the sequel, we abbreviate *receive* $= a$, *inspect* $= b$, *record* $= c$, *inform* $= d$, *fault1* $= b_1$, *fault2* $= b_2$, *fault3* $= b_3$, *alarm* $= b_4$. A *timeout* event is labeled with action τ since it is internal. Moreover, we assume $k(a) = 2$, $k(b) = 6$, $k(c) = 6$, $k(d) = 3$ and $k(b_1) = k(b_2) = k(b_3) = k(b_4) = 1$.

By $init(\mathcal{E})$ we denote the set of initial events of $\mathcal{E}$, and $exit(\mathcal{E})$ its set of successful termination events, i.e.,

$$init(\mathcal{E}) = \{e \in E \mid \neg(\exists X \subseteq E : X \vdash e)\}, exit(\mathcal{E}) = \{e \in E \mid l(e) = \sqrt{}\}.$$

We denote by $TAES$ the set of taes's. $\mathcal{E} = (E, \sharp, \vdash, l, \mathcal{D}, \mathcal{R}, \mathcal{U})$, possibly subscripted and/or primed, stands for a member of this set. When necessary, we also use $E_\mathcal{E}, \sharp_\mathcal{E}, \vdash_\mathcal{E}, l_\mathcal{E}, \mathcal{D}_\mathcal{E}, \mathcal{R}_\mathcal{E}$ and $\mathcal{U}_\mathcal{E}$ to represent the components of $\mathcal{E}$.

2.2   Partial Order Semantics

We first consider the functional behavior of a taes, then take the time aspect into account and define their semantics, taking care of both the functional and timing issues.

Functional Behavior. Let $\Phi = e_1, \cdots, e_m$ be a sequence of events (of $\mathcal{E}$), where e_i and e_j are distinct whenever $i \neq j$. $E(\Phi) = \{e_1, \cdots, e_m\}$. Assume $\Phi_{i-1} = e_1, \cdots, e_{i-1}$ is the $(i-1)$-th prefix of Φ $(1 \leq i \leq m)$.

In a run of a system, any two events that occur should not be in conflict, and if an event occurs in a run its causal predecessors should have occurred before. Let

$$en(\Phi_{i-1}) = \{ \, e \in E \setminus E(\Phi_{i-1}) \mid (\forall e_j \in E(\Phi_{i-1}) : e \, \#e_j) \wedge$$
$$(\forall X \vdash e : X \cap E(\Phi_{i-1}) \neq \emptyset)\}.$$

$en(\Phi_{i-1})$ is then the set of events *enabled after* Φ_{i-1}. If $e_i \in en(\Phi_{i-1})$ for all $1 \leqslant i \leqslant m$, then $C = E(\Phi)$ is called a *frame configuration* of $\mathcal{E}$.

The event sequence Φ in the definition of frame configurations is usually called a *trace* of $\mathcal{E}$. Traces describe actually the possible functional runs of a taes, whereas the frame configuration is the underlying event set of it. Frame configuration C is usually said to be *obtained from trace* Φ. By $C(\mathcal{E})$ we denote the set of all the frame configurations of $\mathcal{E}$.

A frame configuration C of $\mathcal{E}$ *successfully terminates* if there exists $e \in C$ such that $l(e) = \sqrt{}$. $\mathcal{E}$ is called *well-labeled* if for each $C \in C(\mathcal{E})$, $C \cap exit(\mathcal{E})$ is empty or a singleton.

When causal ambiguity exists, as argued in [14], frame configurations or traces do not sufficiently describe the system behavior, and partial ordered sets are used to represent the causal relations between the events that occurred so far in a system run.

For $e_i, e_j \in E$, by $e_j \mapsto e_i$ we mean that e_j is a *causal predecessor* of e_i, i.e., there exits an $X \subseteq E$ such that $e_j \in X$ and $X \vdash e_i$. Let $C \in C(\mathcal{E})$, and $\mapsto |_C$ denotes the restriction of $\mapsto$ to C, namely $\mapsto |_C = \mapsto \cap (C \times C)$.

Let $\mapsto_C$ be a subset of $\mapsto |_C$, such that $\overset{*}{\mapsto}_C$ is a partial order on C. Here, as usual $\overset{*}{\mapsto}_C$ represents the relation on C by the elements of $\mapsto_C$ as generators, namely its reflexive and transitive closure. $P = \langle C, \overset{*}{\mapsto}_C \rangle$ is called a *poset of $\mathcal{E}$*. The *cause* of event $e \in C$ (in this poset) is defined as $\mathcal{A}_e = \{e' \in C \mid e' \mapsto_C e\}$. The elements of $\mathcal{A}_e$ constitute indeed all the direct predecessors of e in this poset, namely the events that cause e to happen. A *maximal event* in a poset P is defined as an event $e \in C$, satisfying that there does not exist an event $e' \in C$ with $e \mapsto_C e'$.

Taking Time into Account. If event e_j causes event e_i in a system run of $\mathcal{E}$, and two time instants t_j and $t_i \in \mathbb{R}^+$ are associated to events e_j and e_i respectively $(t_j \leq t_i)$, then e_j and e_i start at time points t_j and t_i, and t_j and t_i are required to be in the time instant sets labeled to e_j and e_i, respectively. $t_i - (t_j + k(l(e_j)))$ is then the transition delay from the end of e_j to the start of e_i. It is required to be in the time instant set attached to the corresponding bundle. Bearing this in mind, we see that if an event e is enabled by its cause $\mathcal{A}_e$ in a poset P then

$$T_P(e) = \mathcal{D}(e) \cap \bigcap_{e_j \in \mathcal{A}_e \wedge X \vdash e, e_j \in X} (t_j + k(l(e_j)) + \mathcal{R}(X, e))$$

consists of all the potential time instants at which event e may start to happen. Here, for $t \in \mathbb{R}^+$ and $T \subseteq \mathbb{R}^+$, $t \pm T$ denotes the set $\{t \pm t_i \mid t_i \in T\} \cap \mathbb{R}^+$ respectively. $T \pm t$ is defined in a similar way, and we say $t \leq T$ if t is not greater than any element of T. Furthermore, the fact that event e_i occurs implies also that the starting time of e_i must not be greater than the time at which e_0 may occur, where e_0 is an urgent event in conflict with e_i and enabled by e_j. We define $T_P(e) = \mathcal{D}(e)$ if $\mathcal{A}_e = \emptyset$.

Formally, we assume hereafter that event sequence $\Phi = e_1, \cdots, e_m$ is a trace of $\mathcal{E}$, from which a frame configuration C is obtained. For event $e \in C$, all bundles pointing to e in $\mathcal{E}$ are given by $X_1 \vdash e, \cdots, X_n \vdash e$. Furthermore, $P = \langle C, \stackrel{*}{\mapsto}_C \rangle$ is a poset. Let $TP = T\langle C, \stackrel{*}{\mapsto}_C \rangle$ associate with each event $e \in C$ in poset $\langle C, \stackrel{*}{\mapsto}_C \rangle$ a time instant $t \in \mathbb{R}^+$, and let $time(C, e)$ denote the time instant associated to event e in TP.

$TP = T\langle C, \stackrel{*}{\mapsto}_C \rangle$ is called a *timed poset* of $\mathcal{E}$, if for all $e \in C$ and $e_0 \in \mathcal{U}$ the following conditions hold:

(1) $time(C, e) \in T_P(e)$;
(2) $time(C, e) \leq T_P(e_0)$ if $e, e_0 \in en(\Phi_{i-1})$ for all $1 \leq i \leq m$ and $e \sharp e_0$.

The first condition requires that the time at which e is enabled to happen cannot be smaller than the execution time of its causal events. The second condition ensures that an event in conflict with a timeout should not occur later than the timeout.

A non-empty timed poset TP is often graphically denoted, where only the generators of $\stackrel{*}{\mapsto}_C$, i.e. the elements of $\mapsto_C$, together with the time instants associated with the events are depicted explicitly. That is, if $e_j \mapsto_C e_i$ is one of the elements of $\mapsto_C$, then an arrow from $(e_j, time(C, e_j))$ towards $(e_i, time(C, e_i))$ is drawn.

Let $Maxt(\mathcal{E})$ consist of all the time instants at which a successful termination run of the system finishes. That is,

$$Maxt(\mathcal{E}) = \{t \in \mathbb{R}^+ \mid \text{there is a timed poset } T\langle C, \mapsto_C \rangle \text{ of } \mathcal{E} \text{ and an event}$$
$$e \in C \text{ with } l(e) = \sqrt{} \text{ and } t = time(C, e)\}.$$

The Semantics. Motivated by a large variety of applications, partial order semantics for taes's is defined on the basis of different viewpoints on the causality in a frame configuration. We only present here the definition of timed lib-posets (timed liberal posets). For the similar details of *timed bsat-posets* (timed bundle satisfaction posets), *timed min-posets* (timed minimal posets), *timed early-posets* and *timed late-posets*, as well as their relationships, the reader may consult [14].

A timed poset $T\langle C, \stackrel{*}{\mapsto}_C \rangle$ of $\mathcal{E}$ is said to be a *timed lib-poset*, if for all $e \in C$ the cause $\mathcal{A}_e$ of e meets the conditions below:

(1) Each $e' \in \mathcal{A}_e$ occurs before e in Φ;
(2) $X_i \cap \mathcal{A}_e \neq \emptyset$ for all $i \in \{1, \ldots, n\}$.

Timed lib-posets model the least restrictive notion of causality. It says that each set of events from bundles pointing to event e that satisfies all bundles is a cause of e.

From now on, we assume $x \in \{lib, bsat, min, early, late\}$, and by $TP_x(\mathcal{E})$ we denote the set of all timed x-posets of $\mathcal{E}$.

2.3   Equivalence Notions

For concurrency models such as timed event structures with causal ambiguity, the possible executions of systems may be represented as partially ordered multi-sets of actions (pomsets). Based on this consideration, a linear-time equivalence similar to pomset trace equivalence [2] is defined. A branching-time equivalence similar to history preserving bisimulation equivalence [19] can be defined as well to further record where choices are made, and the idea is to relate two events only if they have the same causal history.

For $x \in \{lib, bsat, min, early, late\}$ and $i = 1, 2$, let $TP_i = T\langle C_i, \stackrel{*}{\hookmapsto}_{iC_i}\rangle$ be timed x-posets of taes $\mathcal{E}_i$, where $C_i \in C(\mathcal{E}_i)$, and $\hookmapsto_{iC_i} \subseteq \hookmapsto_i |_{C_i}$. Moreover, let $l_i|_{C_i}$ denote the restriction of l_i on C_i, namely $l_i|_{C_i}(e) = l_i(e)$ for $e \in C_i$.

TP_1 and TP_2 are said to be isomorphic, if they differ only in the event names, while the associated time instants, the action labels, the causality relations of events as well as the urgency of events in the two timed x-posets remain the same. Formally, TP_1 and TP_2 are *isomorphic*, denoted $TP_1 \approx TP_2$, if there exists a bijection $h : C_1 \longrightarrow C_2$ such that for arbitrary $e, e' \in C_1$,

(1) $l_1|_{C_1}(e) = l_2|_{C_2}(h(e))$;
(2) $e \hookmapsto_{1C_1} e'$ iff $h(e) \hookmapsto_{2C_2} h(e')$;
(3) $time(C_1, e) = time(C_2, h(e))$;
(4) $e \in \mathcal{U}_1$ iff $h(e) \in \mathcal{U}_2$.

By $TP_x(\mathcal{E}_1) \approx TP_x(\mathcal{E}_2)$ we mean that $\mathcal{E}_1$ and $\mathcal{E}_2$ have isomorphic timed x-posets. That is, for any $TP_1 \in TP_x(\mathcal{E}_1)$ $[TP_2 \in TP_x(\mathcal{E}_2)]$ there exists $TP_2 \in TP_x(\mathcal{E}_2)$ [resp. $TP_1 \in TP_x(\mathcal{E}_1)$] such that $TP_1 \approx TP_2$.

Two taes's $\mathcal{E}_1$ and $\mathcal{E}_2$ are said to be *x-pomset trace equivalent*, denoted $\mathcal{E}_1 \cong_{px} \mathcal{E}_2$, if $TP_x(\mathcal{E}_1) \approx TP_x(\mathcal{E}_2)$.

Let $TP = T\langle C, \stackrel{*}{\hookmapsto}_C\rangle$ and $TP' = T\langle C', \stackrel{*}{\hookmapsto}_{C'}\rangle$ be two timed x-posets of taes $\mathcal{E}$, where $C, C' \in C(\mathcal{E})$, and $\hookmapsto_C$ and $\hookmapsto_{C'}$ are subsets of $\hookmapsto |_C$ and $\hookmapsto |_{C'}$, respectively. For action $a \in Act$, $t \in \mathbb{R}^+$, we say $TP \xrightarrow{a,t} TP'$ (or $\xrightarrow{a,t}_i$ when necessary) if $C' \setminus C = \{e\}$ with $l(e) = a$ and $time(C', e) = t$.

A relation $H \subseteq TP_x(\mathcal{E}_1) \times TP_x(\mathcal{E}_2) \times 2^{E_1 \times E_2}$ is called an *x-history preserving bisimulation* between $\mathcal{E}_1$ and $\mathcal{E}_2$, if $(\emptyset, \emptyset, \emptyset) \in H$, and when $(TP_1, TP_2, h) \in H$ then

(1) h is an isomorphism between TP_1 and TP_2,
(2) $TP_1 \xrightarrow{a,t}_1 TP_1' \Rightarrow \exists TP_2', h' :$
$\quad TP_2 \xrightarrow{a,t}_2 TP_2', (TP_1', TP_2', h') \in H$ and $h'|_{C_1} = h$,
(3) $TP_2 \xrightarrow{a,t}_2 TP_2' \Rightarrow \exists TP_1', h' :$
$\quad TP_1 \xrightarrow{a,t}_1 TP_1', (TP_1', TP_2', h') \in H$ and $h'|_{C_1} = h$.

Here $h'|_{C_1}$ denotes the restriction of h' on C_1. h is an isomorphism between TP_1 and TP_2 if it is the bijection in the definition that TP_1 and TP_2 are isomorphic.

Two taes's $\mathcal{E}_1$ and $\mathcal{E}_2$ are said to be x-history preserving bisimulation equivalent, denoted $\mathcal{E}_1 \cong_{bx} \mathcal{E}_2$, if there exists an x-history preserving bisimulation between $\mathcal{E}_1$ and $\mathcal{E}_2$.

x-pomset trace equivalence is coarser than x-history preserving bisimulation equivalence for any $x \in \{lib, bsat, min, early, late\}$. We refer the reader to [6] for this in the non-ambiguous case.

3   Refinement of Actions

We follow the methodology to treat refinement of actions as an operator. Before refining a given taes, we have first to modify the taes's that are used to implement actions.

3.1   Introducing Start-Events

Every system has a start point, which is usually supposed to be performing the internal silent action at time instant zero. Here, in the taes used to refine an action we introduce a new event to explicitly represent this point.

Let $r(\mathcal{E})$ be the taes obtained by adding to taes $\mathcal{E}$ a new event e_0 as well as new bundles from e_0 to all the events of $\mathcal{E}$, and transferring all the absolute time attachments of events to relative time attachments of the corresponding newly introduced bundles, where e_0 is labeled with the internal action τ and associated with time instant 0, imitating the start point of system, which is executing the internal silent action at time instant 0. Formally,

$$r(\mathcal{E}) = (E \cup \{e_0\}, \sharp, \mapsto_r, l \cup \{(e_0, \tau)\}, \mathcal{D}_r, \mathcal{R}_r, \mathcal{U}), \text{ where } e_0 \notin E, \text{ and}$$

$$\mapsto_r = \mapsto \cup (\{\{e_0\}\} \times E),$$
$$\mathcal{D}_r = \{(e_0, \{0\})\} \cup (E \times \{\mathbb{R}^+\}),$$
$$\mathcal{R}_r = \mathcal{R} \cup \{((\{e_0\}, e), \mathcal{D}(e)) \mid e \in E\}.$$

We call $r(\mathcal{E})$ the *rooted taes* associated with $\mathcal{E}$. The newly introduced event e_0, denoted by $o_{r(\mathcal{E})}$, is called the *start-event* of $\mathcal{E}$ or $r(\mathcal{E})$.

Example 3.1.1 Let $\mathcal{E}_b$ be the taes of Figure 1(b) of Example 2.1.1. Then $r(\mathcal{E}_b)$ is the taes of Figure 2.

3.2   Refining a Taes

Let Act_0 be a subset of Act that contains τ and $\sqrt{}$, representing the set of actions which need not or cannot be refined. Function $f : Act \setminus Act_0 \longrightarrow TAES$ is called a *refinement function*, if for any action $a \in Act \setminus Act_0$ it satisfies the following conditions:

$$(1)\ f(a)\ \text{is well-labeled};$$
$$(2)\ Maxt(f(a)) = \{k(a)\}.$$

$f(a)$ is called *a refinement of action a*.

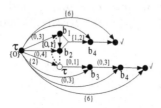

Fig. 2. The rooted taes associated with Figure 1(b)

Example 3.2.1 Assume $Act \setminus Act_0 = \{b\}$, and $\mathcal{E}_b$ the taes of Figure 1(b) of Example 2.1.1. Then $f(b) = \mathcal{E}_b$ is a refinement of action b.

Throughout the paper, we use f to denote a refinement function. The current question is how this refinement function can be applied to a given taes to obtain a refined one. Our basic idea, as illustrated in Figure 3, is that an action say a is replaced by $r(f(a))$ in the original taes. For simplicity, we use in the following $rfl(e)$ and $rf(a)$ to abbreviate $r(f(l(e)))$ and $r(f(a))$, respectively.

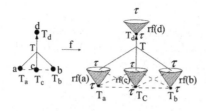

Fig. 3. Illustration of refining a taes

Definition The *refinement of taes* $\mathcal{E}$ is defined as
$$f(\mathcal{E}) = (E_f, \sharp_f, \vdash_f, l_f, \mathcal{D}_f, \mathcal{R}_f, \mathcal{U}_f), \text{ where}$$

• *Event set*
$$E_f = \{(e, e') \mid (e \in E) \wedge (l(e) \notin Act_0) \wedge$$
$$(e' \in E_{rfl(e)})\} \cup \{(e, e) \mid (e \in E) \wedge (l(e) \in Act_0)\},$$

- *Conflict relation*

for $(e_1, e_2), (e_1', e_2') \in E_f$, $(e_1, e_2) \sharp_f (e_1', e_2')$ iff

if $e_1 = e_1'$ then $e_2 \sharp_{rfl(e_1)} e_2'$,

if $e_1 \neq e_1'$ then

if $e_2 = e_1$ and $e_2' = e_1'$ then $e_1 \sharp e_1'$,

if $e_2 \neq e_1$ and $e_2' = e_1'$ then $e_1 \sharp e_1'$ and $e_2 = o_{rfl(e_1)}$,

if $e_2 = e_1$ and $e_2' \neq e_1'$ then $e_1 \sharp e_1'$ and $e_2' = o_{rfl(e_1')}$,

if $e_2 \neq e_1$ and $e_2' \neq e_1'$ then $e_1 \sharp e_1'$, $e_2 = o_{rfl(e_1)}$ and $e_2' \in \{o_{rfl(e_1')}\} \cup$
$exit(rfl(e_1'))$ or $e_2 \in \{o_{rfl(e_1)}\} \cup exit(rfl(e_1))$ and $e_2' = o_{rfl(e_1')}$,

- *Bundle relation*

for $X \subseteq E_f$ and $(e_1, e_2) \in E_f$, $X \vdash_f (e_1, e_2)$ iff

if $e_2 \neq e_1$ and $e_2 \in E_{rfl(e_1)} \setminus \{o_{rfl(e_1)}\}$ then $\pi_1(X) = \{e_1\}$ and
$\pi_2(X) \vdash_{rfl(e_1)} e_2$,

if $e_2 \neq e_1$ and $e_2 = o_{rfl(e_1)}$ or $e_2 = e_1$ then $\pi_1(X) \vdash e_1$ and
$\pi_2(X) = \bigcup_{e \in \pi_1(X), l(e) \notin Act_0} exit(rfl(e)) \cup (\bigcup_{e \in \pi_1(X), l(e) \in Act_0}) \{e\}$,

- *Action labeling function*

for $(e_1, e_2) \in E_f$ if $e_2 \neq e_1$ then

if $e_2 \notin exit(rfl(e_1))$ then $l_f(e_1, e_2) = l_{rfl(e_1)}(e_2)$,

if $e_2 \in exit(rfl(e_1))$ then $l_f(e_1, e_2) = \tau$,

if $e_2 = e_1$ then $l_f(e_1, e_2) = l(e_1)$,

- *Event delay function*

for $(e_1, e_2) \in E_f$ if $e_1 = e_2$ then $\mathcal{D}_f(e_1, e_2) = \mathcal{D}(e_1)$,

if $e_1 \neq e_2$ then

if $e_2 = o_{rfl(e_1)}$ then $\mathcal{D}_f(e_1, e_2) = \mathcal{D}(e_1)$,

if $e_2 \neq o_{rfl(e_1)}$ then $\mathcal{D}_f(e_1, e_2) = \mathbb{R}^+$,

- *Bundle delay function*

for $X \subseteq E_f$ and $(e_1, e_2) \in E_f$, if $X \vdash_f (e_1, e_2)$ then

if $e_2 \neq e_1$, $e_2 \in E_{rfl(e_1)} \setminus \{o_{rfl(e_1)}\}$ and $\pi_1(X) = \{e_1\}$ then
$\mathcal{R}_f(X, (e_1, e_2)) = \mathcal{R}_{rfl(e_1)}(\pi_2(X), e_2)$,

if $e_2 \neq e_1$ and $e_2 = o_{rfl(e_1)}$ then $\mathcal{R}_f(X, (e_1, e_2)) = \mathcal{R}(\pi_1(X), e_1)$,

if $e_2 = e_1$ then $\mathcal{R}_f(X, (e_1, e_2)) = \mathcal{R}(\pi_1(X), e_1)$,

- *Urgent events*

for $(e, e') \in E_f$, $(e, e') \in \mathcal{U}_f$ iff $e \in \mathcal{U}$ or $e' \in \mathcal{U}_{rfl(e)}$ if $e' \neq e$.

Here, $\pi_1(X) = \{e \mid (e, e') \in X\}$, and $\pi_2(X) = \{e' \mid (e, e') \in X\}$.

Example 3.2.2 Suppose that $\mathcal{E}$ is the taes of Figure 1(a) of Example 2.1.1. Let
$Act \setminus Act_0 = \{b\}$, and $f(b)$ the refinement of action b defined in Example 3.2.1
(Figure 1(b)). Then $rf(b)$ is the taes of Figure 2 of Example 3.1.1, and the
refinement $f(\mathcal{E})$ of $\mathcal{E}$ is the taes of Figure 4.

$f(\mathcal{E})$ satisfies the definition of taes's. From this fact, the following theorem follows.

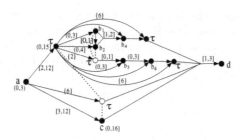

Fig. 4. The refinement of Figure 1(a)

Theorem 3.2.1 Let $\mathcal{E} \in TAES$, and f a refinement function. Then $f(\mathcal{E}) \in TAES$.

4 Correctness and Congruence Results

We show that our operation of action refinement is correct and furthermore, the equivalences defined in the preceding section are congruences under the refinement.

Assume again $x \in \{lib, bsat, min, early, late\}$. Let $TP_f = T\langle C_f, \overset{*}{\mapsto}_{fC_f}\rangle$ be a timed x-poset of $f(\mathcal{E})$, where C_f is a frame configuration of $f(\mathcal{E})$, and $\mapsto_{fC_f} \subseteq \mapsto_f |_{C_f}$. Let

$$\pi_1(TP_f) = T\langle \pi_1(C_f), \overset{*}{\mapsto}_{\pi_1(C_f)}\rangle, \text{ where}$$
$$\pi_1(C_f) = \{e \in E \mid (e, e_j) \in C_f\},$$
$$\forall e \in \pi_1(C_f), time(\pi_1(C_f), e) =$$
$$\quad \text{if } l(e) \in Act_0 \text{ then } time(C_f, (e, e)) \text{ else } time(C_f, (e, o_{rfl(e)})),$$
$$\mapsto_{\pi_1(C_f)} \subseteq E \times E : e \mapsto_{\pi_1(C_f)} e' \text{ iff } \exists(e, e_1) \mapsto_{fC_f} (e', e_1').$$

Moreover, for event $e \in \pi_1(C_f)$ with $l(e) \notin Act_0$, let

$$\pi_e(TP_f) = T\langle \pi_e(C_f), \overset{*}{\mapsto}_{\pi_e(C_f)}\rangle, \text{ where}$$
$$\pi_e(C_f) = \{e_j \in E_{rfl(e)} \mid (e, e_j) \in C_f\},$$
$$\forall e_j \in \pi_e(C_f), time(\pi_e(C_f), e_j) = time(C_f, (e, e_j)) - time(C_f, (e, o_{rfl(e)})),$$
$$\mapsto_{\pi_e(C_f)} \subseteq E_{rfl(e)} \times E_{rfl(e)} : e_1 \mapsto_{\pi_e(C_f)} e_2 \text{ iff } (e, e_1) \mapsto_{fC_f} (e, e_2).$$

$\pi_1(TP_f)$ is the projection of timed x-poset TP_f on taes $\mathcal{E}$, and $\pi_e(TP_f)$ the projection of TP_f on taes $rfl(e)$. We have then the following Lemma 4.1, which indicates that the projection of TP_f on $\mathcal{E}$ is a timed x-poset of $\mathcal{E}$, and the projection of TP_f on $rfl(e)$ is a timed x-poset of $rfl(e)$.

Lemma 4.1 (1) $\pi_e(TP_f) \in TP_x(rfl(e))$; (2) $\pi_1(TP_f) \in TP_x(\mathcal{E})$.

We have also the following simple Lemma 4.2, which demonstrates that $\pi_e(TP_f)$ successfully terminates if e is causally necessary for some other events. Notice that a timed x-poset is said to successfully terminate, if the frame configuration on which this timed x-poset is based successfully terminates.

Lemma 4.2 If $e \in \pi_1(C_f)$, $l(e) \notin Act_0$ and e is not maximal in $\pi_1(TP_f)$, then $\pi_e(TP_f)$ successfully terminates.

Now, we suppose $TP = T\langle C, \overset{*}{\mapsto}_C\rangle$ is a timed x-poset of $\mathcal{E}$, where $C \in C(\mathcal{E})$, and $\mapsto_C \subseteq \mapsto |_C$. Furthermore, $e \in C$ with $l(e) \notin Act_0$, and $TP_e = T\langle C_e, \overset{*}{\mapsto}_{rfl(e)C_e}\rangle$ a timed x-poset of $rfl(e)$, where $C_e \in C(rfl(e))$, $\mapsto_{rfl(e)C_e} \subseteq \mapsto_{rfl(e)} |_{C_e}$, and C_e successfully terminates if e is not maximal in C. Let

$$f(TP, \triangleright_e TP_e) = T\langle f(C, \cup_e C_e), \overset{*}{\mapsto}_{ff(C,\cup_e C_e)}\rangle, \text{ where}$$
$$f(C, \cup_e C_e) = \{ (e, e_j) \mid e \in C, \text{ if } l(e) \in Act_0 \text{ then } e_j = e \text{ else } e_j \in C_e\},$$
$$\forall(e, e_j) \in f(C, \cup_e C_e), \; time(f(C, \cup_e C_e), (e, e_j)) =$$
$$\text{if } l(e) \in Act_0 \text{ then } time(C, e) \text{ else } time(C_e, e_j) + time(C, e),$$
$$\text{for } (e_1, e_1'), (e_2, e_2') \in E_f \times E_f, \; (e_1, e_1') \mapsto_{ff(C,\cup_e C_e)} (e_2, e_2') \text{ iff}$$
$$e_1 \mapsto_C e_2, \text{ and either } e_1' = e_1 \text{ and } e_2' = e_2, \text{ or}$$
$$\text{if } e_1' \neq e_1 \text{ and } e_2' = e_2 \text{ then } e_1' \in exit(rfl(e_1)),$$
$$\text{if } e_1' = e_1 \text{ and } e_2' \neq e_2 \text{ then } e_2' = o_{rfl(e_2)},$$
$$\text{if } e_1' \neq e_1 \text{ and } e_2' \neq e_2 \text{ then}$$
$$\text{if } e_1 = e_2 \text{ then } e_1' \mapsto_{rfl(e_1)C_{e_1}} e_2',$$
$$\text{if } e_1 \neq e_2 \text{ then } e_1' \in exit(rfl(e_1)) \text{ and } e_2' = o_{rfl(e_2)}.$$

We call it a *refinement of TP*. By $f(TP_x(\mathcal{E}))$ we represent the set of all refinements of timed x-posets of taes $\mathcal{E}$. We have then Lemma 4.3, which states that a refinement of a timed x-poset of taes $\mathcal{E}$ is a timed x-poset of the refined taes $f(\mathcal{E})$.

Lemma 4.3 $f(TP, \triangleright_e TP_e) \in TP_x(f(\mathcal{E}))$ for $x \in \{lib, bsat, min, early, late\}$.

From Lemmas 4.1, 4.2 and 4.3, the following two theorems follow.

Theorem 4.1 Suppose that $\mathcal{E}$ is a taes, and f a refinement function. Then $TP_x(f(\mathcal{E})) = f(TP_x(\mathcal{E}))$ for $x \in \{lib, bsat, min, early, late\}$.

This theorem indicates that timed x-posets of the refined taes $f(\mathcal{E})$ can be obtained by replacing event e with $e \notin Act_0$ in timed x-posets of the original taes $\mathcal{E}$ by timed x-posets of taes $rfl(e)$ used to refine action $l(e)$. The behavior of the refined taes can thus be inferred compositionally from the behavior of the original taes and from the behavior of those used to substitute actions, where the system starts are explicitly represented. The refinement keeps correct.

Theorem 4.2 Let $\mathcal{E}_1$ and $\mathcal{E}_2$ be two taes's, and f_1 and f_2 two refinement functions. If $\mathcal{E}_1 \cong_{eq} \mathcal{E}_2$, and for any $a \in Act \setminus Act_0, f_1(a) \cong_{eq} f_2(a)$, then $f_1(\mathcal{E}_1) \cong_{eq} f_2(\mathcal{E}_2)$, where $eq \in \{px, bx\}$ and $x \in \{lib, bsat, min, early, late\}$.

This theorem shows that x-pomset trace and x-history preserving bisimulation equivalences are both congruences under the refinement. Our refinement notion is therefore well-defined under these equivalences.

5   Concluding Remarks

In this paper, we developed an approach of action refinement for real-time concurrent systems with causal ambiguity, where timed event structures with causal ambiguity are used as the system model. Furthermore, the following correctness and congruence results were certified under a certain partial order semantics:

- The behavior of the refined system can be inferred compositionally from the behavior of the original system and from the behavior of the systems used to refine actions, where new events are introduced to model the system starts.
- The variants of pomset trace and history preserving bisimulation equivalences are both congruences under the refinement.

We adopt again in this paper the basic refinement methodology proposed by us in [4, 5, 15, 16, 17]. We believe that the methodology for the probabilistic and stochastic cases proposed in [5, 17] applies to the corresponding cases when causal ambiguity exists. This is in fact our immediate future work. We also want to define a suitable process algebra to specify taes's, develop an approach of action refinement at this language level, and try to make the syntactic refinement and the semantic refinement presented in this paper conform to each other.

References

1. H. Bowman, J-P. Katoen. A True Concurrency Semantics for ET-LOTOS. *Proceedings Int. Conference on Applications of Concurrency to System Design,* 228 - 239, 1998.
2. L. Castellano, G. Michelis, and L. Pomello. Concurrency vs Interleaving: An Instructive Example. *Bull. EATCS,* 31: 12- 15, 1987.

462   M. Majster-Cederbaum et al.

3. H. Fecher, M. Majster-Cederbaum, and J. Wu. Bundle Event Structures: A Revised Cpo Approach. *Information Processing Letters*, 83: 7 – 12, 2002.
4. H. Fecher, M. Majster-Cederbaum, and J. Wu. Refinement of Actions in a Real-Time Process Algebra with a True Concurrency Model. *Electronic Notes in Theoretical Computer Science*, 70(3), 2002.
5. H. Fecher, M. Majster-Cederbaum, and J. Wu. Action Refinement for Probabilistic Processes with True Concurrency Models. *Lecture Notes in Computer Science*, 2399: 77 – 94, 2002.
6. R. van Glabbeek, U. Goltz. Refinement of Actions and Equivalence Notions for Concurrent Systems. *Acta Informatica*, 37: 229 - 327, 2001.
7. U. Goltz, R. Gorrieri, and A. Rensink. On Syntactic and Semantic Action Refinement. *Lecture Notes in Computer Science*, 789: 385-404, 1994.
8. R. Gorrieri, A. Rensink. Action Refinement. *Handbook of Process Algebra*, Elsevier Science, 1047 - 1147, 2001.
9. J-P. Katoen. *Quantitative and Qualitative Extensions of Event Structures*. PhD thesis, University of Twente, 1996.
10. J-P. Katoen, C. Baier, and D. Latella. Metric Semantics for True Concurrent Real Time. *Th. Comp. Sci.*, 254(1-2): 501 - 542, 2001.
11. J-P. Katoen, R. Langerak, E. Brinksma, D. Latella & T. Bolognesi. A Consistent Causality Based View on a Timed Process Algebra Including Urgent Interactions. *Formal Meth. in Sys. Design*, 12: 189 - 216, 1998.
12. J-P. Katoen, R. Langerak, D. Latella & E. Brinksma. On Specifying Real-Time Systems in a Causality-Based Setting. *Lecture Notes in Computer Science*, 1135: 385 - 405, 1996.
13. R. Langerak. Bundle Event Structures: A Non-Interleaving Semantics for LOTOS. In M. Diaz and R. Groz editors, *Formal Description Techniques V, IFIP Transactions*, C-10: 331 - 346, 1993.
14. R. Langerak, E. Brinksma, and J-P. Katoen. Causal Ambiguity and Partial Orders in Event Structures. *CONCUR'97*, Lecture Notes in Computer Science, 1243: 317 – 331, 1997.
15. M. Majster-Cederbaum, J. Wu. Action Refinement for True Concurrent Real Time. *Proc. ICECCS 2001*, IEEE Computer Society Press, 58 - 68, 2001.
16. M. Majster-Cederbaum, J. Wu. Towards Action Refinement for True Concurrent Real Time. *Acta Informatica*, 39(8): 531 - 577, 2003.
17. M. Majster-Cederbaum, J. Wu. Adding Action Refinement to Stochastic True Concurrency Models. *Lecture Notes in Computer Science*, 2885: 226 - 245, 2003.
18. D. Murphy. Time and Duration in Noninterleaving Concurrency. *Fundamenta Informaticae*, 19: 403 - 416, 1993.
19. A. Rabinovich, B. A. Trakhtenbrot. Behavior Structures and Nets. *Fund. Info.*, 11(4): 357 - 404, 1988.
20. M. van Sinderen, L. Ferreira Pires, C. A. Vissers, and J-P Katoen. A Design Model for Open Distributed Processing Systems. *Computer Networks and ISDN Systems*, 27: 1263 - 1285, 1995.
21. M. K. de Weger, H. Franken, and C. A. Vissers. A Development Model for Distributed Information Systems. In: *Proceedings of the 1st Int. Distributed Conference on High Performance Networking for Teleteaching (IDC'95)*, 1995.

22. J. Wu and H. Yue. Towards Action Refinement for Concurrent Systems with Causal Ambiguity. *Proc. SEFM 2004*, IEEE Computer Society Press, to appear, 2004.
23. A. Yakovlev, M. Kishinevsky, A. Kondratyev, and L. Lavagno. On the Models for Asynchronous Circuit Behaviour with OR causality. *Technical Report 463*, University of Newcastle upon Tyne, 1993.

From Durational Specifications to TLA Designs of Timed Automata

Yifeng Chen and Zhiming Liu

Department of Computer Science,
University of Leicester, Leicester LE1 7RH, UK
{Y.Chen, Z.Liu}@mcs.le.ac.uk

Abstract. Different temporal logics tend to emphasise different aspects of a hybrid system. In this paper, we study the predicative interpretation of Duration Calculus (DC) and Temporal Logic of Actions (TLA) and the link between them. A notation called *generic composition* is used to simplify the manipulation of predicates. The modalities of possibility and necessity become generic composition and its inverse of converse respectively. The transformation between different temporal logics is also characterised as such modalities. The formalism provides a framework in which human experience about hybrid system development can be formalised as refinement laws. A high-level durational specification can be decomposed to two durational specifications driven by an automaton. In such a stepwise design process, durational features are reduced while automaton features increase gradually. The application of the technique is demonstrated in the case study of the gas burner problem.

1 Introduction

An embedded system consists of both continuous components that observe continuous physical laws and discrete components that execute digital instructions. Hybrid systems inevitably involve time as an observable and can be naturally specified using temporal logics. Different temporal logics tend to emphasise different aspects of an embedded system. For example, interval logics such as Duration Calculus (DC) [20], emphasising properties over intervals, are more suitable for describing high-level continuous properties and hence closer to the continuous aspects of embedded systems. On the other hand, Linear Temporal Logics (LTL) [14], emphasising the properties of states at discrete time points, are more suitable for modelling discrete aspects of embedded systems and can be easily verified as a timed automaton [15]. A straightforward specification in one logic may become less intuitive in another logic. In the past, all aspects of an embedded system are normally specified in one logic [10, 21]. Traditional method of combining logics is to collect syntactical constructs together and identify the axioms of the system. This usually results in a complicated axiomatic system difficult to handle. For example, the design of an embedded system may involve an abstract specification of the requirements in DC and a concrete LTL specification that describes the behaviour of the system of implementation. Existing development techniques do not support such refinement. A more natural approach is to unify the different logics at a common semantic level.

Predicative interpretation is a standard technique in modal logic [2, 18]. A proposition with modal operators can be interpreted as a predicate. The modality of possibility (or necessity) is represented as an existential (or universal) quantifier. Predicates are also used in semantic modelling of programming languages. Each program or specification permits a certain set of observations over some observable aspects of the computation and is represented as a predicate on the corresponding logical variables that denote the observables. This approach is often known as *predicative semantics* [6, 8].

We use a notation called *generic composition* [3] to simplify the manipulation of predicates. A generic composition is a relational composition with a **designated interface consisting of several logical variables**. Generic composition has an inverse operator. With the help of the two operators, we no longer need the existential and universal quantifiers. The modality of possibility then becomes a generic composition, while the modality of necessity becomes its inverse of converse [5]. Temporal logics have been characterised algebraically using Galois connections [1, 13, 19]. In our approach, the accessibility relation of modal logics is directly parameterised. The link between two specifications in different temporal logics is characterised as a pointwise relation between the possible observations of the specifications. Such a pointwise relation also determines a pair of modalities and can be defined with a generic composition and its inverse. Our approach is essentially a relational semantics and directly corresponds to Kripke semantics [9]. Using relations to link two semantic spaces is an entirely natural idea, because all implementable system compositions are essentially relational (and hence distribute the universal nondeterministic choice) in observation-based semantics. The advantage of our approach is that it is based on predicative semantics and is more convenient to represent the link between only the related observables of two distinctive specification spaces, and unrelated observable aspects are not linked. An alternative approach is to adopt predicate transformers, which may permit more high-order manipulation, but their implementable cores are still relational. Compared to the predicate-transformer approach, relational semantics is more specific, intuitive and implementable.

For unification, we model different temporal domains such as real time, traces, timed traces, forests (for branching time) and intervals under a notion called *resource cumulator* [4]. A cumulator is a quintuple compromising a monoid, a corresponding partial order and a volume function that measures the amount of resources. A cumulator provides the "type" for a logical variable of a particular temporal domain. The integration of different temporal logics will not be useful unless we provide the knowledge about how specifications in one logic can be approximated or refined by specifications in another logic. Such knowledge can be formalised as the refinement laws of modalities. Identifying these laws can make the design process more systematic.

In this paper, we will demonstrate this by studying the refinement from DC specifications to TLA implementations. An automaton with two states can be readily specified in TLA. A high-level durational specification can be decomposed to two durational specifications "driven" by an automaton. Such decomposition can be repeated several times and create a hierarchical structure of two-state automata. The rest of the design is to combine the automata in a single flat one. The advantage of this approach is that implemental features are introduced step by step gradually. This allows each development step to preserve more nondeterminism from the original specification and thus keep more flexibility in the following design steps.

In previous works, Schenke and Olderog [17] studied the direct refinement transformation from DC to a language similar to CSP [7]. Since the gap between DC and TLA specifications is smaller than that between DC and a real programming language, our approach yields stronger algebraic properties. The result TLA implementations can be verified with model-checking tools.

Section 2 studies the predicative semantics of modal logic using the notation of generic composition and its inverse. Section 3 unifies different temporal domains under the notion of resource cumulator and defines the predicative semantics of temporal logic in general and discusses several temporal logics including DC and TLA. The relationship between DC and TLA is studied in Section 4. The refinement laws identified in Section 4 are then applied to the case study in Section 5.

2   Predicative Semantics of Modal Logics

Manipulating Predicates

We assume that there are two types of logical variables: non-overlined variables such as $x, y, z, \cdots$ and overlined variables such as $\overline{x}, \overline{y}, \overline{z}, \cdots$. Overlining is only used to associate corresponding logical variables syntactically. We use a notation called *generic composition* [3] to manipulate predicates. A generic composition is a relational composition with a designated interface of non-overlined variables.

Def 1. $P :_x R \ \widehat{=} \ \exists x_0 \cdot P[x_0/x] \wedge R[x_0/\overline{x}]$.

A 'fresh' variable x_0 is used to connect x of P and $\overline{x}$ of R and hidden by the existential quantifier. Generic composition is a restricted form of relational composition. It relates two predicates on only some of their logical variables. For example, the following composition relates two predicates on only x (and $\overline{x}$):

$$(x = 10 \wedge y = 20) :_x (\overline{x} \leqslant x \wedge z = 30) \ = \ (10 \leqslant x \wedge y = 20 \wedge z = 30).$$

The existential quantifier $\exists x \cdot P$ is simply represented as $P :_x true$, and variable substitution $P[e/x]$ as $P :_x (\overline{x} = e)$. An interface x may split into several variables, e.g. (y, z). For example, the generic composition $P :_{(y, z)} true$ is the same as the predicate $\exists y \exists z \cdot P$. If the vector is empty, a generic composition becomes a conjunction: $P : R = P \wedge R$.

Generic composition has an inverse operator denoted by $P/_x R$, which is the weakest predicate X such that $(X :_x R) \subseteq P$. It can be defined by a Galois connection:

Def 2. $X \subseteq P/_x R$ *iff* $X :_x R \subseteq P$ *for any predicate* X.

Generic composition and its inverse satisfy a property:

$$P/_x R \; = \; \neg(\neg P :_x \widetilde{R}) \; = \; \forall x_0 \cdot (R[x_0/x, x/\overline{x}] \Rightarrow P[x_0/x])$$

where $\widetilde{R} \; \hat{=} \; R[\overline{x}/x, x/\overline{x}]$ is the converse of R for the variable x. Universal quantifier $\forall x \cdot P$ can then be written as $P/_x$ *true*. Negation $\neg P$ becomes *false* $/P$ whose interface is empty. Implication $P \Rightarrow Q$ becomes Q/P with an empty interface. Disjunction $P \vee Q$ is a trivial combination of negation and implication. Thus all connectives, substitution and quantifiers become special cases of generic composition and its inverse [3].

Theorem 1.   *Generic composition and its inverse are complete in the sense that any predicate that does not contain overlined free variables can be written in terms of generic composition and its inverse using only the constant predicates and predicate letters.*

The theorem shows the expressiveness of generic composition for predicate manipulation. Generic composition and its inverse form a Galois connection and satisfy the algebraic laws of strictness, distributivity and associativity.

Law 1.

(1) $A \subseteq (A :_x R)/_x R$ (2) $(A/_x R) :_x R \subseteq A$
(3) *false* $:_x R = $ *false*   (4) *true* $/_x R = $ *true*
(5) $A :_x (R \vee S) = (A :_x R) \vee (A :_x S)$ (6) $(A \vee B) :_x R = (A :_x R) \vee (A :_x R)$
(7) $A/_x (R \vee S) = (A/_x R) \wedge (A/_x S)$ (8) $(A \wedge B)/_x R = (A/_x R) \wedge (A/_x R)$
(9) $(A :_x R) :_x S = A :_x (R :_x S)$ (10) $(A/_x R)/_x S = A/_x (S :_x R)$.

The notation is especially useful when the interfaces of the operators in a predicate are not identical. For example, in the following law we assume that x, y and z are three different logical variables, $A = \exists z \cdot A$ (independence of the variable z) and $C = \exists \overline{y} \cdot C$ (independence of the variable $\overline{y}$).

Law 2. $(A :_{(y,x)} B) :_{(x,z)} C \; = \; A :_{(y,x)} (B :_{(x,z)} C)$.

Generic composition and its inverse can be used to define modalities. These properties make the composition a useful technical tool for linking temporal logics. Generic composition has also been applied to define a variety of healthiness conditions and parallel compositions. The above laws and a series of other laws can be found in [3].

Interpreting Modalities

Under Kripke semantics [2], modal logics are logical systems of relations (called "accessibility relations"). Here, we represent a specification as a predicate on a *modal variable* (e.g. x) and an *auxiliary variable* (e.g. y). The modal variable records the observable aspect related to the accessibility of the modalities, while the auxiliary variable records the unrelated observable aspect. For now, the variables are left untyped. These logical variables will later be typed in temporal logics. A logical variable may split into several ones, and its type becomes the product of several types. The semantic space is the set of all such specifications (e.g. denoted by $\mathcal{A}$). An accessibility relation $R = R(\overline{x}, x)$ is denoted by a predicate on two variables: the modal variable x and the overlined modal variable $\overline{x}$. Overlined variables only appear in the accessibility relations. Each accessibility relation determines a pair of modalities.

Def 3. $\Diamond_\mathcal{A} P \cong P :_x \tilde{R}$ *and* $\Box_\mathcal{A} P \cong P /_x R$.

The operator $\Diamond_\mathcal{A} P$ informally means that "*the predicate P may be true*" and is defined as a generic composition of the specification P and the converse relation $\tilde{R}$; its dual modality $\Box_\mathcal{A} P$ informally means that "*the predicate P must be true*" is defined with an inverse operator.

   If we replace the accessibility relation with its converse, we will obtain a pair of converse modalities.

Def 4. $\tilde{\Diamond}_\mathcal{A} P \cong P :_x R$ *and* $\tilde{\Box}_\mathcal{A} P \cong P /_x \tilde{R}$.

Generic composition and its inverse can be regarded as parameterised modal operators. They have a designated interface and are more convenient than traditional relational composition in this context for two reasons. Firstly, the observable aspects (described by the auxiliary variable) unrelated to the accessibility relation can be excluded from the interface of the relational composition. Secondly, the predicate on the left-hand side of a generic composition (or its inverse) can be either a specification (without overlined variables) or an accessibility relation (with overlined variables). Thus the operators can be directly used to represent the composition of accessibility relations (i.e. the composition of modalities).

   The converse/inverse relationships between these modalities are illustrated in a diagram (see Figure 1). The four modalities form two Galois connections.

Law 3. $\Diamond_\mathcal{A} P \subseteq Q$ *iff* $P \subseteq \tilde{\Box}_\mathcal{A} Q$ *for any* $P \in \mathcal{A}$ *and* $Q \in \mathcal{B}$
              $\tilde{\Diamond}_\mathcal{A} P \subseteq Q$ *iff* $P \subseteq \Box_\mathcal{A} Q$ *for any* $P \in \mathcal{A}$ *and* $Q \in \mathcal{B}$.

Transformer Modalities

The transformation between two temporal logics also becomes modalities. Let $\mathcal{A}$ (or $\mathcal{B}$) be a semantic space of specifications, each of which is a predicate on modal variable x (or x') and auxiliary variable y (or y'). The transformation

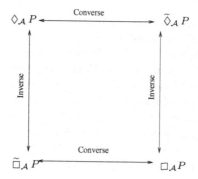

Fig. 1. Diagram of converse/inverse relationships

from $\mathcal{A}$ to $\mathcal{B}$ is characterised as a transformation predicate $T = T(\overline{x}, \overline{y}, x', y')$ on four variables. The predicate determines a transformer modality $\Diamond_{\mathcal{A} \to \mathcal{B}}$ from $\mathcal{A}$ to $\mathcal{B}$ and a corresponding inverse transformer $\Box_{\mathcal{B} \to \mathcal{A}}$ from $\mathcal{B}$ to $\mathcal{A}$. In the following definition, we assume that $P = P(x, y)$ and $Q = Q(x', y')$.

Def 5. $\quad \Diamond_{\mathcal{A} \to \mathcal{B}} P \;\widehat{=}\; P \mathbin{:}_{(x,y)} T$

$\quad\quad\quad \Box_{\mathcal{B} \to \mathcal{A}} Q \;\widehat{=}\; Q /_{(x', y')} T.$

Note that $\Diamond_{\mathcal{A} \to \mathcal{B}}$ and $\Box_{\mathcal{B} \to \mathcal{A}}$ form just one pair of transformers based on the predicate T. Other transformers between the two logics can be denoted as $\Diamond_{\mathcal{A} \to '\mathcal{B}}$ and $\Diamond_{\mathcal{A} \to ''\mathcal{B}}$ etc. Let $\Diamond_{\mathcal{A} \to \mathcal{B}}$ and $\Diamond_{\mathcal{B} \to \mathcal{C}}$ be two transformers. Their composition $\Diamond_{\mathcal{A} \to \mathcal{B}} \Diamond_{\mathcal{B} \to \mathcal{C}}$ is also a transformer (from $\mathcal{A}$ to $\mathcal{C}$), so is the composition of their inverses.

If the modal variable and the auxiliary variable are untyped, the above predicative semantics is contained in predicate calculus and hence complete. A well-formed formula is always true if and only if it can be proved using the laws of generic composition and its inverse (or equivalently, the axioms of predicate calculus).

3 Temporal Logic of Resource Cumulation

Resource Cumulation

Many aspects of computing can be modelled as the cumulation of resources. In real-time computing, *time* is a kind of resource. A process "consumes" a non-negative amount of time. A computation may also produce resources. For example, a reactive process generates an increasingly longer sequence of intermediate states called a *trace*. Resource cumulation can be formalized as a quintuple called a *cumulator*: $(X, \leqslant \,;\, 0, \,\widehat{}\; \,;\, |\cdot|)$, which consists of three parts: a well-founded partial order $(X, \leqslant)$ in which each element is called a *cumulation* and the greatest lower bound exists for any non-empty subset, a monoid $(0, \,\widehat{}\,)$ in which 0, or zero cumulation is the least cumulation, and a monotonic and associative binary operation *concatenation* $\widehat{}$ corresponds to the addition of cumulations, and a monotonic and strict *volume* function $|\cdot| : X \to [0,\infty]$: We assume that the partial order and the monoid are consistent: $a \leqslant b \Leftrightarrow \exists c \in X \cdot a \,{}^\frown c = b$. The unusual part of a cumulator is the volume function. A volume function measures the amount of resource cumulated. With such additional information we can then reason about the dynamics of resource cumulation. For example, a resource is exhausted when its volume reaches infinity ∞. The use of volume functions can substantially simplify the reasoning of limit points, continuity, and other topological properties. Such modelling is aimed at avoiding complicated domain construction and has reflected our pragmatic view on resources.

For a more complete account of resource cumulation, please refer to [4].

Example: The amount of time that a computation consumes can be modelled as a cumulator: $RTime \;\hat{=}\; ([0,\infty], \leqslant ; 0, + ; id)$ where $+$ is addition. id is the identity function.

Example: In some applications, we are interested in temporal properties over a period of time and thus need to reason about temporal intervals. Intervals form a cumulator $Interval \;\hat{=}\; (I, \leqslant ; \emptyset, {}^\frown ; |\cdot|)$ where I denotes the set of intervals, each of which is a convex subset i of the real domain $[0,\infty]$ (such that for any $t_1, t_2 \in i$ and $t_3 \in T$, $t_1 \leqslant t_3 \leqslant t_2$ implies $t_3 \in i$). For example, $[1,2]$, $[1,2)$, $(1,2]$, $(1,2)$ and the empty set $\emptyset$ are intervals. Let I denote the set of all intervals. $a \,{}^\frown b \;\hat{=}\; a \cup b$ if $a \cap b = \emptyset$, $\sqcup a = \sqcap b$ and $a \cup b \in I$. The volume of a non-empty interval is its length: $|a| \;\hat{=}\; \sqcup a - \sqcap a$ where $\sqcup a$ and $\sqcap a$ denote the lub and glb of the interval a respectively. The volume of the empty set is zero $|\emptyset| = 0$. The orders $a \leqslant b$ means that b is a right-hand extension of a, i.e. $\exists c \in I \cdot a \,{}^\frown c = b$.

Example: Finite and infinite traces form a typical cumulator: $Trace(X) \;\hat{=}\; (X^\dagger, \leqslant ; \langle\rangle, {}^\wedge ; |\cdot|)$ where X is the type of each element, and $X^\dagger$ the set of all sequences of elements (including the infinite ones). For two sequences $a, b \in X^\dagger$, $a \,{}^\wedge b$ denotes their concatenation. If a is an infinite sequence, then for any b, $a \,{}^\wedge b = a$. $a \leqslant b$ iff a is a *prefix* (i.e. pre-cumulation) of b. $|a|$ denotes the length of a. For exampe, the length of the empty sequence $\langle\rangle$ is 0. a_i denotes the i-th element of the sequence where $1 \leqslant i \leqslant |a|$.

Example: A timed trace is a trace with non-decreasing time stamps. The sequence $\langle (1,p),(2,q),(4,p)\rangle$ is one example. In general, a timed trace is a trace of pairs in the form $\langle (t_1,s_1),(t_2,s_2),\cdots,(t_n,s_n),\cdots\rangle$. Timed traces form a cumulator: $TimedTrace(X) \;\hat{=}\; (T(X), \leqslant ; \langle\rangle, {}^\wedge ; |\cdot|)$ where

$$T(X) \;\hat{=}\; \{ tr \in ([0,\infty] \times X)^\dagger \mid \forall i, j < |tr| \cdot (i \leqslant j \Rightarrow t_i \leqslant t_j) \}.$$

Temporal Logic of Resource Cumulation

Temporal logic of resource cumulation is a modal logic. Let $(X, \leqslant ; 0, {}^\frown ; |\cdot|)$ be a cumulator. A general cumulative specification is a predicate on a modal variable $x \in X$ whose type is a cumulator and an untyped auxiliary variable y. We let $\mathcal{R}$ denote the semantic space of such specifications. The general cumulator gives rise to a number of accessibility relations, each of which determines two pairs of modalities. A common accessibility relation corresponds to the left-hand contractions: $R \triangleq \exists z \in X \cdot (\overline{x} = z^\frown x)$.

The modality $\Diamond_{\mathcal{R}} P$ informally means that "*the predicate P becomes true after some pre-cumulation of resources*". More precisely, the behaviours of $\Diamond_{\mathcal{R}} P$ are the behaviours of P extended with arbitrary cumulations on the left-hand side. The modality $\Box_{\mathcal{R}} P$, instead, means that "*the predicate P is true for any left-hand extensions of the behaviours of P*". The pair of converse modalities $\widetilde{\Diamond}_{\mathcal{R}} P$ and $\widetilde{\Box}_{\mathcal{R}} P$ are actually the corresponding "past-tense" modalities. All properties of general modalities are inherited.

There exists a dual accessibility relation for right-hand contractions: $R' \triangleq \exists z \in X \cdot (\overline{x} = x^\frown z)$. Again, it determines two pairs of modalities $\Diamond_{\mathcal{R}'} P$, $\Box_{\mathcal{R}'} P$, $\widetilde{\Diamond}_{\mathcal{R}'} P$ and $\widetilde{\Box}_{\mathcal{R}'} P$. The modalities of left-hand and right-hand extensions/contractions commute with each other respectively. Their respective compositions (e.g. $\Diamond_{\mathcal{R}} \Diamond_{\mathcal{R}'} P$) becomes a bi-directional contractions/extensions.

The most commonly used temporal operator $\Diamond P$ in LTL means that "*the predicate P eventually becomes true in finite steps*". Its dual operator $\Box P$ means that "*the predicate P is always true after finite steps*". They correspond to $\Diamond_{|L|<\infty} P$ and $\Box_{|L|<\infty} P$ respectively (with the cumulator *Trace*).

In general, temporal logic of resource cumulation is not complete, since the temporal domain (i.e. the cumulator) of the modal variable may not have a complete axiomatic characterisation. Nevertheless, it is still possible to reason about temporal specifications manually based on the semantic properties of the underlying temporal domain.

Examples of Temporal Logics

The amount of time that a computation consumes corresponds to the cumulator *RTime*. A real-time specification is a predicate on a typed modal variable $t \in [0, \infty]$ that denotes time and an untyped auxiliary variable s that denotes the system's state at the time. We let $\mathcal{T}$ denote the space of such specifications. Since addition is commutative i.e. $a + b = b + a$, it makes no difference whether time is extended from the left-hand side or the right-hand side. For example, $e^t = x$ described a system's temperature growing exponentially over time.

Intervals within a time domain form the cumulator *Interval*. A specification on intervals is a predicate on a variable $i \in I$ that denotes the interval and an auxiliary variable x that denotes some system feature related to the interval. We let $\mathcal{I}$ denote the space of all temporal specifications on intervals. An interval can be extended from either left-hand side or right-hand side.

Traces of elements of X form a cumulator *Trace*(X). A trace specification is a predicate on a single variable $tr \in X^\dagger$. We let $\mathcal{S}$ denote the space of trace specifications. For example, the specification $\Box_{|\mathcal{S}|<\infty} (tr_1 = 1)$ states that the first element of every suffix is 1, *i.e.* every state is 1. We introduce a dependent variable $s \triangleq tr_1$. The specification can then be simplified as $\Box_{|\mathcal{S}|<\infty} (s = 1)$.

Such semantic notation directly corresponds to LTL, although here we use a non-standard notation and allow finite traces.

If another dependent variable $s' \; \widehat{=} \; tr_2$ is used to denote the second element of the trace, we can then specify *infinite traces* of actions. For example, let X be the set of natural numbers. The specification $\Box_{|S|<\infty} \, (s < s')$ describes a trace of increasing numbers. Temporal Logic of Actions (TLA) [11] is a logic of stuttering-closed specifications on actions. The stuttering closure $[P]_s \; \widehat{=} \; (P \vee s = s')$ of a specification P is a disjunction. For example, the specification $\Box_{|S|<\infty} \, [s < s']_s$ describes a trace of non-decreasing natural numbers.

The link between the original variables and the dependent variables can also be characterized as a transformer. For example, let $P(s, s')$ be a specification on the current state s and the next state s'. It corresponds to a specification $P :_{(s,s')} (\overline{s} = tr_1 \wedge \overline{s}' = tr_2)$ on traces.

Timed traces form the cumulator $TimedTrace(X)$. We let $\mathcal{K}$ denote the space of specifications on timed traces. For TLA of timed traces, we consider only infinite traces, introduce dependent variables $s \,\widehat{=}\, s_1$, $s' \,\widehat{=}\, s_2$, $t \,\widehat{=}\, t_1$ and $t' \,\widehat{=}\, t_2$, and assume that $t \leqslant t'$. The stuttering closure is defined: $[P]_{(s,t)} \; \widehat{=} \; P \vee (s = s' \wedge t = t')$. For example, the following specification requires the state to change from 1 to 0 after no more than 4 seconds or from 0 to 1 after no less than 26 seconds:

$$\Box_{\mathcal{K}} \, [(s = 1 \wedge s' = 0 \wedge t' - t \leqslant 4) \vee (s = 0 \wedge s' = 1 \wedge t' - t \geqslant 26)]_{(s,t)} . \qquad (1)$$

The above example can be generalised to an automaton with two (composite) states (see Figure 2): from a state satisfying p (i.e. $s = 1$ in the above example), the automaton moves into another state satisfying $\neg p$ in some time $t \in U$ and then moves back to a state satisfying p in some time $t \in V$ where $U, V \subseteq [0, \infty]$. The two-state automaton can be formalised as follows:

$$Automaton(p, U, V) \; \widehat{=} \qquad\qquad\qquad\qquad\qquad\qquad (2)$$
$$\Box_{\mathcal{K}} \, [(p(s) \wedge \neg p(s') \wedge t' - t \in U) \vee (\neg p(s) \wedge p(s') \wedge t' - t \in V)]_{(s,t)} .$$

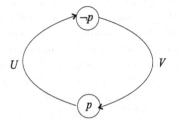

Fig. 2. Automaton with two states

Duration calculus (DC) is a special interval logic. A durational specification is a predicate on a variable $i \in I$ that denotes the interval and an auxiliary variable $x : [0, \infty] \to S$ that denotes a real-time Boolean function. We use a boolean function $p: S \rightarrow \{0, 1\}$ to denote whether a state $x(t)$ at the time t satisfies the predicate $p(\cdot)$. The space of durational specifications is denoted by $\mathcal{D}$.

Again, we may introduce some dependent variables. For example, instead of specifying the relation (i.e. a predicate) between the interval and the real-time function, we may specify the relation between the length of the interval and the integral of the real function in the interval. Although not all computation can be specified in such a restricted way, it has been expressive enough for most applications and covers most common design patterns [16]. The following table lists the primitives of DC:

$P(\ell, \int p)$	general pattern
$\lceil p \rceil$	lift
$\Box_{\mathcal{D}} P$	modality of sub-interval closure
$P \,\fatsemi\, Q$	chop operation
$P \vee Q$	logical disjunction
$\neg P$	negation

For example, the Gas Burner problem [16] includes a requirement that gas leak is bounded by 4 for any interval no longer than 30. This can be formalised as a specification in DC:

$$\Box_{\mathcal{D}} \, (|i| \leqslant 30 \Rightarrow \int_i Leak(x(t)) \, dt \leqslant 4) \tag{3}$$

where $Leak$ is a predicate denoting whether there is leaking in a state. For simplicity, we rewrite the specification using standard abbreviations:

$$\Box_{\mathcal{D}} \, (\ell \leqslant 30 \Rightarrow \int Leak \leqslant 4)$$

where $\ell \,\hat{=}\, |i|$ and $\int Leak \,\hat{=}\, \int_i Leak(x(t)) \, dt$.

The following two concrete DC specifications form a common design implementing the above abstract specification:

$$\Box_{\mathcal{D}} \, (\lceil Leak \rceil \Rightarrow |i| \leqslant 4) \quad \text{and} \quad \Box_{\mathcal{D}} \, (\lceil Leak \rceil \,\fatsemi\, \lceil \neg Leak \rceil \,\fatsemi\, \lceil Leak \rceil \Rightarrow |i| \geqslant 26) \tag{4}$$

where the real-time function $x(t)$ records the state at the time point t, the specification $\lceil Leak \rceil \,\hat{=}\, (\int Leak = \ell)$ describes a period with gas leak (at "most" time points of in the period [20]), and $\lceil \neg Leak \rceil \,\hat{=}\, (\int Leak = \ell)$ describes a period almost without leak. The first specification requires any leaking period to be bounded by 4 seconds; the second specification states that, during any interval, the period of non-leak between two periods of leak should be no less than 26 seconds. The sequential composition $\,\fatsemi\,$ (also known as the *chop operation*) is the pointwise concatenation of the intervals of specifications:

$$P \,\fatsemi\, Q \,\hat{=}\, \exists i_1 i_2 \cdot (P[i_1/i] \wedge Q[i_2/i] \wedge i = i_1 \! \frown \! i_2).$$

The similarity between the TLA specification (1) and the DC design (4) is obvious. They essentially describe the same controlling strategy. Their link will be captured by a transformer between the two logics.

4   Linking Duration Calculus and TLA

The Transformer from TLA to DC

We now study a technique to link DC specifications with TLA designs. Indeed each timed trace of 0s and 1s determines some real-time Boolean function in $[0, \infty] \to \{0, 1\}$. For example, the timed trace $\langle (1.0, 0), (2.0, 1), (4.0, 0) \rangle$ corresponds to a Boolean real-time function whose value is 0 from time 1.0 to time 2.0 when the value becomes 1 until time 4.0. The state between any two consecutive time points is constant. For example, the DC abstract specification (3) can be implemented with a TLA specification of timed traces (1). The TLA design is arguably more intuitive than (3) in DC alone. Such interpretation of a timed trace also directly corresponds to a timed automaton.

The link between timed-trace TLA and durational calculus can be characterised as a predicate of weak inverse on timed trace $\overline{tr}$, interval i and real-time function $x(\ell)$:

$$T(\overline{tr}, i, x) \ \widehat{=} \ \bigwedge_k (\ell = \int (x = \overline{s}_k) \, /_i \, (i \subseteq [\overline{t}_k, \overline{t}_{k+1}] \cap \overline{i})).$$

Each timed trace determines a real-time function whose value may only change at the time points of the trace. The value between two consecutive time points is "stable" in the sense that the values at "most" time point (except for isolated ones not affecting the integral) during the period are the same. The transformer requires that in any sub-interval segment of the timed trace, the real-time function x matches the stable states generated by the timed trace.

A timed trace may contain arbitrarily-many consecutive state transitions at a single time point. Since the above transformer allows nondeterminism at isolated time points, such zero-time transitions cause no difficulty.

Def 6. $\lozenge_{\mathcal{K} \to \mathcal{D}} P \ \widehat{=} \ P :_{tr} T$ *and* $\square_{\mathcal{D} \to \mathcal{K}} P \ \widehat{=} \ P /_{tr} T$.

It is easy to show that any DC specification transformed from a TLA specification is always sub-interval closed.

Law 4. $\square_{\mathcal{D}} \lozenge_{\mathcal{K} \to \mathcal{D}} P = \lozenge_{\mathcal{K} \to \mathcal{D}} P$.

An automaton can be easily specified using a TLA formula (2). We introduce a notation for DC-specified automata in which $U, V \subseteq [0, \infty]$ are two closed non-empty sets of time points such that the lub and glb of any of their non-empty subsets are contained in them. For example, they can be closed intervals like $[0, 1]$.

Def 7. $\langle U \uparrow p \downarrow V \rangle \ \widehat{=} \ \lozenge_{\mathcal{K} \to \mathcal{D}} Automaton(p, U, V)$.

An automaton is symmetric and monotonic in the sense that reducing the range of timing restrictions leads to the reduction of nondeterminism.

Law 5.   (1) $\langle U \uparrow p \downarrow V \rangle = \langle V \uparrow \neg p \downarrow U \rangle$
              (2) $\langle U \uparrow p \downarrow V \rangle \ \supseteq \ \langle U' \uparrow p \downarrow V' \rangle$ $(U \supseteq U', V \supseteq V')$.

We use ∞ to denote the singleton range $[\infty, \infty]$. Lift and chop operators can then be expressed with special automata. Note that the chop operation implies a certain synchronisation between the system and the observer: the chopping point must always fall in the interval of observation. This is achieved by eliminating the possibility that the chopping point falls out of the observation interval.

Law 6.   (1) $\lceil p \rceil = \langle \infty \uparrow p \downarrow [0, 0] \rangle$
     (2) $\langle \infty \uparrow p \downarrow \infty \rangle = \lceil p \rceil \vee \lceil \neg p \rceil$
     (3) $\lceil p \rceil \, \S \, \lceil \neg p \rceil = \langle [0, \infty] \uparrow p \downarrow \infty \rangle \wedge \neg \langle \infty \uparrow p \downarrow \infty \rangle$.

We use an abbreviation $P \lhd p \rhd Q$ of choice to denote that two durational specifications P and Q are controlled by a boolean p: during any interval in which p is always true, P must hold; during any interval in which $\neg p$ is always true, Q must hold. There is no restriction for those intervals in which p is sometimes true and sometimes not true.

Def 8. $P \lhd p \rhd Q \; \hat{=} \; \lceil p \rceil \Rightarrow P \wedge \lceil \neg p \rceil \Rightarrow Q$.

The following law shows that the chop composition of any two durational specifications can be implemented as a choice between the specifications, and the change of the choice is made sometime during an interval. If p is independent of P and Q and becomes hidden, the two sides will be equal.

Law 7. $P \, \S \, Q \; \supseteq \; P \lhd p \rhd Q \wedge \langle [0, \infty] \uparrow p \downarrow \infty \rangle \wedge \neg \langle \infty \uparrow p \downarrow \infty \rangle$.

General Patterns of Specifications and Their Refinement

A durational specification is a predicate $P(i, x)$ on the interval i and the real-time function $x: [0, \infty] \rightarrow S$. A common durational specification is a predicate $P(\ell, \int p)$ on the length $\ell \hat{=} |i|$ of the interval and the integral of a boolean function p during the interval. This reflects the fact that the controlling of a system is normally independent of the starting time and insensitive to state changes at isolated time points.

A durational specification $\Box_D \int p \leqslant f(\ell)$ requires the total time of the state satisfying p in any interval with length ℓ to be bounded by a *characteristic function* $f(\ell)$. For example, the specification $\Box_D (\ell \leqslant 30 \Rightarrow \int leak \leqslant 4)$ is a special case of this pattern with the characteristic function $f(\ell) \hat{=} 4 \lhd \ell \in [4, 30] \rhd \ell$ where we use $a \lhd b \rhd c$ to denote the value a if b is true, or the value c otherwise. The dual pattern $\Box_D \int p \geqslant g(\ell)$ is equal to $\Box_D \int \neg p \leqslant (\ell - f(\ell))$.

The following law shows that two specifications with different characteristic functions may describe the same requirement.

Law 8. $\Box_D \int p \geqslant f(\ell) = \Box_D \int p \geqslant f'(\ell)$, *if any of the following condition is satisfied* ($\ell, \ell_0, \ell_1 \geqslant 0$):

1. $f'(\ell) = \min(\ell, f(\ell))$,
2. $f'(\ell) = \min \{ f(\ell') \mid \ell' \geqslant \ell \}$,
3. *or* $f'(\ell) = \min \{ f(\ell_0) + f(\ell_1) \mid \ell_0 + \ell_1 = \ell \}$.

Refinement of General Patterns

The durational specification $\langle U \uparrow p \downarrow V \rangle$ describes an automaton with two composite states satisfying p and $\neg p$, respectively. A common durational specification may be implemented with an automaton, if the timed transitions are determined properly. For example, the durational specification of gas burner[16] can be implemented as follows:

$$\Box_{\mathcal{D}} (\ell \leqslant 30 \Rightarrow \int leak \leqslant 4) \supseteq \langle [0,4] \uparrow leak \downarrow [26,\infty] \rangle.$$

In each cycle of the automaton, the designed system must stay in a state satisfying p in no more than 4 seconds and then must stay in a state satisfying $\neg p$ in no less than 26 seconds. Note that the above implementation is not unique. We may easily replace it with an automaton $\langle [0,2] \uparrow leak \downarrow [13,\infty] \rangle$ twice as fast.

The fact that general durational specifications may have different implementations reveals the considerable gap between DC and TLA. The former is more suitable for higher-level specification on continuous properties expressible with integrals, while the latter naturally describes the properties of automata. Not every non-zero durational specification can be implemented as a non-trivial automaton. For example, the specification $\Box_{\mathcal{D}} \int p = \ell/2$ describes a system whose density of states satisfying p is 0.5 everywhere. However, it can not be implemented with any automaton as it does not allow the state to be stable in any short period of time.

The different natures of the two formalisms suggest that we should incorporate both in most parts of the system development. A design process starts from an abstract durational specification, which is refined in a number of steps. In each step, transitional features will be enriched, with durational features reduced. The design process eventually reaches an automaton system without durational features.

A durational specification in the common pattern can be decomposed into two such specifications "driven" by an automaton:

$$\Box_{\mathcal{D}} \int p \leqslant f(\ell) \supseteq (\Box_{\mathcal{D}} \int p \leqslant g(\ell) \vartriangleleft q \vartriangleright \Box_{\mathcal{D}} \int p \leqslant h(\ell)) \wedge \langle U \uparrow q \downarrow V \rangle. \qquad (5)$$

The automaton $\langle U \uparrow q \downarrow V \rangle$ switches between q and $\neg q$ according to the time restrictions U and V. If the automaton is in a state satisfying q, the system behaves like $\Box_{\mathcal{D}} \int p \leqslant g(\ell)$; or if it is in $\neg q$, the system behaves like $\Box_{\mathcal{D}} \int p \leqslant h(\ell)$. Note that the above refinement only holds when the characteristic functions f, g, h and the sets U, V of time points satisfy some constraints, which can now be identified in seperate laws.

We first consider the most general case of refinement. If an automaton switches between two states in exactly a and c seconds respectively, the maximum number of *full* segments contained in an interval of length ℓ is identified as follows:

$$segnum(\ell, a, c) \mathrel{\widehat{=}} \max\{m+n \mid ma+nc < \ell, |m-n| \leqslant 1\}.$$

Since a slower automaton can only produce less segments in an interval, the number $segnum(\ell, \inf U, \inf V)$ has provided the maximum number of segments for a general automaton $\langle U \uparrow q \downarrow V \rangle$. Note that we assume $(\inf U + \inf V) > 0$ and consider only non-Zeno automata. Besides full segments, an interval may include partial segments on both ends. Their lengths are bounded by $\sup U$ or $\sup V$, depending on the state. This is why according to the definition, we have $segnum(a + c, a, c) = 1$ so that the last segment on either end can be regarded as a partial segment. The purpose is to enumerate all possibilities for each interval and ensure that in every case, the right-hand side of (5) refines the left-hand side. In the following laws, we use $a \triangleleft b \triangleright c$ to denote the value a if $b = 1$, or the value c if $b = 0$.

Def 9. *A characteristic function f can be decomposed as two functions g and h under the restrictions of U and V, if $(\inf U + \inf V) > 0$ and for any $t \geqslant 0$ and any $n \leqslant segnum(t, \inf U, \inf V)$ and any $t_0, t_1, \cdots, t_{n+1}$ and $t'_0, t'_1, \cdots, t'_{n+1}$ such that $t_0, t_{n+1} \leqslant \sup U$, $t'_0, t'_{n+1} \leqslant \sup V$, $t_1, \cdots, t_n \in U$ and $t'_1, \cdots, t'_n \in V$, we have: if $\sum_{k=0}^{n+1} (t_k \triangleleft 2 \mid k \triangleright t'_k) = t$ then $\sum_{k=0}^{n+1} (g(t_k) \triangleleft 2 \mid k \triangleright h(t'_k)) \leqslant f(t)$; and if $\sum_{k=0}^{n+1} (t'_k \triangleleft 2 \mid k \triangleright t_k) = t$ then $\sum_{k=0}^{n+1} (h(t'_k) \triangleleft 2 \mid k \triangleright g(t_k)) \leqslant f(t)$.*

Law 9. *If the function f can be decomposed as g and h under the restrictions of U and V, the law (5) holds.*

The following theorem reveals that if g and h are maximally minimised (see Law 8.), then Law 9. is complete.

Theorem 2 (Completeness). *If (5) holds but the function f cannot be decomposed as g and h under the restrictions of U and V, then there exist g' and h' such that $\Box_{\mathcal{D}} \int p \leqslant g(\ell) = \Box_{\mathcal{D}} \int p \leqslant g'(\ell)$ and $\Box_{\mathcal{D}} \int p \leqslant h(\ell) = \Box_{\mathcal{D}} \int p \leqslant h'(\ell)$ and $\Box_{\mathcal{D}} \int p \leqslant f(\ell) \supseteq (\Box_{\mathcal{D}} \int p \leqslant g'(\ell) \triangleleft q \triangleright \Box_{\mathcal{D}} \int p \leqslant h'(\ell)) \wedge \langle U \uparrow q \downarrow V \rangle$, and f can be decomposed as g' and h' under the restrictions of U and V.*

Unfortunately the precondition of the complete law is too complicated to check in practice. We must consider its useful special cases. If the abstract specification is related to only intervals no longer than the sum of the minimum lengths of the two phases, then the precondition of the decomposition can be reduced to a constraint on at most three segments.

Law 10. *If $a + c > 0$, $U = [a, b]$, $V = [c, d]$, $t \leqslant f(t)$ for any $t > a + c$, and for any t, we have $g(t_0) + g(t_1) + h(t_2) \leqslant f(t)$ for any $t_0, t_1 \in [a, b]$ and $t_2 \in [c, d]$ such that $t_0 + t_1 + t_2 = t$, and $h(t_0) + h(t_1) + g(t_2) \leqslant f(t)$ for any $t_0, t_1 \in [c, d]$ and $t_2 \in [a, b]$ such that $t_0 + t_1 + t_2 = t$, then the law (5) holds.*

If the abstract specification is related to only intervals no longer than any phase, then the precondition can be reduced to a constraint on at most two segments.

Law 11. *If $a, c > 0$, $U = [a, b]$, $V = [c, d]$, $t \leqslant f(t)$ for any $t > \min(b, c)$, and for any t, we have $g(t_0) + h(t_1) \leqslant f(t)$ for any $t_0 \in [a, b]$ and $t_1 \in [c, d]$ or $t_0 \in [c, d]$ and $t_1 \in [a, b]$ such that $t_0 + t_1 = t$, then the law (5) holds.*

The above laws introduce an automaton as the structure of refinement and leave the parameters to be decided later. System developers need to determine the parameters according to their own design strategy.

Refinement of Basic Patterns

If the driven specifications are the extreme ones either almost true or almost not true, the refinement laws can be further simplified. For example, the durational specification

$$\Box_{\mathcal{D}} \left(\ell \leqslant A \Rightarrow \int p \leqslant B \right) \tag{6}$$

requires a system not to stay in the a state satisfying p longer than B during any period no longer than A. This is illustrated in Figure 3 (a) as sets of coordinates (t, s) where t denotes ℓ and s denotes $\int p$. We assume that $s \leqslant t$.

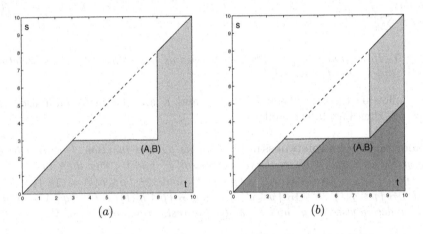

Fig. 3. The basic pattern and its refinement $(b = B/2)$

Such a durational specification is directly implemented with an automaton, instead of being decomposed to a mixture of intermediate specifications.

Law 12. *If* $0 < b \leqslant B$ *and* $c \geqslant \frac{A-B}{\lfloor B/b \rfloor}$, *then*

$$\Box_{\mathcal{D}} \left(\ell \leqslant A \Rightarrow \int p \leqslant B \right) \supseteq \langle [0, b] \uparrow p \downarrow [c, \infty] \rangle .$$

Figure 3(b) illustrates the refinement of the basic patterns. The grey area indicates the requirements, while the dark area (contained in the grey area) illustrates the TLA design.

The following law is a generalisation of Law 12. for general functional restrictions.

Law 13. *If* $\ell \leqslant f(\ell)$ *for any* $\ell \leqslant b$, $f(\ell) > b$ *for any* $\ell > b$, *and* $c \geqslant \sup_{\ell > b} \frac{\ell - f(\ell)}{\lfloor f(\ell)/b \rfloor}$, *then* $\Box_{\mathcal{D}} \int p \leqslant f(\ell) \supseteq \langle [0, b] \uparrow p \downarrow [c, \infty] \rangle .$

5   Case Study: The Gas Burner

The Gas Burner problem was first stated in [16] and has been a standard example of hybrid system design. A gas burner can be in any state of being idle, purging (waiting the leaked gas to disperse), attempting to ignite, monitoring flame when igniting, or burning after successful ignition. There is no leak in idling or purging, but there is always leak in any attempt of ignition before burning. In this paper, we consider a challenging version of the example in which the burning phase may have some leak due to the possibility of disturbance from the environment (see [12]).

The main requirement is to ensure that the total gas leak in every 30 seconds does not exceed 4 seconds. This can be neatly specified in Duration Calculus as follows:

$$\Box_{\mathcal{D}} \left(\ell \leqslant 30 \Rightarrow \int Leak \leqslant 4 \right).$$

Our treatment of this problem consists of several steps of automata decomposition hierarchically. This process may be viewed as "refinement", as each step corresponds to a reduction of nondeterminism. On the other hand, if the target automaton is constructed and model-checked first, the reversed process can be used to establish the link between the checked model and the original specification for verification purposes.

We first decompose the original requirement into burning and non-burning phases generated by a cyclic automaton. For simplicity, we intend to use the 2-segment refinement Law 11. and thus need to construct a slow automaton that takes at least 30 seconds to change state. Since the original specification is in a special form, we need to consider only intervals of length 30 and choose $g(\cdot)$ and $h(\cdot)$ (to characterise the amount of leak) such that for any t_0 and t_1, if $t_0 + t_1 = 30$ $g(t_0) + h(t_1) \leqslant 4$. For convenience, we choose $g(t) \stackrel{\frown}{=} B_1 \lhd t \in [B_1, 30] \rhd \ell$ and $h(t) \stackrel{\frown}{=} B_2 \lhd t \in [B_2, 30] \rhd \ell$. We now obtain our first refinement (illustrated in Figure 5).

$$\Box_{\mathcal{D}} \left(\ell \leqslant 30 \Rightarrow \int Leak \leqslant 4 \right) \sqsupseteq$$
$$\Box_{\mathcal{D}} \left(\ell \leqslant 30 \Rightarrow \int Leak \leqslant B_1 \right) \lhd Burn \rhd \Box_{\mathcal{D}} \left(\ell \leqslant 30 \Rightarrow \int Leak \leqslant B_2 \right)$$
$$\wedge \langle\, [a, \infty] \uparrow Burn \downarrow [b, \infty] \,\rangle$$

where the parameters satisfy the following condition:

Restriction 1. $a \geqslant 30$, $b \geqslant 30$ and $B_1 + B_2 \leqslant 4$.

According to Law 12., the non-burning phase $\Box_{\mathcal{D}} \left(\ell \leqslant 30 \Rightarrow \int Leak \leqslant B_2 \right)$ can be further decomposed to another automaton driven by the first one with leaking and non-leaking phases (illustrated in Figure 5):

$$\Box_{\mathcal{D}} \left(\ell \leqslant 30 \Rightarrow \int Leak \leqslant B_2 \right) \sqsupseteq \langle\, [0, c] \uparrow Leak \downarrow [d, \infty] \,\rangle.$$

where the parameters satisfy the following condition:

Restriction 2. $0 < c \leqslant B_2$ and $d \geqslant \frac{30 - B_2}{\lfloor B_2/c \rfloor}$.

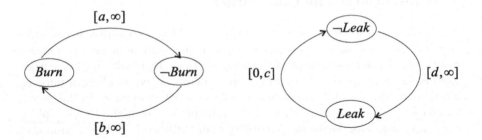

Fig. 4. Design of automata

The two automata run independently. The second automaton only takes effect when the system is not burning. Further refinement of the non-burning phase can be done using standard automaton techniques. For example, the two automata can be combined in one in Figure 5.

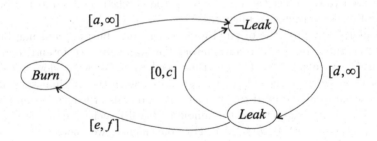

Fig. 5. Combined design

Restriction 3. $e \leqslant B_2$, $e+d \geqslant b$ and $f \leqslant B_2$.

There are many possible solutions to the restrictions. We take the following combination: $a = b = 30$, $B_1 = B_2 = 2$, $c = 2$, $d = 30$, $e = 0$, $f = 2$. Note that we could let d be 28 and then $e = f = 2$, but that means the control of the ignition must be exactly in 2 seconds — a requirement difficult to meet in practice. By extending the purging phase, we allow more flexibility for the ignition. Once an automaton is obtained, the transition restrictions can be strengthened to reduce nondeterminism. For example, the restriction $[d, \infty]$ can be replaced with $[30, 30 + \varepsilon]$ where ε indicates a tolerantable timing inaccuracy.

In the final step, we split the state of non-leaking into idling and purging and the state of leaking into two states of ignition, and restrict the timing nondeterminism to obtain a reasonable design. Again the verification of this step can be conducted in TLA.

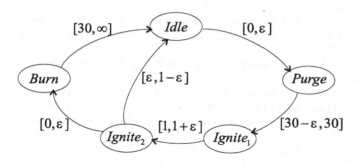

Fig. 6. Combined design

In the above design, the state of burning must be no less than 30 seconds. This additional requirement is introduced by Law 11. and can be avoided if we decided to use Law 10. instead, although this alternative design would generate more complicated restrictions for the parameters.

6   Conclusions

This paper studies a formal framework in which our knowledge about the relationships between different temporal logics can be formalised in the form of algebraic or refinement laws. In the case study on DC and TLA, we have identified refinement laws for several design patterns. Some of the laws are general and cover most types of refinement with a particular target implementation. More specific laws are introduced for the most common patterns, and their parameters can be more readily determined. The technique is applied to the design of gas burner problem. It is not a trivial task to identify general but at the same time practically useful laws. However once such laws are identified, they genuinely make the design process more systematic, especially on the determination of parameters.

The formalism of the framework was first presented at IFM'04. The main focus of this paper is, however, on the relationship between DC and TLA. In particular, the decomposition of durational specifications (into automata) is the main new contribution.

References

1. R. Back and J. von Wright. *Refinement Calculus: A Systematic Introduction.* Graduate Texts in Computer Science. Springer, 1998.
2. P. Blackburn, M. de Rijke, and Y. Venema. *Modal Logic.* Cambridge University Press, 2001.
3. Y. Chen. Generic composition. *Formal Aspects of Computing*, 14(2):108–122, 2002.
4. Y. Chen. Cumulative computing. In *19th Conference on the Mathematical Foundations of Programming Semantics*, volume 38 of *Electronic Notes in Theoretical Computer Science*. Elsevier, 2004.

5. Y. Chen and Z. Liu. Integrating temporal logics. In *4nd International Conference on Integrated Formal Methods*, volume 2999 of *LNCS*, pages 402–420. Springer-Verlag, 2004.
6. E.C.R. Hehner. Predicative programming I, II. *Communications of ACM*, 27(2):134–151, 1984.
7. C. A. R. Hoare. *Communicating Sequential Processes*. Prentice Hall, 1985.
8. C. A. R. Hoare and J. He. *Unifying Theories of Programming*. Prentice Hall, 1998.
9. S. Kripke. Semantical considerations on modal logic. *Acta Philosophica Fennica*, 16:83–94, 1963.
10. L. Lamport. Hybrid systems in TLA+. In *Hybrid Systems*, volume 736 of *LNCS*, pages 77–102. Springer-Verlag, 1993.
11. L. Lamport. A temporal logic of actions. *ACM Transctions on Programming Languages and Systems*, 16(3):872–923, 1994.
12. Z. Liu, A. P. Ravn, and X. Li. Unifying proof methodologies of duration calculus and linear temporal logic. Technical Report 1999/14, Department of Maths and Computer Science, University of Leicester, July 1999. To appear in *Formal Aspects of Computing* (19 pages).
13. C.C. Morgan. The cuppest capjunctive capping, and Galois. In A. W. Roscoe, editor, *A Classical Mind*, pages 317–332. Prentice Hall, 1994.
14. A. Pnueli. The temporal semantics of concurrent programs. *Theoretical Computer Science*, 13:45–60, 1981.
15. A. Pnueli and E. Harel. Applications of temporal logic to the specification of real-time systems. In M. Joseph, editor, *Formal Techniques in Real-Time and Fault-Tolerant Systems, Lecture Notes in Computer Science 331*, pages 84–98. Springer-Verlag, 1988.
16. A.P. Ravn, H. Rischel, and K.M. Hansen. Specifying and verifying requirements of real-time systems. *IEEE Transactions on Software Engineering*, 19(1):41–55, 1993.
17. M. Schenke and E. Olderog. Transformational design of real-time systems part I: From requirements to program specifications. *Acta Informatica*, 36(1):1–65, 1999.
18. H. Shalqvist. Completeness and correspondence in the first and second order semantics for modal logic. In *Proceedings of the third Scandinavian logic symposium*, pages 110–143. North Holland, 1975.
19. B. von Karger. A calculational approach to reactive systems. *Science of Computer Programming*, 37:139–161, 2000.
20. C. Zhou, C. A. R. Hoare, and A. P. Ravn. A calculus of durations. *Information Processing Letters*, 40(5):269–276, 1991.
21. C.C. Zhou, A.P. Ravn, and M.R. Hansen. An extended duration calculus for hybrid real-time systems. In R.L. Grossman, A. Nerode, A.P. Ravn, and H. Rischel, editors, *Hybrid Systems, Lecture Notes in Computer Science 736*, pages 36–59. Springer-Verlag, 1993.

Timed Patterns: TCOZ to Timed Automata

Jin Song Dong[1], Ping Hao[*,1], Sheng Chao Qin[1], Jun Sun[1], and Wang Yi[2]

[1] National University of Singapore
{dongjs,haoping,qinsc,sunj}@comp.nus.edu.sg
[2] Uppsala University, Sweden
yi@docs.uu.se

Abstract. The integrated logic-based modeling language, Timed Communicating Object Z (TCOZ), is well suited for presenting complete and coherent requirement models for complex real-time systems. However, the challenge is how to verify the TCOZ models with tool support, especially for analyzing timing properties. Specialized graph-based modeling technique, Timed Automata (TA), has powerful mechanisms for designing real-time models using multiple clocks and has well developed automatic tool support. One weakness of TA is the lack of high level composable graphical patterns to support systematic designs for complex systems. The investigation of possible links between TCOZ and TA may benefit both techniques. For TCOZ, TA's tool support can be reused to check timing properties. For TA, a set of composable graphical patterns can be defined based on the semantics of the TCOZ constructs, so that those patterns can be re-used in a generic way. This paper firstly defines the composable TA graphical patterns, and then presents sound transformation rules and a tool for projecting TCOZ specifications into TA. A case study of a railroad crossing system is demonstrated.

Keywords: Modeling and specification formalisms.

1 Introduction

The specification of complex real-time systems requires powerful mechanisms for modeling state, concurrency and real-time behavior. Integrated formal methods (IFM) are well suited for presenting complete and coherent requirement models for complex systems. An important research agenda in IFM is the combination of Z/Object-Z [6] with CSP/TCSP [13] such as Timed Communicating Object Z (TCOZ) [9], Circus [16] and Object-Z + CSP [14]. However, the challenge is how to analyze and verify these models with tool support. We believe one effective approach is to project the integrated requirement models into multiple domains so that existing specialized tools in these corresponding domains can be utilized to perform the checking and analyzing tasks.

TCOZ is an integrated formal specification language which builds on the strengths of the Object-Z and TCSP notations for modeling both the state, process and timing

---

* Author for correspondence: haoping@comp.nus.edu.sg

J. Davies et al. (Eds.): ICFEM 2004, LNCS 3308, pp. 483–498, 2004.
© Springer-Verlag Berlin Heidelberg 2004

aspects of complex systems. Rather than to develop a single tool support for TCOZ from scratch, we believe a better approach is to reuse existing tools. The specialized graph-based modeling technique, Timed Automata (TA) [1], is powerful in designing real-time models with multiple clocks and has well developed automatic tool support i.e., KRONOS [4] and UPPAAL [2]. However, one weakness of TA is the lack of high level composable graphical patterns to support systematic designs for complex real-time systems. The investigation of possible links between TCOZ and TA may be beneficial to both techniques. For TCOZ, TA's tool support can be reused to check real-time constraints. For TA, a set of composable graphical patterns can be defined based on the semantics of the TCOZ constructs so that those patterns can be used as a generic framework for developing complex TA design models.

This paper is organized as follows. Section 2 introduces TCOZ and Timed Automata. Section 3 presents a set of composable TA patterns with their formal definitions (specified in Z). Section 4 presents the transformation rules with their correctness proof and a Java tool for projecting TCOZ (in XML format) to TA (also in XML of UPPAAL). Section 5 conducts a case study of a railroad crossing system. The last section gives the conclusion.

2   TCOZ and TA

2.1   TCOZ

TCOZ is essentially a blending of Object-Z with TCSP, for the most part preserving them as proper sub-languages of the blended notation. The essence of this blending is the identification of Object-Z operation specification schemas with terminating CSP [12] processes. Thus operation schemas and CSP processes occupy the same syntactic and semantic category; operation schema expressions can appear wherever processes appear in CSP and CSP process definitions can appear wherever operation definitions appear in Object-Z. In this section we briefly consider various aspects of TCOZ. A detailed introduction to TCOZ and its TCSP and Object-Z features may be found elsewhere [9]. The formal semantics of TCOZ (presented in Z) is also documented [10].

Timing and Channels: In TCOZ, all timing information is represented as real valued measurements. TCOZ adopts all TCSP timing operators, for instance, *timeout* and *wait*. In order to describe the timing requirements of operations and sequences of operations, a deadline command has been introduced. If *OP* is an operation specification (defined through any combination of CSP process primitives and Object-Z operation schemas) then *OP* • DEADLINE *t* describes the process which has the same effect as *OP*, but is constrained to terminate no later than *t* (relative time). If it cannot terminate by time *t*, it deadlocks. The WAITUNTIL operator is a dual to the deadline operator. The process *OP* • WAITUNTIL *t* performs *OP*, but will not terminate until at least time *t*. In this paper, when the term TCOZ timing constructs is mentioned, it means TCSP constructs with extensions, i.e., DEADLINE and WAITUNTIL.

CSP channels are given an independent, first class role in TCOZ. In order to support the role of CSP channels, the state schema convention is extended to allow the declaration of communication channels. Contrary to the conventions adopted for internal state attributes, channels are viewed as shared (global) rather than as encapsulated entities. This is an essential consequence of their role as communication interfaces *between* objects. The introduction of channels to TCOZ reduces the need to reference other classes in class definitions, thereby enhancing the modularity of system specifications.

Active Objects and Semantics: Active objects have their own thread of control, while passive objects are controlled by other objects in a system. In TCOZ, an identifier MAIN (non-terminating process) is used to determine the behavior of active objects of a given class. The MAIN operation is optional in a class definition. It only appears in a class definition when the objects of that class are active objects. Classes for defining passive objects will not have the MAIN definition, but may contain CSP process constructors. If ob_1 and ob_2 are active objects of the class C, then the independent parallel composition behavior of the two objects can be represented as $ob_1 \;|||\; ob_2$, which means $ob_1.$MAIN $|||$ $ob_2.$MAIN.

The details of the blended state/event process model forms the basis for the TCOZ denotational semantics [10]. In brief, the semantic approach identifies the notions of operation and process by providing a process interpretation of the Z operation schema construct. Operation schemas are modeled by the collection of those sequences of update events that achieve the state change described by the schema. This means that there is no semantic difference between a Z operation schema and a CSP process. It therefore makes sense to also identify their syntactic classes.

A Railroad Crossing Gate Example: The use of TCOZ is illustrated by a railroad crossing gate class as following (later a case study on this system will be conducted). The essential behaviors of this railroad crossing gate are to open and close itself according to its external commands (events) *up* and *down*. A free type *GateS* is used to capture the status of a gate:

$$GateS ::= ToUp \mid Up \mid ToDn \mid Down$$

┌─ *Gate* ──
│ ┌──────────────────────────┐ ┌─ *Init* ─────────────
│ │ *status* : *GateS*   │ │ *status* = *Up*
│ │ *up*, *down* : **chan**   │ └──────────────────────
│ └──────────────────────────┘ ┌─ *Raise* ────────────
│ ┌─ *Lower* ─────────────────┐ │ $\Delta(status)$
│ │ $\Delta(status)$ │ │ ──────────────────
│ │ ──────────────────   │ │ $status' = ToUp$
│ │ $status' = ToDn$ │ └──────────────────────
│ └──────────────────────────┘ ┌─ *Up* ───────────────
│ ┌─ *Down* ──────────────────┐ │ $\Delta(status)$
│ │ $\Delta(status)$ │ │ ──────────────────
│ │ ──────────────────   │ │ $status' = Up$
│ │ $status' = Down$ │ └──────────────────────
│ └──────────────────────────┘
│
│ *Open* $\widehat{=}$ *up* $\rightarrow$ (*Raise* • WAITUNTIL 1; *Up*) • DEADLINE 2
│ *Close* $\widehat{=}$ *down* $\rightarrow$ *Lower* • DEADLINE 1; *Down*
│ MAIN $\widehat{=}$ $\mu\, G$ • *Close*; *Open*; *G*
└───

The interface of the *gate* class is defined through channels *up* and *down*. The DEADLINE and WAITUNTIL expressions are used here to capture its timing properties, which constrain that the gate takes less than 1 time unit to come down and between 1 and 2 time units to come up.

2.2   Timed Automata

Timed Automata [1, 3] are finite state machines with clocks. It was introduced as a formal notation to model the behavior of real-time systems. Its definition provides a general way to annotate state-transition graphs with timing constraints using finitely many real-valued clock variables. The set of clock constraints $\Phi(X)$ is defined by the following grammar:

$$\varphi := x \leq c \mid c \leq x \mid x < c \mid c < x \mid \varphi_1 \wedge \varphi_2$$

A timed automaton A is a tuple $(S, S_0, \Sigma, X, I, E)$, where S is a finite set of states; S_0 is a set of initial states and a subset of S; Σ is a set of actions/events; X is a finite set of clocks; I is a mapping that labels each location s in S with some clock constraint in $\Phi(X)$; E, a subset of $S \times S \times \Sigma \times 2^X \times \Phi(X)$, is the set of switches. A switch $\langle s, s', a, \lambda, \delta \rangle$ represents a transition from state s to state s' on input symbol a. The set λ gives the clocks to be reset with this transition, and δ is a clock constraint over X that specifies when the switch is enabled.

For example, the railroad crossing gate can be designed in Figure 1. The gate is open in state *Up* and closed in state *Down*. It communicates with its controller through the events *up* and *down*. The states *ToUp* and *ToDown* denote the opening and the closing of the gate. The gate responds to the event *down* by closing within 1 time unit, and responds to the event *up* within 1 to 2 time units.

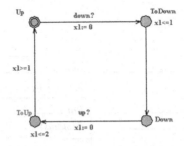

Fig. 1. The gate automaton

UPPAAL. UPPAAL [2] is a tool for modeling, simulation and verification of real-time systems. It consists of three main parts: a system editor, a simulator and a model checker. The system editor provides a graphical interface of the tool, to allow easier maintenance. Its output is an XML representation of time automatons. The simulator is a validation tool which enables examination of possible dynamic executions of a system during early design (or modeling) stages and thus provides an inexpensive mean of fault detection prior to verification by the model checker which covers the exhaustive dynamic behavior of the system. The model checker is to check invariant and bounded liveness properties by exploring the symbolic state space of a system. UPPAAL is appropriate for systems that can be modeled as a collection of non-deterministic processes with finite control structure and real-valued clocks, communicating through channels or shared variables. Typical application areas include real-time controllers and communication protocols in particular, those where timing aspects are critical.

3   Composable TA Patterns

High level real-time system requirements often need to state the system timing constraints in terms of *deadline, timeout, waituntil* and etc which can be regarded as common timing constraint patterns. For example, "task A must complete within t time period" is a typical one (*deadline*). TCOZ is a good candidate for specifying the requirements of complex real-time systems because it has the composable language constructs that directly capture those common timing patterns. On the other hand, if TA is considered to be used to capture real-time requirements, then one often need to manually cast those timing patterns into a set of clock variables with carefully calculated clock constraints, which is a process that is very much towards design rather than specification. One interesting question is the following: Can we build a set of TA patterns that correspond to the TCOZ timing constructs? If such a set of TA patterns can be formulated, then not only the transformation from TCOZ to TA can be readily achieved (one objective of this paper), but also TA can sysmatically capture high level requirements by utilizing those composable TA patterns.

Since the current semantics of TCOZ [10] is specified in Z, we define a set of composable TA patterns also in the same meta notation Z. First of all, we give the definition of TA in Z as follows.

$$[\mathbb{T}, State, Event, Clock]$$
$$\Phi ::= (\_ \leq \_)\langle\!\langle Clock \times \mathbb{T}\rangle\!\rangle \mid (\_ \geq \_)\langle\!\langle Clock \times \mathbb{T}\rangle\!\rangle \mid$$
$$\quad (\_ < \_)\langle\!\langle Clock \times \mathbb{T}\rangle\!\rangle \mid (\_ > \_)\langle\!\langle Clock \times \mathbb{T}\rangle\!\rangle \mid$$
$$\quad (\_ \wedge \_)\langle\!\langle \Phi \times \Phi\rangle\!\rangle \mid true$$
$$Transition \mathrel{\widehat{=}} State \times Label \times State$$
$$Label \mathrel{\widehat{=}} \mathbb{P}\, Event \times \mathbb{P}\, Clock \times \Phi$$

$\mathcal{S}_{TA}$
___
$S : \mathbb{P}\, State;\quad i, e : State$
$I : State \nrightarrow \Phi$
$T : \mathbb{P}\, Transition$

$i, e \in S \wedge \operatorname{dom} I = S$
$\forall s, s' : state;\ l : label \bullet (s, l, s') \in T \Rightarrow s, s' \in S$

There are four basic types, i.e., $\mathbb{T}$, *State*, *Event*, and *Clock*, in which $\mathbb{T}$ is the set of positive real numbers; Φ defines the types of clock constraints, in which a *true* type is added to represent the empty clock constraints; *Label* models transition conditions, in which $\mathbb{P}\,Event$ is a set of enabling events, and $\mathbb{P}\,Clock$ gives a set of clocks to be reset, and Φ specifies clock constraints. $\mathcal{S}_{TA}$ defines a timed automaton, in which i and e represent its initial states and terminal states respectively; I defines local clock invariants on states; and T models transitions.

   Some TA patterns together with their formal definitions in Z are presented in Figure 2 - Figure 5, the rest can be found in the technical report [5]. In these graphical TA patterns, an automaton A is abstracted as a triangle, the left vertex of this triangle or a circle attached to the left vertex represents the initial state of A, and the right edge represents the terminal state of A. For example, Figure 2 demonstrates how two sequential timed automatons A_1, A_2 can be composed together. By linking the terminal state of A_1 with the initial state of A_2, the resultant automaton passes control from A_1 to A_2 when A_1 goes to its terminal state. Figure 3 shows one of the common timing constraint patterns – *deadline*. There is a single clock x. When the system switches to the automaton A, the clock x gets reset to 0. The local invariant $x <= t$ covers each state of the timed automaton A and specifies the requirement that a switch must occur before t time unit for every state of A. Thus the timing constraint expressed by this automaton is that A should terminate no later than t time units.

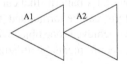

Fig. 2. Sequential Composition

$$seqcom : \mathcal{S}_{TA} \times \mathcal{S}_{TA} \to \mathcal{S}_{TA}$$

$\forall A_1, A_2 : \mathcal{S}_{TA} \bullet$
$\quad seqcom(A_1, A_2) = ($
$\quad S \cong A_1.S \cup A_2.S,$
$\quad i \cong A_1.i, e \cong A_2.e, I \cong A_1.I \cup A_2.I,$
$\quad T \cong A_1.T \cup A_2.T \cup \{(A_1.e, (\tau, \varnothing,$
$\quad\quad true), A_2.i)\})$

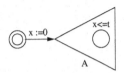

Fig. 3. Deadline

$$deadline : \mathcal{S}_{TA} \times \mathbb{T} \to \mathcal{S}_{TA}$$

$\forall A : \mathcal{S}_{TA}; \ t : \mathbb{T}; \ \exists x : Clock; \ i_0 : State \bullet$
$\quad deadline(A, t) = ($
$\quad S \cong A.S \cup \{i_0\}, i \cong i_0, e \cong A.e,$
$\quad I \cong \{s : A.S \bullet (s, x <= t \wedge A.I(s))\},$
$\quad T \cong A.T \cup \{(i, (\tau, \{x\}, true), A.i)\})$

   These timed composable patterns can be seen as a reusable high level library that may facilitate a systematic engineering process when TA is used to design the timed systems. Furthermore, these patterns provide an interchange media for transforming TCOZ specifications into TA designs.

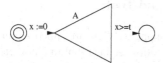

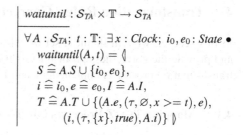

Fig. 4. Waituntil

$$waituntil : S_{TA} \times \mathbb{T} \rightarrow S_{TA}$$

$\forall A : S_{TA};\ t : \mathbb{T};\ \exists x : Clock;\ i_0, e_0 : State\ \bullet$
$waituntil(A, t) = ($
$\quad S \mathrel{\widehat{=}} A.S \cup \{i_0, e_0\},$
$\quad i \mathrel{\widehat{=}} i_0, e \mathrel{\widehat{=}} e_0, I \mathrel{\widehat{=}} A.I,$
$\quad T \mathrel{\widehat{=}} A.T \cup \{(A.e, (\tau, \varnothing, x >= t), e),$
$\qquad\qquad (i, (\tau, \{x\}, true), A.i)\}\ )$

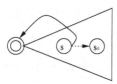

Fig. 5. Recursion

$$recursion : S_{TA} \times State \rightarrow S_{TA}$$

$\forall A : S_{TA};\ s_0 : State \mid s_0 \in A.S\ \bullet$
$recursion(A, s_0) = ($
$\quad S \mathrel{\widehat{=}} A.S, i \mathrel{\widehat{=}} A.i, e \mathrel{\widehat{=}} A.e, I \mathrel{\widehat{=}} A.I,$
$\quad T \mathrel{\widehat{=}} \{s : State, l : Label \mid (s, l, s_0) \in A.T$
$\quad \bullet (s, l, i)\} \cup A.T - \{s : State,$
$\quad l : Label \mid (s, l, s_0) \in A.T \bullet (s, l, s_0)\}\ )$

Composing TA Patterns

New patterns can be composed from the existing ones. For example, given a specification "Task A' is repeated every t_0 time units provided that A' is guaranteed to terminate before t_0 time unit", obviously, the TA model of this specification can be seen as a new pattern which can be composed by three existing patterns - *deadline*, *waituntil* and *recursion*, as shown in Figure 6, in which clock x is used to give time constraints for both the *deadline* pattern and the *waituntil* pattern, assuming A is the automaton equivalent to the TCOZ process A'.

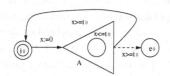

Fig. 6. Periodic Repeat

$$PeriodicRepeat : S_{TA} \times \mathbb{T} \rightarrow S_{TA}$$

$\forall A, A_0 : S_{TA};\ t_0 : \mathbb{T};\ e_0 : State \mid e_0 = A_0.e$
$\quad \wedge A_0 = waituntil(deadline(A, t_0), t_0)\ \bullet$
$\quad PeriodicRepeat(A, t_0) = recursion(A_0, e_0)$

According to the definition of *deadline*, *waituntil* and *recursion* patterns, the resultant automaton can be derived as follows:

$\mathcal{A}(P) = PeriodicRepeat(A, t_0) = ($
$\quad S \mathrel{\widehat{=}} A.S \cup \{i_0, e_0\}, i \mathrel{\widehat{=}} i_0, e \mathrel{\widehat{=}} e_0,$
$\quad I \mathrel{\widehat{=}} \{s : A.S \bullet (s, x <= t_0 \wedge A.I(s))\},$
$\quad T \mathrel{\widehat{=}} \{(i, (\tau, \{x\}, true), A.i)\} \cup \{A.e, (\tau, \varnothing, x >= t_0), i)\} \cup A.T - \{A.e, (\tau, \varnothing,$
$\qquad x >= t_0), e_0)\}\ )$

4   Transformation Rules, Correctness and Tool

In this section, we will define a set of rules for mapping TCOZ to Timed Automata and provide the correctness proof for this transformation. A Java tool to automate the transformation process is implemented and illustrated.

4.1   Mapping TCOZ Processes into TA Patterns

Since the timed composable patterns are defined according to TCOZ process constructs, the transformation rules are straightforward:

Definition 1. *We define the mapping function $\mathcal{A}$ from TCOZ processes to TA as follows.*

- *If $P = $ SKIP, then $\mathcal{A}(P) = \langle\!\langle S \mathrel{\hat{=}} \{i_0, e_0\}, i \mathrel{\hat{=}} i_0, e \mathrel{\hat{=}} e_0, I \mathrel{\hat{=}} \varnothing, T \mathrel{\hat{=}} \{(i, (\tau, \varnothing, true),$ $e)\} \rangle\!\rangle$*
- *If $P = $ STOP, then $\mathcal{A}(P) = \langle\!\langle S \mathrel{\hat{=}} \{i_0, e_0\}, i \mathrel{\hat{=}} i_0, e \mathrel{\hat{=}} e_0, I \mathrel{\hat{=}} \varnothing, T \mathrel{\hat{=}} \varnothing \rangle\!\rangle$*
- *If $P = a@t \rightarrow P_0$, then $\mathcal{A}(P) = tprefix(a, t, \mathcal{A}(P_0))$*
- *If $P = P_0 \bullet $ DEADLINE t, then $\mathcal{A}(P) = deadline(\mathcal{A}(P_0), t)$*
- *If $P = P_0 \bullet $ WAITUNTIL t, then $\mathcal{A}(P) = waituntil(\mathcal{A}(P_0), t)$*
- *If $P = $ WAIT t, then $\mathcal{A}(P) = wait(t)$*
- *If $P = P_1 \{t\} P_2$, then $\mathcal{A}(P) = timeout(\mathcal{A}(P_1), \mathcal{A}(P_2), t)$*
- *If $P = P_1 \triangledown\{t\} P_2$, then $\mathcal{A}(P) = tinterrupt(\mathcal{A}(P_1), \mathcal{A}(P_2), t)$*
- *If $P = \mu N \bullet P(N)$, then $\mathcal{A}(P) = recursion(\mathcal{A}(P(N)), N)$*
- *If $P = P_1; P_2$, then $\mathcal{A}(P) = seqcom(\mathcal{A}(P_1), \mathcal{A}(P_2))$*
- *If $P = P_1 \sqcap P_2$, then $\mathcal{A}(P) = intchoice(\mathcal{A}(P_1), \mathcal{A}(P_2))$*
- *If $P = P_1 \square P_2$, then $\mathcal{A}(P) = extchoice(\mathcal{A}(P_1), \mathcal{A}(P_2))$*
- *If $P = P_1 \|[X]\| P_2$, then $\mathcal{A}(P) = \mathcal{A}(P_1) \parallel \mathcal{A}(P_2)$*

In these mapping rules, channels, events and guards in a TCOZ model are viewed as triggers which cause the state transitions. They match the definition of actions and timed constraints in Timed Automata, thus, they are directly projected as transition conditions. Note that UPPAAL also adopts channels as its synchronization mechanism for the interaction between automatons, which is equivalent to the approach taken in TCOZ. Clock variables will be generated in the target automaton to guard its transition if the process of TCOZ to be translated has any timing constraints such as the DEADLINE. For example, the translation rule on the DEADLINE primitive, $P_0 \bullet $ DEADLINE t describes the process which has the same effect as P_0, but is constrained to terminate no later than t.

The above rules apply to all the TCOZ time primitives and its basic composition of events, guards and processes, through which all the important dynamic information with time constraints in TCOZ specification can be completely translated into timed automata. The following provides the transformation rules for TCOZ classes/ objects:

- In UPPAAL, every object is represented by an automaton. To fully represent behaviors of all the instances of a class, every instance (object) of a TCOZ class is projected as a timed automaton.

- The *INIT* schema in TCOZ class is used to appoint one of those identified states to be an initial state. It will not be projected as a new state because it does not trigger any transition.
- Each operation schema in a TCOZ class is projected as an atomic state in its associated automaton instead of a triangle.

4.2 Correctness

This subsection is devoted to the soundness proofs for our mapping rules from TCOZ processes to structuralized Timed Automata. We shall prove that any source process in TCOZ and its corresponding target Timed Automaton preserve the same semantics under a bisimulation equivalence relation.

The operational semantics for TCOZ processes is captured by the labelled transition system (LTS)

$$TS_{\mathrm{TCOZ}}^1 \cong (\mathcal{C}, \Sigma^\tau \cup \mathbb{T}, \longrightarrow_1)$$

where $\mathcal{C} \cong \mathcal{P} \times \mathbb{T}$ is the set of configurations. A configuration $c = \langle P, t \rangle$ comprising process P and time t denotes a state in the transition system. Σ^τ is the set of possible communication events including the silent event τ. While $\longrightarrow_1 \subseteq (\mathcal{C} \times (\Sigma^\tau \cup \mathbb{T}) \times \mathcal{C})$ is the set of transitions. The operational rules are given in our technical report [5].

In order to derive observable behaviors of TCOZ processes, we define a new abstract transition system as follows:

$$TS_{\mathrm{TCOZ}}^2 \cong (\mathcal{C}, \Sigma \cup \mathbb{T}, \Longrightarrow_1)$$

Note that the set of configurations remains the same as that in TS_{TCOZ}^1, but the transition relation abstracts away from internal actions. That is, for any states c, c',

$$c \stackrel{a}{\Longrightarrow}_1 c' \cong \exists c_1, c_2 \cdot c \stackrel{\tau}{\longrightarrow}_1^* c_1 \stackrel{a}{\longrightarrow}_1 c_2 \stackrel{\tau}{\longrightarrow}_1^* c'$$
$$c \stackrel{\delta}{\Longrightarrow}_1 c' \cong \exists c_1, c_2 \cdot c \stackrel{\tau}{\longrightarrow}_1^* c_1 \stackrel{\delta}{\longrightarrow}_1 c_2 \stackrel{\tau}{\longrightarrow}_1^* c'$$

where the relation $\stackrel{\tau}{\longrightarrow}_1^*$ is the sequential composition of zero or finite number of $\stackrel{\tau}{\longrightarrow}_1$.

Now we construct an abstract transition system for our target formalism, Timed Automata. A "normal" transition system associated with timed automata ([1, 3]) can be

$$TS_{\mathrm{TA}}^1 \cong (\mathcal{S}, s_0, \Sigma^\tau \cup \mathbb{T}, \longrightarrow_2)$$

Notice that $\mathcal{S} \cong S \times V$ denotes all possible states of the transition system. Each state is composed of a state of the timed automaton and a clock valuation (interpretation). The initial state $s_0 = \langle i, v_0 \rangle$ comprises the initial state i and a zero valuation v_0. While the set $\longrightarrow_2 \subseteq \mathcal{S} \times (\Sigma^\tau \cup \mathbb{T}) \times \mathcal{S}$ comprises two kinds of transitions: a time passing move or an action move (Please refer to [5] for more details).

Based on TS_{TA}^1, a new abstract transition system is defined as follows.

$$TS_{\mathrm{TA}}^2 \mathrel{\hat{=}} (\mathcal{S}, s_0, \Sigma \cup \mathbb{T}, \Longrightarrow_2)$$

The only difference from TS_{TA}^1 lies in the transition relation $\Longrightarrow_2 \subseteq \mathcal{S} \times (\Sigma \cup \mathbb{T}) \times \mathcal{S}$, which abstracts away from all internal (τ) actions. That is, for states s, s',

$$s \overset{a}{\Longrightarrow}_2 s' \mathrel{\hat{=}} \exists s_1, s_2 \cdot s \overset{\tau}{\longrightarrow}_2^* s_1 \overset{a}{\longrightarrow}_2 s_2 \overset{\tau}{\longrightarrow}_2^* s'$$
$$s \overset{\delta}{\Longrightarrow}_2 s' \mathrel{\hat{=}} \exists s_1, s_2 \cdot s \overset{\tau}{\longrightarrow}_2^* s_1 \overset{\delta}{\longrightarrow}_2 s_2 \overset{\tau}{\longrightarrow}_2^* s'$$

Now we define a bisimular relation between TS_{TCOZ}^2 and TS_{TA}^2 as below:

Definition 2 (Bisimulation). *The relation $\approx \subseteq \mathcal{C} \times \mathcal{S}$ between states of TS_{TCOZ}^2 and states of TS_{TA}^2 is defined as follows, for any $c \in \mathcal{C}$ and $s \in \mathcal{S}$, $c \approx s$ if and only if the following conditions hold:*
(1) $c \overset{\alpha}{\Longrightarrow}_1 c'$ implies there exists s' such that $s \overset{\alpha}{\Longrightarrow}_2 s'$, and $c' \approx s'$;
(2) $s \overset{\alpha}{\Longrightarrow}_2 s'$ implies there exists c' such that $c \overset{\alpha}{\Longrightarrow}_1 c'$, and $c' \approx s'$.

The following theorem shows that our mapping rules preserve the bisimulation relation between the source and target transition systems. Since the two transition systems employ the same set of observable actions (events), the theorem thus demonstrates that each source TCOZ process and its corresponding target timed automaton are semantically equivalent under the bisimulation relation.

Theorem 1 (Correctness). *For any TCOZ process P and its corresponding timed automaton $\mathcal{A}(P)$, $\langle P, t \rangle \approx \langle i, v_0 \rangle$ for some t, where i is the initial state of $\mathcal{A}(P)$, v_0 is the zero valuation.*

Proof. By structural induction on process P.

– $P = \textsc{Skip}$, or $P = \textsc{Stop}$. The proof is trivial.
– $P = \textsc{Wait}\, t_0$. We know $\mathcal{A}(P) = wait(t_0)$. We show the condition (1) holds in Definition 2. The condition (2) can be demonstrated similarly. The process P can perform a time passing move (δ). The automaton $wait(t_0)$ can also advance a corresponding δ-step.
  If $\delta < t_0$, $\langle P, t \rangle$ moves to $\langle \textsc{Wait}(t_0 - \delta), t + \delta \rangle$, while $\langle i, v_0 \rangle$ moves to $\langle w_0, v_0 + \delta \rangle$. By hypothesis, we know $\langle \textsc{Wait}(t_0 - \delta), t + \delta \rangle \approx \langle w_0, v_0 + \delta \rangle$.
  If $\delta = t_0$, both $\langle P, t \rangle$ and $\langle i, v_0 \rangle$ moves to their terminal states and preserve the bisimulation as well.
– Other cases are presented in the report [5] due to space constraints.   □

4.3 Implementation

The translation process can be automated by employing XML/XSL technology. In our previous work [15], the syntax of Z family languages, i.e., Z/Object-Z/TCOZ, has been defined using XML Schema and supported by the ZML tool. As the UPPAAL tool can read an XML representation of Timed Automata, the automatic projection of the TCOZ model (in ZML) to TA model (in UPPAAL XML) can be developed as a tool in Java.

The tool takes in a TCOZ specification represented in XML, and outputs an XML representation of a Timed Automata specification which has its own defined style file DTD by UPPAAL. The transformation is achieved firstly by implementing a ZML parser, which will take in a ZML specification and build a virtual model of the system in the memory. A TA interface is then built according to the UPPAAL document structure, e.g. each TA document contains multiple templates and each template contains some states, their transitions and transition conditions. A transformation module is built to get information from the ZML parser, apply the right transformation rule and feed the outcome of the transformation to the TA interface. Note that TCOZ process expression can be defined recursively, i.e, a process expression may contain one or more other process expressions, our transformation modules are built to take care of all valid TCOZ specifications and the transformation rules are applied recursively. The outcome of our transformation tool is UPPAAL's XML representation of TA, which is ready to be taken as input for verification and simulation.

5   Case Study: Railroad Crossing System

In this section, we will use a Railroad Crossing System (RCS) specified in TCOZ as a driving example to illustrate our approach to model-checking TCOZ models of real-time systems. The concept of the Railroad Crossing Problem was primarily evolved by Heitmeyer [7] and used as a case study in many formal systems. It is a system which operates a gate at a railroad crossing safely. Based on the above features, we define some assumptions and constraints as follows:

1. The train sends a signal to the controller at least 3 time units before it enters the crossing, stays there no more than 2 time units and sends another signal to the controller upon exiting the crossing.
2. The controller commands the gate to lower exactly 1 time unit after it has received the approaching signal from the train and commands the gate to rise again no more than 1 time unit after receiving the exiting signal.
3. The gate takes less than 1 time unit to come down and between 1 and 2 time units to come up.

5.1   TCOZ Model of RCS

According to the requirement description, an RCS consists of three components: a central controller, a train, and a gate to control the traffic. The basic types for the status of the train and controller are defined as follows:

$TrainS ::= ToIn \mid In \mid Out$
$ControllerS ::= TrIn \mid TrOut \mid GtClose \mid GtOpen$

The TCOZ specification of *Gate* class has been presented in Section 2, the following provides the formal specification of *Train* and *Controller* class.

Train: The basic behavior of the train component is to communicate with controller with its passing information.

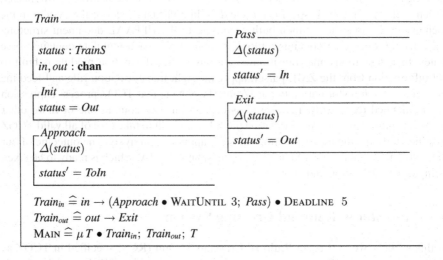

Train
_____

| status : TrainS |
| in, out : **chan** |

Pass
_____
$\Delta(status)$

$status' = In$

Init
_____
$status = Out$

Exit
_____
$\Delta(status)$

$status' = Out$

Approach
_____
$\Delta(status)$

$status' = ToIn$

$Train_{in} \hat{=} in \rightarrow (Approach \bullet \text{WaitUntil } 3; \; Pass) \bullet \text{Deadline } 5$
$Train_{out} \hat{=} out \rightarrow Exit$
$\text{Main} \hat{=} \mu T \bullet Train_{in}; \; Train_{out}; \; T$

Central Controller: The central controller is the crucial part of the system, actively communicating with the train, light and gate. The *Controller* class is modeled as follows:

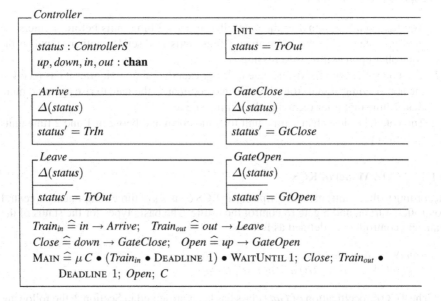

Controller
_____

| status : ControllerS |
| up, down, in, out : **chan** |

Init
_____
$status = TrOut$

Arrive
_____
$\Delta(status)$

$status' = TrIn$

GateClose
_____
$\Delta(status)$

$status' = GtClose$

Leave
_____
$\Delta(status)$

$status' = TrOut$

GateOpen
_____
$\Delta(status)$

$status' = GtOpen$

$Train_{in} \hat{=} in \rightarrow Arrive; \quad Train_{out} \hat{=} out \rightarrow Leave$
$Close \hat{=} down \rightarrow GateClose; \quad Open \hat{=} up \rightarrow GateOpen$
$\text{Main} \hat{=} \mu C \bullet (Train_{in} \bullet \text{Deadline } 1) \bullet \text{WaitUntil } 1; \; Close; \; Train_{out} \bullet$
$\qquad \text{Deadline } 1; \; Open; \; C$

The attribute *status* keeps the records of the train's passing information in the system. When the train sends an *in* signal, the *status* of the controller changes from *TrOut* to *TrIn*. When the train has passed the crossing and sent an *out* signal to the controller, the *status* of the controller changes from *TrIn* to *TrOut*. The main processes of the controller are receiving the train passing information and manipulating the gate operations at the same time. If the gate is open then instructions on closing the gate will be sent to the *Gate*. On the other hand, when the train has passed the gate, the controller will open the gate.

RCS Configuration: After specifying individual components, the next step is to compose them into a whole system. The overall system is a composition of all the communicating components.

__*RCSystem*_____

> *t* : *Train*; *g* : *Gate*; *c* : *Controller*
> _____
>
> MAIN $\widehat{=}$ $\Big\|$ $(t \xleftarrow{in,out} c \xleftarrow{up,down} g)$

Two essential properties of RCS are: first, the gate is never closed at a stretch for more than a stipulated time range (suppose 10 time units); second, the gate should be down whenever a train is crossing. These properties can be formally expressed as:

$RCSystem \bullet \Box(g.status = ToDn \rightarrow \Diamond_{\leq 10}\ g.status = Up)$
$RCSystem \bullet t.status = In \Rightarrow g.status = Down$

5.2   Translation

In this section, we show how the given translation rules can be applied to map TCOZ specification into Timed automatons.

First of all, for the whole RCS system, three automatons can be identified in the Timed Automata model, i.e., gate, train and controller.

We use the gate class as an example to show the identification of the states, transitions, guards and synchronization mentioned above. According to the translation rules for TCOZ classes/objects, four states can be identified through the static view of *Gate* class, it has four operation schema, each one is mapped into a state, namely, *Up*, *ToDown*, *Down*, and *ToUp* as shown in Figure 1, among which *Up* is the initial state as indicated by the *INIT* schema in the *Gate* class. Synchronization and clock conditions on the transitions are constructed by transforming the *Open* and *Close* process of *Gate* class according to the translation rules on DEADLINE and WAITUNTIL primitives. A clock is generated to guard the atomic process *Lower* to be finished no later than 1 time unit, then it is reused to guard *Raise* and *Up* process to meet their timing constraints by resetting its value to 0. The initial and terminal states generated for every non-atomic process due to those translation rules, if they are linked by a transition with a τ event, are incorporated into one state to simplified the resultant automaton.

This gate automaton can be automatically generated by our translation tool and visualized in UPPAAL as "process gate" in Figure 7. In the same way, we can get the train and controller automatons as "process train" and "process controller".

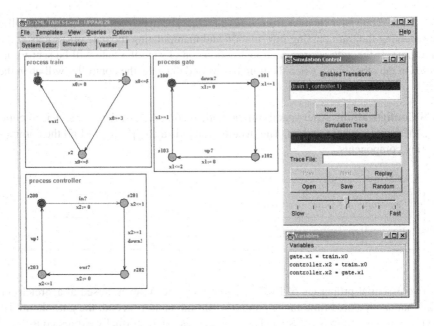

Fig. 7. Simulation

5.3   Model-Checking RCS

Now we can use the UPPAAL tool to simulate the system as well as to model-check some invariants and real-time properties. In UPPAAL correctness criteria can be specified as formulas of the timed temporal logic TCTL [8], for which UPPAAL implements model-checking algorithms.

From a safety critical perspective, the key point of the RCS is to provide guaranteed safety and efficient services. These properties can be formally interpreted from our model as:

- safety properties - The properties state that whenever the train is in, the gate is down. It can be translated into the TCTL formula in UPPAAL as follows:

    ```
    A[] train.s2 imply gate.s102
    ```
- efficient service properties - the gate is never closed at a stretch for more than 10 time units. To verify this property, we add a clock x to record the time the gate takes to reopen itself:

    ```
    gate.s101 --> (gate.s100 and gate.x<=10)
    ```

UPPAAL verified that these properties actually hold for this given model.

6   Conclusion

TCOZ and TA lie at each end of the spectrum of formal modeling techniques. TCOZ is good at structurally specifying high level requirements for complex systems, while TA is good at designing timed models in simple clock constraints but with highly automatic tools support.

The investigation on the strengths and links between those two modeling techniques leads us to an interesting research result, i.e., timed composable patterns (reminiscence of 'design patterns' in object-oriented modeling). In this paper, these patterns are formally defined in Z and the process algebra-like compositional nature are preserved in the graphical representations. These timed composable patterns.

- not only provide a proficient interchange media for transforming TCOZ specifications into TA designs
- but also provide a generic reusable framework for designing real-time systems in TA alone.

One possible future work would be to encode those timed patterns as icons in the model checker tool, such as UPPAAL, so that the complex timed models can be built systematically in UPPAAL.

Since TCOZ is a superset of TCSP, one consequence of this work is that a semantic link and a practical translation tool from TCSP to TA has been achieved so that TA tools i.e. UPPAAL can also be used to check TCSP timing properties. In this context, this work complements the recent pure theoretical investigation [11] on the expressiveness of TCSP and closed timed automata.

Acknowledgements

We would like to thank Hugh Anderson, Sun Jing and Wang Hai for their helpful comments on this work.

References

1. R. Alur and D. L. Dill. A theory of timed automata. *Theoretical Computer Science*, 126:183–235, 1994.
2. J. Bengtsson, K. G. Larsen, F. Larsson, and P. Pettersson avd Y. Wang. UPPAAL - a tool suite for automatic verification of real-time systems. In *Hybrid Systems III: Verification and Control*, pages 232–243. Springer, 1996.
3. Albert M. K. Cheng. *Real-time systems : scheduling, analysis, and verification*. John Wiley and Sons, 2002.
4. C. Daws, A. Olivero, S. Tripakis, and S. Yovine. The tool KRONOS. In *Hybrid Systems III: Verification and Control*, pages 208–219. Springer, 1996.
5. J. S. Dong, P. Hao, S. C. Qin, J. Sun, and W. Yi. TCOZ to Timed Automata. Technical report TRC6/03, School of Computing, National University of Singapore, 2003. http://nt-appn.comp.nus.edu.sg/fm/tcoz2ta/tr.zip.
6. R. Duke, G. Rose, and G. Smith. Object-Z: a Specification Language Advocated for the Description of Standards. *Computer Standards and Interfaces*, 17:511–533, 1995.
7. C. L. Heitmeyer and N. Lynch. The Generalized Railroad Crossing: A Case Study in Formal Verification of Real-Time Systems. In *Proceedings of RTSS'94, Real-Time Systems Symposium*, pages 120–131, San Juan, Puerto Rico, December 1994. IEEE Computer Society Press.
8. T. A. Henzinger, X. Nicollin, J. Sifakis, and S. Yovine. Symbolic model checking for real-time systems. *Information and Computation*, 111(2):193–243, 1994.

9. B. Mahony and J. S. Dong. Timed Communicating Object Z. *IEEE Transactions on Software Engineering*, 26(2):150–177, February 2000.
10. B. Mahony and J. S. Dong. Deep Semantic Links of TCSP and Object-Z: TCOZ Approach. *Formal Aspects of Computing*, 13(2):142–160, 2002.
11. J. Ouaknine and J. Worrell. Timed CSP = Closed Timed Automata. In *Proceedings of EXPRESS 02*, volume 38(2) of *ENTCS*, 2002.
12. A. W. Roscoe. *The Theory and Practice of Concurrency*. Prentice-Hall, 1997.
13. S. Schneider, J. Davies, D. M. Jackson, G. M. Reed, J. N. Reed, and A. W. Roscoe. Timed CSP: Theory and practice. In J. W. de Bakker, C. Huixing, W. P. de Roever, and G. Rozenberg, editors, *Real-Time: Theory in Practice*, volume 600 of *Lect. Notes in Comput. Sci.*, pages 640–675. Springer-Verlag, 1992.
14. G. Smith. An integration of real-time object-z and csp for specifying concurrent real-time systems. In M. Butler, L. Petre, and K. Sere, editors, *IFM 2002*, page 267¨C285. Springer-Verlag, 2002.
15. J. Sun, J. S. Dong, J. Liu, and H. Wang. A formal object approach to the design of zml. *Annals ol Software Engineering*, 13:329–356, 2002.
16. J. Woodcock and A. Cavalcanti. The Semantics of Circus. In *ZB 2002: Formal Specification and Development in Z and B*, volume 2272 of *Lecture Notes in Computer Science*, pages 184–203. Springer-Verlag, 2002.

Author Index